The Rise and Fall of ...
1483–1...

B

Blackwell Classic Histories of Europe

This series comprises new editions of seminal histories of Europe. Written by the leading scholars of their generation, the books represent both major works of historical analysis and interpretation and clear, authoritative overviews of the major periods of European history. All the volumes have been revised for inclusion in the series and include updated material to aid further study. *Blackwell Classic Histories of Europe* provides a forum in which these key works can continue to be enjoyed by scholars, students and general readers alike.

Published

Forthcoming

THE RISE AND FALL OF RENAISSANCE FRANCE

1483–1610

Second Edition

R. J. Knecht

Copyright © R. J. Knecht 1996, 2001

The right of R. J. Knecht to be identified as author of this work has been asserted in accordance with the Copyright, Designs and Patents Act 1988.

First published by Fontana Press in 1996.
Second edition published by Blackwell Publishers Ltd 2001

2 4 6 8 10 9 7 6 5 3 1

Blackwell Publishers Ltd
108 Cowley Road
Oxford OX4 1JF
UK

Blackwell Publishers Inc.
350 Main Street
Malden, Massachusetts 02148
USA

British Library Cataloguing in Publication Data

A CIP catalogue record for this book is available from the British Library.

Library of Congress Cataloging-in-Publication Data is available for this book.

ISBN 0 631 22728 8
     0 631 22729 6 (pbk)

Typeset in 10pt on 12pt Sabon by
Rowland Phototypesetting Ltd, Bury St Edmunds, Suffolk
Printed in Great Britain by T.J. International, Padstow, Cornwall

This book is printed on acid-free paper.

In memory of Jean Jacquart (1928–98)

Contents

A Note on Coinage and Measures

Two types of money existed side by side in sixteenth-century France: money of account and actual coin. Royal accounts were kept in the former; actual transactions carried out in the latter. The principal money of account was the *livre tournois* (sometimes called the *franc*) which was subdivided in *sous* (or *sols*) and *deniers*. One *livre* = 20 *sous*; 1 *sou* = 12 *deniers*. This was the French equivalent of the English system of pounds, shillings and pence. The *livre tournois* was worth about two English shillings.

Actual coin was either gold, silver or billon: e.g. the *écu au soleil* was gold, the *teston* silver and the *douzain* billon. From 1500 to 1546 gold coins constituted on average two-thirds of the total annual coinage of the royal mints; thereafter till the end of the century that average fell to 17 per cent. Rulers who did not have enough coin at their disposal were naturally tempted to devalue the money of account and also to debase the precious-metal content of the coinage itself. Francis I's successors resorted with mounting frequency to devaluation. Thus the gold *écu* which was valued at 40 *sous* in 1516, was set at 46 *sous* in 1550, 50 *sous* in 1561 and 60 *sous* in 1575. Over the same period, the value of the *teston* rose from 10 *sous* to 14 *sous*. In addition to royal coins, provincial and foreign coins circulated in France.

France had no unified system of weights and measures in the sixteenth century. Each region had its own. In Paris the *setier* of grain = 156 litres. Twelve *setiers* = 1 *muid*.

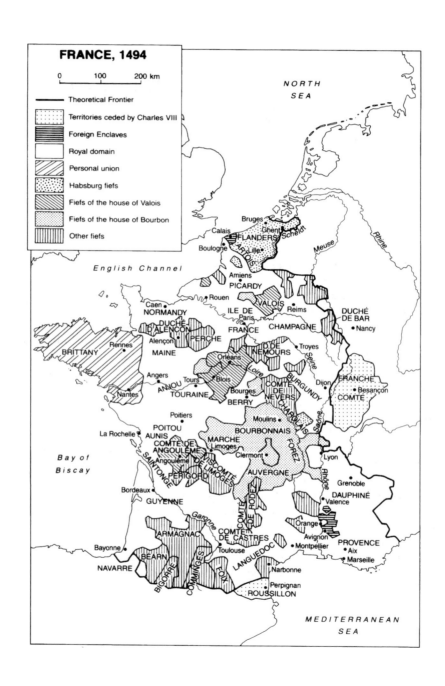

FRANCE, 1494

0   100   200 km

Theoretical Frontier
Territories ceded by Charles VIII
Foreign Enclaves
Royal domain
Personal union
Habsburg fiefs
Fiefs of the house of Valois
Fiefs of the house of Bourbon
Other fiefs

NORTH SEA

Bruges
Calais
Ghent
Scheldt
FLANDERS
Boulogne
ARTOIS
Lille
Meuse
Rhine

English Channel

Amiens
PICARDY
Rouen
ILE DE
VALOIS
Reims
DUCHÉ DE BAR
Caen
NORMANDY
Paris
FRANCE
CHAMPAGNE
Nancy
DUCHÉ-
D'ALENÇON
PERCHE
Troyes
Rennes
Alençon
ILE DE
NEMOURS
FRANCHE
BRITTANY
MAINE
Orléans
Seine
Besançon
COMTÉ
Angers
Tours
Blois
Loire
Dijon
Nantes
ANJOU
BURGUNDY
TOURAINE
Bourges
COMTÉ
DE
NEVERS
BERRY
CHAROLAIS
Poitiers
Moulins
POITOU
BOURBONNAIS
La Rochelle
AUNIS
MARCHE
COMTÉ DE
ANGOULÊME
Limoges
Bay of
Biscay
Angoulême
VICOMTE
Clermont
FOREZ
Lyon
SAINTONGE
DE LIMOGES
AUVERGNE
PÉRIGORD
Bordeaux
Grenoble
GUYENNE
COMTÉ
DAUPHINÉ
Garonne
DE RODEZ
Valence
Rhône
ARMAGNAC
COMTÉ
Orange
Bayonne
DE CASTRES
Avignon
PROVENCE
BÉARN
BIGORRE
Toulouse
Montpellier
Aix
NAVARRE
COMMINGES
FOIX
LANGUEDOC
Marseille
Narbonne
Perpignan
ROUSSILLON

MEDITERRANEAN SEA

FRANCE, 1585-98

0   100   200 km

—— Lands of Henry of Navarre in 1585,
(Henry IV of France 1589-1610)

▨ Greatest extent of the Catholic League

▨ Areas governed by the Huguenots

▲ Chief recognized Huguenot centres 1598-1629
according to the Edict of Nantes 1598

■ Towns with a Reformed Government

⊙ Courts for trying Huguenot cases

• Sites of important battles or treaties

NORTH SEA

KINGDOM OF ENGLAND

English Channel

Calais
Scheldt
Meuse
Cambrai
BP. OF CAMBRAI
Doullens
Dieppe
Amiens
Arques
Folembray
Vervins
Rouen
Laon
Verdun
Metz
Senlis
Mantes-la-Jolie
Ivry
Paris
Lagny
Toul
Falaise
La Ferté Vidame
Corbiel
Joinville
Chartres
Dourdan
Auneau
Nemours
Rennes
Jargeau
Vimory
Sully
Fontaine-Française
Nantes
Plessis-les-Tours
Blois
Saumur
Loudun
Châtellerault
Maillezais
Marans
Niort
La Rochelle
Issoire
St.-Jean-d'Angély
Lyon
Jarnac
MAR. OF SALUZZO

Bay of Biscay

Coutras
Ste.-Foy-la-Grande
Grenoble
Castillon
Bergerac
Albiac
Privas
Die
Briançon
Bordeaux
Monségur
Figeac
Gap
Embrun
Clairac
Vezins
Nérac
Montauban
Alais
Uzès
Mont-de-Marsan
Villemur
Millau
Lunel
Nîmes
Lourmarin
Lectoure
Montpellier
Alguesmortes
Castres
Garonne
BÉARN
NAVARRE
Foix
Tarascon

Gulf of Lions

KINGDOM OF SPAIN

MEDITERRANEAN SEA

THE EMPIRE

Rhine
Seine
Loire
Saône
Rhône

Preface to the Second Edition

Since 1996 much research has been done on sixteenth-century France and I have amended my text accordingly. Thus, I have tempered praise of Francis I as 'father of letters'; given more notice to French policy towards the Council of Trent; pointed to the difficulties of implementing the peace of Amboise; underlined the significance of the Peace of Longjumeau; and stressed Henry III's aloofness from his subjects. The bibliography has been brought up to date. A sad loss of the past four years has been the death of Jean Jacquart, as much loved as he was eminent in sixteenth-century French studies. To his memory this edition is dedicated.

BIRMINGHAM, 2001

Preface to the First Edition

The title of this book requires a gloss. 'Rise' may be construed as a move towards political order, economic prosperity and social contentment; 'fall' as a lapse into political confusion, economic depression and social unrest. France in the sixteenth century experienced both conditions. This book attempts to describe and, I hope, to explain this duality in the period often called 'the Renaissance'. Fixing the chronological limits has not been easy, for history can never be strictly compartmentalized. The division traditionally drawn between the Middle Ages and modern times is nothing more than an academic convenience; historically it makes no sense. French institutions in the sixteenth century were rooted in the Middle Ages. The significance which historians have traditionally attached to the year 1494 as ending the Middle Ages has little validity. It was then that King Charles VIII invaded Italy, setting in train a series of French wars in the peninsula which lasted on and off until the Peace of Cateau-Cambrésis in 1559. I have chosen to begin my story with Charles VIII's accession in 1483. Ideally, I should have traced the origins of the 'rise' back to the formative reign of Louis XI, often regarded as the founder of French national unity, but this would have lengthened the book too much. As for the 'fall', I might have ended with the assassination of the last Valois king in 1589. Henry IV's reign that followed is often taken to mark the recovery of France, but there is a strong case for thinking that the real recovery did not start till 1651, after the Fronde.

In the early sixteenth century France seemed set to become the most powerful nation in Europe, yet by 1600 she had sunk to one of the lowest points in her history. Half a century of more or less continual civil conflict, allegedly over religion, had brought desolation and despair to her inhabitants. Her economy had been almost destroyed, her society was in disarray and her political system was on the brink of collapse. The very origins of a monarchy, which had once been revered as God's lieutenancy on earth, were being questioned. Much of the interest that springs from studying sixteenth-century France resides in probing the causes of her precipitous decline. Was religion the only cause of dissension among her people, or were they responding to other factors? Why was a monarchy which had seemed so strong under Francis I and Henry II reduced to little more than an impotent figurehead? These are merely two questions among many that the reader might care to ponder. I hope to provide some answers, but the subject is vast and controversial.

The past cannot change, but history does. The last fifty years have seen considerable changes in historical thinking, particularly in France, where the *Annales* school has turned away from 'the history of events' (*histoire événementielle*) to that of a wide-ranging interdisciplinary study of the past. This has led to a greater preoccupation with socio-economic issues, *mentalités* and other aspects of human activity which historians traditionally had overlooked or not seen as their concern. Recently, however, there has been a reaction. A new school of historians, less doctrinaire than their elders, have returned to the 'history of events' with a sharpened awareness of its complexities. The massacre of St Bartholomew's day, for example, is no longer seen simply as the slaughter of Protestants by Catholics. The sociology of denominational violence as well as its psychological context have come under close scrutiny.

This book along with its companions in the series adheres to a chronological, not a thematic, plan, for the reader needs to be made aware of the sequence of events. However, I have tried, wherever possible, to feed analysis into the narrative, taking into account modern research. For example, the nature and effectiveness of the French monarchy has become controversial. Was it 'absolute', as the kings often claimed, or was it subject to limitations? The crucial importance of finance at a time when the technology of war was making unprecedented demands on the traditional resources of the state is now recognized. The French Reformation is no longer seen simply as a German import; its indigenous roots have been brought to light. We also know far more about the problems posed for the crown by the upsurge of religious dissent and about the policies by which it hoped to solve them. Religion was once dismissed as a cause of the civil wars that bear its name. It was alleged that the nobility used religion as a cover for their internecine greed. Modern research has demonstrated that religion was indeed a major source of conflict, and also an important component of popular culture, which until recently was virtually a closed book. Those pages have now been opened, and historians are better able to probe the thoughts of ordinary French men and women during the Renaissance. The psychology of denominational conflict, as reflected in a vast pamphlet literature, has been exhaustively analysed. The Wars of Religion also provided a fertile soil for political thinkers. While some upheld the doctrine of absolutism, others championed resistance to a monarchy they viewed as ungodly and therefore tyrannical. Under the cumulative impact of persecution, Protestants, who had for long adhered to the Pauline doctrine of obedience to 'the powers that be', turned into revolutionaries willing to condone even tyrannicide.

During the past half-century French historians have been more interested in looking at French society and *mentalités* than at political events. Two great pioneering works by E. Le Roy Ladurie (*Les Paysans de Languedoc*) and Jean Jacquart (*La Crise rurale en Ile-de-France, 1550–1670*) have revolutionized knowledge of the countryside and its inhabitants who made up the bulk of the population. We know far more now about the economic difficulties they had to face and also about the impact on their lives of natural disasters and war. The towns too have received much attention lately. Their social structure has been examined as well as their administrative, economic and religious role. Demographic historians have considered the reasons for the growth of towns during the century. Notarial registers have yielded information about humble Frenchmen who, one might have assumed, had vanished without trace. Scholars now know that the Parisian League, which was once identified with the rabble, was far from proletarian. Another major source of interest has been the nobility. The old notion of a complete economic collapse of the class under the mounting pressure of inflation has been exploded, while the importance of clientage as a bond between great and lesser nobles has been stressed. So has the importance of provincial governors in either buttressing the crown's authority or undermining it. The careers and fortunes of several individual noblemen have recently been the subject of detailed studies. Another welcome development of recent years has been the use which art historians have made of history. No longer are they content to judge style without reference to the historical context. Patronage and iconography are now seen as crucially important to the study of Renaissance art. A royal château was designed for use, not merely as decoration.

In the course of writing this history I have incurred debts to many scholars. Among them are Bernard Barbiche, Joseph Bergin, Richard Bonney, Monique Chatenet, Denis Crouzet, Robert Descimon, Mark Greengrass, Philippe Hamon, Jean Jacquart, Anne-Marie Lecoq, Nicole Lemaitre, David Nicholls, David Parker, David Parrott, David Potter, and Penny Roberts. John Bourne and W. Scott Lucas have guided me through the mysterious world of the computer. My copy-editor, Betty Palmer, has been a model of efficiency and tact. They all have my warmest thanks, as does my old friend and colleague Douglas Johnson, who kindly invited me to contribute to this series and for his helpful advice as general editor. I am also deeply grateful to Philip Gwyn Jones of HarperCollins for his patience and generosity. My biggest debt, as always, is to my wife, Maureen, without whose tolerance this book could never have been written.

Note

The names of French kings are given in French before their accession and in English thereafter: e.g. François d'Angoulême becomes Francis I, Henri duc d'Orléans becomes Henry II and Henri de Navarre becomes Henry IV.

BIRMINGHAM, February 1996

I

France in 1500

At the beginning of the sixteenth century France was still only partially developed as a nation. She still lacked well-defined borders, a common language and a unified legal system. The eastern frontier, in so far as it existed at all, followed roughly the rivers Scheldt, Meuse, Saône and Rhône from the North Sea to the Mediterranean. People living west of this line were vassals of the French king; those to the east owed allegiance to the Holy Roman Emperor. French suzerainty over Artois and Flanders was purely nominal, effective control of these areas having passed to the house of Burgundy. Further east, the frontier cut across the duchy of Bar whose ruler, the duke of Lorraine, did homage for half the territory to the king of France and for the other half to the emperor. In the south, Dauphiné and Provence, being east of the Rhône, were still not regarded as integral parts of the French kingdom: the king was obeyed as 'Dauphin' in the one, and as count in the other. The south-west border more or less followed the Pyrenees, avoiding Roussillon, which belonged to the kingdom of Aragon, and the small kingdom of Navarre, ruled by the house of Albret. Within France, there were three foreign enclaves: Calais belonged to England, the Comtat-Venaissin to the Holy See and the principality of Orange to the house of Chalon. Some great fiefs also survived, including the duchies of Brittany and Bourbon.

France also lacked a common language. Modern French is descended from *langue d'oïl*, a dialect spoken in northern France during the medieval period; in the south, *langue d'oc* or *occitan* was used. The linguistic frontier ran from the Bec d'Ambès in the west to the col du Lautaret in the east, passing through Limoges, the Cantal and Annonay. South of this line, even educated people used the local idiom or Latin; *langue d'oïl* was spoken by feudal magnates when addressing the king. After 1450, as the French crown asserted its authority following the expulsion of the English, *langue d'oïl* began to make deep inroads in the south-west. The parlements of Toulouse, Bordeaux and Aix used it, and noblemen from the south who took up offices at court adopted it. They continued to speak it when they returned home, passing the habit to their servants. By 1500 the southward expansion of *langue d'oïl* was gathering pace, at least among the upper classes, but the linguistic unity of France still lay far in the future. Nor was the divide simply between north and south. Within each linguistic half there were whole families of provincial patois, not to mention such peripheral languages as Breton, Basque or Flemish.

The law was another area lacking national unity. Each province, each *pays* and often each locality had its own set of customs. Broadly speaking, Roman law prevailed in the south while customary law existed in the north, but patches of customary law existed in the south, while Roman law penetrated the north to a limited extent. For a long time customs were fixed only by practice, which made for flexibility but also uncertainty; so from the twelfth century onwards charters were drawn up listing the customs of individual lordships or towns. The first serious attempt to codify customs was made by Charles VII, but no real progress was made till Charles VIII set up a commission in 1495. It was under Louis XII, however, that codification really got under way.

The surface area of France in 1500 was far smaller than it is today: 459,000 square kilometres as against 550,986. Yet it must have seemed enormous to people living at the time, given the slowness of their communications. The speed of road travel may be assessed by consulting the guide-book published by Charles Estienne in 1553. One could cover 15 or 16 leagues in a day where the terrain was flat, 14 where it rose gently and only 11 to 13 where it rose steeply. Thus it took normally two days to travel from Paris to Amiens, six from Paris to Limoges, seven and a half from Paris to Bordeaux, six to eight from Paris to Lyon and ten to fourteen from Paris to Marseille.

The social and political implications of distance were far-reaching. Fernand Braudel has suggested that it made for a fragmented society in which villages, towns, *pays*, even provinces 'existed in sheltered cocoons, having almost no contact with one another'. Yet the immobility of French life in the late Middle Ages should not be exaggerated. In spite of the distances involved, people were continually moving in and out of towns. 'We would be wrong to imagine', Bernard Chevalier has written, 'our ancestors as immobile beings, riveted to their fields or workshops.'

By 1500, France had largely rid herself of the two great scourges of plague and war which had proved so devastating between 1340 and 1450. Outbreaks of plague did still take place, but there were no pandemics of the kind that had swept across the kingdom between 1348 and 1440. Epidemics

were limited to one or two provinces at most, and destructive ones were
less frequent. War had also largely receded: except for certain border areas,
there was little fighting within France between the end of the Hundred
Years War in 1453 and the start of the Wars of Religion in 1562. Large
companies of disbanded soldiers and brigands continued to terrorize the
countryside from time to time, but in general the fear and uncertainty that
had discouraged agricultural enterprise before 1450 were removed. Nor
was there any major grain famine between 1440 and 1520.

The recession of plague, war and famine served to stimulate a recovery
of France's population after 1450. In the absence of a general census for
this period it is impossible to give precise figures. We have to rely on
evidence supplied by a relatively few parish registers, mainly relating to
Provence and the north-west, which are often in poor condition, do not
provide complete baptismal lists, seldom record burials and mention marriages only occasionally. But certain general conclusions may be drawn. It
is unlikely that France's population exceeded 15 million around 1500, but
it was growing. Having been reduced by half between 1330 and 1450, it
seems to have doubled between 1450 and 1560. In other words, the numerical effects of the Black Death and Hundred Years War were largely made
up in the century after 1450. The rise was by no means uniform across the
kingdom: some villages, even regions, maintained a high annual growth
rate over a long period, while others made more modest advances.

The need to feed more mouths stimulated agricultural production after
1450. This was achieved by means of land clearance and reclamation rather
than by improved farming techniques. The reconstruction began in earnest
about 1470 and lasted till about 1540. The initiative rested with individual
seigneurs, who had to overcome enormous obstacles. On countless estates
nothing was visible except 'thorns, thickets and other encumbrances'; the
old boundaries had vanished and people no longer knew where their patri-
monies lay. The compilation of new *censiers* and terriers was costly and
time-consuming. Labour was also in short supply to begin with, forcing
lords to offer substantial concessions to attract settlers on their lands.

Reclamation, like the resettlement of the countryside, was subject to many
regional variations. It began sooner in the Paris region and the south-west
than in the Midi, where it took up almost the entire first quarter of the
sixteenth century. Pastoral farming was often damaged in the process, as
many village communities, anxious to maximize their arable production,
tried to restrict grazing. Peasants were forbidden to own more than a specified number of animals, but the need for manure precluded a complete ban
on livestock. In mountain areas, where arable farming was less important,
steps were taken to protect pastures from excessive land-clearance.

The rise of France's population after 1450 was reflected in urban growth.
Although evidence for this is often selective (like tax returns) or incomplete,

*it doesn't explain where he got all of
of his information should this
diminish his credibility)*

4   FRANCE IN 1500

all of it points upwards. Thus at Périgueux the population rose gently between 1450 and 1480, then steeply, reaching a peak in 1490. Using the base index of 100 for the number of known families, this had fallen to 29 in 1450, before rising to 87 in 1490 and levelling off at 79 in 1500. Paris, which was by far the largest town in France, had some 200,000 inhabitants by 1500. A document of 1538 distributing the cost of 20,000 infantry among the cities in accordance with their ability to pay enables us to rank them in order of size. Below Paris were four towns (Rouen, Lyon, Toulouse and Orléans) of between 40,000 and 70,000 inhabitants, then perhaps a score of towns of between 10,000 and 30,000 inhabitants, then another forty or so of between 5000 and 10,000. Finally there were many more small towns with fewer than 5000 inhabitants. The line distinguishing a small town from a large village was often difficult to draw. A town was usually walled. It also possessed certain privileges and comprised a wider variety of occupational and social types than a village.

The character of a town was determined by its main activity. Trade was important to all of them, but some were also administrative, intellectual and ecclesiastical centres. Seven had parlements; about 90 were capitals of *bailliages* and *sénéchaussées*, 15 (Paris, Toulouse, Montpellier, Orléans, Cahors, Angers, Aix, Poitiers, Valence, Caen, Nantes, Bourges, Bordeaux, Angoulême and Issoire) had universities, and about 110 were archiepiscopal or episcopal sees. Virtually the only industrial towns were Amiens, where the making of cloth kept half the population employed, and Tours, where silk was important.

By 1500 the walled towns, commonly described as 'good towns' (*bonnes villes*) to distinguish them from the large villages or *villes champêtres*, were active politically. In 1482, King Louis XI asked the people of Amiens to endorse a treaty, giving as his reason 'the need to secure the consent and ratification of the men of the estates and communities of the *bonnes villes* of our kingdom'. The towns have been described as a fourth power in the kingdom along with the king, the church and the nobility. The crown and the towns worked together as allies, while watching each other closely.

The walls of many towns had fallen into disrepair by the thirteenth century and, consequently, many had been taken by the English during the Hundred Years War. To protect themselves, many towns by 1500 had repaired their walls at their own cost and the process continued in the sixteenth century. In order to qualify as a *bonne ville* a town needed not only a curtain wall, but also human and material resources with which to defend itself. In the words of Claude de Seyssel, writing in 1510) 'a *bonne ville* or *place forte* that is well supplied, well equipped with guns and with all things necessary to sustain a siege and nourish a garrison and relief force is the safeguard of an entire kingdom.' A recent survey has traced the remains of 1700 *places-fortes* in France dating from before 1500.

primary source →

The topography of Paris was determined by the River Seine, which divided it into three parts: the *Cité* on the island in the middle of the river; the *Ville* on the right bank and the *Université* on the left bank. The city was encircled by medieval walls, but only the left bank remained within the wall built in the twelfth century by King Philip Augustus. The right bank had outstripped it long ago, and was now hemmed in by a fourteenth-century wall. Beyond the walls lay suburbs or *faubourgs*, the most important having grown around the abbey of Saint-Germain-des-Prés. The area within the walls was small and densely built up, the inhabitants crammed into narrow houses of two or three storeys. All the streets, except a few axial ones, were narrow and virtually impassable to wheeled traffic. They also stank because of the ordure that was thrown into them. Among the few open spaces were the Cemetery of the Innocents and the Place de Grève, both on the right bank. Two bridges linked the *Ville* to the *Cité*: the Pont-au-Change, a wooden bridge built in 1296 which was lined with shops owned by goldsmiths, jewellers and money-changers, and the Pont Notre-Dame, which collapsed in 1499 and was rebuilt. Two bridges linked the *Cité* to the left bank – the Petit Pont and Pont Saint-Michel. In addition to being a thriving business community, the *Cité* was also a judicial and ecclesiastical centre. At the eastern end of the island stood the cathedral of Notre-Dame. Close by were the fortified bishop's palace and a gated close of 37 canons' houses. At the opposite end of the island stood the *Palais* or old royal palace, now occupied by the parlement, which was the highest court of law, and other sovereign courts. Its business attracted a vast number of councillors, barristers, procurators, solicitors, ushers and so on, in addition to the many litigants and people who came to shop at the stalls set up by tradesmen within the palace. Also on the island was the Hôtel-Dieu, the city's main hospital.

The *Ville* was the business quarter of Paris. It comprised the markets of the Halles, expensive shops in the rue Saint-Denis and mixed commerce around the rue Saint-Martin. Many streets were organized by trades. The Place de Grève, in addition to being a port, was the place where the militia assembled and the site of civic ceremonies and public executions. On the square's east side stood the Maison aux Piliers, the seat of the municipal government or *Bureau de la Ville*. Other important secular buildings in the *Ville* were the Louvre, a medieval fortress with a tall central keep, and the Châtelet, seat of the *prévôt* of Paris and his staff. The palace of the Tournelles was the only royal residence within the capital that was still used by the king and his court.

The University of Paris, which had been founded in the twelfth century, was best known for its faculties of theology and arts. It also had faculties of canon law and medicine. In the fifteenth century its reputation declined and it ceased to attract as many foreign students as in the past. While degrees were conferred by the faculties, teaching was done in fifty or so colleges. The most famous were the Sorbonne and the colleges of Navarre, Cardinal Lemoine, Sainte-Barbe and Montaigu. Not all students lived in them; many lodged in 'digs' some of which were run by their tutors. For physical exercise the students could use the Pré-aux-Clercs, a large meadow just outside the Porte de Nesle.

The rise in population, growth of urbanization and a general rise in the standard of living were mainly responsible for an economic boom that lasted from the 1460s until the 1520s. France was fortunate in being largely self-sufficient in respect of basic necessities. Grain was her chief product. Though she sometimes had to import foreign grain, this was only in times of famine; normally she produced enough for her own needs and exported any surplus. Wine consumption increased hugely during the sixteenth century, as shown by the rapid expansion of vineyards around Paris, Orléans, Reims and Lyon, by the yield from duties on wine and by the multiplication of taverns. Then as now, wine was produced not only for the home market, but for export. Several major vineyards were developed along the Atlantic coast around Bordeaux, La Rochelle and in the Basse-Loire. England and the Netherlands were the best customers.

Salt, like wine, was produced for markets at home and abroad. From marshes along the Mediterranean coast, it was sent up the Rhône and Saône to south-east France, Burgundy, Switzerland and Savoy. Another group of salt marshes along the Atlantic coast supplied a much wider area, including northern France, England, the Netherlands and Baltic states.

Metalware, especially of iron or steel, was not widely used in late medieval France. Agricultural and industrial tools were still usually made of wood. Apart from a few basic iron pots, the greatest demand was for nails and pins. For non-ferrous metals, France depended largely on foreign imports: copper, brass and tinplate from Germany, pewter and lead from England and steel from Italy.

As trade developed in France around the close of the Middle Ages, no fewer than 344 markets and fairs were set up under royal licence between 1483 and 1500. A fair was given privileges designed to attract foreign merchants: for example, foreign money was allowed to circulate freely, the goods of aliens were guaranteed against seizure and distraint, and the *droit d'aubaine*, whereby an alien's inheritance was liable to forfeiture by the crown, was set aside. Some fairs were exempted from entry or exit dues and sometimes special judges were appointed to hear the suits of merchants, thereby sparing them the delays of ordinary justice.

By 1500 most big towns and many smaller ones had fairs. The most famous were the four annual fairs of Lyon, which drew many foreigners, especially Italians, Germans and Swiss. They were also important to the history of banking. Though banks had existed in France since the thirteenth century, they only became important as agencies of credit and exchange in the fifteenth century. They fixed themselves in Lyon because of the large amount of business transacted there, and threw out branches in other trading centres. The use of bills of exchange eliminated the need to carry large amounts of cash, and the fairs of Lyon became a regular clearing house for the settlement of accounts. At the same time, bankers took money on deposit, lent it at interest and negotiated letters of credit.

French overseas trade had recovered from the stagnation it had suffered during the Hundred Years War. The annexation of Provence in 1481 was extremely significant for French trade in the Mediterranean. Although Marseille failed to wrest the monopoly of Levantine trade from Venice, it established useful links with the ports of the Ligurian coast, Tuscany, Catalonia, Sicily, Rhodes and the Barbary coast. The chief traders were Italians who looked to the bankers of Lyon for capital. The French Atlantic and Channel ports also recovered in the late fifteenth century and traded actively with England, Spain, the Netherlands and Scandinavia. As land communications were poor, harbours developed along the west coast, along navigable rivers and even far inland. As many as 200 ships might be seen at any time along the quays at Rouen. The most important port of the south-west was Bordeaux which was visited by an English wine-fleet each year.

The expansion of trade was linked to industrial growth. Cloth-making, which was centred in northern France but becoming entrenched in other areas, notably Languedoc, was France's chief industry. Although often named after the towns from which the cloth-merchants operated, the various kinds of cloth were produced mainly in the countryside. French cloth was, generally speaking, of ordinary quality and cheap, serving the day-to-day needs of the lower social strata. Even the best French cloth could not compete with such foreign imports as Florentine serges. The finest wool was imported from Spain, England, the Barbary coast and the Levant. An important development was the establishment of a luxury textile industry, first at Tours, then at Lyon. But France alone could not satisfy the increasingly sophisticated tastes of the court and nobility. For the finest linen she looked to the Netherlands and South Germany and for silks to Italy – velvet from Genoa, damask and satin from Florence and Lucca, and cloth of gold from Milan.

An industry that was developing fast in France around 1500 was printing. After its importation from Germany in 1470, it spread to Lyon in 1473, Albi in 1475 and Toulouse and Angers in 1476. By 1500 there were 75 presses in Paris alone. France still lagged behind Italy in book production, but it was catching up fast. Thus between 1480 and 1482, Venice produced 156 editions and Paris 35; between 1495 and 1497, Venice produced 447, Paris 181 and Lyon 95. Whereas in 1480 only nine French towns had printing presses, by 1500 the number had risen to 40. Although French printers began by targeting academic clients, they soon branched out in pursuit of bigger profits. In addition to classical and humanistic texts, they published all kinds of religious works and also secular works, like tales of chivalry.

French society in the late Middle Ages was far simpler structurally than it is today. It consisted mainly of peasants, who lived in the kingdom's 30,000 villages. A village was largely self-contained: if it looked outwards at all, it was only to the neighbouring parishes or to the nearest *bourg* with its market and lawcourt. Yet some peasants did venture further afield. Each year, for example, thousands of Auvergnats took up seasonal work in Spain while teams of Norman peasants helped to bring in the grain harvest in Beauce and the Ile-de-France. But most peasants stayed in or near their birthplace.

Each village had its own hierarchy. At the top was the *seigneur*, who was usually but not always a nobleman, for a *seigneurie* was purchasable like any other piece of property. It comprised a landed estate of variable size and a judicial area. The estate was usually in two parts: the demesne, which included the seigneur's house and the tribunal as well as the lands and woods he cultivated himself; and the *censives* or *tenures*, lands which he had entrusted in the past to peasants so that they might cultivate them more or less freely in return for numerous obligations, called *redevances*. The main one was the *cens*, an annual rent, often quite light, which was paid on a fixed day. The seigneur usually retained the mill, wine-press and oven, and expected to be paid for their use. He took a proportion of any land sold, exchanged or inherited by a *censitaire*, and exacted *champart*, a kind of seigneurial tithe, at harvest time. The seigneur also had certain judicial powers. Usually he had surrendered his criminal authority to the royal courts, but he continued to act in civil cases through his *bailli* and other officials. His court judged cases arising among the *censitaires* but also between them and himself. Almost inevitably in a country as large as France, *seigneuries* did not exist everywhere: in the centre and south there were freehold lands (*alleux*) which were totally free of seigneurial dominance. By contrast, Brittany and Burgundy were oppressively seigneurial.

The closing years of the Middle Ages witnessed two important social changes in the French countryside: a reduction in the wealth and authority of the seigneur, and the rise of a village aristocracy. During the period of agricultural recovery the seigneur had been obliged to make concessions to his tenants: new leases laid down precisely their obligations to the seigneur. By 1500 serfdom had all but disappeared. However, as the demographic rise created land hunger, the seigneurs tried to back-track on concessions, usually without success. At the same time, their authority was being eroded by the crown. A long series of royal enactments rode roughshod over local customs. The king's judges heard appeals from decisions taken in the seigneurial courts and pardons were often granted by the crown. Another blow to seigneurial prestige was the responsibility assigned to most village communities to allocate and collect the main direct tax, the *taille*.

The peasantry, too, underwent a significant transformation in the century after 1450. At the top of their social scale were the *fermiers or coqs de village*, who frequently acted as intermediaries between the seigneur and the rest of the peasants. With at least thirty hectares at his disposal, the *fermier* could produce in a year more than he needed to feed his family and pay his dues to the seigneur. The surplus enabled him to set up as a grain-merchant or cattle-breeder. He lent tools, seed and money to less fortunate peasants and offered them seasonal work or artisanal commissions. At the same time, the *fermier* collected leases, levied seigneurial dues and monopolized positions of influence in the village or parish. The rise of this village aristocracy did not affect the whole of France. The west, for example, was hardly touched by it; yet it was a development of great importance for the future.

Urban society was more varied, open and mobile than rural society. For one thing, it was continually being renewed: the death rate in towns was higher than in the countryside because of overcrowding and poor standards of hygiene. Even a mild epidemic could decimate a town, so that a regular flow of immigrants was essential to maintain and increase its population. Such incomers might include apprentices, journeymen, domestic servants, wet-nurses, students and clerics. They would converge on a town each day from the rural hinterland looking for a better life and perhaps opportunities of social advancement. Beggars came expecting more effective alms-giving, and the rural poor looking for work, when the rise in population reduced the chances of employment on the land. The number of immigrants could be huge. At Nantes, for example, the population might jump in one year from 20,000 to 30,000. Most immigrants helped to swell the ranks of the urban poor which remained vulnerable to any famine.

Contemporaries tended to divide urban society into two groups: the *aisés*, or well-to-do, and the *menu peuple*, or proletariat. The reality, however, was more complex. The well-to-do were themselves divided between merchants and office-holders. In towns like Bordeaux or Toulouse, which were important trading centres as well as having a parlement, these two groups were fairly evenly balanced, but in Lyon, where trade was all-important, merchants were pre-eminent. They lived in comfortable town houses and added to the profits of their trade the revenues from their estates in the neighbouring countryside. In towns which were primarily administrative centres, the office-holders were preponderant. They were often as rich as merchants, from whose ranks many of them had risen. The core of urban society consisted of artisans and small to middling merchants. They worked for themselves, served in the urban militia, paid taxes, participated in general assemblies of the commune, and owned enough property to guarantee their future security. Artisans were mainly of two kinds: those who employed large numbers of workmen and those who employed no labour other than their own families.

The lower stratum of urban society – the *menu peuple* – consisted of manual workers, who were excluded from any share in local government and lived in constant fear of hunger. They included journeymen, who were paid in money or money and kind, *manoeuvres* (paid by the day) and *gagne-deniers* (paid by the piece).

Whereas we tend to divide society into groups according to their place of residence, occupation or wealth, Frenchmen in the early sixteenth century used quite different criteria. They classified people, great and small, rich and poor, into one of three estates: clergy, nobility and third estate, which were regarded as divinely ordained and permanently fixed. Each estate had its distinctive function, life-style and privileges, which were acknowledged in both law and custom. Social peace rested on respect for this sacred hierarchy, yet the possibility was admitted that merit and/or wealth might enable an individual or family to pass from one estate into another.

Of the three estates, the most clearly defined was the clergy, whose members had to be ordained or at least to have taken minor orders. It had its own hierarchy and code of discipline. At the top were the archbishops, bishops, abbots and priors. Then came the canons of cathedrals and collegiate churches, and below them the great mass of parish priests, unbeneficed clergy, monks, friars and nuns. In terms of wealth the gulf between a prelate and a humble parish priest or *curé* was enormous. The bishop often disposed of large temporal revenues. Thus the bishop of Langres was also a duke, the *seigneur* of 100 villages and he owned seven châteaux. Seigneuries were also held by cathedral chapters and collegiate churches. By contrast, the humble *curé* was often desperately poor. The *dîme* or tithe paid to him by his parishioners was so meagre that he was often obliged to run a small business on the side or to serve as the seigneur's agent in order to make ends meet. Theoretically, under the Pragmatic Sanction of Bourges (1438), bishops and abbots were elected by their chapters, but in practice the church had difficulty resisting the demands of royal patronage. When the crown did not directly dispose of major benefices, elections were often disputed and the crown had to act as arbiter. Many lesser benefices were in the gift of a patron, ecclesiastical or lay. The secular clergy may have numbered 100,000, made up of about 100 bishops, many suffragan bishops and canons, about 30,000 parish priests and a huge crowd of unbeneficed clergy. The regular clergy cannot be quantified but was obviously substantial: there were 600 Benedictine abbeys, 400 mendicant houses, more than 100 commanderies of St John and 60 charterhouses.

The second estate, or nobility, was widely envied for its prestige and life-style. The noble condition was identified with perfection, while juridically and politically it implied a special status. Heredity was essential to the concept: a nobleman was born rather than made. Many nobles flaunted pedigrees going back to 'times immemorial'. Yet it was also possible for a nobleman to be created. The king could ennoble someone who had served him well. At first this was an exceptional favour, but in the fifteenth century the holders of certain offices (for instance royal notaries and secretaries) were automatically ennobled and the practice spread to other offices. This development was accompanied by the widespread acquisition of *seigneuries* by office-holders. Some nobles simply usurped their status by 'living nobly' (i.e. avoiding any business activity), holding a public office, fighting for the king, owning a fief or *seigneurie* and living in a house large enough to be a manor. But a false nobleman had to ensure that his name was dropped from the tax rolls over a long period so that, if his claim to tax exemption was challenged, he could summon witnesses who would testify that his family had lived nobly for as long as anyone could remember. It is impossible to quantify the nobility exactly, but it may have numbered between 120,000 and 200,000.

The bulk of France's population consisted of the third estate, made up of people of widely different fortunes and occupations. Seyssel in his *La Monarchie de France* (1519) made a useful distinction between middling people (*peuple moyen*) and the lesser folk (*peuple menu*). The former, he explained, were merchants and officers of finance and justice. The *peuple menu* were people principally engaged in 'the cultivation of the land, the mechanical arts and other inferior crafts'. Seyssel believed that such people should not be 'in too great liberty or immeasurably rich and especially not generally trained in the use of arms', otherwise they might be tempted to rise against their betters. The third estate had its own hierarchy defined by custom and expressed in certain honorific titles, such as *noble homme* or *honorable homme*, in notarial documents, but most Frenchmen did not qualify for such titles. As one historian has written: 'four-fifths of Francis I's subjects fell into anonymity'.

The government of France

At a meeting of the Estates-General in 1484 Philippe Pot, representing the Burgundian nobility, described kingship as 'the dignity, not the property, of the prince'. The crown, according to the jurists, was handed down to the nearest male kinsman of the deceased monarch. The king was not free to give it away or to bequeath it to anyone; he was only the temporary holder of a public office. Yet the concept of the king as head of the state already existed. The word 'state' did not come into current usage till the mid-sixteenth century, but the idea existed under the name of 'commonwealth' (*chose publique*) or 'republic'. Although official documents distinguished between the king and the state, the interests of both were closely identified. Thus in 1517, Chancellor Duprat said: 'The kingdom's interest is the king's interest, and the king's interest is the kingdom's interest. For it is a mystical body of which the king is the head.' As head of state, the king was not bound to assume the obligations entered upon by his predecessors; the debts of a king could be legitimately repudiated by his successor. A corporation or individual holding privileges from the crown needed to have them confirmed at the start of a new reign. The same rule applied to office-holders.

'The king never dies'. This adage embodied an important principle of French constitutional law: the king succeeded from the instant of his predecessor's death. No interregnum, however brief, was deemed possible. Nor could a lawful king be denied the full exercise of his authority for reasons of age or health. If he were a minor or unfit to rule for some other reason, his authority was exercised in his name by his council, although in practice a regent was appointed. Contemporary opinion favoured the king's nearest adult male kinsman for this role, but in the sixteenth century it was repeatedly filled by a woman: Louise of Savoy under Francis I and Catherine de' Medici under Charles IX.

In the sixteenth century the coronation or *sacre* at Reims was no longer regarded as essential to the exercise of kingship, yet it remained important as a symbol of the supernatural powers of kingship and of the close alliance between church and state. The coronation service began with the oath. Standing over the Gospels, the king promised to promote peace in Christendom, to protect Christians against injury, to dispense justice fairly and mercifully, and to expel heretics from his dominions. This was followed by the anointing, the most important part of the ceremony. Thrusting his hand through slits in the king's garment, the archbishop of Reims anointed his body with a chrism allegedly handed down from heaven by a dove at the baptism of King Clovis in 496 and used ever since to consecrate France's kings. The anointing set the king apart from other men, giving him a quasi-sacerdotal character. Although no French king ever claimed the right to celebrate mass, he did take communion in both kinds, a privilege enjoyed only by priests.

By virtue of his anointing the king of France, who bore the title of 'Most Christian King', was deemed to possess thaumaturgical powers, that is to say powers of healing the sick. The only other Christian ruler to claim this power was the king of England. In time, it became restricted to the curing of scrofula, or tuberculosis of the lymph nodes on the side of the neck, a disease more repulsive than dangerous and subject to periods of remission.

The king touched the victim's sores and tumours with his bare hands, and, making the sign of the cross, said: 'The king touches you and God cures you.' Each victim was then given two small silver coins.

France at the end of the Middle Ages was still a largely feudal country: many towns, corporations and individuals enjoyed a degree of autonomy, regarding themselves as parties to a contract in which mutual obligations were laid down and complete submission to the king was ruled out. But a school of thought existed which advocated royal absolutism. Its chief exponents were the royal jurists, who found in Roman law the idea of absolute power vested in one man and of subjects equally subservient to him. The doctrine was backed up by the Christian concept of the king as God's vicegerent on earth. It was claimed that he could legislate, dispense justice, revoke all lawsuits to his own court, levy taxes and create offices. He could also annul any concession detracting from his authority, and local privileges could survive only if he chose to renew them at his accession. The authority of Cicero was invoked to show that the king was entitled to sacrifice private interest to the public good.

Roman legal concepts, as elaborated by medieval commentators, were accepted in sixteenth-century France. Jurists identified the king with the Roman *princeps* and declared him to be emperor within his own kingdom. This simply meant that he was independent of both pope and Holy Roman Emperor in temporal matters. The idea of his absolute authority was universally accepted in French law, but he was not expected to rule absolutely without his subjects' consent as expressed through certain institutions, notably the Parlement of Paris, which was commonly regarded as the modern equivalent of the ancient Roman Senate.

The best-known statement of the constitutionalism that prevailed in sixteenth-century France was *La Monarchie de France* by Claude de Seyssel, who became bishop of Marseille after long years of service to the crown as a councillor, administrator and diplomat. Like Machiavelli he was a realist, who viewed politics as a science distinct from morality and religion. Being an Aristotelian, he valued moderation in a constitution, and believed that the French kings owed their greatness to their voluntary acceptance of three constraints (*freins*) – religion, justice and *la police* – on their power. Writing of justice, Seyssel affirms that it is 'better authorized in France than in any other country we know in all the world. This is especially owing to the parlements, which have been instituted to put a bridle on the absolute power that our kings would have wished to use.'

However absolute, the monarch needed an administrative machinery at the centre of the kingdom and in the localities, to carry out his policies. Its chief component was the king's council, which in 1500 was still evolving. In theory its members comprised the princes of the blood, the peers of the realm and the great officers of state, but in practice admission was by royal invitation. Before 1526 the council was a large body. Between August 1484 and January 1485 there were 120 councillors, but only a small proportion of them attended with any degree of frequency. It is likely that a core of working councillors existed within the larger body. In 1502 this core consisted of only four members, of whom three belonged to the house of Amboise. Financial business was apparently dealt with separately by experts, who nevertheless continued to attend the council when non-financial matters were being discussed, The council might also divide for administrative convenience. Thus in 1494 part of the council followed Charles VIII to Italy while the rest stayed in Moulins with Pierre de Bourbon. The situation has been described as 'one of relative informality and of response to immediate royal needs. Some councillors were specialists and the disposition of personnel in terms of location was fluid, but these were not structural arrangements within the council as an institution.'

There were many routes to membership of the council: birth, skill in law, diplomacy or administration, regional importance, ecclesiastical dignity and the influence of patrons and relatives. Councillors served at the king's pleasure, not for life, and membership was not hereditary. Some councillors served under all three kings from 1483 to 1526, but membership was usually for shorter periods. The council was not only a point of contact between the crown, the nobility and local communities; it was also a tool which the crown used to secure the obedience of the governing classes and to arbitrate between them.

The body responsible for turning the council's decisions into laws was the chancery, headed by the Chancellor of France. He was invariably an eminent jurist, who had served his apprenticeship in a parlement, and sometimes he was also a high-ranking churchman. His powers and duties ranged more widely than those of any other great officer of the crown. In effect, he was a kind of prime minister. As head of the royal chancery, he kept the Great Seal and other seals of state. All documents emanating from the king and his council were drawn up in the chancery and sealed in the chancellor's presence. He had to ensure that the text of each document matched the orders received, and could refuse to seal any that seemed incorrect. This power, moreover, extended to all the other chanceries in the kingdom, including those of the 'sovereign courts'. The chancellor's authority was, therefore, nation-wide. His influence on legislation was also crucial. He exercised it not only as a councillor but also by drafting royal edicts himself. As head of the judicial administration, he was by right entitled to preside over any sovereign court, including the parlement. He appointed judges and received their oaths of office unless they had already sworn them before the king. The chancellor attended the king's council regularly and took the chair in the king's absence. He helped to determine policies and explained them, if necessary, to the parlement. Now and again he served on major diplomatic missions. He was appointed for life by the king, but, if necessary, his functions could be performed by a Keeper of the Seals, who did not have his prestige or influence.

The chancery was the nearest equivalent to a modern ministry. In 1500 it had a staff of 120 which grew even larger during the sixteenth century. Unlike the 'sovereign courts', it continued to follow the king on his travels. Originally, all the chancery clerks drew up documents to be sealed by the great seal, but during the Middle Ages they began to specialize: the *clercs du secret* drafted documents emanating directly from the king; in time they became known as secretaries. Under an ordinance of 1482 notaries of the chancery were effectively granted a monopoly of drawing up and signing all royal acts, chancery letters, conciliar decisions and decrees of the 'sovereign courts'. They were automatically ennobled and enjoyed the privilege of *committimus* as well as numerous tax exemptions. The quantity of documents processed by them was enormous.

Closely associated with the chancellor were the masters of requests (*maîtres des requêtes de l'hôtel*). There were eight of them about 1500, but their number increased rapidly thereafter. Under an edict of 1493 they were authorized to preside at the courts of the *bailliages* and *sénéchaussées*, to receive complaints against local officials and to correct abuses. They could preside at the *Grand conseil* and sit in the parlement, where they ranked immediately below the presidents. The masters of requests were often given temporary commissions in financial, diplomatic and judicial affairs. They were the ancestors of the *intendants*, who became the principal agents of royal centralization in the seventeenth century.

The Great Council (*Grand conseil*) was an exclusively judicial body which had taken over part of the work formerly exercised by the king's council: it investigated complaints against royal officials, intervened in conflicts of jurisdiction between other courts and could revoke enactments that the parlement had registered. It also acted as a court of appeal and of first instance for a wide range of lawsuits. Though the Great Council's procedure was fairly simple and relatively cheap, it had one serious disadvantage for suitors: like the king's council, it continued to follow the king on his travels through the kingdom. It carried its records around, and suitors had to change their lawyers as it moved from place to place. Because of its closeness to the king's person, the Great Council was more susceptible to his influence than was the parlement, and he often used it to bend the law to his interest.

The king of France was first and foremost a judge, and the earliest form of royal intervention at the local level had been the establishment of officials charged with exercising justice in his name. At the bottom of the hierarchy, but above the judges of the feudal courts, were magistrates, called *prévôts*, *viguiers* or *vicomtes*, whose powers were limited to the simplest cases. The basic unit of local government was the *bailliage* (sometimes called *sénéchaussée*). The kingdom comprised about 100 such units, which could vary enormously in size. By the sixteenth century, the official in charge of the *bailliage*, the *bailli* (or *sénéchal*), had purely honorific or military duties (for example, he summoned the feudal levy, called the *ban et arrière-ban*), but the tribunal of the *bailliage*, under the *bailli*'s deputy or *lieutenant* and his staff, was a hive of activity, bustling with barristers, solicitors, sergeants and ushers. The *bailliage* judged on appeal cases sent up from inferior courts and in first instance cases concerning privileged persons or *cas royaux*. These were crimes committed against the king's person, rights and demesne, ranging from treason and *lèse-majesté* to rape and highway robbery. In addition to their judicial competence, the *bailliages* had important administrative powers: they published royal statutes and issued decrees of their own.

Above the *bailliages* were the *parlements* of which there were seven in 1500: Paris, Toulouse, Grenoble, Bordeaux, Dijon, Rouen and Aix-en-Provence. The oldest and most prestigious was the Parlement of Paris which had 'gone out of court' in the thirteenth century and was now permanently based in Paris in the old royal palace on the Ile de la Cité. Though separate from the king's council, the parlement was still considered to be part of it: thus peers of the realm were entitled to sit in it and when the king came to the parlement, accompanied by his ministers and advisers to hold a *lit de justice*, the old *Curia regis* was in effect reconstituted for the occasion. The parlement's view of royal absolutism differed from the king's: while admitting that authority resided in the king's person, it did not believe that he could treat the kingdom as he liked. He was its administrator, not its owner, and was bound to observe the so-called 'fundamental laws' governing the succession to the throne and preservation of the royal demesne. The parlement's view implied a distinction between the sovereign as an ideal and the fallible creature who occupied the throne. It saw its own function as that of protecting the interests of the ideal sovereign from the errors that the human king might commit. The parlement's magistrates liked to compare themselves to the senators of ancient Rome, an analogy resented by the king. In 1500 the Parlement of Paris consisted of five chambers: the *Grand' chambre*, two *Chambres des enquêtes*, the *Chambre des requêtes* and the *Tournelle criminelle*, with a combined personnel of about sixty lay and clerical councillors.

Originally, the parlement's *ressort* or area of jurisdiction had been the whole kingdom, but as this had been enlarged a number of provincial parlements had been created. Yet the Parlement of Paris retained control of two-thirds of the kingdom. It was responsible for the whole of France, excluding Normandy, as far south as the Lyonnais and Upper Auvergne. Within this area it judged a wide variety of cases in first instance and on appeal. But it was not just a court of law: it regulated such matters as public hygiene or the upkeep of roads, bridges and quays; it ensured that Paris received enough grain and fuel, controlled the quality, weight and price of bread, fixed wages and hours of work, punished shoddy workmanship, and intervened in academic matters. As printing came into its own, the parlement began to control the book trade. Not even the church escaped its vigilance. No papal bull could be applied to France if it had not been registered by the parlement. The court also kept an eye on the conduct of royal officials in the provinces.

Finally, the parlement played a significant role in politics by ratifying royal legislation. If it found an enactment satisfactory, this was registered and published forthwith; if not, the parlement submitted remonstrances (*remontrances*) to the king, either verbally or in writing, whereupon he would either modify the enactment or issue a *lettre de jussion* ordering the court to register the act as it stood without delay. Such a move might lead to more remonstrances and more *lettres de jussion*. In the end, if the parlement remained obdurate, the king would hold a *lit de justice*, that is to say, he would resume the authority he had delegated to the parlement by coming to the court in person and presiding over the registration of the controversial measure himself. Only the *Grand' chambre* was entitled to register royal enactments or issue decrees (*arrêts*). Its official head was the chancellor of France, but its effective head was the First President (*Premier président*) of the parlement, who was assisted by three other presidents and about thirty lay and clerical councillors.

The provincial parlements developed out of the courts that had existed in the great fiefs before their absorption into the kingdom. Modelled on the Paris parlement, they exercised a similar jurisdiction within their respective areas. All claimed equality of authority and jurisdiction with the Parlement of Paris, but the latter had privileges that made it unique. Each parlement was sovereign within its own area in respect of registering royal enactments: thus a law registered by the Parlement of Paris could not be applied in Languedoc unless it had been registered by the Parlement of Toulouse.

A major figure in French local government around 1500 was the provincial governor. There were eleven governorships (*gouvernements*) corresponding roughly with the kingdom's border provinces. The governors were normally recruited from princes of the blood and high nobility. Although closely identified with the person and authority of the monarch, the governor was only a commissioner who could be revoked at the king's will. His powers, as laid out in his commission or letters of provision, were seldom clearly defined. While it was customary for his military responsibilities, such as the securing of fortresses and the supplying or disciplining of troops, to be stressed, there was also often a clause open to wide interpretation. Thus in 1515, Odet de Foix, governor of Guyenne, was instructed 'generally to do . . . all that we would see and recognize as necessary for the good of ourselves and our affairs . . .' which amounted to a general delegation of royal authority. But the commissions lacked uniformity: the king, it seems, was more concerned with adapting to local circumstances than establishing functional harmony among his senior provincial representatives. A governor seldom resided in his province as he was often at court or fighting for the king. The exercise of his local duties was therefore delegated to a *lieutenant*, who was usually a lesser nobleman or prelate. But a governor could still do much for his province, even at a distance. He could, for example, ensure that its grievances received the attention of the king's council.

A governor's presence at court gave him unique opportunities of patronage which he might use to build up a powerful clientele within his province. This comprised three elements: the regular army (*compagnies d'ordonnance*), household officers and servants, and local gentlemen. Nearly all the governors were captains of the *gendarmerie* – the heavily armoured cavalry – and as such controlled recruitment and promotion within its ranks. A governor also had a large private household which provided employment for local noblemen and education for their children. All of this clearly made him potentially dangerous to the crown, for he might use his personal following within his province to undermine royal authority.

The most complex and least efficient part of French government at the end of the Middle Ages was the fiscal administration. This was built essentially around two kinds of revenue: the 'ordinary' revenue (*finances ordinaires*), which the king drew from his demesne, and the 'extraordinary' revenue (*finances extraordinaires*) which he got from taxation. The 'extraordinary' revenue owed its name to the fact that originally it had been levied for a special purpose and for a limited time, usually in wartime. By 1500, however, it came from regular taxes levied in peace and war. The 'ordinary' revenue consisted not only of fixed and predictable feudal rents, but also of a wide range of variable dues owed to the king as suzerain.

The 'extraordinary' revenue comprised three main taxes: the *taille*, the *gabelle* and the *aides*. The *taille* was the only direct tax. It was levied annually, the amount being decided by the king's council, and it could be supplemented by a *crue* or surtax. There were two sorts of *taille*: the *taille réelle* was a land tax payable by everyone irrespective of social rank, and the *taille personnelle* fell mainly on land owned by unprivileged commoners. The former was obviously fairer, but it was found only in a few areas, notably Provence and Languedoc. The nobility and clergy were exempt from the *taille*, but it does not follow that all the rest of society was liable. Many professional groups (for example, royal officials, military personnel, municipal officials, lawyers, university teachers and students) were exempt, as were a large number of towns, called *villes franches*, including Paris.

Thus if the peasantry was *taillable*, the same was not true of the bourgeoisie as a whole.

The *gabelle* was a tax on salt. By the late Middle Ages the salt trade had become so important in France that the crown decided to take a share of the profits by controlling its sale and distribution. But royal control was strongest in the northern and central provinces (*pays de grandes gabelles*), which had constituted the demesne of King Charles V (1346–80). Here the salt was taken to royal warehouses (*greniers à sel*), where it was weighed and allowed to dry, usually for two years. It was then weighed again and taxed before the merchant who owned it was allowed to sell it. As a safeguard against illicit trading in salt, the crown introduced the system of *sel par impôt*, whereby every household had to purchase from a royal warehouse enough salt for its average needs. Outside the *pays de grandes gabelles*, the salt tax was levied in different ways: in the west of France it was a quarter or a fifth of the sale price, while in the south a tariff was levied as the salt passed through royal warehouses situated along the coast near areas of production.

The *aides* were duties levied on various commodities sold regularly and in large quantities. The rate of tax was one *sou* per *livre* on all merchandise sold wholesale or retail, except wine and other beverages which were taxed both ways. An important *aide* was the levy on livestock raised in many towns; another was the *aide* on wine, called *vingtième et huitième*. But indirect taxation was, like the *taille*, subject to local variations; several parts of France were exempt from the *aides*.

The usual method of tax collection in respect of the *taille* was for the leading men of a parish to elect from among themselves an assessor and a collector. The assessment, once completed, was read out in church by the local priest; a week later the parishioners paid their taxes to the collector as they left church. The assessor and collector were not inclined to be lenient, for they were liable to be imprisoned or to have their property sequestered if the sum collected fell short of the anticipated total. Indirect taxes were usually farmed by the highest bidder at an auction.

The most lucrative tax was the *taille*, which amounted to 2.4 million *livres* out of a total revenue of 4.9 million in 1515. It was followed by the *aides*, which brought in about a third of the *taille*. As for the *gabelle*, it was bringing in 284,000 *livres* (about six per cent of the total revenue).

The fiscal administration in 1500, like the tax system, had not changed since the reign of Charles VII (1422–61). It comprised two administrations corresponding with the two kinds of revenue. The *Trésor*, which was responsible for the 'ordinary' revenue, was under four *trésoriers de France* who had very wide powers. Each was responsible for one of four areas, called respectively Languedoïl, Languedoc, Normandy and Outre-Seine-et-Yonne. The *trésoriers* supervised the collection and disbursement of revenues, but did not handle them. This task was left to the *receveurs ordinaires*, who were each responsible for a subdivision of the *bailliage*. The receiver-general for all revenues from the demesne was the *changeur du Trésor*, who was based in Paris, but only a small proportion of the revenues actually reached him, for the crown settled many debts by means of warrants (*décharges*) assigned on a local treasurer. This avoided the expense and risk of transporting large amounts of cash along dangerous, bandit-infested roads, while passing on the recovery costs to the creditor.

The four *généraux des finances*, who had charge of the 'extraordinary' revenues, had virtually the same powers as the *trésoriers de France*, each being responsible for an area, called *généralité*. These were subdivided into *élections*, of which there were 85 in 1500, but in general there were no *élections* in areas which had retained their representative estates (*pays d'états*). The *élection* owed its name to the *élu*, an official whose main function was to carry out regular tours of inspection (*chevauchées*) of his district, checking its ability to pay and the trustworthiness of his underlings.

The personnel responsible for the administration of the *gabelles* varied according to the different kinds of salt tax. In the *pays de grandes gabelles*, each royal warehouse was under a *grenetier* assisted by a *contrôleur*; elsewhere the tax was farmed out by commissioners.

On the same level as the *changeur du Trésor* and performing the same duties, though in respect of the 'extraordinary' revenue, were the four *receveurs généraux des finances*, one for each *généralité*.

The two fiscal administrations were not entirely separate, for the *trésoriers de France* and *généraux des finances* (known collectively as *gens des finances*) were expected to reside at court whenever they were not carrying out inspections of their respective areas. They formed a financial committee, which met regularly and independently of the king's council, and were empowered to take certain decisions on their own. They also attended the king's council whenever important financial matters were discussed. However, their most important duty was to draw up at the start of each year a sort of national budget (*état général par estimation*), based on accounts sent in by each financial district.

Popular representation

The French monarchy after the Hundred Years War was stronger than it had been earlier, when it had had to share power with the great feudal magnates, yet it was not strong enough to ignore the traditional rights and privileges of its subjects. The king's army rarely reached 25,000 men in peacetime and twice that number in war. Such a force could not be expected to hold down a population of around 15 million, particularly as the king could not depend on the loyalty of his troops; mercenaries were notoriously unreliable. The royal civil service was also minute by modern standards. In 1505 there were only 12,000 officials, or one for each 1250 inhabitants. Consequently, the monarchy could be effective only by enlisting the co-operation of its subjects. This could be done in various ways: by protecting their privileges, by keeping in close contact with them, by controlling a vast system of patronage and by using representative institutions.

At the national level the only representative institution was the Estates-General, made up of elected representatives of the three estates: clergy, nobility and third estate. But the king was under no statutory obligation to call them and in 1484 during the minority of Charles VIII they met for the last time before 1560. It does not follow that the people ceased to have a voice. At the national level, the king often called meetings of one or two estates to discuss particular questions, although such assemblies seem to have been primarily intended for propaganda purposes. As Russell Major has written, they 'served more to keep alive the idea that the wise king acted only upon the advice of his leading subjects than they did to develop new deliberative techniques'.

However, many French provinces continued to have representative estates of their own during the long period when the Estates-General were in abeyance. They were known as *pays d'états* and the principal ones were Normandy, Languedoc, Dauphiné, Burgundy, Provence and Brittany. Most of the estates consisted of prelates, nobles with fiefs and representatives of the chief towns, but there were numerous exceptions. In Languedoc, for instance, only the bishops and 22 noblemen were allowed to represent their respective estates. At the opposite end, there were local assemblies where only villages and small towns were represented. The estates depended for their existence on the king: he called them, fixed the date and place of their meeting, appointed their president and determined their agenda. Royal commissioners put forward demands, negotiated with the delegates and met some of their demands. Usually the estates met once a year, but they could meet more often. The estates did not exist simply to vote taxes demanded by the king. Through the petitions they submitted to him, they could have an influence on his policies. They played a major role in legal, legislative and administrative matters. The codification of customs, for example, was done in assemblies of the estates. They had their own perma-nent staff supported out of special taxes. The estates apportioned and col-lected royal taxes within their province; they also voted money to build roads and bridges and to support various activities beneficial to the local economy. They raised troops, repaired fortifications, built hospitals and engaged in poor relief.

2

The Minority Rule of
Charles VIII, 1483–94

When Louis XI died on 30 August 1483, his son Charles was only thirteen years old – ten months short of the age of majority for a king of France as laid down by an ordinance of 1374. It was consequently necessary to provide a regent for the intervening period. Four people could claim this role: the queen mother, Charlotte of Savoy; the king's cousin, Louis duc d'Orléans; and the king's sister and brother-in-law, Anne and Pierre de Beaujeu. Charlotte could point to the precedent set by Blanche de Castille during the minority of Louis IX, but she was a meek woman who had been allowed only a minor political role by the late king. Orléans was old enough to rule (he was twenty-two years old), but lacked the necessary qualities, being flighty, dissolute and a spendthrift. Anne and Pierre de Beaujeu were better qualified. Anne, who was also twenty-two years old, was intelligent and proud, albeit vindictive and grasping. Her husband Pierre was her senior by twenty-one years and had gained administrative experience under Louis XI. The Beaujeus had important advantages over their rivals: they had custody of the young king and enjoyed the support of the royal civil service; but they could not be sure of the military backing of the great nobles.

Not much is known about the first year of Charles VIII's reign. Historians have generally assumed that the Beaujeus kept a tenuous hold on the government till the duc d'Orléans fled from the court in 1485. This has been questioned by J. Russell Major, who believes that the Beaujeus were 'supplanted' by a council made up of great nobles and their protégés. 'Supplanted' seems too strong a word. The Beaujeus retained control while having to co-operate with members of the nobility. Their rival, Louis d'Orléans, became president of the king's council and lieutenant-general of the Ile-de-France. His uncle, Dunois, was appointed governor of Dauphiné, Valentinois and Diois. Within their orbit were Charles comte d'Angoulême,

who was next in line to the throne after Louis, and Jean de Foix, vicomte
de Narbonne and comte d'Etampes. Jean duc de Bourbon, elder brother of
Pierre de Beaujeu, was showered with favours: he became lieutenant-general
of the kingdom, constable of France and governor of Languedoc. Among
other prominent nobles who flocked to the court of Charles VIII in 1483
in quest of offices, privileges, gifts and pensions were René II, duc de Lorraine, Alain le Grand, sire d'Albret and Philippe of Savoy, comte de Bresse.

The Estates-General of 1484

The decision to call the Estates-General was taken soon after the death of
Louis XI, no one knows by whom. Some historians believe that it was
taken by Louis d'Orléans at the instigation of Dunois; others ascribe the
responsibility to the Beaujeus. Both parties needed popular support. The
estates were due to meet at Orléans on 1 January 1484, but they were
moved to Tours because of the threat of plague and did not begin till 15
January. The 287 deputies were drawn from all parts of the kingdom. They
were elected in the various *bailliages* and *sénéchaussées* without, it seems,
any undue pressure being exerted on the electors by Orléans or the Beaujeus.
'When all is said', writes Major, 'neither side made a concerted effort to
influence all the elections or to bribe all the deputies when once they were
chosen.' Among them was Jean Masselin, who has left us a uniquely
detailed, if somewhat one-sided, account of the proceedings; another was
Philippe Pot, *sénéchal* of Burgundy, who made a remarkable speech on 9
February.

The estates opened, as was the custom, with a speech from the Chancellor
of France, Guillaume de Rochefort. The French people, he said, had always
been devoted to their rulers, unlike the English who had just crowned the
murderer of Edward IV's young sons, Richard III. He tried to calm the
deputies' fears about the age of their own monarch. Such was the trust that
the king placed in them that he would ask them to share in the government:
they were to inform him of their grievances, report any oppression by public
officials, and advise on how peace, justice and good government might be
achieved.

After dividing into six sections, the deputies set up a committee to prepare
a general *cahier* for presentation to the king. This was read out on 2
February. It contained a sweeping denunciation of the government of Louis
XI and a call for a return to the practices of Charles VII. The clergy wanted
the Pragmatic Sanction of Bourges to be enforced. The nobility complained
that they were being impoverished by excessive use of the feudal levy (*ban
et arrière-ban*). They wanted to see foreigners excluded from military commands and from offices in the royal household. They also complained of

infringements of their hunting rights by royal officials. Poverty loomed large
in the third estate's submission: the current scarcity of money was blamed
on wars and the export of bullion to Rome; taxation was described as
excessive. The king was urged to remove the need for the *taille* by revoking
all alienations of domain made by his father, reducing the size of the army,
stopping or curbing pensions and decreasing the number and pay of royal
officials. The longest chapter of the *cahier* was concerned with justice: it
called for the replacement of officials who had been appointed by Louis XI
out of favour rather than on merit.

The government of the kingdom was also considered by the estates. The
Beaujeus were anxious to prevent Louis d'Orléans becoming regent and
their cause was championed by Philippe Pot on 9 February. 'The throne',
he declared, 'is an office of dignity, not an hereditary possession, and as
such it does not pass to the nearest relatives in the way a patrimony passes
to its natural guardians. If, then, the commonwealth is not to be bereft of
government, its care must devolve upon the Estates-General of the realm,
whose duty is not to administer it themselves, but to entrust its administration to worthy hands.' A Norman deputy put forward Orléans's claim:
'If the king needs a governor and tutor, or, as it is said, a regent, the duke
intends no one other than himself to hold that office.' Having listened to
both sides, the deputies decided that 'the lord and lady of Beaujeu should
remain with the king as they have been hitherto'. The king was given neither
regent nor tutor, his intellectual maturity being deemed sufficient. In the
chancellor's words: 'Our king, young as he is, is of an extraordinary wisdom
and seriousness.' On 6 February the estates were given a list of possible
members of the king's council, but they left the choice to the monarch and
the princes.

The assembly of 1484 exerted relatively little influence on the future
development of France, but the deputies were reasonably satisfied with their
achievements. The *taille*, which had reached 4.5 million *livres* under Louis
XI, was reduced to 1,500,000 *livres*. The nobility regained hunting rights
on their own lands. Only the clergy were disappointed: their efforts to get
the Pragmatic Sanction reinstated were successfully opposed by a pro-papal
lobby of cardinals and prelates.

The Estates-General came to an end on 7 March. Orléans felt disgruntled
that he had not been given the regency. In May he was awarded the lands
of Olivier le Daim, Louis XI's hated barber, but this was not enough to
satisfy him. He continued to intrigue with the duke of Brittany, Richard
III of England and Maximilian of Habsburg, who ruled Austria and the
Netherlands. However, the threat inherent in such a coalition was temporarily averted by the recall of the nobles to attend the coronation of Charles
VIII on 30 May. But a new danger arose for the Beaujeus. The young king
became infatuated with Orléans's athletic prowess and may have pleaded

to be rid of his sister's domination. The duke plotted to abduct Charles, but was forestalled by the Beaujeus who fled with the king from Paris to the security of the small fortified town of Montargis. Here various members of the Orléans faction were dismissed from court. The duke, after protesting about this action, retired to his *gouvernement* of Ile-de-France.

The 'Mad War', 1487–8

The princely revolts, which cast a shadow across the early years of Charles VIII's reign, have sometimes been read as the sequel to the War of the Public Weal of 1465. The two movements, however, were quite different. The rising of 1465 had been aimed at Louis XI's overthrow and had lasted only a few months. The Mad War (*Guerre folle*), by contrast, was not directed at Charles VIII but at the Beaujeus; it also developed surreptitiously over a period of two years, erupting in 1487. A major reason for the long gestation was the independence of the duchy of Brittany, which offered a safe haven to malcontents from the French court. The rising was given its pejorative name soon afterwards by the contemporary historian Paolo Emilio, in his *De rebus gestis Francorum*.

Brittany's independence of France manifested itself in various ways. Duke Francis II had paid only a simple homage to King Louis XI which entailed none of the obligations customarily incumbent on a vassal to his suzerain; he had not even gone this far in respect of Charles VIII. Brittany seemed bent on becoming a second Burgundy. Yet it was poor, and militarily far inferior to its French neighbour; it could only hope to defend itself by calling in foreign help, especially from England. But paradoxically the duchy's independence was undermined by its own subjects, for many Breton nobles chose to serve the king of France, attaching themselves to his court. They retained important estates in Brittany and longed to unite the duchy to the kingdom which provided them with offices, honours and wealth. Another Breton weakness was Duke Francis II, a feckless dilettante who became senile about 1484. His only offspring were two daughters, Anne and Isabeau. The affairs of the duchy fell into the hands of Pierre Landais, its treasurer and a much hated parvenu.

In October 1484 the Breton exiles in France came to an agreement at Montargis with the French government. They swore to recognize Charles VIII as their duke's successor, should the latter die without male issue. The king, for his part, promised to respect Breton privileges and to arrange good marriages for the duke's two daughters. Francis's riposte was to take an oath from his subjects acknowledging his daughters as his heirs. On 23 November he also made a treaty with Louis d'Orléans aimed at freeing Charles VIII from Beaujeu tutelage. The duke, at the same time, won the support of a number of French malcontents and courted the Parisians. Early in 1485, Dunois, Orléans's evil genius, produced a manifesto condemning the government's financial management. Orléans begged Charles to emancipate himself from the Beaujeus and return to Paris. The king refused, whereupon Orléans left the capital and started raising troops. He appealed to all his friends, including Francis II, for armed assistance, but the first fires of rebellion were soon put out by the Beaujeus. In February, Charles VIII returned to Paris and measures were taken against the rebels: Orléans was deprived of his governorships of Ile-de-France and Champagne, and Dunois of that of Dauphiné. On 23 March the duke made his submission and was readmitted to the council.

Orléans, however, was biding his time. On 30 August he issued a new manifesto critical of the government's financial policy. In league with him were Beaujeu's brother Jean, Constable of Bourbon, the comte d'Angoulême, the comte d'Etampes, Cardinal Pierre de Foix, the sire d'Albret and, of course, Dunois. The rebels hoped to have a larger army than the Beaujeus, who had just sent 4000 men to help Henry Tudor gain the English throne; but their hopes were soon dashed. Charles VIII besieged Orléans and Dunois in Beaugency and within a week the revolt was over. By mid-September the duke was again penitent and had to accept royal garrisons in the towns of his apanage. Dunois lost his office of great chamberlain and was banished to Asti for a year. Bourbon and the other rebels also capitulated. The Peace of Bourges (2 November) gave France several months of domestic tranquillity.

In June 1486, Maximilian of Habsburg, who had recently been elected King of the Romans, launched a surprise attack on France's northern border. It soon ran out of steam because Maximilian was, as usual, unable to pay his troops, but it triggered off another rebellion within France. The pretext was again fiscal: the Beaujeus had imposed a new *crue de taille* of 300,000 *livres* in October. In January 1487, Orléans joined Dunois in Brittany, but Charles VIII and Anne de Beaujeu decided to deal with the rebels in Guyenne before attending to Brittany. Their campaign, which lasted a month and a half, comprised a series of successful sieges. The leading rebel in the southwest, Charles d'Angoulême, surrendered on 19 March and was married off to Louise of Savoy. The future King Francis I was their son.

The Breton Wars, 1487–91

In March 1487 an important treaty was signed at Châteaubriant between the king of France and some sixty Breton nobles, led by Marshal de Rieux. The king promised to supply them with an army of not more than 400 lances and 4000 foot, and to withdraw it once the French rebels left Brittany. Charles also undertook not to attack Duke Francis in person or any town where he might be residing. The Bretons, for their part, agreed to serve in the king's army. But the Beaujeus were keen to overrun Brittany swiftly before any foreign power could come to its aid. In May a French army, much larger than that envisaged in the treaty, moved into the duchy. By 1 June it had reached Vannes, forcing the dukes of Brittany and Orléans to escape by sea to Nantes. On 19 June the French broke the treaty again by laying siege to Nantes. The operation was directed by Charles VIII from his headquarters at Ancenis. On 6 August, however, the siege was lifted, possibly because word had reached the king of Rieux's impending betrayal. On 20 February 1488, after returning to Paris, Charles presided over a meeting of the parlement which sentenced Orléans to the confiscation of all his property and also punished his accomplices. From the government's point of view these were timely confiscations, since it was in urgent need of money.

Early in 1488, Rieux recaptured most of the Breton towns that had fallen into French hands. On 11 March, La Trémoïlle was appointed by Charles as his lieutenant-general in the duchy. Their correspondence survives, revealing the king, though still only eighteen, in full charge of military operations from his headquarters in Anjou: he gathered in supplies, armaments and troops and sent them into Brittany. The decisive phase of the campaign began when La Trémoïlle captured Châteaubriant. Fougères, which was reputed impregnable, fell to the French on 19 July. The Bretons received some armed assistance from the sire d'Albret, but nothing from Henry VII of England or from Maximilian. On 28 July the French won a decisive victory at Saint-Aubin-du-Cormier, capturing the duc d'Orléans along with many Bretons.

The Bretons sued for peace soon afterwards, but a majority of the French king's council wanted to press on with the war; they reckoned that Brittany would be conquered in a month. The chancellor, however, warned against alienating the Bretons by using violence instead of investigating the legal rights of both sides, and the king, rather surprisingly, accepted this view. Peace was accordingly signed at Le Verger on 20 August. In exchange for the withdrawal of the French army from Brittany, Francis II promised to expel all foreign troops from his own soil. He also agreed not to marry his daughters without Charles VIII's consent and to hand over four Breton towns to the French as securities, pending an examination of the claims of both parties. A few days later he died.

Anne, the duke's elder daughter, was only eleven and a half at this time and the question of her guardianship immediately caused friction between the Bretons and the French. Francis II in his will had entrusted his daughters to the custody of Marshal de Rieux and the sire de Lescun; but on 18 September, Charles VIII claimed it for himself by virtue of his kinship with the girls. Matters were complicated further when Anne fell out with Rieux, who was planning to marry her off to Alain d'Albret. While Anne shut herself up in Rennes with Dunois and a force of German mercenaries, Rieux occupied Nantes, seizing the ducal treasury.

The French threat to the independence of Brittany was a matter of serious concern to other European powers, especially Spain, Maximilian of Habsburg and England. They used the respite provided by the Treaty of Le Verger to draw closer together. The Iberian peninsula had recently become more unified as a result of the marriage of Ferdinand of Aragon with Isabella of Castile. As each was a monarch in his or her own right, they were known as 'the Catholic Kings'. But the unification of Spain still had a long way to go. It needed to annex the Moorish kingdom of Granada in the south, and the counties of Cerdagne and Roussillon, not to mention the small kingdom of Navarre in the north. Ferdinand had claimed Roussillon since the accession of Charles VIII, but France did nothing to oblige him as long as she knew that the bulk of his army was engaged in the conquest of Granada. Yet if Ferdinand could not act himself, he could obstruct French designs by using other European powers, such as England. Though Henry VII was indebted to the French government for assistance in gaining his throne, he was unable to resist Ferdinand's tempting offer of a matrimonial alliance. This was concluded in 1489, when Ferdinand's daughter Catherine married Arthur Prince of Wales.

Maximilian of Habsburg viewed himself as the heir to Charles the Bold, duke of Burgundy (d. 1477), who had built up a powerful state stretching from the North Sea to Switzerland and sandwiched between France in the west and the Holy Roman Empire in the east. He had been succeeded by his daughter Mary, but some of her territories, notably Burgundy, had been forcibly annexed by Louis XI of France. He had wanted to win her by any means for his son, the future Charles VIII, but she would marry only Maximilian who thus acquired his claim to the old Burgundian territories. His efforts to regain those that had been taken by France, however, were hampered by his chronic insolvency and by the need to defend his patrimonial domain in central Europe (Austria and Bohemia) against the Hungarians and Turks. France, for her part, sought to embarrass Maximilian by meddling in the Low Countries. When he attacked France in 1484, the Beaujeus sent troops into Flanders. Some had to be recalled at the start of the Mad War, but in 1487 the French captured Saint-Omer and Thérouanne. In an engagement at Béthune on 27 July they captured the count of Nassau and the duke of Guelders, narrowly missing Maximilian himself. In the following year, Flanders rose in revolt. The inhabitants of Ghent declared themselves subjects of the king of France, while the people of Bruges seized Maximilian; they kept him prisoner for a few months and put to death his Flemish councillors. In May 1488 he regained his freedom as a result of French arbitration, and in 1489 he signed the Peace of Frankfurt.

England kept a close watch on continental events from her vantage point in Calais. In 1485 the Beaujeus had helped to place Henry Tudor on the English throne: they had supplied him with ships, troops and money. He was not ungrateful, but his subjects regarded the independence of Brittany as essential to their security. As the archbishop of Sens reported in 1489: 'The English, in their king's presence, told them [the French ambassadors] that Brittany was "little England". They will send there up to the last man in England in spite of the king.'

On 11 December 1488, France declared war on Brittany. Within a few weeks her troops overran the duchy, occupying Brest, Concarneau and Vannes, but swift as it was, the French campaign was not quite swift enough. Troops sent by Brittany's allies – Henry VII, Ferdinand of Aragon and Maximilian – soon arrived in the duchy. Encouraged by this help, Breton resistance stiffened; and by May all of Lower Brittany save Brest had reverted to the duchess Anne. Yet the Bretons were by no means united: several nobles went over to the French side during the year, while Rieux tried to win power for himself by isolating Anne from her allies. On 22 July 1489, Maximilian signed a peace treaty with France in which the question of Brittany was referred to a court of arbitration in Avignon chaired by the papal legate, Giuliano della Rovere, who at this time was a notorious Francophile. In October 1490 a truce ended the fighting in Brittany until 1 May 1491.

Rieux now abandoned Albret as a prospective husband for Anne and rallied to the idea of marrying her off to Maximilian, King of the Romans. This project became something of a reality in March 1490 when Maximilian appointed four proxies to marry the duchess. The ceremony, which had the approval of the Breton estates, took place in Rennes cathedral on 19 December. Such a marriage was in breach of the Treaty of Le Verger, which had forbidden the duchess to marry without the consent of the king of France, and gave serious offence to Alain d'Albret who had hoped to marry her himself. As captain of Nantes, he was well placed to influence events in the duchy. He began secret talks with Charles VIII and, on 2 January 1491, offered him the keys of Nantes in return for major concessions which the king was unlikely ever to implement. French troops entered Nantes on 19 March and, after elaborate preparations, Charles made his own entry on Palm Sunday (4 April). As soon as the truce expired the French resumed their military operations in the duchy, capturing Vannes on 19 May and Concarneau on 6 June. La Trémoïlle, who had once again become lieutenant-general, took Redon and Guingamp. Only Rennes and the duchess remained independent.

Charles VIII now staged a *coup d'état*. Realizing that Louis d'Orléans might help a settlement of the Breton question, he ordered his release from prison in Bourges and pardoned his treason. The duke, for his part, was glad to make his peace with Charles. Much as they disliked this turn of events, the Beaujeus resigned themselves to it. On 4 September, Pierre de Beaujeu (now duc de Bourbon) and Orléans were formally reconciled and, according to Commynes, became inseparable. Meanwhile, the war in Brittany drew to a close. In mid-June 1491, 15,000 French troops encircled Rennes, and Anne, finding herself without money or effective allies, had to seek a settlement. On 27 October she was advised by the Breton estates to marry the king of France, but Anne was only prepared to exchange Rennes for her own personal freedom. Charles, meanwhile, waited patiently. On 15 October, Rennes capitulated. Under a treaty the town was declared to be neutral and handed over to the dukes of Orléans and Bourbon and the prince of Orange, Anne's freedom being respected.

The king did not ask for Anne's hand. Instead, he offered her an escort should she wish to join Maximilian and 120,000 *livres* for her upkeep. He even offered to settle the wages of her foreign auxiliaries. When Anne refused to go into exile, Charles, invoking his rights of suzerain, offered her marriage to a high-ranking French nobleman, but she declared that she would marry only a king or the son of a king. Eventually, under strong pressure from members of her entourage, Anne, who was not yet fifteen, agreed to meet the French king. He came to Rennes on 15 November and, although his first impressions of the duchess were unfavourable, he agreed to take her as his wife. After the betrothal on 17 November, Charles returned to Plessis-lez-Tours.

His conscience was not, it seems, untroubled. In 1483 he had solemnly promised to marry Margaret of Austria, the daughter of Maximilian, and he was afraid that his breach of promise might stain his honour as head of the knightly Order of St Michael. What is more, he seems to have had tender feelings for the princess, who reciprocated them. She wept bitterly on hearing of the king's marriage and kept his portrait for the rest of her life. When she eventually left France he gave her a valuable chain symbolizing eternal friendship. Another source of anxiety for Charles was the proxy marriage between Anne and Maximilian. Theologians were divided on its validity, though all agreed that an unconsummated marriage could easily be annulled by the church. The necessary dispensation was obtained without difficulty from Pope Innocent VIII.

Charles VIII and Anne of Brittany were married at the château of Langeais on 6 December 1491. Both parties renounced their rights of ownership in Brittany. If Charles predeceased Anne, she was to remarry his successor. If he died without male issue, she was to regain possession of her duchy. On 4 January a Milanese diplomat reported from the French court: 'There is no sign of rejoicing over this marriage on the part of the king or anyone else.' Yet Bretons and Frenchmen were evidently pleased to see an end to their conflicts. Anne was welcomed by her French subjects, though doubts regarding the validity of her marriage were not immediately dispelled. They were confirmed by the accidental death of Dunois, one of its architects, shortly before it took place. Doubts were also to be raised by the premature deaths of children born of the marriage.

The Breton marriage, which effectively destroyed Brittany's independence of France, was naturally viewed with concern by France's neighbours. However, Maximilian was too preoccupied in central Europe to react forcefully. He was, it seems, far more irritated by the slowness with which the French returned Margaret of Austria and her dowry than by the overthrow of his own Breton marriage. Instead of resorting to arms, he tried to turn international opinion against Charles by branding him as an adulterer. Ferdinand of Aragon was too busy besieging Granada to react strongly to the Franco-Breton marriage. He gladly accepted an offer from Charles to open serious talks on the future of Roussillon. By contrast, Henry VII of England protested at the marriage and assembled a fleet, but, as a French observer pointed out, this did not necessarily presage an English invasion of France.

Three peace treaties

In 1492 and 1493, Charles VIII signed three important treaties with neighbouring powers in which he gave away some territories and rights. Historians have commonly assumed that these sacrifices were intended to clear the path for his invasion of Italy in 1494. This explanation, however, may be too simple. While the treaties may have contributed to a European peace essential to the launch of Charles VIII's campaign, they were concerned with problems unconnected with Italy.

In January 1491, soon after his marriage with Anne of Brittany, Charles VIII disbanded his army in the duchy. This was as much for financial as for political reasons: the Breton wars had been a heavy drain on his resources. Only by periodically appealing to the generosity of the 'good towns' had he been able to keep the *taille* at a constant level since 1489 (i.e. 2,300,000 *livres* per annum). Yet England continued to threaten French security. In the autumn of 1491, Henry VII announced his intention of asserting his claim to the French crown and persuaded Parliament to vote him subsidies. During the following summer an English invasion of northern France seemed imminent. Charles reluctantly levied a *crue de taille* and again called on the 'good towns' to help. On 2 October, Henry VII landed at Calais with a large army and soon afterwards laid siege to Boulogne; but the campaigning season was almost over and it soon became clear that the king had come to bargain, not to fight. He was fortunate to find Charles similarly disposed. On 3 November they signed the Peace of Etaples, the first perpetual peace between England and France since the Hundred Years War. In 1478, France had agreed to pay England an annual pension of 50,000 gold *écus* for the lifetime of the signatories and for a hundred years after the death of either of them. This pension had lapsed on the death of Louis XI so that France owed England 450,000 *écus* in 1492. This matter was now settled to France's advantage. She agreed to pay 750,000 gold *écus* in twice-yearly instalments of 25,000 *écus* and her obligation to pay a tribute over a much longer period than fifteen years was dropped. All of this was in addition to an earlier undertaking by Charles to settle his wife's English debt of 620,000 gold crowns.

Though expensive, the Treaty of Etaples was beneficial to France. Apart from its financial provisions, which represented a reduction of the burden incurred in 1478, it entailed no loss of French territory. The settlement of Brittany's English debt freed the duchy's towns that had served as securities for this debt, while denying Henry VII any pretext for intervention in Brittany's affairs. In the words of an English historian: 'The treaty of Etaples was a major setback to English interests. Brittany's independence was gone. The entire southern shore of the Channel, except for Calais, had become French.'

On 3 November 1492, Charles VIII informed the inhabitants of Perpignan of his intention to hand back Roussillon and Cerdagne to Spain. His move may have been prompted by his father's deathbed wish that the two counties, which he had seized unlawfully in 1463, should be restored to their rightful owner. Spanish prestige was riding high at the French court in 1492 following the conquest of Granada by Ferdinand and Isabella. Yet negotiations between France and Spain dragged on into the autumn and, losing patience, Ferdinand urged his allies Henry VII and Maximilian to invade France. It was partly to avert the danger of a triple invasion that Charles concluded the Treaty of Barcelona on 19 January 1493. The perpetual alliance between France and Castile was renewed and given precedence over all other treaties entered upon by the parties, save with the Holy See. No marriage was to be arranged between the children of the Catholic Kings and any of France's enemies without her permission. Roussillon and Cerdagne were ceded to Spain without prejudice to the rights and claims of future kings of France. The Catholic Kings did not promise to remain neutral in the event of a French invasion of Naples. Such a commitment was requested by Charles VIII in March 1493 and conceded in August; it was additional to the treaty, not part of it.

The King of the Romans was displeased by the treaties of Etaples and Barcelona. In December 1492 he claimed the whole of his Burgundian inheritance and invaded Franche-Comté. He did not advance into the Lyonnais, however, and in March 1493 agreed to negotiate with France. The upshot was the Treaty of Senlis, published on 23 May. Charles promised to return Margaret of Austria to her father and the bulk of her dowry, including Artois and Franche-Comté, to her brother, the archduke Philip. The king retained the county of Auxonne and provisionally Hesdin, Aire, Béthune and Arras. These towns, except Arras, were to be returned to Philip on his twentieth birthday (23 June 1498). A court of arbitration was to decide who owned the counties of Mâcon, Auxerre and Bar-sur-Seine. The treaty was completed by clauses guaranteeing freedom of trade and restoring property lost in the wars since 1470. An important aspect of the treaty was the implicit recognition of the marriage of Charles VIII and Anne of Brittany. The Treaty of Senlis, like that of Barcelona, contained no agreement in respect of a future French intervention in southern Italy. Maximilian did allow Charles VIII a free hand in Naples, but this was not part of the treaty which was mainly prompted by the need to regularize Margaret of Austria's position in the wake of the Franco-Breton marriage. However, it did not solve all the issues dividing the parties. Neither Maximilian nor Margaret ever forgot that Burgundy was the cradle of Charles the Bold's power. All their efforts were later directed towards its reconquest, but, as long as Charles VIII was alive, Burgundy was not seriously threatened. The Peace of Senlis gave France five years of peace on her eastern frontier.

Although France did not as yet think of pushing her eastern frontier to the Rhine, Charles did not ignore the eastern and northern borders of his kingdom. Like his father and sister, he sought allies in Flanders, first the large communes, then the nobles running the government. In 1494, Philip the Fair, governor of the Low Countries, paid homage to the king for Flanders, thereby effectively guaranteeing much of France's northern frontier. In 1492, Charles VIII was offered the suzerainty of Liège, but he wisely refused. Had he accepted, he would have had to intervene countless times in Flemish and German affairs.

A comparison of the three treaties of 1492 and 1493 suggests that the best for France was the Treaty of Etaples, for it disposed of England's traditional enmity without loss of territory. France's acquisition of Brittany made up for the loss of Franche-Comté and Artois in the Treaty of Senlis. She also scored a diplomatic triumph by obtaining implicit recognition of Charles VIII's marriage. Only the Treaty of Barcelona was seriously damaging. The return of Roussillon and Cerdagne to Spain, though legally justified, failed to ensure stable Franco-Spanish relations: the two powers were soon to fall out in Italy. Yet, in exchange for her sacrifices, France, including Brittany, gained domestic peace for the remainder of Charles VIII's reign.

3

Charles VIII and the Italian Wars, 1494–8

In 1494, King Charles VIII invaded Italy and conquered the kingdom of Naples. His action marked the beginning of a series of French campaigns south of the Alps which have come to be known as the Italian Wars. They lasted on and off till the Peace of Cateau-Cambrésis of 1559.

Italy at the end of the fifteenth century was a tempting prey to a more powerful neighbour, for it was divided into a large number of more or less independent states which could be played off against each other. The most important were Venice, Milan, Florence, the States of the Church and Naples. The Venetian republic, though threatened by the westward expansion of the Ottoman empire, was at the height of its power. In addition to an extensive territory on the mainland, it controlled lands along the Adriatic seaboard, in the Aegean and in the eastern Mediterranean. The Venetian constitution was the most stable in Italy, being vested in an aristocratic oligarchy and exercised through a well-balanced system of councils. To the west lay the duchy of Milan which the house of Visconti had created out of a collection of cities; it was now ruled by the house of Sforza under which it continued to prosper economically. A strong Milan was regarded by other Italian states as a necessary bulwark against foreign invasion and Venetian expansionism. Florence was ruled in theory by a popular government, but effective authority was in the hands of the Medici family. Though weak militarily, the republic was influential among the other Italian states on account of the Medicis' extensive banking connections and genius for diplomacy. The States of the Church stretched diagonally across the Italian peninsula from the Tiber to the Po and comprised a number of virtually autonomous towns and districts. The city of Rome was continually disturbed by the feuds of its leading families, while dreams of republican government still stirred among its inhabitants. A principal aim of the Renaissance popes was to establish their authority firmly throughout their territories, a policy which often led them into nepotism. Naples, the only feudal monarchy in the peninsula, was a land of large estates ruled by turbulent barons. It was divided into two parts: Sicily belonged to the house of Aragon, while Naples and the mainland were ruled by an illegitimate branch of the same house. Notable among the lesser Italian states were the duchy of Savoy, sitting astride the Alps and under the shadow of France; the republic of Genoa, which had lapsed into political insignificance as a result of domestic squabbles; and the duchy of Ferrara, serving as a buffer state between Venice and the States of the Church.

Following the Peace of Lodi (1454) the preservation of order in Italy was made to depend on a close understanding between Milan, Florence and Naples, which Lorenzo de' Medici strove untiringly to maintain. His son Piero, however, who succeeded him in 1492, lacked political judgement. By leaning too heavily on the side of Naples he upset the tripartite axis and precipitated a breakdown of relations between Milan and Naples. Isabella of Aragon, duchess of Milan, was the daughter of Alfonso duke of Calabria and granddaughter of Ferrante I, king of Naples. She and her husband, Giangaleazzo Sforza, felt overshadowed by the regent, Lodovico Sforza. Alfonso was always looking for an opportunity to extend his power in Italy. He also remembered that his grandfather, Alfonso I of Naples, had been named by Filippo Maria Visconti duke of Milan (d. 1447) as his heir. As the duke prepared to attack Milan, Lodovico turned to France for help. He probably did not wish to bring the king of France into the peninsula, only to shelter beneath the threat of a French invasion. But there were others, apart from Lodovico, who were urging the king of France to make good his own claim to the kingdom of Naples.

French intervention in the area had a long history. The emperor Charlemagne had carried the defence of Christendom to the heart of Italy. The Capetian kings, on the other hand, had been content to observe Italian affairs from afar. St Louis refused the kingdom of Sicily, but allowed his brother Charles comte d'Anjou to respond to calls for help from the papacy and to accept for himself and his heirs territories in southern Italy. In 1481, Louis XI inherited the Angevin lands, including the county of Provence and the kingdom of Naples, but was too near death to take possession of them. In 1486 the annexation of Provence to the kingdom of France was formally ratified by the Parlement of Paris; but the claim to Naples was disputed between the king of France and the duke of Lorraine.

An additional complication was the fact that Naples was a papal fief. Its hereditary transmission was determined by a bull of investiture of 1265 which conferred the kingdom on Charles d'Anjou and his heirs in the direct or collateral line up to the fourth degree of kinship. Charles VIII was too far removed in kinship from Charles d'Anjou to qualify, but this did not deter him from pressing his claim. In 1493, Naples was ruled by Ferrante

I, the brother-in-law of Ferdinand of Aragon, as part of a kingdom comprising the whole of Italy south of the States of the Church except Sicily which belonged to Ferdinand. Ferrante was hardly a docile vassal of the papacy: he had been excommunicated by Pope Innocent VIII and had opposed the election of Alexander VI, who repeatedly called on the French king to attack Naples.

Charles VIII wanted Naples not only for itself but as a springboard from which to launch a crusade against the Turks. The fifteenth century had seen a rapid expansion of Turkish power westward under Sultan Mehmet II. After capturing Greece and Albania, the Turks established a foothold in southern Italy in August 1480. The death of Mehmet in May 1481 was followed by a respite. In 1482 the Turks were driven out of southern Italy, but they remained a threat. There was general agreement among the Christian powers of the need for a new crusade aimed ultimately at freeing Constantinople and the Holy Places; but there was no consensus as to who should lead it. Two possible candidates were Charles VIII and Maximilian, King of the Romans. Although Philippe de Commynes doubted Charles's sincerity in proposing a crusade, ample evidence suggests otherwise. As Robert Gaguin, on an embassy to England, explained: the king, his master, was anxious to follow the example set by Henry IV of England, who at the end of his life had planned to lead an expedition to the Holy Land. He was also much impressed by the efforts of Ferdinand of Aragon to wrest the kingdom of Granada from the Saracens. A Venetian envoy wrote from Rome in June 1495: 'You may be sure that the king's intention is to attack the Turks. He has made the vow to God and would already have launched his enterprise if so many troubles had not befallen him. I, who have spoken to His Majesty, know this to be true.'

In planning a crusade Charles was almost certainly influenced by a number of legends. One was that of Charlemagne, who had allegedly freed the Holy Places and handed them over to the emperor in Constantinople. Another was that of a king of France, called Philip 'le despourveu', who had travelled incognito to Naples in order to rescue the king of Sicily and his daughter from the Saracens. A prophecy popular in the 1490s forecast that a French prince called Charles, crowned at fourteen and married to Justice, would destroy Florence and be crowned in Rome after purging it of bad priests. He would then sail to Greece, become its king, defeat the Turks and end his life as king of Jerusalem.

Charles was also subject to less fanciful influences. There were Neapolitan exiles at his court, such as Antonello San Severino, who wanted his help to return to their native land. He gave them pensions and the use of a fortress in Burgundy until he could raise an army in support of their cause. Alongside the Neapolitans were Frenchmen, like Etienne de Vesc or Guillaume Briçonnet, who could see opportunities of personal enrichment or advancement arise out of a French intervention in Italy. Briçonnet was anxious to get a red hat. Even outside the court there was support for a French expedition south of the Alps. The bankers of Lyon and the merchants of Marseille wanted to expand their commercial interests in the Mediterranean at the expense of the Venetians and Aragonese.

Even within Italy there were forces working for a French intervention. Lodovico Sforza, nicknamed Il Moro, the effective ruler of the duchy of Milan, urged the king of France as early as 1491 to make good his claim to Naples. He suggested that Genoa might serve as a base for an attack on the southern kingdom. In January 1494 he was much alarmed when Alfonso, who had tried several times to have him assassinated, became king of Naples. His appeals to the king of France became desperate. Among Italian states, Florence was the only ally of the king of Naples, for the silk trade on which much of its prosperity depended passed through his territories, yet even there support for a French invasion existed. Many Florentines, who resented the autocratic ways of Piero de' Medici, looked favourably towards France. For example, the Dominican preacher Savonarola prophesied Charles VIII's coming in his Lenten sermon of 1493. 'I have seen', he exclaimed, 'in the sky a suspended sword and I have heard these words: *Ecce gladius Domini super terram cito et velociter*. The sword fell bringing about wars, massacres and numberless ills.' As for the Venetians, their foreign policy was primarily dictated by commercial interests: they wanted to maintain the status quo in the Adriatic and were, in general, opposed to any move which might antagonize the Turks. Yet they needed French help against the Habsburgs, who, having gained control of Trieste and Fiume, were entertaining maritime ambitions. Thus the Venetians were among the first to encourage Charles VIII to seize Naples. Another Italian who exerted similar pressure upon the king was Cardinal Giuliano della Rovere. He came to France shortly after his defeat in the papal conclave of 1492. Hoping to use a French invasion to topple his successful rival, Pope Alexander VI, he assured the French of the support of the Colonna faction which controlled the port of Ostia and several castles in the Roman Campagna.

Yet if Charles was under heavy pressure at home and abroad to invade Italy, support for such an enterprise among his own subjects was far from unanimous. According to a Florentine envoy it was opposed by the princes of the blood, most other nobles, royal councillors, prelates, finance ministers and all the people. Belgioioso, the Milanese ambassador, remarked: 'It is truly a miracle that the king, young as he is, has persevered in his design in spite of all the opposition he has encountered.' Charles himself informed the Italians in 1494 that he had left his kingdom 'against the wishes of the princes and great nobles'. The opposition, however, was not united. Some great nobles resented the influence exercised by de Vesc and Briçonnet over the king. Louis d'Orléans wanted to divert the expedition from Naples to Milan, to which he had inherited a claim from his grandmother Valentina Visconti. The Bourbons showed no enthusiasm for the enterprise, yet took part in it. Nobles generally believed that the costs of equipping themselves for such a distant campaign would not be offset by the results. However, the main focus of opposition lay in the towns of northern France which refused royal demands for a subsidy. Many French people disapproved of the king leaving his kingdom when the Dauphin was still only an infant.

Commynes tells us that the French invasion of Italy in 1494 was poorly prepared. 'All things necessary to so great an enterprise', he writes, 'were lacking.' But Guillaume de La Mare, a usually reliable eyewitness, wrote on 27 March: 'the Neapolitan campaign . . . is being prepared with the utmost prudence and zeal . . . There is nothing that the king is not putting into execution with extreme activity and care.' Collecting the funds necessary to such a campaign was a matter of primary importance. Marshal d'Esquerdes informed Charles that he would need one million gold *écus* before the start of the campaign and another million once the army had crossed the Alps. The king managed to raise the first million by resorting to various expedients. The great nobles were asked for a loan of 50,000 ducats and contributions were also requested from the *Chambre des comptes* and other state departments. What the clergy offered is unknown, but a number of *bonnes villes* responded with varying generosity. Lyon offered 10,000 *livres*, while Paris refused to give anything. Amiens gave 3000 *livres*, half as much as the king had demanded. Parts of the royal domain were sold or mortgaged to the tune of 120,000 *livres*. The wages of royal officials and pensioners were delayed for six months. Finally, the *taille* was increased to 575,000 *livres*. As far as the second million was concerned, Charles relied mainly on contributions from various Italian cities.

On 13 February 1494, shortly after the death of Ferrante of Naples, Charles VIII travelled to Lyon and assumed the title of King of Sicily and Jerusalem. He dispatched an ambassador to the pope asking for the investiture of Naples, but on 18 April, at a secret consistory, Alexander conferred it on Ferrante's son Alfonso. This volte-face by the pope, who had previously been hostile to Ferrante, did not cause the king to change his plans. On 29 July he reaffirmed his determination to go to Italy and appointed Pierre de Bourbon as lieutenant-general of the kingdom in his absence. Meanwhile, Charles assembled his army.

At the start of the summer of 1494 the king's *gendarmerie* comprised slightly more than 1500 *lances*: that is to say, about 6000 to 8000 troops reinforced by the cavalry, archers and crossbowmen of the royal household. In addition there were some Italian *lances*, comprising fewer men than the French ones (one auxiliary and one page per man-at-arms). The infantry consisted of 4000 to 5000 men raised in France and about as many Swiss mercenaries. Thus it was an army of about 16,000 to 20,000 men which Charles led into Italy. To this number must be added the sizeable amount of non-combatants such as valets and pages, secretaries, merchants, camp followers and vagabonds in quest of loot. An important component of the French army was the artillery, which was larger and more advanced technically than any other and accounted for 8 per cent of the king's total military expenditure. In 1489, Charles had about 150 pieces, dozens of gunners and large quantities of gunpowder. He was allegedly the first to use in Italy cannon balls made of iron instead of stone.

Charles crossed the Alps at the end of August, using the Mont Genèvre pass. His principal lieutenants were Stuart d'Aubigny, Louis d'Orléans and Gilbert de Montpensier. The army's passage through the mountains was eased by the fact that the artillery was sent to Genoa by sea. On reaching Piedmont the army marched on Asti, which belonged to the duc d'Orléans, before advancing on Turin. The house of Savoy had for some time distanced itself from France, but the duke was a child and his mother, Blanche, could only welcome her cousin the French king, backed, as he was, by such a considerable force. On 5 September he was magnificently received in Turin. Meanwhile, at Rapallo, the first serious engagement of the campaign took place, when a Neapolitan attack on Genoa was repulsed by a fleet commanded by Louis d'Orléans. After spending nearly a month in Asti, Charles moved to Milan. On 22 October, following the death of Giangaleazzo Sforza, the citizens asked Lodovico to become their duke. Although there were other claimants to the duchy, including Louis d'Orléans, Charles did not oppose Lodovico for fear of prejudicing his own campaign.

Meanwhile, in Florence, news of the French invasion revived the myth of liberty so closely associated with the French crown. Piero de' Medici, unlike his father, had failed to remain *primus inter pares*. His government had become increasingly arbitrary. Without the consent of the Signoria he had drawn closer to Naples and broken the city's alliance with France, a move seen by the Florentines as a serious abuse of power. Their civic tradition was deeply rooted in the Carolingian legend. According to Villani, Charlemagne had given them independence and freedom while Charles d'Anjou had caused the Guelf cause to triumph over imperial tutelage. Charles VIII was regarded as their descendant and his coming was taken by the Florentines as an opportunity to demonstrate their unshaken loyalty to the French alliance. As the French army penetrated Tuscany there was panic in Florence. On 30 October, after a show of resistance, Piero handed over to Charles the *Signoria*'s fortresses. His caution or cowardice precipitated his downfall. On 9 November the Medici regime was toppled.

The French invasion of Italy also coincided with a widely felt eschatological vision. Many people believed that the old world was coming to an end and a new Golden Age was about to begin. This seemed confirmed by a profusion of natural phenomena such as eclipses, floods and thunderbolts. Charles VIII appeared as the man of Providence chosen to bring peace, liberty and justice, to purify the church, to drive the infidel out of Jerusalem and to rid Italy of her shame. He was still in Pisa when he was visited by a deputation from Florence headed by Savonarola, who, claiming to be God's spokesman, acclaimed him as 'an instrument in the hands of the Lord'. The friar urged Charles to fulfil his divine mission of purification, begging him at the same time to show mercy to the people of Florence. Meanwhile, the Pisans asked to be released from Florentine tutelage, but Charles would give them only vague promises; the support of Florence was more precious to him at this moment than the gratitude of the Pisans. On 17 November he entered Florence in triumph. However, his accord with the republic alienated the duke of Milan who had hoped to recover two former Genoese towns – Sarzana and Pietrasanta – which Florence had seized in the past. He recalled 6000 troops who were serving alongside the French and began to intrigue against them with other powers.

From the moment Charles crossed the Alps until his arrival in Naples, his march through Italy was a triumphal progress. Wherever he passed, large crowds flocked to acclaim him. Each town received him in the same way: an official deputation, made up of senior churchmen and representatives of the local government, would come forward to meet him, they would hand him the keys of the town, and a length of its wall would be destroyed as a mark of subservience. Great efforts were also made to decorate the streets in the king's honour. Precious hangings adorned the façades of houses and temporary monuments, such as triumphal arches, were erected in his path. Inscriptions comparing him to Caesar or Alexander the Great stressed the sacredness of his mission as well as his invincibility. Many coins bearing his effigy were struck. Wherever the king made his entry he was accompanied by a large military contingent. Italian spectators were much impressed by the sheer size of the French army and by the colourful costumes worn by the king and his nobles.

The unanimous capitulation of towns to Charles VIII was inspired not only by his reputation as a divinely appointed liberator but also by fear of the force at his disposal. The size of the French army, its formidable armament and the fighting qualities of its troops were awesome to the Italians. Although the invasion met with little resistance and was, therefore, largely bloodless, a few incidents, such as the sack of a fortress at Fivizzano, revealed the cruelty of the French. They took no prisoners, and massacred everyone regardless of sex or age. They seemed to have respect neither for God nor the devil. The *furia francese* was compared by some observers to a tempest. Not content with shedding blood, the French liked to set fire to everything. An eyewitness, Passaro, described them as worse than the Turks and the Moors, worse even than savages.

The French invasion divided Italy rather than helping to unify it. The various states fell into two camps as they sided with or against Charles. His coming created a climate of tension in the peninsula in which antagonisms hitherto latent became manifest. A wind of revolt blew across the peninsula, reviving old conflicts between Guelfs and Ghibellines. Mercenary captains offered their services to the highest bidder. Towns of the *contado* rid themselves of the tutelage of the *Signoria*. In Tuscany, revolts broke out in Pisa, Montepulciano and Arezzo. The fragile edifice of the States of the Church also collapsed: at Perugia, the Baglioni strengthened their authority at the pope's expense. The towns of the papal states capitulated to the French in rapid succession. Partisans of the Colonna harried the pope up to the gates of Rome. Alexander VI, finding himself abandoned by his court and the people of Rome, prepared to fortify Castel Sant'Angelo in self-defence.

The pope had every reason to be fearful as the French drew closer to Rome. He was not unduly worried about the threat to the Aragonese regime in Naples, which had not always been submissive to his suzerainty, but he did not wish to see the French permanently established in the southern kingdom. On the other hand, he could not risk opposing the king of France for fear of provoking a Gallican reaction and reviving an earlier threat that a General Council would be created bent on reforming the church in its head and members. Charles, for his part, did not wish to incur excommunication which would harm his international standing. So both sides played a devious game. In a bid to avoid Charles's presence in Rome, Alexander offered to meet him on the way, but the king declared himself unworthy of such an honour. His Christian duty, he explained, was to do the pope reverence in his own apostolic palace. He assured him of his desire to lead a crusade against the Turks after reconquering his Neapolitan inheritance.

As the king pressed on through Orvieto, Viterbo and Bracciano, his army occupied Civitavecchia. On 20 December the French vanguard was joined outside Ostia by 2000 infantry that had come from Genoa by sea. The talks with the pope, meanwhile, dragged on. Charles wanted the investiture of Naples and the surrender into his own hands of Djem, the sultan's brother, who was being held hostage in Rome. Alexander wriggled for as long as possible, but eventually gave way. On 29 December the French army entered Rome as a few Neapolitan troops who had come to defend the pope left the city. Charles made his entry by torchlight on the night of 31 December. He had cause to feel satisfied with his progress to date. Within four months he had reached the Holy City without encountering any major obstacle; his army was more or less intact.

On 15 January, Charles and the pope came to an agreement and next day the king knelt before the Vicar of Christ after attending mass at St Peter's. On 20 January, Alexander celebrated mass in the basilica before the king and a congregation of 15,000 people. Among the cardinals present was the newly created Guillaume Briçonnet. The service lasted five hours, after which the pope blessed the French troops and gave them general absolution. Charles took his leave of the pope on 28 January. He had gained right of passage for his army through the States of the Church, but Alexander had not given him the investiture of Naples.

The French now resumed their southward advance. On 4 February they attacked the fortress of Monte San Giovanni. As the king wrote:

> My cousin Montpensier had arrived before me with my artillery . . . and after firing for four hours my said artillery had made a breach wide enough for an assault. I ordered it to be made by men-at-arms and others, and though the place was held by 5–600 good fighting men as well as its inhabitants, they went in in such a manner that, thanks to God [the town] has been taken with little loss to me, and to the defenders great loss, punishment and great example to those others who might think of obstructing me.

As the French were entering the kingdom of Naples, its people rose in rebellion. King Alfonso fled to Sicily after abdicating in favour of his son Ferrandino, who, finding himself abandoned by most of his followers, shut himself up in the Castel Nuovo in Naples. On 19 February the first French troops entered the city. Soon afterwards Ferrandino accepted the offer of honourable retirement in France.

Charles VIII had improved on Caesar's achievement for, as Guicciardini wrote, the king had conquered even before he had seen. This he owed largely to the reputation which had preceded him, clearing obstacles from his path. Without exception every town on his march south had opened its gates to him, making possible the spanking pace of his progress. In the words of Marsilio Ficino, Charles 'had shaken the world by a nod of his head'. Chroniclers were dumbfounded by the effortlessness of his victory. One remarked that he had conquered Naples with a falcon on his wrist. Some contemporaries looked for rational explanations of his triumph; others just called it a miracle.

The king's first task was to reward all the people who had assisted him in his campaign. They were showered with offices and lands. Eleven Frenchmen and only one Neapolitan were appointed to the council of state (*sacro consilio*). Frenchmen also acquired the principal offices of state, the only notable exceptions being the prince of Salerno and Giacomo Caracciolo, who recovered their offices of admiral and chancellor respectively. The governorships of provinces and towns were distributed in the same way. Etienne de Vesc, one of the main promoters of the Neapolitan expedition, acquired a veritable principality: he became duke of Nola and Ascoli, count of Avellino, great chamberlain and president of the *Sommaria* or chamber of accounts. The Colonna family was rewarded with dozens of fiefs. Several profitable marriages were also concluded between French noblemen and Neapolitan heiresses. Thus Louis de Luxembourg married Eleonora de Guevara, whose lands in Apulia yielded an annual income of 30,000 to 40,000 ducats, and Pierre de Rohan, marshal de Gié, married Eleonora's younger sister.

However, the French conquest of Naples was not acceptable in the long term to other Italian states. In March 1495, as the king of France and his troops were enjoying the pleasures, reputable and disreputable, of Naples, four states – Milan, Venice, the papacy and Mantua – formed a league aimed at their expulsion from the peninsula. They planned to sever Charles's communications with France. The king's position was made all the more critical by the material aid promised to the league by Maximilian (who had succeeded as emperor in 1493) and King Ferdinand of Aragon. Maximilian recalled that the French expedition had been intended as a crusade, not a conquest, while Ferdinand argued that Charles had broken the Treaty of Barcelona. The league was the beginning of official interference by Spain in Italian affairs and more generally of foreign domination of the peninsula; it soon reached out beyond Italy, becoming a European coalition. Not all the Italian states joined the league. Florence and Ferrara abstained, and the hostility that divided the latter from Venice showed that the league could not eradicate internal rivalries. In spite of the challenge posed by the French conquest of Naples, Italian politics continued to focus on local interests. However, contemporary historians and chroniclers argued that the Italian states needed to work more closely together. As from 1494 the political outlook of many Italians, notably Machiavelli, was not entirely devoid of a certain national consciousness.

Charles wisely decided not to linger in his southern kingdom but to return home as quickly as possible. He divided his army into two parts: one to defend Naples under Gilbert de Montpensier as viceroy, the other to escort him back to France. On 20 May, Charles left Naples and travelled to Rome in only ten days. To avoid meeting him the pope retired first to Orvieto, then to Perugia. Meanwhile, in northern Italy, Louis d'Orléans, acting on his own authority, pre-empted a move by Lodovico Sforza against Asti by attacking the Milanese town of Novara. As this was an imperial fief, Louis's move offered Maximilian a legitimate pretext for armed intervention. Charles, much alarmed by this turn of events, asked Pierre de Bourbon to send reinforcements in haste to Asti. Meanwhile, the king continued his march northward: he was at Siena on 13 June and at Pisa on the 20th, having by-passed Florence. While part of his army moved on Genoa, the bulk crossed the Appenines. Waiting for them on the north side was the league's much larger army commanded by the marquis of Mantua. Charles was inclined to seek terms for a free passage, but Marshal Trivulzio argued successfully in favour of engaging the enemy. On 6 July the armies collided at Fornovo during a thunderstorm. Charles was nearly captured several times in the course of the battle which was extremely bloody, especially for the league. The marquis of Mantua claimed it as a victory, but it was really a draw; the French got through, admittedly with the loss of much baggage.

After covering 200 kilometres in seven days, Charles reached Asti on 15 July. Although annoyed with his cousin Louis for his unauthorized attack on Novara, he went to his assistance early in September. As he marched on Vercelli, the league opened talks which ended in a treaty (9 October): Novara was handed back to Milan, Orléans kept Asti, and Genoa was 'neutralized', though the French were still allowed to use its harbour facilities. Even more important, however, was Lodovico's decision to abandon the league which promptly fell apart. On 15 October the situation in north Italy was sufficiently settled for Charles to undertake his homeward journey across the Alps.

Meanwhile, in the kingdom of Naples, the French under Montpensier found themselves subjected to mounting pressure as the Venetians attacked several towns along the Adriatic coast, and Ferrandino reoccupied Naples itself and laid siege to a number of fortresses within the city. Charles sent a fleet to Naples, but it was scattered by storms and never reached its destination. On 5 October, Montpensier signed a truce which prepared for his capitulation on 2 December unless he received help by that date. When it failed to materialize, several French garrisons surrendered. Gaeta and a few strongholds in Apulia held out longer, but they gradually fell to Ferrandino. Charles VIII clung to his rights in the kingdom, but the death of his infant son, Charles-Orland, prevented him from leading a rescue operation, for the king was traditionally bound to stay at home as long as his succession was not assured. He was also short of money. Even so, he spent the spring of 1496 in Lyon trying to organize two expeditions: one to relieve Montpensier, who was besieged in Atella, the other to defend Asti against attack by the duke of Milan. Early in 1498, Charles managed to win over his erstwhile opponent, the marquis of Mantua; but the king died on 7 April, before he was able to send a new expedition to Italy.

It is difficult to regard Charles's Italian campaign as anything other than a disaster for France. One of its consequences was the demystification of the French king in Italian eyes. They had looked up to him as the heir of Charlemagne and as a benefactor chosen by God to bring them freedom and liberty. Instead, they had found him to be a repulsively ugly little man betraying a character not much better than his physique. His policies too upset them by their waywardness. The Florentines, in particular, felt betrayed by his apparent encouragement of the Pisan rebellion. In Naples he came to share in the execration aroused by the viciousness of his entourage. Italians everywhere believed that Charles had failed in his mission: he had brought them neither liberty nor justice; he had not reformed the church;

and, far from leading a crusade, he had exacerbated the Turkish threat. The war he had unleashed had brought famine and inflation in its wake. In brief, Charles now appeared not as a benefactor but as an oppressor. As for the French soldiers and their captains, they had shown themselves to be worse than Turks or Moors: they were barbarians without regard for human life, who desecrated churches and turned palaces into pigsties.

The French were to pay a heavy price for their debauches in Naples. They brought home a new and terrible disease, syphilis, which they called the 'Neapolitan sickness' while the Italians called it the 'French sickness'. The first descriptions of it date from the battle of Fornovo. Cumano, a military doctor to the Venetian troops, relates that he saw 'several men-at-arms or foot soldiers who, owing to the ferment of the humours, had "pustules" on their faces and all over their bodies'. Benedetto, another Venetian doctor, reported: 'Through sexual contact, an ailment which is new, or at least unknown to previous doctors, the French sickness, has worked its way in from the West to this spot as I write. The entire body is so repulsive to look at and the suffering is so great, especially at night, that this sickness is even more horrifying than incurable leprosy or elephantiasis, and it can be fatal.' Charles VIII's mercenaries, who were disbanded in the summer of 1495, spread the new disease when they returned to their own countries. France was the first affected. Jean Molinet, the official historian of the house of Burgundy, blamed the king for bringing home the 'pox'. In Lyon an agreement was made in March 1496 between the city magistrates and the king's officers to expel from the city 'persons afflicted with the great pox'. In Besançon, in April, the municipal authorities granted compensation to several victims of 'what is known as the Neapolitan sickness'. Paris was affected by the autumn of 1496 at the latest, as we are informed by a ledger at the *Hôtel-Dieu*. Although by 1497 almost the entire kingdom was experiencing the epidemic, certain towns were particularly badly hit, such as Bordeaux, Niort, Poitiers and Rouen. Less than ten years after Fornovo the whole of Europe was affected. The scourge stimulated various theories as to its origin. Ambroise Paré, along with many others, was to invoke 'God's wrath, which allowed this malady to descend upon the human race, in order to curb its lasciviousness and inordinate concupiscence'.

4

Louis XII, 'Father of the People', 1498–1515

Louis duc d'Orléans was 36 years old when he succeeded his cousin as king of France on 7 April 1498. He was physically unattractive and subject to frequent bouts of ill-health, yet he was always a keen huntsman and took part in much violent exercise. From the start of his reign he sought popularity. He showed goodwill to the house of Bourbon by allowing the marriage of Suzanne, daughter of Pierre and Anne de Beaujeu, to her cousin, Charles de Bourbon-Montpensier, and he sought the loyalty of former opponents like Louis de La Trémoïlle. When delegates from Orléans excused themselves for not giving him more support in the past, Louis said that a king of France ought not to avenge the quarrels of a duc d'Orléans.

Louis XII ruled with a small council of less than ten members. Foremost among them was Georges d'Amboise, archbishop of Rouen, an old friend of the king whom he had served in various capacities. He had been imprisoned for two years (1487–90) for his part in Louis's rebellion against the Beaujeus, and during Charles VIII's Italian campaign he had helped to relieve Louis in Novara. Amboise became one of Louis XII's most influential advisers. He combined a long experience of public affairs with dogged loyalty, but he lacked the duplicity needed for success in politics. That may be why he failed in his ambition to become pope. Another important member of the council was Florimond Robertet, an experienced civil servant with an unusual competence in foreign languages. After serving Charles VIII as a notary and secretary, he was drawn into the orbit of the house of Orléans by his marriage to the daughter of the treasurer, Michel Gaillard. Louis XII confirmed him as councillor and *maître des comptes* and Robertet later became *secrétaire des finances* and *trésorier de France*; but it was as the king's personal secretary that he exercised an influence which may have been at least equal to that of Georges d'Amboise.

The king's remarriage

One thought preoccupied Louis XII at his accession: to rid himself of his barren and deformed wife, Jeanne de France, and remarry Charles VIII's widow, Anne of Brittany. He had been forced to marry Jeanne by her father Louis XI as a sinister ploy to ensure the early termination of the Orléans branch of the royal family and the absorption of its lands into the royal domain. For a long time Louis had refused to live with Jeanne, preferring a life of unrestrained debauchery, but eventually he had accepted the mar- riage to the extent of seeing his wife from time to time. He even slept with her, despite the physical revulsion which she inspired in him. He made no attempt to repudiate her during her father's lifetime or that of her brother, Charles VIII, but only his conscience could stop him now that he was king if the pope would declare his marriage null and void.

Fortunately for Louis, Pope Alexander VI was prepared to subordinate spiritual values to his own temporal interests, notably the advancement of his illegitimate son Cesare Borgia, who was looking for a wife and rich fiefs. France could provide both, so Alexander sent Cesare to congratulate Louis on his accession and acceded to his matrimonial designs: on 29 July he issued a brief listing eight reasons for regarding the king's marriage as null and void and Louis expressed his gratitude by making Cesare duc de Valentinois. The pope next set up a tribunal in France. It was generally assumed that Queen Jeanne would not face up to the ordeal of litigation, but she decided to defend herself. Many people, however, refused to assist her for fear of offending the king. When the tribunal met at Tours on 10 August 1498, the *procureur du roi* asked for the annulment of Louis's marriage and that he should be allowed to remarry. Jeanne denounced the *procureur*'s statements as unworthy of refutation. Even so, she answered intimate questions with dignity. She denied that violence had been used to extort Louis's consent to the marriage and, while conceding that she lacked the beauty of most other women, denied that she was incapable of sexual intercourse. While the tribunal was still sitting, Cesare Borgia arrived in Lyon bearing papal gifts: a cardinal's hat for Georges d'Amboise and the dispensations required by Louis XII to marry Anne of Brittany. But, perhaps deliberately, Cesare did not reach the French court till judgement had been given in the king's matrimonial suit.

Between 25 September and 15 October the tribunal examined witnesses – four for the queen and twenty-seven for the king. Jeanne's counsel pointed out that Louis had frequently slept with her. He also produced a dispen- sation from Sixtus IV which had removed impediments to their marriage. On 27 October, Louis was himself interrogated, but his answers were so inconclusive that he had to be questioned again, this time under oath. He solemnly swore that he had never had intercourse with Jeanne. Since royal perjury was unthinkable, the tribunal felt bound to accept his word.

On 17 December the cardinal of Luxemburg announced the court's verdict: the king's marriage had never taken place. Not everyone, however, would accept this outcome. Some well-known preachers spoke in support of Jeanne, who had won much public support during her ordeal. Rather than stifle such opinions, Louis allowed time to silence them. He was also generous to Jeanne. She was promised for the rest of her life 'the fine and honest train' due to the daughter, sister and ex-wife (even though the marriage was allegedly non-existent) of three successive monarchs. She was also given the duchy of Berry and devoted the rest of her life to the service of God. She founded an order of nuns, the *Annonciades*, and began building a convent in Bourges. In 1503 she took the veil herself and won admiration by her self-mortification. She died two years later and was canonized in 1950.

Louis was now free to marry Charles VIII's widow. Anne attracted him for at least two reasons: first, she was only twenty-two years old and had proved herself capable of childbearing; secondly, by marrying her he would retain control of Brittany. While mourning her late husband, Anne asserted her independence as duchess. She appointed Jean de Chalon, prince of Orange, to administer Brittany in her name and instructed various towns in the duchy to send representatives who would accompany her to Paris for her meeting with the king.

Anne could drive a hard bargain. When Louis first proposed to her, she reminded him that he was not yet free to marry and seemed doubtful about his chances of getting his marriage annulled. She even declared that no verdict on this matter, however authoritative, would satisfy her conscience. Yet Anne's religious scruples were, it seems, less strong than her desire to become queen for the second time. On 19 August she and Louis reached an agreement at Étampes. He promised to hand over to her representatives three Breton towns which had been under French occupation. Anne, for her part, promised to marry Louis as soon as he was free. Shortly afterwards she returned to Brittany.

On 7 January 1499, Anne and Louis signed their marriage contract in Nantes. This laid down that in the event of issue from the marriage, the second male child, or a female in default of a male, would inherit Brittany. If only one son were born, the heir to the duchy would be his second son. In any event, Anne would administer the duchy in her lifetime and draw its revenues. If she died first, Louis was to administer Brittany during his life; it would then revert to Anne's relatives and heirs exclusively. On 19 January, Louis undertook to respect all the rights and privileges traditionally enjoyed by the Bretons.

Meanwhile, on 8 January, Louis and Anne were married in the château of Nantes. Though often praised for her beauty, Anne had one leg shorter than the other, an infirmity which she concealed by wearing a high heel. Her genetic antecedents were poor, which doubtless explains why so many of her pregnancies failed. Her first child by Louis, Claude, born on 13 October 1499, was for eleven years the only child in the royal nursery and the pivot of Louis's matrimonial diplomacy. Though plain, Claude was a desirable match on account of her rich dowry which included the Orléans patrimony, the duchy of Brittany, and the French claims to Asti, Milan, Genoa and Naples.

The conquest of Milan, 1499

On becoming king, Louis XII acquired the Angevin claim to Naples. He also regained the county of Asti which he had ceded to Charles VIII in 1496; but he was mainly interested in the duchy of Milan, to which he had a personal claim dating back to the marriage of his grandfather Louis to Valentina, daughter of Giangaleazzo Visconti, duke of Milan. The house of Sforza now ruled Milan and Louis XII, as duc d'Orléans, had tried on several occasions to make good his claim.

Milan was among the richest, most powerful states in Italy. It had a flourishing agriculture and its arms industry enjoyed a reputation equalled only by that of Germany. Strategically, the duchy was well situated: in the north it controlled the mountain passes leading to the rich cities of south Germany; in the east its influence extended to the middle Po valley; and in the south it exercised a semi-protectorate over Genoa, giving it an outlet to the Mediterranean and access to Genoese banking facilities. For all these reasons, Milan was the envy of its neighbours. The Swiss wanted to annex the area near Lake Como controlling access to the Alpine passes; and Venice, having seized Brescia and Bergamo, was not averse to a further westward expansion of her *terra firma*.

In seeking to make good his claim to Milan, Louis needed allies in Italy. He won over Pope Alexander VI by conniving at the creation of a new principality in the Romagna for Cesare Borgia, at the expense of lesser Italian states. From his own resources Louis gave Cesare the duchy of Valentinois, as we have seen, and also a pension and the hand of Charlotte d'Albret. He secured the neutrality of Venice by agreeing to her annexation of Cremona. Success also smiled on his diplomatic efforts outside Italy. Henry VII of England, who needed to consolidate his position at home, was easily persuaded to renew the Treaty of Etaples. Ferdinand of Aragon was glad to see the French king concerning himself with Milan rather than Naples. Philip the Fair, who ruled the Netherlands, took the unusual step in July 1499 of doing homage to Louis for the fiefs of Flanders, Artois and

Charolais. The Swiss allowed him to raise troops in the cantons in return for a perpetual pension and an annual subsidy. As for Philibert duke of Savoy, he granted the king free passage through his territories in return for an annual pension of 22,000 *livres* payable after the conquest of Lombardy and a monthly payment of 3000 gold *écus* during the campaign. Within Milan itself, Lodovico Sforza was seen by many as a usurper. He claimed that he had assumed the dukedom in 1494 by popular invitation, but was widely suspected of having poisoned his predecessor. Unlike the king of France, he could count on little outside support.

While Louis's diplomats paved the way for a new French invasion of Italy, he reorganized his army. Some companies were disbanded and new ones formed. In the spring of 1499 he recruited infantry, mainly in Switzerland: eventually he built up an army of more than 6000 horse and 17,000 foot. After coming to Lyon on 10 July 1499, Louis inspected his troops but decided not lead them himself. His council apparently thought it would be beneath the dignity of a king of France to measure himself against a mere Sforza, but perhaps more important was the tradition that the king should not leave France as long as he had no direct male heir to succeed him. Command of the army was accordingly entrusted to three captains: Gian Giacomo Trivulzio, Stuart d'Aubigny (soon to be replaced by Charles de Chaumont) and Louis de Ligny.

The vanguard entered the Milanese on 18 July, on the same day as the artillery and the rest of the cavalry left Lyon. A fortnight later the whole army regrouped in the Lombard plain. Sforza played for time by offering Louis the Milanese succession. His proposal, however, was rejected, and the French penetrated the Milanese from Asti. Their savage sacking of two small towns, Rocca d'Arezzo and Annona, was calculated to spread terror across the duchy. At Valenza they employed a different tactic. Three captured Italian captains were set free without a ransom being exacted, an act of royal clemency which encouraged other towns to surrender. Alessandria, however, after resisting a three-day siege, suffered terribly at the hands of the Swiss. Meanwhile, Genoa rallied to Louis, the Venetians marched on Lodi and a number of Lombard towns rebelled. On 2 September, Sforza fled to the imperial court. The citizens of Milan, anxious to avoid a sack, capitulated soon afterwards. Amidst popular rejoicing, the arms of Sforza were replaced by those of King Louis.

On 6 October, Louis made his entry into 'his city of Milan' for the first time. He passed under a triumphal arch bearing the inscription: 'Louis king of the Franks, duke of Milan'. Representatives of various Italian states came to congratulate him. Louis spent barely two months in the Milanese during which he tried to win the hearts of the people by severely punishing his troops for any excesses. He also abolished some old hunting laws, which were resented by the local nobility. While important families that had been persecuted by the Sforzas were given back their privileges and property, favours were showered on Sforza's followers in the hope of winning them over. But Louis showed less concern for humble folk. He reduced direct taxation but raised indirect taxes. He also distributed offices, lands and lordships to captains who had distinguished themselves in the recent campaign.

With men of trust occupying key posts in the duchy and a sizeable number of garrisons planted in various towns, Louis felt able to return home. But no sooner had he left Milan than his troops began to misbehave. The Milanese soon regretted Sforza's rule and when he invaded in January 1500 he was acclaimed almost everywhere as a liberator. On 25 January the people of Milan threw out the French (except for a garrison in the castle), forcing them to withdraw to Novara, but Sforza obliged them to go further still. Early in March a new French army commanded by La Trémoïlle invaded Italy and advanced on Novara, where Sforza lay in wait. A battle seemed imminent, but his Swiss soldiers refused to fight their compatriots on the French side. La Trémoïlle allowed them to return to Switzerland. Sforza tried to conceal himself among them, but was recognized, taken to France and imprisoned at Loches, where he died a few years later.

Georges d'Amboise, meanwhile, reorganized the administration of Milan. He pardoned the citizens in the king's name and reduced the fine they had been asked to pay. A new French-style government was set up comprising two governors – one civil, one military – working alongside a senate with a Franco-Italian membership, its functions similar to those of a parlement in France. In May 1500 he handed over the government of Milan to his nephew, Chaumont d'Amboise.

The reconquest of Naples, 1501

Louis next turned his attention to Naples, where many of his courtiers had lordships they hoped to recover. He revived the idea, first mooted under Charles VIII, of taking the king of Aragon into partnership. In the secret Treaty of Granada (11 November 1500) the two monarchs agreed to conquer Naples jointly and then divide it between them. Louis was to get Naples, Campania, Gaeta, the Terra di Lavoro, the Abruzzi and the province of Campobasso along with the titles of king of Naples and of Jerusalem; Ferdinand was to get Apulia and Calabria and the titles of king of Sicily and duke of Calabria and Apulia. However, for some unknown reason, two provinces – Basilicata and Capitanata – were overlooked in the treaty.

In the spring of 1501, Louis raised a new army and placed it under the command of Stuart d'Aubigny. After a general muster at Parma on 25 May, the army crossed the Appenines. Meanwhile, Ferdinand sent an army under

Gonzalo da Cordoba to establish a foothold in Calabria and along the coast of Apulia. Early in July, the French invaded the kingdom of Naples using the same terror tactics as in the Milanese. Any town offering resistance, however slight, was brutally sacked. The worst massacre was at Capua where all the defenders were put to the sword and the entire population – estimated at 8000 – was wiped out. The streets flowed with blood as the French and Swiss raped, looted and burned. Against such barbarity Federigo III of Naples offered no resistance. On 4 August the French entered Naples. Federigo, who threw himself on their mercy, was better treated than Sforza had been. He was allowed to travel to France in regal style and given a pension and the county of Maine, spending his last years peacefully in the Loire valley.

While planting garrisons in the kingdom of Naples, d'Aubigny sent La Palice to occupy the Abruzzi and the provinces of Capitanata and Basilicata. The period between August 1501 and June 1502 was marked by the greatest expansion of French power in Italy. Louis XII's Italian dominions, including Milan and Asti, covered an area of 75,000 square kilometres. No king of France had ever owned as much territory since the start of the Capetian dynasty in AD 887; none was to have as much again before 1789. Realizing the economic potential of his new dominions, Louis took steps to exploit them. Early in August 1501 he appointed Louis d'Armagnac, duc de Nemours, as viceroy in Naples. Nemours, however, was a mediocrity incapable of standing up to his Spanish rival, Gonzalo da Cordoba.

The Spaniards had carefully avoided collaborating with the French in the conquest of Naples. Working strictly for themselves they had occupied the territories – the two Calabrias and Apulia – given to them by the Treaty of Granada. Soon, however, squabbles developed between the allies. A major difficulty concerned the two provinces that had been overlooked by the treaty. After the French had occupied them, Gonzalo claimed them for Aragon. In the spring of 1502 he entered Capitanata and expelled the French from several forts. Following the breakdown of talks between Nemours and Gonzalo, on 9 June the Spaniards captured Tripalda. There followed months, even years, of desultory warfare without, it seems, any overall strategy. Each captain did more or less as he thought best. Certain engagements caught the imagination of chroniclers. One was the famous duel between the French knight Bayard and the Spanish captain Alonso de Sotomayor, which ended in the latter's death. Another was the epic encounter between French and Spanish knights – eleven on each side – which was watched by a thousand people from the walls of Trani.

Louis XII returned to Italy in the summer of 1502. His presence raised the morale of his troops. They invaded Apulia in July and soon afterwards Calabria. By the end of the summer the Spaniards held only a few towns along the Adriatic coast, including Barletta, where Gonzalo had his headquarters. Though Nemours disposed of larger forces, he allowed them to succumb to disease, hunger and desertion. As his army dwindled in size, the Spaniards received reinforcements by sea. Gonzalo was not only a brave soldier but a brilliant tactician. His military reforms led to the creation of the *tercio* in the sixteenth century. Abandoning the use of light cavalry, he relied mainly on infantry and provided it with better protection than in the past. The old companies which were too small for modern warfare were grouped into larger *coronelias*, each supported by cavalry and artillery.

In April 1503, Gonzalo launched an offensive. He defeated d'Aubigny at Seminara on 21 April and a week later crushed Nemours at Cerignola. The duke was killed and the bulk of his army had to retreat to the Capua region where it awaited reinforcements. A relief army under La Trémoïlle arrived in Rome just as a new pope was being elected and remained there for three months, supposedly to protect the conclave. Meanwhile, the French position in the south crumbled away. In mid-July, Gonzalo entered Naples effortlessly. He failed, however, to capture Gaeta where the two French armies joined forces at the end of the summer. During the harsh winter that followed both sides suffered hardships. Eventually, Gonzalo offered the French generous surrender terms which they accepted, much to Louis XII's dismay. He ordered Chaumont d'Amboise to detain troops returning from southern Italy who had served him 'so badly', and rounded on his own fiscal officials, accusing them of not paying the army. About twenty were tried and two at least were executed. The disaster in southern Italy, however, was irreversible. On 31 March 1504, Louis and Ferdinand signed a truce of three years.

The succession problem

By marrying Anne of Brittany, Louis XII had hoped to produce a son. So far, however, the queen had borne him only a daughter whom the Salic law debarred from the throne. The king's nearest male heir was his second cousin, François d'Angoulême, who in 1500 was six years old. He was being brought up at Amboise by his mother, Louise of Savoy. Both were closely supervised by Pierre de Gié, a marshal of France of Breton origin. Being firmly committed to Brittany's union with France, Gié hoped to see it maintained by a marriage between the king's daughter Claude and François. But Anne was determined to protect her duchy's independence and, for this reason, favoured an alternative match between Claude and Charles of Ghent, the infant son of Archduke Philip the Fair and grandson of the Emperor Maximilian. Finding himself caught in the crossfire between Anne and Gié, Louis pursued contradictory policies. Whether he did so out of weakness or duplicity is not easy to unravel.

On 30 April 1501 the king signed a secret declaration nullifying in advance any marriage between his daughter and another than François. Meanwhile, the idea of marrying Claude to Charles of Ghent was strongly canvassed by Anne with the backing of Georges d'Amboise. Claude's dowry was to comprise Milan, Asti and Naples, the duchies of Burgundy and Brittany and the county of Blois. Had this marriage taken place, France would have been dismembered. That Louis XII should have entertained such a possibility is difficult to understand. He may have agreed to Anne's proposal simply in order to extort the investiture of Milan from the emperor. He may also have felt covered by the secret declaration made in April 1501. Be that as it may, the betrothal of Claude and Charles was celebrated in August 1501, and Philip the Fair and his wife, Juana of Castile, visited France in November and met their prospective daughter-in-law. As for Maximilian, he promised to confer Milan's investiture on Louis, but only verbally and within the secrecy of his own chamber.

Early in 1504, as Louis fell seriously ill, Gié persuaded him to confirm his declaration of April 1501. He also ordered a strict watch to be kept on all river traffic and roads leading to Brittany, so as to prevent Anne from returning there with her daughter in the event of Louis's death. The king, however, recovered, and Gié came under fire from both Anne and Louise of Savoy. The latter's servant, Pierre de Pontbriant, brought damaging charges to the king, which were subsequently used to prepare Gié's indictment. He was accused *inter alia* of ordering the queen's detention and of alienating her from Louise. In July a royal commission was appointed to investigate the charges.

Maximilian, in the meantime, drew closer to Louis. On 22 September the Treaty of Blois was concluded. It consisted of three separate agreements. The first was an alliance between Maximilian, Philip the Fair and Louis XII which Ferdinand of Aragon was conditionally invited to join. Louis renounced his claim to Milan in return for an indemnity of 900,000 florins, and Maximilian promised to give him the investiture of Milan within three months. The second agreement was a league against Venice which involved Pope Julius II. The third revived the projected marriage between Claude de France and Charles of Ghent. If Louis died without a direct male heir, the couple were to get Milan, Genoa, Brittany, Asti, Blois, Burgundy, Auxonne, the Auxerrois, the Mâconnais, and Bar-sur-Seine! On 7 April 1505, Maximilian conferred the investiture of Milan on Louis and his male descendants. However, the accord between the two rulers was upset in November by the death of Isabella of Castile. She bequeathed her kingdom to her husband, Ferdinand of Aragon, thereby setting aside the rights of her daughter Juana. Philip the Fair, taking umbrage, assumed the title of king of Castile. He also accused Louis XII of betrayal, a development which naturally threatened the marriage recently arranged between his son and Claude. Another setback for Anne was the trial of Marshal Gié. He appeared before the *Grand conseil* in October 1504 and was relentlessly interrogated. The magistrates, impressed by his testimony, refused the queen's demand for an additional enquiry to be held in Brittany. Once all the evidence had been gathered, the prosecuting counsel called for the death sentence to be passed on Gié, whom he accused of *lèse-majesté*. However, on 30 December, the marshal was set free, his case being adjourned till April.

In April 1505, Louis XII made his will. He ordered his daughter's marriage to François d'Angoulême as soon as she was old enough, notwithstanding the earlier agreement with Charles of Ghent. He also forbade her to leave the kingdom in the meantime for any reason and set up a council of regency which included a number of royal servants capable of standing up to the queen. These arrangements infuriated Anne, and when the king had a relapse she again demonstrated her ducal independence by withdrawing to Brittany for five months. At the same time she brought pressure to bear on Gié's trial. On 14 March it was transferred to the Parlement of Toulouse, a body noted for its severity. Anne employed an army of barristers to press her case against the marshal and sought the backing of jurists from as far afield as Italy. Her efforts, however, proved unavailing. Although Gié was found guilty of various offences, the sentence passed on him on 9 February 1506 was surprisingly mild. He lost the governorship of François d'Angoulême, his captaincies of the châteaux of Angers and Amboise and his company of a hundred *lances*. He was also suspended as marshal for five years and banished from court for the same length of time. Though he was refused a royal pardon, Gié was allowed to retire to his château at Le Verger, where he died in 1513.

The queen's absence in Brittany gave Louis a chance to secure his position. In May he formally announced his daughter's forthcoming marriage to François d'Angoulême whom he instructed to join him at Plessis-lez-Tours. The captains of all the kingdom's fortresses were made to swear an oath to obey the king's will when the time came. Before the marriage could take place, however, the Treaty of Blois had to be repudiated. It contained a penalty clause whereby Burgundy, Milan and Asti were to be forfeited to Charles if his marriage to Claude were broken off by Louis, Anne or Claude herself. Louis got round the difficulty by putting the responsibility for his breach of faith on the shoulders of his subjects. He called an Assembly of Notables consisting of representatives from the parlements and towns, which met at Plessis-lez-Tours in May 1506. Through their spokesman Thomas Bricot, a doctor of the University of Paris, the delegates implored the king, whom they addressed as 'Father of the people', to gratify them by marrying his daughter to François d'Angoulême, who, being 'wholly French' (*tout français*), was most acceptable to them. Simulating surprise, the king requested time for reflection and to consult the princes of the blood. A few days later, the chancellor signified Louis's willingness to concede his subjects' request. He asked them to promise in return to see that the marriage took place and to recognize François as king should Louis die without male issue. On 21 May, Claude and François were formally betrothed; Louis had averted the damage that the kingdom would have suffered if the Treaty of Blois had been implemented.

On 3 August 1508, François d'Angoulême left Amboise to settle permanently at court. At fourteen he was old enough for kingship, but could not yet be sure of the throne. In April 1510 the queen was again pregnant, but on 25 October she gave birth to another daughter, called Renée. Anne did produce a son in 1512, but he died almost at birth. The king, it seems, now abandoned hope of perpetuating his line. François, now known as the Dauphin, was admitted to the king's council and made captain of a hundred *lances*.

Domestic policies

Historians have given so much attention to the Italian Wars that they have barely noticed the government of France under Charles VIII and Louis XII. Yet, as Russell Major has shown, it was under these kings that the monarchy which had begun to take shape under Charles VII was 'cemented'. Louis XII's contribution was especially notable: he provided France with 'the most efficient government that it enjoyed during the Renaissance'. His reign produced a large number of edicts and ordinances aimed for the most part at improving the administration of justice. How far they represented his own ideas or those of his ministers is hard to say. There is not enough evidence to support the view of one historian (J.-A. Neret) that Louis came to the throne with a plan of reform inspired by Machiavelli. He certainly combined maturity with a long experience of variable political fortunes.

From the start of his reign Louis tried to be popular. This could best be done by sparing his subjects' pockets. Charles VIII had left a treasury so empty that it could not even pay his funeral costs (estimated at 45,000 *livres*), so Louis announced that he would pay for them out of his private purse. He also paid for the festivities marking his own entry into Paris on 2 July and released royal officials and pensioners from the traditional obligation of making an accession gift. Louis announced that he would limit taxes to the minimum required by the defence of the realm, and kept his word for as long as possible. Except for a few years, he kept down the level of the *taille* almost till the end of the reign, and even lowered it on occasion. Around 1500, the *taille* amounted to only about 2.3 million *livres* annually, as compared with 3.9 million under Louis XI. Louis once ordered his agents to stop collecting a surtax when the reason for it – the Genoese revolt – had ended. When he came under pressure, he preferred to alienate parts of the royal domain or rely on loans or forced loans rather than raise taxes. He was able to do this because for many years his campaigns in Italy more than paid for themselves through plunder. At the end of his reign Louis ran into difficulties and taxes rose; yet he continued to be regarded, even as late as the seventeenth century, as a king who had spared his subjects.

Believing that a king should 'live of his own' (i.e. on the income from his domain), Louis avoided excessive expenditure on his court and on gifts to courtiers. He reduced the annual total of gifts and pensions from over 500,000 *livres* around 1500 to less than half that sum by 1510. However, in the last two years of the reign it went up again. Disappointed courtiers called Louis '*le roi roturier*' (the commoner king) and his parsimony was mocked in satirical plays staged in Paris by the *Basoche*. But Louis was unrepentant. 'I much prefer', he said, 'to make dandies laugh at my miserliness than to make the people weep at my open-handedness.' Apart from curbing expenditure, he trebled the revenue from his domain by more efficient accounting. It reached a total of 231,000l. annually, or 6.3 per cent of the total royal revenues.

The sale of offices was a fiscal expedient used by Louis XII. By the end of the fifteenth century a distinction was made between financial and judicial offices: only the sale of the former was tacitly allowed. The ban on the sale of judicial offices had been affirmed by Charles VIII in July 1493: a candidate for office was only to be admitted after swearing an oath that he had paid nothing for it. Louis XII repeated the ban in March 1498. He admitted that he had allowed such sales in the past and foresaw that he might do so again 'out of importunity or otherwise'. The chancellor was instructed not to seal such letters of provision, and royal officers were not to implement them if the letters had been sealed inadvertently. However, Louis could hardly expect his servants to obey a law which he had broken himself. In April 1499 he appointed Jean le Coq as *conseiller général des aides* 'notwithstanding ... his promise to pay a certain sum'. Office-holders, notably members of the Parlement of Paris, were allowed by Louis to resign their offices in return for a payment. Sometimes a fiction was used – such as the exchange of one office for another – to conceal an original payment.

Louis XII was one of the last kings of France to listen to pleadings in the parlement. The great Ordinance of Blois (March 1499) was aimed at 'upholding justice, shortening trials and giving relief to the people'. Its 162 clauses dealt with many matters, not all judicial. While prescribing severe penalties for vagabonds and accepting the need for interrogation under torture, the ordinance sought to promote fair and prompt justice. Magistrates were to be worthy of their responsibilities; they were not to delegate them or be absent without leave. Proper legal qualifications were laid down for service on the judicial bench. No fathers, sons or brothers were to serve in the same court, and the sale of offices was banned, not for the first time. However, the ordinance seems to have been poorly enforced, for several of its provisions had to be repeated in another ordinance of 1510. This contained new clauses directed against usurers and regulations concerning notaries.

One of Louis XII's major reforms was the reorganization of the *Grand conseil*, or king's council acting as a lawcourt. It can be traced back to 1469 and a continuous series of archives, starting in 1483, shows that by then the council was meeting regularly and beginning to acquire a distinct identity. But it was Louis who, in August 1497, gave it a permanent staff of legal experts capable of coping with its growing legal business. Their competence included disputes between sovereign courts, complaints levelled at royal officials, quarrels over fiefs or ecclesiastical benefices, as well as appeals in civil and criminal cases. Being directly under the king, the council facilitated his intervention in criminal cases which touched him personally, such as that of Marshal Gié. Regarding the *Grand conseil* as a rival, the parlement showed its hostility on several occasions; but Louis placated it by giving it precedence and allowing its members to sit in the *Grand conseil* whenever they wished.

Louis's concern to streamline the judicial system extended to France's newest provinces. In Normandy the highest court of law, dating from the time of the dukes, was the *Echiquier* which met occasionally and had no permanent staff. Louis turned it into a permanent body with four presidents and 28 councillors. Under Francis I it became the Parlement of Rouen. In Provence, the *Conseil éminent* of the old counts of Provence was turned by Louis into a parlement with one president and eleven councillors. Finally, in Brittany justice was administered by the *Grands Jours*, a commission renewable each year. The members were partly Bretons and partly recruits from the Parlement of Paris. It functioned alongside a council, which was an administrative and judicial body. Gradually the commission developed at the expense of the council: in 1491 it acquired a permanent staff and fixed annual sessions. However, it did not become a parlement till 1554.

A major obstacle to judicial efficiency in early modern France was the survival of unwritten customary law. This varied from one locality to another; it was entirely pragmatic, serving particular needs as they arose. Because customs were variable and ill-defined, they needed to be validated by a judge before they could be used as evidence. In the Middle Ages attempts had been made by various kings to distinguish good customs from bad ones. Royal intervention took the form of a written declaration establishing what customs were to apply to a particular area. Professional jurists also produced *coutumiers* in which the customary law of whole provinces was written down. But it was only in the fifteenth century, when the kingdom was sufficiently unified politically, that the crown was able to think of providing an official, authenticated and coherent set of customs. The lead was given by Charles VII, but little further progress was made till 1497, when Charles VIII altered the procedure by which definitive customary laws were arrived at. Henceforth, a royal judge in a given area drew up a tentative list of customs after consulting his colleagues and local worthies. Representatives of the three estates then met to discuss the draft, which had to be approved by a majority of each estate's representatives before being published in the king's name. Much of this work was done under Louis XII, who commissioned two distinguished *parlementaires* – Roger Barme and Thibaut Baillet – to write down the customs of northern France. Till the end of the reign these two legists, acting in concert with the *baillis*, *sénéchaux* and representatives of the three estates in each area, verified and confirmed many customs after weeding out accretions. Georges d'Amboise signed the first *rédaction* at Tours on 5 May 1508 and many others quickly followed, but the task was unfinished when Louis died. Several provinces had to wait a century before their customs were verified.

In 1506, Louis was acclaimed by the spokesman of the notables at Blois as 'father of the people'. He became renowned for his efforts to spare his subjects taxes, to give them justice and to provide them with security. His praises were sung throughout the sixteenth century. Even after Henry IV's reign there were demands for a return to the time of Louis XII. His role, according to Russell Major, was 'more to make the monarchy beloved than to change its character'.

The Genoese rebellion, 1506

Although Louis XII had relinquished his rights in Naples, he had not abandoned all his Italian interests. His authority as duke of Milan had been legitimized in April 1505 by the emperor's investiture and he was also count of Asti and 'protector' of Genoa. Early in 1506 a popular rising in Genoa against the rule of the local patricians turned into a revolt against the French. At first Louis tried to temporize, but the rebels set up a new administration headed by a doge. On 12 March they massacred Frenchmen who had taken refuge in a fort. Taking this as a personal affront, Louis gathered a large army in the spring of 1507 and invaded Genoa. The doge fled and the city surrendered. Louis annexed Genoa to his domain, destroyed its charters, executed sixty rebels and threatened to impose a huge fine on the inhabitants. Later he relented: most of the citizens were allowed to keep their lives and property, and their fine was reduced. A new governor, Raoul de Lannoy, was ordered to run the city humanely and fairly. The king appreciated Genoa's importance as a commercial and financial centre. He did not want to see it destroyed and therefore refused to allow the bulk of his army into it. He did, however, impose his authority in an entry acclaimed by contemporaries as the ceremonial climax of his reign. Wearing full armour, a helmet with white plumes and a surcoat of gold cloth, he rode a richly caparisoned black charger beneath a canopy carried by four Genoese notables dressed in black. Along the route young girls holding olive branches begged for mercy.

France and Venice had been allies since 1500. The Venetians had taken advantage of the French conquest of Milan by nibbling at the eastern edge of the duchy. But the long-term objectives of the allies were not necessarily identical. The Venetians were alarmed by the closeness of the French to their own *terra firma*. The two powers also differed about the emperor. In February 1508, Maximilian attacked the Venetians. Louis was about to send a force to help them, when he learned that they had signed a truce with Maximilian. He felt badly let down as they had not consulted him. The pope, meanwhile, had his own reasons for falling out with the Venetians. His desire to extend the States of the Church into the Romagna ran counter to Venice's territorial ambitions. Moreover, Venetian policy towards the Turks contradicted the pope's aim of mounting a crusade.

In December 1508 representatives of the emperor, the kings of France and Aragon, and the pope met at Cambrai. However divergent their individual aims may have been, they all wanted to abase the pride of Venice. Anticipating her defeat, they agreed to share the spoils: Verona and control of the Adige valley would go to Maximilian, Brescia to Louis XII, Ravenna to the pope and Otranto to Ferdinand of Aragon, now king of Naples. For some unknown reason, Louis decided to fire the opening shot, while his allies undertook to declare themselves one month later. The pope simply placed Venice under an interdict.

On 16 April 1509, three days after declaring war on Venice, Louis crossed the Alps to take charge of military operations. An important innovation was the decision to place infantry under the command of noblemen, who previously would have considered such a role beneath their dignity. In addition to 20,000 infantry (including 8000 Swiss mercenaries) the king disposed of about 2000 men-at-arms. His lieutenants included names familiar from earlier campaigns such as Gian Giacomo Trivulzio, La Trémoïlle, La Palice, Chaumont d'Amboise and San Severino. Among younger men, going into action for the first time, were the king's cousin, Charles de Bourbon-Montpensier, and his nephew, Gaston de Foix. The Venetian army was larger: it comprised, according to Guicciardini, 2000 Italian *lances*, 3000 light cavalry (including Albanian stradiots) and 20,000 infantry. The commanders included Bartolomeo d'Alviano and Niccolò Orsini, count of Pitigliano.

On 14 May the two armies faced each other at Agnadello. Instead of attacking the French as they crossed the river Adda, Pitigliano preferred to wait for them within a well-fortified camp. He was ordered, however, to move to higher ground, and this gave the French a chance to attack him in the open. D'Alviano, commanding the Venetian vanguard, bore the brunt of the attack and repulsed it, but the rest of the Venetian army was too widely spread out to come to his aid. He and his cavalry were consequently surrounded and captured. His infantry fought on bravely, only to be annihilated by a much larger force of Swiss and Gascons.

Following their victory the French captured Cremona, Crema and Brescia. The pope, meanwhile, pushed towards Ravenna with his army, but Maximilian failed to appear in Italy. So Louis returned to France after celebrating his triumph in Milan. Venice, for its part, allowed imperial troops to occupy Treviso, Verona and Padua, handed over ports in southern Italy to Ferdinand of Aragon, released the people of the *terra firma* from their allegiance and accepted the pope's occupation of towns in the Romagna. The Venetians, however, had enough experience of foreign affairs (their diplomats were the best in Europe at the time) to know that time was on their side: they felt sure that sooner or later the coalition against them would break up.

Early in July the Venetians recaptured Padua from the emperor. He appealed for help to Louis XII, who promptly sent a force under La Palice, which was soon joined by a large army led by Maximilian himself; but he did not lay siege to Padua till mid-September. After breaching its wall, he prepared an assault, but the French nobles refused to fight as infantry as long as the German nobles remained mounted. In the end, the assault was abandoned. On 30 September, Maximilian angrily lifted the siege. He left that night for Austria, soon to be followed by the rest of his army. La Palice and his men returned to Milan.

Julius II, meanwhile, began to detach himself from the league; he did not wish to see Venice destroyed, for her maritime co-operation was essential to his crusading plans. Nor was he keen to see France or the Empire strongly entrenched in north Italy. In February 1510 he lifted the interdict on Venice. He then detached Ferdinand of Aragon from the coalition. In return for the investiture of Naples, Ferdinand agreed to be neutral for the present. Henry VIII of England was also won over. But the pope's most resounding diplomatic coup was to persuade the Swiss to debar France from raising mercenaries in the cantons. In the summer of 1510, Julius attacked Ferrara, seemingly an easy prey. The duke, Alfonso d'Este, appealed to Louis XII for help. Having recently abandoned the siege of Padua, the French army under Chaumont returned to the Milanese. They had to face a Swiss invasion, but it did not last long. Fighting around Ferrara continued for more than a year without giving the pope a decisive victory. Following the death of Chaumont on 11 February 1511, command of the French army in Italy was given first to Trivulzio, then to Gaston de Foix, duc de Nemours.

He was young, handsome and brave, and his presence in Italy raised French morale, putting new life into the campaign.

So far the pope had failed to detach Maximilian from his alliance with France. What is more, Louis and Maximilian were in agreement over the need to reform the church in its head and members. They supported the idea, put forward two hundred years earlier, that a General Council of the church was superior in authority to the pope. At their bidding five cardinals who had fallen out with the pope called a General Council to Pisa for the autumn of 1511. Julius was ordered to appear before this body under threat of deposition, but he was not easily intimidated: he replied by summoning an alternative council to Rome for April 1512.

The battle of Ravenna, 11 April 1512

Meanwhile, the French army in north Italy, now commanded by Gaston de Foix, invaded the Romagna, relieving Ferrara and capturing Mirandola. As it drew near to Bologna, the pope's army fell back on Ravenna. Early in October 1511 a so-called Holy League was formed between the pope, Ferdinand of Aragon and Venice. Its avowed aim was to reconquer the lands recently taken from the Holy See, but its real purpose was to drive the French out of Italy.

Gaston reorganized his army to face the threat of a triple invasion of Lombardy: by the Swiss in the north, by papal and Spanish forces from the south and by the Venetians in the east. The Swiss were the first to attack, capturing Bellinzona in December; but Gaston wisely remained inside Milan instead of coming out to meet them. He knew that if he left the city, the people of Milan would rebel. His caution was justified when the Swiss returned home of their own accord. The army of the Holy League, meanwhile, tried to win back lost ground in the Romagna, prompting Gaston to send reinforcements to Bologna. In February he marched to the relief of Brescia which was under attack from the Venetians. A fierce struggle ended in their defeat. When the pope heard the news, he is said to have torn off his beard. He could draw comfort, however, from the dismal failure of the Council of Pisa. It had been unable to gather international support and was disbanded soon after moving to Milan.

In November, Henry VIII joined the Holy League and prepared to invade Picardy. The threat of such an attack, coupled with indications that Maximilian might change sides, impressed upon Louis XII the need for a decisive victory in Italy. While Gaston de Foix had been fighting near Brescia, a Hispano-papal army under Ramon de Cardona, viceroy of Naples, had reconquered most of the Romagna. Gaston marched on Ravenna in the hope of luring the enemy into the open. Although the viceroy's army was smaller than that of the French, he came down from Imola and pitched camp on marshy ground outside Ravenna. It was protected by a deep trench, behind which was arrayed a battery of thirty guns and strange war machines which contemporaries compared to the scythed chariots used in antiquity. Gaston's artillery consisted of thirty French guns and twenty-four supplied by the duke of Ferrara.

At dawn on 11 April, Gaston, after crossing the River Ronco, formed his army into a crescent with infantry in the middle and cavalry on the wings. Closing in on the viceroy's camp, he began a fierce bombardment. The Spanish guns responded, inflicting heavy losses on the French infantry. Eventually the Spanish cavalry came out and engaged the French men-at-arms in a bloody encounter which ended in a Spanish rout. The infantry, meanwhile, moved into action. More fierce fighting ended in victory to the French. But as Gaston tried to intercept some Spaniards who were fleeing from the field, his horse stumbled, enabling the enemy to fall on him and wound him fatally. Thus ended the career of a military leader of great promise. His death, Bayard wrote, made the victory seem like a defeat.

The battle of Ravenna was one of the bloodiest on record. Both sides suffered heavily. Ramon de Cardona returned to Naples with only 300 horse and 3000 foot, having started out with 16,000 men. Among Spaniards taken prisoner were Fabrizio Colonna, general of the horse, and Pedro Navarro, general of the foot. A more unusual captive was the papal legate, Giulio de' Medici, the future Pope Clement VII. French losses, though fewer, were none the less severe: 3000 to 4000 infantry, 80 men-at-arms, several gentlemen of the king's household and nine archers of his guard. From the tactical standpoint, Ravenna is remembered as the first Italian battle in which cannon decided the day. Gaston de Foix saw that Spanish tactics could be overcome by superior artillery strength. His only serious mistake was to bring his infantry too far forward at the start so that it suffered heavier losses than necessary.

Even if Gaston had survived, it is doubtful if the French could have taken advantage of their victory, for the odds were heavily against them. On 6 May, 18,000 Swiss troops led by Cardinal Schiner descended into Italy and joined the Venetian army near Verona. Together they marched on Milan. La Palice, the new French commander, retreated westward from Ravenna with an army much reduced in size after the recent battle to which disease and desertion had added their toll. The retreat soon turned into a headlong flight. By the end of June, France had lost the Milanese and her army was back in Dauphiné. The few French garrisons that had been left behind in Italy gradually capitulated.

Ferdinand took advantage of Louis's difficulties to invade Navarre in pursuit of the claim which his wife, Germaine de Foix, had inherited from her brother Gaston. Louis, who had supported Gaston's claim against the ruling house of Albret, was obliged to support the rival claim of Jean d'Albret. However, Ferdinand, having occupied Spanish Navarre, declared himself its lawful sovereign. Louis despatched an army under the nominal command of François d'Angoulême, the effective commanders being marshals La Palice and Lautrec. They laid siege to Pamplona, but the arrival of Aragonese reinforcements forced them to withdraw. Spanish Navarre was irretrievably lost. All that remained to Jean d'Albret was a small portion of his kingdom on the French side of the Pyrenees.

In Italy, meanwhile, important political changes were taking place. In November 1512 the emperor joined the Holy League, causing the Venetians to abandon their hostility to France. Within the Milanese, the departure of the French released the conflicting ambitions of former allies. The Swiss wanted Como and Novara; the marquis of Mantua claimed Peschiera; the pope wanted Parma and Piacenza; the duke of Savoy asked for Vercelli; and the Venetians were keen to recover Brescia. In December 1512 the Swiss set up Massimiliano Sforza, the son of Lodovico il Moro, as duke of Milan. Soon afterwards, in February 1513, Pope Julius II died. He was succeeded by Cardinal Giovanni de' Medici, who took the name of Leo X. Although no friend of France, he was more peaceable than his predecessor. Louis skilfully exploited the changed situation. In March 1513, Venice reached an agreement with him regarding the partition of north Italy. France renewed her 'Auld Alliance' with Scotland in the hope of containing Henry VIII, who was anxious to cut a dash on the Continent. Louis also signed a truce with Ferdinand: each agreed to respect the status quo in Navarre. All that remained of the Holy League was a coalition of England, the Empire and the Swiss Confederation.

A disastrous year, 1513

Louis XII might have been expected to leave Italy alone after his last disastrous campaign, particularly as Henry VIII and Maximilian were now threatening his northern frontiers, but he would not accept the loss of Milan. His new treaty with Venice encouraged him to launch another trans-Alpine campaign. He gathered an army 12,000 strong in April 1513 and placed it under the command of Louis de La Trémoïlle, who was assisted by d'Aubigny and Trivulzio. It crossed the Alps in May and captured Alessandria. Four thousand Swiss shut themselves up in Novara. The French, meanwhile, seized Milan with the help of the anti-Sforza faction within the city. Heartened by this success, La Trémoïlle laid siege to Novara. The town was bombarded and its walls breached, but, hearing that a Swiss relief army was approaching, La Trémoïlle withdrew to Trecate. Here he pitched camp and, believing that he was not being pursued, allowed his troops some rest.

The Swiss, however, launched a furious attack, taking the French by surprise. The main blow fell on the German mercenaries, the landsknechts, who were nearly all wiped out. One of the few survivors was the future Marshal Florange, who allegedly received forty-six wounds. The *gendarmerie* was never seriously engaged in the battle. La Trémoïlle, it seems, waited for an attack that never came, allowing his infantry to be cut to pieces. When he realized that all was lost, he ordered his men to retreat. By the end of June they were back in France. After the French débâcle all the towns in the duchy of Milan, except those under Venetian occupation, submitted to Sforza.

The French defeat in Italy coincided with an invasion of northern France. In mid-June a huge English army commanded by the earl of Shrewsbury and the duke of Suffolk landed in Calais. After joining an imperial army, it laid siege to Thérouanne. Louis XII hurriedly sent an army to Artois under the seigneur de Piennes with orders to relieve Thérouanne but to avoid a pitched battle. He managed to get supplies through to the beleaguered garrison, but as his men-at-arms were returning from their mission, they were intercepted near Guinegatte. Obeying orders, they avoided an engagement, but as they retreated they spread confusion among the French reserve. The retreat became a headlong flight, hence the name 'Battle of the Spurs' given to the action. Among the captains who fell into English hands were the duc de Longueville and Bayard. Thérouanne surrendered on 23 August, but instead of marching on Amiens and Paris, the English seized Tournai which they kept until 1521.

More misfortunes soon befell Louis XII. Early in September, 20,000 to 30,000 Swiss invaded Burgundy and laid siege to Dijon. The town's governor, La Trémoïlle, knowing that his men were outnumbered and that no relief could be expected soon, opened talks with the enemy. They were strong enough to bid for high stakes. Under the Treaty of Dijon, which La Trémoïlle signed in his master's name, Louis gave up all his claims to Milan and Asti. He also promised to buy off the Swiss for 400,000 *écus*. La Trémoïlle handed over hostages as security for the treaty's execution, and the Swiss returned to their cantons. Dijon and Burgundy had been saved, but Louis disavowed La Trémoïlle and refused to ratify the treaty. His breach of faith was not soon forgiven by the Swiss.

The winter of 1513 brought no relief to France's ailing monarch. Anne of Brittany died without giving him the son he had wanted so much. Her claim to Brittany passed to her daughter, Claude. On 18 May 1514 she married François d'Angoulême. The ceremony at Saint-Germain-en-Laye was a simple affair, as the court was still in mourning for the queen. Eyewitnesses, noting Louis's sickly appearance, did not give him long to live, but he was about to spring a surprise. In January 1514 he drew closer to Pope Leo X by recognizing the Fifth Lateran Council and in March he renewed his truce with Ferdinand of Aragon. His master stroke, however, was to drive a wedge between Henry VIII and Maximilian. An Anglo-French treaty, signed in London in August, was sealed by a marriage between Louis and Henry's sister Mary. Public opinion was shocked that a girl of eighteen, universally acclaimed for her beauty, should marry a gouty dotard of fifty-three, but she was ready to pay a heavy price to become queen of France. Henry had also promised to allow her to choose her second husband, a likely prospect, given Louis's age and health.

Louis and Mary were married at Abbeville on 9 October. After the wedding night Louis boasted that he had 'performed marvels', but few believed him, least of all François d'Angoulême, who stood most to lose from the king's remarriage. 'I am certain,' he declared, 'unless I have been told lies, that the king and queen cannot possibly have a child.' Within a short time, Louis began to show signs of wear and tear. The *Basoche* put on a play in which he was shown being carried off to Heaven or to Hell by a filly given by the king of England. Soon after Christmas, Louis fell ill at the palace of the Tournelles in Paris. He died on 1 January 1515 and was immediately succeeded on the throne by François d'Angoulême. Soon afterwards Mary Tudor secretly married the duke of Suffolk, whom Henry VIII had sent to France to congratulate François on his accession.

5

The Church in Crisis

The French or Gallican church faced a serious crisis at the end of the Middle Ages, which was constitutional as well as moral. The papacy had become an absolute monarchy: it controlled appointments to ecclesiastical benefices by means of 'provisions' and 'reservations' and it taxed the clergy by means of annates, tenths, and so on. All this caused much discontent among the clergy. Cathedral and monastic chapters resented the loss of their traditional right to elect their bishops and abbots; the clergy begrudged paying taxes to the papal Curia. The demand arose for the reform of the church in its head and its members. But who was to carry out that reform? Could the papacy be trusted to reform itself?

During the fourteenth century some churchmen began to argue that the responsibility for reform lay not with the papacy but with a General Council. The Dominican John of Paris put forward the theory that a council, since it represented the whole church, was superior in authority to the pope and might depose him if he misused his power. Marsilio of Padua, in his *Defensor Pacis*, denied Christ's institution of the papal primacy and argued in favour of the superiority of a council since it represented the people. Supporters of the conciliar theory were able to put it into practice following a disputed election to the papacy in 1378. The only way of solving the problem of two rival popes seemed to be to call a General Council. This offered a chance, not merely of healing the Great Schism, but also of bringing about reform through a limitation of papal authority. The Council of Constance (1414–18) managed to heal the schism, but otherwise was a disappointment. It issued two decrees: one laid down that a General Council derived its authority directly from Christ; the other provided that such a council should meet at regular intervals. Both decrees represented a victory for the conciliar party, but not a decisive one. It was difficult to see how a General Council, meeting occasionally, could assert its authority over a permanent and powerful papacy. The traditional concept of the papacy remained intact, and the new pope, Martin V, did not confirm the decrees of the council. By banning appeals from the pope to another tribunal, he implicitly rejected the doctrine of conciliar supremacy.

This, however, was not the end of attempts to put a General Council above the pope. The decisive battle between the pope and the conciliarists was fought at the Council of Basle (1431–49). In May 1439 it declared as a dogma of the Christian faith that 'the General Council is above the pope'. It deposed Pope Eugenius IV, replacing him with Felix V; it abolished annates and reservations; and it passed a decree providing for regular provincial and diocesan synods. Yet it failed to defeat the pope for two reasons. First, the radicalism of the council alienated some of its best members; many bishops withdrew when they saw representatives of the lower clergy and universities gaining the ascendancy. Secondly, the princes of Europe failed to give the council their full support, knowing that they could secure more political advantages from the pope than from a council. A few European states, including France, adopted some of the reform decrees of the Council of Basle without even considering the papacy.

Representatives of the Gallican church, meeting at Bourges in 1438, drew up a constitution called the Pragmatic Sanction, which King Charles VII promulgated in July. It declared a General Council to be superior in authority to the pope, abolished annates, forbade appeals to Rome before intermediate jurisdictions had been exhausted, abolished papal reservations, except in respect of benefices vacated at the Curia, and restored the election by chapters of bishops, abbots and priors. The papacy was allowed to collate to a small proportion of benefices, but all expectatives were banned save in respect of university teachers and students. The Pragmatic Sanction guaranteed the latter a third of all prebends while regulating their rights. It also tried, albeit more timidly, to protect the church from royal interference in its affairs: the king was asked to avoid imperious recommendations and to desist from violence in supporting his protégés. Yet he was allowed to present 'benign solicitations' from time to time on behalf of candidates showing zeal for the public good.

The Pragmatic Sanction, however, was not strictly applied after 1438. The French crown used it to check papal pretensions without showing respect for the liberties it enshrined. The king commonly disposed of benefices as he wished, his 'benign' solicitations all too often being brutal commands. Louis XI abolished or restored the Pragmatic for his own political ends. A delegate at the Estates-General of 1484, after the accession of Charles VIII, complained that under the late king the church had declined: elections had been annulled, unworthy people had been appointed to benefices, and holy persons had been relegated to a 'vile and ignominious' condition. The deputies demanded the restoration of the Pragmatic

Sanction, but the government of the Beaujeus was unwilling to renounce Louis XI's authoritarian ways. Equally opposed to the Pragmatic were the bishops who owed their sees to royal favour. In May 1484 the Beaujeus sent a delegation to Rome with the aim of securing a Concordat. The pope, however, insisted on a formal condemnation of the Pragmatic Sanction; and in November 1487, Innocent VIII demanded its abolition. The French crown was unwilling to give way – the Pragmatic was potentially useful against the papacy without seriously threatening royal authority – and the talks with the Holy See accordingly foundered. In the absence of an agreement, the crown did as it wished, sometimes allowing the Pragmatic to operate, sometimes conniving with the papacy at its violation.

Meanwhile, the idea of a General Council lived on. During the second half of the fifteenth century people in many European countries demanded one. The appeal to a council in France came mainly from two directions: first, from the Gallican church whenever the king for political reasons violated the Pragmatic Sanction or threatened to replace it by a Concordat with the papacy; secondly, from the crown itself, whenever it wanted to put pressure on Rome. This had unfortunate consequences: the more the conciliar idea was exploited for political ends, the less the papacy felt inclined to call a council, fearing that it would revive the old question of authority in the church. In 1460, Pius II forbade any future appeal to a council in the bull *Execrabilis*.

On 12 November 1493, King Charles VIII summoned a reform commission to Tours. The members, who were drawn from abbeys and university colleges where discipline had been maintained or restored, called for the enforcement of the Pragmatic Sanction, but failed to get the support of high-ranking churchmen who had a vested interest in the old order. In 1494 the Gallican church was as sick as it had been at the end of Louis XI's reign. The pope and the king continued to dispose of benefices without regard for the rights of chapters or patrons. While rival candidates for benefices fought each other in the parlements, the benefices themselves were sometimes left vacant for years. Bishops, who were often primarily courtiers, soldiers and diplomats, enriched themselves by accumulating benefices, including monasteries which they could hold *in commendam*.

Charles VIII wrote to the French bishops from Italy on 29 October 1494: 'We hope to go to Rome and be there around Christmas. Our aim is to negotiate over the Gallican church with a view to restoring its ancient liberties and to achieving more if we can.' In Florence he met Savonarola, who urged him to rescue Christendom from its current distress, and in Rome he was pressed by Cardinal della Rovere to depose Pope Alexander VI and call a General Council. But the king's position in Italy was too precarious to allow him to tackle church reform seriously. Louis XII was also hamstrung at the start of his reign. He needed the pope to obtain the

annulment of his marriage to Jeanne de France, and was therefore obliged
to give up the idea of a General Council at least for the time being. He was
also unwilling to allow free elections to church benefices or to abstain
from imposing his own candidates on chapters. His chief minister, Georges
d'Amboise, archbishop of Rouen, belonged to one of those rich bourgeois
families which were accustomed to securing the finest abbeys and wealthiest
bishoprics for their members. He was devoted to the king's person and
opposed any reduction of his authority.

In March 1499 an Assembly of Notables, meeting at Blois, was asked
by Louis to look into ways of improving the administration of justice;
but the ordinance that resulted from its deliberations failed to address the
questions of burning concern to church reformers. While proclaiming the
king's determination to uphold 'the fine constitutions contained in the sacred
decrees of Basle and the Pragmatic Sanction', it made no mention of elections, reservations, expectatives and commends. When the parlement registered the ordinance, the university, whose objections had been disregarded,
went on strike. The chancellor ordered the strike to be lifted unconditionally
and the parlement imposed sanctions on the university, which appealed
directly to the king without success. In the end the university capitulated
and the sanctions were lifted.

A matter of serious concern to Gallicans was the authority conferred on
Georges d'Amboise as papal legate. The parlement registered his powers in
December 1501, provided he undertook in writing not to prejudice the
king's rights and prerogatives. In February 1502 the legate made a speech
in the parlement in which he declared his commitment to monastic reform.
By so doing he may have hoped to gain support for his candidature to the
papacy following the death of Alexander VI; but he was unable to rally
enough support within the Sacred College. After the brief pontificate of
Pius III, Giuliano della Rovere became Pope Julius II. As a consolation
prize, Amboise asked for more than a limited extension of his legateship.
Julius duly obliged by extending it indefinitely, thereby conferring on
Amboise an almost absolute authority over the Gallican church.

On 19 March 1504 the university opposed registration of the legate's
new powers by the parlement and pressed the court to foil any attempt by
Amboise and other prelates to give benefices to their own protégés. The
parlement refused to extend the legate's powers beyond the limit previously
set by Alexander VI and demanded his written consent to the limitations
previously imposed on him. But Louis XII insisted on the papal bull being
registered without further discussion or delay. On 20 April the parlement
confirmed the legate's powers, but made them depend on the king's pleasure.
Amboise was asked for a written undertaking that he would respect the
Gallican liberties and the Pragmatic Sanction. During the last six years of
his life he carefully avoided offending Gallican feelings. His powers, how-

ever, were merely tolerated and the old animosities of the French clergy towards the Holy See continued to feed on the same grievances as before.

Meanwhile, agitation for a new council continued, forcing the popes to take evasive action. They developed the idea of a council of selected prelates under papal control in Rome. The popes could not ignore the demand for a council. Even within the college of cardinals there was a strong movement of opposition to papal absolutism. In 1511, as we have seen, a group of mainly French cardinals summoned a General Council to Pisa and, after proclaiming its own superior authority, suspended Julius II. But the pope took the wind out of its sails by calling a council of his own at the Lateran. The question was no longer 'council or no council?' but 'which council?' The majority of Christendom declared in favour of the Lateran council, and the council of Pisa petered out.

The Pre-Reformation

At the Estates-General of 1484, Jean de Rely, who spoke for the Parisian clergy, painted a grim picture of the contemporary French church. 'Everyone knows', he declared, 'that among the monks of Cîteaux, St Benedict and St Augustine, as among the rest, there is no longer any rule, devotion or religious discipline.' Among the secular clergy, he went on, pastoral duties were generally neglected. The clergy ought to be setting an example to the laity, yet the roles were now reversed.

The disorderly state of the Gallican church was exemplified in Paris, where the chapter of Notre-Dame claimed exemption from all episcopal jurisdiction. When Tristan de Salazar, metropolitan archbishop of Sens, tried to assert his authority, he was violently attacked by the canons. As he left the cathedral on 2 February 1492, after celebrating mass in the king's presence, two canons seized the processional cross. In the ensuing scuffle the cross was damaged, the archbishop butted in the stomach and his mitre torn to shreds. The incident prompted a lawsuit in the parlement which lasted thirteen years. In 1504 the archbishop's right to officiate at Notre-Dame was recognized and the canons were ordered to restore the damaged cross.

The authority of the bishop of Paris, though less feeble than that of his metropolitan, was none the less weak. His jurisdiction was undermined by appeals to Rome or to the parlement and by the judicial activities of the cathedral chapter. His right to nominate to benefices in and around Paris was strictly limited. The chapter and most religious houses were exempt from his jurisdiction. In 1492 the canons refused to accept the king's nominee, Jean de Rely, as bishop. They elected Gérard Gobaille, who was himself challenged by Jean Simon. As the two rivals fought over the episcopal revenues, their quarrel came before the parlement. When Gobaille died in September 1494 the pope, acting at the king's request, confirmed Simon as bishop, but the chapter set about electing a new bishop. Only Simon's willingness to stand as candidate averted a major confrontation between the crown and the chapter. Even after he had won, however, some canons refused to obey him.

There was also much disorder among the parish clergy of the diocese. Within Paris itself priests seemed more interested in their revenues than in the discharge of their spiritual duties. These they habitually unloaded on vicars whose disorderly conduct was a matter of continual concern to the bishop's official. Rural parishes were even worse off. Their incumbents tended to reside in the capital, leaving indigent clergy to perform their duties. As yet there were no seminaries for the training of rural clergy. They picked up the rudiments of Christian dogma haphazardly while retaining the manners and tastes of their social background. The upper clergy despised them for their ignorance and uncouth ways.

Deficient as it was, the secular clergy was far superior to the regular one. Yet Paris and its suburbs had some of the wealthiest abbeys in the kingdom. During the Hundred Years War suburban monasteries and the rural estates of the great Parisian abbeys had been ravaged by passing armies. Though some had managed to repair their losses, many monasteries and convents in the countryside around Paris were ruinous and poverty-stricken. Even in Paris, except among the Cordeliers and Jacobins, the number of regular clergy had declined, and the monastic rule was no longer being generally observed. At Saint-Martin des Champs, a reform commission in 1501 noted that life in common had vanished: the monks owned property without regard for their rule. The same was true of Benedictine houses. There was disorder too among the Cordeliers and in 1502 the Jacobins claimed the right to seek refreshment outside the cloister. A similar state of affairs existed among the Carmelites and the Augustinians. Everywhere monks deserted the dormitory and refectory: each had his own room where he entertained friends. Apostolic poverty and the common ownership of goods were memories; everyone had his own purse. Monks roamed the streets mingling with boatmen and jugglers.

How far could the French crown be relied upon to assume responsibility for church reform in the absence of a serious papal initiative? King Charles VIII, unlike his father, was interested in reform. He sponsored the Synod of Sens (July–August 1485), which produced a comprehensive programme of reform covering worship, monastic discipline, fiscal abuses and disorder among the secular clergy, but a renewal of political troubles in France between 1485 and 1491 prevented that programme from being implemented. In November 1493 a reform commission met at Tours. It proposed a number of sensible practical remedies for the church's ailments. Avoiding doctrine or worship, it concentrated on clerical discipline and the results were not insignificant. The French government sent the proposals to the pope with a demand that he should back the reform movement. In July 1494, Alexander VI empowered three abbots to visit and reform the Benedictine houses in France. Charles VIII's interest in church reform could not be sustained once he had decided to invade Italy, yet the impetus he had provided was not lost: in many parts of France reformist activity continued till the end of the reign. Although no concerted action was taken by heads of the Gallican church, a number of bishops did reform their dioceses. At Langres, Chartres, Nantes and Troyes, they called synods and drew up or renewed episcopal statutes.

One of the loudest voices for reform in late fifteenth-century Paris was that of Olivier Maillard, a Franciscan friar, whose brutal frankness in the pulpit earned him enormous popularity. He poured scorn on unworthy priests and bewailed the decline of the church. Other champions of reform were Jean Raulin, principal of the collège de Navarre, Jean Quentin, penitentiary of Notre-Dame, and Jean Standonck. All three had come under the influence of Francis of Paola, an Italian hermit who had been invited to France in 1482 by Louis XI. He had founded in Italy a new order of friars, called Minims, who, in addition to the normal vows of poverty, chastity and obedience, promised to observe a perpetual Lent. In 1491, Charles VIII built a monastery for Francis at Montils-lès-Tours and another at Amboise. In the same year two Minims were allowed to set up a house in Paris. Francis was canonized in 1519, only twelve years after his death.

While preachers in Paris demanded reform, a slow movement of renewal was taking place in provincial monasteries. At Cluny in 1481, the abbot Jacques d'Amboise, brother of the cardinal, continued reforms that had been undertaken some twenty years earlier by his predecessor, Jean de Bourbon. Cluny's example was followed by the nuns of Fontevrault where a reform programme initiated in 1458 by the abbess, Mary of Brittany, was continued by her successors and extended to other houses in 1475. In 1483, Charles VIII gave the convent of the Filles-Dieu in Paris to the abbess Anne d'Orléans, the sister of duke Louis. Benedictine reform also reached Marmoutier, near Tours, and Chezal-Benoist in Berry. Among the Cistercians a revival was also under way: in 1487, Innocent VIII commissioned Jean de Cirey, abbot of Cîteaux, to reform the order. He reorganized studies at the Cistercian college in Paris in August 1493, and laid down new rules for all the order's houses at a general chapter in February 1494.

Reform among the mendicant orders was weaker. The Franciscans were bitterly divided between the Observants and Conventuals and the ferocity with which they fought each other in the courts seriously damaged their moral authority. Among the Dominicans reform was imported from the Low Countries. The Dutch Dominicans attached less importance to theological speculation than to mystical contemplation. In this respect they differed from the Jacobins, who adhered to the scholastic tradition. The missionary activities of the Dutch Dominicans tended to be excessively militant and consequently encountered stiff opposition.

In 1496, Standonck visited the canons regular of Windesheim, who practised the ideals of the Brethren of the Common Life. Following his visit, six brothers from Windesheim led by Jean Mombaer went to Château-Landon. They encountered resistance but, with the support of powerful patrons, they gained the upper hand, Mombaer becoming prior. In March 1497, Jean Simon, bishop of Paris, looked to Windesheim as he tried to reform the abbey of Saint-Victor. Writing to the general chapter of his order, Mombaer underlined the importance of the task in hand: 'It is not simply a matter of reforming a once famous abbey,' he said, 'but eventually the entire Gallican church.' In October, Windesheim sent seven brothers to Saint-Victor and two others visited the Augustinian house at Livry. Their rule gradually penetrated the French kingdom, although they suffered some serious setbacks under Louis XII: at Saint-Victor they made themselves so unpopular by their tactlessness that they had to leave.

Louis XII appreciated the urgent need to reform the French church. To bring this about he relied on Cardinal Georges d'Amboise, who, as papal legate, was empowered to visit religious houses, to depose and replace delinquent heads and to impose discipline on the monks. Although the reform programme of November 1493 had envisaged a reform of the whole Gallican church, Amboise concentrated his efforts on the regular clergy. With the help of energetic men like Maillard, reform of religious houses in Paris was carried out promptly, often in the face of stiff resistance. This was particularly strong among the Jacobins and Cordeliers. Sometimes the legate had to impose order by armed force. As for the nunneries, where reform had marked time in the face of countless difficulties, they too were visited, reformed and repaired. The famous abbey of Fontevrault received special attention. Under Amboise, communal life was restored, visitors sent out to daughter houses and reformed nuns introduced where necessary. New rules recently adopted at Fontevrault were extended to daughter houses between 1502 and 1507. Among other important abbeys reformed at this time were Chelles, Montmartre and Roye. In 1506 it was the turn of the great abbey of Poissy. Finally, the legate fought against the isolation of monasteries. They were grouped together and placed under the control of large and wholesome ones. In 1508, for example, the Jacobins of Paris, Rouen, Blois, Compiègne and Argenton were linked to the Dutch congregation.

Thus much was done to improve conditions in the Gallican church under Charles VIII and Louis XII. Although both kings backed reform, the initiative was mainly taken by individual churchmen, including some prelates.

Georges d'Amboise, in his dual capacity of royal minister and papal legate, was a powerful force. In a large number of monasteries discipline was restored. Yet the results, as many contemporaries complained, did not go far enough. Only the surface wounds of the church had been bandaged; the real sickness within the body remained to be cured. The main cause of trouble was the government of the church itself. Although the Renaissance popes paid lip-service to the cause of church reform, they were generally far more interested in advancing their family or princely interests. The Fifth Lateran Council, which Julius II had called, was too unrepresentative of the church as a whole to be an effective vehicle of reform. It produced only half-measures aimed at reducing, not extirpating, abuses. Once the council had been dissolved, its decisions were quickly forgotten.

Reform in France was strongly resisted and frequently overturned. Monks and nuns took refuge in endless lawsuits, piling appeal upon appeal, in defence of their exemptions. In many places they rose against the reformers, driving them out by force. At every turn, episcopal agents were obstructed, threatened or subjected to physical abuse. Among the mendicants a positive state of war existed between the Conventuals and the Observants – they fought each other in the courts, with their fists or by means of censures and pamphlets. In 1506, Julius II tried to reconcile the two branches of the Franciscan order. No sooner had this been accomplished than the effort had to begin afresh. In 1511 the convent of Saint-Pierre in Lyon was reformed by the grand prior of Cluny; two years later, royal officials noted that the abbess and the nuns had destroyed the walls, scrapped the new rules and sued the archbishop and his officials. Only by deporting the nuns could order be restored. At Saint-Sansom in Orléans, in 1514, the monks refused to live in common. Only after five years of quarrels, lawsuits and revolts was reform imposed by royal decree in January 1519. Almost everywhere reform had to fight every inch of the way. Even where it struck root, it often needed to be replanted.

In the past the church had put its own house in order. Now the reformers were frequently obliged to seek the assistance of the secular authorities. Municipal bodies were sometimes asked to help, but they seldom wanted to be drawn into a situation likely to trigger off public disturbances. They were particularly cautious regarding the mendicants, who, even in their unreformed state, had much popular support. Nor could the parlements be depended upon to assist reform. They were traditionally suspicious of any interference by Rome, as they showed by challenging the powers of legates. They also denied bishops freedom of action. In 1486 the *avocat du roi* Le Maistre denied that bishops could exercise any jurisdiction over exempt churches. The parlement claimed the right to judge all suits involving privileged monasteries. In 1483 it demanded the reinstatement of the Conventual friars who had been expelled from Tours by Maillard and the Observants.

In 1501 it received an appeal from the monks of Saint-Victor against the bishop of Paris who was trying to reform them. All too often, reform of the French church degenerated into a kind of police operation. By placing too much reliance on force and not enough on conversion, it created a large body of discontent among regular clergy who were forced to accept a life-style with which they had grown unfamiliar or be thrown out of their monasteries and convents.

By 1515, therefore, much still remained to be done. The constitutional argument between conciliarism and papalism was unresolved. The Pragmatic Sanction, though still in force, was often disregarded by the king. Disputes over appointments to benefices were still coming before the parlement with undue frequency. Abuses among the clergy were still rife, offering much scope to popular satirists like Pierre Gringore. His *Folles Entreprises* (1505) and *Abus du monde* (1509) attacked the debauchery and avarice of the secular clergy, the ambition of prelates and the corruption of monks. He even accused reformers of hypocrisy. As for the theologians, they remained divided into two broad camps: the schoolmen and the humanists. While the former dispensed the dry subtleties of Scotus and Ockham, the latter tried to build a new faith on a basis of sound scriptural studies. At the same time a wave of mysticism, reaching back to Thomas à Kempis, Cusa, Lull and beyond, caused many Christians to turn away from the formal observances of the church in favour of private prayer and ecstasy. It was this partially reformed, often rebellious and ideologically divided Gallican church which was soon to be faced by the Protestant challenge.

6

Francis I: The First Decade, 1515–25

'Kingship is the dignity, not the property, of the prince.' These words spoken by a deputy at the Estates-General of 1484 embody the theory of royal succession which prevailed in late mediaeval France. The king, however absolute he might deem himself to be, was not free to dispose of the crown; he had to be succeeded by his nearest male kinsman. It was in accordance with this principle that François duc de Valois and comte d'Angoulême, Louis XII's cousin, succeeded to the throne on 1 January 1515 at the age of twenty-one. His right to do so was unimpeachable, for it was a clearly established principle that 'the king never dies'; he was to be followed immediately by his lawful successor. There was no possibility of an inter-regnum.

In the words of the English chronicler Edward Hall, Francis I was 'a goodly prince, stately of countenance, merry of chere, brown coloured, great eyes, high nosed, big lipped, fair breasted and shoulders, small legs and long feet'. Ellis Griffith, a Welsh soldier in the service of Henry VIII, who was able to observe the French king closely at the Field of Cloth of Gold in 1520, tells us that he was six feet tall. His head was rightly pro-portioned for his height, the nape of his neck was unusually broad, his hair brown, smooth and neatly combed, his beard of three months' growth darker in colour, his nose long, his eyes hazel and bloodshot, and his complexion the colour of watered-down milk. He had muscular buttocks and thighs, but his legs below the knees were thin and bandy, while his feet were long, slender and completely flat. He had an agreeable voice and, in conversation, an animated expression marred only by the unkingly habit of continually rolling up his eyes.

Contemporaries often remarked on Francis's eloquence and charm. He would talk easily on almost any subject, though sometimes with more self-assurance than knowledge; he could also write well. The letters he wrote to his mother during his first Italian campaign are spontaneous and vivid; his verses display emotional sincerity. But Francis was first and foremost a man of action: he delighted in hunting, jousting and dancing. Dangerously realistic mock battles capable of inflicting serious injuries were a stock entertainment at his court. In hunting, as in war, Francis showed outstanding courage. During celebrations at Amboise in June 1515 he had to be dissuaded from engaging a wild boar in single combat.

Francis has gone down in history as a great lover. Women certainly loomed large in his life, though many stories about his amours are pure fantasy. That is not to say that his morals were irreproachable. He was dissolute and had probably contracted syphilis before 1524. About the time of his accession he was having an affair with the wife of Jacques Disomme, a distinguished *parlementaire*. Truth, however, is not easily distilled from gossip. Even the king's first official mistress, Françoise de Foix, comtesse de Châteaubriant, is a shadowy figure. She seems to have had little or no political influence.

Three women were pre-eminent at Francis I's court in the early part of his reign: his mother, his sister and his wife. Louise of Savoy, being a widow in her early forties, was free to devote herself to her son's service. She was given a powerful voice in government and her influence was felt especially in foreign affairs. The king's sister Marguerite was intelligent, vivacious, and quite attractive. In 1509 she married Charles duc d'Alençon, but the match proved unhappy. Marguerite found consolation in pious meditation and good works. She became attracted to the ideas of Jacques Lefèvre d'Etaples, leader of an evangelical group known as the *Cercle de Meaux*, and wrote religious poems which offended the narrowly orthodox 'Sorbonne', as the Paris Faculty of Theology is commonly known. Marguerite shared her mother's interest in public affairs; foreign ambassadors often mentioned her in their dispatches. As for Queen Claude, she was widely renowned for her sweet, charitable and pious nature. Over a period of nine years she bore the king three sons and four daughters.

The new administration

The funeral of Louis XII took place at the abbey of Saint-Denis on 12 January 1515. Francis meanwhile organized his administration. Though not bound by the obligations of his predecessor, he chose to confirm many existing office-holders and privileges. On 2 January, for example, he confirmed members of the Parlement of Paris. Among members of Louis XII's administration who were kept in office was Florimond Robertet, 'the father of the secretaries of state'. The new reign also brought new blood into the administration. Antoine Duprat became Chancellor of France. The son of a merchant of Issoire, he had entered the law and had risen from the Parlement of Toulouse to that of Paris, becoming its First President. He gained the favour of Anne of Brittany and, after her death, joined the service of Louise of Savoy. It was doubtless with her support that he became chancellor. Duprat was hard-working and shrewd, but also ruthless and grasping. He became almost universally unpopular. Another great office that had fallen vacant was the constableship of France. Charles III duc de Bourbon, the king's most powerful vassal, was now given the office. He had a distinguished war record, having fought bravely at Agnadello in 1509 and against the Swiss in 1513. Bourbon was also governor of Languedoc and *Grand chambrier de France*. The marshals of France, though subordinate to the constable, were on a par with dukes and peers. At Francis's accession they numbered only two: Stuart d'Aubigny and Gian Giacomo Trivulzio. Francis created two more: Odet de Foix, seigneur de Lautrec, and Jacques de Chabannes, seigneur de Lapalice. On becoming marshal, Lapalice relinquished the office of Grand Master of France (*Grand maître de France*), which was given to Francis's erstwhile governor, Artus Gouffier, seigneur de Boisy.

In distributing favours Francis did not forget his relatives and friends. He allegedly handed over to his mother all the revenues accruing from the confirmation of existing office-holders. Her county of Angoulême was raised to ducal status and she was also given the duchy of Anjou, the counties of Maine and Beaufort-en-Vallée and the barony of Amboise. Her half-brother René, 'the great bastard of Savoy', was appointed *Grand sénéchal* and governor of Provence. Francis's brother-in-law, Charles d'Alençon, officially recognized as 'the second person of the kingdom', was made governor of Normandy. The house of Bourbon was also honoured: the *vicomté* of Châtellerault, which belonged to François, the constable's brother, was turned into a duchy. The county of Vendôme, belonging to a second brother called Charles, was likewise elevated in status. Guillaume Gouffier, seigneur de Bonnivet, one of Francis's childhood companions at Amboise, was appointed Admiral of France, though at this time the office did not imply service at sea.

On 25 January, Francis was crowned in Reims cathedral. Though no longer regarded as essential to the exercise of kingship, the coronation or *sacre* remained an important symbol of the monarchy's supernatural quality and close alliance with the church. From Reims, Francis went first to the shrine of Saint-Marcoul at the priory of Corbeny, a pilgrimage closely connected with his thaumaturgical powers, then to the shrine of the Black Virgin at Notre-Dame de Liesse. At Saint-Denis, burial place of his royal predecessors, he confirmed the abbey's privileges and underwent another, less elaborate, coronation. Finally, on 15 February, he made his joyful entry (*entrée joyeuse*) into Paris.

Marignano, 13–14 September 1515

By January 1515, France had lost all her Italian conquests. The house of Sforza held Milan in the person of Massimiliano Sforza, Genoa was an independent republic, and the kingdom of Naples belonged to Aragon. Francis I was expected to regain the ground lost by his immediate predecessors and to avenge the defeats recently suffered by French arms. Veterans of the Italian wars whose reputations had been dented and young noblemen anxious to show their valour looked to him for satisfaction. His youth and powerful physique seemed perfectly suited to the part they expected him to play. But before he could launch a new Italian campaign, Francis needed to neutralize his more powerful neighbours. Charles of Habsburg, a shy and unprepossessing youth of fifteen, was the son of Archduke Philip the Fair and the grandson of the Emperor Maximilian and Ferdinand of Aragon. On his father's death in 1506 he had inherited the territories of the house of Burgundy (Franche-Comté, Luxemburg, Brabant, Flanders, Holland, Zeeland, Hainault and Artois) as well as a claim to the duchy of Burgundy, which France had annexed in 1477. A Burgundian by birth and upbringing, Charles longed to rebuild his mutilated inheritance, hoping eventually to be buried in Dijon cathedral. He was encouraged by his aunt Margaret of Savoy, who ruled the Low Countries in his name. Shortly after Francis's coronation, ambassadors from Charles came to Compiègne with their master's homage for Flanders and other fiefs. An alliance soon followed: under the Treaty of Paris (24 March 1515), Charles was promised the hand of Louis XII's infant daughter Renée.

Henry VIII, king of England, a robust young man of twenty-four, was anxious not to be outshone by the new king of France, yet did not wish to pick a quarrel with him at this stage. Having recently tasted victory on the Continent, he was content to enjoy himself at home and leave policy-making to his chief minister, Thomas Wolsey. On 5 April the Anglo-French Treaty of London was given a new lease of life, Francis promising to honour his predecessor's debt to England of one million gold *écus* over ten years.

In Italy, Francis's diplomacy was less successful. The Venetians agreed to help him militarily in return for assistance against the emperor, and the Genoese reverted to their allegiance to France in exchange for local concessions, but other powers proved less co-operative. The Swiss, in particular, had not forgotten Louis XII's refusal to ratify the Treaty of Dijon; nor were they prepared to surrender territories in Lombardy which Sforza had ceded to them or the pension they received from him in return for their armed protection. Sforza was also supported by Ferdinand of Aragon and Pope Leo X. Ferdinand did not wish to see any change in the Italian situation which might endanger his hold on Naples, while Leo was anxious to avoid a repetition of the events of 1494 which had led to the overthrow of his Medici kinsmen in Florence. He was also keen to retain the towns of Parma and Piacenza which Sforza had ceded to him. As for the emperor, being at war with the Venetians, he was not prepared to treat with their ally the king of France.

The most urgent military task facing Francis I in 1515 was to raise enough infantry. France had the largest standing army in Christendom, but it consisted almost entirely of cavalry. By the early sixteenth century wars could no longer be won by cavalry alone, as had been demonstrated by the victories of the Swiss infantry over the Burgundians in the late fifteenth century. But infantry of good fighting quality was not easily raised. The king could rely to some extent on native volunteers, called *aventuriers*, but the best infantry were foreign mercenaries. Until 1510, France had been able to hire the Swiss, but, as they were now employed by the enemy, he had to look elsewhere. In 1515 he raised 23,000 German landsknechts, who were less disciplined than the Swiss.

Mercenaries made heavy demands on the royal purse. The main source of royal revenue was the *taille* which fell on commoners, especially the peasantry. The king also asked his subjects for a contribution of 2,900,000 *livres* in celebration of his accession, but this took a long time to collect. Francis thus had to resort to various expedients: his gold plate was melted down, forced loans were exacted from the 'good towns', financial officials advanced loans to the crown, and parts of the royal domain were mortgaged. By such means the king managed to create a sizeable army, which in April began to assemble near Lyon and Grenoble. It consisted of about 6000 cavalry and 31,500 infantry, but its pride was the artillery, comprising some sixty large cannon and many lighter pieces.

On 26 June, Francis informed the 'good towns' of his imminent departure for Italy and of his mother's regency in his absence. At the same time he obtained from his wife Claude formal cession of her rights to Milan. Next day the king left Amboise for Lyon, where a spectacular entry awaited him on 12 July. Francis spent nearly three weeks there putting the finishing touches to his invasion plan. On 15 July he appointed his mother as regent, but her powers were limited as the chancellor accompanied the king to Italy, taking the Great Seal with him. The enemy, meanwhile, prepared to bar the king's way. They assumed that he would cross the Alps by way of either the Mont Genèvre or Mont Cenis pass. On 17 July the duke of Milan, the pope, the king of Aragon and the emperor signed a league for the defence of Italy. As the Swiss had no cavalry, the pope sent 1500 horse under Prospero Colonna to Piedmont. Francis had either to fight his way past the Swiss or by-pass them. He decided to use the Col de Larche, a pass frequented only by peasants, and sent a force of sappers ahead of the army to bridge torrents and remove obstacles. On 11 August the vanguard under Bourbon crossed the mountains and, entering the plain of Piedmont, surprised and captured the papal commander Colonna and his men at Villafranca. The Swiss thus lost their cavalry support.

The king of France, in the meantime, set off with the rest of the army. He found the crossing of the Alps arduous. The descent into Italy was so precipitous that many horses and mules fell into ravines, while cannon had to be dismantled and lowered on ropes. On reaching the plain, Francis advanced rapidly eastward. The Swiss, meanwhile, fell back to Lake Maggiore and Francis agreed to negotiate with them through his uncle, René of Savoy. A treaty was drafted, but a new round of talks began at Gallarate. The king, meanwhile, drew closer to Milan, hoping to effect a junction with the Venetian army under d'Alviano. On 9 September, Francis received the text of a treaty signed at Gallarate. The Swiss agreed to give up their Milanese territories, except Bellinzona, in return for a subsidy of one million gold écus of which 150,000 were to be paid in cash immediately. Sforza was to surrender Milan in exchange for the duchy of Nemours. Francis was to be allowed to raise troops in Switzerland in return for a subsidy to each canton. He immediately obtained the sum of 150,000 écus from his entourage and sent it to Gallarate. Meanwhile, he encamped at Marignano (now Melegnano), a village situated between Milan and Pavia.

However, not all the Swiss wanted peace. While the men of Berne, Fribourg and Solothurn were keen to go home, those from other cantons refused to give up the fruits of their recent victories without a fight. They were encouraged by Cardinal Schiner, a bitter enemy of France, who made a stirring speech in Milan on 13 September. A minor skirmish with French scouts outside the city precipitated an armed decision. About midday the Swiss, most of them barefoot, hatless and without armour, swarmed out of the city. Their artillery consisted of only eight small guns; Schiner and about 200 papal horse followed in the rear. Hoping to catch the French by surprise, the Swiss marched briskly and in silence, but inevitably they threw up a cloud of dust.

A party of French sappers, spotting the cloud, alerted the French camp, which was soon ready for action. As usual, the Swiss advanced in an echelon of three compact squares of 7000 or 8000 pikemen each. The first crossed a ditch protecting the French guns and scattered the infantry, leaving the gunners isolated. The landsknechts then moved forward, and two gigantic squares of pikemen collided. Once again the Swiss broke through. A counterattack by the French cavalry was thrown back. The fighting continued until midnight, when the moon vanished, plunging the field into complete obscurity. The two armies then separated, the French responding to shrill trumpet calls and the Swiss to the deep bellowing of their war-horns. Francis used the interval to redeploy his army. Duprat, meanwhile, wrote to Lautrec, instructing him not to hand over the money to the Swiss at Gallarate. When battle was resumed at dawn, the Swiss adapted their tactics to the new French formation. Instead of advancing in echelon, they engaged the entire French line. Braving the fire of the French guns, they forced back the landsknechts in the centre, but were themselves driven back by Francis and the *gendarmerie*. On the left, however, the Swiss overwhelmed the French guns, scattered the infantry and lunged into the landsknechts. The French left was about to collapse when the Venetian cavalry arrived, shouting: 'San Marco! San Marco!' Their spirits revived, the French mounted a counter-attack. By 11 AM the Swiss had been routed.

Marshal Trivulzio, a veteran of seventeen battles, described Marignano as a 'battle of giants' beside which the others were but 'children's games'. The gravediggers reported burying 16,500 corpses, but the exact number of French and Swiss losses is not known. Many French noblemen lost their lives; their bodies were embalmed and sent back to their estates for burial. Reviewing the battle, Francis singled out for praise Galiot de Genouillac, whose guns had slowed down the Swiss attack, and Pierre du Terrail, seigneur de Bayard. The king allegedly crowned his victory by having himself knighted by Bayard on the battlefield as a tribute to his bravery.

The immediate result of Marignano was the capitulation of Milan on 16 September. Sforza gave up its castle on 6 October and retired to France, where he died in May 1530. Francis entered Milan in triumph on 11 October and stayed there till the end of the month, when he entrusted the city to Bourbon and Duprat. The latter was appointed chancellor of Milan in addition to his existing office, and the Senate originally set up by Louis XII was revived. The citizens were asked to pay a huge fine as a punishment for their rebellion and to surrender hostages.

No sixteenth-century ruler could afford to alienate the Swiss. As Charles V once said, the 'secret of secrets' was to win them over. In October, therefore, Francis sent an embassy to thank the cantons that had pulled out of the war and to seek a settlement with the others. On 7 November the Treaty of Geneva was signed with ten cantons, but only eight ratified it; the rest offered their services to the emperor.

No one was more upset by Francis's victory than Pope Leo X, who had backed the wrong horse; but he had nothing to fear as Francis needed his friendship. Recent history had shown that a king of France could not establish a lasting foothold in Italy without papal co-operation. Despite his victory, Francis's position in Italy remained precarious. He was faced by the possibility of a coalition between the hostile Swiss cantons, the emperor and England. This threat made it all the more urgent for Francis to gain the pope's friendship, or at least his neutrality. Thus a treaty was soon arranged: in exchange for Parma and Piacenza, the king gave the duchy of Nemours to Leo's brother Giuliano, along with a fat pension, and another pension to the pope's nephew Lorenzo. This, however, was only the first step. The two rulers needed to discuss other matters, notably the Pragmatic Sanction of Bourges (1438) whose abrogation the papacy had long demanded. They arranged to meet in Bologna.

Francis reached Bologna on 11 December, three days after the pope. Both resided at the Palazzo Pubblico. Though shrouded in secrecy, their talks were, it seems, much concerned with Italian affairs. Leo may have hinted at the possibility of Francis being given Naples on the death of Ferdinand of Aragon in return for a promise of French aid to the Medici in Florence. Agreement was also reached on the need for a crusade, Francis being allowed to levy a clerical tenth, but the most important decision taken at Bologna was to substitute a Concordat for the Pragmatic Sanction of Bourges.

The Concordat of Bologna, 1516

The Concordat of Bologna was approved by the pope on 18 August 1516, but before it could become law in France it had to be registered by the Parlement of Paris, and Francis I was allowed six months in which to get this done. The parlement, however, was deeply suspicious of a settlement which threatened to undermine, if not to destroy, the liberties of the Gallican church, as enshrined in the Pragmatic Sanction. Although it was asked on 5 February 1517 to register the Concordat, it took more than two years to comply and Francis had to obtain an extension of the deadline he had been given. The parlement's delaying tactics angered him so much that in June 1517 he ordered his uncle, René of Savoy, to attend the court's debates. The parlement protested at this infringement of its liberties, but had to submit when Francis threatened to replace its members by 'gens de bien' (worthy men). Despite René's presence, the parlement still would not register the Concordat. Its refusal was conveyed to the king at Amboise by two *parlementaires*, who had to face his wrath. There would be only one king in France, he declared, and no Senate as in Venice. He threatened to make the parlement 'trot after him like the *Grand conseil*' and accused it of neglecting its judicial duties. When the envoys asked for permission to delay their departure until local floods had subsided, they were told that if they had not left by morning they would be thrown into a deep pit and left there for six months. On 6 March 1518 the king again demanded registration of the Concordat. He was said to be planning to set up a rival parlement at Orléans. The threat achieved its purpose and on 22 March the parlement finally gave way: the Concordat was registered, albeit with the addition of a phrase indicating duress. At the same time, the parlement secretly declared that it would continue to apply the Pragmatic Sanction in ecclesiastical disputes.

No sooner had the parlement capitulated than the University of Paris began to agitate, fearing that its graduates would lose the privileged position given to them by the Pragmatic Sanction in respect of collation to ecclesiastical benefices. The university suspended its lectures, forbade anyone to print the Concordat, and appealed to a future General Council. A memorandum denouncing the Concordat was circulated to preachers for use in their Lenten sermons. Placards to the same effect were put up in colleges and public places. Francis ordered the parlement to intervene; otherwise, he threatened to apply the severest measures. A few days later he appointed a special commission to enquire into the disorders. College principals were ordered to restrain their students. On 25 April the university was forbidden to meddle in state affairs under pain of loss of its privileges and banishment from the kingdom.

It is commonly assumed that the main purpose of the Concordat was to increase the king's control of the Gallican church and that, having won the battle of Marignano, he had imposed his terms on Leo X. Both assumptions, however, are questionable. The crown, as we have seen, already had extensive control of the church before 1516. After 1438 the church was governed in theory by the Pragmatic Sanction, which allowed chapters the right to elect bishops and abbots; but the monarchy often determined the outcome of elections. By 1515 royal control of the ecclesiastical hierarchy was an accepted fact. This was acknowledged by the president of the parlement in March 1515, when he begged Francis to appoint worthy men of sufficient years to administer sees and religious houses.

Marignano did not give Francis mastery of Italy. He remained vulnerable in the north, nor could he impose terms on the pope. The king needed Leo not merely to safeguard his own gains in north Italy but also to acquire territory farther south. In February 1516, on learning of the death of Ferdinand of Aragon, Francis 'decided to try to recover the kingdom of Naples'. To achieve this, however, he needed the pope's help. As temporal ruler of the States of the Church, Leo controlled the overland route south; as suzerain of Naples, he alone could grant its investiture. So Francis decided to satisfy the long-standing papal demand for the annulment of the Pragmatic Sanction, even though this meant offending his subjects. It was primarily to win papal support for his Italian policy that he signed the Concordat.

As a political move, the Concordat was a failure. After supporting the king of France, Leo X ditched him in 1521. Yet Francis was never tempted to revoke the Concordat. As long as he hoped to re-establish his rule in Italy he tried to remain on good terms with the Holy See. As an ecclesiastical settlement, the Concordat was a bargain struck by the king and the papacy at the expense of the Gallican liberties. It restored papal authority in France while legalizing and enlarging royal control of church appointments. Yet the king was not given unlimited control: the pope retained the right of instituting royal nominees and of setting aside any whose qualifications fell short of the canonical requirements. Some churches were also allowed to continue electing their superiors. In practice, however, the Concordat was not strictly applied: the king imposed his candidates on churches claiming the privilege of election, and in June 1531 he obtained from the pope the annulment of this privilege, except in respect of religious houses. Francis also sometimes ignored canonical requirements. Very occasionally the pope refused to institute a royal nominee, but this was exceptional. In general the Concordat strengthened royal control of the Gallican church.

Naples and Navarre

On 23 January, after Francis had returned to the south of France, Ferdinand of Aragon died leaving his kingdom to his grandson Charles. This upset the balance of power in Europe, for Charles already ruled the Netherlands and Franche-Comté. By gaining the kingdoms of Castile, Aragon and Naples, he became France's most powerful neighbour. What is more, Francis had an interest in Naples and Navarre, two of the territories now acquired by Charles. Having inherited the Angevin claim to Naples, he ordered the archives of Provence to be searched for documentary proof of his title. Part of the small Pyrenean kingdom of Navarre had been seized by Ferdinand from its king, Jean d'Albret, in 1512 and had since been absorbed into Castile. Jean looked to the king of France for redress. As duke of Burgundy, Charles had implicitly recognized Jean's claim to Navarre, but he was unlikely to do so in his new role of Spanish monarch. He was equally unlikely to give up Naples.

For a time, however, trouble between Francis and Charles was contained. For Charles, who was in the Netherlands at the time, still had to take possession of his Spanish realm, where, as a Fleming by birth, he could expect opposition. He needed assurance that France would not invade the Netherlands during his absence in Spain. On 13 August, therefore, he and Francis signed the Treaty of Noyon. Charles was promised the hand of Louise, Francis's infant daughter, and Naples was to be part of her dowry. Pending the marriage, Charles was to pay Francis an annual tribute for Naples of 100,000 gold *écus* thereby implicitly recognizing the French claim to that kingdom. He also promised to compensate Jean d'Albret's widow, Catherine de Foix, for the loss of Spanish Navarre.

The 'Perpetual' Peace of Fribourg, 29 November 1516

In Austria, meanwhile, Cardinal Schiner had been urging the Emperor Maximilian to invade Milan and restore the Sforzas to power. The emperor could count on the support of some Swiss and of Henry VIII, whose jealousy had been aroused by the French victory at Marignano. Early in March 1516, Maximilian invaded north Italy. He reached the outskirts of Milan, but two days later he suddenly decamped, leaving his troops in the lurch. His ignominious flight enabled Francis to come to terms with the Swiss. On 29 November the so-called 'Perpetual Peace of Fribourg' was signed. Francis agreed to pay a war indemnity of 700,000 écus to the cantons. He also promised them 300,000 écus for the castles of Lugano and Locarno and fortresses in the Valtelline, and an annual subsidy of 2000 écus to each canton. The Swiss, for their part, promised not to serve anyone against France. Although less than a complete alliance, the treaty gave Francis the right to hire Swiss mercenaries in the future. The peace was called 'perpetual' because it was never formally broken. Swiss troops still guarded the king of France during the French Revolution.

On 11 March 1517, Francis, Maximilian and Charles of Spain signed the Treaty of Cambrai in which they agreed to assist each other if attacked and to join a crusade. Christendom needed to unite against the westward expansion of the Turks. Under Mehmet II they had captured Constantinople, penetrated deep into the Balkans and expelled the Venetians from Euboea. Now, under Selim the Grim, they were advancing once more: after overrunning Syria in August 1516, they invaded Egypt early in 1517. 'It is time', Leo X declared, 'that we woke from sleep lest we be put to the sword unawares.' In March 1518 he proclaimed a five-year truce among Christian powers and sent nuncios to the courts of Europe to gather support for a crusade, but they were more interested in problems nearer home than in the Balkans or eastern Mediterranean.

In September 1517, Charles arrived in Spain with an entourage of Flemings and took control of his kingdom. The Treaty of Noyon had become an embarrassment to him: he could not afford to pay the Neapolitan tribute and seemed disinclined to honour his pledge regarding Navarre. Yet Charles continued to assure Francis of his good intentions. In May 1519 a conference was held at Montpellier to sort out differences between the two monarchs, but it soon became a slanging match over the question of Navarre and collapsed altogether following the death of Boisy, who had led the French delegation.

The imperial election, 1519

On 12 January 1519 the Holy Roman Emperor, Maximilian I, died, causing another major upheaval of Europe's power structure. The Empire was an elective dignity, not a hereditary one, the emperor being chosen by seven Electors: the archbishops of Mainz, Cologne and Trier, the king of Bohemia, the Elector-Palatine, the duke of Saxony and the margrave of Brandenburg. They were not obliged to choose a Habsburg or even a German, for the Empire was a supra-national dignity, the secular counterpart of the papacy. Thus it was possible for a Frenchman to be a candidate.

In 1516, even before Maximilian's death, the archbishops of Mainz and Trier had invited Francis to stand for election, promising him their votes. They had soon been joined by Joachim of Brandenburg and the Elector-Palatine, so that the king could reasonably expect a majority in his favour in the electoral college. The Empire attracted him not only for its international prestige, but also because he wanted to keep it out of the hands of Maximilian's grandson Charles, who was already powerful enough. As he explained, 'The reason which moves me to gain the Empire . . . is to prevent the said Catholic King from doing so. If he were to succeed, seeing the extent of his kingdoms and lordships, this could do me immeasurable harm; he would always be mistrustful and suspicious, and would doubtless throw me out of Italy.'

The Electors were less interested in Francis's candidature than in promoting a contest. Under rules laid down in the Golden Bull, an imperial election was supposed to be free of corruption. In practice, however, it resembled an auction. As the Habsburgs marshalled their resources, Francis did likewise. He sent envoys to the Electors with 400,000 écus to distribute as bribes. When Charles Guillart suggested that persuasion might be preferable to bribery, Francis strongly disagreed. He was better placed than his rival to win the election, for he was closer to Germany and allowed his agents a free hand, whereas Charles was far away in Spain and would not allow his agents to concede anything without his prior approval. But Francis was denied the co-operation of the German bankers, who sided with the Habsburgs if only because they controlled the silver mines of central Europe. Consequently, he was denied exchange facilities and obliged to send ready cash to Germany at a time when the roads were infested with brigands.

German public opinion was also strongly anti-French. Habsburg agents used every means, including sermons and illustrated broadsheets, to stir up suspicion and hatred of the French. Germans were led to believe that the bribes Francis was distributing had been forcibly taken from his subjects and that a comparable fate would befall themselves if he were elected. Francis countered this propaganda by claiming that he, rather than Charles, would be the more effective champion of Christendom against the Turkish Infidel.

On 8 June 1519 the Electors gathered at Frankfurt under the shadow of the army of the Swabian League. No Frenchmen, said Henry of Nassau, would enter Germany save on the points of spears and swords. At the eleventh hour Leo X, who had so far supported Francis as the lesser of two evils (he did not wish to see a union of the imperial and Neapolitan crowns), changed his mind. Even Francis gave up hope of winning. On 26 June he withdrew his candidature and, two days later, Charles was chosen unanimously.

Historians have often assumed that the rivalry which developed between Francis and Charles stemmed from the imperial election. Francis was undoubtedly vexed by the result, particularly as he had wasted some 400,000 *écus* on bribes. But his disappointment was dwarfed by the political implications of the election. Before Charles could be a fully-fledged emperor, he needed to be crowned by the pope in Italy. He was likely to go there in force and would almost certainly threaten Francis's hold on Milan, particularly as the emperor was the duchy's suzerain. The pope, too, had reason to fear Habsburg domination of the peninsula. On 22 October he signed a secret treaty with Francis. While the king promised to defend the States of the Church against Charles, Leo undertook to deny Charles the investiture of Naples.

The Field of Cloth of Gold, June 1520

The imperial election brought France and England closer together. Whereas in the past there had been four major powers in Europe, France, Spain, England and the Empire, now there were only three, Spain and the Empire having become joined in the person of Charles V. As France and the new Habsburg state seemed of roughly equal weight, England's position was enhanced. Cardinal Wolsey, who directed Henry VIII's foreign policy, revived the idea, first mooted in 1518, of a meeting between Henry and Francis. On 12 March he laid down the conditions of what has become known as the Field of Cloth of Gold. Charles, whose aunt Catherine of Aragon was Henry's queen, tried hard to prevent the meeting or to secure its postponement. He visited England on his way from Spain to Germany and held talks with Henry VIII, but no one knows what they decided.

The Anglo-French meeting took place in June at a site between the English town of Guînes and the French town of Ardres. Providing suitable accommodation for the large number of participants was probably the biggest headache for the organizers. Henry erected a large temporary palace outside Guînes castle, while Francis put up a superb tent covered with gold brocade

and striped with blue velvet powdered with gold fleur-de-lys. It was the
tallest of some 300 or 400 pitched in a meadow outside Ardres.

The Field of Cloth of Gold consisted of two events: the initial meeting
of the kings on 7 June and a tournament or feat of arms scheduled to last
twelve days. Henry and his court crossed the Channel on 31 May. Soon
afterwards, Wolsey with a magnificent escort called on Francis at Ardres
and signed a treaty which provided for the marriage between the Dauphin
and Mary Tudor. On 7 June, at an agreed signal, the two kings, each
accompanied by a large escort, moved towards the Val Doré, where they
faced each other on two artificial mounds. After a fanfare, Henry and
Francis rode towards the bottom of the valley. They spurred their mounts
as if about to engage in combat, but instead embraced each other. After
dismounting, they retired to a tent where they were joined by Wolsey and
Bonnivet. An hour later they emerged and presented their respective nobles
to each other.

The 'feat of arms', which began on 11 June, lasted till the 24th. Complicated regulations had been drawn up to prevent accidents. The two kings
did not fight each other: they competed each with his own team. The famous
story of Henry being worsted by Francis in a wrestling match is probably
apocryphal. What is certain is that the king of France soon tired of the
rigid etiquette that had been prescribed. On 17 June he paid Henry a surprise
visit. Bursting into his chamber, he exclaimed: 'Brother, here am I your
prisoner!' Not to be outdone, Henry turned up in Francis's bedroom two
days later. This put everyone in a good mood. On 23 June mass was
celebrated by Wolsey amidst great pomp on the tournament field. The two
royal chapels sang alternate verses of hymns accompanied by an organ,
trombones and cornets. Afterwards the pope's blessing was conferred on
both kings. Louise of Savoy announced that her son and Henry intended
jointly to build a palace in the Val Doré where they might meet each year,
and also a chapel dedicated to Our Lady of Friendship.

Money matters

Francis I incurred heavy expenses from the start of his reign. Having
inherited a deficit of 1.4 million *livres* from Louis XII, he had to pay for
that king's funeral and for his own coronation. The overall cost of the
Marignano campaign has been estimated at 7.5 million *livres*. The Peace
of Fribourg cost the French crown one million *écus* and inaugurated a
system of pensions to the Swiss. In 1518, Francis paid 600,000 *écus* for
the return of Tournai. The imperial election campaign may have cost him
another 400,000 *écus* and the Field of Cloth of Gold at least 200,000l.
In June 1517 the king's council decided to levy supplementary taxes

worth 1,100,043l. in an attempt to reduce the government's deficit of 3,996,506l.

Francis did not substantially change either the burden or the structure of taxation during his reign. Royal income from taxes rose by an annual average of 1.44 per cent, which is moderate by comparison with the average of 2.38 per cent per annum under Louis XII and 5.7 per cent per annum under Henry II. The *taille* rose most in absolute terms: from about 2.4 million *livres* in 1515 to some 4.6 million in 1544–5 with a fall to 3.6 million in 1547. The rate of the *gabelle* in north and central France trebled during the reign, but over the whole kingdom its value was only 700,000l. in 1547 as compared with less than 400,000 in the early part of the reign. The *aides* and other indirect taxes are said to have risen from about 1.2 million to 2.15 million. Domainal revenues did not rise at all. The only tax created by Francis was one on walled towns to pay for infantry.

However, taxation estimates based on the central records are misleading, for a high proportion of the receipts were disbursed at the collection point and never reached the royal treasury. The actual burden of taxation was also heavier than is suggested by the central records, the sums imposed by local collectors being often in excess of the legal limits. The yield was also eroded by the costs of collection.

Although in theory the French church was exempt from direct taxation, the reality was different. In theory the clerical tenth or *décime* was a voluntary gift to assist the king in an emergency, yet in practice it became virtually a regular tax. Following the Concordat of Bologna, the pope allowed Francis to levy a tenth on the French clergy and he did so again in 1527 and 1533, but papal authorization was not regarded as essential; the initiative was often taken by the king alone. Altogether 57 tenths were levied under Francis and may have yielded a total of 18 million *livres*.

It was outside his regular income that Francis innovated most. To meet his immediate needs, he borrowed from merchants and bankers, most of them Italians who had settled in Lyon. They lent to the crown sometimes under constraint or in exchange for commercial concessions, but usually as a result of free speculative choice. The king was often prepared to pay high rates of interest. For example, a loan of 100,000 *écus* raised for the Field of Cloth of Gold carried an annual interest of 16.2 per cent. By 1516 the crown was already heavily in debt to the Lyon bankers.

Francis also borrowed heavily from his own tax officials, who were invariably men of substance. If for some reason the tax yield was lower than expected, a tax official might be asked to advance money from his own pocket. In return, he would be allowed to reimburse himself from the next year's tax receipts. This was how taxes were 'anticipated'. On a number of occasions the king helped himself to the inheritance of a wealthy subject. His first victim was the seigneur de Boisy who died in May 1519.

Although many towns were exempt from the *taille*, they were often asked
for forced loans, which could be even more burdensome. In 1515 and 1516,
for example, Francis asked for sums ranging from 1500 to 6000 *livres* each
from Toulouse, Lyon, Troyes and Angers. Paris was asked for 20,000l. to
help pay for the defence of the kingdom. Sometimes a town was allowed
to recoup by levying a local tax or *octroi* on some commodity such as wine.
An expedient much used by Francis was the alienation of crown lands by
gift or sale. This was repeatedly opposed by the parlement, which pointed
to the adverse effect on the king's 'poor subjects' of any diminution of his
'ordinary' revenue, but Francis always managed to get his way.

Two other expedients were the sale of titles of nobility and of royal
offices. As far as is known, Francis issued 183 letters of ennoblement during
his reign of which 153 were sold. They cost between 100 and 300 *écus*
before 1543 and considerably more afterwards. As for offices, Francis
turned their sale into a veritable system. They were sold directly to bourgeois
anxious to acquire them as a means of social advancement (for many offices
conferred noble status on the holders) or were given away as rewards for
services rendered or as repayment of loans, leaving the recipients free to
sell them if they wished. Francis also sold *résignations* and *survivances*
which enabled office-holders to nominate their successors. The price of a
councillorship in the Parlement of Paris was fixed by 1522 at 3000 *écus*;
other offices commanded variable amounts. The sale or venality of offices
created a dangerous situation in the long term as they tended to be monopolized by a limited number of families.

The *trésoriers de France* and *généraux des finances* (known collectively
as *gens des finances*), who administered the crown's finances between 1515
and 1527, were closely related to each other and shared their interests.
Alongside their royal duties they ran very profitable businesses of their
own. Consequently, their public and private functions overlapped, offering
speculative temptations. An outstanding member of this financial oligarchy
was Jacques de Beaune, baron of Semblançay, the son of a rich merchant
of Tours, who became the king's chief financial adviser after serving his
mother and, before her, Anne of Brittany. As *général* of Languedoïl, he
played a leading role in funding the Marignano campaign. In January 1518
he was given overall powers of supervision over all the king's revenues, but
it was probably as an agent of credit that he proved most useful to the
crown. Important as they were, the *gens des finances* did not have ultimate
control of the crown's financial policy. This was vested in the king's council
among whose members one, usually the Grand Master, was singled out to
oversee financial business. The king himself was by no means uninterested
in such business. In April 1519 he spent three days with his *gens des finances*
looking for ways to fund the army.

War with the emperor, 1521

Charles of Habsburg was crowned King of the Romans at Aachen on 23 October 1520. Two days later Pope Leo X allowed him to use the title of 'Roman emperor elect'. Charles hoped to go to Italy soon for his imperial coronation, but various matters detained him in Germany, among them the Lutheran Reformation. Francis hoped to return to Italy himself, but was prevented by a serious accident. However, he added to Charles's problems in order to keep him out of Italy. Among visitors to the king's bedside were Robert de La Marck, seigneur de Sedan, and Henri d'Albret, king of Navarre. Soon afterwards they invaded Luxemburg and Navarre respectively. Francis disclaimed any responsibility for their actions, but Charles was not deceived. He accused the king of waging war covertly and warned him of the risks involved. Soon afterwards an imperial army led by the count of Nassau threw La Marck out of Luxemburg, overran Sedan and threatened France's northern border. In the south, Marshal Lescun's army was routed at Ezquiros, and Spanish Navarre, which he had invaded, reverted to Castilian rule.

In Italy, too, Francis ran into serious trouble. On 29 May, Leo X came to terms with Charles V. The latter promised to restore Parma and Piacenza to the Holy See, to assist the pope against the duke of Ferrara and to take the Medici under his protection, while Leo promised to crown Charles emperor in Rome and signified his willingness to invest him with Naples. The treaty, however, was kept secret until Leo was given a pretext to break his alliance with France. In June, Lescun, who had been left in charge of Milan, invaded the States of the Church in pursuit of some rebels. His action gave the pope the pretext he had been waiting for. When an ammunition dump in Milan exploded, killing many French soldiers, Leo acclaimed the event as an act of God and made public his treaty with Charles. Soon afterwards they formed a league for the defence of Italy. Denouncing the pope's ingratitude on 13 July, Francis banned the export of all ecclesiastical revenues to Rome and imposed heavy fines on Florentine merchants in France. He boasted that before long he would enter Rome and impose laws on the pope.

By the summer of 1521, Francis had cause to rethink his policies. The emperor was threatening his northern border, Navarre was again under Castilian rule, the pope had turned imperialist and the French hold on Milan was precarious. On 9 June the king accepted an offer of mediation from Henry VIII, and in July an international conference met at Calais under Wolsey's chairmanship. Francis wanted peace, not a truce, but Mercurino di Gattinara, the imperial chancellor, wanted neither. He was anxious to prove that Francis had been the aggressor as the first step towards forming an Anglo-imperial alliance.

On 20 August the emperor invaded northern France. For three weeks Mézières was heavily bombarded, but the garrison, commanded by Bayard, put up a stout resistance. This gave Francis time to gather an army near Reims. He still hoped for peace, but the Calais conference was getting nowhere. Wolsey, who had paid a mysterious visit to the emperor in Bruges, seemed to be playing for time. In late September the tide of war suddenly turned in France's favour. On 26 September, Nassau lifted the siege of Mézières and retreated into Hainault; in Italy, Lautrec relieved Parma; and on 19 October, Bonnivet captured Fuenterrabía on the Franco-Spanish border. These French victories naturally affected the talks in Calais. When Wolsey suggested a truce, Francis was no longer interested. He planned to relieve Tournai which was being besieged by the imperialists, but on 23 October he missed a unique opportunity of defeating the enemy, and on 1 November he began retreating towards Arras. Nine days later he disbanded his army; soon afterwards Tournai capitulated. Francis was hoping for better news from Italy, but on 19 November the league's army captured Milan. The French were then driven out of other towns in the duchy. The Calais conference, meanwhile, came to an end. On 24 November, in the Treaty of Bruges, Wolsey committed England to enter the war on the emperor's side in 1522.

The financial crisis of 1521–3

It was only in 1521, after Francis had gone to war with the emperor, that the gap between his income and expenses became almost unbridgeable. For war had become very expensive, especially the hire of Swiss mercenaries. 'These people', wrote Anne de Montmorency, 'ask for so much money and are so unreasonable that it is almost impossible to satisfy them.' Yet Francis could not dispense with them. Within a few months his indebtedness to moneylenders rose alarmingly. By the spring of 1522 he owed them one million *livres*. At the beginning of 1521, Semblançay had in his keeping 300,000 *écus* which the king had received from Charles V as part of the Neapolitan pension and 107,000 *livres* belonging to Louise of Savoy. When she implored Semblançay to do everything in his power to assist her son, he assumed that she meant him to use her savings as well as the king's. But this money was very soon swallowed up. On 13 September, Semblançay informed the king that he had only enough money left for one month. As the war dragged on through the winter, Francis created offices, and in February 1522 alienated crown lands worth 200,000 *livres*. The *taille* of 1523 was anticipated to the tune of 1,191,184l. The king called on a number of towns to pay for infantry. He also seized church treasures worth 240,000l. The silver grille enclosing the shrine of St Martin at Tours was torn down by royal agents, melted down and turned into coin. At Laon cathedral four statues of apostles in gold were given the same treatment.

On 22 September the government raised a loan of 200,000l. from the Parisian public against the security of the municipal revenues. This marked the beginning of the system of public credit, known as the *Rentes sur l'Hôtel de Ville*. Each contributor to the loan was assured of a life annuity or *rente*, carrying a rate of interest of 8 per cent which was paid out of the receipts from various local taxes. As the interest was paid by municipal officials of the same social background as the lenders, the system rested on a fair measure of mutual trust, yet Parisians showed little enthusiasm for the scheme.

The battle of La Bicocca, 27 April 1522

The sudden death of Leo X on 1 December 1521 changed the situation in Italy. As the flow of money from papal coffers to Colonna's army dried up, the French under Marshal Lautrec reorganized themselves. Much, however, hung on the result of the next papal conclave. Francis threatened to sever his allegiance to the Holy See if Cardinal Giulio de' Medici, leader of the imperial faction in the Sacred College, were elected. In the event, the cardinals chose Adrian of Utrecht, Charles V's old tutor and regent in Spain. Francis was understandably furious, but Adrian, who took the name of Hadrian VI, approached his new duties in a truly Christian spirit. Denying that he owed his election to Charles, he refused to be drawn into the anti-French league. His main objective was to pacify Christendom as the first step towards arranging a crusade against the Turks, who now threatened Rhodes, the last Christian outpost in the eastern Mediterranean. Francis, however, was more interested in regaining Milan.

In March 1522, Lautrec, whose army had been reinforced by 16,000 Swiss, laid siege to Milan, but, finding the city too strong, he turned his attention to Pavia. Francesco Sforza was thus able to put more troops into Milan, much to the chagrin of Francis who accused his captains in Italy of incompetence. He declared his intention of returning there himself, but was overtaken by events. Emerging from Milan, Colonna threatened Lautrec's rear, whereupon the marshal lifted the siege of Pavia and marched to Monza. Colonna followed at a safe distance and encamped in the grounds of a villa north-west of Milan, called La Bicocca. He fortified his camp with ditches, ramparts and gun platforms. Lautrec saw the madness of attacking it, but his Swiss troops, who had grown tired of marching and counter-marching to no purpose, threatened to leave unless he engaged the enemy at once. He begged them to think again, but eventually conceded their demand. On 27 April they attacked the imperial camp only to be decimated. Some 3000 were killed, leaving the rest to return to Switzerland utterly humiliated. Lautrec, after a vain attempt to hang on to Lodi, returned angrily to France. His brother Lescun surrendered Cremona soon afterwards. On 30 May, Genoa capitulated. Only the castles of Milan and Cremona remained in French hands. The French débâcle in Italy was soon followed by England's entry into the war. On 29 May an English herald appeared before Francis in Lyon and declared war in Henry VIII's name. Hostilities began in July when the earl of Surrey raided Morlaix. In September he led an army out of Calais and tried unsuccessfully to provoke the French into giving battle. Within a month, however, his supplies ran out, forcing him to withdraw to Calais.

While the princes of Christendom were fighting each other, Rhodes fell to the Turks. Hadrian VI urged the princes to sink their differences and join a crusade; but Francis insisted on Milan being restored to him first. The pope, he said, had no canonical right to impose a truce under threat of spiritual sanctions. He reminded Hadrian of the fate that had befallen Pope Boniface VIII in the fourteenth century when he had opposed the French king Philip the Fair. In June he banned the export of money from France to Rome and dismissed the papal nuncio from his court. These measures only served to drive Hadrian into the imperial camp. On 3 August he joined a league for the defence of Italy.

The enquiry commissions of 1523–4 and fiscal reform

By 1523 there was not enough money in the king's coffers to pay for the war. Francis had to look for new sources of income. He suspected that he was being cheated by his own fiscal officials, and set up a commission to audit their accounts and to punish any malpractices. Not even Semblançay, who had done so much to assist the king out of his difficulties, was spared, yet his only fault had been not to distinguish between the king's purse and his mother's. At the end, the commissioners found that he owed Louise 707,267 *livres*, but that he was owed 1,190,374 *livres* by the king.

Francis and his ministers also began reforming the fiscal administration. The revenues most susceptible to corruption were the irregular ones, which were collected and handled in an *ad hoc* way by many officials. A measure of centralization was needed to ensure that they were properly collected, used and accounted for. The first step taken in this direction was the creation on 18 March of the *Trésorier de l'Epargne* with powers to collect and disburse all royal revenues save those from the demesne and from regular taxation. Alone among the fiscal officials, he was exempt from supervision by the *trésoriers de France* and *généraux des finances*. He took his oath of office to the king alone. The first man appointed to the post was Philibert

Babou. In December his powers were considerably enlarged. He was now to receive all royal revenues after deduction of customary local expenses and authorized to make disbursements sanctioned only by royal warrants. This, however, was too heavy a burden. In June 1524, Babou was made responsible only for revenues from the demesne and taxation, while another official, called *Receveur des parties casuelles*, was put in charge of the rest.

In July 1524 an edict claimed that the new fiscal system had proved a success. The king had apparently been spared the need to cut back wages and pensions and had cleared many debts. Although part of his revenues continued to be spent locally, the fact that all payments now had to be authorized by a single official instead of a dozen meant that the king had a tighter control of expenditure. He was also better able to know how much cash he disposed of for emergencies. Another effect of the reforms was the destruction of the influence of the *trésoriers de France* and *généraux des finances*. Their offices survived, but their powers were drastically reduced: they continued to carry out inspections in their respective districts, but policy-making was left firmly in the hands of the king and his council.

The treason of Bourbon, 1523

Francis now prepared to lead a new invasion of Italy. On 23 July he went to Saint-Denis and, as was the custom, placed the relics of the patron saint on the high altar, where they were to remain for the duration of the military campaign. On 12 August, at Gien, he appointed his mother as regent for the second time. Four days later, however, he received a letter from Louis de Brézé, *sénéchal* of Normandy, warning him of a treason plot by the Constable of Bourbon.

Charles duc de Bourbon was Francis I's most powerful vassal. He owned three duchies, seven counties, two *vicomtés* and seven *seigneuries*. All these territories, save three, formed a compact bloc in central France. In addition to his French fiefs, Bourbon also had three lordships within the Holy Roman Empire, making him the vassal of both the emperor and the king of France. Within his domain he was virtually all-powerful: he raised troops, levied taxes, dispensed justice and summoned the estates. His château at Moulins was one of the finest in France. As constable, Bourbon had charge of the king's army in peacetime: he enforced discipline, supervised supplies, appointed commissioners of musters, authorized military expenditure and allocated troops to garrison towns. In wartime he commanded the army in the king's absence or the vanguard in his presence. On ceremonial occasions he carried the king's naked sword. Bourbon was also *Grand chambrier*, responsible for the smooth running of the king's chamber, and governor of Languedoc, where he represented the king though he delegated his functions

to a lieutenant. The duke was related to Francis by marriage, for his wife
Suzanne was Louise of Savoy's first cousin.

Relations between Francis and Charles de Bourbon were good, if not
intimate, during the first five years of the reign. No special significance need
be attached to the fact that Bourbon was recalled from Milan in 1516 and
replaced as lieutenant-general by Marshal Lautrec. He continued to appear
at court fairly often. In 1521, however, he was not chosen to lead the
vanguard during the campaign in northern France, his rightful place being
taken by the king's brother-in-law, Alençon. This was a snub, which it is
tempting to link to the death of Bourbon's wife in April of that year. She
had made a will in her husband's favour, which was challenged by the king
and his mother.

Charles de Bourbon belonged to the younger branch of the house founded
in the fourteenth century by Robert de Clermont, sixth son of King Louis
IX. In 1443 its lands were divided between the two sons of duc Jean I and
it looked for a time as if the two branches would go their separate ways;
but in 1488 the lands of the elder branch passed into the hands of Pierre
de Beaujeu, who, having no son, bequeathed them to his daughter Suzanne.
When she married Charles the lands of both branches were reunited. Even
so, her inheritance comprised lands of three kinds: first, lands which had
originally been detached from the royal demesne as apanages and which,
in theory, were to revert to it on the extinction of the family for which they
had been created; secondly, lands due to escheat to the crown in the event
of a failure of the direct or male line; and thirdly, lands that could be passed
on to heirs male or female, direct or collateral.

In April 1522, Louise of Savoy claimed Suzanne's inheritance as her first
cousin and nearest blood relative. At the same time Francis claimed the
return to the crown of all her fiefs that were only transmissible to male
heirs. The two claims were contradictory, but Francis and his mother were
obviously working towards the same end: the dismantling of the Bourbon
demesne. As the duke was a peer of the realm, it was up to the parlement
to decide the rights and wrongs of the various claims, but on 7 October,
before it could pass judgement, Louise paid homage to the king for most
of the disputed lands. By accepting her oath, he implicitly recognized her
claim, and soon afterwards he gave her lands and revenues pertaining to
the inheritance of Suzanne's mother, Anne de France, who had died in
November. On 6 August 1523 the parlement ordered the sequestration of
Bourbon's lands.

The death of Suzanne had also created another problem. As her only son
had died, Charles needed to remarry in order to perpetuate his line. At
thirty-one he was a most eligible widower. Even in Suzanne's lifetime he
had been offered the hand of one of the emperor's sisters, an offer that
was now renewed. Such a marriage would seriously threaten the territorial

integrity of France. At the same time, it seems, Bourbon found himself under pressure to marry a French princess of royal blood. Louise herself may have been a suitor. Be that as it may, the duke grew increasingly restless. Early in 1523, during a visit to Paris, he allegedly quarrelled with the king, who had accused him of planning a secret marriage. In fact, Bourbon had been dabbling in treason for some time.

In August 1522 the imperial chamberlain, Beaurain, was informed that Bourbon was prepared to lead a rebellion and eight months later was empowered to negotiate with him on behalf of Charles V and Henry VIII. He met the constable secretly at Montbrison on 11 July and signed a treaty. Bourbon was promised the hand of one of Charles's sisters and a dowry of 100,000 *écus*. The emperor was to invade Languedoc from Spain and place 10,000 landsknechts at Bourbon's disposal. Henry was to invade Normandy and subsidize the constable to the tune of 100,000 *écus*. Bourbon's plan was to wait for Francis to invade Italy, then to rise in his rear, using the emperor's landsknechts. But news of the plot soon leaked out. Two noblemen informed their confessor, the bishop of Lisieux, who passed the information to Louis de Brézé. On 10 August he wrote the letter which Francis received as he was travelling south to join his army.

The king's reaction to the disclosure of Bourbon's plot was remarkably cool. He went to Moulins with an armed escort and, finding the duke ill in bed, told him of the warning he had received. Pretending not to believe it, he made various promises to Bourbon on condition that he accompanied him to Italy. The constable agreed, but asked for time to recover from his illness. This was granted and the king continued his journey to Lyon. A few days later Bourbon left Moulins, only to turn back almost at once. On 6 September he met Henry VIII's envoy, Sir John Russell, at Gayette and formalized his relations with England. By now Francis was convinced of the duke's treason. On 5 September three of Bourbon's accomplices – Jean de Poitiers, seigneur de Saint-Vallier, Antoine de Chabannes, bishop of Le Puy, and Aymar de Prie – were arrested. Two days later Bourbon, who had retired to the fortress of Chantelle, severed his allegiance. Next day he fled with a few companions and, after wandering through the mountains of Auvergne, crossed the Rhône into imperial territory.

The plot had failed, but Francis was unsure of its extent. He decided to remain in France to face developments and handed over his command in Italy to Bonnivet. The wisdom of his change of plan was soon demonstrated when a large English army under the duke of Suffolk invaded Picardy on 19 September. Suffolk's initial objective was Boulogne, but he was persuaded to march on Paris instead. By late October he was only fifty miles from the capital. Francis dispatched Philippe Chabot to reassure the panic-stricken population, but the English withdrew of their own accord. By mid-December they were back in Calais. Bourbon, meanwhile, prepared to invade Franche-Comté, but he failed to receive the landsknechts he had been promised by Charles V. So he retired to Italy, hoping eventually to join the emperor in Spain.

In the meantime, a special commission was set up by Francis to try Bourbon's accomplices. The four judges were ordered to use torture if necessary to gain information and to mete out exemplary punishments to all the plotters save the constable, whose fate was reserved to the king's judgement. The commissioners thought the parlement was the appropriate tribunal, and Francis eventually deferred to their wishes. In December, Bourbon's accomplices were moved from their prison at Loches to Paris for trial. Saint-Vallier was sentenced to death on 16 January 1524, but was reprieved just as he was about to be beheaded and remained a prisoner at Loches until his release in 1526. Legend has it that his daughter, Diane de Poitiers, had given her favours to the king in return for her father's life. Other plotters were treated even more leniently, presumably because they incriminated friends who had fled abroad.

Francis needed to regain the confidence of Parisians, who felt that he had left them defenceless while pursuing his Italian adventures. On 6 March, at the Hôtel de Ville, he presented himself as the innocent victim of Bourbon's treachery. Many Parisians, it seems, sympathized with the constable, whose trial *in absentia* opened in the parlement on 8 March. Pierre Lizet, the *avocat du roi*, demanded that he be sentenced to death and all his property confiscated, but the parlement merely ordered his arrest and imprisonment along with the seizure of his property. At a *lit de justice* on 9 March, Francis expressed dismay that the property of Bourbon's accomplices had not been seized. Their crime, he said, ought not to be treated merely as a civil case. On 16 May he ordered a retrial and appointed nineteen new judges to sit alongside the original ones. Yet Bourbon's accomplices were not sentenced till July. While De Prie, Popillon and d'Escars were lightly punished, savage, albeit unenforceable, sentences were passed on the constable's men who had fled abroad. The only sentence left outstanding was Bourbon's own which had to await the king's pleasure.

Meanwhile, Bonnivet made some headway in northern Italy: after crossing the Ticino on 14 September, he forced the imperialists under Colonna to fall back on Milan. But, failing to press home his advantage, he allowed Colonna time to prepare Milan's defences. When Bonnivet resumed his advance, the city was too strong to be stormed; he tried to starve it out, but, as winter closed in, he withdrew to Abbiategrasso. In March 1524, Charles de Lannoy, viceroy of Naples, launched a powerful counteroffensive. After suffering terrible hardship during the winter, Bonnivet's army lacked food and ammunition; so many horses had died that the men-at-arms were reduced to riding ponies. As Bonnivet retreated across the River Sesia, he was badly wounded by a sniper's bullet and had to hand over his command to the comte de Saint-Pol. On 30 April, Bayard, the *chevalier sans peur et sans reproche*, was fatally wounded. On reaching the Alps, the French and the Swiss parted on the worst possible terms. Their defeat had been truly crushing.

In May 1524, Henry VIII and Charles V signed a new treaty. Each agreed to contribute 100,000 crowns towards an invasion of France led by Bourbon, who somewhat reluctantly agreed to put the crown of France on Henry's head. On 1 July, acting as the emperor's lieutenant-general, he invaded Provence from Italy. The French under Lapalice were too weak to offer resistance. Town after town fell to the invaders. Bourbon entered Aix on 9 August and declared himself count of Provence. Ten days later he laid siege to Marseille as Francis brought an army to Avignon. On 21 September the constable ordered his men to storm Marseille through a breach in its wall which his guns had opened up, but, seeing the obstacles that awaited them beyond, they refused. On the brink of despair, Bourbon thought of engaging Francis in battle, but was persuaded by his captains not to be so reckless. So, lifting the siege of Marseille, he retreated along the coast towards Italy, leaving the way clear for Francis to cross the Alps once more.

Success can smile on a monarch too soon. The victory Francis had won at Marignano in 1515 had given him an inflated view of his generalship. Believing that only the incompetence of his lieutenants had lost him Milan, he now imagined that he would only need to reappear in Italy at the head of his troops to win back all the lost ground. Events were to prove him wrong.

7

The New Learning and Heresy, 1483–1525

The late fifteenth century was marked by a deep spiritual malaise throughout Christendom. It would be wrong, however, to imagine that the Renaissance had created a mood of scepticism among the laity in respect of the traditional teachings of the church. Piety still flourished. Pilgrimages and the cult of saints were as popular as ever. However, on a more sophisticated level, that of the theologians in the universities, sharp differences existed regarding the philosophical foundations of Christian belief. Three currents of thought existed simultaneously: scholasticism, mysticism and humanism.

The University of Paris on the eve of the Reformation

The University of Paris comprised four faculties: Theology, Canon Law, Medicine and Arts. The first three were graduate faculties, whose members had to be doctors. The Faculty of Arts was made up of those who had obtained the degree of Master of Arts, a prerequisite for doctoral study in the other faculties. The beginner in arts was usually about fifteen years old. He attached himself to a master, registered with one of four 'nations' and paid a means-tested fee. By 1500 nearly all the teaching took place in one of about forty secular colleges. The mendicants were taught in their own convents, while other religious orders maintained residential colleges (*studia*) where their members lived while pursuing the arts course. The usual period of study in arts was three and a half years, which was commonly followed by a trial regency of a year and a half, making five in all. Following this *quinquennium*, the student became a regent master. A Master of Arts who wished to become a doctor of theology had to study for another thirteen or fifteen years. The Bible and the *Book of Sentences* of Peter Lombard (c.1100–64) formed the core of the long curriculum. Lectures took place in several colleges and in the *studia* of the religious orders. Each bachelor lectured in the college or convent to which he was affiliated.

In theory, doctors of theology were licensed to 'read, dispute, deliberate, and teach' in the faculty; in practice, few did all of these things. Many were content to give simply one annual lecture on the feast of St Euphemia. Their main function was to preside over the disputations and inaugural lectures of students. Another major duty was attendance at regular meetings of the faculty, especially those called to deal with important matters. From 1506 to 1520 the average number of meetings was 27 per annum and they normally took place in the chapel or refectory of the convent of Saint Mathurin. A doctor's income, made up of fees from students and fringe benefits, barely compensated for his long years of training. The main attraction of the doctorate in theology was prestige: it enabled the holder to deliberate on the highest matters of faith and to help decide matters of religious and political significance. Both church and state were in the habit of consulting the university's theologians on various issues. They were consulted about 70 times on matters of doctrine or morals between 1500 and 1542 and such deliberations sometimes led the doctors to challenge papal authority.

Scholasticism

The Faculty of Theology of the University of Paris was, by virtue of its teaching, the preaching of its masters and the doctrinal judgements of its assembly, the sovereign interpreter of dogma. All its learning was drawn from the Bible, the only source of divine knowledge, and Lombard's *Book of Sentences*. However in the fifteenth century all notion of a critical study of Scripture had been lost. A decision of the council of Vienne of 1311 that oriental languages should be taught in the principal European universities had been ignored, so theologians were unable to read the Old Testament in the original Hebrew or the New in the original Greek. They were content instead with the quadruple method of exegesis, historical, allegorical, analogical and tropological. In applying this method they preferred the interpretations of medieval scholars, like Nicholas of Lyra, to those of the early church fathers. Above all they relied on the *Book of Sentences*, a compendium of answers to metaphysical and ethical problems written in the twelfth century.

The Faculty of Arts regarded Aristotle's writings as the fount of all knowledge, but, as the Parisian masters knew no Greek, they had to rely on mediocre Latin versions. They used the gloss by Averroes, the twelfth-century Arab philosopher, to build up their own theories on the world and on man. Outstanding among thirteenth-century doctors at the university was St Thomas Aquinas, whose philosophy was largely shaped by Aristotle's metaphysical writings. In his judgement, knowledge of God was attainable through reason with the assistance of Scripture and the traditional teaching of the church. However, the certainties inherent in his teaching were challenged by Duns Scotus (*c.*1265–1308) and, more recently, by William of Ockham (*c.*1285–1347). The latter denied that spiritual concepts could be grasped merely through reason. Divine truth, in his opinion, lay beyond the reach of the human intellect; obscurely expressed in Scripture, it was held in trust by the church and could only be apprehended through its teaching.

The new doctrine, called Nominalism, as distinct from the Realism of Aquinas, seemed to demote knowledge into a mere study of ideas and for this reason it was twice condemned by the University of Paris, but during the second half of the fourteenth century it managed to gain dominance. The Nominalists, instead of building on Ockham's ideas, were content merely to repeat them. They even narrowed their scope, withdrawing into a study of formal logic that was both abstract and sterile. They created a new philosophy, called Terminism, which became for the sixteenth-century humanists the epitome of intellectual backwardness and confusion. The triumph of Nominalism effectively paralysed the study of theology in the university. Christianity was reduced to a collection of affirmations that had to be accepted without thought or love, and the Christian life to the observance of formal practices and performance of good works.

By the second half of the fifteenth century the University of Paris no longer had the philosophical mastery which for three centuries had been its glory and pride. It seemed uninterested even in publishing the works of its greatest doctors. Scholars who wanted them had to turn to printers outside France. Biblical studies also languished. The first Bible to be printed in Paris appeared in 1476, twenty-five years after Gutenberg's Mainz edition. Studying the Bible occupied less of the working time of teachers and students of theology than debating Lombard's *Sentences*. Nor did patristic studies make up for the poverty of speculation. The Parisian presses largely neglected the writings of the Fathers. Theologians seemed interested only in the Immaculate Conception, a doctrine that had gained wide popular currency since the thirteenth century.

Mysticism

Terminism was too dry and formal a doctrine to satisfy many Christians; sooner or later it was bound to provoke a reaction. A strong mystical tradition existed in Paris, reaching back to such fourteenth-century teachers as Pierre d'Ailly and Jean Gerson, but it was in the Low Countries that late medieval mysticism underwent a remarkable flowering. A major ascetic movement which drew large numbers of laity was the *Devotio Moderna*. Its followers, the Brethren of the Common Life, avoided formal vows while sharing a life in common dedicated to poverty, chastity and obedience. Their founder, Geert Groote (1340–84), wanted religion to be simple, devout and charitable. By the early fifteenth century the Brethren had numerous houses in the Low Countries, Germany and the Rhineland. Their ideals were best expressed in the *Imitation of Christ* by Thomas à Kempis. The Brethren were closely associated with a house of Canons Regular founded at Windesheim in 1387. Rejecting the Nominalists' dumb acceptance of the church's teaching, they found the truth of Christianity in the Bible and liked to read St Augustine and St Bernard, the two great exponents of the inner life and divine love.

An important link between the mysticism of the Low Countries and France was Jean Standonck, a pupil of the Brethren who eventually settled in Paris. After completing the arts course, he entered the collège de Montaigu to study theology and in 1483 became its principal. Though French was not his native tongue, he became a popular preacher. He relinquished the personal use of money and, chastising his body relentlessly, gave all he had to the poor. At Montaigu he imposed a harsh discipline on the students, hoping to develop among them an active and mystical piety. The rule he drew up for a college of poor students which he set up alongside Montaigu has been described as 'one of the capital monuments of the Catholic reformation at the start of the sixteenth century'.

While the Faculty of Theology continued its arid Nominalist teaching, many Parisian clergy turned to St Bernard and St Augustine for spiritual comfort. The mystical writings of d'Ailly and Gerson were also popular, as were books produced by the Brethren of the Common Life and the canons of Windesheim. However, it was mainly through the *Imitation of Christ* that theologians in Paris were influenced by Dutch religious thought. Many editions were available after 1490: a partial French version was printed in 1484 and a full translation in 1493. It was the antidote to the arid discipline of the the Terminists and Scotists; it sustained and satisfied the desire for a more personal faith which scholastic teaching threatened to stifle.

Humanism

Scholasticism and mysticism were only two components of Parisian thought at the close of the Middle Ages. The third was humanism. Parisian teachers of the fourteenth century were not ignorant of classical antiquity, but it was only gradually that Italian humanism penetrated the University of Paris. An early sign was the appointment of Gregorio di Città di Castello, also known as Tifernate, to a chair of Greek. Around 1470, Guillaume Fichet, who visited Italy several times, was the central figure of a group professing a love of ancient Rome. Its members keenly felt the need for accurate texts of the Latin classics, especially the works of Cicero, Virgil and Sallust. In 1470 the first Parisian press was set up in the cellars of the Sorbonne. It was entrusted to two young Germans, Ulrich Gering and Michael Friburger, who within three years printed several humanistic texts, including Fichet's *Rhetoric*. Fichet's aim was to introduce to Paris not simply the eloquence of humanism but also its philosophy. He and his followers combined a respect for the two traditions of Aquinas and Scotus with a love of Latin letters and an interest in Platonic ideas.

Among Fichet's heirs in Paris the most important was Robert Gaguin (b. 1433), general of the the Trinitarian order. Around him gathered a small number of scholars sharing an interest in ancient letters. They discussed literary and ethical questions and, when writing to each other, tried to recapture the charm of Cicero's letters. Yet they never allowed their enthusiasm for ancient letters to undermine their adherence to Christian dogma. Many were churchmen who retained a strict, almost monastic, ideal. They were helped in their labours by a number of Italian humanists. In 1476, Filippo Beroaldo, a young scholar from Bologna, came to Paris where he remained for two years, lecturing on Lucan. Paolo Emilio, who came to Paris in 1483, was patronized by Cardinal Charles de Bourbon, received at court and did a little teaching at the university. He was followed in 1484 by Girolamo Balbi, who soon became famous for his teaching, his Latin epigrams and his edition of Seneca's tragedies. A vain and quarrelsome man, he became involved in a bitter dispute with Fausto Andrelini, another Italian who came to Paris. When Balbi took flight in January 1491 after being charged with sodomy, Andrelini celebrated his triumph in an elegy.

The early Parisian humanists also developed an interest in ancient philosophy, but, as they did not know enough Greek to read the original works of Plato and Aristotle, they had to obtain good Latin translations from Italy. A few were also published in Paris. These developments, however, were only first steps. Parisian teachers and students also needed to become acquainted with the philosophical speculations of the leading Italian humanists. One of them, Pico della Mirandola, visited Paris between July 1485 and March 1486. His major goal was to reconcile and harmonize Platonism and Aristotelianism. He was well acquainted with the traditions of medieval Aristotelianism, and also with the sources of Jewish and Arabic thought.

Parisian teachers and students needed to know Greek before they could become seriously acquainted with the ancient philosophers. In 1476, Greek studies received a boost when George Hermonymos, a Spartan, settled in

Paris. For more than thirty years he lived by copying Greek manuscripts and teaching the language. His pupils included Erasmus, Beatus Rhenanus and Budé, who all complained of his mediocre teaching and avarice. In 1495, Charles VIII brought back from Italy an excellent Hellenist in the person of Janus Lascaris (c.1445–1535) who taught Greek to a number of humanists, Budé being among his pupils. Lascaris also began organizing the royal library at Blois. After about 1504 excellent teachers of Greek were available in Paris. The first Greek printing there was in 1494, but until 1507 it consisted only of passages in a few works. The most significant were in Badius's edition of Valla's *Annotationes in Novum Testamentum* (1505). Greek typography began in 1507 with François Tissard's edition of the *Liber Gnomagyricus* (published by Gilles de Gourmont). He stressed the necessity of Greek to men of learning and urged Frenchmen to combat Italian charges of barbarism. In May 1508, Girolamo Aleandro arrived in Paris recommended by Erasmus and began giving private lessons in Greek to people rich enough to afford the expensive books produced by the Aldine press. In 1509 he went public, and published three small works by Plutarch. His intention, as he grandly announced, was to edit all the works of Greek authors.

Despite the humanists, scholasticism remained firmly entrenched at the University of Paris in the early sixteenth century. Outstanding among the new generation of teachers was the Scottish theologian John Mair or Major (c.1470–1550), who taught at the collège de Montaigu. He resented the charge of barbarousness levelled at the schoolmen by humanists, yet his works exemplified some of the worst traits of scholasticism, notably the endless chewing over of insignificant problems. Statutes drawn up for Montaigu by Noël Béda in February 1509 did not forbid humanistic texts, but they provided for the teaching of only Latin, not Greek. No attempt was made to develop an enthusiasm for the ancient world among the students.

In the autumn of 1495, Gaguin acquired a new disciple: Erasmus of Rotterdam. He first came to Paris in 1493 to study theology and entered the collège de Montaigu, where Standonck's regime instilled in him a deep and lasting aversion to abstinence and austerity. His *Colloquies* contain a grim description of life at Montaigu: bad sanitation, poor and inadequate food, and infected water undermined the health of the students, some becoming blind, mad or leprous within a year. Many promising young minds were, according to Erasmus, blighted by such terrible privations. During his stay at Montaigu, Erasmus attended lectures on the Bible and the *Book of Sentences*, gave some lessons on Scripture, and preached a few sermons, perhaps in the abbey of Sainte-Geneviève. But he derived no satisfaction, intellectual or spiritual, from the teaching of the schoolmen. 'They exhaust the mind', he wrote, 'by a certain jejune and barren subtlety, without fertilizing or inspiring it. By their stammering and by the stains of their impure style they disfigure theology which had been enriched and adorned by the eloquence of the ancients.'

The schoolmen, however, were not entirely to blame for Erasmus's attitude: his mind was not well suited to philosophical or dogmatic speculation. For the present, he was interested in ancient letters, not in philosophy or theology. He attached himself to the circle of Gaguin whose Latin history of France, *De Origine et gestis Francorum Compendium*, was in the press. It was the first specimen of humanistic historiography to appear in France. The printer had finished his work on 30 September 1495, but two leaves remained blank. Erasmus helped to fill the gap by providing a long commendatory letter, his earliest publication.

By the spring of 1496, Erasmus had had enough of the rigours of Montaigu. He fell ill and returned to the Low Countries, but in the autumn he reappeared in Paris. This time, however, he gave the collège de Montaigu a wide berth and earned his living by teaching rich young men. Among them was William Blount, Lord Mountjoy, who took him to England in the summer of 1499. At Oxford, Erasmus met John Colet, under whose influence he broke with the theological systems of the Middle Ages and with the monastic ideal. But Colet's intuitive interpretation of Scripture, without knowledge of the original languages, failed to satisfy him and he decided to improve his own knowledge of Greek. Following his return to Paris in February 1500, he completed the first edition of his *Adages*. In the preface, he castigated the schoolmen for their ignorance of ancient culture and their conceit.

While staying at Saint-Omer in 1501, Erasmus met Jean Vitrier, the warden of the Franciscan monastery, whom he grew to admire as much as Colet. It was under his influence that he composed his *Enchiridion Militis Christiani*, first published in Antwerp in February 1504. In this work Erasmus developed for the first time his theological programme, calling essentially for a return to Scripture. Every Christian, he argues, must strive to understand Scripture in the purity of its original meaning. Before he can do so, he must study the ancient orators, poets and philosophers, especially Plato. Avoiding the Scotists, he must follow the guidance of St Jerome, St Augustine and St Ambrose. Assisted by grammar and languages, he will seek the precise meaning, both literal and allegorical, of Scripture. Erasmus also develops his concept of the Christian life as a continual meditation on Scripture, not as a series of external observances. He no longer identifies Christian holiness with strict observance of the monastic rule, and rejects the notion that the perfect Christian needs to shun the world. Above all, he calls for the wider diffusion of the Gospel.

At the end of 1504, Erasmus returned to Paris after two years spent in Louvain. He set about restoring the New Testament to its original purity, and in March 1505, Badius printed Valla's *Annotationes* as a kind of model for him. But in the autumn of 1505, Erasmus went back to England. Henry VII's physician was looking for a master to accompany his sons to Italy. Erasmus accepted the post and in June 1506 found himself once more among his humanist friends in Paris. He translated two dialogues by Lucan and resumed work on his *Adages*. Two months later he continued his journey to Italy. As he crossed the Alps, he wrote a poem for Guillaume Cop in which he declared his intention to devote himself wholly to sacred studies.

In April 1511, Erasmus was back in Paris mainly in order to see his *Encomium Morae* (Praise of Folly) through the press. This famous work contains a satiric attack on current abuses, especially on worthless monks, vain schoolmen and warring popes. The message of the book is similar to that of the *Enchiridion*: we should look to realities rather than names, to a man's life rather than his words, to the spirit rather than the letter of the law. Erasmus makes merciless fun of the schoolmen with their 'Magisterial Definitions, Conclusions, Corollaries, Propositions Explicit and Implicit', and of ignorant and conceited monks with their meticulous observance of tiny rules of dress and their total disregard of purity of life or apostolic example. The *Praise of Folly* was a huge popular success. Erasmus left Paris in June, never to return, but his influence lived on. His works continued to be published and read in the French capital for many years.

Jacques Lefèvre d'Etaples

A leading French humanist of the late fifteenth century was Jacques Lefèvre. He was born at Etaples in Picardy about 1450, but we know little about his early life. After becoming an MA in Paris, he learnt Greek from Hermonymos while studying mathematics, astronomy and music. Like all keen scholars of his day he travelled to Italy, visiting Pavia, Padua, Venice, Rome and Florence. Wherever he went, he made friends with humanists and other scholars. After teaching in Paris for a few years, he returned to Rome, then visited Germany. On his return he took up a lodging at the abbey of Saint-Germain-des-Prés under the protection of the abbot, Guillaume Briçonnet, the future bishop of Meaux.

At first Lefèvre devoted himself mainly to the study of philosophy. In his approach to the subject he combined mystical tendencies with the precision of a mathematician. In February 1499 he published an edition of the *Mystical Theology* of Dionysius the Pseudo-Areopagite, a work that describes the ascent of the soul to union with God. Lefèvre's admiration for Dionysius was unbounded: 'Never', he wrote, 'outside Scripture, have I met anything which has seemed to me as great and as divine as the books of Dionysius.' In April he published some works by Raymond Lull expressing the horror which he himself felt for Islam and Averroistic materialism. By 1501, Lefèvre had fallen under the influence of the fifteenth-century German cardinal and philosopher Nicholas of Cusa, from whom he learnt that Truth is unknowable to man and that it is only by intuition that he can discover God wherein all contradictions meet.

Lefèvre gave himself heart and soul to Aristotle, whom he translated and explained with boundless enthusiasm and whose many texts he edited after careful expurgations. He wrote commentaries for nearly all the Aristotelian works on the curriculum of the Paris schools. His aim was to set Christian doctrine on the firm foundation of an Aristotelianism freed from scholastic sophism. Yet, even as he explained Aristotle, his mysticism expressed itself. 'While Aristotle writes of things that are deciduous and transitory', he explained, 'he is also treating of the divine mysteries. All this philosophy of tangible nature tends towards the divine things, and, starting from elements that can be sensed, opens the way to the intelligible world.'

He also looked to Plato. During his visit to Florence in 1492 he fell under the influence of Marsilio Ficino (1433–99), founder of the Florentine Academy, who interpreted the contemplative life as a gradual ascent of the soul towards always higher degrees of truth and being, culminating in the immediate knowledge and vision of God. Closely related to Ficino's moral doctrine were his theories of the immortality of the soul and of Platonic love. Another Florentine humanist much admired by Lefèvre was Pico della Mirandola (1463–94), who sought to reconcile ancient philosophy with modern doctrines and Christian dogma. With Pico, as with Marsilio, philosophical speculation was fused with divine love. Like many of his contemporaries, Lefèvre was fascinated by the Hermetic Books. Thus, in 1494, he published Ficino's Latin translation of the *Liber de potestate et sapientia Dei*, attributed to the Egyptian priest Hermes Trismegistus.

The ideas and theories which Lefèvre drew from so many sources ancient and medieval turned him from a philosopher into a theologian, but he remained a humanist. He was firmly committed to textual purity, proclaiming that 'one should only ascribe to God what Scripture teaches about Him'. Thus he looked for the precise meaning of Scripture after ridding it of the barbarous language and useless subtleties of the schoolmen. Yet Lefèvre's command of Latin was always heavy and clumsy. He also condemned most pagan poets, even preferring Battista Spagnuoli to Virgil.

Lefèvre placed his learning at the service of religion. His purpose was 'to give souls the taste for and understanding of Scripture'. He saw philosophy and learning not as ends in themselves but as assisting the triumph of a purer, more enlightened faith. In an edition of Aristotelian works (August 1506) he set out a complete educational programme, but one that was very different from that contained in Erasmus's recently published *Enchiridion*. Lefèvre and Erasmus stood for different Christian ideals. Both wanted their students to write pure and correct Latin, but their attitude to ancient writers differed. Whereas Erasmus believed that their wisdom could lead to a reception of Christian revelation, Lefèvre regarded them simply as models of style. Whereas Erasmus found in Plato the most suitable introduction to the Gospel, Lefèvre regarded Aristotle as the superior teacher. Both men wanted to return to the Bible as interpreted by the church fathers, not by the schoolmen. But Erasmus was no mystic; he turned to Scripture for practical counsel. He ceased to believe in the virtues of monasticism, while Lefèvre wished that his health would allow him to enter a Benedictine or Carthusian monastery and neglected none of the traditional religious observances which Erasmus dismissed as useless.

In July 1509, Lefèvre published his edition of the Psalter. Like Erasmus, he insisted on the need for doctrine to be based on accurate editions of Scripture, but he was not content with a purely literal interpretation, believing that a reading of Scripture had to be prepared by meditation and prayer; also by a close familiarity with the writings of the prophets and apostles. In December 1512 his edition of St Paul's Epistles was published. This set out to explain the apostle's ideas simply, rejecting the scholastic notion that every passage in Scripture requires a quadruple interpretation. In Lefèvre's opinion, Scripture has a literal and a spiritual meaning. Before this can be grasped, it is essential to enter the mind of St Paul, an exercise calling for divine inspiration. Lefèvre read St Paul as a mystic committed to the inner life rather than as a dogmatic theologian or logician. He did not deduce the idea of predestination from his work. His aim was to reconcile grace and free will; not to abolish the autonomy of the human will.

Lefèvre's study of St Paul did not lead him to the same conclusions as those drawn by Erasmus or Luther. He remained loyal to Roman observances. Good works, he says, cannot save by themselves, but they are not useless: they attract, hold and enlarge grace. Nor does faith ensure salvation: it opens the way to God who alone justifies and absolves. Good works make us better men, faith converts us, justification illuminates us. At the same time, his interpretation of dogma was at times extraordinarily free. He denied the magical properties of the sacraments, seeing them rather as signs of spiritual grace, and viewed the mass not as a sacrifice but as a memorial of Christ's sacrifice on the cross. Yet he timidly accepted the new doctrine of the Immaculate Conception, and was surprisingly conservative regarding church reform. He did not suggest the abolition of clerical celibacy or the introduction of prayers in the vernacular.

Guillaume Budé

In 1497, Lefèvre's circle of friends and disciples at the collège du cardinal Lemoine was joined by Guillaume Budé. He belonged to a family of the well-to-do Parisian bourgeoisie, which over three generations had risen to the highest offices in the royal chancery. About 1483 he had been sent to study civil law at Orléans. On returning to the capital he seemed only interested in hunting and other pleasures, but in 1491 he became disgusted with his way of life. Resuming his studies, he began to learn Greek. He also got to know Andrelini, who in 1496 dedicated a work to him. Even after becoming a royal secretary in 1497, Budé continued to read classical and patristic texts. He translated some works of Plutarch, dedicating one to Pope Julius II.

In November 1508, Budé published his *Annotations on the Pandects* which laid down the principle that Roman law can only be understood through the study of Roman history, literature and classical philology. It was also a scathing attack on scholastic jurisprudence as represented by the work of Accursius and Bartolus. Using both philology and history, Budé undermined their assumption that the *Corpus Iuris* was an authoritative system of law adaptable to the needs of all time. The effect of this onslaught on current legal thinking was comparable to that on theology of Valla's exposure of the 'Donation of Constantine' (a document fabricated in the 8th–9th century to strengthen the power of the Holy See). Yet Budé was more interested in restoring the text of Justinian's Digest as literature than in using it for legal education and practice. His polemic against contemporary jurisprudence was the first of many similar legal works of the sixteenth century, the best known being Rabelais's caricature of legal terminology and practice. Almost the entire legal profession was attacked by Budé. He accused its members of using the law not to establish equity or justice but simply to sell and prostitute their words. Deploring the lack of public spirit among his compatriots and the loss of ancient virtues, he expressed the hope that a revival of letters would reawaken their consciences. A theme which assumed importance in Budé's later work – his absolutist theory of the state – was already present in his *Annotations*. While refuting Accursius, he showed the invalidity of equating the parlement with the Roman senate.

The *Annotations* was France's first great work of philology and its impact, notably on Alciati's teaching of law at the University of Bourges, was considerable. Budé followed Valla in his use of a philological-historical method and in his opposition to the Bartolists, but he went further by reviving the Aristotelian concept of equity. This was to have a lasting effect on legal practice in France and elsewhere. Budé's scholarship, though profound, was long-winded and undisciplined. His *De Asse* (1515), a treatise on ancient coinage, is full of absurdly patriotic digressions in which he seeks to elevate Paris above Athens as a centre of ancient learning.

Like Lefèvre d'Etaples, Budé repudiated the vocabulary and methodology of the schoolmen and wanted Christianity to rest solely on the correct study of Scripture. But he did not share Lefèvre's mysticism. He despised devotions that were purely formal or smacked of superstition. He equated Christianity with obedience to Christ's commands and the imitation of His life on earth. As a scholar Budé was well aware of errors in the Latin Vulgate and favoured a return to the original Greek text of the New Testament. His objective was to revivify religion by uniting the Christian faith and humanism. His admiration for the classics did not persuade him that compromise was possible between Hellenism and Christianity. Given the choice, he preferred the latter and in his last work, *De transitu Hellenismi ad Christianismum*, he even denied the value of ancient philosophy.

The Reuchlin affair

In 1514 the Faculty of Theology of the University of Paris was drawn into a conflict which had been raging for three years between the German humanist Johann Reuchlin (1455–1522) and the German Dominicans. Reuchlin had promoted the Talmud, the Cabala and other Jewish studies as essential to a true understanding of biblical revelation; he also believed that the Bible and all its traditional glosses and interpretations should be re-examined in the light of recent exegetical advances and of the new expertise in Greek and Hebrew. His programme, however, if implemented, was likely to disrupt the traditional curriculum of theological faculties. He was accordingly censured by a special inquisition at Mainz in October 1513, and by another in Cologne four months later. The bishop of Speyer, however, acting for the pope, cleared Reuchlin of all charges and ordered an end to the inquisition, whereupon the Cologne theologians decided to consult their colleagues in Louvain and Paris.

The Parisian doctors received the message from Cologne at the end of April 1514 and promptly set up a committee comprising representatives of the scholastic tradition and friends of humanism to examine extracts from Reuchlin's *Augenspiegel*. Numerous meetings followed in the course of which the Cologne theologians sent another book by Reuchlin for examination. There was also an intervention by Duke Ulrich of Württemberg, who asked the faculty to drop its proceedings. On 2 August, however, the faculty decided against Reuchlin. His writings were described as 'strongly suspect of heresy, most of them smacking of heresy and some actually heretical'. The faculty asked for the suppression of the *Augenspiegel* and the author's unconditional retraction. What happened next is not clear. The faculty received a letter from the papal Curia in April 1515, which probably expressed surprise at the decision passed in August, and it ceased to discuss Reuchlin after 2 May. Traditionally, historians have seen the Reuchlin affair as marking a decisive break in the University of Paris between the 'Old Learning' and the 'New'. It was the first serious conflict between schoolmen and humanists. Henceforth Erasmus and Lefèvre d'Etaples were seen by their friends as pursuing the same quest for a deeper faith, and by their enemies as sharing the same heresy.

'Father of Letters'

Francis I was anxious to be seen as a great patron of learning as well as a great soldier. Though primarily a man of action, he liked books and enjoyed being read to at mealtimes. His baggage train included two chests of books whose titles point to his main interests: Roman history and the heroic deeds of antiquity. Like many other princes of his day, he was also interested in astrology, alchemy and the Cabala, occult sciences which were believed to hold the key to the universe. Francis asked Jean Thenaud to write two works for him on the Cabala, but the author warned him of its dangers: 'It is far better', he wrote, 'to be ignorant than to ask or to look for what cannot be known without sinning.'

In the early sixteenth century the crying need for humanists in France was an institution in which classical languages that were excluded from the universities' curriculum could be taught. In February 1517, Francis announced his intention to found such a college. He invited Erasmus to take charge of it, but the great Dutchman was far too keen on his own intellectual freedom to tie himself to the service of any prince. So Francis had to fall back on Janus Lascaris, who was now head of the classical college recently founded in Rome by Pope Leo X. As a first step towards establishing a college in France, the king asked Lascaris to set one up in Milan and provided him with some funds, but these soon ran out and Lascaris had to abandon the venture. In January 1522, Francis decided to establish a college for the study of Greek at the Hôtel de Nesle in Paris, but before this could get under way, his attention was absorbed by his war with the emperor which had begun in 1521.

The beginnings of heresy

Heresy was not unknown in France at the close of the Middle Ages, but except in parts of the south which had been infiltrated by Waldensianism (see below p. 188), it was not an organized movement. Thus Erasmus was broadly correct when he described France in 1517 as the only part of Christendom that was free of heresy. But this happy state was short-lived. In 1519, only two years after Martin Luther had posted up his ninety-five theses in Wittenberg, Lutheranism first appeared in Paris. John Froben, the Basle printer, reported on 14 February that he had sent 600 copies of Luther's works to France and Spain. They were being avidly read, even by members of the Paris Faculty of Theology. In July 1519, Luther and Eck held their famous debate in Leipzig, and soon afterwards they agreed to submit their propositions to the judgement of the universities of Erfurt and Paris. While the Paris theologians were pondering the matter, Luther gave them further food for thought by publishing three radical tracts. On 15 April 1521 the faculty published its *Determinatio* condemning 104 Lutheran propositions. On 13 June the faculty and the parlement assumed joint control of the book trade in and around Paris. It became an offence to print or sell any religious book without the faculty's prior approval. On 3 August a proclamation was read out in the streets to the sound of trumpets, calling on all owners of Lutheran books to hand them over to the parlement within a week on pain of imprisonment and a fine.

Whatever his private beliefs may have been, Francis I repeatedly expressed his opposition to heresy, sharing the view, almost universally held in his day, that religious toleration undermined national unity. The oath he had taken at his coronation bound him not only to defend the faith, but to extirpate heresy from the kingdom. However, at this early stage of the Protestant Reformation heresy was not easily recognized; the boundary between Christian humanism, as expressed in the works of Erasmus or Lefèvre, and Lutheranism was far from clear. Nor was the king obliged to endorse any definition of heresy, not even that of the Faculty of Theology. Having already committed himself to the cause of humanism, Francis must have found it difficult to accept Béda's view that 'Luther's errors have entered this [kingdom] more through the works of Erasmus and Lefèvre than any others.' The king was also much influenced by his sister Marguerite, a deeply devout person, who corresponded with Guillaume Briçonnet, bishop of Meaux, from June 1521 until October 1524, and through his teaching imbibed the ideas of Lefèvre.

Sooner or later trouble was likely to break out between the king and the faculty. While Francis was ready to suppress Lutheranism, he was unwilling to silence the voice of Christian humanism. The first sign of conflict occurred in November 1522, when Guillaume Petit, the king's confessor, complained to the faculty about the sermons of Michel d'Arande, an Augustinian hermit who had become Marguerite's almoner. By 1523 the Faculty of Theology and the parlement were seriously worried about the growth of heresy. Lutheran books were being reported from many parts of the kingdom, and evangelical preachers were increasingly active. In June 1523 the faculty was told of scandals provoked by the publication of Lefèvre's *Commentarii initiatorii in IV Evangelia*, but it decided not to examine the work after a warning received from Chancellor Duprat. In July it summoned Mazurier and Caroli, two members of the *Cercle de Meaux*, to answer a complaint arising from their sermons. This marked a change of policy by the faculty: hitherto it had been content to judge doctrine; now it was encroaching on episcopal jurisdiction. The faculty's action was, in effect, an attack on the entire *Cercle de Meaux*. In August, prompted by the publication of Lefèvre's edition of the New Testament, Béda forced through the faculty a condemnation of all editions of Scripture in Greek, Hebrew and French, causing Francis to intervene again. In April 1524 he forbade any discussion of Lefèvre's work, alleging that he was a scholar of international renown. In October he nipped in the bud a move by the faculty to condemn Erasmus.

By 1523 heresy was so firmly entrenched in France that the Faculty of Theology and the parlement decided that censoring books was not enough: it was time to make an example of the heretics themselves. On 13 May the home of Louis de Berquin, a young nobleman-scholar, was searched by the parlement's officials. On his shelves they found books by Luther and other reformers as well as Berquin's own writings. These the faculty was asked to scrutinize, but the king, after giving his consent, changed his mind: he appointed a special commission, headed by Duprat, to carry out the examination. But the faculty, having already examined Berquin's books, condemned them, and on 1 August he was imprisoned by the parlement. Four days later he was sent for trial on a heresy charge by the bishop of Paris, but Francis evoked the case to the *Grand conseil*. Meanwhile, Berquin was set free by royal command and allowed to go home. His books, however, were burnt outside Notre-Dame.

8

Defeat, Captivity and Restoration, 1525–7

In September 1524 everything seemed set fair for the king of France. The threat of internal rebellion had been removed; Bourbon was beating a hasty retreat to Italy after failing to capture Marseille. Though advised to wait until the spring before invading Italy, Francis was keen to reach Lombardy before the imperial forces could regroup. On 17 October he appointed his mother as regent and soon afterwards led a powerful army across the Alps. The weather being exceptionally mild, he accomplished the crossing in record time. As he pressed forward into Lombardy, the imperialists retreated to Lodi, abandoning Milan. Francis now had the choice of either pursuing them to Lodi or besieging Pavia. He chose the latter, prompting the imperial captain, the marquis of Pescara, to exclaim: 'We were defeated, soon we shall be victorious.' For Pavia was a hard nut to crack, protected on three sides by a wall and on the south side by the River Ticino. The garrison, consisting of German and Spanish veterans, was commanded by Antonio de Leyva, one of the ablest captains of his day.

The battle of Pavia, 24 February 1525

The French began bombarding Pavia on 6 November. Within three days they had breached the wall, but an assault by them was repulsed with heavy losses. They then tried to divert the Ticino by building a dam, but it was washed away by torrential rains. The siege degenerated into a blockade punctuated by skirmishes and artillery duels. Francis then made a controversial move: he detached 6000 troops from his army and sent them under the duke of Albany to conquer Naples. The idea may have been to draw the viceroy of Naples away from Lombardy, but he chose to stay put. Had Albany moved faster, he might have taken advantage of popular unrest in

Naples; but instead he allowed himself to get bogged down in Sienese politics. His expedition, however, did help to bring the new pope into the war on the French side. Clement VII had so far remained neutral in order not to jeopardize the rule of his Medici kinsmen in Florence, but on 25 January 1525 he allowed Albany free passage through the States of the Church.

The siege of Pavia was a grave tactical error. Though Francis was advised to retire to Milan for the winter, he refused on the ground that no king of France had ever besieged a town without capturing it. Believing that Pavia would soon capitulate, he sentenced his men to spend four months in appalling conditions outside the town. Their main camp on the east side of Pavia was strongly fortified. They also occupied the walled park of Mirabello to the north of the town. Within the park the terrain was open and rolling with clumps of trees and shrubs; it was also criss-crossed by numerous brooks and streams. On 22 January the imperialists marched out of Lodi as if they intended to attack Milan. Then, as the French failed to react, they veered south-west and pitched camp within a stone's throw of the French. Only the Vernavola, a small tributary of the Ticino, kept the two armies apart.

On 23 February the imperial commanders, Charles de Lannoy, viceroy of Naples, and Bourbon, tried to break the deadlock. They moved out of their camp after nightfall, leaving only a token force behind, and marched north along the east wall of the park. Two hours later they halted near the north side, and sappers, using only picks and battering rams, opened up three gaps in the wall. At dawn the first troops entered the park. Despite a heavy mist they were spotted by the French, who opened fire with their guns. The rest of the imperial army, meanwhile, had entered the park. The sequel is not clear, but it seems that Francis and his cavalry had formed up within the park. As the imperialists advanced, the king led a cavalry charge and got in the way of his artillery which had to stop firing. His infantry was left far behind. After breaking through the enemy line, Francis and his men-at-arms came within range of Spanish arquebusiers who had been carefully concealed in copses around the northern edge of the park. The French nobles with their suits of armour, plumed helmets and distinctive horse trappings offered easy targets. As they were picked off by the arque-busiers they crashed to the ground like so many helpless lobsters. After the king's horse had been killed, he continued to fight on foot, valiantly striking out with his sword (now on display at the Musée de l'Armée, Paris), but was gradually surrounded by enemy soldiers anxious to earn a king's ransom. In their eagerness to snatch pieces of his armour as evidence for their claim, they might easily have killed him. At this juncture Lannoy appeared and Francis surrendered to him. Meanwhile, the battle raged in various parts of the field. As huge blocks of French and imperial infantry collided there was terrible carnage, and many Swiss troops were drowned as they tried to ford the Ticino. By noon on 24 February the battle was over. The imperialists had won the day and Francis was their prisoner.

Pavia was the greatest slaughter of French noblemen since Agincourt. Among the dead were many illustrious captains and also close friends of the king. They included Bonnivet, Giangaleazzo da San Severino, Marshal Lapalice, François de Lorraine and Richard de la Pole, the so-called 'White Rose'. Marshal Lescun and the king's uncle, the Bastard of Savoy, had been fatally wounded. Apart from the king, prisoners included Henri d'Albret, king of Navarre, Louis comte de Nevers, Anne de Montmorency, and the seigneurs of Florange, Chabot de Brion, Lorges, La Rochepot, Annebault and Langey. Among important French nobles only the king's brother, Charles d'Alençon, escaped death and capture. He died on 15 April, soon after returning to France, some said of shame, others of sorrow. About 4000 French prisoners who were not worth a ransom were freed on parole.

After the battle, Francis was taken to the Certosa at Pavia and allowed to write to his mother. 'All is lost', he said, 'save my honour and my life.' He asked Louise to take care of his children and allow free passage to a messenger whom he was sending to the emperor in Spain. In his letter, Francis appealed to Charles's magnanimity: by accepting a ransom, he said, Charles would turn his prisoner into a lifelong friend.

The emperor was in Madrid when he received news of his victory on 10 March. He instructed the viceroy of Naples to treat Francis well and to give Louise frequent news of him. The king was, in fact, well treated. He was imprisoned at first in the castle of Pizzighettone, near Cremona, where he remained for nearly three months in the custody of a Spanish captain called Fernando de Alarçon. He was allowed companions, visitors and physical exercise. Montmorency, who shared the king's captivity, kept his sister Marguerite informed about his health. She urged Francis to stop fasting and sent him the Epistles of St Paul to read. On 18 May he was taken to Genoa, where a fleet of Spanish galleys waited to carry him off to Naples. The prospect terrified Francis, for Naples had the reputation among Frenchmen of being a graveyard. He begged Lannoy to take him instead to Spain, where he hoped to win over the emperor by exercising his charm. The viceroy agreed on condition that French galleys were placed at his disposal. This was duly arranged, and on 19 June Francis landed at Barcelona to a tumultuous welcome. He attended mass in the cathedral and hundreds of sick people came to be touched by him. The king was then taken by sea to Tarragona, where he was nearly killed by a stray bullet as he looked out of a castle window. At the end of June he was moved to Valencia, then to an agreeable Moorish villa at Benisanó.

In the meantime, Montmorency carried three requests from Francis to the emperor in Toledo. The first was for a safe-conduct for the king's sister

Marguerite d'Angoulême to come to Spain as a peace negotiator; the second
was for Francis to be brought nearer to the peace table so that he might
be more easily consulted; and the third was for a truce to last as long as
the talks. All three requests were conceded. At the end of July, Francis was
taken to Madrid. His journey, which lasted three weeks, was like a royal
progress. At Guadalajara he was lavishly entertained by the duke of
Infantado, a leading Spanish grandee; at Alcalá de Henares he visited the
university recently founded by Cardinal Jimenez de Cisneros. In Madrid,
where he arrived on 11 August, the king was given a room in the Alcázar,
which stood on the site of the present royal palace.

The regency of Louise of Savoy

Francis's captivity lasted just over a year, until 17 March 1526. In his
absence France was governed by his mother from the abbey of Saint-Just,
near Lyon, assisted by Duprat and by Robertet. Their first task was to
provide for the kingdom's defence. Pavia had not ended the war. France
continued to be threatened with invasion for several months, mainly from
England. 'Now is the time', Henry VIII wrote, 'for the emperor and myself
to devise means of getting full satisfaction from France. Not an hour is to
be lost.' He sent an embassy to Spain with proposals for the dismemberment
of France. Henry hoped to be crowned in Paris and to recover all that was
his 'by just title of inheritance'. At the very least, he expected to acquire
Normandy or Picardy and Boulogne.

   Henry assessed the situation correctly: France had been largely denuded
of troops, armaments and supplies in the interest of Francis's Italian campaign. Such troops as remained in the north were unpaid and lived off the
countryside, striking terror in villages and even in the suburbs of Paris. In
the south the situation was less critical, as remnants of the royal army
drifted back across the Alps. In April, Albany's troops returned home by
sea almost intact. But the regent could only pay some of them; the rest she
sent north to swell the marauding bands. A joint invasion by Henry VIII
and Charles V would almost certainly have brought the kingdom to its
knees; but Henry failed to get the co-operation of Charles, who had to cope
with many urgent problems in various corners of Europe. His troops in Italy
were unpaid and mutinous, if they had not already deserted. In Germany the
Peasants' War was threatening the very fabric of society, while further east
the Turkish threat loomed large. The Sultan Suleiman, having conquered
Rhodes in 1522, was preparing to attack Hungary whose king, Louis II,
was Charles V's brother-in-law.

   In providing for the defence of France, Louise of Savoy concentrated her
efforts on Burgundy. She posted lookouts along the River Saône and sent

the comte de Guise to inspect the province's fortifications. However, in June 1525 her cousin Margaret of Savoy, governor of the Netherlands, renewed the truce neutralizing the frontier dividing the two Burgundies. In the north, Louise relied on help from the parlement. It purchased and sent grain to towns in Picardy and persuaded the Parisian authorities to send arms and ammunition.

Perhaps the most important task facing the regent was to maintain the king's authority. Some people believed that the regency should be exercised by the king's nearest adult male kinsman and an attempt was apparently made to put the duc de Vendôme in Louise's place, but he refused to act in a way likely to divide the kingdom. In March 1525 the parlement assured Louise of its support, but it was keen to reverse the trend towards a more absolute, less consultative, monarchy.

On 23 March the parlement set up a commission to draw up remonstrances for presentation to the regent. Normally, remonstrances were concerned with a particular piece of legislation, but the commissioners chose to examine a wide range of royal policies. They saw the hand of God in the misfortunes that had befallen the kingdom. Penitence and prayer were needed to put matters right, but also measures to root out heresy. Here the parlement was tilting at Marguerite d'Angoulême's protection of the *Cercle de Meaux* and at royal interference with the Berquin trial. The parlement also called for the annulment of the Concordat with the Holy See and for a return to the Pragmatic Sanction. It objected to the government's use of *évocations* whereby lawsuits were referred to the *Grand conseil*, which was under the king's immediate influence. Another area of concern was the fiscal administration. The parlement believed that fiscal officials were thieves and that public money was being wasted. It deplored alienations of the royal demesne regardless of the 'fundamental law' that forbade the practice.

When the regent received the remonstrances on 10 April she described them as 'to the honour of God, exaltation of the faith, and very useful and necessary to the good of the king and commonwealth'. She explained that the Concordat could be revoked only by the king, but promised to satisfy the parlement's other demands. However, Louise never again spoke about the remonstrances, and only in respect of heresy did she go some way towards meeting the parlement's wishes. Recent disturbances at Meaux had alarmed the parlement. Bishop Briçonnet was ordered to set up a tribunal comprising two *parlementaires* and two theologians to try heresy cases. Its competence, which was at first limited to his diocese, was soon extended to include all dioceses within the parlement's *ressort* or area of jurisdiction, in effect removing heresy cases from the episcopal courts which had traditionally judged them. The parlement also wanted the new court to try bishops suspected of heresy, but this required papal consent. On 29 April, Louise asked Clement VII for the necessary rescript, which he duly conceded. As the new judges thus exercised papal jurisdiction, they became known as the *juges délégués* (delegated judges). An appeals procedure was set up from them to the parlement, which consequently achieved overall control of heresy cases.

The parlement took advantage of the king's absence to launch an attack on religious dissenters. In February 1526 heresy was defined so broadly as to take in even the smallest deviation from religious orthodoxy. The censorship of books was tightened up, printers and booksellers being forbidden to publish or stock religious works in French. The parlement was particularly anxious to seize copies of Lefèvre d'Etaples' *Epitres et évangiles des cinquante et deux dimanches* which had been published anonymously. However, books were not the only victims of the persecution. The *juges délégués* were asked to prosecute Lefèvre, Caroli, Mazurier and Roussel. This attack on the *Cercle de Meaux* prompted Francis's only known intervention in the domestic affairs of his kingdom during his captivity. In November 1525 he ordered the parlement to suspend proceedings against Lefèvre, Caroli and Roussel, holding them to be innocent victims of persecution by the 'Sorbonne'. But the parlement stuck to its guns: on 29 November the *juges délégués* were instructed by the court to press on with their activities regardless. Lefèvre and Caroli fled to Strassburg, while Mazurier recanted. As for Briçonnet, he decided to fall into line with orthodoxy. Another victim was Berquin, who was rearrested in January 1526, found guilty of heresy and sent to the parlement to be sentenced, but the court desisted when it learned that Francis was about to come home.

A serious bone of contention between the regent and the parlement was the Concordat. On 24 February 1525, Etienne Poncher, archbishop of Sens and abbot of Saint-Benoît-sur-Loire, died. In response to a request from Chancellor Duprat, who had recently taken holy orders, Louise appointed him to both benefices. However, both Sens and Saint-Benoît were exempt from the Concordat's provisions and the chapters proceeded to elect their superiors: Jean de Salazar at Sens and François Poncher (Etienne's nephew) at Saint-Benoît. Duprat promptly appealed to the papacy which quashed the elections; the chapters appealed to the parlement. A protracted legal struggle ensued which was inflamed when Duprat sent an armed force to occupy Saint-Benoît, and the parlement tried to dislodge it. The regent evoked both lawsuits to the *Grand conseil* which consequently found itself in dispute with the parlement. On 24 June the two courts were ordered to hand over the lawsuits to a special commission appointed by Louise. At the same time she sent troops to Paris, presumably to force the parlement's compliance.

The quarrel was given a dangerous new twist in July, when the parlement mounted an attack on Duprat, whom it had never forgiven for his part in securing the Concordat. He was summoned to Paris to answer certain charges, but the regent would not let him go. She asked for an explanation of the parlement's conduct and kept its representatives waiting several weeks before granting them an audience. Her procrastination paid off. The parlement dropped its attack on the chancellor and agreed not to judge the affairs of Sens and Saint-Benoît if the *Grand conseil* would do likewise. This satisfied Louise, who allowed matters to rest there until her son's return.

The Treaty of Madrid, January 1526

Foreign policy was the most successful aspect of Louise of Savoy's regency. While negotiating with Charles V for her son's freedom, she worked to break up the Anglo-imperial alliance and stirred up trouble for the emperor in Italy and elsewhere. His terms for the release of Francis were anything but generous. The king was to give up Burgundy and all other territories owned by Charles the Bold in 1477; also Thérouanne and Hesdin. Bourbon's property was to be restored; an independent kingdom, including Provence, was to be created for him; and his accomplices were to be pardoned. Henry VIII's French claims were to be satisfied and Francis was to settle an indemnity owed by the emperor to Henry. The prince of Orange, whom the French had taken prisoner, was to be released and his principality restored. Peace was to be sealed by a marriage between Charles's niece Mary and the Dauphin. Finally, the king's release was to be conditional on the peace treaty being ratified by the French estates and parlements.

When these terms were laid before Francis in April 1525, he refused to discuss them, and referred the imperial envoy Beaurain to Louise. She appointed François de Tournon, archbishop of Embrun, as ambassador. His instructions stated that no part of France was to be ceded to the emperor. Tournon was soon joined in Spain by Jean de Selve. Both men saw Charles V in Toledo on 17 July, when he refused ever to accept a ransom for Francis. Burgundy was the main stumbling-block in the negotiations. On 16 August, Francis made a secret declaration to the effect that he would never cede the duchy of his own free will, and that if he were compelled to do so his action would be null and void.

Louise, meanwhile, set about destroying the Anglo-imperial alliance. The English government, fearing a separate peace between Francis and Charles, resumed secret negotiations with the regent which Pavia had interrupted. On 30 August the Treaty of the More was signed, restoring peace between England and France and drawing them together in a defensive alliance. Henry VIII undertook to use his influence with Charles to obtain Francis's release. Francis, for his part, promised to pay Henry two million *écus* in annual instalments of 100,000 *écus*. Maritime disputes between the two countries were to be settled. The Scots were to stop armed raids across the border and Albany was banned from Scotland during James V's minority. France agreed to indemnify Louis XII's widow Mary, now duchess of Suffolk, for losses she had incurred during the war. Because Francis was not free to ratify the treaty, the English demanded special guarantees in the form of registration by four parlements and two provincial estates as well as financial pledges from nine major towns, including Paris, and eight noblemen. Louise asked the parties concerned to signify their acceptance of these terms, but they viewed them as a serious breach of their privileges. The Parlement of Paris waited till 28 October before ratifying the treaty and the estates of Normandy never did so. The eight noblemen complied with the regent's request, but the towns, especially Paris, proved troublesome. Fortunately for Louise, she was able to persuade the English government to postpone the deadline for the surrender of the pledges.

In June 1525, Louise offered the pope and Venice an alliance aimed at driving the imperialists out of Italy and forcing Charles to release her son. It was not concluded, however, because Louise was only willing to give financial help to her allies: she was afraid of alienating the emperor permanently by offering them military aid. Her diplomacy also encompassed the eastern Mediterranean. John Frangipani was dispatched to the sultan with an appeal for aid from Francis and his mother. Suleiman promised in reply to lead an expedition against the emperor.

On 11 September, Francis fell gravely ill and the emperor, who so far had avoided seeing him, hastened to his bedside. The two rivals embraced and exchanged friendly greetings. Next day Marguerite arrived, after travelling post-haste from France. On 22 September, Francis lapsed into a semi-coma, but a 'miracle' suddenly occurred: an abscess inside the king's head burst, his fever dropped and his spirits revived. His companions were soon able to inform the regent and the parlement that he was out of danger.

Marguerite now went to Toledo to negotiate her brother's release; but the imperial council held out no hope of concessions. Francis declared that he would rather remain a prisoner for good than dismember his kingdom. In November he abdicated in favour of his seven-year-old son, the Dauphin François, but the deed of abdication was not sent to the parlement for registration. It was almost certainly nothing more than a ploy aimed at frightening Charles into making concessions. In November, after Marguerite had decided to go home, Louise instructed her envoys to make peace at any price. 'What was the point of losing a kingdom', she asked, 'for the sake of a duchy?' Francis apparently came round to this view: he accepted the emperor's terms on condition that his release preceded the surrender of Burgundy; as he explained, he alone could persuade his subjects to give up the duchy. Going against Gattinara's advice, Charles agreed to this condition in return for guarantees: Francis had to swear on the Gospels and give his word as a nobleman that he would hand over the Dauphin and his brother as hostages and would return to prison in the event of the treaty not being fulfilled. Charles needed peace, for he was in dire financial straits. He also knew that a new coalition, including England, Venice and the papacy, was being formed against him. The German situation remained bleak and, further east, the Turks were preparing the offensive which was to destroy the Hungarian monarchy on the field of Mohácz.

On 14 January 1526 the text of the Treaty of Madrid was brought to Francis. In it, he agreed to abandon Burgundy and Tournai, give up his rights in Italy, and rehabilitate Bourbon and his accomplices. He also deserted his allies, the king of Navarre, the duke of Guelders and Robert de La Marck. His two sons were to replace him as hostages in Spain. However, on the eve of signing the treaty, Francis formally protested before several French witnesses, including two notaries, that the concessions he was about to make were null and void. That afternoon, in front of all the plenipotentiaries, he swore to observe the treaty and to return to prison within four months if its ratification failed to materialize.

Francis was detained at the Alcázar, probably for health reasons, till mid-February. On 20 January he was betrothed by proxy to Charles's sister Eleanor, and on 13 February, Charles came to Madrid and spent six days in his company. The two monarchs went to Illescas where Francis was introduced to Eleanor. On 19 February, Charles left for Seville to marry Isabella of Portugal, while Francis set off on his journey back to France. He was exchanged for his sons on 17 March on an island in the River Bidassoa. After setting foot on French soil, he rode full tilt to Bayonne where his mother, sister, ministers and friends were waiting for him. On 20 March he attended a service of thanksgiving in Bayonne cathedral.

The second accession

Following his return home, Francis spent several months touring south-west and central France. It was probably at Mont-de-Marsan in March 1526 that he first met Anne de Pisseleu, who was to replace Françoise de Châteaubriant in his affections. She was eighteen and admired for her beauty, intelligence and vivacity. By 1527 she had joined the king's 'fair band' of ladies. In 1531 she became the governess of his daughters, Madeleine and Marguerite, and about 1534 Francis married her off to Jean de Brosse, soon to become duc d'Etampes. Thus did Anne become duchesse d'Etampes, the name by which she is best remembered. Despite her marriage, she remained at court where she came to exert a powerful political and artistic influence.

In October 1526 the bodies of Queen Claude and her infant daughter Louise, whose funerals had been postponed on account of the war, were taken from Blois to the abbey of Saint-Denis, where they were buried on 7 November. And on 30 January 1527 the king's sister Marguerite took as her second husband Henri d'Albret, king of Navarre, who had escaped from prison in Pavia. The marriage was politically significant, since Henri's claim to Spanish Navarre had yet to be satisfied by the emperor. After visiting her small kingdom, Marguerite returned to court where in June 1528 she attended the wedding of her sister-in-law Renée with Ercole d'Este. On 16 November, Marguerite gave birth to a daughter, Jeanne, who was to become the mother of King Henry IV.

Francis's homecoming in March 1526 was followed by a distribution of honours comparable to that of 1515. Bourbon's treason and the slaughter of so many noblemen at Pavia had created numerous vacancies in the royal administration. The king also wished to reward people who had been loyal to him during his captivity. Foremost among the new appointees were Anne de Montmorency and Philippe Chabot de Brion. Both had been brought up with Francis, had shared his captivity and had helped to bring about his release. Montmorency was thirty-one years old and a scion of one of the oldest and richest aristocratic houses. In August 1522, after serving in several military campaigns, he had become a marshal of France, a knight of the Order of St Michael, and a royal councillor. Now, on 23 March 1526, he was appointed *Grand maître de France* (in place of René of Savoy) and governor of Languedoc (in place of Bourbon). As the official head of Francis's household, Montmorency became one of his principal advisers. He was a strict disciplinarian and a religious conservative. In January 1527 he married Madeleine of Savoy, daughter of the king's deceased uncle, René. She brought Anne a large dowry which increased his already considerable fortune.

Philippe Chabot, seigneur de Brion, was appointed Admiral of France on 23 March 1526 in succession to Bonnivet, the king's deceased favourite. Early in the reign Chabot had become a gentleman of the king's chamber, captain of a company of *lances*, a knight of the Order of St Michael and mayor of Bordeaux. Among his military exploits was the successful defence of Marseille against Bourbon in 1524. In addition to the admiralship of France, he became governor of Burgundy. Though he received many gifts of land and money, he never became as wealthy as Montmorency. In January 1527 he married Françoise de Longwy, daughter of Francis I's bastard sister.

Among other important appointments made by Francis in 1526, Galiot de Genouillac became *Grand écuyer* (Master of the Horse) in place of Giangaleazzo da San Severino; Robert de La Marck, seigneur de Florange, became a marshal of France; Jean de La Barre became comte d'Etampes and *prévôt* of Paris; and François de Tournon was promoted to the archbishopric of Bourges.

The king breaks his word

The first clear indication of Francis's intentions regarding the Peace of Madrid was his refusal to ratify it. The imperial envoy, de Praet, who came to fetch the ratification, was sent home empty-handed. On 2 April 1526 the king complained that the treaty had been prematurely published in Antwerp, Rome and Florence. His subjects, he said, were angry and asked to be heard before the treaty was ratified. Early in May the viceroy of Naples, to whom Francis had surrendered at Pavia, came to Cognac hoping to persuade Francis to ratify the treaty. He was warmly welcomed by the king, who had not forgotten that he owed him both life and freedom, but he did not allow gratitude to stand in the way of his interests. On 10 May, Lannoy was informed by the king's council that Burgundy could not be handed over because the king's subjects would not allow such a diminution of his patrimony. Francis also argued that promises made under duress were null and void. However, since he wished to remain the emperor's friend, he was willing to honour parts of the treaty which were acceptable to him and to pay a cash ransom. On 4 June the estates of Burgundy, meeting under the presidency of Chabot, endorsed the decision taken by the king's council. Denouncing the treaty as 'contrary to all reason and equity', the deputies affirmed their wish to remain French. A similar declaration was made a few days later by the estates of Auxonne. In July a royal apologia intended for international consumption was published. It stressed the 'fundamental law' which forbade the king to alienate any part of his demesne, and enunciated the novel principle that no province or town could change ownership without the consent of its inhabitants. In addition to justifying his breach of faith, Francis acted to prevent an imperial conquest of Burgundy. Chabot inspected the province's defences and put them on a war footing, but this proved unnecessary as Charles V lacked the means to invade. After an unsuccessful attempt by the prince of Orange to capture Auxonne, Charles disbanded his army. His dream of reuniting the two Burgundies had vanished for ever.

The League of Cognac, 22 May 1526

Francis's repudiation of the Treaty of Madrid did not imply a readiness to resume hostilities with Charles V, at least for the time being. His chief aim was to recover his sons. To do this, he needed to put pressure on Charles by drawing closer to other European powers. On 15 May he ratified the Treaty of the More and on 22 May formed the 'Holy' League of Cognac with Venice, the papacy, Florence and Milan. Though ostensibly directed against the Turks, its real purpose was to expel imperial forces from Italy. Charles V had intended to go there to be crowned emperor by the pope. Now, because of the league, he felt obliged to stay in Spain and prepare for a new conflict. The allies were confident of success: the imperial army in Italy was penniless and disorganized, so Francis still hoped to recover his sons for a cash ransom. Charles, however, would not hear of this. 'I will not deliver them for money,' he declared. 'I refused money for the father: I will much less take money for the sons. I am content to return them upon reasonable treaty, but not for money; nor will I trust any more the king's promise, for he has deceived me, and that like no noble prince.'

By the autumn of 1526, Francis had come to realize that he needed to step up pressure on Charles. He made warlike noises, which encouraged the pope to act against the pro-imperial Colonna family in the States of the Church. French assistance, however, failed to materialize, and Clement VII's situation soon grew desperate. In March 1527 he made a truce with the viceroy of Naples, who had landed in Tuscany with 9000 troops. Meanwhile, Francis looked to friendship with England rather than military involvement in Italy as the most economical way of bringing the emperor to heel. On 30 April, in the Treaty of Westminster, he and Henry VIII agreed to send a joint embassy to Charles to negotiate the release of Francis's sons. If Charles refused their terms, war was to be declared on him.

From the pope's point of view, the Anglo-French entente came too late. Despite his truce with Lannoy, the main imperial army under Bourbon invaded the States of the Church. On 6 May the Sack of Rome began. Bourbon was fatally wounded as he scaled the walls of the city, but his troops poured into it like a torrent, destroying everything in their path. Clement and some cardinals took refuge in the castle of Sant' Angelo. On 5 June the pope signed a humiliating treaty which left him virtually a prisoner in imperial hands.

Francis restores his authority

Although the king's authority had not been seriously threatened during his captivity, various bodies, notably the Parlement of Paris, had caused the regent enough embarrassment to justify a tightening up of that authority.

One of Francis's first moves on returning home was to intervene in Berquin's trial for heresy. He forbade the parlement to pass sentence and tried to alleviate Berquin's prison conditions. The parlement submitted without demur when Jean de La Barre, acting for the king, released Berquin from prison. Francis also came to the rescue of the *Cercle de Meaux*. Lefèvre, Caroli and Roussel returned from exile: Lefèvre became the king's librarian, Caroli resumed preaching in Paris and Roussel was appointed almoner to

Marguerite de Navarre. The king also defended Erasmus after the Faculty of Theology had condemned his *Colloquies*. He ordered the parlement to ban publication of any work by the faculty which had not been previously examined and approved by the court and early in 1527 he abolished the *juges délégués*.

Reformers imagined that the king of France was coming over to their side. 'The king favours the Word,' Capito wrote to Zwingli, but Francis was simply reasserting his authority after the parlement and Faculty of Theology had tried to deal with heresy in their own way. While they defined heresy narrowly, he was evidently prepared to tolerate a fair measure of evangelicalism, especially within his court.

Francis also vindicated his authority in another sphere. In April 1526 he authorized Duprat to take possession of Saint-Benoît-sur-Loire and soon afterwards confirmed the *Grand conseil*'s decree conferring the see of Sens on the chancellor. In December, during a debate between representatives of the parlement and *Grand conseil* in front of the king's council, Duprat tried to justify the government's action at Saint-Benoît. On 10 December the king's council decided that the parlement had acted illegally and nullified its decrees regarding Saint-Benoît. In January 1527, Francis ordered the parlement to hand over the minutes of its debates during his captivity. The court complied after deleting passages about Duprat. Among churchmen involved in the Saint-Benoît affair, the most severely punished was Duprat's rival, François Poncher, bishop of Paris. He was charged with sedition and imprisoned at Vincennes, where he died in September 1532.

Following his return from Spain, Francis did not reappear in Paris till 14 April 1527. He may have wanted to show his displeasure with the inhabitants' behaviour during his absence. They had obstructed his mother's peace-making efforts and had indulged in various disloyal pranks. When the king did eventually reappear, he did not give the customary notice. His entry was preceded by the arrest of eight citizens who had opposed the guarantees required under the Treaty of the More – a canon of Notre-Dame, three *parlementaires*, a notary and three merchants. The notary and merchants were soon freed, but the others were left to languish in prison for two years.

The quarrel between king and parlement was finally settled at a *lit de justice* on 24 July 1527. It has been suggested that this was, in fact, the first *lit de justice*, that all previous meetings of the parlement in the king's presence had been merely 'royal séances', and that the phrase *lit de justice* was used in the Middle Ages simply to describe the trappings – throne, drapes and cushions – associated with the royal presence. Yet there is ample evidence that the medieval *lit de justice* had a distinctive judicial purpose. In July 1527, Francis acted as supreme judge, as his predecessors had done before him. The notion that he was creating a new forum dedicated to upholding 'French public law' is false. Francis needed to punish the parlement for its opposition to the regent during his captivity, to vindicate his own authority and that of his chancellor, and to remind the parlement of its rightful place in the constitution. The full majesty of kingship was reflected in the elaborate staging. Francis appeared on an elevated throne beneath a blue canopy embroidered with gold fleur-de-lys. On either side of him on raised tiers sat peers, nobles and prelates, *maîtres des requêtes*, and the three presidents of the parlement. Beneath the king, sharing in his majesty, sat the chancellor. The floor of the *Grand' chambre* was occupied by 75 councillors of the parlement and numerous courtiers. As the king took his throne, the *parlementaires* fell upon their knees until ordered to rise.

In a long opening speech, the president Charles Guillart criticized many aspects of royal policy, especially the evocation of lawsuits from the parlement to the *Grand conseil*. The true seat of royal justice, he claimed, was the parlement which had originated as 'a public assembly like a convention of estates'. Justice, he declared, was indivisible: just as there was only one sun, so there was only one king of France and one justice. If two were allowed to exist, division would arise between the nobles, communities and subjects. Yet Guillart disclaimed any desire to question the king's authority. 'We know well', he said, 'that you are above the laws and that laws and ordinances cannot constrain you and that no coactive authority binds you to them. But we wish to say that you do not or should not wish to do all that lies in your power, but only that which is good and equitable, which is nothing else than justice.'

That afternoon Francis and his council drew up an edict which subordinated the parlement to his authority. In particular, it was required to seek annual confirmation of its delegated authority. Moreover, by ordering the parlement to register the decree without imposing it by his presence, Francis manifested his authority more powerfully than if the court had been able to shelter under the customary formula implying duress.

The edict marked a turning-point in the parlement's relations with the crown. It continued to remonstrate from time to time till the end of the reign, but never again did it seriously encroach upon the king's authority.

The condemnation of Bourbon

Another loose knot needed to be tied: namely, the case of the Constable of Bourbon. Francis had promised in the Treaty of Madrid to reinstate him, but this proved to be another broken promise. No legal action, however, was taken against Bourbon until two months after his death. In July 1527 two indictments were presented to a special commission. The first repeated accusations which had been levelled in 1523 and subsequently disproved; the second focused on Bourbon's more recent 'crimes', including the invasion of Provence and the Sack of Rome. On 26 July his trial by the court of peers began in the king's presence. Although only five peers were present, the scene was given solemnity by the attendance of the whole parlement. An usher summoned Bourbon to appear at the bar of the court. When no one responded, the state prosecutor demanded that Bourbon's memory be condemned, his coat-of-arms effaced and his property seques-tered. After a purely formal debate, the court announced its verdict: Bourbon was declared guilty of felony, rebellion and *lèse-majesté*. He lost his coat of arms and title, his fiefs were formally annexed to the royal demesne and all his personal property was confiscated.

Bourbon's accomplices were treated more leniently. By March 1526 only three remained in prison. Saint-Vallier was released in July and recovered his property and titles the following year. The bishop of Autun was pardoned in 1527. The fate of the bishop of Le Puy is unknown.

The condemnation of Semblançay

Francis liked to blame others for his own mistakes. In particular, he blamed the *gens des finances* for his defeat at Pavia and its aftermath. They formed a wealthy oligarchy cemented by close matrimonial ties. While helping the state with one hand, they built up private fortunes with the other. The chief culprit in the king's eyes was Semblançay. His accounts had been examined by a commission in 1523, as we have seen, and he had been largely exoner-ated. The enquiry had found that, far from being indebted to the king, Semblançay was owed more than a million *livres* by Francis. That was enough to seal his fate. On 13 January he was thrown into the Bastille and his goods were seized. He was accused of various malpractices and tried by judges who were his personal enemies. Though Semblançay produced documentary evidence refuting the charges against him, he was found guilty on 9 August and sentenced to death. He wrote to the king, reminding him of his past services, but Francis was unmoved. On 11 August, Semblançay was taken through crowded streets to the gibbet at Montfaucon where he was made to wait six hours before being hanged. His age (he was about eighty at the time) and dignified bearing earned him popular sympathy. A chronicler wrote: 'He was much pitied and mourned by the people, who would have been pleased if the king had seen fit to spare him.'

9

War and Peace, 1527–38

An immediate consequence of the Sack of Rome was a rapprochement between France and England, for Henry VIII was afraid that the pope, who was now Charles V's prisoner, would not be able to grant him a divorce from Catherine of Aragon, the emperor's aunt. Peace remained the objective of Wolsey's foreign policy, but he also wanted to liberate the pope. It was primarily with this end in view that the cardinal met Francis at Amiens in August 1527. Their talks resulted in a treaty, signed on 18 August, under which the eleven-year-old Mary Tudor was promised to the duc d'Orléans, and Henry waived his objection to Francis marrying the emperor's sister. Both parties agreed not to attend a General Council as long as Clement VII remained a prisoner. The talks were rounded off with an exchange of honours: Francis conferred the Order of St Michael on Henry VIII and received from him the Order of the Garter.

Francis, in the meantime, decided to increase pressure on Charles V to release his sons by intervening militarily in Italy. In August an army led by Marshal Lautrec overran Lombardy, except Milan, while Andrea Doria, who had entered the service of France, seized Genoa. In the autumn Lautrec occupied Parma. Meanwhile Alfonso d'Este, duke of Ferrara, joined the league and his son Ercole was promised the hand of Princess Renée, Louis XII's daughter.

On 16 December, Francis held an Assembly of Notables in Paris, representing the nobility, the clergy, the parlements and the city of Paris. The purpose of the meeting was twofold: to legitimize the king's decision to break the Treaty of Madrid, and to raise enough money either to pay a ransom for his sons or to make war on the emperor, should he persist in demanding Burgundy as the price of their release. On 20 December the treaty was declared null and void, and each estate agreed to contribute to the ransom for the king's sons. The clergy's contribution was fixed at 1.3

million *livres* to be shared among the clergy at their provincial assemblies. The nobles of the Ile-de-France offered 10 per cent of the annual revenues of their fiefs and rear-fiefs. Elsewhere the nobles responded with varying degrees of enthusiasm. Paris was appalled when asked for 100,000 gold *écus* and secured a reduction to 150,000l. on condition this was kept secret from other towns, where the response to the king's demand was also unenthusiastic. The provincial estates, like the towns, had to contribute to the ransom. The heaviest burden, 400,000l., was imposed on Burgundy as the price of remaining part of France. Finally, various methods were used to raise money from royal office-holders. Savings were also made by cutting the wages of public servants; in certain instances they were stopped altogether.

Charles V, however, refused to release Francis's sons at any price as long as Lautrec's army was not recalled from Italy and its conquests restored. This condition being unacceptable to both France and England, they declared war on Charles on 22 January 1528. Yet even at this stage the enemies engaged in an archaic ritual. On 20 March, Francis accepted a challenge from the emperor to fight a duel on the Franco-Spanish border, but created so many difficulties that it was in Italy, not on the River Bidassoa, and not in person but with their armies, that the rulers fought each other. On 9 February, Lautrec invaded the kingdom of Naples and soon swept across it, conquering towns in the Abruzzi and also Apulia. At the end of April he threatened Naples from the landward side, while the city was blockaded at sea by Andrea Doria's nephew, Filippino. But in June, Andrea defected to the imperial side and persuaded Filippino to remove his fleet from the Bay of Naples. As the flow of supplies to Naples was restored, an outbreak of plague began to decimate the French camp. Lautrec was himself carried off by the epidemic on 27 August, and the remnants of his army capitulated soon afterwards. The French disaster was completed by the loss of Genoa and the entire Ligurian coast. An attempt by the comte de Saint-Pol to retake Genoa in June 1529 was defeated at Landriano.

The French collapse in Italy convinced Pope Clement VII, who had escaped to Orvieto in December 1528, that neutrality would gain him nothing. Only the emperor could provide the military support needed to restore the Medici to power in Florence; only he could halt the progress of Lutheranism in Germany and the westward advance of the Turks. On 29 June, therefore, Clement signed the Treaty of Barcelona with Charles. This provided for the restoration of Medici rule in Florence and the return of Ravenna, Cervia, Modena and Reggio to the pope. Clement promised to crown Charles emperor and to absolve all those responsible for the Sack of Rome. A marriage was arranged between the pope's nephew Alessandro and the emperor's illegitimate daughter Margaret. On 16 July, Clement revoked Henry VIII's divorce suit to Rome, thereby precipitating Wolsey's fall and England's breach with Rome.

The fight against heresy

In December 1527, Francis, possibly out of gratitude for the clergy's handsome offer of 1.3 million *livres* at the Assembly of Notables, promised to demonstrate that he was 'The Most Christian King'. He was soon given an opportunity to do so, when a statue of the Virgin and Child at a street corner in Paris was vandalized by persons unknown. The king expressed his revulsion by offering a large reward for information leading to the arrest of the culprits. He also commissioned a new statue and took part in a public procession to invoke God's forgiveness. Between 3 February and 9 October 1528 the Synod of Sens met in Paris under Duprat's chairmanship. After pronouncing their unanimous support for orthodoxy, the assembled prelates laid down stringent measures for the suppression of heresy.

Yet even now Francis protected certain scholars and preachers from persecution. In March 1528 the trial of Louis de Berquin, which had been suspended at the time of the king's return from Spain, was resumed, and on 15 April he was found guilty of heresy and sentenced to life imprisonment. Berquin should have been content with this sentence, but instead he decided to appeal to the parlement. Two days later, while the king was absent from the capital, the appeal was rejected and the sentence changed to one of death. We do not know if Francis would have saved Berquin's life for a third time, had he been given the chance. What is certain is that Berquin was hastily burned on the Place de Grève.

In May 1530 the king's sister Marguerite de Navarre asked the Grand Master to allow Lefèvre to leave Blois, where the climate did not suit his health. 'He has put the royal library in order,' she explained, 'classified the books, and drawn up an inventory which he will give to whomsoever the king pleases.' The permission was readily granted and Lefèvre moved to Nérac where he spent his last years peacefully under Marguerite's protection.

The *Grande Rebeyne*, April 1529

The reign of Francis I marked the end of the 'golden age' of cheap bread. After 1520 nominal wages began to lag behind grain prices and poor people began to go hungry. The most serious outbreak of popular disorder was the *Grande Rebeyne* of Lyon. In April 1529 posters appeared in the city calling on the people to rise against speculators who were blamed for the high price of bread. A mob, mainly of poor people, ransacked the Franciscan monastery and the homes of notables. The municipal granaries were broken into as well as that of the abbey of l'Ile Barbe. The municipal government

(*Consulat*) promised concessions, but a few weeks later it was busier hanging and whipping the leaders of the revolt than reducing the price of bread.

The *Grande Rebeyne* was more than a grain riot. It was also a protest against new taxes on imports of wine and grain, and it may have had a religious motivation, though this has been disputed. Lyon's population of artisans included many Germans, who doubtless brought news of Lutheran activities in their own country. Symphorien Champier, whose house was wrecked by the mob, believed that heretics were largely responsible. What is certain is that the riot coincided with a sharp decline in the living standard of the common people. It also expressed dissatisfaction with the self-interested fiscal policies of the wealthy oligarchy ruling the city.

The rioting generated a deep fear of the *menu peuple* among the ruling élite of Lyon, which found expression in its policies regarding the poor, notably the creation of the *Aumône générale*, a system of publicly funded poor relief, in 1531. It also contributed to the establishment in 1536 of the silk industry which was expected to offer opportunities of employment to humble folk, including women and children. Finally, it strengthened the alliance between the crown and the patriciate of Lyon. It marked 'a stage in the history of the eclipse of urban liberties in the face of the rise of royal authority'.

Lyon may have been an exceptionally volatile city, but other towns experienced social disturbances in the 1520s. Unrest at Meaux, for example, was not just religious: it also stemmed from worsening economic and political conditions. In 1521–2 and again in 1524–5, Brie and Ile-de-France had been hit by plague and famine. These afflictions, coupled with war and brigandage, drove many peasants to seek shelter within walled towns. At the same time, artisans in the cloth industry became unemployed. The crisis had ignited a revolt in October 1522 against the ruling oligarchy.

Royal concern with the increase of vagabondage was reflected in legislation. Several edicts forbade soldiers to take on vagrants as 'servants', while others ordered vagabonds to move only in small groups under threat of being cut to pieces. Such measures, however, were ineffective. In January 1536 the responsibility for arresting and punishing vagrants was transferred from the *baillis* to the *prévôts des maréchaux*, and in May 1537 anyone was authorized by the crown to kill vagabonds as rebels. Coercion, however, was only one method of coping with poverty. As from 1519, Francis I set about reforming hospitals and leper houses. The laicization of hospitals was also encouraged, but clerical opposition limited the effectiveness of such measures.

Sixteenth-century legislation insisted on each town and village caring for its own poor. The existing hospitals, however, were generally inadequate, so municipal authorities set up organizations specifically to bring relief to the poor in their own homes. Such schemes were funded by taxing the well-to-do (*aisés*). In Paris, poor relief was traditionally administered by the parlement, but in November 1544, Francis transferred this responsibility to the Bureau de la Ville. A *Bureau des pauvres* was established with powers to collect a poor tax and receive donations. The impotent poor were allowed to share in public handouts and to receive medical treatment at home. At the same time sergeants were used to look for sturdy beggars and to assign them to public works.

The *Aumône générale*, founded in Lyon after a famine in 1531, was at first a temporary measure, but in 1534 it became permanent. It comprised eight commissioners and a treasurer with wide discretionary powers. Unlike medieval hospitals, the *Aumône* had no endowment: it drew its funds from police fines, legacies, collections in churches and inns, and especially a tax on a wide spectrum of Lyonnais society. Two major aspects of the *Aumône*'s work were the care of orphans and foundlings and bread handouts to the public.

The Ladies' Peace, 3 August 1529

By December 1528 both Francis and Charles V were anxious to end their conflict, but, instead of negotiating directly, they entrusted the task to Louise of Savoy and Margaret of Austria, who was not only the emperor's aunt but also Louise's sister-in-law. Their talks, which opened at Cambrai on 5 July, proved far more gruelling than had been anticipated and culminated in a treaty, signed on 3 August, which has come to be known as 'the Ladies' Peace'. In all essentials it was a revision of the Treaty of Madrid. In place of Burgundy, the emperor accepted a ransom of two million gold *écus*. Francis gave up all his Italian claims, the towns of Hesdin, Arras, Lille and Tournai, and his suzerainty over Flanders and Artois. He agreed to lend Charles twelve galleys for six months and guaranteed the rights of Bourbon's heirs. The emperor, for his part, promised to send his sister Eleanor to France and to return Francis's sons.

Early in November, Charles V and Clement VII met in Bologna, where they spent four months negotiating against a backcloth of civic revelry. The emperor was afraid that Francis would break the peace once he had recovered his sons and to avert this danger a league of Italian states was formed on 23 December. Venice agreed to restore Ravenna and Cervia to the pope, while Francesco Sforza was restored to power in Milan. The duke of Ferrara was to be admitted in due course. Only Florence was excluded from the league, because it refused to restore the Medici. Charles placed his army at the pope's disposal and, after a siege that lasted eight months, Florence surrendered. Eighteen months later Clement's nephew Alessandro became its hereditary duke. Meanwhile, Charles achieved his greatest ambition: on

24 February 1530, his birthday and the anniversary of his victory at Pavia, he was crowned Holy Roman Emperor in Bologna.

Meanwhile, Francis ratified the peace and appointed Montmorency and Tournon to collect his sons' ransom. They arrived in Bayonne on 22 March 1530 and collaborated for the next three months, assisted by a large team of financial experts. The ransom was to be paid in three ways: a single lump sum of 1.2 million *écus*; a reimbursement of Charles V's debts to Henry VIII, estimated at 290,000 *écus*; and an annuity of 25,500 *écus* to be raised from the lands of the duchesse de Vendôme in the Netherlands. Francis managed to get some alleviation of the debt to Henry VIII in return for help in getting the English king's divorce. Even so, he had great difficulty raising the sum demanded by Charles. The task was hampered by corruption and inefficiency within the French fiscal administration; also by much quibbling on the part of the imperial commissioners charged with receiving the ransom. Because of all the complications, the date for the return of the princely hostages had to be postponed several times. But on 10 June, Don Alvares de Lugo acknowledged receipt of the ransom, and on 1 July it was exchanged for the Dauphin and his brother, and also for Eleanor of Portugal. On 3 July, Francis met his new queen at Roquefort-de-Marsan, and they were formally married on 7 July in a chapel adjoining the monastery of Beyries. Thus was the Ladies' Peace sealed: Francis was now the brother-in-law of his great enemy and chief rival.

The successful talks at Bayonne greatly enhanced Montmorency's prestige at court. Already a very rich man, he became even richer when his father, Guillaume, died in May 1531. Anne acquired two-thirds of the paternal inheritance, the rest going to his brother François. Early in 1531 he supervised arrangements for Eleanor's coronation at Saint-Denis on 5 March, which was soon followed by her entry into Paris. But Francis seemed far more interested in his mistress, Anne de Pisseleu, the future duchesse d'Etampes. People were shocked to see him flirting with her at an open window during the queen's entry. Two years later the king's sister told the duke of Norfolk that Francis could not bear to share his wife's bed. 'When he lieth from her', she said, 'no man sleepeth better.' Eleanor's relations with her mother-in-law Louise of Savoy were also none too happy, but she did not have to put up with her for long. On 22 September 1531, Louise died at Grez-sur-Loing. Her inheritance was large: the moveables alone were valued at 150,000 *écus*, and the lands now became part of the royal demesne.

The annexation of Brittany, August 1532

Ever since 1515 the duchy of Brittany had been administered by the king of France in the right of his first wife, Claude. Then, in 1524, shortly before her death, Claude bequeathed the duchy to her eldest son François, but, as he was a minor, the king continued to administer it. When François came of age in 1532 it became necessary to regularize the duchy's status. As a first step, Chancellor Duprat invited some influential Bretons to Paris. They included Louis des Désers, president of the *Grands Jours* or sovereign court of Rennes (soon to become a parlement), who advised that the demand for permanent union with France should emanate from the Breton estates themselves and that a few well-placed bribes would achieve this. His advice was followed, and in August 1532 Francis took up residence at a castle near Vannes, where the estates met to debate the proposed union with France.

Ardent patriots among the deputies argued that union with France would drag Brittany into foreign wars and subject it to heavy taxation; their opponents pointed to the hardships that had befallen the duchy when independent. But even the partisans of union wanted certain guarantees. On 4 August the estates made four demands: the Dauphin was to be sent to Rennes as duke and owner of the duchy; its administration and usufruct were to be reserved to the king; its rights and privileges were to be respected after the union; and the Dauphin was to take an oath to this effect. Francis agreed to all four demands and issued an edict annexing Brittany irrevocably to France. On 12 August the Dauphin made his entry into Rennes; two days later he was crowned as Duke François III. He was to be the last holder of the ducal title – at his death in 1536, Brittany became an ordinary French province. By completing the process begun by Charles VIII in 1491, Francis I made a notable contribution to France's territorial unification. A small, independent yet vassal state, which in the past had often called in the foreigner to defend its independence, was no more. From Calais to the Pyrenees, the Atlantic seaboard now belonged to France.

German Protestants and Turks

Even after the Ladies' Peace, Francis still wanted to recover the duchy of Milan. The treaty merely provided him with a breathing space in which to replenish his coffers, rebuild his armed forces and consolidate his alliances. Between 1530 and 1534 he stirred up more trouble for Charles V in Germany and the Mediterranean without, however, openly violating the peace. At the same time he built up an anti-Habsburg coalition. But his

task was made difficult by the Protestant Reformation, which divided the
Holy Roman Empire into two rival religious camps, and also by Henry
VIII's divorce, which was condemned by the pope. These impediments to
a unified opposition to the emperor obliged Francis to take on the role of
religious peacemaker.

The election of Charles V's brother Ferdinand as King of the Romans
in January 1531 alienated many German princes from the emperor. No
constitutional warrant existed for such a choice during the emperor's lifetime, and the Protestant princes were naturally alarmed by the election of
a Catholic dedicated to the defence of his faith. On 16 February they
appealed to the king of France for help, and eleven days later six princes
and ten cities formed the Schmalkaldic League to defend their interests.
Although Francis had promised at Cambrai not to meddle in German affairs,
he was unable to resist the appeal from the German princes. But the situation
in Germany was far from clear-cut. As a first step, Francis's agent, Gervase
Wain, mediated between the Catholic dukes of Bavaria and the Schmalkaldic
League. On 26 October they formed an alliance at Saalfeld, which was the
foundation-stone of Francis's future policy beyond the Rhine. After refusing
to join the alliance, he changed his mind and backed a plan for the
reconquest of Württemberg, which the Habsburgs had seized in 1519. He
signed an alliance with Saxony, Hesse and Bavaria at Scheyern on 26 May
1532 and promised to contribute 100,000 écus towards the forthcoming
war. Before this could be declared, however, the Turks invaded central
Europe.

Francis had been intriguing with the Turks for some time. The disputed
succession to the Hungarian throne which had followed the death of Louis
II at Mohácz enabled him to undermine Habsburg interests in central
Europe. In February 1527 a Spanish renegade called Antonio Rincon had
offered French aid to John Zápolyai, Voivode of Transylvania, who had
been elected king in opposition to Ferdinand of Habsburg. By the end of
1527, Zápolyai had been defeated, but he had not given up the struggle.
In 1529 the Turkish sultan confirmed Zápolyai as king, as he overran
Hungary on his way to besiege Vienna. In July 1530, Rincon went to
Constantinople, allegedly to persuade the sultan to attack Charles V in
Italy. As Thomas Cromwell remarked, no Christian scruple would deter
Francis from bringing the Turk and the devil into the heart of Christendom
if they could help him regain Milan.

A Turkish attack on central Europe always had the effect of uniting
German opinion in support of the Habsburgs. From the French standpoint
a Turkish attack on Italy was preferable. Thus in March 1532, Francis sent
Rincon to the sultan, who was preparing a new offensive in the west, to
persuade him to attack Italy, not Hungary, but the envoy arrived too late.
The Turks, after sweeping through the Balkans, pushed towards the Danube

valley, but they retreated after being held up at Güns for three weeks. On
23 September, Charles V entered Vienna in triumph.

Henry VIII's 'Great Matter'

Henry VIII, meanwhile, tried to put pressure on Pope Clement VII to concede his divorce by consulting the theologians of various universities, including Paris. The task of canvassing support for Henry among the Paris
theologians fell to Guillaume du Bellay, seigneur de Langey, who was probably less interested in the theological aspects of the case than in the political
advantages to be gained for Francis: a decision favourable to Henry was
likely to drive a wedge between him and Charles V. The debates among
the theologians proved stormy, but in the end a majority supported the
divorce. Satisfactory as it was for Francis in his dealings with England, the
decision did not solve the problem posed by the widening rift between
England and the Holy See, for the king of France wanted both to be his
friends. In April 1531, Cardinal Gramont was sent to Rome to help solve
the problem of Henry's divorce and to propose a marriage between Francis's
second son, Henri duc d'Orléans, and the pope's niece, Catherine de'
Medici.

In October 1532, Francis and Henry met for the second time. Their
meeting, which was divided between Calais and Boulogne, lasted only a
week and was far less elaborate and costly than the Field of Cloth of Gold.
Ostensibly it was directed against the Turks, but in reality it was intended
to co-ordinate the kings' policies in Germany and in Rome. While Francis
wanted Henry to share the burden of subsidizing the League of Scheyern,
Henry, who had recently got rid of Wolsey, looked to French cardinals to
advance his cause at the Curia. Following the arrival of cardinals Gramont
and Tournon in Bologna in January 1533, the pope agreed to meet Francis
and accepted his proposal for a marriage alliance. Clement also issued the
bulls Cranmer needed to become archbishop of Canterbury, but Francis's
efforts to forward the royal divorce were frustrated by Henry's impatience.
He married Anne Boleyn in secret around 25 January and only informed
Francis in March. The marriage was made public in May, but it was already
common knowledge because Anne's pregnancy could not be concealed.
Henry wanted his marriage to be legalized by the pope before the birth of
Anne's child, but Francis refused to put pressure on Clement which might
simply drive him into the emperor's arms. He was certainly not prepared
to put at risk the marriage between his son and the pope's niece. Henry's
fate depended to some extent on the forthcoming meeting between Francis
and Clement, but this had to be postponed for various reasons. On 23
May, Cranmer, usurping the pope's jurisdiction, declared Henry's remar-

riage lawful and, on 1 June, crowned Anne Boleyn. The pope's reponse
was to condemn the union and to order Henry to take back Catherine of
Aragon before September or face excommunication.

On 1 September, Catherine de' Medici sailed from La Spezia to Villefranche, where she was joined a few weeks later by her uncle the pope. On 11
October the papal fleet reached Marseille and next day Clement entered the
town escorted by fourteen cardinals. Francis prostrated himself at his feet on
the 13th, and on the 28th, Henri duc d'Orléans and Catherine, aged fifteen
and twelve respectively, were married amidst great pomp. The Franco-papal
alliance, however, was not formalized in a treaty. The pope created four
French cardinals and allowed Francis to levy another clerical tenth.

No one knows for certain what the king and the pope decided at
Marseille, but they certainly discussed three topics: the spread of heresy in
France, the calling of a General Council and Henry VIII's divorce. Francis
allegedly promised to eradicate heresy from his kingdom, and on 10 November, Clement issued a bull against the French Lutherans. Regarding the
General Council, Francis said that it could serve no useful purpose as long
as he remained on bad terms with the emperor, and Clement was very
happy to be offered an excuse to postpone it indefinitely. As for Henry's
divorce, Francis asked Clement to wait six months before excommunicating
Henry, but the pope would only concede one month's delay. On 23 March
1534 he fulminated his anathema, whereupon Henry completed his breach
with Rome.

The Affair of the Placards, October 1534

On 25 August 1530, writing to Luther, Bucer reported that the Gospel was
making good progress in France. The king, he explained, 'is not opposed
to the truth, and now that he has received back his children, he will cease
to be so dependent on the pope and the emperor.' In a certain region of
Normandy, Bucer explained, 'so many have now professed the Gospel that
the enemy has begun to call it "little Germany".' In Lent 1531, Gérard
Roussel, Marguerite de Navarre's almoner, was accused by the Paris Faculty
of Theology of preaching heresy in her presence at the Louvre. The king
ordered him in future to give advance notice of whatever he intended to
say in his sermons, which pacified the faculty for the time being, but in 1533
the accusation was repeated. A committee of theologians was appointed on
9 May to draw up a list of heretical articles preached by Roussel for submission to the king. But Francis was angry with the theologians after they
had publicly accused his brother-in-law, the king of Navarre, of heresy. On
13 May he banished Noël Béda, the faculty's syndic, from the capital,
prompting several days of demonstrations for and against Béda.

Much of the university's resentment was focused on the king's sister. In October 1533, during Francis's absence from the capital, students of the collège de Navarre put on a satirical play in which Marguerite was shown preaching heresy at the instigation of a Fury, called *Mégère*, and tormenting anyone who would not listen. The play came to the notice of the royal authorities and the college was searched. The playwright was not discovered, but two senior members of the college were arrested.

Later that month Marguerite again came under fire when her poem *The Mirror of a Sinful Soul*, which she had published anonymously, was banned by the university. Francis demanded an explanation, whereupon the newly elected rector, Nicolas Cop, called a meeting of all the faculties. The theologian who had blacklisted the poem explained that he had intended no offence against Marguerite; her poem had been published without his faculty's *imprimatur* which was essential for all religious works. On 8 October fifty-eight theologians signed a statement to the effect that they had never read the poem and had, therefore, neither condemned nor approved it. This settled the matter.

On 1 November 1533, Nicolas Cop preached a sermon in the church of the Mathurins to an academic congregation. It opened on an Erasmian note of appreciation for 'the philosophy divinely given to man by Christ to show forth the true and surest felicity'. Cop urged his audience to pray that Christ should flow into their souls and shower them with 'the dew of spiritual grace' and went on to compare the Gospel and the Law in a manner characteristic of evangelical humanism. He also attacked salvation by good works.

Though not especially radical, Cop's sermon offended some members of his audience who complained to the parlement. Meanwhile he called a meeting of the entire university. Claiming to have been misrepresented, he demanded that his critics be called to account. But failing to get support, he suddenly vanished, taking with him the university's seal. Three months later he turned up in Basle. Another fugitive was Cop's friend John Calvin, who may have had a hand in his sermon. He retired to the home of Louis du Tillet, a canon of Angoulême, where he may have begun writing his *Institutes*.

At the end of November the parlement made a number of arrests. It warned the king of the growth of heresy in the capital. 'We are angry and displeased', he replied, 'to learn that ... this damned heretical Lutheran sect is flourishing in our good town of Paris.' He ordered the publication of two papal bulls against heresy and the appointment of two *parlementaires* to judge heresy suspects. This measure was resisted by the bishop's vicar-general, René du Bellay, who argued that the threat of heresy in the capital had been much exaggerated.

For nearly two decades the Reformation in France offered no clear-cut confessions of faith; its followers felt at liberty to switch doctrines in their search for the truth. Some abandoned Luther's doctrine in favour of Zwingli's which was more radical, notably in its interpretation of the Eucharist. Both reformers rejected the Catholic doctrine of transubstantiation, but Luther continued to believe in the Real Presence whereas Zwingli rejected it. All religious dissenters, however, continued to be branded as 'Lutherans' by the French authorities regardless of their differences.

In 1534 an event occurred which pointed to the radicalism of certain French reformers. On 18 October, Parisians on their way to Sunday mass were startled to find that Protestant placards or broadsheets had been put up overnight in various public places. Each consisted of a single sheet of paper printed in Gothic type and entitled: *True articles on the horrible, great and insufferable abuses of the papal mass*. The mass was attacked on four grounds: first, there has only been one sacrifice, that of Christ on the Cross, which, being perfect, cannot be repeated; secondly, the mass implies the Real Presence of Christ in the host, yet Scripture tells us that He is with God the Father till the Day of Judgement; thirdly, transubstantiation is a human invention contrary to Scripture; lastly, communion is a memorial service, not a miracle. The placard, in short, stated the Zwinglian or Sacramentarian position on the mass, not the Lutheran one. The author was Antoine Marcourt, a Frenchman exiled in Switzerland, who had become pastor of Neuchâtel. Copies of the placard, which had been printed in Switzerland, had been smuggled into France by Guillaume Feret, a servant of the king's apothecary.

The discovery of the placards caused hysteria to sweep through Paris as rumours circulated of an impending massacre of Catholics. Fear was heightened by reports that similar placards had been found in various provincial towns and even on the door of the king's bedchamber at the château of Amboise. Within twenty-four hours the parlement ordered a general procession and began a search for culprits. On 10 November the first sentences were passed and three days later a shoemaker's son was burned at the stake. He was soon followed to the pyre by Jean du Bourg, a rich draper. By the end of the month a printer, a weaver, a bookseller and a stonemason had become Protestant martyrs.

Francis, meanwhile, returned to Paris from Amboise. On 9 December he wrote to the chancellor, signifying his approval of the police measures so far taken. On 21 December he set up a commission to try suspects, thereby earning a vote of thanks by the Faculty of Theology. However on 13 January, soon after the king's return to the capital, the dissenters struck again. Copies of Marcourt's *Small treatise* – an elaboration of the placards' doctrine – were found in the streets of Paris. Francis responded by banning all printing till further notice and ordering a procession on 21 January. Such processions, as Benedict has shown, 'served as a rite of purification for a city soiled by heresy, thereby conveying very clearly to the onlooking crowds the message that the Protestants formed a force within society whose polluting actions required community atonement'.

The procession on 21 January was one of the most spectacular ever seen in the French capital, with the king's court, the sovereign courts, university, religious orders, municipal government and trade guilds all taking part. A notable feature was the large number of shrines and relics brought out from churches. The most precious were from the Sainte-Chapelle and included the Crown of Thorns. At the centre of the procession was the Blessed Sacrament, which the bishop of Paris carried reverently beneath a canopy borne by the king's three sons and the duc de Vendôme. Immediately behind it walked Francis, bareheaded and dressed in black, holding a lighted candle. After mass at Notre-Dame, he and the queen were given lunch at the bishop's palace. Then, in front of a large and distinguished crowd, Francis urged all his subjects to denounce heretics, even if they were kinsmen or friends. The day ended with six more burnings. On 24 January, 73 so-called Lutherans, who had gone into hiding, were ordered to give themselves up, among them the poet Clément Marot. Five days later harbourers of heretics were made liable to the same penalties as the heretics themselves.

The king's anger over the discovery of the placard on his bedchamber door at Amboise has traditionally been blamed for the savagery of the persecution that ensued. But it was in Paris, not in Amboise, that the extreme response was unleashed. Furthermore, it happened immediately, before the king could have made known his wishes: even a fast messenger would have taken a day or two to reach the capital from Amboise. Nor do the original orders carry the king's signature. All the available evidence suggests that it was the parlement, not Francis, which initiated the persecution: he merely endorsed it after it had got under way. The real reason for the measures was almost certainly the doctrinal content of the placard – the violent attack on the mass and on priests – rather than the alleged offence to the royal person. Unlike Cop's sermon in 1533, which had been addressed to an academic audience, the placard was directed at the general public. Even by sixteenth-century standards its invective was exceptionally abusive and likely to provoke public disturbances.

The 'Affair of the Placards' revealed the existence in France of a group of Protestant radicals whose views were far more extreme than any which had yet been publicly expressed. It did not mark the end of Lucien Febvre's 'long period of magnificent religious anarchy', when, in the absence of clear confessions of faith, the boundary between orthodoxy and heresy was easily crossed, but it brought it into sharper focus. Frenchmen who previously had crossed it with a certain insouciance now became more circumspect. The coming of sacramentarianism to France helped to polarize religious opinion, yet French Protestantism continued to be 'largely formless' until the late 1550s. The term 'Lutheran' continued to be applied indiscriminately to all sorts of dissenters.

The persecution seriously damaged Francis's reputation in Germany. Imperial agents pointed to the shameful contrast between his harsh treatment of French Protestants and his friendly reception of Turkish envoys. The king defended himself in a manifesto addressed to the imperial estates (1 February 1535). The persecution, he explained, was political, not religious; its aim was the suppression of sedition. But imperial propaganda needed to be countered by deeds as well as words, which doubtless explains the promulgation of the Edict of Coucy (16 July 1535) ordering the release of all religious prisoners and allowing religious exiles to come home, both categories being offered a pardon. But the edict did not offer toleration, for sacramentarians were specifically excluded from the amnesty. Dissenters who failed to abjure within six months were to be hanged.

Francis and the German Protestants

The Edict of Coucy coincided with a resumption of talks between Francis and the German Protestants. On 16 July he invited Philip Melanchthon to take part in a debate with doctors of the Paris faculty. But they were unco-operative: 'One must not listen to heretics', they said, 'or have any dealings with them.' When Langey submitted to the faculty twelve articles which he had received from Melanchthon, Bucer and Hedio in response to questions he had put to them in 1534, the doctors were unimpressed. If the Lutherans wanted a settlement, they said, they had only to submit to the church's teaching. In Germany, too, Francis's hopes of achieving a religious compromise were dashed. Johannes Sturm, the Strassburg reformer, urged Melanchthon to accept Francis's invitation, but he was forbidden to go by his overlord, the Saxon Elector.

Yet Francis persisted in his efforts. With Bucer's encouragement he sent Langey to the diet of the Schmalkaldic League. He urged the deputies to send representatives to France, before accepting the pope's invitation to a General Council in Mantua. Langey even led the German reformers to believe that Francis shared most of their doctrinal opinions. Only their attitude to Purgatory and good works, he said, was likely to cause difficulty, but he did not think it would be insuperable. The deputies, however, were not persuaded. They turned down the pope's invitation and evaded the debate in France. Nor would they admit Francis to the Schmalkaldic League: they merely promised not to assist his enemies in any dispute that did not involve the emperor.

The growth of persecution

Despite its limitations, the Edict of Coucy encouraged reformers to hope that Francis was still open to persuasion. This hope was eloquently expressed by John Calvin in the preface to his *Institutes* (Basle, 1536), which he addressed to the king. The evangelicals, he explained, had been falsely accused of sedition. It was the king's duty to listen to what they had to say in self-defence. They were the true heirs of the primitive church. 'Although your heart is at present alienated from, even inflamed against, us,' Calvin wrote, 'I trust that we may regain its favour, if you will only read our confession once without indignation or wrath.' Reformers were encouraged on 31 May 1536, when Francis extended the Coucy amnesty to all heretics, including sacramentarians, provided they abjured within six months. Francis's deeds, however, did not always match his words. He promised to set free religious dissidents, yet in November two were martyred at Nîmes. Religious persecution was sustained in spite of the edicts of 1535 and 1536.

On 1 June 1540 the Edict of Fontainebleau gave the parlements overall control of heresy jurisdiction. The preamble explained the need to eradicate 'evil errors' which, after being purged, were reappearing in the kingdom. They were being spread partly by religious exiles who had come home, partly by heretics who had lain low during the repression. Royal judges were empowered to enquire into the activities of all persons, lay and ecclesiastical, except clergy in major orders. Suspects were to be tried by the sovereign courts regardless of any privilege or franchise. The church courts were to deal with clergy in major orders with the assistance of the secular arm. Finally, all subjects were ordered, on pain of *lèse-majesté*, to denounce heretics 'just as each is bound to run in order to put out a public fire'.

The provincial legions, July 1534

A difficult problem facing the king of France was how to raise a large force of infantry that was effective and reliable yet cheap. The Swiss were efficient, but not always reliable (witness their conduct at La Bicocca) and certainly not cheap. Francis could not do without them altogether, but he tried to lessen his dependence by establishing seven legions of infantry within his kingdom. Under an ordinance of 24 July 1534, Normandy, Brittany, Picardy, Languedoc and Guyenne were to raise one legion each. The sixth was to be provided by Burgundy, Champagne and Nivernais, and the seventh by Dauphiné, Provence, the Lyonnais and Auvergne. Everyone serving in a legion was supposed to be a native of the province that raised it. Recruitment was probably by voluntary enlistment, in return for which noblemen were promised exemption from the *ban et arrière-ban* and commoners exemption from the *taille*.

Each legion was divided into six *bandes* of a thousand men under a captain, who was to be a nobleman chosen by the king. One of the six captains was also the colonel commanding the whole legion. Each captain was to be paid 50 *livres* per month in peacetime and 100 in wartime; the rank and file were to be paid only in wartime. Legionaries were armed with pikes, halberds and arquebuses, the distribution of weapons varying with each legion. The defensive armour consisted of a gorget of mail and a light helmet. Musters were to be held twice a year and were intended partly as training exercises. The ordinance of 1534 laid down a strict code of discipline: a legionary below the rank of officer was to have his tongue pierced if he shouted; one who stole from a church was to be hanged; one who blasphemed was to wear a heavy iron collar for six hours. Punishments were balanced by rewards. A gold ring was to be awarded for outstanding valour, and a legionary who achieved this distinction was to be allowed to rise through the ranks. On becoming a lieutenant, he was to be ennobled.

The ordinance was swiftly given effect. Francis inspected the Normandy, Picardy and Champagne legions between April and August 1535. Other legions were, in the meantime, raised in the south, but the Breton legion was never formed. In spite of all the publicity they received, the legions proved a disappointment. Their discipline left much to be desired, and they showed up badly in action. They were soon relegated to the secondary role of guarding fortresses and border towns.

The invasion of Savoy, November 1536

Western Europe stood on the brink of war in the spring of 1535. While Francis was inspecting his legions, his diplomats were active throughout Europe. In February 1535, Jean de la Forêt was sent to Constantinople to win the sultan's help in a future war with the emperor. Stopping in North Africa on the way, he offered the Barbary corsair Khair-ad-Din Barbarossa fifty ships as well as victuals and munitions in return for help against Genoa. In Constantinople he may have signed a treaty, called the *Capitulations* (February 1536), but its existence has been called into question. Meanwhile, Jean du Bellay was sent to Italy mainly to win over the new pope, Paul III, and to dissuade him from calling a General Council. In Germany, Francis tried to salvage something from Langey's negotiations with the Protestants in 1534.

In June 1535, Charles V led an expedition against the Moors of North Africa. He captured Tunis, and Barbarossa fled to Algiers with part of his fleet. On 22 August the emperor landed in Sicily and began a triumphal progress that was to take him up the entire length of the Italian peninsula.

Francis, in the meantime, did nothing. This angered the war party at his court led by Admiral Chabot, but Montmorency had given his word to the imperial ambassador that his master would not attack the emperor while he was fighting the Infidel. A more important reason for Francis's inertia may have been his unpreparedness. By the time his legions were mobilized, the fighting season was almost over.

On 1 November, Francesco Sforza, duke of Milan, died without leaving a male heir. Francis, who had given up his claim to the duchy in the Ladies' Peace, immediately proposed that Milan should be given to his second son, Henri duc d'Orléans. This, however, was unacceptable to the emperor, who was suzerain of Milan. Henri was too close to the French throne and also had a claim to the duchy of Urbino through his wife, Catherine de' Medici; if he acquired Milan, he would need only Naples to become master of Italy. But Charles did not rule out the possibility of conferring Milan on Francis's third son, Charles duc d'Angoulême.

Matters stood thus in February 1536, when Francis suddenly invaded the duchy of Savoy, ruled by his uncle Charles III. The duke was too weak to resist: on 24 February he lost Bourg-en-Bresse and, five days later, Chambéry. The conquest of Savoy was completed in March when Chabot seized the capital, Turin. Francis claimed that he had acted in self-defence. He only wanted territories that he had inherited from his mother, Louise of Savoy, but this was merely an excuse: his purpose was to acquire either a bargaining counter for use in his talks with the emperor on Milan's future or a springboard from which to invade that duchy should the talks fail. However, Charles III was also the emperor's brother-in-law and ally. By conquering Savoy, Francis gave serious offence to Charles V, who denounced his aggression in a speech on 17 April to the pope and college of cardinals. He offered Francis the choice of either accepting Milan unconditionally for his youngest son or meeting him, the emperor, in single combat. If he chose the second option, the prize would be Burgundy on the one side and Milan on the other. Francis gave his reply on 11 May. Denying that he had broken the peace, he offered to submit his claim to the duchy to papal arbitration and accepted the emperor's challenge to a duel.

In north Italy, meanwhile, an undeclared state of war existed between France and the Empire. In April, Chabot was replaced as the French lieutenant-general in Piedmont by Francesco marquis of Saluzzo. In May the imperial commander de Leyva invaded Piedmont, and soon afterwards Saluzzo turned traitor. This event nearly caused the collapse of the French cause in Piedmont, but the garrison in Fossano held out for a month, thereby enabling Francis to prepare the defence of south-east France against a possible imperial invasion. On 11 June he dismissed the imperial ambassador. The pope, meanwhile, attempted to mediate, but Charles was determined to teach Francis a lesson.

The emperor invaded Provence on 24 July. Montmorency, the French lieutenant-general in southern France, could either engage the enemy or wait for him in fortified positions. He ordered the evacuation of Aix-en-Provence as part of a strategy of creating a vacuum in front of the enemy. Lower Provence was systematically laid waste: mills were destroyed, wells blocked, stocks of wood and fuel destroyed, wine barrels smashed open, salt ruined and farm animals let loose. Only fruit trees and vines were spared in the hope of encouraging dysentery among the enemy. At the same time, Montmorency took steps to prevent a link-up between the invading army and another which might enter France from Spain. Thus towns along the Rhône were fortified. The hub of the French defensive system was Montmorency's camp outside Avignon. 'No camp', he declared, 'was ever seen in our time which was stronger, more beautiful, more disease-free or well supplied with victuals.' The king, meanwhile, set up his headquarters at Valence, which became a major assembly point for troops, artillery and supplies bound for Avignon.

While Charles V overran Provence, Henry of Nassau invaded the north and on 12 August laid siege to Péronne. The defence of northern France was entrusted to Charles duc de Vendôme, governor of Picardy, Claude duc de Guise, governor of Champagne, and Cardinal Jean du Bellay, governor of Paris and Ile-de-France. Their task was made difficult by the absence in the south of the *gendarmerie*, and by a shortage of funds. Even so, Nassau was eventually forced to lift the siege of Péronne and retire to Flanders. Meanwhile, Charles V ran into serious difficulties. Having captured Aix, he had to decide where to go next. It would have been risky to push northwards without first taking Marseille. He decided for the present to stay put, but his troops began to succumb to sickness and hunger. On 7 September, Antonio de Leyva, Charles's chief lieutenant, died.

In the meantime, on 10 August the Dauphin François died at Tournus, almost certainly of natural causes. However, poison was suspected and Sebastian de Montecuculli, one of the Dauphin's servants, was accused of murder. After admitting the charge under torture, he retracted, but was none the less executed with great cruelty in Lyon on 7 October. The French government tried to politicize the Dauphin's death by accusing the emperor and Ferrante Gonzaga, the imperial governor of Milan, of having instigated his murder. The papal legate, Cardinal Trivulzio, pointed out that the Dauphin's death had removed the main obstacle to a peaceful resolution of the Milanese succession: Henri duc d'Orléans was now too near the French throne to be acceptable as duke, while the emperor had already expressed a willingness to accept Henri's younger brother, the duc d'Angoulême.

On 11 September, Charles V began to retreat towards Italy along the coast of Provence, but Francis resisted the temptation to set off in pursuit. He toured Provence instead and saw for himself the terrible effects of the recent campaign on the lives of the inhabitants. In mid-October he returned to Paris and on the way met James V of Scotland to whom he gave the hand of his daughter Madeleine. The marriage was celebrated in Paris on 1 January 1537. Then, at a *lit de justice* on 15 January, Francis proclaimed the annexation to France of Flanders, Artois and Charolais. His aim was to consolidate the northern frontier of his kingdom by annexing Thérouanne. Early in March he and Montmorency overran the county of Saint-Pol. But Francis soon called off the campaign in order to assist his army in Piedmont. This prompted the emperor to launch a counteroffensive in northern France. After capturing Saint-Pol and Montreuil, he laid siege to Thérouanne. Montmorency was immediately sent back to Artois and most of the troops intended for Piedmont were recalled. However, the northern campaign came to an abrupt halt when the regent of the Netherlands called a truce. This was signed at Bomy on 30 July and the siege of Thérouanne was lifted. The truce enabled Francis to assist his army in Piedmont. On 8 October, Montmorency crossed the Alps and relieved the garrisons at Savigliano, Pinerolo and Turin. Within a few days the French had occupied the whole of Piedmont.

Financial matters

Royal expenditure continued to rise during the 1530s. War, as usual, was the most expensive item: in 1536–8 it may have cost Francis some 15 million *livres*. Following the defection of Andrea Doria, he had to spend more than before on his navy. He also incurred heavy diplomatic costs. The Boulogne interview with Henry VIII cost 86,469l. Alliances, too, drained royal resources: more than 4 million *livres* were paid to the Swiss between 1516 and 1546, not counting secret bribes. Sums paid to Henry VIII in the course of Francis's reign totalled 1,784,643 *écus*. The king also had to subsidize his allies in Italy and Germany. In 1534 he supported his friends beyond the Rhine to the tune of 100,000 *écus* by purchasing the county of Montbéliard from the duke of Württemberg and selling it back to him at a heavy loss. The largest single disbursement Francis made in the 1530s was the ransom of two million gold *écus* imposed on him by the Ladies' Peace.

To meet these and other obligations Francis made more demands on his subjects. Direct taxation failed to keep pace with inflation, and the yield continued to suffer from corrupt practices. To compensate for inadequate tax yields, Francis resorted to expedients. Between 1535 and 1537 he obtained 3,173,000 *livres* by way of clerical tenths. Towns too were heavily mulcted. In 1533 and 1535 he seized municipal revenues and in 1537 imposed many forced loans. In 1538 the infantry tax (*solde des 20,000 hommes de pied*) of 1520–21 was revived and imposed on 227 towns. In the 1530s Francis was again able to borrow from Italian bankers, whose confidence had been shaken by the disastrous 1520s, but he had to accept high rates of interest. By 1536 his finances were in better shape: Francis had even paid off some old debts. He could also count on the services of Cardinal Tournon, who won the trust of the Lyon bankers by repaying loans punctually.

On 7 February 1532, Francis regulated the Epargne. The coffers in which the *Trésorier de l'Epargne* kept his cash were no longer to follow the court but to remain at the Louvre in Paris and all the king's revenues, except the *parties casuelles*, were to be paid into them. Various regulations were also laid down for the coffers' safekeeping. However, the 1532 ordinance was not strictly applied. Important sums in the hands of the *receveurs-généraux* never reached the Louvre. They were used by the *Trésorier de l'Epargne* to pay the king's day-by-day expenses wherever he might be.

During the 1530s the *Commission de la Tour Carrée*, which had been set up in November 1527, continued to harass financiers and fiscal officials. Gaillard Spifame, for instance, was thrown into prison on a charge of 'having cheated the king of more than three or four hundred thousand francs when he had been in charge of the *extraordinaire des guerres* ... thereby causing the loss of the war and of the battle in which the king had been captured because the men at arms had not been paid'. Altogether about 40 out of 118 senior fiscal officials were prosecuted by the *Tour Carrée* and other tribunals and at least eighteen were condemned over a period of ten years. Only one, Jean Poncher, was executed. The last known victim, Jean Ruzé, was sentenced on 12 April 1536.

Francis and his ministers doubtless hoped for huge financial gains from these trials. A large amount of property was confiscated, but it has to be set against the substantial legal costs incurred by the crown and also the cost of administering the confiscated lands. Nor was it easy for the crown to recover the debts of convicted financiers. In August 1533 two million *livres* arising from sentences imposed by the *Tour Carrée* still needed to be collected. Yet the trials did yield additional revenue to the crown. In many cases the king accepted lump sums ranging from 20,000 to 150,000 *livres* by way of commutation for fines. Altogether such settlements amounted to 707,082l. Sometimes they were in kind: the Ponchers, for example, ceded Limours to the king, and the heirs of Thomas Bohier gave up Chenonceaux with its beautiful château.

10

The Court and Patronage of Francis I

The court of France was much larger than the king's family circle. It took in his household, the households of members of his family, and an amorphous mass of hangers-on. Though less magnificent than the Burgundian court, it had nevertheless become an important political institution by the fifteenth century. Whoever had the king's ear shared to some extent in his power. Nobles went to court in the hope of securing offices, pensions or other favours. The king, for his part, welcomed a trend which increased aristocratic dependence on his authority.

The growth of the royal household (*maison du roi*) can be traced back to the thirteenth century through a series of royal ordinances. By 1261 it had already been divided into six departments, each with its own staff. A distinction existed between services to the king's person (*bouche*) and to his entourage (*commun*). Household officers were paid in money, kind or both. Remuneration in kind included the right to eat at court and to receive allowances of fuel, candles and fodder.

The evidence provided by an incomplete series of payrolls suggests that the size of the court increased significantly from 1494 onwards. In 1523 the household of Francis I comprised 540 officials of various kinds distributed across a number of departments, each with its distinctive function. The three main ones were the chapel, the chamber and the *hôtel*. The chapel, under the Grand Almoner, attended to the king's spiritual needs; the chamber, under the Great Chamberlain or First Gentleman of the Chamber, was concerned with the day-to-day routine of the king's bedchamber; the *hôtel*, under the Grand Master, was responsible for feeding the court. Bread, wine, fruit, and candles were provided by three sub-departments: the *paneterie*, *échansonnerie* and *fruiterie*. There were two kitchens, one for the king, the other for the courtiers in general. The *fourrière* was responsible for transporting the court and its furniture. A team of quartermasters allocated lodgings according to a strict order of precedence. The stables (*écurie*), under the Master of the Horse (*Grand écuyer*), cared for the king's horses and also had a staff of messengers and a riding school for pages. Two departments, the *vénerie* and *fauconnerie*, organized the royal hunts.

Alongside the royal household there was a military establishment made up of units created in different reigns. The oldest was the Scottish guard, created under Charles VII, which provided the king's bodyguard. The archers comprised three companies, each of one hundred men. The Hundred Swiss (*Cent-suisses*) were set up by Charles VIII. Lastly there were the Two Hundred gentlemen of the household, divided into two companies. All these troops, except the Swiss, were mounted.

Law and order at court were maintained by the provost (*prévôt*) and his staff of three lieutenants and thirty archers. He could punish crimes committed in a royal residence or within five miles of the king's person. When the court was on progress, he had the duty of ensuring that supplies were adequate and unscrupulous victuallers were not overpricing them.

The finances of the household were administered by the *Chambre aux deniers* whose annual budget was subject to the approval of the chamber of accounts (*Chambre des comptes*); but the king's privy purse escaped this control.

The queen's household, though smaller than the king's, was none the less sizeable. It had more or less the same number of departments, but the chamber staff was entirely female. Francis's mother and children also had their own households.

The court included many permanent or semi-permanent guests, such as princes of the blood, foreign princes, high church dignitaries and ambassadors, each with his own retainers. When the young Federico Gonzaga stayed at the court in 1516 and 1517 his suite numbered 50 persons and 41 horses. Many people who were not part of the court had to go there on business. They included members of the king's council, masters of requests, notaries and secretaries. Lastly there were numerous hangers-on, including merchants and artisans, who were exempted from tolls and guild regulations as long as they served only the court. Under Louis XII they had numbered 100; Francis I raised their number to 160 in March 1544. There were also the camp-followers or *filles de joie suivant la cour*.

Overall control of the court was vested in the Grand Master. He drew up the annual roll of the household staff, supervised appointments, kept the keys of the royal residence and ensured the king's safety. Such an important office needed to be held by someone enjoying the king's complete trust. Under Francis I it was first held by his old governor, Artus Gouffier, then by his uncle, René of Savoy, and finally by Anne de Montmorency, who held it for more than thirty years. He was also Constable of France and virtually ran the government from 1528 until his fall in 1541.

Francis did not fundamentally alter the court's structure. However, in 1515 he created the new title of Gentleman of the Chamber for his closest male companions, releasing the older title of *valet de chambre* for use by commoners. The head of the chamber was now the First Gentleman (*Premier gentilhomme*), an office held for most of the reign by Jean de La Barre, comte d'Etampes and *Prévôt de Paris*. His duties included custody of the crown jewels, holding money for the king's private use and signing contracts for work on royal palaces.

Although the gentlemen of the chamber were the king's constant companions, they were not always at court. They served according to a roster and some were employed on a variety of missions which might take them away from the court for considerable periods of time. For example, Guillaume du Bellay, seigneur de Langey, served on embassies in England, Italy, Switzerland and Germany. In the 1540s he administered Piedmont for the king.

The chamber was an important centre for the exchange and dissemination of ideas and impressions gathered by the gentlemen in the course of their travels. One of the ways in which monarchs demonstrated mutual friendship and trust was by exchanging gentlemen of their respective chambers. For example, Francis invited Sir Thomas Cheney, one of the gentlemen of Henry VIII's chamber, to enter his as freely as if it were that of his own master.

By 1535 the number of household officials at Francis's court had risen to 622, and the amount spent on wages from 65,915 *livres* in 1517 to 214,918l. But the overall population of the court was much larger, though it fluctuated wildly. As a general rule, it was larger in peacetime than during a war, when the king and his courtiers went on campaign leaving behind a rump of women, old men and ecclesiastics. Even in peacetime the court's population was variable. As it travelled across the kingdom it would attract nobles from one area, who would tag on for a few days or even weeks. They would then go home and nobles from another region might fill their places, also for a limited period. Few noblemen chose to reside permanently at court. Life there was expensive and not always rewarding. Even the greatest nobles liked to return to their estates from time to time. Yet the court at its fullest extent might contain as many as ten thousand people – it was like a medium-sized town on the move. About 1550 only twenty-five towns in France had a larger population.

Francis I's court was not only larger than its predecessors; its manners were also more polished, at least on the surface. This change has been generally ascribed to the growth of Italian influence. As the French king became a key political figure south of the Alps, Italians looked to him more and more for aid or protection. They came in waves that reflected the variable fortunes of Italian political life. Among early arrivals were the Fregosi of Genoa, the San Severini and Caraccioli of Naples and the Trivulzi of Milan. Not all came to France as political exiles; some came in response to the king's matrimonial diplomacy. The marriage of Catherine de' Medici to Francis's second son, Henri duc d'Orléans, in October 1533 brought a substantial number of Florentines to the French court.

Traffic between France and Italy was not simply one-way. Frenchmen were given many opportunities as soldiers, administrators or diplomats for observing Italian life and manners at first hand. They noted that in Italy women were an essential adornment of court society; also that close attention was given to patronage of literature and the arts. In the light of this experience they tried to bring greater refinement to the French court. But extravagance came in its wake, as courtiers spent lavishly on clothes, jewels and entertainment. This made them unpopular with Frenchmen in general, who began to look upon the court as a centre of expensive frivolity, not to say debauchery. The extravagance of courtiers was seen as a symptom of physical and moral decay. Literary criticism of court life became more barbed than before.

Our knowledge of the day-to-day routine of the French court rests largely on a letter of 1576 written by Catherine de' Medici to her son, Henry III, in which she urged him to restore the routine which had been observed by his father and grandfather. The day began with the king's *lever* in the presence of the principal courtiers and distinguished guests. The king's shirt would be handed to him by the most honoured person present. He would then retire to his study with his secretaries to deal with state papers or would hold a meeting of his council. At 10 AM he would go to mass escorted by all the princes and lords. At 11.00 he would have his lunch alone, albeit 'in public', in the main reception room, during which he might be read to aloud. Twice a week, lunch would be followed by an audience in which people would approach him individually or in groups. After spending an hour or so with his queen (or mistress?) he would withdraw to his study until about 3 PM, when he would take part in some sport such as tennis or a hunt. In the evening he would sup with his family; then perhaps offer a ball or masque. The day ended with the king's *coucher*, again in the presence of great nobles.

Except when an outbreak of plague forced the king to keep to his room, he was extraordinarily approachable. Anyone who was properly dressed or could claim acquaintance with someone at court was readily admitted. Such accessibility carried risks. Thus in November 1530, Francis complained that ornaments had been stolen from his chapel, and silver plate and clothes from his wardrobe. Such thefts were to be punished by death in future.

The court in the sixteenth century, as in the Middle Ages, continued to be nomadic; indeed, as the kingdom increased in size and became more peaceful internally, the court travelled more than before. 'Never during the whole of my embassy', wrote a Venetian ambassador, 'was the court in the same place for fifteen consecutive days.' However, this was not always so; in winter and spring, when the roads turned into quagmires, the court tended to stay put. Its nomadic way of life was more than a medieval survival: in an age of growing political centralization, the king needed to show himself to his subjects. His wanderings were far from haphazard. At the start of his reign Francis visited several French provinces: Provence (1516), Picardy (1517), Anjou and Brittany (1518), Poitou and Angoumois (1519), Picardy again (1520) and Burgundy (1521). As he engaged in war, his movements were determined by military needs. When peace returned in 1526 he resumed his progresses, and even when his health failed at the end of his life he continued to travel extensively. His most extensive progress lasted from November 1531 till February 1534.

Travel enabled Francis to hunt in a wide variety of places. He was never happier, it seems, than when he shed cares of state and vanished into some deep forest with a few companions. By comparison with the cramped and unhygienic conditions of sixteenth-century towns, the lure of the open must have been irresistible. Yet Francis could not ignore Paris. The kingdom had, in effect, two capitals: the court and Paris. While the king's council continued to follow the court, some of the principal departments of state, notably the parlement, had 'gone out of court' during the Middle Ages and become fixed in Paris. Only by coming to the parlement and holding a *lit de justice* could the king override its opposition to legislation. He also needed the financial support of wealthy Parisians. As the capital was a *ville franche*, a town exempt from direct taxation, he needed to make personal appeals to the generosity of its inhabitants. Paris was also the traditional venue for important public ceremonies, such as a royal entry, a visit by a foreign dignitary, an aristocratic wedding or a religious procession, and Francis liked to go shopping there for luxury goods such as jewellery.

Whenever the king visited a major town for the first time he was given an entry or *entrée joyeuse*. From a relatively simple affair in which the townspeople offered him victuals and sometimes fodder, a royal entry had become a spectacular pageant by the close of the Middle Ages. The king was met outside the town by the leading citizens, wearing colourful liveries, and escorted into it to a musical accompaniment. While he solemnly promised to maintain the town's privileges, the inhabitants swore obedience to him. A gift in the form of money or some valuable work of art was then offered to the king. After receiving the town keys, he would ride under a rich canopy along a carefully prepared route. Tapestries usually adorned the façades of the houses. By the early sixteenth century roadside theatricals had become the rule. The reign of Francis marked an important transition in the development of the royal entry in France. Whereas in 1515 the symbolism was still mainly medieval, by 1547 it had incorporated many classical elements. The transition was gradual, with medieval and classical elements existing side by side or overlapping, but after 1530 the classical began to dominate. Instead of being acclaimed as a second David or Solomon, Francis was now hailed as the new Caesar. Allegories inspired by medieval romances were displaced by the Roman triumph. The chariot, equestrian statue and triumphal arch became part of the normal trappings of a royal entry.

Moving the court was like moving an army. According to Benvenuto Cellini, the Florentine artist, who visited the French court in the 1540s, as many as 18,000 horses were used to transport it. An Englishman who witnessed the court's arrival in Bordeaux in 1526 reported that stabling had been provided for 22,500 horses and mules. The court's baggage train was enormous: it contained furniture, gold and silver plate and tapestries. Only châteaux regularly frequented by the court were kept permanently furnished; the rest remained empty from one visit to the next.

Feeding the court could be a problem. In May 1533 the Venetian ambassador reported that Lyon could not accommodate so many men and horses. There was a great scarcity of lodgings, bread, corn and stabling, and the presence of the court had caused a steep rise in the price of essential foodstuffs. In August 1540 an ambassador described the plight of the court as it travelled to Le Havre: there was neither fodder for the horses nor wine or cider for the men. As all the wells were dry, courtiers were forced to drink polluted water and many fell seriously ill.

Finding lodgings was often difficult. The king stayed in one of his own châteaux wherever possible or at the home of a courtier. If neither was available, he would stay at an abbey or inn. However, relatively few courtiers could hope to share his roof. They had to look for alternative accommodation, usually over a wide area; if all else failed they could always pitch tents. 'Sometimes', writes Cellini, 'there were scarcely two houses to be found and then we set up canvas tents like gipsies, and suffered at times very great discomfort.'

Francis as a builder

The early years of Francis's reign were marked by much architectural activity all over France. Until the mid-fifteenth century the country houses of the nobility had been built for defence rather than comfort: they had thick walls, few windows, massive angle towers, machicolations, portcullises and moats filled with water. However, with the return of domestic peace following the end of the Hundred Years War, the need for military features largely disappeared. They were not abandoned overnight, but were treated more as decorations or status symbols. Large windows appeared in the walls, angle towers were transformed into graceful turrets and machicolations became friezes. At the same time, French nobles who fought in Italy became acquainted with classical architecture. Even if they did not fully understand its rules, they appreciated some of the decoration, notably the columns, pilasters, pediments and medallions, which they proceeded to apply to the façades of their own, structurally Gothic, homes. Pioneers of this movement were Charles VIII, who employed Italian craftsmen at Amboise, and Cardinal Georges d'Amboise, who did likewise at Gaillon.

Under Francis I, the classical influence began to permeate the structure of buildings. Three châteaux were favourite residences of the court in the first part of his reign: Amboise, Blois and Saint-Germain-en-Laye. The most interesting construction was the wing built by Francis at Blois with the Façade of the Loggias on one side and an external spiral staircase on the other. The inspiration behind the façade was evidently Bramante's loggias at the Vatican palace in Rome, which were under construction at the time. By choosing them as his model, Francis showed that he wished to keep abreast of fashion at its best.

Even more interesting is the château of Chambord, one of several palaces which Francis built from scratch. They were not intended as residences so much as glorified hunting lodges, where he and his companions could live informally. The overall plan of Chambord is essentially medieval, consisting of a square keep flanked by four round towers from which run lower buildings with towers at the corners. But the internal plan of the keep has no French precedent: it is divided into four parts by a Greek cross, of which the arms lead from entrances to a double spiral staircase in the middle. This arrangement leaves a square in each corner subdivided into a lodging of three rooms. The origin of this plan, which is repeated on each of three storeys, is Italian. Except for the spiral staircase, it recalls the plan of the villa built by Giuliano da Sangallo at Poggio a Caiano, near Florence, in the 1480s. This architect had a pupil, Domenico da Cortona, who worked in France during Francis's reign. He was paid for wooden models of various buildings, including Chambord, and was also commissioned to build a new town hall in Paris. So he may have been the architect of Chambord, but architectural historians doubt if he had the necessary genius. Some believe that Chambord was inspired by Leonardo da Vinci, although he died in 1519 before the building had actually got under way.

In March 1528, two years after his return from Spain, Francis I announced that he would henceforth reside more often in or near Paris. Although the court continued to travel about France, the king's main building activities were transferred from the valley of the Loire to Paris and its region. He began rebuilding the Louvre, erected the château of Madrid in the Bois de Boulogne, remodelled that of Saint-Germain-en-Laye, built the château of Villers-Cotterêts and began transforming Fontainebleau.

The Louvre at this time was a decrepit medieval fortress without a court-yard. In 1528, Francis created one by demolishing the keep. The moat was also filled in, approaches to the castle improved and an embankment built along the Seine to allow the passage of horses pulling barges along the river. However, the rebuilding of the Louvre took a very long time. It was only at the end of his reign that Francis ordered Pierre Lescot to demolish the west wing of the present *Cour carrée*. The work was continued after the king's death in 1547 by his son and successor Henry II.

Nothing survives of the château of Madrid, which Francis built just outside Paris. Work on it began in the spring of 1528 and lasted more than twenty years. It had neither courtyard nor moat. In plan, the château was a rectangular mass made up of five blocks. The centre block was occupied by a large reception room or *salle*, flanked by open loggias. At each end of the building were large square pavilions containing four lodgings per floor, which were reached by spiral staircases housed in square or round towers. Altogether there were 32 identical lodgings. The elevation comprised, on the ground and first floors, two horizontal tiers of open loggias running round the entire building, with a terrace on the second floor. High pitched roofs covered the various blocks and towers. The tall mullioned windows were regularly distributed. But the most unusual feature at Madrid was the decor-ation of brightly coloured glazed terracotta. According to a document of 1530, two men supervised the building: Pierre Gadier, a master mason from Touraine, and Girolamo della Robbia, a member of the famous Florentine family of ceramists. The latter was evidently responsible for the château's dis-tinctive decoration, but it cannot be assumed that he was its architect.

Various ingenious explanations have been advanced to explain the château's curious name, but a link has now been firmly established with the Casa de Campo, a country house built outside Madrid in Spain. Francis had probably seen this building (which no longer exists) during his captivity and had decided to reproduce a larger version of it outside Paris for his own use.

According to Jacques Androuet du Cerceau, the sixteenth-century French architect, Francis was so knowledgeable about architecture that he could almost be regarded as the sole architect of Saint-Germain-en-Laye. This suggests a close collaboration between the king and the Parisian master mason Pierre Chambiges, who began rebuilding the château in September 1539. Keeping as much as possible of the medieval building, Chambiges added two storeys and completely renovated the inner façades. His principal innovation was the terraced roof, constructed of large, superimposed stone slabs, which proved so heavy that the supporting edifice had to be strength-ened with large buttresses and held together by long iron tie-bars.

Architecturally, Saint-Germain is not a particularly exciting château, yet along with the Louvre and Fontainebleau it was one of the palaces used most frequently by Francis. In the nearby forest stood an ancillary residence, called La Muette, built at a spot where he liked to watch the deer retire 'exhausted from the labours of the chase'. Another small château built by him in the Ile-de-France was Challuau, which had a cubic central block and four square angle pavilions. In 1533 he also began work on the château of Villers-Cotterêts, 85 kilometres north-west of Paris.

A set of building accounts for Saint-Germain, covering the period from 1 January 1547 to 30 September 1550 indicates how the rooms within the château were used by Henry II's court. There were 55 lodgings within the château and 25 in outbuildings. The royal apartments were on the second floor, no one except a member of the royal family being allowed to reside above the king. His lodging comprised a reception room, a chamber, wardrobe and *cabinet*. It was reached by means of a staircase leading directly from the château's courtyard. When important guests came, a guard of honour formed a line from the courtyard to the king's chamber. This was deliberately located at some distance from the chapel, so as to give as many people as possible the chance to see the king as he went to mass. Other occupants of the second floor were the queen, Montmorency, the king's sister and daughter and marshal Saint-André. Henry II's mistress, Diane de Poitiers, lived on the first floor directly below the queen. Rooms at Saint-Germain were allocated according to strict rules of precedence. Ladies, princes who were accompanied by their wives, and most cardinals were accommodated in the château itself, while single nobles, royal secretaries, and officers of the household were relegated to outbuildings.

The most important château built by Francis I in the last two decades of his reign was Fontainebleau. In December 1529 he said that he planned to spend more time there because of the pleasure he derived from hunting deer and wild boar in the neighbouring forest. Fontainebleau did, in fact, become his favourite residence. He 'liked it so much', writes du Cerceau, 'that he spent most of his time there . . . all that he could find of excellence was for his Fontainebleau of which he was so fond that whenever he went there he would say that he was going home.'

A castle, oval in shape with a gatehouse, keep and flanking towers. had existed at Fontainebleau since the twelfth century, but it was too small to serve the needs of a Renaissance court. Francis enlarged it by building on the site of a nearby monastery which he purchased in 1529. Gilles Le Breton, a Parisian master mason, agreed to restore the old château and to build a new one on the monastic site as well as a gallery projecting westward from the keep of the old château. The medieval gateway was transformed into the *Porte Dorée* with two superimposed loggias. Instead of the beautiful white stone used for building in the Loire valley, Le Breton used the local *grès*, a hard stone not easily carved.

A great deal of what Francis built at Fontainebleau has been destroyed. Only the north wing of the *Cour du Cheval Blanc* is more or less in its original state. The west wing was destroyed by Napoleon and the south wing was rebuilt by Louis XV, who swept away the *Galerie d'Ulysse*, the longest gallery in France with murals by Primaticcio. The only part of the south wing that survives is the *Grotte des Pins* with its giants emerging from a rocky background, built about 1543 as a summer-house. In the seventeenth century the *Cour du Cheval Blanc* (named after a plaster copy of the statue of Marcus Aurelius on the Capitol in Rome which Catherine de' Medici set up in the middle) was used for equestrian purposes. It may have been similarly used under Francis, whose stables occupied part of the south wing till 1537. The horses were then moved to Monceau and the stables turned over to merchants and artisans attached to the court. The courtyard was entered through a central pavilion of the west wing which was traditionally occupied by the Swiss guard. Another pavilion may have housed the foundry used to cast bronzes of ancient statues; it later became a tapestry workshop.

Today the most important survival of Renaissance Fontainebleau is the *Galerie François Ier*, which occupies the first floor of the wing Lescot added to the medieval keep. Originally it served as a passage from the royal apartments to the church of the Trinitarians. The present building is twice as wide as the original, which was lit from both sides. A terrace was also added on the south side in 1535 to accommodate kitchens and larders. The ground floor housed a bathroom and sweating rooms. The vault and lunettes of the baths were decorated with paintings and stucco.

It was in the *Galerie François Ier* that the Florentine artist Giovanni Battista Rosso evolved a distinctive style of interior decoration. He was followed in March 1532 by Francesco Primaticcio, a pupil of Giulio Romano, who came recommended by the duke of Mantua. Between them Rosso and Primaticcio decorated many parts of the château. Sometimes they collaborated; more often they worked independently, each with a team of assistants. Much of their work has, alas, been destroyed; it is known thanks to preliminary drawings which have survived and a large number of contemporary etchings and engravings copied from or inspired by their designs.

All that remains of Rosso's work at Fontainebleau is contained in the *Galerie François Ier*. The walls are divided into two roughly equal horizontal parts: the lower contains carved wood panelling by Scibec de Carpi, and the upper a combination of stucco and painting. Each space between two windows has a painted panel in the middle, flanked by stucco decorations representing nudes, herms, putti, garlands of fruit and strapwork (i.e. stucco made to look like rolls of leather cut into fantastic shapes). The meaning of these decorations has been the subject of endless speculation by art historians. Some of it has been disproved by a fairly recent restoration which revealed that the frescoes were executed between 1534 and 1538, after the stucco had been completed. Much haste was apparently applied to finishing the gallery before the emperor's visit in 1539. The frescoes were clearly intended to glorify Francis's reign.

The frescoes contain many reminders of the triumphal art of ancient Rome, but historians have tried, so far unsuccessfully, to grasp the underlying theme or programme of the gallery as a whole. H. Zerner has suggested a possible connection between that programme and the book of emblems, a genre created by Andrea Alciati which became very popular in sixteenth-century France. Alciati, who taught jurisprudence in France between 1529 and 1534, may well have influenced Rosso. A similar spirit seems to underlie the emblems and the gallery's programme. In the case of the emblem, only the author could supply the link between the image and the motto. This role may have been played by Francis I when he showed guests his gallery, the key of which he kept on his person. It would have gratified him to dazzle them by revealing the enigma of the gallery's programme. This may have been what his sister, Marguerite, had in mind, when, after a visit to Fontainebleau, she wrote to him regretting that he had not been there to guide her: 'for to see your buildings without hearing what your purpose is, is like reading Hebrew'.

All that survives of Primaticcio's work at Fontainebleau before 1540 is part of a fireplace in the *Chambre de la reine*. His originality may first have been manifested in the stuccos, a technique he had already practised in Mantua. It was later in the reign that he asserted his own distinctive style at Fontainebleau. In 1540 he was sent to Rome to collect works of art for the king of France. This mission brought him into contact with ancient sculpture and the art of Parmigianino. Following his return to France, he developed a style of figure-drawing exemplified by the caryatids in the *Chambre de la duchesse d'Etampes* with their long, tapering limbs, thin necks and small heads with classical profiles. Primaticcio's main work after 1540 was done in the *Salle de Bal* and *Galerie d'Ulysse*. The gallery was destroyed in 1739 and none of its superb murals survives, but scholars have been able to reconstruct the iconographical programme. Primaticcio's choice of the story of Ulysses is not surprising, for Homer was popular at the French court around 1540; but the *Odyssey*, unlike the *Iliad*, had not yet been exploited as a source of illustrations. By choosing it as his inspiration, Primaticcio broke new ground, while enlarging his scope for illustrating the twenty-nine panels on either side of the gallery.

By the 1530s correct usage of the classical Orders was becoming more widely known in France. Master masons were able to use the first popular works of Geoffroy Tory and an abridgement in French of Vitruvius by Diego de Sagredo, published in Paris between 1526 and 1537. Nobles were consequently less dependent on the king's example in pursuing classical correctness in building. A veritable building frenzy took hold of the French aristocracy in the 1530s and 1540s. By 1538, Montmorency's new château at Chantilly was among the finest in France. A long arcaded gallery built at Châteaubriant by Jean de Laval is an almost perfect example of the Italian style. At La Rochefoucauld, François and Anne de Polignac built a courtyard with superimposed galleries reminiscent of an Italian *cortile*. At Assier, Galiot de Genouillac adorned his château with a carved frieze displaying military emblems. Finally, at Pagny, Admiral Chabot erected a magnificent palace which was unfortunately destroyed in 1774.

Francis I as an art patron

Francis I is remembered as one of the world's outstanding art patrons. In addition to building magnificent châteaux, he built up a fine collection of paintings and statues and employed a number of leading artists, whom he recruited mainly in Italy. Even as a boy he was interested in art, for Niccolò Alamanni wrote from Blois to the marquis of Mantua in June 1504 asking for pictures by 'those excellent Italian masters' which gave so much pleasure to the young count. He was particularly anxious to obtain a work by Andrea Mantegna. At that time French painting was at a low ebb. The only native artists of any significance were Jean Bourdichon and Jean Perréal; Italian artists hardly ever visited France. In 1515, however, Francis I's conquest of Milan brought him into direct contact with some masterpieces of the Italian Renaissance and their creators. In particular, he got to know Leonardo da Vinci and invited him to France.

Leonardo was 65 years old in March 1516, when he accepted the king's invitation. He was given the manor of Cloux near Amboise and an annuity. What he did in return is uncertain. Drawings in his notebooks show that he was interested in canal-building, town-planning and architecture. He may have designed a new palace for Louise of Savoy at Romorantin, and some of his ideas may have been adopted at Chambord. He seems to have painted no pictures in France, yet the king held him in the highest esteem and enjoyed frequent conversations with him. Twenty years after Leonardo's death (2 May 1519), Francis declared that no one had known as much about painting, sculpture and architecture.

Another important Italian artist who visited the French court early in the reign was Andrea del Sarto. He painted a portrait of the Dauphin and a *Charity* (now in the Louvre). According to Vasari, Francis gave him a large pension and hoped to retain his services, but Andrea asked for permission to return to Florence which the king granted on the understanding that Andrea would soon return. He also gave him money with which to purchase works of art on his behalf; but the artist pocketed the money and never came back. For a long time afterwards, Francis apparently distrusted Florentine artists.

It was not till 1531 at Fontainebleau that Italian artists began to be regularly employed by the king. The first to arrive was Rosso, who had come under the influence of Michelangelo and Raphael while working in Rome. About 1529 he moved to Venice and did a drawing of *Mars and Venus* for Pietro Aretino, who presented it to Francis. The drawing is an allegory on the Peace of Cambrai: for 'Mars' read Francis and for 'Venus' read Eleanor of Portugal whom the king married as a result of the treaty. The drawing shows Mars discarding his weapons and his clothes in order to make love. It may have paved the way for Rosso's invitation to France. Being not only a good painter but a cultivated man, he made a good impression on Francis who appointed him First Painter with a large salary and a house in Paris. He also received letters of naturalization and became a canon of the Sainte-Chapelle.

Rosso's art at Fontainebleau was widely diffused in different forms. A number of engravings were executed there between 1542 and 1548 by artists such as Antonio Fantuzzi. Another Parisian studio run by Pierre Milan and René Boyvin produced engravings between 1545 and 1580, the best known being the *Nymph of Fontainebleau*. Six of Rosso's frescoes in the *Galerie François Ier* were also reproduced as tapestries. They were woven at Fontainebleau by Jean and Pierre Le Bries between 1540 and 1547 and are now in Vienna.

From the beginning of his stay in France, Rosso did more than paint murals. He designed costumes for various spectacles, tableware, horse-trappings and a tomb. He may also have served as an architect. For the emperor's visit in 1539 he designed costumes, festival decorations and a large silver statue of Hercules given to Charles V by the Parisian authorities. Sometimes he worked for other patrons: he designed a tapestry for Cardinal de Lorraine and painted the *Pietà*, now in the Louvre, for Montmorency.

Francis's artistic interests were not exclusively Italian. For portraiture he turned mainly to Jean Clouet, who hailed from the Netherlands. Many chalk drawings survive of the king, members of his family and entourage, the best of which are usually attributed to Clouet; others are contemporary copies of variable quality. They were originally used in various ways: some were sent to friends or relatives, as photographs are today, or they were gathered into albums. Though Clouet had almost certainly been trained in France, his use of parallel diagonal hatching strokes to achieve a three-dimensional effect was of Italian origin. When he died in 1540 he was succeeded as royal painter by his son François, who continued the series of court portraits into the second half of the century.

Francis also employed agents to buy works of art, including sculpture, for his collection. Some were French diplomats, like Guillaume du Bellay;

others were Italians, like Battista della Palla or Pietro Aretino. Della Palla
was a Florentine, who had come to France as a political exile between 1522
and 1527. He had established close links with the court, especially the
king's sister. In 1528, when he returned to France as an envoy of the new
Florentine republic, he was commissioned to buy works of art for the French
king. He failed to strip the Borgherini nuptial chamber of painted panels
by various artists, but managed to secure other works, including a multi-
breasted statue of *Nature* by Niccolò Tribolo (now at Fontainebleau). Della
Palla sent to Francis at least two other statues by contemporary artists:
Bandinelli's *Mercury holding a flute* and Michelangelo's *Hercules*, an early
work by the master which had belonged to the Strozzi family. It was set
up at Fontainebleau as part of a fountain, but disappeared about 1714.

Venetian artists were not completely overlooked by Francis. In 1538,
Aretino sent him two pictures, 'one magnifying the honour of man, the
other magnifying the glory of God'. The former was Titian's portrait in
profile of the king (taken from a medal); the latter has been identified
with his *Penitent Magdalene* (now in Bordeaux). It was presumably on the
strength of these works that the artist was invited to France by the king,
but he refused to abandon Venice. Aretino's artistic services to Francis
began in 1529 when he attached himself to the circle of scholars and artists
formed by Lazare de Baïf, the French ambassador to Venice. He was
rewarded with the gift of a gold chain and the promise of an annuity.

Sculpture entered the royal collection later than painting. Cardinal
Bibbiena reported in 1520 that it contained no statues, ancient or modern.
This prompted Cardinal Medici to order a copy of the newly discovered
Laocoön from Bandinelli, but it was never sent. In 1540, Francis dispatched
Primaticcio to Rome to buy and copy antiquities on his behalf. The artist
returned in the following year with plaster casts of many famous statues,
most of them in the Vatican collection. Some were turned into bronzes by
Vignola, the future architect, who set up a foundry at Fontainebleau; others
were reproduced in plaster only.

Among other works of art in Francis's collection were a perfume burner
designed by Raphael (of which only the design survives in an engraving)
and a jewel casket with crystal panels representing scenes from the life of
Christ by Valerio Belli. This was given to the king by Pope Clement VII on
the occasion of Catherine de' Medici's marriage in 1533; it is now in the
Pitti palace in Florence.

Some of the most valuable objects in Francis I's collection were made by
Benvenuto Cellini, whose fame rests not only on his artistic achievement
but also on his autobiography, which incidentally sheds much light on the
nature of Francis's artistic patronage. Cellini visited France twice, in 1537
and 1540. The first visit proved a disappointment as the king was too busy
fighting the emperor to give Cellini any attention. The artist, however, did

win the patronage of Cardinal Ippolito d'Este, who paved the way for his return. This second visit lasted five years. The king provided Cellini with a workshop in the Petit Nesle, a medieval building on the left bank of the Seine opposite the Louvre, where he and members of the court would visit the artist from time to time. The first work produced by Cellini for the king was a statue of *Jupiter* in silver. Francis asked for twelve such statues, six gods and six goddesses, to serve as candlesticks for his table. Each was to be six feet tall, like the king. Cellini toiled for five years on this commission, but only managed to complete the *Jupiter* which he presented to Francis at Fontainebleau. It does not survive.

Another work made by Cellini for Francis I is the famous salt-cellar, now in Vienna. It has been described as 'an allegory of consummate naturalness ... a paragon of virtuosity ... an evocative and memorable work of art' (J. Pope-Hennessy). The only other major work to survive from the artist's French period is the bronze relief of the *Nymph of Fontainebleau*, now in the Louvre. This was part of a decorative scheme designed for the *Porte Dorée*, but the nymph never did adorn that gateway; she was eventually given by Henry II to his mistress, Diane de Poitiers, and placed over the gateway of her château at Anet. In February 1542, Cellini showed Francis a model for a fountain at Fontainebleau. In the middle stood a male figure which was intended to stand 54 feet above the ground and was meant to represent the king in the guise of Mars. At each angle of the fountain sat a figure representing one of the arts and sciences that he was patronizing.

Cellini's autobiography shows that Francis delegated much of his patronage to underlings who did not always carry out his wishes to the letter. The artist complained of not receiving some rewards which he had been promised, yet he did not do badly. In addition to cash payments, he was given letters of naturalization. His stay in France, however, was far from peaceful. Attempts were made to dislodge him from the Petit Nesle and he was attacked in the streets and in the courts. His arrogance, bombast and violent temper earned him many enemies including Francis's mistress, the duchesse d'Etampes, who tried to poison the king's mind against him and even to sabotage the presentation of his *Jupiter*.

Less attention has been given to Francis's patronage of music than to his support for the visual arts, yet it was important to him. His chapel played a prominent part at his meetings with the pope at Bologna in December 1515 and with Henry VIII at the Field of Cloth of Gold in 1520. On this occasion the English and French royal chapels sang alternate sections of the mass, each being accompanied by its own organist. An expense account of 1532–3 distinguishes between the *chapelle de musique* and a chapel of plainchant, the first with a staff of 27 and the latter of 14. The master of the *chapelle de musique* was Cardinal Tournon and the sub-master Claude de Sermisy, one of the best-known composers at the time. Other court musicians were attached to the king's chamber and to the *écurie* or stables. The chamber musicians included lutenists, cornettists, fifers and drummers. The distinguished lutenist Alberto da Ripa, who hailed from Mantua, bore the title of *valet de chambre* held by other artists who were members of the royal household. It was a purely honorary title and did not imply domestic duties. About 1535, Francis created a small vocal ensemble to sing *chansons*. Musicians of the *écurie* were not soloists: playing viols, hautbois and sackbuts, they performed as a band on state occasions and in courtly entertainments.

The most important composer employed by Francis before 1522 was Jean Mouton, a disciple of Josquin des Prés. He wrote about a hundred motets in a style distinguished by a serene and smoothly flowing polyphony, great technical finish and a superb contrapuntal command. He also composed about fifteen masses and twenty *chansons*. The latter are in various styles: some were canonic, others three-part popular arrangements and others still witty, imitative pieces influenced by popular tunes of the day.

The first half of the sixteenth century produced some major developments in French music. While some composers developed techniques first explored by Josquin and his contemporaries, others developed new ones which transformed the sound of music. They looked for ways of expressing the meaning as well as the form of the words they set. An autonomous instrumental music grew up independently of literary associations or the dance. At the same time, the distribution of music was revolutionized by a new printing method, probably invented by Pierre Attaingnant. Whereas previously the note had been printed separately from the stave, both were now printed in a single punch, thereby greatly speeding up the printing of music. Attaingnant published vast amounts of music, mostly by Parisian composers.

The reign of Francis corresponds closely with the first period of the sixteenth-century *chanson*. Its textual charm, of varying degrees of respectability, was calculated to delight the king and his courtiers. Despite the broad humour evinced, many *chanson* composers were churchmen. Claude de Sermisy's 160 *chansons* were so popular that they were arranged for lute and keyboard accompaniment and adapted to sacred texts. They are characterized by terseness, precision, simplicity, airiness and a generally dance-like quality.

The Renaissance liking for realistic tone-painting is exemplified by the programme *chansons* of Clément Janequin, who enjoyed the patronage of Jean de Guise, Cardinal of Lorraine, before joining the chapel royal in 1555. In 1530 he provided a song of welcome, 'Chantons, sonnons, trompetes' for the return from captivity of Francis's sons. His most famous *chanson*, 'La Guerre', imitates vividly the sounds of battle. Some 286 *chansons* by Janequin survive, not all programme pieces; many are graceful works of a more conventional kind, such as 'Qu'est ce d'amour', one of several settings of poems by or attributed to Francis I.

The *lecteurs royaux*

In the first part of his reign, as we have seen, Francis I showed an interest in humanism. He took steps to found a college for the study of classical languages, but the outbreak of war with the emperor in 1521 caused the project to be abandoned. In 1526, following his return from Spain, Guillaume Budé reminded Francis of his promise, and in March 1530 he set up four royal lectureships in Greek and Hebrew – the so-called *lecteurs royaux*. Erasmus declared that France was more fortunate than if she had conquered the whole of Italy, while Rabelais acclaimed the coming of a new age in *Pantagruel*:

> Thanks be to God, learning has been restored in my age to its former dignity and enlightenment . . . Now every method of teaching has been restored, and the study of languages has been revived: of Greek, without which it is disgraceful for a man to call himself a scholar, and of Hebrew, Chaldean and Latin.

The creation of the *lecteurs royaux*, for all the enthusiasm which it aroused among humanists, was an informal measure. No royal charter has ever been found. There is a letter from the king, dated 29 November 1529, asking the bishop of Bayeux to release the hellenist, Jacques Toussain, so that he might occupy the chair of Greek in the college which Francis is planning to set up. Otherwise, the archives are silent except for entries in the accounts of the king's household relating to the *lecteurs'* salaries. They often had to wait four or five years to be paid and only survived, it seems, thanks to the generosity of some humanist bishops, who conferred on them ecclesiastical benefices. They also had cause to complain of their teaching conditions. As they had been given no building of their own, they had to teach in existing colleges or even in the street.

The creation of the *lecteurs royaux* has often been interpreted as an enlightened blow struck by the crown in support of humanism against the scholastic obscurantism of the University of Paris. This view, however, is no longer tenable for two reasons. First, the king's role may have been exaggerated. Humanists liked to think of him as their patron, but his personal involvement in the encouragement of classical learning may have been less important than that of Budé and other court humanists. Secondly, the status of the *lecteurs* is unclear: did they belong to the king's household or to the University of Paris? Several of them are known to have taught in the university. The notion of a bitter struggle between the *lecteurs royaux* and the Faculty of Theology needs correction. The *lecteurs* were never accused of teaching heresy. Four were prosecuted by the Parlement in 1534, not because they taught ancient languages, but because their courses on the Bible breached the faculty's monopoly of religious teaching. As grammarians and rhetoricians, they were not licensed to teach religion. Far from being a 'great and decisive victory for the spirit of the Renaissance', as Abel Lefranc once claimed, no verdict, it seems, was reached in the affair, and the faculty emerged from it without loss of prestige. The crown continued to seek its guidance in matters of doctrine.

The word 'college' was never applied to the *lecteurs royaux*. It was used, however, in connection with a project which Francis I allegedly had in mind but never implemented. Whatever may have been the shortcomings of his patronage, Francis was acclaimed as 'the father of letters' by contemporary humanists. Their eulogies found expression in one of Rosso's frescoes at Fontainebleau. This shows the king, sword and book in hand, striding through the open portal of the Temple of Jupiter into its brightly lit interior. Behind him writhe the demons of ignorance, their eyes bandaged and their arms lifted in despair.

Poetry and prose: Clément Marot and François Rabelais

Under Francis I poetry emancipated itself from the allegorical excesses and rhythmic straitjacket which had been imposed upon it by the *rhétoriqueurs*, poets who held the field in the reigns of Charles VIII and Louis XII. A shift took place from old forms to new, while contact with classical sources fostered a reappraisal of rhetorical techniques. On all of this the influence of the court was decisive. Poetry was essential to royal propaganda. Every public event released a flood of encomiastic verse. But the court was not the only centre of poetic activity in France: another was the circle of Marguerite de Navarre. For part of the sixteenth century Lyon was the pace-setter of poetic development.

The most important court poet under Francis I was Clément Marot, who became Marguerite's secretary in 1518. He did not succeed his father Jean, the last of the *rhétoriqueurs*, as court poet till about 1526. From this time onwards he celebrated several public events in verse, but his career was punctuated by spells of imprisonment or exile occasioned by his Protestant sympathies. Thus in 1526 he was imprisoned for breaking the Lenten fast and released thanks to the king's intervention. In October 1534 he fell under suspicion following the 'Affair of the Placards' and took refuge first at the court of Marguerite in Navarre, then at that of Renée duchess of Ferrara. In June 1536 he moved to Venice whence he obtained permission to return to France. Official poetry once more occupied Marot, but in 1542 he again offended the religious authorities and fled to Geneva where he continued translating the Psalms, a task begun some years earlier. In spite of his beliefs, Marot did not find Geneva congenial: he compared it to Hell in a poem dedicated to Francis. He moved to Turin, where he died in September 1544. His last epistle was a celebration of the French victory at Ceresole.

Marot's originality as a poet did not become manifest till after 1526. Rejecting the genres of the *rhétoriqueurs*, he showed a new sensitivity toward classical sources. In his poem *L'Enfer* he revealed a gift for satire which never left him. He promoted classical influences on French poetry by the range of genres he exploited and by the themes he handled. Some of his earliest works involved translations of Virgil; later he turned to Ovid and, more importantly, to the Psalms. But it was in the *épitre* that he really excelled. This genre helped to bring poetry more into line with everyday life by eliminating allegorical comments and reducing the number of metrical fireworks. Most of Marot's epistles are concerned with his personal circumstances and needs. In the final resort, however, his success depended on his use of a more flexible language than that of the *rhétoriqueurs*. Critics sometimes complain of a lack of inner feeling in Marot's poetry, yet no one can dispute his significance as a transitional figure. He took poetry beyond the limits set by the *rhétoriqueurs*, anticipated the Pléiade's use of the ode and was one of the first Frenchmen to compose a sonnet.

François Rabelais, the greatest literary figure of the reign of Francis I, never held office at court, but the king knew his work. He had Rabelais's *Chronicles* read out to him after they had been condemned as heretical by the Sorbonne, and failed to discover anything wrong with them. Rabelais's learning brought him to the notice of Budé as early as 1523, when he was still a Franciscan friar at Fontenay-le-Comte. Budé wrote expressing envy of Rabelais's intellectual freedom, but he was less free than Budé imagined. After his books had been confiscated by his superior, he moved to the Benedictine house of Maillezais and secured the patronage of the local bishop, Geoffroy d'Estissac. For three years he accompanied the bishop on various journeys in Poitou. Then, after visiting several universities, including Paris, Rabelais entered the medical faculty at Montpellier. Two years later he became a physician at the *Hôtel-Dieu* in Lyon.

In 1533, Francis stopped in Lyon on his way south to meet the pope. Among his entourage was Jean du Bellay, bishop of Paris, who invited Rabelais to accompany him to Rome. From this time on he was closely associated with the bishop and his brother Guillaume. He became wedded to their interests and less directly to those of the king. His *Chronicles* are, in part, works of propaganda, which need to be set in their historical context if they are to be fully understood. They were designed not only to win the ear of courtiers and diplomats, but also to amuse and influence the king.

In particular, Rabelais was anxious to buttress the religious policies of his patrons. *Gargantua* mocks those aspects of Catholic worship which stood in the way of an ecumenical rapprochement with the Protestants. The greatest influence on Rabelais's life was Guillaume du Bellay, whom he followed to Piedmont in 1540. It was in Turin that Rabelais tempered the satire of his *Chronicles*. Yet in December 1546 the Sorbonne condemned his *Tiers Livre* although it bore the royal privilege. By this time Rabelais had moved to Metz, an imperial free city noted for its tolerant administration.

Francis I has been credited with the creation of a superb library at Fontainebleau, but the evidence for this is inconclusive. The royal library remained at Blois for much of his reign. In 1518 it contained 1626 volumes, including forty-one in Greek, four in Hebrew and two in Arabic. Some of these books had been acquired by Francis I's predecessors, others had come from his parents. Francis, like Shakespeare, had 'small Latin and less Greek', yet at the instigation of scholars in his entourage, notably Guillaume Budé who became Master of the King's Library in 1522, and Pierre du Chastel, he commissioned agents in Italy to acquire Greek books. These were intended for 'a fine and sumptuous library', which the king wanted to found alongside a college of three languages on the site of the Hôtel de Nesle in Paris, but the college was never built. The books, both manuscript and printed, were nevertheless acquired and sent. Among the most assiduous book collectors for the king were his diplomats in Rome and Venice. While Georges d'Armagnac, bishop of Rodez, had fourteen Greek manuscripts copied during his four years in Rome, Guillaume Pellicier employed twelve copyists continually during his Venetian embassy. In addition to the library at Blois, a second library followed the king around in two chests. Reading aloud to him was the role of the *lecteur du roi*, a post held in 1529 by Jacques Colin, translator of Castiglione's *Courtier*, and in 1537 by du Chastel. The contents of the king's mobile library tell us much about his reading tastes. They contained works by Justinus, Thucydides, Appian and Diodorus Siculus as well as the *Destruction de Troie la Grant*, the *Roman de la Rose* and other romances.

Though rich in manuscripts, the king's library contained relatively few printed works. It was presumably to overcome this that the Ordinance of Montpellier, generally regarded as the first law of legal deposit, was issued on 28 December 1537. All printers and booksellers were required to deliver a copy of every new book, ancient or modern, to the king's librarian at Blois. Imported books were to be examined and, if found suitable, purchased. The ordinance, however, was not strictly applied. In 1544 the library at Blois had only 109 printed books. By this time, the king had seen the expediency of gathering all his books in one place and ordered his library to be moved to Fontainebleau. The books were received there on 12 June by Mathieu Lavisse, the king's private librarian, and in 1546 a Greek copyist and publisher called Nicander of Corcyra reported that the king had established close to his lodging a library containing a large number of books, many of them in Greek, Latin, Hebrew or Arabic. About the same time, Francis ordered many of his books to be rebound, a task that was to be continued more lavishly by Henry II. In 1567 Pierre Ramus petitioned Catherine de' Medici to bring the library from Fontainebleau to Paris so as to make it more accessible to scholars; it thus became the nucleus of the present Bibliothèque nationale.

Francis was anxious to make his library available to scholars, hence his interest in printing. Robert Estienne, who was appointed in 1539 as the King's Printer in Hebrew and Latin and in 1542 as his Printer in Greek, explained Francis's intentions as follows: 'Far from grudging to anyone the records of ancient writers which he at great and truly royal cost has procured from Italy and Greece, he intends to put them at the disposal and service of all men.' For this purpose three special founts of Greek type – the *grecs du roi* – cut by Claude Garamond were financed by royal grants. The first work to be published with the new type was Eusebius's *Ecclesiastical History* (1544) and the most influential was an edition of the New Testament (1550).

Francis I: The Last Decade, 1537–47

In 1538 the foreign policy of Francis I underwent an extraordinary change: after years of bitter hostility towards the emperor, the king suddenly decided to become his friend. His objective remained the same as before: the recovery of the duchy of Milan; but instead of using force to achieve this end, he now tried conciliation. The architect of this change of policy was the Constable of France, Montmorency.

No one wanted peace more earnestly than Pope Paul III, for it was the essential prerequisite to a General Council and to a crusade. In December 1537, Rodolfo Pio, cardinal of Carpi, persuaded Francis to meet the pope at Nice in the summer. The emperor also agreed to come, but Francis refused to meet him in the pope's presence unless Milan were restored to him first. Between 15 May and 20 June the pope met the emperor four times and Francis twice. The main result was a ten-year truce between the parties concerned. Paul III left Nice on 20 June and travelled to Genoa, where he met Charles again before returning to Rome. The emperor then sailed to Aigues-Mortes in Languedoc, where he met Francis on 14 July. Observers could hardly believe their eyes. 'It seems', one wrote, 'that what we are seeing is but a dream, considering all that we have seen in the past.' King and emperor agreed to co-operate in defending Christendom and bringing heretics back into the church. In October, Francis met his sister-in-law Mary of Hungary, regent of the Netherlands, in northern France, and on the 23rd they signed the Treaty of Compiègne. Francis promised not to aid the anti-imperial rebels in the Netherlands; and Mary undertook to compensate certain French nobles whose lands in the Netherlands had been seized during the war.

The meetings at Aigues-Mortes and Compiègne paved the way for new peace talks. In December, French ambassadors submitted the following proposals to the emperor: the king's second son, Charles duc d'Orléans, would marry Charles V's daughter or niece, and his son Philip would marry Francis's daughter Marguerite. The king, for his part, would sever relations with England and join a crusade. Charles's acceptance of these proposals was interpreted in France as almost the equivalent of an alliance. Montmorency felt sure that the peace would last for the lives of Francis and Charles.

The French government, under Montmorency's direction, did in fact honour the Aigues-Mortes accord. Francis scrupulously abstained from any new involvement in German domestic affairs. An embassy from the Schmalkaldic League, which visited France in August 1538 hoping for an alliance, left empty-handed. The German Protestant princes were so convinced of a change in the king's attitude that they turned to England for support.

Henry VIII was afraid that the Franco-imperial entente was the first stage of a Catholic offensive aimed at his deposition. There were signs pointing in that direction. In December 1538, for example, Paul III confirmed Henry's excommunication which had been suspended for three years; he also sent Cardinal Pole to Spain and France in search of secular backing for his bull. Early in 1539 rumours of a Franco-imperial offensive against England caused Henry to make frantic defensive preparations. Yet he had nothing to fear: Charles was preoccupied with the Turks, and Francis did not wish to alienate England simply to please the pope.

The emperor visits France, 1539–40

The climax of the Franco-imperial entente forged at Aigues-Mortes was the emperor's visit to France in the winter of 1539–40. The idea originated with Charles V, who needed to reach the Netherlands from Spain as quickly as possible in order to suppress a tax revolt in Ghent. The sea route across the Bay of Biscay was hazardous in winter, and the alternative routes across the Mediterranean and overland through Italy, Switzerland and Germany were too long. By crossing France, Charles would also save money, which was always in short supply, but he needed to convince his council that he would be safe, and that no attempt would be made by Francis to extort concessions from him. Montmorency was only too anxious to reassure the imperial authorities on this score, as he hoped that the emperor's visit would pave the way to a peaceful resolution of the Milanese question.

Charles accepted Francis's invitation and arrived in Bayonne on 27 November. From this moment onwards he and his small retinue were magnificently entertained. At Bordeaux, Poitiers, Orléans and Paris, the emperor was given an entry and the privilege of setting prisoners free. The street decorations in Paris symbolized 'Peace' and 'Concord', and in every town Charles received magnificent gifts. For example, at Poitiers he was given a silver eagle and lily on a rock, and in Paris a life-size statue, also in silver, of Hercules holding two pillars, which Rosso had designed. The emperor's itinerary from Loches northwards had obviously been planned to show him the principal artistic achievements of the reign. Thus he visited Chenonceaux, Chambord, Fontainebleau, Madrid, the Louvre, Villers-Cotterêts and Chantilly. No expense was spared to make his stay memorable.

Before Charles left France for the Netherlands, he and Francis discussed the Turks and matters touching the faith, but they carefully avoided any mention of their differences. The emperor merely promised to deal with them after meeting his brother Ferdinand in Brussels. He took his leave of Francis at Saint-Quentin on 20 January 1540, and it was generally assumed at the French court that he would open peace talks soon. But Francis and his ministers waited in vain, while Charles put down the Ghent revolt. In March, however, he sent peace proposals: his daughter Mary would marry the duc d'Orléans and both would eventually inherit the Netherlands, Burgundy and Charolais. They would administer these territories in the emperor's lifetime, albeit under his supervision. Two other marriages were proposed: one between Francis's daughter Marguerite and Ferdinand's eldest son; the other between Charles's son Philip and Jeanne d'Albret, the heiress of Navarre. Francis would surrender his claim to Milan as well as Hesdin and the lands he had taken from the duke of Savoy. He would ratify the treaties of Madrid and Cambrai, and join a league for the defence of Christendom.

The proposals caused consternation at the French court. In his reply, Francis explained that the Netherlands were no substitute for Milan, which was his by right. Their future enjoyment was a poor exchange for the immediate possession of Milan which had been promised to the duc d'Orléans on condition he married the Infanta. Francis wished to delay the marriage of his daughter Marguerite, but was ready to accept the match proposed for Jeanne d'Albret. He was willing to exchange Hesdin for Tournai, Mortagne and Saint-Omer, but refused to ratify the treaties of Madrid and Cambrai. He was prepared to hand back parts of Savoy if it could be proved that he held them unlawfully and if the duke would return lands he held without valid title. On 24 April, Francis modified his terms in response to new proposals from Charles, but he still refused to ratify the treaties of Madrid and Cambrai. The two rulers continued to bandy proposals for several weeks, but their basic positions remained unchanged: Milan was still the principal stumbling block. By June their talks had finally collapsed.

The breakdown of the Franco-imperial entente played into the hands of Montmorency's enemies at the French court, who had longed for a chance to topple him. 'He is a great scoundrel,' said the duchesse d'Etampes, 'for he has deceived the king by saying that the emperor would give him Milan at once when he knew that the opposite was true.' The constable continued to attend the king's council for a time, but ceased to influence the conduct of foreign policy. The king began to attend the council more frequently and listened to the advice of such men as Guillaume Poyet and Tournon. On 11 October, Charles V invested his own son, Philip, with the duchy of Milan. This precipitated Montmorency's fall. Princes and ambassadors stopped writing to him; royal secretaries were forbidden to use his cyphers. On 14 June 1541 he appeared at court for the last time, when he attended the wedding of William duke of Cleves and Jeanne d'Albret. He retained his offices, but in May 1542 he was deprived of his governorship of Languedoc.

The Ordinance of Villers-Cotterêts, 30 August 1539

Chancellor Poyet was responsible for the Ordinance of Villers-Cotterêts, which is remembered today mainly for four of its 192 clauses: 1) that French instead of Latin be used in legal documents, 2) that registers of births and deaths be kept by all parish priests, 3) that the accused in criminal cases be denied legal counsel and 4) that all confraternities be abolished. The main purpose of the act was to reform the judicial system. Thus the use of French in legal documents was to remove the need for retrials by eliminating from judgements all 'ambiguity, uncertainty and reason to demand an interpretation', the registration of births and deaths was to facilitate verification of the rights of parties to a lawsuit, and the denial of counsel was to 'shorten proceedings'.

Historians are sometimes inclined to assume the effectiveness of legislation. Villers-Cotterêts is a good example. Can we be so sure that it achieved all that it set out to do and throughout France? Much research needs to be done before this question can be answered. Evidence provided by Alain Croix in his work on the demography of Nantes and its region suggests that the edict was imperfectly applied. The registers of births kept by parish priests were not submitted, as the new law required, to the clerk of the nearest *bailliage*. Only in Nantes itself were they signed by a notary. As for the date and time of birth, they went unrecorded. In short, the ordinance was applied only as far as it endorsed existing routine. As for the use of French in legal documents, the evidence points to a less than comprehensive response to the legislation. In both urban and rural parishes the use of Latin actually increased in the first half of the sixteenth century, perhaps reflecting an improvement in clerical education. French took precedence in urban parishes after 1550, but Latin survived in rural ones till the early seventeenth century. One cannot assume that the ordinance led to the immediate adoption of French in legal records throughout France.

It seems to have been even less effective in respect of the abolition of confraternities. These were associations of masters, apprentices and journeymen formed principally for religious or charitable purposes, which incurred the displeasure of the state by becoming the focus for political and religious unrest. Almost certainly the decision to ban confraternities was prompted by a strike of journeyman printers in Lyon in April 1539, which had caused the local *sénéchal* to ban all gatherings of more than five journeymen. But confraternities generally survived. In Paris the cloth-workers' confraternity was reprieved in April 1541 and other trades subsequently got similar concessions. In 1561 confraternities were reminded by the crown that their funds were to be used only for charitable and religious purposes, a clear indication of their survival.

Francis I and the Parlement of Rouen, 1540

Francis I claimed absolute sovereignty over all the parlements: their role, he affirmed, was to administer justice, not to question his decisions. But members of the provincial parlements saw themselves not only as the highest judges under the king, but as the defenders of local rights and privileges. They opposed the king's creation of offices and his imposition of extraordinary taxes, and were often more successful in their opposition than the Parlement of Paris because their remoteness from the centre of government caused delays in the sending of *lettres de jussion* and made the holding of *lits de justice* difficult, if not impossible. Yet the king could make life difficult for a provincial parlement if he set his mind to it, as Rouen discovered in 1540.

The Rouen magistrates had an unsavoury reputation. It was said that they were dissolutely dressed, arrived late in court (sometimes suffering from hangovers), spent too much time playing tennis or games of chance, frequented bawdy-houses, took bribes and allowed sexual attraction to affect their judgements. Having set up the parlement in Rouen, Francis was all the more aggrieved by its reputation. But no action was taken against the magistrates until August 1540 when they registered the Ordinance of Villers-Cotterêts, omitting sixteen of its clauses. In August the king made threatening noises. The magistrates offered excuses, but were sharply rebuked by Poyet. They then registered the ordinance in its entirety, but Francis was not placated. On 10 September he closed the parlement till further notice, cancelling several of its recent decrees.

There was, however, too much crime in Normandy to allow a complete suspension of royal justice, so some of the Rouen magistrates were allowed to continue judging criminal cases in the town, and others to hold *Grands Jours* at Bayeux. *Grands Jours* were commissions of *parlementaires* sent out from time to time to various parts of the kingdom to buttress the administration of justice and relieve parlements of their heavy workload.

The two commissions enabled the Rouen magistrates to redeem themselves. In January 1541, Francis allowed the Parlement of Rouen to resume its functions, albeit with the exclusion of nine members. But he made it clear that the magistrates were expected to work diligently and equitably, and also to obey royal ordinances.

The return to war, 1542-4

The failure of Montmorency's foreign policy and his consequent fall from power revived the fortunes of the war party at the French court. Publicly, Francis continued to speak of his friendship with Charles V; privately, he boasted of his preparations for a new war with the emperor. In May he sought an alliance with the Schmalkaldic League, but its leaders were too suspicious of his motives to respond positively to his advances. He was more successful in the Levant, where his ambassador managed to restore the sultan's confidence which had been rudely shaken by the emperor's recent visit to France.

Charles V, in the meantime, launched an attack on the Barbary corsairs of north Africa who had been preying on Spanish shipping in the Mediterranean, but his campaign soon met with disaster. After his fleet had been battered in a storm, he called off the siege of Algiers and, in November, returned to Spain, leaving behind his horses and guns. Meanwhile, two French diplomats were murdered by imperial troops as they travelled through north Italy on their way to Constantinople.

On 12 July 1542, Francis declared war on Charles. In a widely publicized proclamation, he listed the injuries he had suffered at the emperor's hands. The murder of his two envoys was described as 'an injury so great, so detestable and so strange to those who bear the title and quality of prince that it cannot be in any way forgiven, suffered or endured'. Having thrown down the gauntlet, Francis launched an offensive on two fronts: in the north an army officially led by the duc d'Orléans conquered Luxemburg, while in the south a larger army under the Dauphin and Anne-bault laid siege to Perpignan. But the offensive soon ran out of steam. The siege of Perpignan was called off after an assault on the town had been repulsed, while Luxemburg was recaptured by the imperialists. With the approach of winter Francis sent his army to reinforce the hard-pressed French garrisons in Piedmont, while he himself put down a revolt at La Rochelle.

The *gabelle* revolt, 1542

On 1 June 1541, Francis I introduced a new tax on salt (see above, p. 19), reorganized its levy, and prescribed severe penalties for fraud and smuggling. In effect, he abolished the system of *greniers* in the *pays de grandes gabelles*, shifting the apparatus of state control to the area of production. Henceforth the west of France would have to pay the same amount of tax as the *pays de grandes gabelles* whereas in the past it had paid less. In April 1542 the tax was reduced in amount, but extended to salt for export and fish curing, which had been previously exempt. The purpose of the legislation was to simplify the *gabelle* and improve its yield, but it was bitterly opposed by the people of the salt marshes along the Atlantic coast who felt that their privileges were under attack. In September large numbers were reported to have taken up arms and resisted the royal commissioners who had been sent to enforce the legislation. The feudal levy was mobilized, but the rebels, knowing that the king was engaged on several fronts at once, stepped up their agitation. At the same time trouble erupted in La Rochelle after the king had imposed a mayor on the citizens and reduced the number of aldermen. A riot between royal troops and the citizens caused the mayor to impose a curfew and disarm the inhabitants.

On 30 December, Francis came to La Rochelle and two days later sat in judgement on the rebels. Offering no excuses for the salters, a barrister expressed their remorse and asked the king to pardon them. The lieutenant of La Rochelle did likewise on behalf of the Rochellois. Francis, in his reply, stressed the seriousness of the rebellion at a time when he was busy defending the kingdom against the foreign aggressor. The rebels, he said, deserved to lose their lives and property, but he could not refuse to pardon those who were truly contrite; nor did he wish to treat them as harshly as the people of Ghent had been treated by Charles V. He therefore pardoned them, and La Rochelle rejoiced. The church bells rang out, bonfires were lit everywhere and the castle's guns thundered. 'I believe that I have won your hearts,' the king declared as he took his leave of the citizens, 'and I assure you, *foi de gentilhomme*, that you will have mine.'

Magnanimity was Francis's only practical option for, as he was still engaged in a foreign war, he would have been unwise to create bitterness in a part of France so vulnerable to English intervention. What is more, his magnanimity was not unconditional. The owners of the salt marshes of Guyenne and Saintonge were ordered to deliver large quantities of salt to the royal *grenier* at Rouen, which doubtless enabled the king to pay off some of his creditors in salt. Nor did he drop his plans for the *gabelle*. Although the ordinance of 1542 was revoked, the idea of a unified salt tax was not abandoned. In 1544 two ordinances extended the system of royal warehouses to the whole kingdom except four provinces, and in March 1546 the government decided to farm out the *gabelle* for ten years. By July 1548 it had become so oppressive that another revolt broke out in Angoumois and Saintonge, which had to be crushed by Henry II.

The growth of faction

Although Francis I continued to impose his authority in the 1540s, despite his failing health, divisions began to appear among his courtiers. A powerful stimulus to faction was the rivalry of his two sons, the Dauphin Henri and Charles duc d'Orléans. This had begun in 1536 after the death of Francis's eldest son François, when Charles had become the king's favourite. The rift widened in 1541 as a result of Montmorency's fall. Henri stayed loyal to the constable during his period of disgrace, whereas Charles became the darling of the duchesse d'Etampes. Each prince became the focus of a group of courtiers: while Montmorency's friends gathered round Henri, the constable's enemies, including Chabot, Marguerite de Navarre and Madame d'Etampes rallied to Charles. Following the outbreak of war in 1542, the rivalry of the brothers was exacerbated by their military performance: Charles gained laurels by conquering Luxemburg, while Henri suffered humiliation by retreating from Perpignan.

In March 1541, after Montmorency's fall, Philippe Chabot was restored to his offices; a year later he was cleared of the charge of *lèse-majesté*. An inevitable consequence of his rehabilitation was the fall of Chancellor Poyet. He was arrested on 2 August 1542 and sent to the Bastille. On 10 October, Chabot collapsed as he was talking to the king. He died on 1 June 1543 and was given a magnificent funeral by Francis. Poyet's fall and Chabot's death cleared the way for the ascendancy of two younger members of the king's council: Claude d'Annebault and Cardinal François de Tournon. Both had been prominent in the administration since the 1530s, but it was only after 1542 that they virtually ran it under the king. As the Venetian ambassador Cavalli reported in 1546, Francis entrusted all affairs of state to Annebault and Tournon, yet he insisted on being consulted about all matters of importance. Annebault, who became Admiral of France in February 1544, was the senior man. Though subordinate to the admiral, Tournon's contribution to government was distinctive and important. He was the financial expert, and one of his main tasks after becoming lieutenant-general in the Lyonnais was to secure funds for the war.

The Anglo-imperial alliance, 1543

In February 1543, Henry VIII made a secret alliance with the emperor which provided for a joint invasion of France within two years. Early in May, the allies sent an ultimatum threatening Francis with war unless he accepted impossible conditions within three weeks. On 22 June, as the deadline expired, they declared war. Soon afterwards an English army under Sir John Wallop invaded the Boulonnais. Meanwhile, as the emperor attacked France's ally, William duke of Cleves, Francis launched an offensive along the borders of Artois and Hainault. The duc de Vendôme revictualled Thérouanne and captured Lillers; in June, Annebault captured Landrecies. But Francis waited at Reims instead of hurrying to assist the duke of Cleves, who capitulated three days before the French recaptured Luxemburg. By so doing the duke destroyed the *raison d'être* of his marriage to Jeanne d'Albret. It was annulled by the pope in April 1545 and William remarried the emperor's niece. Francis was urged to withdraw from Luxemburg, but refused and celebrated Michaelmas there. He then marched to the relief of Landrecies, which was being besieged by Charles, and relieved the garrison, an event which caused much rejoicing in France. As the emperor retreated, he tried to engage Francis in battle, but on 4 November the king slipped away quietly and soon afterwards put his army into winter quarters. Charles captured Cambrai; meanwhile, Wallop's army returned to Calais.

The Turkish occupation of Toulon, 1543–4

Unusual events were in the meantime taking place in the Mediterranean. In April the sultan informed Francis that he was placing Barbarossa's fleet at his disposal for the coming season. The fleet, including 110 galleys, left the Dardanelles with the French ambassador on board and, after raiding the coasts of Sicily and Italy, appeared off Marseille in July. It was warmly welcomed by François de Bourbon, comte d'Enghien, who had attempted a surprise attack on Nice only to be rebuffed by Doria. On 6 August the combined French and Turkish fleets launched a new attack on Nice, which surrendered on the 22nd. The sight of Christian fighting Christian with the help of the Infidel was bad enough, but there was worse in store. On 6 September, Barbarossa threatened to leave unless Francis gave him the means of refitting his fleet. Rather than lose his naval support, the king placed the port of Toulon at his ally's disposal. The inhabitants except 'heads of households' were ordered to leave with their belongings on pain of death; by way of compensation they were exempted from the *taille* for ten years. Toulon thus became a Turkish colony for eight months, each of Barbarossa's captains being given a house for himself, his servants and slaves. Turks who could not be accommodated in the town were allowed to pitch tents outside. Neighbouring villages provided them with food. The transformation of a Christian town into a Muslim one, complete with mosque and slave market, caused amazement in the rest of Christendom.

On the surface Franco-Turkish relations seemed excellent, but Francis did not trust Barbarossa. He also became embarrassed by the Turkish presence on French soil, which brought him universal opprobrium and elicited many complaints from his Provençal subjects. He was, therefore, much relieved when Barbarossa left Toulon on 23 May 1544. Before departing, however, the Turkish admiral demanded the release of all Turkish and Barbary corsairs serving on French ships. He also revictualled his fleet by pillaging five French vessels in Toulon harbour.

The Anglo-imperial invasion, 1544

On 31 December 1543, Henry VIII and Charles V signed a treaty in which they agreed to invade France in person before 20 June. Henry was to invade Picardy and Charles, Champagne; each army, consisting of 35,000 foot and 7000 horse, was then to march on Paris. However, before the treaty could be given effect, Henry had to safeguard his rear from a possible Scottish attack and Charles had to win the support, military and financial, of the German princes assembled at the Diet of Speyer. Meanwhile, in Piedmont, the French under the comte d'Enghien won a notable victory at Ceresole, but they failed to follow it up.

In May 1544 two imperial armies were poised to invade northern France. The first, under Ferrante Gonzaga, viceroy of Sicily, lay north of Luxemburg; the second, under the emperor himself, waited in the Palatinate. On 25 May, Gonzaga captured Luxemburg and, advancing rapidly southward, took Commercy and Ligny. On 8 July he laid siege to Saint-Dizier where he was soon joined by Charles. Henry VIII, meanwhile, sent a huge army to Calais under the dukes of Norfolk and Suffolk. After invading Picardy, it divided into two parts, Norfolk besieging Montreuil, and Suffolk, Boulogne. On 14 July, Henry himself took charge of operations at Boulogne. The imperialists complained that Henry, by tarrying in Picardy, was breaking his agreement with them; he was supposed to march on Paris. Henry explained that he needed to safeguard his supply lines, but this was an excuse: he was only interested in seizing a piece of French soil near Calais, and was not sorry to see Charles held up at Saint-Dizier, since this gave him an excuse for deferring his own advance eastward.

Saint-Dizier had been well fortified by the Italian engineer Girolamo

Marini; it was also heroically defended by the comte de Sancerre and Captain Lalande. It held out until 17 August, by which time the campaigning season was far advanced. A few days later the emperor held a council of war. Some of his captains advised him to retreat, but, unwilling to lose face, he decided to penetrate further into France. He advanced to the neighbourhood of Châlons, but a French army prevented him crossing the Marne. Instead he captured various towns in Champagne. Observers were puzzled by Francis I's inactivity. 'Who would ever have thought', a Venetian exclaimed, 'that the French would allow the invaders free passage and let them devastate their country?'

Panic gripped the French capital as the enemy drew closer. On 1 September all the religious houses were ordered by the parlement to hold processions and masses for peace. Nine days later the presidents of the court called on the king at the Louvre. He assured them of his determination to defend Paris, yet he did almost nothing to check the imperial advance. When Charles V decided on 11 September to retreat, Francis did not pursue him. His strategy is understandable: Paris would have been exposed to an English attack if he had taken his army into Champagne.

From the start of the invasion Francis put out peace feelers, but Henry would not listen to his overtures until he had captured Boulogne, an objective which he achieved only on 13 September. Charles, on the other hand, had shot his bolt. He was desperately short of money and his main concern was to deal with Germany's troubled religious situation. Thus it was Charles, not Henry, who first responded positively to Francis's overtures. On 18 September the Peace of Crépy was signed between France and the Empire. It consisted of two agreements, one open, the other secret. The first laid down that Francis would help fight the Turks; it also restored the territorial status quo of 1538 and provided for a marriage between the duc d'Orléans and Charles's daughter Mary or his niece Anna. In the first case, he was to get the Netherlands and Franche-Comté as dowry; in the second, Milan. Charles was to decide on the bride within four months. Francis, for his part, was to give his son three duchies (Bourbon, Châtellerault and Angoulême); he also gave up his claims to Savoy and Piedmont, while the emperor did likewise in respect of Burgundy. In the second, secret, agreement Francis promised to help Charles reform the church, to further the meeting of a General Council and to bring back the German Protestants into the Catholic fold.

The peace got a mixed reception in France. Queen Eleanor, who had tried to avert a conflict between her husband and her brother, was delighted. She and the duc d'Orléans promptly went to Brussels to join Eleanor's sister, Mary of Hungary, in peace celebrations. But the Dauphin was far from pleased, for the peace robbed him of the chance to avenge his humiliation at Perpignan; it also advanced his brother's prospects. Charles d'Orléans seemed set to become duke of Milan and to acquire four French duchies as apanages. On 12 December 1544, Henri formally protested about the treaty. The parlement only registered it at the king's second request. Abroad too, it aroused mixed feelings: the pope was pleased, but Henry VIII felt that he had been betrayed by his ally. As for the sultan, he almost had the French ambassador impaled.

The Treaty of Crépy proved little more than a dead letter, for Charles d'Orléans died on 9 September 1545 following a brief and mysterious illness. His death, which left Francis heartbroken, effectively nullified the peace, removing the threat to the Dauphin's inheritance. Francis now drew closer to his second son, admitting him to his council. He also tried to give him a more significant role in government, but Henri preferred to stay in the wings until the stage could really be his.

The war with England, 1544–6

Peace talks with England held in the autumn of 1544 failed to make headway, as Henry VIII refused to hand back Boulogne. The French consequently decided to force his hand by a simultaneous attack on two fronts. While Francis assembled an army in Normandy and a fleet at Le Havre for a descent on southern England, the Scots prepared to invade from the north.

On 16 July 1545 the French fleet, commanded by Admiral d'Annebault, sailed out of Le Havre, and a few days later entered the Solent, as Henry VIII was dining on board his flagship *Great Harry*. An engagement ensued during which the English ship *Mary Rose* sank with the loss of 500 men, not as a result of French action but after a breeze had sprung up, driving sea water through her gun ports. On 21 July the French landed on the Isle of Wight and burned a few villages before they were driven back to their ships. A few days later they landed at Seaford, but again withdrew, this time to Dover. Annebault then crossed the strait and added his troops to the French camp outside Boulogne. On 15 August he came out again and met the English fleet. A brief skirmish took place near Beachy Head, but Annebault, instead of exploiting his numerical superiority, retired to Le Havre. Meanwhile, the Scots withdrew from the Border leaving the way clear for the earl of Hertford to penetrate the Lowlands.

By early September the war had reached stalemate and both sides looked to the German Protestant princes for help. An attempt by the Schmalkaldic League to mediate foundered on the mutual mistrust of the belligerents, who began to rearm, albeit without enthusiasm. On 6 May peace talks were resumed which culminated in the Treaty of Ardres (7 June 1546). France agreed to pay 2 million *écus* for the return of Boulogne. Henry VIII, meanwhile, was to retain the town and its county. France also agreed to

pay all the English pensions she owed under past treaties. England promised
not to attack the Scots without cause. The peace, which was received with
relief on both sides of the Channel, did not remove all mistrust. During the
winter of 1546–7 the French ambassador, Odet de Selve, reported military
preparations in England. He believed that they were aimed at the Scots,
but could not be sure that they were not against his own countrymen.

Fiscal expedients and reforms

The war of 1542–6 was the most expensive conflict of Francis's reign. Its
overall cost has been estimated at more than 30 million *livres*. The maximum
spent in 1544 was not much greater than in 1537, but it was the cumulative
cost over four years which proved crippling: it was twice as heavy as in
1536–8 and 50 per cent more than in 1521–5. The proportion spent on
the navy and fortifications was also greater: 15 per cent in 1542–6 as
against 6 per cent in 1536–8.

Expenditure on this scale necessitated a frantic search for money. The
taille rose to 4,446,000 *livres* between 1542 and 1547, but its yield continued to be eroded by corruption among local collectors. Indirect taxation
rose to 9 million *livres* in 1546. At the same time every known expedient
was pushed to the limits. Between 1542 and 1546 at least twenty clerical
tenths were levied by the crown. Towns, too, were made to contribute: in
1543 they had to pay the *solde des 50,000 hommes de pied*. Their fiscal
contribution between 1542 and 1546 helped to worsen the social crisis
caused by the grain famine of 1545.

In the 1540s, Francis I raised huge loans on the Lyon money market.
Such loans had been raised before, but only exceptionally: as from 1542
they were raised annually and renewed at each of Lyon's four annual fairs.
The amount of interest charged by the lenders was 16 per cent over
the year. Their confidence in the crown had evidently been restored: they
were even willing to defer repayments and were no longer interested in
short-term loans. Their changed attitude may have been due to a growth
of capital and a fall in profits from trade. In 1546, Francis owed them the
colossal sum of 6,860,844 *livres*. Even after making peace with England,
he continued to borrow from the Lyon bankers, for he needed to fill his
war-chests in preparation for the next conflict. According to Bodin, they
contained 500,000 *écus* 'and four times as much'. But why store so much
money bearing interest of 16 per cent? Part of the king's strategy was
undoubtedly to prevent Charles V from raising loans himself, yet Francis
could not hope to soak up all the available foreign capital. His policy
was also risky: it led to the *Grand Parti* under Henry II and the crown's
bankruptcy.

Financial pressures stemming from the war of 1542–6 led Francis to continue reforming his fiscal administration. Until 1542 the old royal demesne was divided into four large fiscal districts or *généralités* (Languedoïl, Normandy, Languedoc and Outre-Seine-et-Yonne). In addition there were four *recettes-générales* (Guyenne, Dauphiné, Provence and Burgundy). Now, under the Edict of Cognac (7 December 1542), the old *généralités* were sub-divided into twelve smaller districts. The sixteen new ones were called *recettes-générales* and each was under a *receveur-général*, who had powers to collect all regular revenues, including those from the demesne. This amounted to the fusion of the old 'ordinary' and 'extraordinary' revenues. Since a special treasurer for domainial revenues was no longer required, the post of *Changeur du Trésor* disappeared.

The fiscal reforms of Francis I have been presented as the fulfilment in three stages of a premeditated campaign to replace the system handed down by Charles VII with one that served the crown's needs more effectively. But the latest authority on the subject, Philippe Hamon, does not believe in the existence of a master plan. In his judgement, Francis and his advisers responded to each situation as it arose and were sometimes forced to backtrack. However, the end result of their reforms was probably a more effective fiscal system, albeit one that was still far from perfect.

The fight against heresy

The 1540s were marked by an intensification of the fight against heresy in France. On 1 July 1542 every Parisian was ordered to hand over to the parlement within twenty-four hours Calvin's *Institutes* and any other book which had been banned by the court. Soon the search for banned books began to yield results. On 13 January 1544, the *Institutes* and fourteen works published by Etienne Dolet were burnt outside Notre-Dame. Other measures were taken to control book production. Every master printer had to have his own mark and was made personally responsible for the conduct of his journeymen. At the same time, the Paris Faculty of Theology compiled an Index of forbidden books. When published in 1543 it included 65 titles, including works by Calvin, Luther, Melanchthon, Dolet and Marot. In spite of the complaints of many booksellers, the Index was enlarged in 1545 and 1546. Between 1541 and 1544 six Parisian booksellers or printers were tried: one was tortured and two were burnt at the stake. In the provinces, too, the book trade was persecuted. The most vulnerable were the *colporteurs* or book-pedlars who, if caught, were burnt with their wares.

Heresy was not confined to the book trade: in the thirties and forties it made deeper inroads into French society. It was particularly rife among the lower clergy, the urban bourgeoisie and the proletariat. The peasantry usually stood 'on the sidelines of religious division'. But, as yet, heresy could take a multiplicity of forms; the advent of Calvinism did not immediately impose uniformity or coherence.

The last seven years of Francis's reign saw a sharp rise in the number of heresy prosecutions by the Parlement of Paris. A purge of the capital's religious houses was undertaken and the parlement's prisons began to fill up. A new round of public burnings took place. Among the martyrs was Etienne Dolet, the printer-publisher, who was burned on the Place Maubert as a relapsed heretic on 3 August 1546. Outside Paris, yet within the parlement's area of jurisdiction, bishops had to delegate their judicial powers in heresy cases to special commissioners drawn from the parlement's ranks. Among the most active was Nicole Sanguin, who arrested 62 people at Meaux in September 1546. Of these fourteen were tortured and burned, four banished and the rest punished in various ways. The punishment of the Meaux heretics became one of the most famous events in Protestant martyrology – thousands of people flocked to watch the spectacle, which lasted two days. The parlement's commissioners were also very active in the Loire valley and along the Atlantic coast. Elsewhere the actions of the parlements were uneven. In Normandy it was so lethargic that the king suspended the parlement in 1540, as we have seen. In Toulouse, on the other hand, the parlement waged a fierce campaign against dissenters. In Provence it was even more militant: more than sixty people were arrested and sentenced in fifteen months. But judicial enquiries were slow and tentative; it was fairly easy for a dissenter to escape notice by going into hiding or simply keeping his mouth shut. Magistrates looked for tangible offences rather than ideas; they tended to use torture only if a suspect refused to answer questions. Frequent clashes over jurisdiction between the secular and ecclesiastical courts resulted in sentences being revised or quashed. Many heretics were given a light sentence, like a public penance or a fine. More serious offenders were flogged; only the incorrigible were banished or burnt. Before 1550 burnings were relatively few. In 1543 the Parlement of Paris judged 43 cases of heresy, yet not one resulted in an execution. Neither the secular nor the ecclesiastical courts wanted to create martyrs.

Given these facts and others, such as the immunity from prosecution enjoyed by foreigners in France and the reluctance of the more liberal prelates to apply the law harshly, it is not surprising that heresy continued to thrive. So-called 'Lutherans' continued to be reported from almost every part of the kingdom. In May 1542 the president of the Parlement of Rouen claimed that the church had never been in so much danger since the days of the Arian heresy. Now and again an incident made the king aware of the peril. In 1542, for example, he questioned François Landry, *curé* of Sainte-Croix-de-la-Cité, whose heretical sermons had caused public disturbances. The preacher was so terrified as to be reduced to complete silence, but others continued to preach, provoking more trouble. In August 1542, Francis I admitted that heresy was growing in France despite the repressive measures. He urged the sovereign courts and the ecclesiastical authorities to redouble their efforts to discover 'the secret practices of the sectarians'. In July 1543 he decided that the power of search and arrest would henceforth be shared by the secular and ecclesiastical courts. Meanwhile, the Faculty of Theology produced clear doctrinal guidelines to assist the authorities. All the university's doctors and bachelors were ordered to subscribe to twenty-five articles reaffirming Catholic dogma, worship and organization. Francis ordered their publication throughout the kingdom; anyone teaching a different doctrine was to be prosecuted.

The massacre of the Vaudois, 1545

In May 1540, Francis I empowered the Parlement of Aix to prosecute the Vaudois or Waldenses of Provence, a religious sect whose origins went back to the twelfth-century Poor Men of Lyon. They had since spread to various parts of central and southern Europe, notably Piedmont and Provence. The Vaudois of Provence in the early sixteenth century were mostly peasants who lived in villages and small towns spread out along the valley of the Durance. Their main centres were Mérindol in Provence and Cabrières in the papal enclave of Comtat-Venaissin. The Vaudois believed that spiritual probity was essential to the administration of the sacraments. They rejected the doctrine of purgatory, oath-swearing, the cult of the Virgin and saints, religious images and many forms of prayer. Believing that the whole of nature was sacred, they did not think that worship had to be centred in a church. Outwardly, however, the Vaudois were not easily distinguished from their Catholic neighbours: they attended the local parish church, paid tithes, confessed to the local priest and took communion from him. It was only at night and in the privacy of their homes that they assumed a distinctive religious identity with the help of itinerant preachers, called *barbes*.

Of peasant stock, like their flocks, the *barbes* had learnt to read and write and earned their living by plying some peripatetic trade. They were celibate and tried to lead apostolic lives. Their aim was not to seek converts, but to confirm existing Vaudois in their faith by preaching to them on biblical texts and taking their confessions. Each year the *barbes* would meet in a secluded Alpine valley to report on their activities and to examine the current state of the Vaudois community. They would bring offerings they had received, parts of which were given to the poor. Intermittent persecution of the Vaudois had taken place since the fourteenth century, but in France it had been stopped by Louis XII. It was resumed, unofficially at first, under Francis I. About 1528, Jean de Roma, the Dominican inquisitor of the faith, had toured Vaudois villages extorting confessions under torture. In 1532 an important meeting of *barbes* took place at Chanforan in Piedmont, its main purpose to consider relations between the Vaudois and the Protestant Reformation. Among those present was Guillaume Farel, Calvin's closest collaborator, and it was almost certainly under his influence that the *barbes* decided to join the Calvinist Reformation. By so doing they renounced all the distinctive tenets of their movement, but the adoption of Calvinism by the Vaudois rank and file did not happen overnight: some thirty years elapsed before their day-to-day lives were affected. Another major decision taken at Chanforan was to commission a new Bible in French based on Greek and Hebrew sources, not on the Latin Vulgate. The translation by Pierre Robert, alias Olivétan, was published in Neuchâtel in June 1535.

On 18 November 1540 nineteen Vaudois who had failed to obey a summons from the Parlement of Aix were sentenced to death by burning. Their families were to be arrested or banished from the kingdom, their property confiscated and their village destroyed. In December, Francis ordered the decree (*arrêt de Mérindol*) to be carried out, but soon afterwards he received a report from Guillaume du Bellay, showing the Vaudois to be hard-working, God-fearing and loyal sujects. The king accordingly pardoned them in February 1541, provided they abjured within three months, but they refused to do so unless they could be shown to be in error by reference to Scripture. In April they begged the parlement to allow them to live in peace. Once again they were invited to abjure, but only one turned up with a demand for an unconditional pardon. The parlement complained to the king, who ordered Grignan, the provincial governor, to wipe them out. But an appeal from the German Protestants led to another stay of execution. In March the parlement again tried to persuade the people of Mérindol to abjure, but in vain. Soon afterwards the bishop of Cavaillon led an armed force against the Vaudois of Cabrières, thereby provoking an intervention in their favour by the people of Mérindol. Francis accordingly revived the *arrêt de Mérindol*, but the Vaudois accused their persecutors of being more interested in seizing their goods than in defending the faith. Suspending the *arrêt* again, Francis ordered an enquiry.

In December 1543, Jean Maynier, baron d'Oppède, was appointed First President of the Parlement of Aix. He hated the Vaudois, not only for religious reasons but also because he had long coveted some of their lands. During the winter of 1544–5 alarming reports of Vaudois activities, deliberately coloured by d'Oppède to suggest sedition, began to reach the king. At the same time the papacy, concerned by the presence of heretics in the Comtat-Venaissin, pressed him to punish the Vaudois. On 31 January 1545 he ordered the *arrêt de Mérindol* to be given effect. In Grignan's absence, responsibility for executing it fell on d'Oppède, who thus assumed the supreme legislative and executive functions in Provence. He enlisted the services of the *vieilles bandes de Piémont*, veterans of the Italian Wars under the command of Antoine Escalin, baron de La Garde, alias Captain Polin, who were about to embark at Marseille as an expeditionary force against England. D'Oppède was also able to count on papal troops from the Comtat-Venaissin.

On 11 April, d'Oppède and de La Garde held a council of war and a week later they unleashed operations against the Vaudois. As their troops converged on Mérindol, the inhabitants fled, whereupon the troops set fire to the houses and slaughtered stragglers. They then sacked Cabrières, killing all the inhabitants except twelve who were taken to Avignon to serve as 'an example'. Four were executed. Elsewhere, too, atrocities were committed. At Murs, twenty-five women and children were suffocated in a cave after troops had set fire to the entrance. The massacre was followed by a wave of looting by peasants from other parts of Provence driven by greed rather than religious zeal, for the province was less prosperous than it had been at the time of the original Vaudois immigration. There were too many mouths to feed for the amount of land under cultivation. Poverty was increasing and towns were groaning under the weight of taxation.

The number of victims of the massacre is not known precisely. A fairly reliable estimate put the number of dead at 2700 and of survivors sent to the galleys at 600. A number of Vaudois managed to escape. Several sought refuge in Geneva, and many eventually returned to Provence. Some even recovered their property, albeit after long delays, but the legacy of the massacre was not easily erased. At Lourmarin, eighteen months afterwards, commissioners found only destruction and despair.

The massacre, whatever its scale, was a monstrous crime, particularly as the victims had never been tried. Yet Francis I was thanked by the papal nuncio for so promptly punishing the heretics. On 18 August the king congratulated d'Oppède for his efficient enforcement of the law and in 1546 allowed him to become a papal count. Protestants abroad were appalled by the massacre. The council of Strassburg protested to the king, only to be sharply rebuked. He had never meddled with their subjects, he said, and was surprised that they should meddle with his.

Under Henry II, in 1549, d'Oppède and his accomplices were brought to justice following a local complaint. A special court, set up at Melun, was dissolved almost at once and the case transferred to the Parlement of Paris. In what soon became a *cause célèbre*, d'Oppède claimed that he had only carried out the king's orders and denied responsibility for the massacre at Cabrières. In October 1551, he and all the accused, save one, were acquitted. Seven years later Polin became governor of Marseille, while D'Oppède was reinstated as First President of the Parlement of Aix and allowed to keep his papal titles. In the words of Jean Crespin, the Protestant martyrologist: 'One might have expected some important judgements after such lengthy pleadings; instead, the mountain produced a mere puff of smoke.'

The Absolutism of Francis I

Was Francis I an 'absolute monarch'? The question has been much debated by historians. According to Pagès (1946), 'Francis I and Henry II were as powerful as any other kings of France; it was at the beginning of the sixteenth century that the absolute monarchy triumphed.' For Doucet (1948), it was under Francis that 'a new system of government' was set up which, 'starting from the traditional and still feudal monarchy of Louis XII, foreshadowed the absolute and centralized monarchy of the following centuries'. On the other hand, Russell Major has argued that 'French Renaissance monarchy' was 'popular and consultative'. In his opinion, it stressed legitimacy on account of its 'feudal-dynastic structure' and tolerated decentralization because of limitations on its power. Ultimately it rested on popular support rather than military power and encouraged the growth of representative institutions.

The theory of absolutism existed, at least in theory, under Francis. Guillaume Budé in *L'Institution du prince* (1518), which he dedicated to the king, expressed his belief in absolute monarchy. He dismissed ordinary folk as politically inept and would only allow the nobility privileges, not a share of authority. Precisely because he believed the king to be all-powerful, Budé stressed the importance of his education. A knowledge of history was, in his opinion, essential to political success, and he tried to point Francis in the right direction by means of stories taken from Scripture and ancient histories. He advised him also to listen to wise counsellors, to respect his predecessors' ordinances, to safeguard his subjects' freedom and prosperity and to abstain from war, but he admitted that the prince was free to reject this advice. The only limit on his power was the judgement of posterity.

Budé's acceptance of royal absolutism was characteristic of the strongly royalist ideology which can be traced back to the reign of Louis XII, when

Jean Ferrault wrote his *Twenty Special Privileges of the Most Christian King*. Under Francis the monarchy was exalted by jurists, like Barthélemy Chasseneuz and Charles de Grassaille. The former in his *Catalogus Gloriae mundi* (1529) lists 208 attributes of majesty culled from the *Corpus juris* and various medieval sources. The flavour of Grassaille's *Regalium Franciae libri duo* (1538) is well conveyed by its chapter headings which describe the king of France as 'more glorious than any other king', 'a second sun on earth' and 'like a corporeal god'.

The most systematic champion of royal supremacy was Charles du Moulin, whose *Commentaries on the Customs of Paris* began to appear in 1539. In his opinion, vassalage, including the notion of personal service, was a Frankish invention of the sixth century and a usurpation of the absolute *imperium* formerly exercised by the French monarchy. A fief, according to du Moulin, was simply a form of land-holding; it implied no rights of personal service from the vassal. No legalized form of personal subjection could be owed by anyone to the king, for he alone was 'the source of all justice, holding all jurisdictions and enjoying full *Imperium*'. Since he had complete control over all temporal lords, secular or ecclesiastical, all were equally subject to his authority in the exercise of their jurisdictions and lordships. Du Moulin's critique of feudal relationships resulted in a new absolutist orthodoxy. Legists began to argue that the king's judicial authority could not be lawfully challenged by the parlement.

Yet historians have sometimes exaggerated the theoretical underpinning of absolutism under Francis I. Du Moulin may have anticipated Bodin in his view of sovereignty as 'indivisible', but in several respects his thinking was conservative. It rested on the distinction between the prince's two bodies: the 'intellectual' and the 'physical'. While sovereignty was uniquely vested in the 'intellectual' prince, its exercise could not be restricted to the 'physical' prince. In this respect, Du Moulin fell into line with traditional thinking of the *parlementaires*. While strongly absolutist in their rejection of feudal limitations on the king's authority, they also believed that, in exercising it, he should take them into partnership. Another thinker whose support for absolutism has been distorted is Pierre Rebuffi, an eminent canon lawyer who taught in Paris in 1533. In respect of secular government his standpoint was constitutionalist. While accepting the catalogue of royal prerogatives put out by jurists, he qualifies them in various ways. Thus again and again he insists that the king must take counsel. 'It is more just for the prince', he writes, 'to follow the advice of all his friends than for them all to follow the will of one sole prince'. Such advice, Rebuffi thinks, should be taken above all from the Parlement of Paris, whom he casts in the role of intermediary between God, monarch and people at large. Because 'the king is in duty bound to preserve the well-being of the commonwealth', he writes, 'when a royal statute touches the people, it should require the consent not of all, but of the people's principal members'. Rebuffi has in mind here the three estates and, failing them, the Parlement.

The realities of power

From the start of his reign Francis showed a strongly authoritarian disposition. He did not apparently consider himself bound by tradition or by existing ordinances, institutions and methods of government and repeatedly rejected the parallel commonly drawn between the parlement and the Roman senate. Chancellor Duprat denied that the parlement had any right to oppose the king's wishes. 'We owe obedience to the king,' he declared, 'and it is not for us to question his commands.' All authority, he claimed, emanated from the king; otherwise the kingdom would be an aristocracy, not a monarchy. Policy was decided by the king alone, though he normally consulted his council. Thus the Concordat of Bologna was imposed on the French people regardless of the parlement's bitter opposition. Nor was popular opinion tested before Francis decided in May 1526 to break the Peace of Madrid.

On a practical level the effectiveness of royal absolutism in early sixteenth-century France may be measured by the amount of fiscal control exercised by the king. Foreign observers imagined that Francis could tax his subjects at will. He certainly had more control over their purses than any fellow monarch in western Europe: ever since the fifteenth century the *taille* had been raised each year without the consent of the people's representatives. The only national representative body in France, the Estates-General, never met during Francis's reign. Meanwhile, the *taille* rose from about 2.4 million *livres* in 1515 to 4.6 million in 1544–5.

The *taille*, however, was inadequate to meet the king's needs, particularly in wartime, so he was forced to use expedients including the sale of offices and crown lands. Both were strongly opposed by the parlements. The sale of crown lands breached a 'fundamental law' which the parlement was committed to defend. By selling off parts of his patrimony, the king inevitably reduced his 'ordinary' revenue, and was likely to recoup his loss by increasing taxation. The parlement pointed to the adverse effect this would have on the lives of the king's 'poor subjects', but he was quite unmoved. In the end, his alienations of crown land were always registered by the parlement, albeit under protest.

The sale or venality of offices was also much used by Francis. In 1546 the Venetian ambassador noted: 'Offices are infinite in number and increase daily ... half of which would suffice.' Existing office-holders naturally viewed with concern the multiplication of offices, which undermined their own status and income. They tried to curb the practice and sometimes obtained the suppression of a new office by buying it up themselves. The parlement often resisted the creation of offices by delaying the registration of the edicts of creation or the admission of royal nominees. Yet the king usually got his way.

The towns of France were a target of fiscal exploitation. The infantry tax (*solde des 50,000 hommes de pied*) introduced in 1543 was not wholly new, except that it was now levied annually even in peacetime. Its impact on certain towns was far-reaching. At Lyon, the *solde* was presented as a forced loan rather than a tax, which the king undertook to repay over three years. It was levied by the municipal government (*Consulat*) on the chief inhabitants. They offered no resistance, as they had been promised reimbursement; but the king broke his word: in 1546 he still owed 33,000 *livres*. The *Consulat* was unable to call on the same lenders again when the crown renewed its demand in 1544 and after. Instead, it borrowed the money from Italian bankers and reimbursed itself by levying two taxes on certain goods entering the city. Such taxes were extremely unpopular, not only with the poor but also among the clergy, who complained that they were being taxed twice since they already paid tenths. Foreign merchants claimed that the taxes breached privileges which they had received from the crown: they threatened to leave Lyon and boycott its fairs. Eventually, the *Consulat* had to drop the indirect taxes and it was left in 1547 with a deficit of 107,000 *livres*.

In other towns, too, the *solde des 50,000 hommes de pied* caused problems. Paris repeatedly asked the king to reduce its contribution, but in vain. In 1546 the municipal government explained that the Parisians, much as they wished to assist the king, could not do so because of the heavy burdens they had been asked to bear in the past. They were now utterly wretched, crushed by taxes and debts and grappling with plague: they implored the king to show them pity and treat them as part of his family. In March 1547 he was reminded of past privileges enjoyed by Paris. 'The capital of Christendom', it was claimed, 'had never been subject to taxation and once enjoyed a reputation for freedom equalling, perhaps surpassing, that of Rome or any other city, but it had now fallen into extreme poverty.' Francis never replied.

Representative assemblies

Provincial estates played an important role in Renaissance France, yet the frequency of their meetings was determined by the fiscal needs of the crown. In theory, the voting of a subsidy was conditional: the king's commissioners were supposed to attend to the estates' grievances before supply was granted, but the deputies knew that important decisions would be taken, not by the commissioners themselves, but by the king and his council long after the granting of supply. In 1538, Francis ordered his commissioners at the estates of Albi not to reply to their demands until supply had been granted. After protesting, the estates sent their *doléances* directly to the king, by-passing the commissioners. In September 1541 the estates of Montpellier were forbidden to send a deputy to the king until they had agreed to a subsidy.

It has been suggested that Francis, far from being absolute, treated the Norman estates 'in the same good-natured way as had his predecessors'. True, he instructed his commissioners to ask them to grant a subsidy of their own free will. But what did this mean? The estates could not refuse the *taille* or even ask for a reduction. They could only resist supplementary taxes or *crues*, usually in vain. In 1516 a delegate wanted a subsidy to be conditional on the king's promise to abolish all 'innovations' created since the start of his reign. These remained, however, and each year the estates voted ever larger *crues*. In Languedoc, the situation was comparable: the estates sometimes delayed a *crue*, but were never able to refuse it completely or to reduce the amount. Their compliance was a foregone conclusion, so that the king often assigned funds on a *crue* still to be voted by the estates.

In Dauphiné, an extension of the estates' administrative jurisdiction granted by Francis in 1537 did not lead to a revival of provincial autonomy. As Van Doren has shown, 'the weight of the war levies during the 1540s and 1550s deepened divisions among and within the communities in ways that prevented the Estates from consolidating an effective defense of provincial liberties.' The estates often complained of the king's fiscal expedients, but they seldom persuaded him to abandon them. In 1517, for example, Francis planned to extend the salt tax to the whole of Normandy. The spokesman for the estates was prosecuted when they protested. Francis dropped the proposal, but only for a time: in June 1546 the salt tax was restored. It also caused trouble in Languedoc, where the estates claimed that they had been exempted in 1488. The king acknowledged their privilege, yet in 1537 the *crue* on salt became permanent. Its purpose was allegedly to fund the wages of the sovereign courts, but, as the estates pointed out, the *octroi* already existed for this purpose. Francis chose to ignore them.

The creation of offices frequently caused trouble between the king and the estates. In 1543 he created a *Chambre des comptes* in Rouen. The members were to buy their offices and be paid their wages out of a local tax on goods. Following a petition from the people of Rouen, Francis called the estates and offered to drop the new court in exchange for a composition of 220,000 *livres*, more than twice as much as he would have got from the sale of the offices concerned. In the end, the estates paid 246,875l. In Languedoc, too, the estates found that the only way of getting harmful offices abolished was to buy them up. However, they could not be sure that they would not reappear after a time.

The king could raise a new tax in the *pays d'états* without the prior consent of the people's representatives. In Languedoc, the towns, clergy and nobility were all taxed regardless of the estates. Most towns were taxed like the countryside: only Carcassonne was totally exempt, and Toulouse and Narbonne partially so. Francis none the less imposed the infantry tax on them. When the estates claimed exemption, he demanded a composition for the privilege. Toulouse, however, was asked for a subsidy. Again the estates protested, claiming that the town was not a *ville franche*. But Francis would not change his mind: 'Where there is a profit to be made in Languedoc', he said, 'the people of Toulouse are always there; but where there is an obligation, they declare themselves exempt.' The infantry tax became a heavy burden on the town. The church, too, was roughly handled by Francis. He levied a series of tenths without the consent of either the estates or the assembly of the French church. As for the nobles, they had to endure the feudal levy (*ban et arrière-ban*) sometimes four or five times a year and they remained under arms at their own expense for months. The estates asked for the length of feudal service to be restricted to forty days: in January 1544 it was fixed at three months within France and forty days abroad. Commoners owning noble fiefs had to compound for military service.

The burden of maintaining garrisons or troops passing through Languedoc was a standing grievance with the estates. In 1522, Francis promised to reimburse their expenditure on his army, but he broke his word: a year later he fixed a tariff for supplies purchased by his troops which was not enforced. The estates did obtain a reduction in the number of garrisons, but it rose again after Montmorency's fall from power in 1541. Attempts by the estates to ensure a fair distribution of the military burden proved unworkable.

Yet even if the king rode roughshod over his subjects' rights, the estates still had a significant part to play. For they did not simply defend local privileges; they also dealt with various administrative and economic matters about which they did not have to disagree with the crown. It was to their mutual advantage, for example, to ensure that royal officials carried out their duties competently and honestly. The estates also made useful suggestions about economic matters, such as trade. Their effectiveness, however, was in the main limited to matters of secondary importance; where the king's financial interest was at stake, they were virtually powerless.

Contemporary observers were loud in their condemnation of Francis I's authoritarian ways. Thus the future Philip II of Spain, writing to his father in 1547, stated that Francis ruled like a despot, following his whim rather than his reason, and that the French were willing to put up with anything. Francis seldom consulted his subjects. When Languedoc claimed exemption from the garrisoning of troops, he replied: 'this kingdom is one body and monarchy'. All his subjects, he explained, needed to be treated alike, since he loved them all equally; if some were exempt, the rest would have to shoulder a proportionately heavier burden. On another occasion Francis declared: 'In times of necessity all privileges cease, and not only privileges but common laws as well, for necessity knows no law.' The estates complained in 1522 that he was treating them 'as if they had never acquired the said privileges'. True, Francis did sometimes bargain with them, but only over ways of raising a sum of money, not over the sum itself. He did not mind suppressing offices as long as he received as much or more money from their suppression as from their sale. In non-fiscal matters he could be more flexible, but in the long term his policy undermined provincial autonomy. His philosophy was summed up by Chancellor Poyet in 1540: 'The king is not asking for advice as to whether or not they [his laws] are to be observed; no one has the right to interpret, adjust or diminish them.'

Yet if Francis was a strong ruler, he could not ignore the foundations of medieval privilege upon which his monarchy rested. His legislation was subject to ratification by the parlements, and in the *pays d'états* his taxation was subject, in theory at least, to the consent of the people's representatives. The enforcement of his laws also depended on the co-operation of the local authorities, which was not always forthcoming. The evidence of the *Grands Jours* of Bayeux shows that, even near Paris, law and order had largely broken down by 1540. However ineffective the provincial estates may have been in resisting the crown's fiscal demands, they nevertheless survived. This suggests that the king was less absolute in practice than in theory. The French crown remained vulnerable in the sixteenth century. Its recent advances, far from resolving the antagonism between the centralizing and decentralizing forces within the body politic, actually made it worse. In the absence of a national representative institution, like the English parliament, the French king had to cope with a multiplicity of local interests. Apart from the provincial estates, many towns retained substantial political and financial privileges. In spite of Francis's fiscal reforms, localism and particularism continued to make an impact on the revenue system. While some fiscal expedients increased royal dependence on financiers, others served to buttress provincialism. The sale of offices, for example, helped to reinforce local autonomy. They became the patrimony of well-to-do provincial families who used them to preserve their privileged status. Likewise, many nobles found opportunities to consolidate their position while serving in the provincial parlements.

The constraints on monarchy were not only institutional and legal but social. The nobles, through their ownership of land, domination of the peasantry and capacity to use force, were the main obstacle in the path of extending royal power. Their loyalty to the crown had to be secured by concessions, notably tax exemption. This was 'a permanent impediment to the mobilization of the kingdom's wealth' (D. Parker). The system of provincial governorships could be used either to extend royal power or to preserve noble interests. Being a patrimonial form of administration, it conferred on governors enormous powers of patronage which they might use against the crown. As captains in the *gendarmerie*, they could make or break the careers of the men who served in it. The *gendarmerie* has been aptly described as 'the Renaissance monarchy's compromise with the indigenous patron-client networks in the provinces'. Effective government depended on the crown's ability to manipulate personal and patrimonial ties.

Under Francis I's strong rule the limits on monarchy were generally contained. Except for the Constable of Bourbon, the high nobility stayed loyal to the crown and even aided its centralizing efforts. The clergy and the towns may have complained about fiscal burdens, but their obedience to the crown never wavered. The parlements and estates were also broadly submissive. And this situation held good until the accidental death of Henry II in 1559 deprived the ship of state of a firm hand on the tiller.

Much needed to happen before absolutism, however imperfect, could develop in France. The doctrine of resistance evolved by the Huguenots in the late sixteenth century, the upheaval of the Fronde and the challenge of Cartesianism, all prompted a hardening of the ideological and institutional fabric of monarchy. This was accompanied by a huge increase in the personnel of government. One has only to compare the number of office-holders in 1515 with that in 1665 to see the gulf that separated Francis's administration from that of Louis XIV: the total number of fiscal and judicial office-holders under Francis has been estimated at 5000 (that is, one per 3000 inhabitants, assuming a total population of 15 million). Louis XIV had eleven times as many to impose his will on 20 million subjects. It follows that Francis must have been less 'absolute' than Louis XIV. He could only point in the direction of the absolutism that developed under Richelieu and later. An 'absolutism' that is complete in theory yet imperfect in practice is best described as 'limited absolutism'.

The death of Francis I, 31 March 1547

In February 1547, Francis set off from Rochefort-en-Yvelines intending to reach Paris in time for a memorial service for Henry VIII who had died on 28 January. On reaching Rambouillet he fell seriously ill, and on 31 March he died at the age of 52. It seems he died of some kind of urinary infection: for a long time historians have argued for and against syphilis as the cause of death. On the same day his son and successor Henry II ordered a triple funeral for his father and two brothers, François and Charles, whose bodies had remained at Tournon and Beauvais respectively since their deaths. The artist François Clouet travelled to Rambouillet to make Francis's death mask and to take measurements for his funereal effigy.

On 6 April the king's heart and entrails were buried in the priory of Haute-Bruyère, near Rambouillet, and five days later his body was taken to the palace of Saint-Cloud. On 24 April the focus of the funeral ceremony shifted from the king's body to his effigy, which was as lifelike as possible and laid out with full royal regalia on a bed of state. For eleven days the king's meals were served as if he were still alive. On 4 May the last was served and the effigy removed. Overnight the great hall of the palace was turned into a funereal chamber with the king's coffin in the centre. On 18 May, Henry II aspersed his father's body. This was his only public appearance between Francis's death and his own coronation: had he appeared while the effigy was still on display, he would have destroyed the illusion that Francis was still alive. On 21 May the king's coffin was taken on a waggon drawn by six horses to Notre-Dame-des-Champs and placed alongside the coffins of his two sons. Next day, the effigies of all three were produced and attached to litters.

Francis's effigy now had a different set of hands: instead of being clasped in prayer, one held the sceptre and the other the hand of justice. In the afternoon the huge funeral cortège set off for the cathedral of Notre-Dame in Paris. As was the custom, the king's effigy was carried by the *hanouars* or salt-carriers of Paris. Alongside marched eight gentlemen of the household who were attached to the litter by a halter. After a short service, the company broke up, only to reassemble next day for the last rites. It was then that Pierre du Chastel, the Grand Almoner, delivered a funeral oration. That afternoon the cortège went to the abbey of Saint-Denis, traditional resting-place of the kings and queens of France. Next day the effigies were removed and the coffins taken to a vault. Francis's stewards threw their wands into his grave and Admiral Annebault dipped the banner of France. 'Le roy est mort! Vive le roy!' cried Normandy herald. The company then retired for supper and Francis's chief steward, Mendoza, broke his wand to signify the dissolution of the late king's household.

Although Henry II's relations with his father had at times been strained, he commissioned a splendid tomb for him. It was designed by the architect Philibert de l'Orme on the model of a triumphal arch, while conforming to the late medieval convention of combining kneeling figures (*priants*) of the deceased and members of his family on the top of the tomb with recumbent figures (*gisants*) on the sarcophagus beneath. The sculptor Pierre Bontemps carved the *gisants* and the bas-reliefs depicting the battles of Marignano and Ceresole round the tomb's base. Bontemps also worked on a monument for the heart of Francis which was set up at Haute-Bruyère in 1556, but is now at Saint-Denis.

Thus ended the life of one of France's greatest kings. In the mid-sixteenth century Francis I was called 'le grand roy Françoys'. He was called great, wrote Brantôme, 'not so much because of his very tall stature and presence or his very regal majesty as on account of his virtues, valour, great deeds and high merits, as were once Alexander, Pompey and others'. De Thou in his *Histoire universelle* wrote of the 'eulogies deserved by that great prince'. These judgements have seldom been endorsed since the sixteenth century. Writing in 1697, Bayle described Francis as 'one of those great princes in whom great qualities were mixed with many faults'. Jules Michelet, writing in the nineteenth century, dismissed Francis as 'a dangerous object who was to deceive everyone'.

Francis had many faults and made many mistakes. He was wilful, impetuous, grasping, profligate, licentious and fickle, but also intelligent, eloquent, brave and, by the standards of his age, humane. Territorially, his many military campaigns achieved little: he annexed parts of Savoy but failed in his lifelong bid to conquer Milan. His last years were overshadowed by the loss of Boulogne to the English. His main territorial achievement was to retain Burgundy in the face of Charles V's efforts to regain the duchy. In other respects, Francis's reign had long-term importance. His obsession with war stimulated administrative change. He had to look for new forms of income, to reorganize the fiscal system and to promote centralization wherever possible. Economically, his reign witnessed the completion of France's agricultural recovery after the Hundred Years War. The population grew, town life flourished and trade boomed. As new horizons were opened up overseas, the ports of the Atlantic coast were developed. Francis's cultural legacy was outstanding. The beautiful châteaux, which he and his courtiers built, bear witness even today to the brilliant intellectual and artistic life of his court. His collection of works of art was the nucleus of the collection now housed at the Louvre and his library of the Bibliothèque nationale. The *Lecteurs royaux* whom he created in 1530 were to become the collège de France. Few royal legacies have been as rich.

13

Henry II, the Victor of Metz, 1547–52

Historians have, on the whole, done less than justice to Henry II. He has been portrayed by Michelet as a gloomy monarch, yet after his accession he shed the melancholia that had marked his unhappy youth. In 1547 a Venetian envoy described him as 'joyful, rubicund and with an excellent colour'. He was fond of practical jokes and, being tall and muscular like his father, loved sports, particularly tennis, riding and jousting. Though less committed intellectually, he was interested in architecture and skilful in using the arts to project his monarchical authority. His private life was only a shade more respectable than Francis's: he shared it with his wife Catherine de' Medici (who after ten childless years of marriage miraculously produced four sons and three daughters in eleven years) and his mistress, Diane de Poitiers. But the king also had a number of affairs (for example with Lady Fleming, one of Mary Stuart's ladies-in-waiting) which produced illegitimate children.

Henry's faults and qualities were fairly evenly balanced: he was kind to his offspring and loyal to his friends (especially those who had stood by him under Francis), but he could be vindictive and stubborn. In the exercise of his kingly duties, he was conscientious and hard-working. He lacked experience, having been excluded from public affairs by his father, and tended to rely heavily on people he trusted. According to the Ferrarese ambassador, Henry trembled whenever Montmorency appeared 'as children do when they see their teacher'. Yet the king was not spineless: at council meetings and in diplomatic audiences, he listened carefully and spoke clearly and sensibly. There are solid grounds for thinking that he has been seriously underrated as a ruler simply because his reign was relatively short.

The palace revolution

Henry II's accession was followed, as widely expected, by a palace revolution. The forces of faction which had been gathering momentum during the last years of Francis I's reign were now allowed free rein. Henry had not forgiven his father's mistress and ministers for the Peace of Crépy, which had been so damaging to his interests, and as the close friend of Anne de Montmorency, he was unwilling to tolerate the presence at court of the constable's enemies.

No one stood to lose as much from Francis's death as Anne duchesse d'Etampes, who had created many enemies by her arrogance and her self-interested patronage. The imperial ambassador, Saint-Mauris, believed that if she had appeared in public she would have been stoned. Having retired to Limours shortly before Francis's death, she now tried to return to her apartment at the château of Saint-Germain-en-Laye, but was informed by Henry that she would need to apply to the dowager Queen Eleanor. In the meantime, the constable occupied her suite. This was only the first of several humiliations suffered by the duchess. She was also made to disgorge jewels given to her by Francis which Henry then gave to his own mistress, Diane, and was charged with conspiring with the emperor in 1544, although her only punishment was to concede lands to the crown. Yet she was not completely ruined. She retired to one of her châteaux and devoted her last years to good works.

The person who triumphed as a result of Madame d'Etampes' overthrow was her arch-enemy Diane de Poitiers. According to Saint-Mauris, Henry discussed all decisions and policy with her each day after lunch, giving her an account of all the business he had transacted that morning. Specific examples of her influence on policy-making are not easily found in the contemporary documentation, but as the king's mistress (she was forty-eight and he only twenty-seven) she became the dominant woman at court. She distributed favours as unscrupulously as the duchesse d'Etampes had done previously. Her son-in-law Robert de La Marck became a marshal of France and a royal councillor, three of her nephews received bishoprics within two years, and her confidant André Blondet became *Trésorier de l'Epargne*. The king pandered to her avarice. He gave her the château of Chenonceaux and conferred on her the title of duchesse de Valentinois with lands to match.

But the most significant feature of the new dispensation was the return to power of the constable, Anne de Montmorency, who had been living on his estates since his fall in 1541. He had not lost his principal offices, but had simply ceased to exercise them or to draw their wages. Henry was grateful to Montmorency for having helped to free him from his long Spanish captivity. As Dauphin, he had remained in close touch with the constable during his disgrace, and his first act on reaching the throne was to call Montmorency to Saint-Germain. After they had talked in private for two hours, Montmorency emerged as president of the king's council. On 12 April he took his oath as constable and was confirmed as Grand Master. His arrears of pay – amounting to 100,000 écus – were settled, and he recovered the governorship of Languedoc. In July 1551, Montmorency was created a duke and a peer, an unprecedented elevation for a mere baron, placing him on a par with the highest noblemen in the land. His brother François, seigneur de La Rochepot, was reappointed governor of Picardy and Ile-de-France.

The constable had a large family – four sons and seven daughters – and he was to provide for them well in the future. However, in 1547, his eldest son was only seventeen, so Montmorency's patronage was initially focused on his sister's sons, the Châtillons. The eldest, Cardinal Odet de Châtillon, shared his uncle's apartment at Saint-Germain and allegedly began to compete with the Cardinal of Ferrara for precedence among the ecclesiastical courtiers. His brother Gaspard was soon appointed colonel-general of the infantry and, following the death of his uncle La Rochepot in 1551, succeeded him as governor of Picardy and Ile-de-France. The third nephew, François seigneur d'Andelot, became one of the new favourites at court.

Montmorency's return to power automatically led to the disgrace of Annebault and Tournon, who had run the government in the last years of Francis I's reign. Annebault was allowed to remain admiral, albeit without pay, but he had to give up his marshalship to Jacques d'Albon de Saint-André, who also became the king's Grand Chamberlain. Though Annebault remained a royal councillor, he ceased to have any political importance, which was probably as well for he was regarded by many as a bonehead. He died in 1552. Tournon's disgrace was, in the short term, more complete than the admiral's. He was excluded from the king's council, forbidden to reside at court, and replaced as chancellor of the Order of St Michael by Charles de Lorraine, archbishop of Reims. Tournon eventually attended the conclave in Rome that elected Pope Julius III, enabling him to serve French interests at the Curia. In 1551 he became archbishop of Lyon. Two years later, he and Montmorency were reconciled.

Henry II's accession was a signal for change not only at the highest ministerial level, but in other departments of state as well. Two of Francis's secretaries of state, Guillaume Bochetel and Claude de L'Aubespine, were retained, but Gilbert Bayard was dismissed for allegedly disparaging Diane de Poitiers' looks. He was replaced by Cosme Clausse, who had served Henry when he was Dauphin. A fourth secretary was appointed in 1547 in the person of Jean du Thier, a 'creature of the constable'. Shortly after his father's death, Henry issued letters patent explicitly setting out the duties of the four secretaries. Each was assigned an area of responsibility: thus

Bochetel was given Normandy, Picardy, Flanders, Scotland and England. In September the king raised their salaries from 1623 *livres* to 3000 *livres* in recognition of their importance and of their need to accompany him on his travels. The four secretaries, who were all related by marriage, were well rewarded for their services, six of their relatives becoming bishops. The change in the nature of the secretaries' duties and competence has been described as 'among the most important and enduring of the administrative decisions of Henry's reign'.

Among newcomers to the king's council, two deserve special notice: François comte d'Aumale and his brother, Charles archbishop of Reims. They were sons of Claude, first duc de Guise, and nephews of another royal councillor, Jean, Cardinal of Lorraine. Their eldest sister Mary had married James V of Scotland in 1538 by whom she had a daughter, also called Mary, the future Queen of Scots. François was a soldier, nicknamed *le balafré* (Scarface) after he had been seriously wounded in the face at Boulogne in 1545. He was not only a brilliant tactician, but also a clever politician. Charles was highly intelligent and a fine orator. His appointment as archbishop of Reims in 1538 gave him the highest position in the Gallican church and one of the richest. Both men had been Henry II's friends before his accession. The story that Francis I on his deathbed warned his son against their ambition is almost certainly apocryphal, but the high favour the Guises enjoyed from the start of Henry's reign is indisputable. Within a few months Charles had become a cardinal and François a duke. Both were in the flower of manhood and immensely ambitious. They also had the backing of Diane de Poitiers, who needed a counterweight to the constable's influence. In December 1549, François married Anne d'Este, the grand-daughter of Louis XII. One of his six brothers, Claude, marquis de Mayenne and duc d'Aumale, married Louise de Brézé, daughter of Diane; another, also called François, was Grand Prior and general of the galleys. The young-est, René, was content to stay within the entourage of his brothers. Louis, like Charles, was made a cardinal. Their sisters also added to their family's prestige: in addition to Mary who ruled over Scotland, there was Louise who was twice married, first to the prince of Orange, then to the prince of Chimay. Two others became abbesses of Farmoutier. A source of strength to the Guise family was their remarkable cohesion: instead of setting up distinct houses, they recognized the superior authority of the eldest brother. Each morning, the four youngest attended on the Cardinal of Lorraine and followed him to the *lever* of the head of the family, François. All would then go to the king's *lever*.

Influential as the Guises were, Montmorency seems to have overestimated their hold on the king. According to a history of Henry II, which may have been written by his secretary l'Aubespine, Montmorency and Diane had absolute power: he over the crown, she over the body. The same source affirms that the Guises by themselves could not shake the king's judgement. They depended largely on Diane.

Scotland and Boulogne

Henry II could not forget the humiliation inflicted on French arms by Henry VIII's capture of Boulogne in 1544, particularly as he had taken part in that campaign himself. His first move towards wiping the slate clean was to punish the captains who had surrendered the town. They were accused of cowardice and tried for treason. The principal accused were Oudart de Biez, the former governor of Boulogne, and the seigneur de Vervins. Both were found guilty of *lèse-majesté*. Vervins was executed in Paris and his head stuck on a post outside Boulogne, his body quartered and the pieces exposed in the four chief towns of Picardy. De Biez was pardoned when the king was persuaded that he had been wrongly convicted. Retribution, however, was not enough to satisfy Henry. He vowed that he would recapture Boulogne 'sword in hand', and in the summer of 1547 he carried out a reconnaissance of the surrounding countryside. He also vowed that he would restore to Boulogne a statue of the Virgin which the English had removed from the main church.

However, it was in Scotland, not in the Boulonnais, that the king made his first significant move against England. This was because Scotland had been for some time under threat of annexation by England. In December 1542 it had been plunged into a royal minority by the premature death of King James V. Scotland had experienced minorities before, but this one was different for the minor was an infant girl, Mary Stuart, who soon became a pawn in the international marriage market. Henry VIII tried to have her sent to England with a view to marrying her off to his own son Edward, thereby uniting England and Scotland. Meeting with resistance, he had unleashed a war against the Scots, which has come to be known as 'the Rough Wooing'.

The Protector Somerset, who ruled England during the first part of Edward VI's minority (Henry VIII having died on 28 January 1547), was inspired by a vision of a united Great Britain in which the Scots and the English would live together in peace and friendship. But the Scots remembered him as the chief executor of Henry VIII's destructive raids across the border. They refused to negotiate with him, but he would not take no for an answer. As he stepped up pressure on the Scots, they looked to France for protection. Henry II had cogent reasons for taking an interest in Scotland. One was the 'Auld Alliance' itself which had offered France many opportunities in the past to divert England's aggressive urges from the Continent; another was the influence of the house of Guise to which the Scottish dowager, Mary, belonged. Her brothers, François duc d'Aumale and Charles de Lorraine, urged Henry to go to her assistance. A third reason was the political advantage to be gained from the marriage of the infant Queen of Scots, who was in line of succession to the English throne. Married to the Dauphin, she would promote French ascendancy not only over Scotland, but perhaps over England as well. However, Henry II was not yet prepared to go to war with England. He also knew that the Emperor Charles V would honour pledges given to Henry VIII in 1543, particularly as he had just routed the army of the Schmalkaldic League at Mühlberg (21 April 1547).

The idea of a marriage between Mary Stuart and the Dauphin François had been openly discussed as early as September 1543, but it was only after the Scots had been defeated by Somerset at Pinkie in September 1547 that they threw in their lot with France. Their regent, the earl of Arran, in return for the promise of a French duchy, reached an agreement with Henry II which provided for the marriage of Mary and the Dauphin. Soon afterwards the king of France sent an army to Scotland. The expedition proved remarkably successful: it captured St Andrews castle and its rebellious garrison. Among the prisoners was the Protestant reformer John Knox, who was sentenced to serve on the French king's galleys. Meanwhile, the Scottish parliament met near Haddington within sight of its English garrison and defiantly ratified Arran's treaty with Henry II: it agreed to the marriage of Mary Stuart and the Dauphin and to her being sent to France beforehand. It also sanctioned the garrisoning of several Scottish fortresses by French troops. Early in August a French fleet picked up Mary Stuart at Dumbarton and, sailing round 'the back of Ireland' to avoid interception by English ships, carried her safely to Brittany. Her arrival on 13 August 1548 was greeted by Henry with jubilation. 'France and Scotland', he declared, 'are now one country.' Although the long-term results of his intervention in Scotland fell short of his expectations, it was hailed at the time as a triumph. French troops were now manning Scottish forts against the English and the Scottish queen was in France pledged to marry the Dauphin. The 'Auld Alliance' had never seemed more secure or auspicious.

Once the English threat to Scotland had been removed, Henry could attend to Boulogne. In June 1549, Protector Somerset tried to persuade the emperor to include the town in the guarantee he had given to Henry VIII in respect of Calais in 1543, but Charles did not wish to be drawn into another conflict with France at this stage. He therefore declined Somerset's proposal, leaving the way clear for Henry II to attack Boulogne. On 8 August 1549, as Somerset's government was faced by serious revolts at home, Henry declared war and invaded the Boulonnais in person, but it was Montmorency who undertook the encirclement of Boulogne. After capturing Ambleteuse and Blackness, the French closed in on Boulogne, but a prolonged bombardment failed to dislodge the garrison. Henry accordingly ordered a blockade and returned to Paris for the winter, leaving Aumale in charge of operations.

The situation in England, meanwhile, took a decisive turn. In October, Somerset was replaced at the head of the government by the earl of Warwick, who decided to end the war with France and Scotland. Peace talks led to an agreement on 24 March 1550, which has been described as 'the most ignominious treaty signed by England during the century'. In return for 400,000 crowns – half the redemption money formally agreed upon – the English handed back Boulogne on 25 April. Pending final settlement of the debt, Henry sent six high-ranking French nobles, including Montmorency, to England as hostages. Under the treaty, English troops were removed from Scotland. On 16 May, Henry II made a triumphal entry into Boulogne and set up a new statue of the Virgin in a temporary sanctuary. Eventually, the original one was returned by the English government along with the hostages.

Following Boulogne's surrender, Henry II and Edward VI became the best of friends, exchanging orders of chivalry. On 19 July 1551 a marriage alliance was signed at Angers between Henry's daughter Elizabeth and the English monarch. Her dowry was fixed at 200,000 crowns. Edward also agreed to be godfather to Henry's son, the future Henry III, who was christened Edouard-Alexandre. These good relations lasted till Edward's premature death in July 1553. Having nothing to fear from England for two years, Henry was free to act as he wished in Italy and Germany.

Italy

Henry II was as determined as his father had been to rule northern Italy. At his accession the French controlled much of Piedmont, including Turin, but Milan was in the hands of the Emperor Charles V. As always, French fortunes in the peninsula hinged on relations with the Holy See. Fortunately for Henry, Pope Paul III had recently fallen out with the emperor and was accordingly keen to draw closer to France. A link already existed in the person of his grandson, Orazio Farnese, who had been brought up at the court of Francis I. Paul now sought to strengthen the French party in the Sacred College and at his instigation seven French cardinals, led by Jean du Bellay, took up residence in Rome. Their number was soon increased by new papal creations: on 27 July 1547, Charles de Lorraine became a cardinal, and he was followed on 9 January 1548 by Charles de Bourbon. The new Franco-papal alliance was sealed on 30 June 1547, when a marriage was arranged between Orazio Farnese and Henry II's natural daughter Diane.

One reason for the hostility that had developed between Paul III and Charles V was the pope's conferment in August 1545 on his son, Pier Luigi

Farnese, of the duchies of Parma and Piacenza, which the emperor regarded as part of the duchy of Milan. On 10 September 1547, Pier Luigi was assassinated at Piacenza by imperial agents who handed over the city to Ferrante Gonzaga, the imperial governor of Milan. Henry II promptly assured the pope of his support. Charles de Lorraine, who had gone to Rome to receive his red hat, was instructed to persuade the pope to sign a defensive alliance with France. The Guises, who had a claim to the kingdom of Naples dating back to the fourteenth-century dukes of Anjou, were keen to see Henry intervene in the peninsula.

The time seemed ripe, in the spring of 1548, for Henry II to stage a show of force south of the Alps. French influence in Italy seemed in the ascendant, and unrest had developed in imperial territories, notably in Genoa and Naples. Charles V was in Augsburg, trying to impose a constitutional and religious settlement on the rebellious German princes. The refusal of Venice to join a defensive alliance dissuaded Henry from going to war, but he decided none the less that his presence in Italy would serve to settle some disputed points in his favour. He left Fontainebleau in April 1548 with many great nobles. His queen, Catherine de' Medici, was appointed regent in his absence. The royal party reached Turin in August. Among Italian princes who came to salute the king was Ercole d'Este, duke of Ferrara, who used the occasion to arrange a marriage between his daughter Anne and François de Guise. This match brought the Guise family into even closer union with the royal family, for Anne was Louis XII's granddaughter.

All seemed to be going well for Henry when news reached him of a tax rebellion in western France. At first he was not too worried. He even issued a pardon to the rebels on condition they laid down their arms within four days. But the unrest grew alarmingly, whereupon the king decided on punitive action and appointed Montmorency and Aumale to take charge of it. However, Henry did not allow the rising to upset his prearranged schedule. He had planned to visit Lyon in the autumn of 1548 and was there, as appointed, on 23 September, when he was given one of the grandest entries ever staged in France followed by a round of festivities that lasted a week. On 21 October, Henry and his court were at Moulins for the wedding of Jeanne d'Albret and Antoine de Bourbon.

The *gabelle* revolt, 1548

Francis I had planned a complete overhaul of salt taxes (*gabelles*) in France. Not only were they to be raised and tax farms introduced, but a system of *greniers* was to be set up in the west. None of these measures was actually taken until 1548, when Henry II ordered the plan to be given effect. Trouble soon followed. In Angoumois, as early as May, peasants (called *pitaux*) rose against the hated salt-tax officials, but they also attacked rich people and royal officials. Lacking enough troops to restore order, the governor of Angoumois appealed for aid to Henri d'Albret, governor of Guyenne. But such troops as he was able to send were routed by 4000 rebels, led by a certain Bois-Menier who called himself 'colonel of Angoumois, Périgord and Saintonge'. Encouraged by this success, the rebellion spread to Saintonge, where a petty nobleman called Puymoreau took the lead. Everywhere bands of rebels searched for tax officials, while pillaging houses of the rich. At Cognac, the receiver of the local *grenier* was cruelly put to death and his body cast into the river. On 12 August the rebels, now numbering some 20,000, captured Saintes, destroying the *grenier* and setting fire to well-to-do houses. What had begun as a tax revolt was turning into a proletarian uprising. Cognac too was seized. The revolt then reached Bordeaux, where the citizens, who were exempt from the *gabelle*, were complaining of an infantry tax that had been imposed upon them. They demanded its remission. Matters came to a head on 21 August, when Tristan de Moneins, Albret's lieutenant, was lynched as he was about to negotiate with local dignitaries. Twenty *gabeleurs* were killed at the same time and their bodies covered with salt as a gesture of derision.

Seriously disturbed by these events, Henry decided to punish severely both the rebels and the authorities in Bordeaux which had been so weak in facing up to them. At Pinerolo, on 3 September, a plan of campaign was worked out. Montmorency and Aumale were instructed to rally troops and converge on western France. On 20 October, Montmorency arrived at Bordeaux. Ten thousand royal troops poured into the city and the constable disarmed the inhabitants, confiscating the city's artillery and stock of gunpowder. He then dissolved the parlement, replacing it with magistrates from other parts of France, who began criminal proceedings against Bordeaux's administration. On 6 November, Bordeaux was deprived of its privileges, exemptions and rights for ever; it was to remain disarmed, meet the cost of the punitive expedition and pay a fine of 120,000 *livres*. The *jurade* and 120 notables were made to attend the exhumation of Moneins' body and to take part in a procession to the cathedral where it was buried anew in an expiatory chapel. As they passed the constable's lodging, they had to fall on their knees and plead for forgiveness. There followed about 150 executions. On 22 November, Montmorency left the city. This, however, did not mark the end of the repression. In areas where the rebellion had begun, the leaders were rounded up and put to death with various refinements of cruelty. Some were broken on the wheel and crowned with red hot irons. Huge fines were imposed on villages and the bells of churches that had called the rebels to arms were destroyed. Troops billeted in Angoumois and Saintonge were instructed to live off the countryside.

Once the revolt had been suppressed, Henry had second thoughts about the measures which had provoked it. In September 1549 he recognized that the salt tax was 'odious to the people' and restored the system of *quart* and *demi-quart* which had existed before 1542. The arrears of tax were fixed at 450,000 *livres* payable in January and July 1556. The annual amount was fixed at 80,000l. and its collection left to the local estates. After further talks, which ended in December 1553, the salt tax was abolished in all provinces paying the *quartage* in return for a composition of 1,194,000l. payable in two instalments in 1554. Thereafter the western provinces were freed from the *gabelle* and separated from the rest of the kingdom by a customs barrier. Until 1789 they were known as *provinces redimées*. In October 1549, Henry issued an amnesty to all who had taken part in the *gabelle* revolt except the murderers of Moneins and the ringleaders. The city of Bordeaux was reinstated, all the punitive measures taken against it being rescinded, including the fine of 200,000 *livres*.

Mounting persecution

By 1547 the French monarchy seemed resolutely committed to defend the Catholic faith against the rising tide of Protestantism. Henry II's personal faith was, it seems, conventionally orthodox. Lacking his father's interest in humanism, he was less sensitive to the subtle differences between evangelicalism and heresy – which was, in any case, becoming more easily identifiable whilst remaining fluid. Calvin did not begin to give Protestantism cohesion in France until after 1555. Henry had also less reason than his father to consider the sensitivities of the German Protestant princes following their decisive defeat at Mühlberg in 1547. He was allegedly encouraged to persecute heretics by Diane de Poitiers and doubtless by others as well. Among his principal advisers, Montmorency was not noted for his liberal sentiments. If Francis I had never witnessed an *auto-da-fé*, his son did so on more than one occasion.

It has been suggested that Henry II's coronation oath did not include the traditional clause vowing to expel heretics from the kingdom, but this seems doubtful given the king's subsequent behaviour. He began by issuing an edict against blasphemy (5 April 1547) and on 8 October set up a special tribunal in the Parlement of Paris to deal with cases of heresy. It is remembered as the *Chambre Ardente* (Burning Chamber) because of the severity of its sentences. The chamber was in fact a second *Tournelle* aimed at relieving the workload of the first, which had had to cope with both heresy and criminal cases. The *Tournelle* now became an exclusively criminal court. Two of the parlement's presidents, Pierre Lizet and François de Saint-André, presided over the new tribunal's fourteen members on a rotating semester system. The *Chambre Ardente* by-passed the ecclesiastical courts completely. Judging both on appeal and in first instance, it received cases of heresy and blasphemy directly from the *baillis* and *sénéchaux* within the parlement's area of jurisdiction, which covered about a third of the kingdom. The provincial parlements were responsible for heresy cases elsewhere.

Between May 1548 and March 1550 the new court handed down 37 death sentences, representing 17 per cent of the 215 cases heard. Thirty-nine persons were acquitted; the rest had sentences ranging from admonition to lead a good Christian life (31), to doing public penance (67), to receiving a public whipping (41). Twenty-one of those found guilty but not executed had their property confiscated and were banished from the realm; two were sent to the galleys. Another 105 cases were undecided when the chamber closed in March 1550. These statistics apply only to a third of the kingdom: other parlements and courts also sentenced heretics to death. Toulouse condemned at least eight in 1550 and 1551, while Bordeaux executed eighteen between 1541 and 1559.

Although the *Chambre Ardente* proved to be a more efficient way of coping with heresy cases than the earlier system, it was opposed by the ecclesiastical courts which, except in cases involving clerics, had lost their traditional jurisdiction. On 19 November 1549 a new edict gave them jurisdiction over cases of simple heresy, where the accused had not voiced opinions publicly. Following this measure, 66 prisoners were released from the Conciergerie and handed over to their respective bishops. However, conflicts over jurisdiction continued, causing Henry to issue the famous Edict of Châteaubriant (27 June 1551). Henceforth, in heresy cases involving laymen, the parlement and the presidial courts were alone empowered to proceed and to judge without appeal; only simple heresy was left to the church courts. In the light of reports that the judiciary itself was being infiltrated by the new doctrines, the parlements were required to review their own personnel every three months in a session called a *mercuriale*. No judicial or municipal appointments were to be made without a certificate of Catholicity. The edict covered in exhaustive detail every aspect of literary censorship. Informing became mandatory: informers were to receive one third of the property of convicted persons. Magistrates were to seek out heretics and search houses for forbidden books. No longer was outward conformity a guarantee of safety. The edict also tried to ensure that all teachers were good Catholics. No one was to correspond with or send money to any exile in Geneva or elsewhere. The property of religious exiles was to be confiscated. Finally, certain religious observances were prescribed: it became obligatory to attend church as often as possible. Bishops were to reside in their dioceses and were to read out in church, every Sunday, the articles of faith which the Paris Faculty of Theology had laid down in 1543. No one who would not adhere to them was allowed to preach.

One effect of the persecution was to swell the ranks of people fleeing to Geneva, where Calvin was seeking to create a city 'governed by God'. Geneva was on France's doorstep, the more so since the duchy of Savoy, which almost encircled the city, had been annexed by France in 1536. Thus it attracted French Protestant refugees in large numbers from the end of the 1540s. In 1549 the city council began to keep a register of those who applied to become *habitants*, which, though incomplete, totalled almost 5000 names before it ceased in January 1560. Other sources suggest that the real figure was closer to 10,000. Although this huge influx did not immediately alter Geneva's political complexion, it did substantially affect its economy. In particular, it greatly boosted the printing industry. Whereas between 1530 and 1540 only 42 titles had been printed in the city, this figure had increased to 500 between 1550 and 1564. The industry employed many French exiles, among them Jean Crespin, Antoine Vincent and Laurent de Normandie.

The *présidiaux*, 1552

In January 1552, Henry II issued an edict with an important bearing on the judicial administration. He created in a number of *bailliages* and *sénéchaussées* a new law court, called *siège présidial*, to judge on appeal certain civil and criminal cases. Altogether there were sixty of these courts, each staffed by two *lieutenants* and seven councillors. In 1557 a president and a chancery were added. The new court stood between the *bailliage* and the parlement, but it did not form part of a new judicial corporation, for existing *bailliages* turned themselves into *présidiaux* simply by adding to their staff the requisite number of magistrates. In respect of civil suits, the competence of the *présidiaux* was limited to those involving property valued at less than 250 *livres*. This limit was raised to 1000 *livres* in 1557, but it was later brought down to the original figure.

The preamble to the edict of 1552 claimed that it was designed to save litigants time and money. They were to be spared long journeys to remote parlements, where they might have to wait endlessly for a decision. But the real reason for the edict was undoubtedly fiscal. The king needed to find new sources of revenue and the creation of the *présidiaux* enabled him to sell more than 500 new offices. Venality was responsible for many of his administrative reforms, including the creation of a parlement at Rennes (1552), and of a semester system in all the parlements.

The *présidiaux* were only a qualified success. Because of the monetary limit set for civil cases, many (including all cases of feudal law) passed them by. When they did not judge on appeal, they were simply an additional rung on the already tall judicial ladder. They were also deeply resented by the parlements, so that conflicts over jurisdiction arose which had to be referred to the *Grand conseil* or *conseil privé*. Thus the new courts were not necessarily the universal blessing which they may have seemed initially.

The War over Parma

Henry II was implacably hostile towards the emperor from the start of his reign – he had never forgiven Charles for the hardship he had suffered as a hostage in Spain – and soon after his accession demonstrated his feelings by ordering Charles to render homage for Flanders in spite of the Treaty of Cambrai (1529) which had ceded it to the emperor. Charles replied that he would only do so at the head of 50,000 troops. But in 1547, Henry was not ready to embark on major hostilities with the emperor. His top priority was to regain Boulogne from the English and, once that had been accomplished, he had to attend to the situation in Italy, where trouble had broken out between the pope and the emperor over Parma and Piacenza.

Towards the end of his life Pope Paul III agreed to endorse Charles V's possession of Piacenza, if he would cede to him Parma and compensate his grandsons, Orazio and Ottavio Farnese. On his deathbed, however, Paul declared Ottavio the rightful heir of both duchies. This judgement was confirmed in February 1550 by his successor, Julius III. But, being committed to reconvening the Council of Trent, the new pope needed imperial support and Charles V made this conditional on his rights to Parma and Piacenza being recognized. Fearing isolation, Ottavio placed himself under France's protection. In April 1551, after the pope had ordered him to surrender Parma, Ottavio disclosed his alliance with Henry II and his resolve to defend himself. Declaring him a rebel and his lands forfeit, Julius asked for Charles V's assistance. The emperor could now invade Parma with the pope's blessing and, after placing Ottavio under the imperial ban, Charles prepared his military campaign.

Henry could not leave Ottavio to his fate. He decided in August to embarrass the emperor by opening another front along the Piedmont-Milan border. The imperial ambassador in France, Simon Renard, warned that unless Parma were neutralized at once there would be a general conflict. But Charles believed that Henry needed more time to raise the money needed to recruit foreign mercenaries; that the fighting season was too far advanced; and that Henry could no longer count on support from the German Protestant princes. He misjudged the situation east of the Rhine. Although he had pacified the Empire, his efforts to impose a constitutional settlement were much resented, as was his order to the Protestant princes that they should send representatives to the Council of Trent. Both Catholic and Protestant princes in Germany accused Charles of subverting their privileges in the interests of his own dynasty.

Henry let it be known that he was ready to support the German rebels. They had approached him in February 1551, and in October a treaty was signed: Henry agreed to provide the princes with 240,000 *écus* immediately and a monthly subsidy of 60,000 indefinitely. In return they allowed him to administer the towns of Cambrai, Metz, Toul and Verdun as imperial vicar. The idea behind the agreement was that Henry should defend them against Charles, who was accused of violating German liberties. However, his ambitions may have been wider, for his propagandists proclaimed him a new Charlemagne, uniting the French and German people. Charles failed to take these developments seriously. He trusted Maurice of Saxony and ignored the warnings of his own sister, Mary of Hungary, who, from the vantage point of the Netherlands, could see clearly the danger clouds on the horizon. Charles's insouciance explains the ease with which Henry invaded the Empire in 1552.

The 'Gallican Crisis', 1551

The war over Parma and the pope's alliance with Charles V almost caused franco-papal relations to break down. Another bone of contention was the decision taken by Pope Julius III to recall the General Council to Trent, the only venue to which the German Protestants might be induced to send representatives. Henry II was opposed to any meeting which might lead to the religious unification of Germany, an outcome which would greatly enhance the emperor's authority. He therefore tried to dissuade Julius from his course by threatening to hold an alternative council in France. Henry even toyed with the idea of setting up a patriarchate. Charles de Guise, a likely candidate for the post, considered it seriously for a time. On 3 September 1551 Henry II banned the export of moneys to Rome for the purchase of benefices. A French breach with Rome seemed imminent. Rumours to that effect circulated in Germany throughout the summer and there was great alarm in Catholic circles. In September, however, franco-papal tension lessened and in May 1552 Henry and Julius signed an agreement. The king sent an apology to the Curia and to the council in which he blamed Charles V for the recent crisis. Julius III informed the emperor that if he had not made peace with Henry, France would have gone Lutheran.

Why did Henry II not follow the example set by Henry VIII of England? Unlike Francis I he cannot have been influenced by the need to retain papal support for his designs in Italy, since Julius III was fighting him there. Other factors are more likely to have weighed with him, such as the strong resistance which he might have encountered from such conservative forces as the Faculty of Theology of the University of Paris, and the Parlement. Gallicans they may have been, but it does not follow that they would have favoured a separation from Rome. Gallicanism was not the crude anti-papal creed often presented by historians. It rested its case on maintaining an equilibrium between various dualities: the spiritual and the temporal, nationalism and universalism, unity and freedom. This equilibrium would have been shattered by a breach with Rome and Gallicanism itself would have suffered as the church would have lost its autonomy in face of the secular power. Even an evangelical sympathizer, like Cardinal Jean du Bellay, showed no enthusiasm for a schism. Nor, it seems, would the French people in general, except for the religious dissenters, have favoured such a radical step. They did not admire Henry VIII, regarding him as a 'tyrant'. Their ideal of 'absolute government' was tempered in their eyes by the king's obligation under his coronation oath to respect the liberties of the church. Finally, the greatest deterrent to schism was probably Henry II's strict dogmatic orthodoxy which never wavered even at the height of the so-called 'Gallican Crisis'. He could not be sure that a schism would not lead to orthodoxy being shaken, as it had been in England. He would also have lost his title of 'eldest son of the church and protector of the Holy See' which enhanced his prestige among his subjects. So the 'Gallican Crisis', grave as it was, blew over. But if Henry remained within the Roman church, he still did not feel bound by the decrees of a General Council in which he had not been represented. He also felt free to ally with the German Protestant princes against Charles V without prejudice to his own religious views.

The 'German Voyage'

On 12 February, Henry, after declaring war on the emperor, held a *lit de justice*. He announced that he would lead his army to the borders of Champagne and if necessary beyond, to avenge the wrongs and injuries he had received from Charles and also to restore German liberties which were being usurped by him. Queen Catherine would be regent in his absence and would be assisted by several royal councillors. In April the king and the constable inspected the army – some 50,000 men in total – at Vitry. On 2 April the van under Montmorency crossed the Meuse; three days later it occupied Toul without encountering resistance. Next to fall was the imperial city of Metz, whose magistrates agreed to admit Montmorency and the Bourbon princes but only two bands of infantry. In fact, many more French troops entered the town, so that it was effectively taken by a ruse. The king, in the meantime, took possession of Toul and visited Nancy, capital of Lorraine, whose duke was both an imperial prince and a vassal of the

French king as duc de Bar. Henry was received as suzerain in spite of the opposition of the duchess, Christina of Denmark, mother of Duke Charles and niece of Charles V. In order to reach the Rhine the king had to violate Lorraine's neutrality. Following his arrival in Nancy (14 April), he took charge of the young duke and sent him to the French court to be brought up with his own children. He planned to marry him off eventually to his daughter Claude. The duke's uncle, M. de Vaudémont, replaced Christina as regent. As 'protector and conservator of the duke's persons and property', Henry received Vaudémont's oath and that of all the duchy's nobles. Then, having effectively taken over Lorraine, he went to Metz, where the constable staged an impressive military parade in his honour. Although Henry promised to respect the city's privileges, he planted a large garrison there under Artus de Cossé.

On 20 April, Henry marched on the Rhine. At Haguenau he encountered the widows and children of German captains who had been executed by the emperor in 1548 for serving the French crown, distributed 10,000 écus among them, and gave their sons commissions in his German companies or places as pages in his household. East of the Moselle, the king encountered growing hostility: Strassburg would only admit him and forty noblemen, but Henry swallowed his pride as the city was too strong to be taken by force. Meanwhile, the German princes warned him not to press on further; otherwise, they said, many Germans would rally to Charles V. The king accordingly withdrew, having 'watered his horses in the Rhine' as he had pledged to do. He entered Verdun on 12 June; later that month he returned to France and resumed his regal powers. He discharged half his army on 26 July and sent the rest under Antoine de Bourbon to invest Hesdin.

Henry II's 'German Voyage' has been described as 'one of the most successful military excursions in French history'. At very little cost in lives or money, he had acquired three strategic bases on France's north-east border and gained a permanent foothold in Lorraine. He did not believe that Charles V, who was ageing rapidly and riddled with gout, was capable of retaliating, but in this he was mistaken. Now that he was no longer threatened by the German princes, the emperor decided to recover Metz. His sister, Mary of Hungary, and his generals pleaded with him to desist, pointing to the lateness of the season and the strength of the fortifications; but Charles would not listen. On 10 November he laid siege to the city and began a bombardment which lasted 45 days. The imperial army consisted of 55,000 men and 150 guns. François de Guise, who defended Metz, disposed of little more than 6000 men and a few guns, but he could rely on excellent technical advice from Jean de Saint-Rémy, an expert on mines, and Camillo Marini, an Italian engineer. As the imperial guns pounded the city, the inhabitants rallied to fill any gaps that were opened up in the walls. Meanwhile, French garrisons based in Lorraine harassed the emperor's supply lines. As the weeks elapsed, his army began to succumb to cold and hunger. His main weakness, however, was lack of money. The Fuggers and Mary of Hungary did their utmost to assist, but they could not keep up with Charles's needs. It was on account of penury as much as for any other reason that he decided to lift the siege. His army, now much reduced in size, began to retreat on 2 January, leaving a trail of wounded behind.

Henry II's victory was widely acclaimed in France. He ordered thanksgiving services throughout the realm, and Guise, before returning to court, held a victory parade in Metz. He had scored a notable personal triumph. 'There is no one among those who were at Metz', wrote the Mantuan ambassador, 'who does not praise the courtesy and good government of Monsieur de Guise so that he is adored today by the whole kingdom.' His victory was compared to David's over Goliath. But the emperor was no Goliath: not only was he a physical wreck, he also suffered acutely from depression and was fast losing his grip on state affairs. In fact, the débâcle at Metz contained the germ of his abdication.

14

The Arts and Literature under Henry II

Henry II may not have been as passionately addicted to the arts as his father had been, yet he undertook a considerable amount of building. In a posthumous panegyric, Pierre Paschal singled out the king's love of architecture. According to Nicolas Houel, Henry's knowledge of building went far beyond what could be expected of a great prince. In the course of his brief reign he continued rebuilding the Louvre, erected the Château-Neuf at Saint-Germain-en-Laye, added a ballroom at Fontainebleau and carried out improvements in other royal châteaux, including Chambord. He also took a close interest in the château which Diane de Poitiers was building at Anet. At the same time, his advisers and friends vied with each other to build houses fit to receive him and the court. Montmorency carried out major works at Ecouen, Chantilly and elsewhere. At Meudon, which the Cardinal of Lorraine acquired in 1552, the famous 'grotto' was created to house his many treasures. 'In this place', wrote Belleforest in 1575, 'no kind of antiquity is missing – columns, architraves, supports, cornices, statues, medals, and other singular things.' At Valléry, near Sens, Marshal Saint-André put up a château which Androuet du Cerceau later compared to the Louvre. Lesser nobles, too, were actively building all over France.

Henry II employed two outstanding architects: Pierre Lescot and Philibert de l'Orme. Lescot was a well-educated man, who seems to have picked up his knowledge of architecture from books. He is chiefly remembered for his rebuilding of the Louvre. Francis I had begun the process of turning the old medieval fortress into a Renaissance palace, but the project had been incomplete at his death; it was left to Henry II to carry it through. Lescot had planned to build on the site of the west wing of the old château a *corps-de-logis* two storeys high with a central projecting pavilion housing a staircase, but during Henry's reign the project was radically altered. The staircase was moved to the north end, leaving space for a much larger reception room or *salle* on each floor. A projecting pavilion was added at each end, one housing the staircase, and also a third storey. At the same time another building, the *Pavillon du roi*, was added in the south-west corner, facing the river. The most striking aspect of Lescot's façade as decorated by the sculptor Jean Goujon is its classicism, notably the correct treatment of the Orders. Yet it is also very un-Italian, the overall effect being one of ornamental beauty rather than monumentality.

The interior decoration of the Louvre is revolutionary. The *salle* on the ground floor is adorned at one end by a gallery supported by four caryatids, 'the first time a passage from Vitruvius had been used to recreate an antique monument on the monumental scale and in a permanent form' (Thomson). At the south end there is a *Tribunal* separated from the main room by sixteen Doric columns in groups of four. As on the façade, the decorations are by Jean Goujon. In another part of the Louvre, Lescot collaborated with the Italian woodcarver Scibec de Carpi, who made the remarkable ceiling of the king's *chambre de parade*. Previously, French ceilings had had beams running across them, usually with painted motifs; this one, by contrast, is coffered. The delicately carved friezes are more correctly Roman than anything seen before in France. The largest motifs were carved separately and the ceiling, which was originally gilded, could be dismantled for cleaning.

Lescot is only known to have accepted six commissions. Among his other buildings two deserve special mention. The Hôtel Carnavalet, begun in 1545, is the only example of a Paris house that survives from the mid-sixteenth century. Much of it has been altered, but certain original features remain, notably the main façade on the court with its bas-reliefs of the four seasons by Goujon. Another work by Lescot is the Fontaine des Innocents which stood at the corner of the rue Saint-Denis, the traditional route for royal entries. It is the only vestige of a royal entry from the *ancien régime*, whose set pieces were usually of wood and canvas.

Though important, Lescot was little more than a talented amateur by comparison with Philibert de l'Orme, 'the first French architect to have something of the universality of the great Italians' (Blunt). Born in Lyon about 1510, he was the son of a master mason. About 1533 he visited Rome where he attracted the attention of the future Pope Marcellus II and of Cardinal du Bellay, Rabelais's patron. After spending three years studying Roman antiquities, de l'Orme returned to Lyon where he built a gallery for the home of Antoine Bullioud. About 1540, du Bellay commissioned him to build the château of Saint-Maur-des-Fossés and through the cardinal he was introduced to the circle of the Dauphin and Diane de Poitiers. In 1547 she commissioned de l'Orme to build her château at Anet, which he completed about 1552. Following Henry II's accession, de l'Orme was appointed superintendent of royal buildings. For the king he designed the tomb of Francis I at Saint-Denis, a chapel at Villers-Cotterêts and the Château-Neuf at Saint-Germain. When Henry died, de l'Orme was dismissed and it seems that for a short time he was maltreated by enemies. However, he was subsequently employed by Catherine de' Medici to build the Tuileries and to complete Saint-Maur, which she had bought from du Bellay's heirs. He died in 1570.

De l'Orme also wrote two books on architecture. The first, called *Nouvelles Inventions pour bien bastir et à petits frais* (1561), is a practical treatise on the building of vaults and roofs. The second, in nine books, is called *Architecture* and was published in 1567. Though indebted to Vitruvius and Alberti, de l'Orme's treatise is original in plan and treatment, combining theory and practice and drawing on his personal experience. This gives his writing freshness and solidity. Yet he is concerned not simply to give practical hints; he believes that an architect should follow the dictates of reason and be sufficiently trained in mathematics, science and music to meet his professional needs. After looking at various practical matters, de l'Orme discusses the use of ornament. In general, he is opposed to richness of decoration or material, except in royal or public buildings. He favours the use of stone as against Italian marble. Stone, in his view, is better suited to the climate of France; it is also less expensive. This reflects de l'Orme's patriotism, which is also present in his refusal blindly to follow an Italian or classical model. His independence of mind and practical sense are combined in his proposal for a new French Order to be added to the five Greek and Roman ones. He justifies it on two grounds: first, the Greeks and Romans invented Orders to meet their practical needs; why should not the French – an equally great nation – do so? Secondly, the Greek and Roman Orders were invented in countries where marble is a natural material, whereas stone is common in France. It is difficult to find a shaft of stone long enough to make a large column; so why not make one out of drums of stone placed one on top of the other? The joints can be concealed by decorated horizontal bands.

Hardly anything of the buildings erected by de l'Orme has survived; knowledge of them rests mainly on contemporary engravings. The château of Saint-Maur, though less individualistic than his more mature works, set a new standard of classicism for its time. The design, recalling the Palazzo Té in Mantua, consisted of one floor only with rooms arranged in a single suite around a square court. On the garden side de l'Orme planned a horseshoe staircase, the earliest example of the kind in France. Saint-Maur was also the first attempt in France to decorate an entire building with a single Order of classical pilasters.

Although much of the château of Anet has been destroyed, its three principal features survive: the frontispiece to the main block, the chapel and the entrance gateway. The frontispiece is remarkable for its monumentality and its correct treatment of the classical Orders. The chapel is the first in France to invoke the Renaissance principle that the circle is the perfect figure and, therefore, suitable for the house of God. The entrance gateway, which was probably built in 1552, is unique. Except for the Doric columns flanking the door, it is almost free of classical elements. A sequence of rectangular blocks builds up to the central feature: a clock consisting of a bronze stag surrounded by hounds, which move at the striking of the hours. On either side are four sarcophagi, and open-work balustrades run round the whole structure. The entrance has been described as 'perhaps the most striking example of Philibert's ability to think in monumental terms while at the same time remaining free from any tendency to imitate the models of the Italian High Renaissance' (Blunt).

The two works executed by de l'Orme for Henry II are less startlingly original than Anet. The tomb of Francis I at Saint-Denis is, in general design, a Roman triumphal arch with the side arches set back from the plane of the principal front. The Château-Neuf at Saint-Germain, which was begun in 1557, consisted of a central *corps-de-logis*, to which were attached four pavilions, preceded by a courtyard enclosed by a wall and intended for festivities. Its unusual shape may have been inspired by Hadrian's villa at Tivoli which was being excavated at the time.

Lescot and de l'Orme were not the only architects active under Henry II. Primaticcio continued to work at Fontainebleau where he designed the grotto in the *Jardin des Pins* and a gate in the *Cour du Cheval Blanc*. He also built the Meudon grotto for the Guises. Serlio continued to write his famous treatise on architecture till his death in 1554. His designs, which often departed wildly from Vitruvian precepts, were influential. Thus a strange design for an Ionic door was closely followed by Lescot at Valléry.

Building activity was also not confined to the Ile-de-France. In the south-west a group of buildings show the influence of Guillaume Philandrier, who accompanied Georges d'Armagnac, bishop of Rodez, to Venice in 1536. He became a pupil of Serlio and studied Vitruvius. On returning to Rodez in 1544, he was given charge of the cathedral's fabric and about 1562 added an extraordinary gable – a complete Roman church façade in miniature – to the Gothic west front. Philandrier's classicism rubbed off on other architects of south-west France, notably at the château of Bournazel, where an impressive double-arcaded screen was erected about 1550. Another centre of classical influence was Toulouse, where Nicolas Bachelier designed some outstanding private houses. Whoever designed the courtyard of the Hôtel d'Assezat was evidently familiar with Book 4 of Serlio's treatise.

The art of decorative painting under Henry II is mainly represented by two artists: Francesco Primaticcio and Niccolò dell'Abbate. Primaticcio continued to work at Fontainebleau after the death of Francis I. He had by this time developed a style characterized by female nudes with long tapering limbs, thin necks and small heads with exaggeratedly classical profiles. Between 1552 and 1556 he painted murals in the ballroom at Fontainebleau which betray the stylistic influence of both Raphael and Parmigianino. More important were his decorations for the *Galerie d'Ulysse*, which were much admired by artists who visited Fontainebleau subsequently, including Rubens. Unfortunately, they disappeared with the gallery in 1739, and modern scholars have been dependent for their knowledge of them on Primaticcio's sketches and on some rather indifferent seventeenth-century engravings. Niccolò dell'Abbate came to Fontainebleau in 1552 with a wide experience of north Italian illusionist painting. Though his personality was partly obscured by Primaticcio's, he did produce distinctive figure compositions deriving ultimately from Correggio. In the field of landscape, Niccolò was an innovator in France: he imported a style akin to that of Dosso but modified it under the influence of the Antwerp school. Another painter at work in France under Henry II, but not connected with Fontainebleau, was Jean Cousin. A native of Sens, he settled in Paris in 1530 and ran a flourishing business as a painter and designer of stained glass until 1560.

Alongside decorative painting, portraiture continued to prosper at this time. Its main exponents were François Clouet, who had succeeded his father, Jean, as royal portraitist in 1541, and Corneille de Lyon. A series of sketches attributed to François Clouet show a more polished technique than that of Jean: he paid closer attention to the accidents of feature and surface; less to simple geometrical volume. As for Corneille de Lyon, very little is known about him except that he was a Dutchman who entered the Dauphin's service in 1540 and continued to work for him as king and for his royal successors until about 1574. He may have been responsible for a series of portraits of French sitters which are characterized by their small size, sensitive naturalistic modelling and usually by a green background.

Engraving in mid-sixteenth-century France stands in sharp contrast to painting. The work of Jean Duvet takes us far away from Fontainebleau. His set of 24 engravings illustrating the 'Apocalypse' was published in Lyon in 1561, but the first plate is dated 1555. They borrow extensively from Dürer's woodcuts, but depart from his preoccupation with clarity of design. Duvet flouts all the canons of classical art in pursuit of an intensely felt mystical vision. His art reflects the atmosphere of growing religious excitement prevalent in his day. He may have spent some time in Geneva, but returned to France where he died about 1561.

Sculpture under Henry II is dominated by Jean Goujon, who worked so closely with Pierre Lescot that their respective contributions are not always easy to separate. Goujon's early work was done in Rouen, where he designed some columns supporting an organ loft, and the tomb of Louis de Brézé, husband of Diane de Poitiers. By 1544 he had settled in Paris where he worked on the rood screen of Saint Germain l'Auxerrois. But his most famous works, produced about the middle of the century, were the Fontaine des Innocents and decoration at the Louvre. The long reliefs of nymphs and tritons which adorn the fountain clearly show the influence of Cellini, particularly in the drapery which is disposed in close parallel folds and floats as a background to the nudes. The figures themselves recall Primaticcio's drawings by their lightness and delicacy. But the essential beauty of the panels resides in Goujon's sense of surface decoration. His work at the Louvre, apart from the purely architectural details like friezes, consists externally of standing figures flanking the *oeils-de-boeuf* on the ground floor (by 1549) and a series of reliefs in the attic (1553). The relationship of the latter to the architecture is remarkably free: the upper figures break out of the field of the pediment and those at the side overlap the zone of the capitals. The reliefs have been described as 'a paean of praise to monarchical government, its pretensions, prerogatives and obligations as well as the blessings it assures' (Wittkower). Goujon's other important work at the Louvre is the gallery supported by four caryatids at one end of the *Salle* on the ground floor of Lescot's wing, a design wholly new to French architecture. The end of Goujon's career is a mystery: he disappears from the royal accounts in 1562 and, as he was a Protestant, it is possible that he left France in the following year.

The only notable sculptor among Goujon's contemporaries in Paris was Pierre Bontemps, who died in 1568. He first worked on decorative sculpture at Fontainebleau under Primaticcio in 1536. From 1540 he made casts from the moulds after Roman statues which Primaticcio had brought back from Rome. About 1550, when he settled in Paris, he was commissioned by de l'Orme to work on Francis I's tomb at Saint-Denis. He was mainly responsible for the *gisants* and executed the bas-reliefs around the base of the tomb (1551–2). His real talent, however, was for decoration, as shown by his monument for the heart of Francis I, one of the finest examples of the decorative style of the Fontainebleau school. He was also the sculptor of the curious tomb of Charles de Maigny (1557) who is shown seated, in full armour and holding a pike, but asleep.

The cult of ancient Rome

Henry II was extremely interested in the impact his image made on his subjects. In 1547 he appointed a 'general engraver of coins' whose task it was to design medals and coins bearing appropriate images, the kind which had helped to carry down the centuries the fame of many a Roman emperor. For each year of his reign Henry ordered first Marc Béchot, then Etienne

Delaune, to produce works that were both commemorative and signals of developing royal aspirations. Henry's device was the crescent moon, a symbol of beneficence which was seen as peculiarly appropriate to a king who took his role as pastor of his people so seriously. The organizers of the Rouen entry (1550) used it to develop Henry's imperial pretensions. Etienne Perlin, writing in 1558, argued that the moon device had magical properties which guaranteed Henry as 'future monarch and emperor of the world'.

Royal image-making was powerfully influenced by the cult of antiquity which swept through the arts and literature in mid-sixteenth-century France. In their wish to become outstanding connoisseurs and patrons of the arts, French nobles imitated their Italian counterparts: when they visited Rome, they filled their trunks with marble and bronze statues, ancient medals, books and paintings. In a gallery at Meudon, the Cardinal de Guise displayed marble busts of Roman emperors and of Cicero and Demosthenes. Symeoni, who visited the 'grotto' in 1558, exclaimed: 'Here is Rome resurrected!' Images of ancient heroes and their deeds were regarded by French nobles as means of stimulating a desire for military glory. Above all they were impressed by the vision of imperial Rome. Serlio inspired many to contemplate and copy Roman remains and new Italian buildings. The enthusiasm for antique forms permeated all the arts, not only buildings. Engravings by Agostino Veneziano of Roman antiquities and of modern Italian works, which flooded into France from the 1530s, provided models for enamellers' designs in the second half of the century. Drawings by Enea Vico inspired cameos of the twelve Caesars adorning a covered agate cup made for Henry II. The motif was also used to decorate marble tables in Montmorency's *hôtel*. Reduced in size, classical cameos became hat jewels and coat buttons; as coins, they were regarded as essential to any art collection. Although Francis I had been identified with Julius Caesar, it was not until Henry II's reign that the essential prerequisites for the reconstruction of a Roman triumph in art and poetry were fulfilled in France. They were a clear perception of what was involved, a deliberate will to link policy and image-making, adequate resources, and properly trained artists with sufficient technical evidence and actual models from which to work. By the mid-1540s all these conditions had come about. Even French nobles who had not been to Rome had a clear vision of its power and triumphal forms. The degree to which this absorption had taken place is best revealed by the royal entries of Henry II.

In 1548, Henry saw in Lyon a re-enactment of a gladiatorial combat as last fought in ancient Rome. It excited him so much that he wished to see it all again six days after his entry. This too was turned into a kind of Roman triumph. As the king entered the city, he was met by some 160 infantry wearing Roman military uniform. One of the triumphal arches along the processional route was nearly sixty feet high and symbolized

INFATUATION WITH ROME

Honour and Virtue. Honour, seated in a triumphal car drawn by two elephants, had a military escort, while Virtue, in a car drawn by two unicorns, was accompanied by nymphs playing musical instruments.

Henry's Parisian entry (1549) was compared to a Roman triumph by learned eyewitnesses, but it was in Rouen in 1550 that the most consistent attempt was made to stage such a ceremony. The citizens chose to honour the king's recent victories with triumphal chariots. The organizers believed that Henry deserved more spectacular triumphs than had been staged in the past because he had brought them peace. The entry fell into two parts: first, a procession of triumphal cars with hundreds of followers; secondly, the king's journey through the city under triumphal arches. These were four in number. Two were at each end of the bridge across the Seine: the first, in rustic style, showed Orpheus, the Muses and Hercules in the act of destroying the Hydra; the other presented the golden age above Henry's device of the crescent moon. In the cathedral square, the figure of Hector in full armour was mounted on a platform held up by four caryatids while at the Fontaine de la Crosse stood an image of Francis I flanked by two columns.

The design of the triumphal cars was an even more potent evocation of a Roman triumph. The first, depicting Fame, was drawn by four winged horses and decorated by battle scenes, spoils of war and representations of death; the second, enriched with statues, showed Vesta enthroned and symbolized religion; and the third displayed the living image of Henry II holding the insignia of state and receiving the imperial crown from the goddess Good Fortune. Each car was preceded by soldiers, cavalry, musicians and standard-bearers wearing Roman armour. The musical instruments imitated the long tubular horns and trumpets of the Romans and, as in Caesar's triumphs, elephants carried the booty. Prisoners of war came dejectedly behind in chains. Priests followed with sacrificial lambs, while Flora and her nymphs scattered flowers of welcome. Wave after wave of citizens dressed *à la romaine* marched past the king, who viewed the triumph seated on a throne in a specially constructed gallery.

The *Pléiade*

The trend towards classicism, which was expressed in the visual arts during Henry II's reign, was also manifested in literature, especially poetry. It was at this time that the *Pléiade*, a group of seven poets led by Pierre de Ronsard, came into being. Ronsard first used the word in 1556 in a homage to Rémy Belleau; in 1564 he recalled that he had once compared seven poets to the stars of the Pleiades. The group grew out of a series of encounters stretching back to 1543, when Ronsard met Peletier at the funeral of Guillaume du

Bellay. In his *Hymne à Henri II de ce nom* (1555), Ronsard names his six companions as du Bellay, Jodelle, Baïf, Peletier, Belleau and Tyard. They all came under the influence of Jean Dorat, who in 1547 had become principal of the collège de Coqueret in Paris. Dorat was a most influential teacher who lectured with great enthusiasm. The intellectual discipline which he imposed on his pupils may be glimpsed in the *Dialogues* of Guy de Bruès (1557), which presents Ronsard and Baïf as natural philosophers discussing the Copernican theory. This shows that their interests were not exclusively 'literary'. The knowledge they imbibed at Coqueret was fed from the great medieval philosophical and scientific tradition as well as Renaissance Platonism. Apart from their foundation knowledge, the poets acquired a poetic method. Dorat showed Ronsard how to hide his own meanings in myth and image.

The *Pléiade* has been described as 'a kind of private, informed academy, the immediate precursor of the officially constituted academies of the reigns of Charles IX and Henry III and linked to them by the closest ties' (Yates). Ronsard and his friends used to meet in Paris at the Hôtel Baïf, a superb house built by Lazare de Baïf, a distinguished humanist who had been Francis I's ambassador in Venice. It had Greek inscriptions under each window which attracted the gaze of learned passers-by. The house stood near the abbey of Saint-Victor, one of the most important centres of medieval mysticism and Platonism, and the university quarter, home of the great rational and Aristotelian tradition. The poets of the *Pléiade* would each bring and read a work of his own so as to receive advice upon it. 'They also discussed Philosophy, Rhetoric, Poetry and any other matter which presented itself; and if at the end of the dispute there seemed any difficulty, the question was raised again at the next conference and was not laid aside until all obscurities had been cleared up' (Sauval).

Dorat directed his pupils' attention not only towards the ancient world, both Greek and Latin, but also towards new models. Thus the *Pléiade* turned to ancient writers such as Homer, Pindar, Aeschylus, on the one hand, or to the *Anthology* and the Alexandrian poets on the other. This is what Ronsard had in mind when he claimed in the preface to his *Odes* (1550) that he had taken 'style à part, sens à part, oeuvre à part' and had 'taken an unknown path . . . showing the way to follow Pindar and Horace'. The *Pléiade* also shared a desire to equal or surpass the Italian poets. Thus they wrote love poems, epic poems and pastoral poems in imitation of Petrarch, Ariosto and Sannazaro respectively. At the same time they were anxious to promote and improve the use of the French language.

The programme of the *Pléiade* was enunciated by Joachim du Bellay in his *Deffence et illustration de la langue française* (1549). This consists essentially of two books: one on linguistics, the other on poetics. The first argues that the French language feels inferior to Greek and Latin. Why then does it need to be defended? Because, du Bellay explains, languages are equal *in nature*, but not necessarily *in fact*, though this inferiority can be overcome. The current inferiority of French is not due to any intrinsic weakness, but to its neglect or misuse. Here du Bellay attacks an earlier generation of poets: the *rhétoriqueurs* and the *marotistes*, who are accused of having wasted their talents on useless games. The remedy, du Bellay argues, is not simply to translate or blindly to imitate the Ancients; they must be studied, but it is also necessary to cultivate the distinctive merits of the French language by giving it rules and enriching it. In other words, the poet is being invited to come to the assistance of the grammarian. Since the beginning the *Deffence* has come in for criticism. Soon after its publication, Barthélemy Aneau criticized its organization, language and argument in his *Quintil Horatian*. More recent critics have pointed to inconsistencies in du Bellay's reasoning. His originality has also been questioned with reference to earlier works by Sébillet (*Art poétique*) and Speroni (*Dialogo delle lingue*). Yet du Bellay, for all his shortcomings, performed a valuable service by providing a cause, which so far had only been expressed in academic treatises, with a fervently patriotic manifesto.

The leader of the *Pléiade* and among the greatest of all French poets was Pierre de Ronsard, who was widely acclaimed even in his own day as France's answer to Homer and Virgil. President de Thou thought that his birth, which coincided with Francis I's defeat at Pavia, made up for that national humiliation. Ronsard's renown was, moreover, achieved within a decade, between his *Odes* (1550) and his *Oeuvres* (1560). His subsequent works, notably the *Franciade*, did nothing to enhance his reputation. At the age of twenty he turned away from a military career in favour of scholarship, allegedly because an illness had left him partially deaf. He learned Greek and Latin, imitated the style, form and matter of ancient writers, and presented the results of his knowledge and art in his first books of *Odes*. In addition to assuring Ronsard of a personal triumph, they gave him a new status: no longer was he just a provider of love songs and amusements for princes, he became a divine prophet, Nature's interpreter, the soul's healer and the recorder of royal deeds. In the *Ode à Michel de l'Hôpital* (1550), Ronsard's aspirations are expressed by Calliope, the muse of epic poetry. His words are heard as the Voice of God, revealing the beauties of nature to people less privileged in their understanding. Not only humble folk but kings will be moved to perform glorious deeds by the power of his words. Such notions had been expressed before, but never by a French poet. The myths that proliferate in Ronsard's early poems are not mere displays of erudition: they are a powerful means of expression. Thus in his *Amours de Cassandre* some well-known stories from antiquity are used to convey the urgency of his passion. At the same time, Ronsard uses myth in pursuit of his aim of reconciling pagan and Christian belief.

Ronsard added his voice to the eulogies addressed to Henry II by artists and poets. His vision of the ideal king in an ideal court is revealed in his *Hymne à Henri II de ce nom* (1555). The climax of the poem is a comparison between the court of France and Olympus. Jupiter and Henry are presented as mirror images reflecting dignity and honour. As the poem unfolds, Ronsard becomes Apollo who sings the praises of Henry's triumphant majesty. His celebration assumes an epic scale as he extols the qualities expected of a prince and found in abundance in Henry. A wonderfully vivid picture of physical strength emerges as Ronsard relates Henry's athletic powers: his superiority as a swordsman and rider. The king's majesty is made to correspond with the abundant energies of his people and the riches of his dominions.

Ronsard achieved success in every branch of poetry, save dramatic verse. He applied his richly varied poetic invention in many different ways, believing that he had renewed the power of poetry by inventing new forms, diversifying his style and discovering new themes. It was as an innovator that he made his principal claim to glory and fulfilled the demands of Du Bellay's *Deffence*. As a true product of the Renaissance, he never forgot the ancient and Italian authors whom he had read and admired, yet his best poems are probably those in which his main concern is not imitation but the expression of his own thoughts and feelings. His themes (nature, love, death, and the transience of life) and images (the rose, the sun, the stars, jewels, the seasons, classical myths) are the conventional ones current in Europe at the time, yet his poetry is distinctively his own. Nature was for Ronsard a constant source of inspiration and solace. He was grief-stricken when his beloved forest of Gatine was threatened with destruction. 'His sense of beauty, his ability to catch at its fragility, its variety, and its vitality, and to record it in the lines of a poem, is his most enduring achievement' (Cruickshank). Ronsard's vision of beauty and of nature is always noble. It is also very formalized: the scene is ordered, the elements of nature are unconsciously beautified and given a pattern. Even in Ronsard's last years, his preoccupation with beauty, as manifested in nature and in woman, remained firm. His desire to feel its delights became all the stronger as he became aware of his own physical weakness. In a sonnet to Hélène, he uses the image of the climbing ivy to describe the urgency of his desires, which are mingled here with confidence in his own immortality.

15

Henry II: The Tragic Peace, 1553–9

In April 1553 the Emperor Charles V invaded Picardy. He besieged Thérouanne, a strategically valuable French enclave hemmed in by Flanders, Hainault and Artois, and, following the town's capitulation in June, razed it to the ground. Among the prisoners taken by him was François de Montmorency, the constable's eldest son. Following the surrender of Hesdin on 18 July, Anne de Montmorency advanced to save Doullens, but the imperialists withdrew. Henry II, meanwhile, entrusted the government of France to his queen and on 1 September reviewed his army. While Guise reconnoitred enemy positions, Montmorency systematically destroyed the countryside as far as Bapaume. He bombarded Cambrai for six days after he had been refused supplies. On 17 September, as the weather deteriorated, the king called off the campaign.

Meanwhile Charles V pulled off a major diplomatic coup in England. Anglo-French relations had improved after the duke of Northumberland had replaced the Protector Somerset at the head of Edward VI's government; but the situation changed radically following the young king's death on 6 July 1554. An attempt by Northumberland to put Lady Jane Grey on the throne was foiled and Mary Tudor became queen. Soon afterwards she married the emperor's son, Philip of Spain. Although the marriage treaty specifically denied him the right to embroil England in his father's war with France, it shattered Henry II's hopes of a possible union of the crowns of France, Scotland and England in the person of Mary Queen of Scots. The future now hinged on Mary Tudor's fertility. If she were to die childless, Philip's rights in England would cease; but if she and Philip were to have children, their eldest son would inherit England, the Netherlands and Franche-Comté; and in the event of Don Carlos, Philip's son by a former wife, having no children, then Spain and her dependencies as well. This was a truly daunting prospect for France.

In June 1554, Henry II invaded the Low Countries. Three French armies penetrated the southern Netherlands, capturing several fortresses, and on 28 June, having outmanoeuvred Charles V, they captured Mariemburg. Soon afterwards the town was rechristened Henriembourg in honour of the king of France. On 12 July he and Montmorency captured Bouvignes and the garrison of 800 Spaniards was put to the sword. As the French closed in on Brussels, they laid waste the countryside. On 10 August they tried to draw the emperor into the open by attacking the fort of Renty. Battle was joined three days later, but Charles held on to the fort, albeit after suffering heavy losses. On 15 August, Henry called off his campaign.

Many Frenchmen were disappointed by the campaign. They thought that Charles should have been captured at Renty and accused Montmorency of not pulling his weight. The Venetian envoy, Capello, wrote: 'He used to be regarded as pusillanimous; now he is seen as a veritable coward, as he has been afraid of chasing an enemy who was beaten and almost fleeing.' Among the constable's chief critics were the Guises. No victory was possible, in their view, as long as he continued to lead the army. The constable, for his part, did not hide his longing for peace: he wanted to liberate his son and consolidate recent territorial gains.

The war between France and the Empire was also fought in Italy. In July 1552 cardinals Tournon and Ippolito d'Este held a conference in Chioggia with France's allies to consider ways of creating a diversion in the peninsula. They focused their attention on Siena, where on 26 July the inhabitants rose and expelled the Spanish garrison. Four days later, Lansac arrived bringing money and an assurance of French support. On 11 August, Paul de Termes, Henry II's lieutenant in central Italy, took command of Siena's defence. Declaring himself the city's 'protector, defender and benefactor', Henry appointed Ippolito as governor; but Cosimo de' Medici, the duke of Tuscany, fearing that Siena would be used as a base by Florentine exiles, intrigued with Charles V to overthrow the Sienese republic. Six months elapsed, however, before the viceroy of Naples was able to gather enough troops and ships. In January 1553 he laid siege to Siena, but was forced to lift it in June when the Turks threatened southern Italy.

In November 1552, Henry had written to Suleiman II asking him to send a fleet against Italy in the spring. Early in 1553 baron de La Garde was sent to Constantinople to arrange a Franco-Turkish attack. In early July the Turkish fleet was off the Tuscan coast where it was joined by French galleys. As Siena seemed out of danger, Henry ordered his commanders in Italy to conquer Corsica. The island, which belonged to Genoa, was a vital staging post between France and central Italy and a favourite port of call for Spanish shipping. The French conquest of the island was easily accomplished, but it drove the Genoese into the imperial camp.

In the absence of de Termes, who had led the Corsican expedition, Henry

II appointed Piero Strozzi, leader of the Florentine exiles, as lieutenant-general in Tuscany. His arrival in Siena in January 1554 was followed by a lengthy dispute between him and the Cardinal of Ferrara. Eventually the cardinal retired to Ferrara. Strozzi's warlike zeal was shared by Catherine de' Medici who mortgaged part of her lands to help his cause. As news of his exploits against Florence reached France, his ultimate triumph was taken for granted. On 2 August, however, he suffered a crushing defeat at Marciano. A few days later the siege of Siena, which Monluc was to describe so vividly in his memoirs, began. By now the Sienese were tired of Strozzi, and Montmorency was having serious doubts about the Tuscan adventure. 'There is much lamentation among the courtiers', wrote an eyewitness, 'over the expenditure in Italy that the complaints would not be louder if the king had lost half his kingdom.' On 17 April, Strozzi's discomfiture was completed by Siena's surrender. He was coolly received by the king on his return to France and the Florentine exiles shared his disgrace. Montmorency now tried to negotiate a general peace.

In northern Italy the war turned to France's advantage in 1555. By capturing Ivrea and Casale, Marshal Brissac became the master of Montferrat and controlled the outlets from the Po valley. In June he tried to relieve Santia, which was being besieged by Alba, but the imperial forces retired before Brissac received reinforcements from France. He used them to besiege Volpiano which threatened Turin's approaches. The operations were entrusted to Claude duc d'Aumale, who was joined by many young noblemen from France. Volpiano's capitulation (24 September) was followed by that of Moncalvo (7 October). By December, Alba was desperate. He accused Charles V of allowing the northern front to receive most subsidies while his forces in Italy were left to bear the brunt of the fighting.

In May 1555 peace talks began at Marcq, near Calais. They made no progress, however, as Henry insisted on preserving the status quo while Charles demanded a return to the pre-war situation. By now the emperor's health was failing, and the readiness of his son Philip to assume the burdens of government encouraged him to lay down his responsibilities. Between October 1555 and January 1556, Charles divested himself of his titles, and in September 1556 he left the Netherlands on his final journey to Spain, where he was to spend his last years in monastic seclusion. The transfer of power from father to son was not universally welcomed, for Philip lacked experience of international and military affairs. He was commonly described as 'spiritless', 'untried', even 'cowardly', and his ministers were not highly rated either. One of Philip's first moves was to buy time by accepting a five-year truce which was signed at Vaucelles on 5 February 1556.

The imperial predicament was such that we may wonder why Henry accepted a truce rather than peace on his own terms? The answer lies almost certainly in his own financial situation. The French crown owed over 2 million *écus* of which only just over 650,000 were secured. In order to find assignments, Henry had to reschedule the debt; he also needed funds with which to pay for the war. In exchange for a new loan of more than half a million *écus*, he agreed to set his finances in order. In a series of edicts issued in 1555, Henry consolidated his debts, converting the short-term, high-interest loans into a long-term debt bearing a uniform rate of interest of 16 per cent. He aimed to discharge it in four annual instalments coinciding with Lyon's fairs between 1555 and 1565. But these measures, collectively called the *Grand Parti de Lyon*, soon became obsolete, for the demands of war and the availability of credit tempted Henry into a new round of heavy borrowing. Between April and October 1555 he borrowed at least 340,000 *écus*. These loans were incorporated into the consolidated debt, throwing existing arrangements into disarray. New revenues had to be assigned to cope with the extra burden. This new situation deterred some bankers from advancing more credit at the end of 1555, yet it was not until August 1556 and January 1557 that Henry was unable to pay the interest due on the new consolidated debt and not until April 1557 that he had difficulty obtaining credit.

The Neapolitan voyage

Charles V's abdication coincided with important changes at the Holy See. Following the death of Julius III on 23 March 1555, Marcellus Cervini was elected pope, but he died after only three weeks. He was succeeded on 23 May by Giampiero Carafa, who took the name of Paul IV. His election satisfied the French court, for he was known to be a bitter enemy of the emperor. Despite his reputation as an ascetic reformer, he used his new-found power to promote his kinsmen, particularly his nephews Carlo Carafa, a soldier turned cardinal, and the duke of Camerino. Paul demanded the see of Naples for the former and Piacenza for the latter. When Philip II refused, Paul reacted angrily: he attacked the Colonna and other Roman nobles who supported Spain, then excommunicated Charles V and his son.

The French were naturally delighted. In August 1555, following the collapse of the peace talks at Marcq, Henry II decided to break imperial intransigence. He proposed 'to force the emperor and his allies to shift the main burden of the war to Italy in order to relieve our territories and subjects on this side [of the Alps]'. On 1 October the Cardinal of Lorraine was instructed to negotiate an alliance with Paul IV which was signed on 15 December. In exchange for French aid, the pope agreed to bestow the kingdom of Naples on one of Henry's two sons and the duchy of Milan on the other. If Henry's son was too young to rule Naples someone (widely assumed to be the duc de Guise) would be chosen to rule in his absence.

Finally, Siena was promised to the pope. However, on 9 February, Lorraine learned of the truce of Vaucelles. 'The constable', he exclaimed, 'has won the day!' On 11 May, Cardinal Carafa left for France, ostensibly 'to complete the holy task of peace', but in reality to urge Henry to make war in Italy. Meanwhile, Paul IV excommunicated the Colonna and seized their property. He told Tournon: 'It is time to break the truce and to give the crown of Naples to the king of France.'

Philip II, in the meantime, decided to launch a pre-emptive strike. On 1 September 1556, Alba invaded the Roman Campagna with a small army, and a fortnight later captured Anagni, opening up a direct route to Rome. Panic gripped the city, which still bore the scars of the sack of 1527. Responding to an urgent appeal for help from Carafa, Henry decided to send an army to Italy. On 14 November he appointed the duc de Guise as lieutenant-general in the peninsula and the duke was soon joined in Paris by some 200 noblemen in search of wealth and adventure. Clear-sighted observers understood that Henry II had not raised a crack army simply to rescue the pope. Ever since 1555, the Cardinal of Lorraine's secret diplomacy had been paving the way for the conquest of Naples.

Guise left Turin on 9 January 1557 with 11,000 infantry, 1800 cavalry and a few guns. Such a force was easy to manage, but its success depended on receiving supplies and reinforcements from Italian allies. As Guise pushed along the Po valley, he ran into terrible weather. 'Never in my life', he wrote, 'have I seen soldiers and horses endure such misery, being up to their bellies in mud.' In mid-February he met his father-in-law, Ercole d'Este, duke of Ferrara, and Cardinal Carafa at Reggio nell'Emilia. Ercole wanted war to be declared on the duke of Parma, but Carafa warned against such a move. Guise thought of attacking Florence, but its ruler, Cosimo de' Medici, managed to avert the threat. The only course left to Guise was to march on Naples. He called on the pope and asked him to cede to him temporarily the ports of Ancona and Civitavecchia so that he might receive reinforcements and supplies by sea. His request, however, was turned down. Further disappointment awaited Guise on 15 March when a creation of cardinals included only two favoured by France. This effectively ruined the prospects of the Neapolitan expedition, for the pope was dying and it seemed unlikely that his successor would confer the investiture of Naples on Henry II's representative. On 10 April, Guise rejoined his army in the March of Ancona. He planned to defeat Alba, then conquer Campania with the help of the French and Turkish navies. But his Italian allies refused him subsidies. Henry II decided that the time had come to pull his troops out of Italy and to leave the pope and his kinsmen to their fate. Guise was accordingly instructed to abandon the march on Naples, though Henry allowed him to remain in the States of the Church for the time being.

In the summer of 1557, following the collapse of the truce of Vaucelles,

Philip II launched an invasion of northern France under Emmanuel-Philibert of Savoy. A huge army under Montmorency awaited the invaders. On 10 August – the feast of St Lawrence – the two armies collided outside Saint-Quentin. The outcome was a shattering defeat for France and her constable, who was taken prisoner. Although the Spaniards chose not follow up their victory by marching on Paris, the inhabitants of the capital were so panic-stricken that Henry had to reassure them by staying among them. 'The Parisians', wrote a Venetian observer, 'in their conversation or broadsheets ceaselessly lacerate the cardinal of Lorraine as the principal author of this war: they recall that he went to Rome to conclude an alliance with the pope and that, aided by his family, he has since pressed the king as hard as possible to go to war.' As the first step towards saving the situation, Henry recalled Guise and his army from Italy.

The conquest of Calais, 7 January 1558

Guise was back at court by 9 October 1557. With him were his best troops: seven companies of arquebusiers and eleven other companies. Henry appointed him lieutenant-general throughout the realm with extraordinary powers. From the duke's standpoint, the battle of Saint-Quentin was indeed fortunate: it enabled him to pose as the kingdom's saviour. Meanwhile his brother, the Cardinal of Lorraine, was put in charge of domestic and foreign policy in place of Montmorency. The Guise brothers thus gained a firm grip on government. Their enemy La Planche described them as 'two heads in one hood'. Whereas the constable and his nephews were associated with ill-luck and failure, the Guises achieved some notable successes early in their careers. The most sensational was the conquest of Calais.

Plans to infiltrate and capture Calais can be traced back to 1547, but they were encouraged by the accession of Mary Tudor and England's obvious drift into the Habsburg camp. According to Brantôme, the French were able to see for themselves the weakness of Calais's defences during the negotiations at Marcq in June 1555, but it was the defeat at Saint-Quentin which galvanized Henry II into an exceptional effort. Part of it consisted in raising money, for the royal coffers were sadly depleted, if not empty. Loans raised on the Lyon bankers or grants voted by the provincial estates could not by themselves sustain the major campaign envisaged by the king. This was why the Estates-General, or something similar, met in Paris in January 1558. The clergy were represented by five cardinals and thirty-five bishops, the nobility by the *baillis* and *sénéchaux* and many courtiers, and the third estate was unusually divided into two parts: the mayors of towns and members of the parlements. The king was warmly thanked by the latter for creating a 'fourth estate of justice'. On 5 January, in a lengthy speech,

Henry explained that he needed money in order to force the enemy into conceding a good and lasting peace. The estates responded with generous promises, but in the end the nobility, as usual, got off scot free, leaving the other estates to shoulder the fiscal burden. The clergy promised to contribute a third of the three million crowns asked for by Henry, while the towns were asked to make up the rest in the form of a loan on which the king would pay 8.3 per cent interest. He also undertook to reduce taxation, both direct and indirect.

In the meantime, Calais came under attack. The unusual idea of attacking it in mid-winter appears to have been Henry's; Guise was doubtful at first, yet he carried out the plan with meticulous care and speed. He was assisted by exceptionally wintry conditions, which facilitated his troops' crossing of the marshy approaches to Calais, and by the complacency of the English commander. The duke entered the Pale about midnight on 31 December and, after cutting off Calais's main outworks, seized the castle. On 7 January 1558 the town fell and a stream of messages conveyed the news to all and sundry. Such was the enthusiasm that greeted it among the deputies of the clergy and towns at the Estates-General that they rashly offered their contributions to the king as gifts rather than loans, though, in the event, their status remained unchanged. On 15 January, Henry appeared before the parlement to obtain registration of edicts against heresy. He then left for Calais, accompanied by the Dauphin and the Cardinal of Lorraine. As the king made his entry into Calais, his chapel sang *In exitu Israel de Egypto*. Meanwhile, on 21 January, Guînes fell to the French.

During his stay in Calais, Henry rewarded the captains who had served him so well. Guise's reward took the form of the king's final commitment to the marriage of the Dauphin and Mary Stuart. Montmorency tried to derail it, fearing that it would enhance the power of the Guises, but Henry found the marriage irresistible: particularly following the death of Edward VI and considering the probable childlessness of Mary Tudor, Mary Stuart's claim to the English throne seemed all the more likely to be realized. So her wedding to the Dauphin took place at Notre-Dame on 21 April. The ceremony was accompanied by magnificent festivities, in which Guise acted as Grand Master in place of the captive Montmorency.

Following his return to court, Guise took control of the kingdom's military administration, while Paul de Termes, the new governor of Calais, took steps to protect the town from a possible English counterattack. He had difficulty gathering enough money, workmen, munitions and timber. His survival depended in large measure on the inability of the enemy to muster their power. In June, Villebon and de Termes took and sacked Dunkirk, Nieupoort and Bergues, but near Gravelines they were defeated with heavy losses, de Termes himself being captured. However, the Burgundians were not in a position to recapture Calais. In late August the last remaining

English garrisons in Picardy were cleared by the Vidame de Chartres. While England mourned the loss of Calais, Scotland seemed to sink deeper under French control. In November 1558 the Scottish parliament granted the 'crown matrimonial' to the Dauphin. Scotland, in fact, remained a serious threat to England. The fall of Calais stirred fears that Berwick would soon follow and led to the town's being equipped with a complete set of angle-bastioned walls to withstand modern artillery.

The Peace of Cateau-Cambrésis, 3–4 April 1559

By the autumn of 1558 both sides in the war badly wanted peace. Henry II was desperate for the return of the Constable of Montmorency, who alone could withstand the rising influence of the Guises. Diane de Poitiers was similarly disposed and formed an alliance with the constable by marrying her granddaughter to his son Henri. The king also knew that he would have difficulty raising enough money to continue the war, and needed to concentrate on the fight against heresy within France. Philip II was equally impecunious and keen to bring the war to an end, particularly as he held a marvellous bargaining counter in the person of the constable. In October 1558, Montmorency was released on parole and commissioners were appointed by both sides to negotiate a peace. They met first at the abbey of Cercamp near the Franco-Flemish border, then at Cateau-Cambrésis.

Two issues dominated the talks: Savoy and Calais. There were other contentious issues, such as Navarre or the three bishoprics in Lorraine (Metz, Toul and Verdun), but neither side chose to make a stand on them. Savoy, however, was different, if only because Italy was still seen as the seat of European supremacy. Philip needed to recover Savoy for two main reasons: first, because it was a barrier to French aggression in Italy; secondly, because he needed to safeguard his international reputation by showing that he could recover lands lost by his allies. He also owed a considerable personal debt to the duke Emmanuel-Philibert. At first, Henry would give up only part of the duchy, but gradually his negotiators agreed to restore it save for a number of fortified places. By mid-November both sides were broadly in agreement.

Talks over the future of Calais proved even more difficult. Philip owed its recovery to his English subjects, but Henry made its retention his minimum condition. The situation seemed hopeless, but Henry suddenly offered to give up almost all his outstanding claims in Italy provided Calais remained French. Philip's advisers were deeply divided on the issue. Alba and Granvelle wanted to continue the war; others, who knew Spain's financial predicament, urged Philip to make peace even without Calais. The death of his wife Mary Tudor on 17 November 1558 persuaded some of Philip's advisers that he no longer had a duty to recover Calais, but the king was desperate to retain the friendship of Elizabeth, England's new queen, lest she should ally with France. Eventually Philip decided on peace regardless of Calais, but the matter was decided by England and France without his knowledge. They agreed to leave Calais in French hands for eight years, after which the French would return it or pay an indemnity of 500,000 crowns.

The Peace of Cateau-Cambrésis (3–4 April 1559) consisted of two treaties: one between France and England; the other between France and Spain. Apart from the compromise regarding Calais, the former provided for the return of sixteen cannon captured by the French in the Pale of Calais and the dismantling of French fortresses along Scotland's border with England. The Franco-Spanish treaty was more complex. In northern France, Henry was to return four fortified places in exchange for an equal number held by Philip. Henry gave the duchy of Bouillon to the bishop of Liège and Philip kept Hesdin. In Italy, France returned Bresse, Savoy and Piedmont to the duke of Savoy, retaining only the small marquisate of Saluzzo and, for a time, five fortified places in Piedmont, including Turin. Spain's rights to Milan and Naples were recognized, and French fortresses in Lombardy were handed over to Spanish forces. In Tuscany, all French positions were ceded to the duke of Mantua or the duke of Florence. Genoa recovered Corsica. Although Spain had pressed for a clause banning Frenchmen from the New World, this was not included in the treaty. Both monarchs promised to support a General Council of the church; otherwise, the treaty was silent on religion. The need to fight heresy was implicitly understood by both parties; there was no need to reaffirm it.

Finally, two marriages were arranged: one between the duke of Savoy and Henry's sister Marguerite; the other between Philip II and Henry's eldest daughter Elisabeth. The eagerness with which Henry had pursued this marriage owed much to his desire to eliminate the prospect of another marital alliance between England and Spain. Much against his will, Philip had been persuaded to offer Elizabeth I his hand. He had been told that unless he did so, the French would establish Mary Stuart and her husband on the English throne, thereby creating a new empire that would destroy the Habsburgs. It was in order to safeguard Catholicism in England that Philip had reluctantly pressed his suit in January 1559. Happily for him, no positive response came from Elizabeth, who was neither keen on marriage nor willing to forgo her Protestant faith, as Philip had requested. This left him under the impression that he was not committed to her and precipitated his marriage to Elisabeth de Valois.

The Peace of Cateau-Cambrésis was denounced as shameful by many Frenchmen, particularly by captains who had fought in the Italian Wars. 'Oh wretched France!' Brissac exclaimed. 'To what ruin and loss have you allowed yourself to fall!' For Monluc, the treaty had lost the king of France nearly two hundred fortresses and almost a third of his kingdom. Yet Henry felt satisfied for several reasons. The peace enabled him to restore his finances, to impose his authority at home and to improve his international position. He and his advisers, it seems, had a more realistic understanding of France's weaknesses than critics of the peace. Nor were the details of the settlement wholly unfavourable to France. After all, Philip failed to recover Calais and the three bishoprics, abandoned for ever all hope of settling his rights to Burgundy, and failed to defend the Iberian monopoly in the New World.

The Calvinist menace

The war had facilitated the progress of heresy in France by drawing the crown's attention away from the domestic scene. As reports from almost every French province offered an alarming picture, Henry II admitted his helplessness. He confessed to the imperial ambassador in April 1556 that he had been unable to cope with heresy because of other business and he denounced Geneva as 'the source of much evil because many heretics are received there and thence disseminate their errors throughout France'. He was much disturbed by the fact that Protestantism, which he had always regarded as a religion of the lower orders, was now attracting many nobles. In 1555 no fewer than 120 fled to Geneva.

French dissenters who had followed Calvin to Geneva were not content simply to practise their faith there; they wanted to bring it home, confident in the belief that its truths would eventually be accepted by their compatriots. In 1555 missionaries trained in Geneva began to slip across the border into France. Research into the archives of the Geneva Company of Pastors has yielded information about 88 missionaries who were sent to France between 1555 and 1562. Sixty-two were French by birth, almost every province being represented among them. Those chiefly represented were Guyenne and Dauphiné. The social background of 42 missionaries is known: they comprised 14 nobles (mostly younger sons), 24 bourgeois and 4 artisans, but not a single peasant. In Geneva the missionaries underwent a rigorous training: they were made to learn Latin, Greek and Hebrew in order that they should know the Bible really well. At first there was no formally organized institution to provide this education; Calvin and Farel tried to fill the need by lecturing themselves. But in 1559 the Genevan Academy was set up under Théodore de Bèze and proved a great success: by 1564 it had 1500 students.

Louis prince de Condé was the most distinguished French nobleman to visit Geneva between 1555 and 1559. Others came not just as visitors but as immigrants. By allowing them to settle within its territory, Geneva almost automatically involved itself in French politics. Some of the future political and military leaders of the Huguenot movement were indoctrinated alongside the pastors who would become its spiritual leaders. A bonding of the two groups thus took place in Geneva before they returned to France.

After completing their studies, the missionaries usually took up pastoral duties in Switzerland. Only after they had become thoroughly attuned to the strict collective self-discipline of the Calvinist church were they sent into France. Before undertaking the journey, a missionary's suitability for the task was examined by the Company of Pastors: he had to expound a selected verse from the Bible at a meeting of the Company; he also had to be a good public speaker and his private life had to be above reproach. After passing all these tests, the missionary was given a letter accrediting him to a particular French church. This was considered essential, for local churches were reluctant to admit a minister without Genevan credentials. They were understandably wary of the many itinerant preachers, unfrocked monks and zany heretics who were floating around. Missionaries were always allocated in response to a request from a church. Thus Jacques l'Anglois was sent in response to a request from the brethren of Poitiers for 'an upright man to administer to them the word of God'.

The distribution of Calvinist missions in France shows where the strength of the new faith was mainly centred. The fact that more pastors were sent to certain towns than to whole provinces points to Calvin's success among the urban middle classes. The main strength of his movement lay in towns like Poitiers and Orléans. Among provinces, Calvinism was strongest in Guyenne, Gascony, Normandy, Dauphiné and Languedoc, areas dominated by Protestant nobles, or in neutral ones. In north-east France, where the Guises or the Constable of Montmorency were all-powerful, Calvinism made little or no headway. No missionaries were sent to Artois, Picardy, Flanders or Burgundy, and only one to Champagne. The church of Paris was one of the earliest and most important of Protestant churches in France. It was founded in 1555 by Jean le Maçon, seigneur de Launay, called La Rivière. He was soon joined by François de Morel and by a young lawyer, Antoine de La Roche-Chandieu. Gaspard Carmel and Nicolas des Gallards arrived in 1557. Jean Macar relieved des Gallards in 1558 and was himself replaced in October by Morel. These frequent changes were necessitated by the dangers that attended the ministers' activities.

Henry II was well aware of the growing threat to his authority presented by the Genevan missionaries. In February 1557 he asked Pope Paul IV for a brief establishing the Holy Office in France. The pope responded by appointing three cardinals – Bourbon, Châtillon and Lorraine – as inquisitors of the faith. The inclusion of Châtillon, whose Protestant sympathies were already apparent, has puzzled historians; but the three cardinals may have been chosen simply because they were those most often at court and sat in the king's council. Montmorency would also have wanted to counterbalance Lorraine's influence by including Châtillon, who was his nephew. Be that as it may, the papal brief was sanctioned by royal edict on 24 July, though this was not registered till January 1558. It was never given effect and was rescinded in April. Also on 24 July 1557, Henry issued the Edict of Compiègne, which increased the penalties which secular courts could impose for heresy. The preamble noted that earlier edicts had failed to achieve religious uniformity because of conflicts over jurisdiction and the malice or lenience of judges. The death penalty was accordingly mandated for obstinate or relapsed sacramentarians (this meant Calvinists, not Lutherans), for people who went to Geneva or had books published there, for blasphemers against images of Christ or the saints, and for illegal preaching and participation in religious gatherings, public or private. The act stated that the number of heretics had grown to such an extent that their offence had become open sedition. Henry accordingly gave notice that he would use force of arms as well as the law courts to deal with it. The edict has been fairly described as 'a declaration of war' (Sutherland), but fierce resistance from the parlement and the French defeat at Saint-Quentin prevented its application.

The Genevan missionaries were thus able to continue making converts in France. They tried at first to operate as secretly as possible: they held services in the homes of prominent Calvinists at night and in heavily curtained rooms. If houses were not available, they used barns or secluded spots in the woods. Sooner or later, however, their activities were bound to come to light. This happened in Paris on 4 September 1557, when an angry mob broke up a Calvinist meeting in a house in the rue Saint-Jacques. The congregation included nobles of both sexes, their children, royal officials, artisans and servants. The noblemen, who had swords, managed to fight their way out of the mêlée, but about 132 people, including many women and children, were arrested and thrown into prison. It was rumoured that they had taken part in orgies, and the parlement put them on trial. On 14 September three, including a noble widow, Philippa de Luns, were burnt on the Place Maubert.

Apart from attracting publicity unwelcome to the Calvinists, the Saint-Jacques affair raised the question of whether or not Protestants could lawfully resist persecution by the crown. In a letter to the Parisian church, Calvin sympathized with its plight, but said that prayer was its only redress. He pleaded with its members to be patient and to attempt nothing against the word of God. His letter ended with the famous warning that it would be preferable for them all to perish than that the Gospel should be accused of driving the people into sedition and tumult.

Meanwhile, however, Calvin asked the German Protestant princes to intercede on behalf of their Parisian co-religionists. They sent an embassy to the king of France with a letter appealing for clemency and assuring him that the Protestants were neither seditious nor fanatical, but he was unimpressed and told the German princes to mind their own business. The prisoners who were still alive were eventually released, but only after continued examination, occasional trials and other kinds of legal pressure.

Although the affair of the rue Saint-Jacques seriously disrupted the activities of the Paris church, it seemed to spur it to further political activity. François d'Andelot, the brother of Admiral Coligny, decided to evangelize his estates in Brittany with the help of Gaspard Carmel, a Parisian pastor. Travelling under a pseudonym, Carmel preached publicly under d'Andelot's armed protection. A permanent church was set up at Le Croisic to which the Paris church sent a young pastor. On their way back to Paris, d'Andelot and Carmel revived the church at Angers. After returning to court, d'Andelot was put under house arrest at Melun and pressured to recant. The Parisian church was most anxious that he should stand firm and thereby display willingness to protect Calvinists who were his social inferiors. Calvin urged him to be steadfast or face eternal damnation. Meanwhile Macar and Chandieu worked hard to win over members of the upper nobility. While Macar was introduced to d'Andelot's brothers, Admiral Coligny and Odet de Châtillon, Chandieu tried to convert members of the house of Bourbon. Long reports of their activity were sent back to Calvin and the Geneva Company of Pastors. In September 1558, Macar was recalled to Geneva, having become too well known in Paris. His successor, François de Morel, showed an even greater interest in court politics.

In May 1558 the Calvinists, taking advantage of an apparent softening of the king's attitude, staged a mass demonstration in Paris. A crowd of between four and five thousand people gathered under the protection of armed nobles to sing psalms in the Pré-aux-Clercs, a meadow on the left bank of the Seine within sight of the Louvre. The demonstration lasted several days in defiance of a ban by the parlement. At least one of the gatherings was attended by Antoine, king of Navarre, whose support the Protestants were most anxious to secure. He was less interested in their plight, however, than in his own small kingdom. He promised to remonstrate with the king about their maltreatment, but did nothing; he did not even abstain from mass. Navarre incurred the contempt of Protestants by spending so much time dancing at court, but as first prince of the blood he could not be overlooked and, in August, Chandieu entered his service, hoping to evangelize his entourage. At the same time, Macar and Chandieu waited upon his brother Condé, who promised them 'mountains and marvels'.

Meanwhile, the king had a violent quarrel with d'Andelot, who had been accused of heresy by the Cardinal of Lorraine. The cardinal secured from Henry a ban under pain of death on all access to the Pré-aux-Clercs. Numerous arrests were made, but Henry did not want to stir up trouble at home just as he was about to leave on a new military campaign, so most of the victims were released and d'Andelot recanted after a fashion. But the rally at the Pré-aux-Clercs had left Henry with the impression that his authority was being seriously challenged. He appointed Monluc colonel-general of the infantry in place of d'Andelot, and declared that as soon as he had settled the foreign situation, he would cause blood to flow and heads to roll at home.

Protestantism was also infiltrating the Parlement of Paris, which delayed registration of the king's repressive edicts and often reduced sentences passed on heretics. Henry did not wish to interfere with the court's judicial procedures, but he expected it to purge heretics from its own ranks. In March 1559 the death sentence passed on three heretics was reduced by the *Tournelle* to one of banishment from the kingdom. This led to the summoning of a special *mercuriale*, which the king attended on 10 June. He was appalled by the opinions expressed by some of the younger councillors, notably Anne Du Bourg, who advocated the suspension of all heresy trials pending a General Council. Du Bourg denounced as evil the burning of people whose only crime had been to call on Christ's name, while adulterers, blasphemers and murderers escaped punishment. Taking the charge of adultery personally, Henry flew into a rage: he asked to see the minutes of earlier sessions of the *mercuriale*, and ordered the arrest of Du Bourg and another councillor, Du Faur. Later that day he ordered the arrest of six more suspects. As a prisoner, Du Bourg wrote an attack on the legitimacy of a monarch who tried to force his subjects to live contrary to the will of God. The text was smuggled out of his prison and published as a pamphlet.

The king's fearsome resolve to wipe out heresy was doubtless also fuelled by a recent attempt upon his life. As he was emerging from the Sainte-Chapelle after a service, a certain chancery clerk, called Caboche, whose brothers had been recently tried and executed in Meaux for various crimes including blasphemy, tried to stab him. Henry wanted to question Caboche, but the would-be assassin was secretly eliminated beforehand, much to Henry's annoyance. It was said that this had been done by Calvinists who did not want their secrets disclosed.

The Peace of Cateau-Cambrésis in April 1559 enabled Henry to pay closer attention to the fast-growing problem of heresy in his kingdom. On 19 June he appointed commissioners to try Du Bourg and Du Faur. It was reported that as soon as the marriage festivities were over, he would lead an army against Protestant strongholds in his kingdom. Henry also considered sending aid to Mary of Guise against the Scottish Calvinists, and toyed with the idea of a Franco-Spanish attack on Geneva.

Meanwhile, the French Calvinists were becoming more unified. In May 1559 they held their first National Synod in Paris. It was held secretly in two private houses under the chairmanship of the Parisian pastor Morel. Nearly all the delegates were pastors from ten other French churches. The synod's main achievement was the drafting of a Confession of Faith and Ecclesiastical Discipline. The former was closely modelled on the Confession which Calvin had drafted in 1557 for presentation to the king of France. The Ecclesiastical Discipline, though less obviously Calvin's work, nevertheless strongly resembled the Genevan ordinances which he had helped to draft. The main effect of the synod's decisions was to tighten the organization of the French Reformed Church. Strict rules were laid down governing the choice of ministers, and church members were forbidden to publish any religious books without the sanction of two or three pastors of known orthodoxy. Nearly every provincial synod which met after 1559 endorsed these Paris decisions. The Calvinist churches in France were thus 'welded into a single instrument under the indirect but real control of Geneva. For the first time in centuries religious dissent in France was organized on a scale and with a centralization that made it a real political power' (Kingdon).

The National Synod's authority was supplemented by provincial synods, regional colloquies, and local consistories, each covering an increasingly small geographical area. The smaller the territory, the more frequently meetings were held. The National Synod was the pinnacle of the organization. Disagreements which could not be settled locally could be sent on appeal to the colloquy, thence to the provincial synod, and finally to the National Synod. In practice, however, the local churches often addressed their appeals directly to Geneva. Provincial synods and colloquies did likewise, as the National Synod met only infrequently. Consequently, the authority of the Geneva Company of Pastors increased through the creation of the new organization. The Company could also exercise discipline by recalling pastors whom it had sent to France. This was often the result of a pastor becoming 'too discovered'. When this happened, he not only risked losing his life but also compromised and endangered all the people with whom he worked. His usefulness would thus be ended and he would be asked to return to Geneva, possibly for a fresh assignment.

The tragedy of the rue Saint-Antoine

Henry's hope that Philip II would come to Paris for his marriage to Elisabeth de Valois was dashed when the Spanish monarch curtly informed him that 'kings of Spain do not go after their brides'. Instead, the duke of Alba came to Paris with a huge aristocratic escort. On 18 June the peace was sworn in Notre-Dame and four days later the marriage was celebrated, Elisabeth's dowry being fixed at 400,000 *livres*. As for the duke of Savoy, he arrived in the French capital on 21 June for his marriage to Henry's sister, Marguerite. This was scheduled for 4 July, her dowry being fixed at 300,000 *livres*. To honour the two marriages, Henry ordered a magnificent tournament, which was to last five days and take place in the rue Saint-Antoine in front of the palace of the Tournelles.

On 30 June, the third day of the tournament, Henry appeared in the lists riding a Turkish stallion given to him by his future brother-in-law, Emmanuel-Philibert. He wore an outfit of black and white as a tribute to Diane de Poitiers, 'the lady whom he served'. Joining a group of nobles, he ran two courses. He vanquished his opponents in the first two, but was seriously jolted in the third by Gabriel de Montgomery, captain of the Scottish guard. Refusing to end on this note, the king challenged his rival to a further contest against the advice of the queen and other members of his circle, who had allegedly received warnings of imminent disaster from soothsayers. The two combatants fell upon each other with great force, splintering each other's lance. Under the rules, they should have dropped their weapons instantly, but Montgomery held on to his, which, glancing upwards, struck the king's visor, and lifting it (had he raised it or forgotten to fasten it?) drove several needle-sharp splinters of wood into his forehead just above the right eye. Some noblemen caught the king as he was about to fall from his mount, and carried him, bleeding profusely, to the Tournelles, where he lay for several days poised between life and death. The famous physician Vesalius hastened to Paris from Brussels and, after experimenting on the head of a murder victim, declared that the king's brain was intact and that he would live. For three days Henry talked and even attended to some state business, but on 4 July he developed a fever. Next day, as he lay dying, Marguerite and Emmanuel-Philibert were married in another part of the palace. At 1 PM on 10 July, Henry died. A post-mortem revealed that a splinter had pierced his brain after all. The Protestants, who had suffered so much at his hands, interpreted his violent death as a divine punishment.

France Overseas

Few royal entries have been as memorably spectacular as that of Henry II into Rouen in 1550. Among the performers were naked bands of Tupinamba Indians, who fought a mock battle in a meadow by the Seine. They had been brought back to France by Norman merchants who had traded regularly with Brazil and they bore witness to France's far-flung commercial interests. Rouen's foreign trade was linked not only to Europe but also to the new worlds being revealed by recent voyages of discovery. Thus between 1531 and 1553 the city imported large amounts of alum from the papal mines at Tolfa, often in exchange for cod fished along the Newfoundland coast. Other products, notably sugar, cotton, pepper, hides and Brazil-wood came from Africa or America. This trade testified to the wealth of the merchants who funded such distant voyages and to the skill of the Norman sailors who manned the ships.

France was among the pioneers of European expansion overseas. She was in the sixteenth century a considerable maritime power endowed with a number of widely dispersed ports. In the south was Marseille which traded with the Levant, the Ligurian coast and Spain. On the Atlantic, France's seaboard, stretching from the Gulf of Gascony to the English Channel, produced seamen hardened by a particularly rough climate and generally reckoned to be second to none. So the appropriate conditions existed for France's early participation in the movement of European expansion overseas, and indeed many Frenchmen were involved in such early Atlantic voyages as the proposed conquest of the Canary Islands in 1344. A Norman adventurer took three of the islands in 1405 and, as he did so, raided the Saharan coast looking for slaves, Christians and gold. From the mid-fifteenth century French seamen were keenly interested in trade with West Africa and also with Central and South America. In 1457 the king of Portugal was so alarmed by French interlopers along the coast of Guinea that he planned to send a fleet to drive them off. In 1504 a Norman captain, Paulmier de Gonneville, went to Brazil and brought back the son of an Indian chief. He said that other Frenchmen had preceded him there in search of dyewood, raw cotton, monkeys, parrots and other exotic products.

French pirates were also active from an early date. They attacked Portuguese ships carrying spices from the Indies and wood from Brazil, and Spanish treasure-ships from America. When war broke out between Francis I and Charles V in 1521, they became corsairs. Outstanding among them was Jean Fleury from Honfleur, who caused a great stir in 1522 by intercepting the ships carrying the Aztec treasure sent by Cortès to Charles V and by sinking two of them.

Knowledge of early French maritime activity in the North Atlantic is vague and incomplete. Bretons were fishing off Newfoundland as early as 1504 and probably long before. Two Normans are said to have explored the coast of Newfoundland in 1506 and 1508, and one of them brought back to Rouen seven Indians complete with their clothes, weapons and canoe. An important person in all this early activity was Jean Ango, a shipowner of Dieppe, who in 1535 entertained Francis I in his country house at Varengeville.

Yet France lagged behind Portugal and Spain in the race to establish colonies overseas, mainly because exploration was left to private enterprise. In the late fifteenth century the French crown was content to revive or develop trade along traditional routes, which the Hundred Years War had disrupted. Louis XI reopened Bordeaux to English ships, gave the spice monopoly to the ports of Languedoc and developed the port of Marseille. Charles VIII was too preoccupied with the conquest of Naples to be interested in American discoveries or to object to the papal bull *Inter caetera*, which allowed the Catholic Kings to claim all the lands beyond a line drawn 100 leagues west of the Azores and Cape Verde islands. It was not until the reign of Francis I that the French crown began to take a serious interest in overseas discoveries.

The voyages of Giovanni da Verrazzano

In 1522 the king of Portugal, warned of a French project that was likely to damage his interests, sent an envoy to persuade Francis to forbid his subjects to attack Portuguese shipping. Almost certainly the project was the first voyage of Giovanni da Verrazzano. This enterprise was apparently initiated by a Florentine syndicate in Lyon, but the king of France was also involved, for Verrazzano, on his return, made a report to Francis in which he stated that the king had sent out four ships 'to explore new lands'. One of the ships, the *Dauphine*, was a royal ship and her captain was paid by the crown during the voyage. This may have been prompted by Sebastiano Elcano's circumnavigation of the world which was widely publicized in 1523. Antonio Pigafetta, one of Elcano's companions, visited the French court soon afterwards and gave 'certain things from the other hemisphere' to the king's mother, Louise of Savoy. So the purpose of Verrazzano's first voyage may have been to find a more direct route to the Far East than the Strait of Magellan used by Elcano.

Verrazzano set sail in January 1524 with four ships, but he soon lost three in a storm. Left with only the *Dauphine*, he crossed the Atlantic and made landfall at Cape Fear (North Carolina), whence he sailed northward along the North American coast for some 160 miles looking for a port. He then returned to his original landfall and set foot on American soil for the first time. After a few days he embarked on a long voyage that took him along the coasts of Virginia and Maryland. After exploring for three days the interior of what he called 'Arcadia', and capturing an Indian boy, Verrazzano resumed his northward voyage, giving the names of various members of the French court to the main topographical features he encountered. Thus he called the bay of New York 'Santa Margarita' after Francis I's sister, and Block Island 'Aloysia' after the king's mother. Beyond Cape Cod, Verrazzano followed the coasts of Massachusetts and Maine until he sighted Newfoundland. Then, as his stores were almost exhausted, he recrossed the Atlantic and reached Dieppe on 8 July 1524.

The expedition had not discovered a northern passage to the Far East; yet Verrazzano's achievement was significant. By exploring, describing and mapping out the east coast of North America from Florida to Cape Breton, he had plugged a major gap in contemporary geographical knowledge. Unfortunately, his return coincided with the invasion of Provence by the Constable of Bourbon, so Francis may not have had time to read his report or to see him. Even so, Verrazzano was commissioned by the king to undertake a second voyage to the Indies. He was given four ships, but soon afterwards they were requisitioned to assist in the defence of the Norman coast. Verrazzano's next moves are unclear – he may have looked for patronage outside France – but in April 1526 he got the backing of Admiral Chabot and Jean Ango, who formed a joint-stock company and fitted out three ships to sail to 'the Spice islands in the Indies'. This time the expedition managed to get away, but where did it go? It may have rounded the Cape of Good Hope and been forced back to Brazil by bad weather. By September 1527, Verrazzano had returned to France. Three months later it was reported that he was about to sail for Brazil. Then in April 1528 he left on another voyage to the Indies which was sponsored by a group of merchants. It seems that he looked for a passage to the Pacific somewhere in central America, but did not live to tell the tale. His ship returned to France in March 1529 with a small cargo of Brazil-wood, but Verrazzano was not on board. It was alleged that he had been killed and eaten by cannibals in the Caribbean.

Franco-Portuguese rivalry

The last two voyages of Verrazzano were part of the long and bitter commercial rivalry between France and Portugal, which was fought out along the West African coast, but mainly in Brazil. Although John III professed to be concerned only with the suppression of piracy, he was, in fact, hostile to all French shipping in Brazilian waters. While ordering its destruction, he asked the French to restore all the Portuguese ships and cargoes which they had seized and to give guarantees for the future. Francis needed John's support in his struggle with the emperor, but the assurances which he gave to the Portuguese monarch were seldom implemented as they ran counter to the private interests of French shipowners.

In 1527 the rivalry reached crisis point when some Breton merchants, who were loading wood at Bahia in Brazil, were captured by the Portuguese authorities and executed. Francis asked for compensation for the relatives of the seamen concerned, but John III offered only a quarter of the sum requested. Once the Peace of Cambrai had been signed in 1529 and Francis had recovered his two sons, who had been held as hostages in Spain, he was better able to support the interests of French seamen. Thus in July 1530 he issued letters of marque to Jean Ango, one of whose ships had been seized by Portuguese coastguards, allowing him to make good his loss by attacking Portuguese ships. Ango tried to prevent all those bound for Flanders from using French ports. John III attempted unsuccessfully to get Ango's letters of marque revoked, but he managed to bribe Admiral Chabot, who agreed to ban all French ships from going to Brazil or Guinea. Ango also had to surrender his letters of marque. Yet, even with the co-operation of the French government, the Portuguese were unable to stop the activities of French interlopers in their waters. Thus about 1531 the baron de Saint-Blancard tried to establish a trading post at Pernambuco, and in the autumn of the same year sixteen ships prepared to sail from Normandy to Guinea and Brazil. Ango, too, continued to trade with both places, and Chabot secretly encouraged such ventures in return for a share of the profits.

John III acknowledged the freedom of seas which had 'always been known to all', but he excluded those which had been recently discovered by his subjects at much cost to themselves. Francis disagreed. All seas, he claimed, should be free and in 1533 he was able to persuade Pope Clement VII to reinterpret Alexander VI's bull *Inter caetera*, which had divided the world between Spain and Portugal without taking effective occupation into account. Clement made it apply only to 'known continents, not to territories subsequently discovered by other powers'. Thus it became possible for the French to challenge the monopoly claimed by the Iberian powers without fear of papal condemnation.

The French in Canada: Cartier and Roberval

In May 1532, Jean Le Veneur, bishop of Lisieux, suggested to Francis I a voyage of discovery beyond Newfoundland to be led by a sea captain called Jacques Cartier. The king agreed and Cartier, who had first-hand knowledge of Newfoundland and Brazil, was commissioned to discover 'certain islands and lands, where it is said he should find rich quantities of gold and other rich things'. He sailed from Saint-Malo in 1534 with two ships of sixty tons each and, after crossing the Atlantic in three weeks, made landfall at Cape Bonavista. On 15 June, Cartier began the first known exploration of the west coast of Newfoundland. On 3 July he inspected Chaleur Bay, which was full of Indians who had come there to fish. They invited Cartier to come ashore by holding up furs on sticks. At first he tried to frighten them off by firing several shots, but by degrees mutual trust was established and the French bartered trinkets and weapons for furs. On 12 July, Cartier began to explore the Gaspé peninsula, where he came across more Indians. With the consent of their chief, Donnaconna, he decided to take two young Indians back to France in the hope of teaching them French and of learning more about their country from them. From Gaspé, Cartier sailed to Anticosti and discovered the strait which he called St Peter's, but as the season was late he decided to postpone further exploration and returned to France, reaching Saint-Malo on 5 September. He had not found gold, but he had collected much useful information. He now knew that there was a sea passage north and south of Anticosti leading to the west, possibly to Asia. The two captured Indians also told him about a rich kingdom, called Saguenay, which lay far inland to the west of their own part of Canada.

Francis was sufficiently impressed by these results to commission a new expedition. This time Cartier was given three ships, each victualled for fifteen months. He was accompanied by the two Indians, who by now had learnt enough French to serve as interpreters and guides. The three ships sailed on 19 May 1535 and, after being separated during the Atlantic crossing, met up at Blanc Sablon on 26 July whence they followed the coast of Labrador and, passing through St Peter's strait, entered the estuary of the St Lawrence river. In September, Cartier set off from Sainte-Croix with one ship and two rowing boats, hoping to explore the kingdom of Hochelaga further upstream. Though he had been warned of hazards ahead, the abundance of flora and fauna beckoned him on. After crossing Lake St Peter, he abandoned his ship and her crew and with a small party made

his way to Hochelaga, where more than a thousand Huron Indians came
to meet him and fraternize. In exchange for fish and corn, the Frenchmen
handed out knives and beads. From the top of a mountain, which he called
Mont Réal, Cartier was shown the Ottawa river, which allegedly flowed
past the kingdom of Saguenay. 'And without our putting any question or
making any sign,' the French reported,' our Indian guides took the silver
chain of the Captain's whistle and the handle of a dagger hanging at the
side of one of our sailors, which was of brass as yellow as gold, and made
signs that such things came from up the said river.' But Cartier decided not
to go further at this stage. He returned instead to Sainte-Croix where the
men he had left behind had built a fort bristling with guns. For five months
Cartier and his companions remained here, frozen in and snowed up. As
their supplies of food and fuel ran short, scurvy began to take effect. The
death toll might have been higher if one of the Indians had not shown
Cartier how to make a healing mixture from the branches of a local tree.
In April 1536 he decided to go home, but not before he had kidnapped
eight Indians, including Donnaconna. He set sail on 6 May in two ships
(the third had been broken up) after setting up a cross and taking formal
possession of the territory he had discovered for France.

Cartier had once again advanced geographical knowledge without bringing back any riches. This must have disappointed King Francis. In September
1538 he authorized two payments to Cartier: one for his past voyages, the
other for looking after the Indians he had brought back. Meanwhile, Cartier
submitted a memorandum to the king setting out his needs for a successful
voyage to Saguenay. He asked for six ships of at least 100 tons each and
two barques of at least 50 tons, all furnished with provisions for two years.
In addition to 120 sailors, Cartier required about 154 artisans and soldiers,
including two goldsmiths 'skilled in handling precious stones' and six
priests. According to the memorandum's preamble, Francis was anxious to
establish Christianity in a remote part of the world that offered little hope
of material gain, but Cartier never showed a strong missionary zeal and his
request for two goldsmiths points to an overriding interest in material gain.
The preamble was probably intended for papal consumption in the hope
that France might be given the same privileges as had already been given
to the Portuguese and Spanish monarchs.

The real motives behind Cartier's third voyage may be deduced from a
conversation between Francis I and a Portuguese pilot called João Lagarto.
After the latter had shown the king two marine charts and an astrolabe,
Francis spoke to him 'with understanding and intelligence' for an hour. On
the following evening, he produced two not very good charts of his own
and pointed to 'a river in the land of Cod'. He spoke of Cartier's two
voyages and explained that the river he had discovered was said to be 800
leagues long. He intended another expedition to be equipped with two

brigantines so that it might reach beyond the falls, where, Francis had been told, there was a large city called Sagana, many mines of gold and silver, men who wore clothes and shoes like Europeans, and an abundance of clove, nutmeg and pepper. Lagarto expressed some doubt about the precious metals and spices, and insinuated that Donnaconna had mentioned them in order to return to his own country, but Francis laughed at this suggestion. The Indian chief, he said, was an honest man who would honour his promises. Never in the course of this conversation was any mention made of the conversion of the Indians to Christianity. The king evidently wanted to imitate the Iberian rulers by having Indies of his own.

In August 1540, Charles V heard that Francis had commissioned Cartier and others to go to the Indies and settle the New Lands. Seeing this as a breach of the truce of Nice, he sent a spy to observe shipping along the Atlantic coast of France. Despite an assurance that his territories would be respected, the emperor ordered all French ships bound for the Indies to be intercepted and their crews thrown into the sea 'as a warning against similar expeditions'. Charles also tried to enlist the support of the king of Portugal and the pope; but John III was only interested in protecting his own interests, and Paul III was unwilling to alienate France for the sake of *Inter caetera*. Francis did not accept the doctrine enshrined in that bull. Popes, he said in December 1540, had no authority to distribute lands among kings. Neither the king of France nor any other Christian ruler had been consulted before the bull had been drawn up, and he rejected any Portuguese or Spanish privileges which failed to take his own interests into account. 'The sun', he declared, 'gave warmth to him as well as to others, and he much desired to see Adam's will to learn how he had partitioned the world.' Yet Francis was ready to respect the emperor's rights wherever he was in effective occupation of a territory.

Undeterred by foreign pressure, Francis commissioned Cartier on 17 October 1540 to go to Canada or Hochelaga 'forming an extremity of Asia on the western side', and if possible Saguenay, in order to convert the natives. Soon afterwards, however, the king changed his mind. Instead of an ostensibly Christianizing mission, he now envisaged the establishment of a French province overseas. This necessitated a change of leadership, for Cartier was a commoner and only a nobleman was regarded as fit to be a royal lieutenant-general. The king's choice for this role fell on Jean-François de La Roque, seigneur de Roberval, a Protestant nobleman from Languedoc who was a soldier and allegedly an expert on fortification. Having lost money by extravagant living at court, he hoped to rebuild his fortune by investing the remainder in the Canadian venture.

On 15 January 1541, Roberval was commissioned to go to Canada, Hochelaga and other adjacent lands and organize them in the king's name provided none was occupied by the emperor, the king of Portugal or any other Christian prince. Although the religious purpose of the expedition was reaffirmed, no particulars were given of any ecclesiastical personnel or institutions. Once the country had been occupied, either peacefully or by force, it was to be settled and organized. There were to be towns, forts and churches. Roberval was to exercise legislative and judicial powers, to appoint to all offices, and to distribute lands as fiefs or lordships. Profits from the expedition were to be divided between the settlers, Roberval and the crown. The expedition was to comprise noblemen, merchants and 'subjects of goodwill and of all qualities, art and industry'.

Cartier was allowed to take fifty prisoners in addition to 'subjects of goodwill', but his efforts to recruit a crew at Saint-Malo and other Breton ports were strongly resisted, perhaps because word had got around of the terrible hardships suffered by his companions during the winter of 1536. By February 1541, following the king's intervention, preparations were far advanced. Roberval was also allowed to take prisoners under sentence of death, who were asked to pay for their transportation to Canada and for their upkeep over two years.

Serving under Roberval, Cartier left Saint-Malo first, on 23 May 1541 with five ships, carrying several hundred men and enough supplies for two years. By 23 August he was back at Sainte-Croix, but this anchorage was unsuitable for his new fleet and crew. So he moved nine miles further up the St Lawrence to a new base, which he called Charles-Bourg-Royal. As the colonists set to work, they found iron and, as they thought, gold and diamonds. Fruit trees were plentiful and vegetables flourished. On 5 September, Cartier travelled upstream to Montreal in two boats. He was hoping to reach Saguenay and managed to by-pass two rapids, but was told that the Ottawa was unnavigable. So he returned to Charles-Bourg, only to find that relations between his men and the Indians had broken down. The French had exploited and ill-treated them instead of returning their friendship, and as a result the small garrison came under almost daily attack. In May 1542, Cartier and his men left for France.

Roberval, meanwhile, had left France on 16 April with three ships carrying about 200 men and women. On 8 June, off Newfoundland, he was surprised to see Cartier's ships heading for France. Roberval ordered him to turn back, but Cartier slipped away during the night, taking with him his experience and possible assistance. Roberval pressed on nevertheless: he arrived at Charles-Bourg at the end of July and renamed it France-Roy. He built two forts and on 14 September sent two of his ships home. As winter approached he imposed food rationing on his company as well as a harsh discipline. Although the colonists were supplied with shad by the Indians, many succumbed to scurvy. By 5 June, Roberval was left with only about a hundred men. Taking seventy with him in eight boats, he began looking for Saguenay, but the expedition encountered difficulties and probably never got further than the Ottawa river. By late June, Roberval was back at France-Roy.

In the meantime, Cartier's return to France had produced major disappointment. The diamonds and gold he brought back proved on closer investigation to be worthless. King Francis, who was again engaged in war with the emperor, had lost interest in Canadian enterprise. He sent two ships to bring back Roberval and the remnants of his colony in the autumn of 1543. Neither Cartier nor Roberval made any profit from their voyages. But whatever contemporaries may have thought of them, modern opinion has been more favourable. The voyages were pioneering attempts to settle Europeans well inside North America and they yielded much experience and knowledge. A tradition had been established that the coastline explored by Verrazzano and the interior explored by Cartier constituted a New France which the motherland could legitimately reoccupy whenever she wished. In other words, the Cartier–Roberval expeditions were 'a standing challenge to the Spanish claim to a monopoly of rights to North America as a whole'.

Villegaignon's colony in Brazil

French maritime activity was sustained during the reign of Henry II. The moving spirit behind it was Admiral Coligny, nephew of Constable Anne de Montmorency. In 1555 he helped to pay for the fitting out of eighteen ships of Dieppe which successfully intercepted a much larger fleet carrying 350,000 crowns from Spain to Charles V's coffers in the Netherlands. The admiral had to cease such activities after the truce of Vaucelles, but he was not similarly constrained with regard to the Portuguese sphere of interest in South America. Being passionately committed to the greatness of France and her king, he was prepared to defy papal bulls which favoured Spain or Portugal in the allocation of overseas territories. In Coligny's judgement, Frenchmen were entitled to take over lands which had not been effectively occupied by a European power. Although he failed in his attempts to colonize Brazil and Florida, he has been fairly acclaimed as 'the first in time of France's colonial statesmen and one of the greatest' (Julien).

In 1553 the chevalier de Villegaignon sought the backing of Coligny for an expedition to Brazil. Villegaignon was a remarkable character who, having been educated in the humanities and theology alongside Calvin at the University of Paris, entered the order of St John of Jerusalem. As a knight of Malta he took part in several military campaigns. He helped to cover Charles V's retreat from Algiers, fought against the Turks in Hungary, was present at the battle of Ceresole, and captained the ship which carried off Mary Stuart from Scotland to France in 1548. This last exploit earned him the title of vice-admiral of Brittany. He was put in charge of harbour works at Brest but, after quarrelling with the local governor, decided to try his luck overseas. What he had in mind, when he asked for Coligny's backing, is controversial. He cannot have hoped to set up a Protestant colony, as some historians have suggested, for Coligny, whatever his private sympathies may have been, had not yet openly declared his conversion to Calvinism. What is more, Villegaignon also secured the backing of the Cardinal of Lorraine. Maybe he was thinking of a place of refuge overseas where all Frenchmen, both Catholic and Protestant, would be free to worship. But this supposition merely rests on the fact that he took Protestants as well as Catholics with him to Brazil.

In March 1555, Villegaignon obtained two fine ships, plentiful supplies, a royal subsidy of 10,000 *livres* and the right to recruit workmen and peasants. He also secured the co-operation of Norman and Breton shipowners who could see commercial advantages to be gained in a Brazilian venture. Villegaignon found it more difficult to recruit men than raise money. He enlisted a few Protestants, a famous pilot, some notable Catholics, including the globe-trotting Franciscan André Thevet, and a doctor of theology from Paris called Jean Cointe. He also had a Scottish bodyguard, but, in general, Frenchmen were reluctant to join his company. In the last resort, he probably had to take released prisoners. His expedition, comprising a motley crew of 600 colonists and adventurers, set off from Le Havre in two ships and a barque loaded with victuals and ammunition on 12 July 1555, but it soon ran into stormy weather and had to put into Dieppe twice, when several volunteers decided to stay behind. The small fleet finally set off on 14 August and, after a terrible crossing of the Atlantic during which the crews suffered from thirst and scurvy, it dropped anchor in the bay of Guanabara (today Rio de Janeiro). Villegaignon chose to occupy an island in the bay, instead of establishing a settlement on the mainland, and strategically this made sense. The island was easily defensible, especially after the construction of a fort, named after Coligny. But from the colonial standpoint, Villegaignon's decision was disastrous, as it condemned his followers to isolation under his own very strict regime. For he was not merely haughty, but also a strict disciplinarian with high standards of morality: he would not allow his men to become intimate with Indian women. So the French island became a kind of Brazilian Malta inhabited by knights without a vocation. Inevitably this produced internal unrest which culminated in a failed attempt to murder Villegaignon. Some of his company did manage to escape ashore, where they ganged up with Frenchmen who had long settled in Brazil with Indian concubines and served passing French traders as interpreters.

The Indians were divided into two rival tribes, the Tomoyo and the Maracaje. The former, under their chief Quoniambec, had long been clients of the French, and Villegaignon used them to supply victuals to his islanders. But the Indians stopped their supplies when they felt that they were being unfairly exploited. As the island faced famine, Villegaignon allowed some of his men ashore, but threatened to hang anyone who broke his strict code of chastity. Meanwhile, more ships arrived from France to trade or deposit emigrants, who settled either on the island or on the mainland where they set up a small trade counter.

By the beginning of 1556, Villegaignon had decided to attract more French settlers to his colony. He had asked Henry II for three or four thousand men with whom to conquer the Indies, but had met with a refusal, so he now turned to his old college acquaintance Calvin. His letter, if it was ever written, has not survived. According to de Bèze, Coligny acted as go-between. Be that as it may, Calvin appointed two pastors, Richer and Chartier, to go to Brazil. He also picked twelve French exiles, including a shoemaker called Jean de Léry, who later wrote a famous account of his Brazilian experiences. This small group called on Coligny on its way through France and picked up a few noblemen in Paris. Meanwhile, Bois-le-Comte who had been sent back to France by Villegaignon soon after his arrival, had been organizing a new expedition. With the help of Coligny and at the king's expense, he had equipped three fine ships and recruited some 290 soldiers, sailors and settlers. Among them were six boys, who were sent to learn the Indian language, and five girls with a governess. Having been joined by the Genevan contingent, the small fleet sailed on 19 November 1556. It reached its destination on 7 March 1557 and was welcomed ashore by Villegaignon, wearing full dress, and his Scottish guard.

At first relations between Villegaignon and the new settlers were cordial. He wrote to Calvin thanking him effusively for the men he had sent. The two pastors, for their part, informed Calvin that they had found in Villegaignon 'a father and a brother'. However, this happy state of affairs did not last. Villegaignon, after responding enthusiastically to the preaching of the pastors, was suddenly beset by Catholic doubts and began to argue with them, principally over the Eucharist. They decided to seek Calvin's arbitration. But in May, Villegaignon lost all self-control and began lashing out in all directions, prompting many defections among his followers. He allowed the Genevans to settle on the mainland, but two months later they left in a leaking ship and managed to reach Brittany after a dreadful voyage of twenty weeks' duration. Their hunger was such that they ate a parrot which they had intended as a gift to Coligny. Five Genevans, who preferred to seek Villegaignon's forgiveness, were punished by him as heretics: two were imprisoned for life; three were thrown into the sea. More than half the settlers left the island: while some looked for ships to repatriate them, others joined the interpreters in the forests.

Villegaignon had no sooner established his authority than he decided to return to France. His enemies accused him of cowardice, but his reason for leaving was almost certainly to defend himself against a charge of heresy. He may also have planned a much larger American venture, for he would not have been content with his puny island. He was not interested in founding an agricultural settlement or a trade counter. As a soldier, he probably envisaged an armed conquest of the Indies and a search for precious metals. He reappeared at the French court in the winter of 1559, after the death of Henry II, when the Guises were dominant. Villegaignon painted a rosy picture of his Brazilian domain which he claimed covered more than 200 leagues. The Cardinal of Lorraine promised the support of the Society of Jesus for a new expedition to Brazil, but an enquiry launched by the General of the Order, Lainez, produced an unexpected result. The Jesuits already established in Brazil denounced Villegaignon and his company as dangerous heretics. Meanwhile a Portuguese expedition, influenced by Father Nobrega, the provincial of the Brazilian Jesuits, laid siege to the French island. After a bombardment lasting twenty days, it fell to the Portuguese and the defenders were made slaves. The fort and its store of gunpowder were destroyed. Many heretical books were found and no religious images, a fact suggesting that a Protestant counter-revolution had followed Villegaignon's departure. The island now became the property of the Jesuits. In a report to the Portuguese regent, the Brazilian governor, Mem de Sá, thanked God for his help in expelling the heretics whose main occupation had been to make war on Christians and to hand them over to the Indians to be eaten.

In January 1563, Villegaignon entered into talks with the Portuguese ambassador in France regarding his rights in Brazil. They resulted in a compromise: in return for 30,000 ducats, Villegaignon gave up all his rights to the island in the bay of Rio de Janeiro. In the meantime he fought a pamphlet war with Calvin and his disciples, which probably did more to publicize America in Europe than any number of cosmographical treatises and books of travel.

The capture of Villegaignon's island marked the end of official French colonization in South America, but not of efforts by individual Frenchmen, allied to local Indians, to oppose the Portuguese. Under Bois-le-Comte they built a fort at Ibiraguaçumirim and occupied the island of Paranapucu. In January 1567, Mem de Sá captured both places and soon afterwards founded the town which was to become Rio de Janeiro. By degrees the Portuguese drove the hostile Indian tribes into remoter corners of Brazil, where the French continued to assist them, albeit without the support of their government. As late as 1597 the Portuguese fought a pitched battle in the Rio Grande with 25,000 Potiguara Indians among whom were fifty French arquebusiers. Forty years after the fall of Fort Coligny, the Jesuits were still denouncing the French with horror.

Admiral Coligny may have had three colonial objectives: to create a safe haven for Protestant exiles, to found a colony which might serve as the nucleus of a French overseas empire, and to break the Iberian monopoly in the New World. The failure of Villegaignon's expedition, though of scant military significance, determined the political, religious and cultural future of the largest South American territory. Yet Coligny did not abandon his vision; less than two years later he switched his attention to Florida, which Spain regarded as her own.

In 1557, André Thevet, Villegaignon's almoner, wrote an account of the ill-fated Brazilian venture in a work entitled *Les Singularitez de la France antarctique*. This also included an account of his alleged experiences in other parts of the western hemisphere, including Newfoundland, Canada, Florida and Mexico. Although the account of Cartier's second voyage had been published in 1545, Thevet claimed that no one had yet written about Canada. His description of that country and its inhabitants offers interesting details of native war customs, hunting methods, medicinal practices, clothing styles and religious beliefs. The *Singularitez* was well received. Other French editions appeared in 1558 and Italian and English translations in 1561 and 1568. Following this success and that of his *Cosmographie du Levant* (1554, 1556), Thevet became almoner to Catherine de' Medici, royal cosmographer to four French kings in succession, a canon of Angoulême cathedral, abbot of Notre-Dame de Masdion (Saintonge) and keeper of the royal collection of curiosities at Fontainebleau. He made no more journeys to America, but continued to write travel books. His most extensive work was his *Cosmographie universelle* (1575). Unlike his earlier works, however, this was not well received. One of its principal critics was Jean de Léry, one of the Genevans Calvin had sent to Villegaignon's colony. He accused Thevet of lies regarding Protestant responsibility for the failure of that enterprise and dismissed his works as 'second-hand rags and tatters'. Another harsh critic was François de Belleforest, a rival cosmographer, who accused Thevet of plagiarizing his own *Cosmographie universelle* published earlier in 1575. Nowadays historians are better disposed towards Thevet's work even if they acknowledge that it must be treated warily. For Charles-André Julien, he had four great qualities: 'a passion for travel that made monastic life unbearable to him, a contempt for danger which led him to face the perils of the sea and forays into "strange" countries, an insatiable curiosity which led him continually to refresh and complete his knowledge, and finally the art of interviewing those in the know and extracting information from them'.

17

The Mid-Century Crisis

The Peace of Cateau-Cambrésis was received with wild rejoicing in western Europe and historians generally have seen it as a watershed. For France it signified the end of more than fifty years of Italian wars; henceforth her rulers could concentrate on overcoming problems at home. Ironically, these problems – economic, social, religious and political – proved far more damaging to the nation than the preceding era of Habsburg–Valois conflict. Frenchmen took to fighting each other with appalling savagery; massacres added to the blood-toll of pitched battles. Neighbours who had previously worked together became implacable foes. The marvellous cultural flowering which marked the reigns of Francis I and Henry II began to wither. The peace, in brief, ushered in a period which can be legitimately seen as one of 'decline'. This, however, should not be taken too literally: the 'rise' had contained seeds of 'decline'.

The historian Fernand Braudel once described the sixteenth century as 'the beautiful century'. But, as Henry Heller has rightly pointed out, it may have been beautiful for some, but not for the commons. As we have already seen, the reign of Francis I was not free of social unrest. There was the *Grande Rebeyne* which shook Lyon in 1529 and the widespread *gabelle* revolt of 1544 in south-west France. But these were only the more important manifestations of discontent among the lower orders of society which was provoked by changing economic and social conditions. Perhaps Heller's revised picture of an early sixteenth century riddled with class warfare is overcoloured; such unrest as there was under Francis I and Henry II did not amount to civil war. But he is right to argue that it did have a bearing on the sinister events that followed the Peace of Cateau-Cambrésis. France in 1559 was a nation in crisis: the economy was showing signs of strain, social tensions were mounting, and religious differences were becoming acute. On top of all this, the death of Henry II created a vacuum at the heart of government which various factions competed to fill.

The economic crisis

The early sixteenth century, as we have seen, saw a significant rise in France's population and a corresponding growth of towns. The demographic rise may not have been more than a recovery of the losses suffered as a result of the Black Death in the fourteenth century; even so it affected both prices and productivity. As the population grew, so land which had been allowed to go to waste was reclaimed and put under the plough by a growing labour force. Pastoral farming, however, did not enjoy a comparable revival: the need to feed more mouths naturally induced peasants to opt rather for arable. But this was a short-sighted policy, for a static or declining stock of farm animals meant less manure which in turn depressed the grain yield. It is also said to have impoverished the diet of humble peasants who had been used to eating meat in the fifteenth century.

A related factor of considerable importance was price inflation. This is particularly well documented in respect of grain. Between the decades 1510–19 and 1540–49 the index figure rose from 100 to 224 in Paris, to 200 in Lyon, and to 173 in Toulouse. From 1558 to 1591 the index figure of 100 rose to 481 for wheat and 530 for rye. Violent fluctuations in the price of grain on the Paris market need to be set against a steady long-term rise, which began about 1525, accelerated after 1550 and reached a peak at the close of the century. About 1600 the average nominal price of grain was five times as high as it had been in 1520. Taking account of successive devaluations of the *livre*, this meant a trebling in real terms. Other goods followed the trend set by agricultural products. Thus, the accounts of the Hôtel-Dieu between 1506–10 and 1539–42 reveal a rise of 60 per cent for metalware, 50 per cent for woollen cloth, 40 per cent for linen and 80 per cent for plaster and tiles.

The reasons for the so-called Price Revolution were controversial even in the sixteenth century. About 1560 the Chambre des comptes ordered an enquiry into the rising cost of commodities which resulted six years later in M. de Malestroit's *Remontrances et paradoxes . . . sur le fait des monnaies*, which argued that the rise was an illusion caused by the depreciation of the *livre*. Two years later this was challenged by Jean Bodin in his famous *Réponse aux Paradoxes de M. de Malestroit*. Prices, in his opinion, had truly risen and, while recognizing the inflationary impact of the demographic explosion, he blamed principally the increased amount of gold and silver in circulation. From Bodin's ideas arose the quantitative theory of money over which modern economists have argued so bitterly. Nowadays historians are generally agreed that the Price Revolution had many causes, not least the currency manipulations of various governments. Even if we acknowledge that the inflationary process began before the discovery of the New World, it cannot be seriously denied that the importation of precious metals resulting from that event did contribute to the rise in European prices. But we must also allow for the operations of supply and demand. Thus the price of grain was primarily determined by the amount harvested and the demand for it, which was in turn regulated by the number of consumers and their capacity to pay. In this respect, we need to remember that agricultural production began to slow down, both quantitatively and qualitatively, about 1525–30. Yet the population continued to rise. The result was a gap between the amount of food available and the number of mouths that required feeding, and this gap widened as the century advanced.

At the same time the demographic rise caused a fall in the standard of living of a growing number of peasant households. Peasant holdings were generally subdivided among heirs, so that they dwindled in size with the passing of each generation as an increasing number of heirs had to be satisfied. Some local customs favoured the eldest son in the matter of inheritance, but the general trend was for the fragmentation of holdings. In time, many fell below the five hectares which were deemed the essential minimum guaranteeing self-sufficiency. Only a minority of peasants (estimated at between a quarter and a fifth of the entire peasant population) managed to stay above this minimum. The rest were forced to buy food at inflated prices which they could not afford.

As many peasants ceased to be independent and were driven to seek paid employment on other holdings, they encountered a lowering of wages. In the fifteenth century, when the labour market had been tight, employers had been forced to offer competitive wages. Now the situation was reversed. As would-be day labourers and farm hands sought employment, the big rural entrepreneurs offered less favourable terms. Nominal wages were more or less fixed while prices rose. Such a situation played into the hands of the grain merchants, but it spelled poverty to the great mass of landless peasants.

There were, of course, three participants in the rural economy: the wage-earner, the farmer and the landlord or *seigneur*. The farmer had to pay rent to the *seigneur*, and he was only better off as a result of the Price Revolution if his rent was fixed by custom. This happened in Languedoc, where a usurer-farmer like Guillaume Masenx was able to rocket into wealth and social prominence. Elsewhere in France, notably in Poitou and the Ile-de-France, rents went up steadily from the start of the sixteenth century. About 1550 they reached a level not even surpassed in the seventeenth century, generally regarded as the golden age of rural rents. It follows that land ownership, in spite of the Price Revolution, remained a worthwhile economic activity – hence the systematic purchase of rural estates by members of the urban bourgeoisie. Such was the importance of this movement that many rich bourgeois from Paris and other towns began to dominate the *plat-pays* or countryside around the towns. They were all the keener to do so as owning land was a passport to social climbing. It enabled them to move out of the mercantile world into that of office-holding, which was itself a door leading to the most prized status of all, that of nobleman. The main victim of this process was the small peasant proprietor who had been forced to sell his holding. It was during the second third of the sixteenth century that the slow movement of expropriation which the majority of peasants were to experience until the eighteenth century first got under way.

The rise in prices naturally affected the cost of government at a time when the scale of war was being enlarged and its technology was advancing. We have already noted the high cost of foreign mercenaries, firearms and fortifications. The need to protect towns from the improved firepower of a more sophisticated artillery necessitated the construction of more effective defences, such as the bastion. All this cost money and the state felt the impact of inflation as did everyone else. The tax system, as we have noted, was chaotic and the fiscal administration, even after Francis I's reforms, was still far from efficient. To meet his growing needs the king had to increase taxation. The figures cited by Clamageran may require correction in the light of current research, but they can be taken as a reliable indicator of a relentless upward trend. Under Henry II the *taille*, which had averaged 4 million *livres* since 1542, rose to 6,755,000l. in 1558. All taxes, including clerical tenths and indirect taxes, which had totalled 5,165,000l. in 1523, reached 13,540,000 under Henry II.

It is sometimes suggested that the real burden of taxation was not as heavy as these statistics suggest, since an allowance has to be made for the fall in the value of money. But much of that burden was carried by the unprivileged members of society – mainly the peasantry – whose standard of living was deteriorating under the impact of inflation. In Dauphiné at least, the absolute increase of the *taille* as it affected the commons has been proved. Furthermore, even if elsewhere the *taille* kept pace with inflation, it is by no means certain that this was also true of additional taxes, like *crues* or the *taillon*, or of forced loans. The cost of billeting, provisioning and supplying royal troops must also be taken into account, for this was imposed unevenly and unpredictably on towns and villages. It was a major grievance, as reflected by many urban records.

The economic changes of the early sixteenth century were undoubtedly a major cause of social unrest. Riots instigated by commoners broke out in many towns. Although hunger was a common motive, it was often tied to other causes. In 1542, for example, a ship being loaded in Rouen with grain for export came under attack from a group of townspeople. They were not all poor, and 1542 was not a year of particular grain shortage. The riot was mainly caused by the war which had interrupted the town's trade with the Low Countries, causing unemployment among merchants and craftsmen. Three years later there was more trouble in Rouen when the *Bureau des Pauvres*, which had been set up to care mainly for unemployed artisans, ran out of funds. A mob of four or five hundred craftsmen surrounded the treasurer's house insulting and threatening him. A similar outbreak occurred at Tours in 1542 when the silk industry was paralysed by the war. At Troyes, in 1529, an outbreak of plague forced the town council to curtail imports of linen and wool. This brought the paper and drapery manufacturers to a standstill. Thousands of workers, finding themselves unemployed, turned to begging. The result was a popular revolt which caused the council hastily to cancel its embargo. A subsistence riot was seen by the great merchants and notables as potentially dangerous since it might develop into a full-scale uprising of craftsmen and lesser merchants. This happened at Meaux in 1522 when a grain shortage linked with unemployment prompted a proletarian revolt. At Agen in 1528 a grain riot among the poor was the catalyst for a revolt leading to the overthrow of the ruling oligarchy.

The food riot in itself was nothing new; such riots had taken place since the Middle Ages. The strike, however, was a quite new phenomenon, which first took place in Lyon's printing industry. It began in the spring of 1539 and involved a dispute over wages, working conditions and the maintenance of the open or closed shop. The strikers defied not only their employers but also the city's consuls and the king's representatives. Violence punctuated the stoppage, which dragged on for two years. A similar clash occurred in the Paris printing industry between 1531 and 1549.

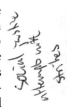

The economic crisis and the rise of Protestantism

What connection, if any, was there between the economic crisis of the sixteenth century and the growth of religious dissent? In 1899, Henri Hauser challenged the view traditionally held by French historians that Protestantism in France originated as an aristocratic movement. Their mistake, in his opinion, was not to look back further than 1560 when the Huguenot movement was indeed taken over by the nobility for political reasons. Previously it had been mainly a movement of the working class, especially in the towns, which had been sorely hit since about the 1520s by rising prices and an oppressive guild system. In Hauser's opinion, the popular classes rose not only against corrupt dogma and the clergy, but also against poverty and injustice; they sought in the Bible not only salvation by faith but the original equality of mankind. This interpretation has recently been endorsed

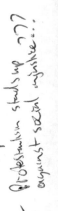

by Henry Heller, who has examined the origins of religious dissent in Meaux. While admitting 'the force of ideas', he argues that this alone cannot account for the Reformation. The economic and social crisis which culminated in the mid-forties was, in his judgement, 'crucial to the evolution of Protestantism at Meaux as elsewhere in France'. The crisis was rural as well as urban. The parcelling of land and the deterioration of rural living standards forced peasants to look for food in the towns, and this rural influx caused a steady fall in the real wages of the working class. The cloth-workers of Meaux suffered economic hardship as the market for their products declined. This, according to Heller, was 'the material basis for their religious estrangement and political bitterness. It was a hostility which was directed at the whole upper stratum of society whose incomes were on the rise. Among the most literate artisans, the upper clergy, the most visible and oppressive element among this upper stratum, became the focal point of anger.' Heller is, of course, aware that evangelical ideas appealed not only to craftsmen but to the élite. But he asserts that 'the artisans were the social base of the French Reformation. Theirs was a religious revolt founded in political and economic protest.'

However, most historians currently working on the origins of French Protestantism are sceptical about linking them too rigidly to socio-economic conditions. As Philip Benedict has shown, 'the essentially impressionistic (and tendentious) methods of the past must be abandoned in favour of a statistical approach which seeks not only to establish a social profile of the movement's adherents, but to compare that with the contours of the larger society from which the converts were drawn.' He has tried to do this for Rouen, within the constraints imposed by the available documentation. Four partial lists of Huguenots survive for the period 1550–72 as well as the membership rolls of a large Catholic association, the General Confraternity of the Holy Sacrament. The Huguenot lists show that Calvinism drew its adherents from virtually all strata of society and from a bewildering variety of occupations, though some of these are represented in numbers disproportionate to their importance within the total city population. As for the membership rolls of the Confraternity, they yield a list of occupations that compares with the evidence about the Reformed church 'as a photographic negative compares with the final print'. Thus where hosiers outnumbered weavers among the Huguenots, cloth-workers outnumbered stocking-makers among the Catholics. Where people in the food and drink trades represented 8 per cent of all artisans in the Protestant lists and élite artisans represented 13 per cent, the figures are reversed in the Catholic list. Benedict finds it 'difficult to know whether to stress the similarities or the differences between Protestant and Catholic in sixteenth-century Rouen'. Both religions attracted adherents from a wide range of occupations and social strata, with the spread being perhaps slightly greater within

Catholicism. There were no perfect correlations between status and religion. Nor is there any evidence that social and occupational rivalries were reflected in religious conflict. Yet if the social differences between adherents of the two faiths show no competing economic interests, they do reveal interesting divergences. Both the Reformed church and the Confraternity appealed most strongly not to the official élite, but to those lower down the social scale. Traditional Catholics tended to come disproportionately from the food and drink trades and from the lowest social level. Cloth-workers and probably lawyers appear to have remained overwhelmingly Catholic. Protestants, by contrast, tended to be recruited from the artisanal élite: more were hosiers than weavers. Among merchants, Calvinists were usually not from the wealthiest families, but from the strata immediately below. There is no evidence of Protestant 'outs' and Catholic 'ins'; for among converts to Protestantism were three of Rouen's six *conseillers-échevins*. The contrasting statistical tendencies visible among the different groups of artisans tend to confirm the views of contemporary observers, such as Ronsard and Florimond de Raemond, as well as those of recent scholars, like Emmanuel Le Roy Ladurie and Natalie Zemon Davis. The more strongly Protestant trades were those in which the literacy rate was higher. This would explain why relatively few women converted to Protestantism, for the rate of literacy was significantly lower among them.

The printing industry of Lyon provides an interesting case study by which to examine the interrelations between 'social forces' and the Reformation in that city. Its personnel of about 600 included men of most social levels: great merchant-publishers, independent publisher-printers, lesser master craftsmen and printers' journeymen. There was much discontent within the industry, masters siding with publishers against journeymen before 1572. There were coalitions, conspiracies, court fights and strikes. And printing supplied many adherents of the Protestant cause, though they were not all on one side of the economic battle. Natalie Davis offers several reasons for the attraction exerted by Protestantism on the printers' journeymen. They were men who spent many years, often all their lives, as wage-earners; they came to Lyon from villages, other cities or abroad; and they worked for a trade that was relatively new and without traditions. Not surprisingly they tried to create traditions for themselves and did what they could to feel less lost and lonely. They worked together and those who were single lived together. All too conscious of the economic gulf that separated them from their masters, they formed a brotherhood of their own, called the Company of the Griffarins. When Protestantism offered them a new style of worship with congregational participation and a liturgy in the vernacular, the journeymen responded: they organized public processions in which they sang the Psalms in French and shouted insults at the canons of the cathedral of Saint-Jean. The journeymen were proud of their skills (about two-thirds could read and write) and believed that their trade was enormously valuable to Christian society. Although among the highest-paid workers in Lyon, they believed that they deserved better and felt no guilt about their militant disobedience. They were encouraged by Protestant preachers who claimed that laymen were being undervalued by the Catholic clergy.

The connection between confidence bred from pride of calling and confidence in one's worth relative to the Catholic clergy may serve to explain the social and vocational distribution of Lyon's Protestants before 1567. The Calvinist movement as a whole was drawn from rich and poor – from Consular families, notable families and families of the *menu peuple* – in numbers roughly proportional to their distribution in the population at large, but certain occupations were over-represented. These were trades which involved skills and often contained some novelty, such as new technology (as in printing), new claims for prestige (as in painting, jewellery and goldsmith's work) and even recent arrival in Lyon (like the silk industry). In contrast, very few grain merchants, vintners, butchers, bakers or ropemakers of any status became Protestant.

But of course, such affinities as may have existed between Calvinism and certain occupational groups cannot alone explain its rise in France. A new religion can only spread if it is allowed social 'space'. Protestantism had existed in France well before the 1550s, yet it only became a major force when the political situation between 1559 and 1562 blurred the lines of authority to such an extent that it could develop without undue harassment. It was also at this time that it gained large numbers of aristocratic converts.

The nobility in crisis?

The political role of the nobility in sixteenth-century France was pre-eminent. In the first half of the century it buttressed the growing power of the monarchy. Historians used to claim that this power was built on the ruins of the old feudal aristocracy with the support of a 'rising' bourgeoisie, but this view is now discredited. As Russell Major has shown, 'the extinction of the great feudal houses and the reunion of their domains to the crown during the fifteenth century was [sic] paralleled by the growth of a new class of powerful nobles, created it is true by royal favor, but none the less capable of actions dangerous to the crown.' Such actions were few under the strong rule of Francis I and Henry II; but as soon as the monarchy passed into the hands of a mere boy, the nobility's potential for troublemaking stood revealed. It was the nobility which provided the leadership and many of the combatants on both sides in the Wars of Religion, hence the concentrated attention currently given to it by historians, for an understanding of the nobility – its status and membership – is crucial to an understanding of sixteenth-century France. We should beware of the historical cliché that the Wars of Religion were fought by nobles under the cloak of faith. This is a crude simplification. Religion was a powerful force in the sixteenth century and some nobles at least may have taken up arms in defence of genuine convictions. But other factors than religion may also have caused dissatisfaction and a spirit of rebellion among them. It is to such factors that we must now turn.

Historians have for a long time believed that the French nobility in the mid-sixteenth century was experiencing a crisis. They have argued that, as a class, it became impoverished as the value of its landed revenues, supposedly fixed by custom, declined. Since nobles were debarred from trade by the law of *dérogeance*, they were less able to adapt to economic change than the bourgeoisie. At the same time they lived extravagantly, fighting for the king or attending his court. Gradually many nobles were forced to sell their lands to members of the rising bourgeoisie, who were keen to raise their social status. Land ownership was generally recognized as a passport to the world of office-holding, and ultimately to the most prized status of all, that of nobleman. According to Lucien Romier (1922), the first half of the sixteenth century witnessed a drastic decline in the real value of noblemen's incomes. By 1560 widespread impoverishment was forcing them to sell their lands and fiefs to merchants and officials who formed a new 'noble' class. Gaston Roupnel (1955) and Henri Drouot (1937) ascribed similar fates to the Burgundian nobility and Paul Raveau (1926) traced the widespread dispossession of nobles in Upper Poitou. In a more general, yet influential, work, Pierre de Vaissière (1925) agreed that, after experiencing a golden age in the first half of the century, many impoverished country nobles had by its end sold or were selling their property to rich merchants and lawyers.

In 1969, Davis Bitton published a book entitled *The French Nobility in Crisis, 1560–1640*, in which he argues that the Price Revolution of the sixteenth century caused most nobles to experience an alarming decline in their real income. Soon incomes of only 1000 or even 500 *livres* were not at all uncommon and the result was heavy indebtedness. Other changes, according to Bitton, also undermined the nobility's social and political standing. 'Almost as painful', he writes, 'were the increasing incursions of non-nobles into the ranks of the nobility', a process which allegedly 'reached a point of extraordinary intensity in the 1550s'. Following the Peace of Cateau-Cambrésis, the nobility suffered 'a galling form of "unemployment"'. Whereas in the past young noblemen had relieved pressure on their family's estates by serving in the army, now they found this outlet closed to them. In 1559 'hundreds of noble sons were thrown back on the home estates, where the family resources were often insufficient to support them. Bands of armed noblemen roamed the countryside, pillaging and plundering.'

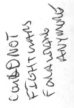

Evidence supporting this picture of the nobility in decline may be found in abundance in contemporary books, pamphlets, tracts and broadsides. The *cahiers* prepared for the Estates-General nearly always contained sections on the nobility. Legal commentaries, collections of lawsuits and royal ordinances had much to say on the subject. The nobility also attracted much popular hostility. In 1560 the third estate denounced nobles who arbitrarily revived old obligations on their peasants and imposed new ones. Other complaints focused on the violence meted out by some nobles against their tenants. The privilege of tax exemption enjoyed by nobles was also much criticized, particularly as its traditional justification no longer seemed valid. In the past nobles had been spared taxes because they had offered their blood fighting for the king, but their military role had changed. Cavalry was no longer as important in war as infantry, which was reckoned to be beneath the dignity of a nobleman. The *ban et arrière-ban*, whereby vassals had previously given military service to their suzerain, had almost died out. According to Bitton this was 'an inevitable result of the large-scale land transfers between 1450 and 1550' which had come to include many commoners (*roturiers*). Nobles avoided serving personally by making a financial payment or hiring a substitute; others neither paid nor served. Those who did serve 'were generally poor country nobles who had been unable to pay the redemption fee'.

Bitton also points to a decline of the nobility's political role. Its traditional rights of seigneurial justice had been drastically curtailed. Many municipal offices, previously held by nobles, had been lost to town dwellers. As the number of sovereign courts was multiplied, most of the judges and councillors were recruited from outside the 'old' nobility and, as venal offices were purchased by commoners, 'the old nobility had a strong sense of being dispossessed of its public functions.' In 1567 an anonymous writer complained that nobles had been turned into villeins and villeins into nobles. This process was ruining the nobility by taking away its income. Another writer blamed the nobility for its predicament: its performance in recent years had been unsatisfactory; if it were improved, the king might employ it again.

The traditional view of the French nobility's decline served historians as an explanation of the social and political conflicts of early modern France. These could be seen as resulting from a conflict between an old declining nobility, and a new rising bourgeoisie. It also helped to explain the rise of the modern absolutist state. Given the assumption that a strong state and a strong nobility were incompatible, the latter's decline in the sixteenth century was seen as the essential precondition of the triumph of the state and its servants – the merchants and the lawyers – in the next century. But as J. B. Wood has shown, the case for a general decline of the French nobility in the sixteenth century rests 'on very weak foundations'. It consists of isolated examples of the sale of fiefs to bourgeois. Romier offers only two examples: the sale of nineteen seigneuries in the Lyon area at an unspecified time in the sixteenth century and the repossession and sale by the crown in 1531 of the Constable of Bourbon's lands. This last example is of doubtful validity anyway, since most of the constable's lands were granted to the king's mother and he had lost them for political, not economic, reasons.

So much for the notion of nobility in crisis. As J. B. Wood has shown, it rests on sources that are literary and general, not archival or specific, and presupposes too monolithic a view of the nobility, which was not a unitary economic group, capable of a single response – rise, decline or fall – to changing economic circumstances. Most nobles were rent-receiving landlords, yet some owned little or no land. Many, even if they had a landed income, had no fief or *seigneurie*. Some nobles worked their holdings themselves; others never set foot in them. Many commoners, too, were landowners and owned fiefs or *seigneuries*. Moreover, office-holding nobles received wages and pensions in addition to their landed income. While some nobles were exceedingly rich, others were virtual paupers. Nor was the nobility functionally unified. Though it considered itself *the* military class, most soldiers were commoners and only a minority of noblemen performed regular military duties. Many were magistrates or financial officers; a few engaged in wholesale trade or industry. Many had no recognizable function at all. Nor were nobles ethnically distinctive: they intermarried with commoners and with recently ennobled families (*anoblis*). Although the nobility formed the second estate, there were nobles in the first estate and some in the third. The only characteristic shared by them all was their legal status, which was both personal and transmissible through the male line. Generally speaking, nobles were allowed to initiate lawsuits directly in a superior court; they enjoyed various kinds of tax exemptions; and they took precedence over and even excluded commoners in various social situations and activities.

Recent research has exploded the notion of an overall economic decline of the French nobility in the sixteenth century. Wood, for example, has examined the changing fortunes of the nobility in the *élection* of Bayeux between the mid-sixteenth and mid-seventeenth centuries. He has used the records of periodic inspections (*recherches*) of noble credentials dating back to the mid-fifteenth century. The *recherches* were fiscal devices aimed at discovering usurpers of noble status and returning them to the tax rolls. They divided nobles into two categories: 'new' and 'old'. Families which had been noble for more than a century were 'old' (*noblesse de race*); the rest were 'new'. The *recherches* show that the sixteenth century was a period of unprecedented expansion for the Bayeux nobility. Its membership doubled in less than sixty years. What is more, the expansion was due as much to the 'old' nobility reproducing itself as to an influx of 'new' nobles.

Upward mobility by commoners was far more limited than is often assumed. Very few of the 477 newcomers in the five *recherches* made between 1523 and 1666 were recently ennobled; the majority (274) were 'old' noble immigrants from other parts of Normandy. The relative number of 'old' nobles remained constant (81 per cent) throughout the century. This suggests that the 'old nobility' was healthier economically than was once thought. The *recherches* also suggest that too much importance has been attached in the past to ennoblement by office-holding. Almost none of the 'new' nobles was ennobled by office; most became noble by being awarded or purchasing letters of nobility.

Wood has also undermined other commonly held assumptions. For example, past historians have often suggested that the nobility was split into two hostile groups: the 'old' nobility of the sword (*noblesse d'épée* or *de race*) and the 'new' office-holding nobility 'of the robe' (*noblesse de robe*). However, in Bayeux the two groups appear to have been largely indistinguishable. Some old nobles held offices, and many new nobles gave up their offices as soon as they had been ennobled and adopted the life-styles of 'old' nobles. The role of military service was also more complex than is often assumed. Many nobles did at some time serve in the army and commanders were almost exclusively recruited from the 'old' nobility; yet more than half the Bayeux nobles never performed any military duties. Once they had been ennobled, 'new' nobles tended to do military service to the same extent as 'old' ones, although few had a military background. No attempt was made by the 'old' nobility to protect its own social identity by excluding 'new' nobles from military service. An examination of marriage patterns among the Bayeux nobility between 1430 and 1669 shows that nobles tended to intermarry and that 'new' nobles married 'old' ones more rapidly than their own kind. Such intermarriage strengthened the cohesion of the whole estate. By opening their ranks to newcomers, 'old' nobles removed any need for them to retain ties with the third estate. The evidence from Bayeux does not confirm the hostility between the nobility of the sword and that of the robe so frequently described in contemporary polemics and memoirs and at meetings of the Estates-General.

The crucial division within the nobility, according to Wood, was not between 'old' and 'new' families, but between the rich and the poor. A comparison of the incomes of nobles has produced three graphs relating to 259 persons in 1552, 459 in 1639 and 553 in 1666. These show no appreciable variation in the distribution of incomes between the mid-sixteenth and the mid-seventeenth centuries. A minority (one-tenth) of very rich nobles received more than half of all the revenue; a relatively poor half received less than a tenth of the total revenue; and between these extremes a well-to-do nobility received about 40 per cent of the total. What is most significant about these statistics is that over the century the number of poor nobles did not increase. In fact, the general tendency was towards enrichment. Available figures for the sixteenth century indicate that nobles of recent creation (i.e. less than a century old) were no better off than older nobles. Of the thirty wealthiest families, 'old' ones were in a majority: 22 as against 7 in 1552.

Recent studies of other French provinces have tended to confirm Wood's findings. In Beauce, seigneurial rents, which were often in kind, and the produce of domains benefited from inflation. Rents rose to such an extent that landlords doubled their capital every six or seven years between 1550 and 1680. The nobility as a whole grew richer and only experienced a crisis at the end of the seventeenth century. In Auvergne, aristocratic wealth as a whole was maintained. In Béarn, the domanial income of the king of Navarre rose seven times between 1530 and 1600 whereas prices in Toulouse only trebled. In Dauphiné, the number of seigneuries owned by the old nobility did recede somewhat, but without causing serious damage to its overall wealth. The same noble houses controlled landed property after the Wars of Religion as before. In Poitou, Louis Merle (1958) has disproved the picture of aristocratic decline originally painted by Paul Raveau. There may have been a crisis in respect of cash revenues, but nobles managed to overcome it by insisting on payments in kind and by a more efficient exploitation of their lands. Having acquired peasant holdings, they had them cultivated by sharecroppers (*métayers*) with whom they shared the produce from the harvests. They also reclaimed and redistributed lands. Thus it seems that the provinces which have yielded evidence of aristocratic decline (Goubert's Beauvaisis, Henri Drouot's Burgundy and Lucien Febvre's Franche-Comté) may have been special cases. The question remains open, but the French nobility in the sixteenth century was evidently more prosperous than was once supposed.

The traditional view of aristocratic decline rested on three assumptions: first, that seigneurial rents were fixed and paid in money; secondly, that war helped to ruin the nobility; and thirdly that extravagant living and a lack of business sense contributed to that ruin. All three are questionable. Many rents were paid in kind and they formed only a part of the seigneur's income which was mainly raised by produce from his domain. J.-M. Constant has shown that only 40 per cent of nobles who served in the army became poorer as a result; 37 per cent grew richer, and the rest did not change. War could sometimes be profitable. A nobleman could make a lot of money by capturing a man of rank and exacting a ransom for his release: Monluc once thought of raising cash in this way to build himself an *hôtel* in Paris. Finally, the idea that noblemen ruined themselves by extravagant living is only partially true. Those who went to court had to spend a great deal to justify their social rank and to serve the king, but most noblemen never went there; they remained on their estates and paid close attention to their management. Nor was a nobleman completely debarred from profitable pursuits: he was allowed to graft and plant trees, and could manufacture glass and produce iron. The day-to-day activities of the *gentil-homme campagnard* are described in detail in the diary of the sire de Gouberville, a petty nobleman from Normandy, who only went to court once in his life. The rest of his time was spent managing his estates and fighting lawsuits in defence of his interests. He kept his accounts very carefully and succeeded in making a profit from his farming, even in lean years.

Some aristocratic families (for example the Nevers) did run up debts, but most of the important houses were extraordinarily resilient. Henri de Montmorency, governor of Languedoc and Constable of France from 1593, ran into serious difficulties at the end of the sixteenth century after inheriting enormous debts from his elder brother François. In May 1598 his treasurer, Nicholas Girard, advised him to sell 100,000 *écus* of forest. Thanks to this sale and also to help from the crown, the Montmorency budget regained its former balance.

The example of the La Trémoïlle family also demonstrates aristocratic powers of recovery from economic hardship. In 1483 the revenues of the La Trémoïlles had been reduced by two-thirds and their debts were huge. Over half a century three of the dukes, Louis I, Louis II and François, restored the situation. They gave up lands in Burgundy and by various means (purchase, inheritance, marriage alliances and royal gifts) built up a considerable and strategically important domain centred on Thouars in western France. Starting as a *vicomté*, it became a duchy in 1563 and a *duché-pairie* in 1595. The dukes ran their estates well and organized the sale of their produce. They exported wheat to Portugal in the second half of the sixteenth century. Louis II bought 160,000 vine roots in Burgundy and transplanted them to his own lands, built ships and took part in maritime trade and piracy. He was the most enterprising of the La Trémoïlles: he continued the restoration of seigneurial rights begun by his father, drained marshes, and repaired mills, presses, ovens and bridges. To combat inflation, he reduced the length of leases and increased rents, changing them from money to kind. His example was followed by his son François, who linked profit-making with honour. He believed that he was enhancing the honour of his family by extending its land-ownership and augmenting its income. The revenues from the family's estates rose 135 per cent between 1486 and 1542 and its total revenues by 99 per cent. This emancipated the family from any dependence on royal largesse.

As Arlette Jouanna has written: 'It would be hazardous, given the extent of our present knowledge, to pass an overall judgement. Yet we should certainly henceforth reject the idea of a general economic decline of the nobility in the sixteenth and seventeenth centuries.' That being so, how do we explain the restlessness which seems to have affected it on the eve of the religious wars? If nobles were not declining economically, were they losing ground politically? There is no doubt that those of the traditional sort were gradually being squeezed out of judicial and financial offices requiring skills which they had not taken the trouble to acquire. They also lost ground because of the diffusion of venality and of the hereditary transmission of offices. But the beneficiaries of change were also nobles – possibly of another kind, but whose pedigrees were often highly respectable. The same process was taking place in the central administration. In the *Conseil étroit*, where the most important decisions were taken, nobles of the sword were being replaced by nobles of the robe. In royal councils of lesser importance, princes of the blood and great magnates managed to retain their right of entry but seldom exercised it. Ministerial offices were also mainly in the hands of *robins*.

A nobleman, however, did not need to hold an office in order to exercise political power. He could still do so by building up a network of well-placed clients. Thus many councillors of the sovereign courts belonged to the clientèle of a great nobleman or *grand*. A nobleman could also exert influence in the king's council, without being actually present, by manipulating a client. Considerable power was still being exercised by the nobility in local government. A *seigneur* wielded much influence locally which was all the greater if he also had jurisdiction. Seigneurial courts existed throughout the *ancien régime* – in Lower Auvergne in the sixteenth century they were virtually the only rural courts – and their staff was usually well trained and competent and five times more numerous than royal judges. Thus it seems that the case for a general political decline of the nobility is as questionable as that for its general economic decline.

French society in the early modern period has been described as a society of *fidélités*. A *fidèle* or client dedicated himself to the service of a patron. In the words of the historian Roland Mousnier, the *fidèle*,

> gives himself completely to the master. He espouses all the latter's ideas, inclinations, ambitions and interests. He devotes himself to him utterly. He serves him in every way possible: he accompanies him, entertains him, speaks, writes, intrigues and argues for him, fights, plots, and rebels for him, follows him into exile, helps him against everyone else, even against the king, against the state; if necessary, he gives his life for his master. In exchange for all of this, the master owes the *fidèle* first and foremost his friendship, his absolute trust, his confidence. He owes him food, clothing, maintenance, and protection in all the circumstances of life, even against the law, even against the head of state. He must see to the advancement of his *fidèle*, arrange a marriage for him, obtain offices and functions for him. If the master has rebelled and is making terms with the king, he must include stipulations on behalf of his *fidèles* in any treaty he signs.

Such a relationship is reminiscent of the 'bastard feudalism' that existed in fifteenth-century England, but in sixteenth-century France there was no indenture whereby the client nearly always reserved a higher loyalty to the king.

The majority of French noblemen probably never became clients, but a minor rural nobleman could occasionally require the support of a courtier. He might turn to a local magnate who was willing to assist him in return for an assurance of future service, or he might apply to the leaders of rival factions at court. Thus, on the eve of the Wars of Religion, some Picard nobles applied to the duc de Montmorency and also to the Guises. A nobleman who bound himself to a magnate might sign documents pledging mutual loyalty and protection or he might take a formal oath or declare his loyalty. Owners of fiefs, of course, had lords to whom they paid homage, though this now implied a social and financial relationship rather than military service.

Mousnier has suggested that the patron–client relationship was more important than the lord–vassal tie because it depended on a free choice. Determined as it was by the chance of inheritance, the relationship of lord and vassal must often have bound together incompatible people. Yet the patron–client relationship, even if it rested on free choice, did not necessarily guarantee loyalty, for it depended more on self-interest than on personal affection. A client whose expectations of reward had not been satisfied, or who felt that his interests lay elsewhere, would often break his bond. Sometimes he would ask his patron's permission to do so, but usually he acted unilaterally.

Sharon Kettering has pointed to the difficulty of measuring the precise extent of reciprocity in patron–client arrangements which were not stated in writing and were often obscured by rhetoric. What is certain is the frequency of misunderstandings and the emotional outbursts resulting from them. Sons might turn against a father because they resented the weight of his authority or were dissatisfied by an uneven distribution of property on his part. A great nobleman did not always have the means to satisfy his clients' expectations. A dissatisfied client often became a 'malcontent' and severed the relationship with his patron in the most resounding way if only to advertise his readiness to serve a different patron. If his rejected patron happened to be the king, the breach would be politically significant. Rulers were so swamped with demands for favours that they allowed their generosity to outstrip their resources. Unless they were strong-willed they might also give only to those petitioners who clamoured loudest, leaving those who did not ask to sulk in the cold. After 1559 the 'Malcontent' was a common type in French society. He might demonstrate his dissatisfaction with the king by stomping out of the court along with his clients. During the Wars of Religion a positive game of musical chairs took place as one great family left the court in high dudgeon to be replaced by another.

Calvinism and the nobility

In 1561 the Venetian ambassador reported that until then Protestantism in France had been limited to the lower orders of society because they had little to lose under persecution other than their lives. But, as we have seen, the situation underwent a change about the mid-century when, much to Henry II's indignation, Calvinism began to make deep inroads among the nobility. One historian has estimated that half the nobility went over to the new faith in the 1560s. This has been explained on economic grounds: the nobles, finding themselves impoverished as a consequence of the Price Revolution, attached themselves to the cause that seemed most likely to bring them quick profits, for Calvinism offered scope for material gain at the expense of the church. But the notion that the French nobility underwent an economic decline has been largely discredited. Many impoverished nobles undoubtedly existed in mid-sixteenth-century France, but the nobility as a class did not collapse economically. What is more, conversion to Calvinism does not seem to have been limited to the poor nobility. In the *élection* of Bayeux more than 200 nobles, or 40 per cent of all nobles in the area, had become Protestants by the end of the 1560s. They represented the nobility as a whole and were not recruited exclusively from a small and socially distinct section. What is more, 41 per cent had fief incomes placing them in the richest quarter of the nobility as a whole.

In other words, Protestantism cut right across noble society from top to bottom economically. This suggests that the mass conversion of nobles to Protestantism may have been due to religious conviction – the power of ideas – rather than materialistic causes. But this is not easily proved. While recognizing the dangers of a purely socio-economic explanation, J. B. Wood has put forward an intriguing suggestion. The fact that Protestantism was mainly adopted in the Bayeux *élection* by relatively affluent nobles made it a serious and dangerous movement, for if it had been composed predominantly of noble dregs it could never have threatened the public order as it did, nor would it have enjoyed the real, albeit short-term, successes that its substantial human, material and spiritual resources made possible. Yet status anxiety or insecurity cannot be ruled out as a prime cause of discontent. A high proportion of the Bayeux nobles were 'new' nobles whose status was less than a century old, and therefore open to challenge by the crown. Indeed, several of them had had their claim to nobility challenged in the courts. Wood suggests that the crown's 'increasingly stringent' attempts to regulate noble status since 1463–4 may have caused an important part of the nobility to use the Protestant movement as a 'logical outlet for its opposition to the legalistic assault on its social position by the crown'. But this theory has yet to be tested across the whole of France.

Another factor which needs to be taken into account when considering the rapid diffusion of Calvinism among the nobility is clientage. A nobleman in sixteenth-century France was never isolated: he had strong provincial and family loyalties. Although feudalism as a system implying military service had long since disappeared, the signs of feudal dependence – the fealty and homage sworn by a vassal to his lord – were still taken seriously. Provincial feudalism, as we have seen, survived in the form of patronage and clientage. No nobleman of middle rank could expect to be admitted to court, the church, the army or the administration without the backing of a patron. This was often a nobleman of greater substance to whom in childhood he had been attached as a page. According to La Noue, a nobleman with an income of 700 or 800 *livres* per year and four or five children on his hands could only provide for their education by sending them to serve as pages to a wealthy neighbour. This would create an indebtedness in later life: the father and his sons would become their benefactor's *créatures*; they would follow him everywhere, be it to court or to war, and a nobleman who converted to Calvinism would carry his clients with him into the new religion. This happened in south-west France, where the process of aristocratic conversion to Calvinism has been compared to the spread of an oil stain. For example, the clientèle of the Gascon nobleman Pons de Polignac, sire des Roys, was 'a veritable religious spider's web'. It included many of the 500 people persecuted for heresy by the Parlement of Toulouse in 1569.

Calvin appreciated the importance of clientage: he knew that the conversion of a single nobleman could lead to multiple conversions among his relatives and dependants. Théodore de Bèze, his principal lieutenant, was himself a nobleman and therefore well-equipped to appeal to his own class. He was sent to Nérac in 1560 and may have brought about the conversion of Jeanne d'Albret, the wife of Antoine de Bourbon and mother of the future Henry IV. A fair proportion of the exiles who went to Geneva were noblemen. They were indoctrinated alongside the pastors so that a close bond was formed between some of the future lay and ecclesiastical leaders of the Huguenot movement. Some nobles returned to France as pastors and played a leading part in setting up Calvinist churches. In 1555, Louis prince de Condé and his suite stopped in Geneva on their way home from a military campaign in Italy. They asked to visit the city and to hear a sermon. We do not know if they met Calvin or any other pastor, but the visit points to Condé's early interest in Calvinism. His Protestantism may not have been simply a matter of political convenience. The religious conscience of any figure of the past is not easily probed by the historian. Adventurism or greed may have caused some French noblemen to embrace Calvinism; others may have been moved by sincere religious sentiment.

An important aspect of the mass conversion of the French nobility to Calvinism around 1560 was the role played by women. Already in the early part of the century Marguerite d'Angoulême had given encouragement and protection to evangelical scholars and preachers. Her influence had rubbed off on some of the ladies of her entourage, who had to face the more serious challenges of the mid-century. They included Louise de Montmorency, sister of the constable and mother of Gaspard de Coligny, the future admiral and leader of the Huguenots; Jacqueline de Longwy, duchesse de Montpensier, who defended Huguenots at the court of Catherine de' Medici; and Michelle de Saubonne, ancestress of the Rohans who led the Huguenots in the later civil wars. Among women of the next generation was Marguerite's own daughter Jeanne d'Albret, who sponsored Calvinist preaching in Béarn and Navarre even before she announced her conversion in 1560. Other important Protestant ladies included Madeleine de Mailly, comtesse de Roye, whose daughter married and converted the prince de Condé; Charlotte de Laval, the wife of Admiral Coligny; Françoise de Seninghen, mother of the prince de Porcien; and Françoise du Bec-Crespin, mother of Philippe Du Plessis-Mornay, a leading spokesman of the Huguenot cause. As many as half the Protestant women arrested following the affair in the rue Saint-Jacques in September 1557 may have been noblewomen. It has been suggested that such women may have found self-fulfilment in the Calvinist faith, but this has been disputed, for Calvinism was no better disposed towards female emancipation than the Catholic faith. In fact, women were given less scope for personal responsibility in Calvin's Geneva than in Counter-Reformation Italy. Calvin, de Bèze and other members of the Venerable Company did not welcome attempts by certain Frenchwomen to get up in church and speak on holy things. They wanted their church to be run by well-trained pastors and sound male members of the Consistories, and they joined Catholic critics in citing Paul's dictum from I Corinthians that 'women keep silence in the churches'.

However, Calvin and his lieutenants appreciated the importance of winning noblewomen to their cause and kept up a lively correspondence with them. Women, as we have seen, were not numerous among the Protestants of Rouen, but noblewomen were often literate; they also had more time to devote to religious pursuits and were susceptible to the influence of a Protestant tutor to their children than were their menfolk, who might be absent at court or fighting in the king's wars.

18
The Failure of Conciliation, 1559–62

Henry II's untimely death revealed the fundamental weakness of a regime whose effectiveness depended on the person of the monarch. Both he and his father had been strong enough to sustain the image of an all-powerful monarchy and to ensure aristocratic loyalty to that ideal. At Henry's death the crown passed to his eldest son Francis, a sickly boy of fifteen. In theory he was old enough to rule, but he lacked maturity and experience. Consequently, the government fell into the hands of his mother, Catherine de' Medici, who had served as regent during her late husband's military campaigns, but had never been allowed much voice in the kingdom's affairs. Henry had relied for advice mainly on his mistress, Diane de Poitiers, and on his principal minister, the Constable of Montmorency. As Catherine hated them both, for different reasons, she chose to rely heavily on François duc de Guise and his brother Charles, Cardinal of Lorraine, the uncles of Francis II's queen, Mary Stuart.

The change of monarch was accompanied by a change of government personnel. Diane de Poitiers was banished from court, made to hand over crown jewels and forced to surrender the château of Chenonceaux to Catherine in exchange for that of Chaumont. Her client Cardinal Bertrand was dismissed as Keeper of the Seals, while the former chancellor, François Olivier, resumed his duties. As for Montmorency, he was allowed to retain his office of constable but was persuaded to hand over the Grand Mastership to the duc de Guise. He ceased to influence the government's policies, but remained a powerful force in the kingdom at large. Montmorency was its richest landowner and, as governor of Languedoc, controlled much of the Midi. His eldest son, François, was governor of Paris and the Ile-de-France, and his nephew Gaspard de Coligny was Admiral of France. Another nephew, François d'Andelot, was colonel-general of the infantry.

Apart from Montmorency and his relatives, the main rivals of the Guises were the Bourbons, who were all descended from the sixth son of Louis IX. The house of Bourbon was divided into the four branches of Vendôme, Condé, La Roche-sur-Yon and Montpensier. Since the treason of the Constable of Bourbon in 1523, his kinsmen had suffered discrimination at the hands of both Francis I and Henry II, who had favoured younger sons of the foreign princely houses like the Guises. Though rich and powerful and also related to the French royal house, the Guises were regarded as aliens by their French enemies because they were not deeply rooted in the old French nobility: their origins lay in the duchy of Lorraine which remained part of the Holy Roman Empire.

Many people in France could see no justification for the authority assumed by the Guises following the death of Henry II. They believed that the right to govern the kingdom rested with Antoine de Bourbon, king of Navarre and first prince of the blood. But he was in Guyenne when Henry died and took a long time reaching the court. Friends urged him to assume his rightful place at the head of the government, but by the time he arrived the Guises were already firmly in control. They found a pretext for not giving him accommodation at court and, although he was admitted to the king's council, he was excluded from the innermost council which decided policy. Navarre feebly accepted this situation. He even agreed to accompany Elisabeth de Valois to Spain in the hope of ingratiating himself with her husband, Philip II, and obtaining restitution of Spanish Navarre. As for his brother, Louis prince de Condé, he accepted a mission to the Netherlands.

The monopoly of power enjoyed by the Guises in 1560 was reflected in the young king's patronage. An examination of secretarial registers for April to June 1560 shows the domination of the Guises and the eclipse of Montmorency and Diane. The *Epargne*'s accounts tell the same story, being filled with gifts of money, payments of arrears and reimbursements of loans to servants of the Guises, as well as to their clients, *gens d'armes* and relatives. For many noblemen the obvious response to this state of affairs was to seek to become Guise clients themselves, but this option was not open to all. Protestant nobles, in particular, could not hope for fair treatment from the family which had championed their persecution under Henry II and continued to do so now. The Guises pressed for the enforcement of the anti-heresy laws and for the punishment of the four *parlementaires* who had been arrested following the *mercuriale* in June 1559. The Huguenots appealed to Catherine de' Medici, who had shown some distaste for the persecution at the end of Henry's reign, to oppose it now. She promised to help them provided they agreed not to assemble or cause scandal, but she did nothing to save Du Bourg, who was burned for heresy. When the Parisian consistory accused her of bad faith, she distanced herself from the Protestant cause, explaining that she had only shown its adherents compassion, not sympathy for their doctrine about which she knew nothing.

[margin notes: "THE GUISE MONOPOLISE THE ROYAL CTL" · "SHE IS WEAK" · "ANTI-PROTESTAND GUISE"]

The queen mother, in fact, did not like the more aggressive posture which the Huguenots seemed to be adopting. Whereas under Henry II they had endured persecution without questioning his right to harass them, they now seemed to be renouncing evangelical patience.

The religious policy of the Guises was only part of a larger and equally controversial government programme. Now that peace had been signed with the Habsburgs, it was necessary to reduce the enormous debt which Henry II had left. Various highly unpopular measures were accordingly taken by Francis II's ministers: royal troops were disbanded, the payment of their wages was deferred, pensions were suppressed, free alienations of royal land revoked and the interest on debts arbitrarily curtailed. Many nobles suspected that these steps were being taken in the interest not of the kingdom but of the Guises and their clients. They wondered if the government's policies truly reflected the wishes of the boy-king, or if he was being manipulated by ministers; and if so, whether it was their right, even their duty, to overthrow the usurpers?

The Tumult of Amboise, March 1560

Soon after Henry II's death, Calvin sent the pastor Antoine de la Roche-Chandieu to the king of Navarre with a message telling him that Providence had cleared his path to the regency. This was in line with Calvin's political thinking as set out in his *Institutes*. But Navarre seemed more interested in reclaiming Spanish Navarre than in challenging the power of the Guises. On 15 August 1559 the pastor François de Morel expressed his disappointment with Navarre in a letter to Calvin. Were there other means, he asked, of delivering the church from its present sufferings? The law laid down that if the king died leaving only minors, the estates should be called to appoint administrators for the realm until they came of age. If Navarre failed to call the estates, could someone else do so in his place, and, if legal means failed, could force be used to win back that which a handful of foreign tyrants had seized? Calvin's reply was uncompromising: only the *first* prince of the blood was empowered by law to act.

Antoine de Navarre's lethargy obliged enemies of the Guises to disregard Calvin's advice. But the origins of the Tumult of Amboise are far from clear. According to Lucien Romier, it was initiated by Condé in August 1559, but a well-informed contemporary, Régnier de La Planche, ascribes it to an unspecified group of persons. After agreeing to restore 'the ancient and lawful government of France', they sought the advice of French and German jurists, who said that a violent coup against the Guises would be lawful provided it was led by at least one prince of the blood. This may have been when Condé was approached. At his suggestion, an indictment of the Guises was prepared and a plan drawn up to arrest them and make them account for their administration to the Estates-General.

Traditionally, historians have tended to focus on the political objectives of the conspirators, but their religious intentions should not be overlooked. Calvinists believed that the people were being 'seduced' by the Catholic church. Beliefs and practices like transubstantiation, the veneration of images, the calendar of feasts and fasts, were seen by them as detracting from the central importance of Christ's sacrifice on the Cross. They also regarded indulgences, anniversary masses, and dispensations for which the church exacted payment as swindling of the laity by an avaricious clergy. Many Calvinists believed that if the king and the parlement would only read the Confession of Faith which their first National Synod had adopted, they would see that their doctrine, far from posing a threat to the established order, embodied the truth of the Gospel. Much Calvinist agitation, therefore, took the form of attempts to present the Confession of Faith to the authorities. According to the historian Jacques Poujol, this was the primary objective of the Amboise conspirators: they were fanatics who planned to present the king with a copy of their Confession of Faith. The attempt to kidnap him and remove him from Guise influence was an afterthought inspired by reckless lesser nobles.

Late in September, La Roche-Chandieu went to Geneva to inform Calvin of the plot, but he advised against it. However, not even Calvin could stop the conspiracy. Whatever Condé's role may have been, the responsibility for its organization was mainly shouldered by Jean du Barry, seigneur de La Renaudie, a petty nobleman from Périgord who had embraced Protestantism in the course of an adventurous career. He was in Paris in September 1559 and in the next five months travelled widely in France and Switzerland gathering supporters and recruiting mercenaries. He seems to have disposed of generous funds of unidentified provenance. In the course of his travels, La Renaudie visited Geneva. He made a bad impression on Calvin, but apparently received encouragement from de Bèze, who gave him a copy of his translation of Psalm 94 ('O Lord God, to whom vengeance belongeth, show thyself . . .') and promised to circulate an anti-Guise booklet, probably written by Hotman, simultaneously with the plot. Among Genevan exiles who rallied to La Renaudie's call were several noblemen who had left France on account of their faith. Though by no means poor, they longed to return to their estates in France. Their hopes had been raised by Henry II's death, then dashed by the Guise administration. Altogether between sixty and seventy such exiles now slipped back into France.

While La Renaudie looked for support in Lyon, Périgord and Brittany, Ardoin de Maillane accomplished a similar mission in Provence and Languedoc. Soon groups of men disguised as merchants or litigants converged on Nantes, where on 1 February 1560 a meeting, purporting to be the

Estates-General, was held in order to legitimize the forthcoming coup. In an opening speech, La Renaudie denounced the government of the Guises. Loyalty to the king was emphasized by the assembled delegates and the purpose of the plot was defined as the dismissal and trial of the Guises. La Renaudie was confirmed as commander of the enterprise and authorized to raise an army. The date of the coup, fixed initially for 10 March, had to be postponed for six days. La Renaudie then moved to Paris, where he remained till the end of February. He dispatched orders, found more recruits and sent arms, horses, supplies and cash to Orléans and Tours, where his troops were due to assemble.

Secrecy was not easily maintained in sixteenth-century France. On 2 March, as reports of a plot were reaching the ears of the king's ministers, Francis II issued the Edict of Amboise, which extended an amnesty to all religious prisoners except pastors and conspirators. A few days later the king ordered the release of all religious prisoners and allowed dissenters to present him with petitions. Historians are divided in ascribing reponsibility for the edict. Nicola Sutherland thinks 'it was the work of Catherine de' Medici and the chancellor L'Hospital'. 'The Guises', she writes, 'would never have issued such a pardon.' L'Hôpital was not appointed chancellor until April 1560. He took up his duties in May and his letters of provision were not signed until June. So his responsibility for the edict is uncertain. Moreover, as Evennett has pointed out, 'it is impossible entirely to dissociate the Cardinal of Lorraine from the Edict of Amboise'; to do so is to fall victim to 'a false *a priori* dogmatism'. Lorraine was a subtle statesman, not the bloodthirsty ogre of Protestant legend: he could adapt to circumstances. When the pope complained of the edict, Lorraine confessed that he had been its chief advocate. Two years later the bishop of Valence, a champion of toleration, declared that recognition of the failure of the persecutions and of the need to devise new methods first came from the Guises in the spring of 1560.

The edict implied no weakness on the part of the government in responding to any challenge to its authority. As groups of conspirators gathered in woods around Amboise, they were set upon by royal troops. Some, including La Renaudie, were killed in ambushes; others were rounded up, tortured and executed. Many were drowned in the Loire or hanged from the château's balconies. The Guises claimed that the plot had been aimed at the crown. They also tried to implicate Condé and 'some preachers of the new doctrine'. The charge was not groundless. Two pastors – La Roche-Chandieu and Boisnormand – were deeply implicated, but most of the Reformed churches in France had followed Calvin's lead. That of Nîmes, for example, had refused to help fund the plot. Apart from a few churches in Provence and some members of the Paris church, almost none had helped the conspirators.

The search for a solution

The aftermath of the tumult is surprising. One might have expected a wave of persecution aimed at wiping out Huguenots. Instead, the policy of moderation initiated by the Edict of Amboise was upheld. At the same time, moves were made to heal the religious division of France. The main challenge facing the crown was to restore unity of belief. Hindsight tells us that this was an unrealistic aim, but contemporaries did not necessarily think so. Many hoped that a General Council might find a way of bringing the Protestants back into the church; but the Council of Trent had failed to win their adherence or respect, and its continuation was likely to confirm the religious split. The French crown consequently favoured calling a new council which might appeal to Protestants of goodwill and point forward to a regained unity. This was the solution favoured by the Cardinal of Lorraine. He did not question the doctrinal decrees of the Council of Trent, but believed that they should be looked at afresh. As for the Gallican church, it was unwilling to entrust its own internal reformation to an international body. Lorraine accordingly revived the idea of a national council, which would reform the French church. He wrote to Pope Pius IV on 21 March, explaining his position. The recent crisis, he wrote, had demonstrated that heretics were a grave threat to Catholicism in France. The international preparations needed for a General Council would inevitably take time. Lorraine therefore asked the pope to send Cardinal Tournon to France as legate *a latere* with powers to reform the French church and to convene, if necessary, an assembly of bishops. Speaking to the papal nuncio, Lorraine painted a grim picture of the condition of the French church and stressed the need for urgent remedies.

News of the Edict of Amboise and of the proposed national council filled the pope with horror and amazement. He saw the growing tendency of the secular powers in Catholic countries to meddle in ecclesiastical matters as a threat to church unity. Not unreasonably, he regarded a national council as heralding a national church. He denounced the council as a 'veritable schism' fraught with perils to both souls and the royal authority, and expressed his displeasure at the French proposals in a letter to the Cardinal of Lorraine, dated 12 May. While agreeing to send Tournon as legate, Pius severely criticized the religious policy of the French crown. The king, he said, had no authority to pardon convicted heretics, and he also condemned the proposed national council, arguing that it was canonically necessary to complete the unfinished Council of Trent.

Meanwhile, as the French court tried to forget its recent troubles, the fires of discontent continued to smoulder in the kingdom at large. From all parts came news of the emergence of Huguenot congregations, while processions celebrated the release of religious prisoners. Public demonstrations against the rule of the Guises also took place. In Paris, the Cardinal of Lorraine was hanged in effigy and publicly burnt. His château of Meudon was attacked by arsonists, and attempts made to set fire to his properties at Dampierre and in Paris. A flood of abusive and obscene pamphlets denounced the Guises and the queen mother. Such pamphlets, including the famous *Epitre au Tigre de la France*, were found even in the apartments of their victims. Fearing assassination, Lorraine surrounded the king and himself with a bodyguard of mounted arquebusiers.

For the present the Guises were fairly secure. The Tumult of Amboise had shown how difficult it was to overthrow them by force. However, a process was beginning which within two years would transform the dissidents into an army. This process, which the great majority of pastors opposed, was already in its initial stages at the time of the tumult. The Edict of Amboise, as qualified by a circular of 31 March, explicitly upheld the ban on illicit assemblies and conventicles. In practice, the government tolerated private meetings, but was ambivalent in respect of public ones. 'Uncertainty became a political system thanks to which the government could extend or restrict toleration without ever defining it precisely' (Romier). Edicts against heresy were often ineffective because the officials responsible for carrying them out, especially those of the *prévôtés* and *bailliage* courts, were themselves Protestants or Protestant sympathizers. Taking advantage of this confused state of affairs, Huguenots demonstrated their faith more or less provocatively. In many places, notably in the Rhône valley, they attacked Catholic churches and religious houses, such acts being frequently committed by turbulent nobles over the heads of the pastors.

Although the amnesty had not improved the situation in the kingdom, the government did not go back on its tracks. On 18 April it reaffirmed the promise of a national council, but it seems that an intensification of coercive measures was also discussed. Be that as it may, the Edict of Romorantin, issued on 18 May, transferred the prosecution of heresy from the royal to the ecclesiastical courts, while the punishment of illicit assemblies and seditious acts was entrusted to the presidial courts. But the church courts had become notoriously slack and the secular courts were so permeated with unreliable officials as to be ineffective; Calvinist communities were left more or less undisturbed. The main obstacle to their expansion came more from Catholic popular violence than from legislation.

Meanwhile, the question of the General Council was not forgotten. On 1 June the French government was informed of the pope's strictures on the idea of a national council and of his plans to resume the Council of Trent. To the Cardinal of Lorraine this seemed very unwise. He insisted that unless a new General Council were to meet elsewhere than in Trent, the national council would have to be carried through. In French eyes the first duty of a General Council was not reform – a task better done at home – but reunion, and this required the co-operation of the Lutheran princes. The French government, it seems, wrongly believed that the Huguenots would echo a favourable Lutheran response to a General Council.

The Fontainebleau assembly, August 1560

In June 1560 a new Chancellor of France was appointed in the person of Michel de L'Hôpital. An Auvergnat, born in 1505, he had studied law at Padua and, during ten years spent in Italy, had developed an interest in humanism. In 1537, following his return to France, he became a councillor in the Parlement of Paris and, after another visit to Italy, entered the service of Marguerite, the sister of Henry II. In 1553 he purchased the office of master of requests and in 1554 that of First President of the *Chambre des comptes*. As Chancellor of France he assumed the highest public office under the king. Like many of his contemporaries, L'Hôpital did not think two religions could coexist within the kingdom without damaging its political unity; but he also knew that Protestantism had become too powerful to be eradicated without violence, which he ruled out as an option. 'Force and violence', he once said, 'pertain to beasts rather than man. Justice derives from that most divine part of our being: reason.' On another occasion he said: 'The knife can do little against the spirit except lose the soul along with the body.' L'Hôpital put state before church in ordering his priorities; he valued national unity more than religious conformity and believed that the best solution to France's domestic problems lay in reform of the church and, above all, of the judicial system.

Before reform at home could be effective, order needed to be restored. This could only be done by giving the great nobles, including the Bourbons, a share in government and by convincing the people that genuine reforms were on the way. It was to achieve these ends that an Assembly of Notables was summoned to Fontainebleau on 20 August. In addition to the king's ordinary councillors, it comprised princes of the blood, great officers of the crown and the knights of the Order of St Michael. Montmorency turned up with a huge escort, but Navarre and his brothers chose to remain in Béarn, thereby weakening their argument that they had been deliberately kept out of the government. The assembly began on 21 August with a speech from L'Hôpital in which he compared the state to a sick man whose cure depended on finding the cause of his ailment. The duc de Guise and the Cardinal of Lorraine followed with an account of their respective ministerial responsibilities: the army and the king's finances.

Two important speeches were then made by Jean de Monluc, bishop of Valence, and Charles de Marillac, archbishop of Vienne. Monluc condemned the persecution of religious dissenters, who were loyal to the crown and merely concerned with their own salvation. He argued in favour of greater toleration, and called for a new General Council or a national council to reform the clergy, a step which he felt would do much to quell the current disorders. As a former diplomat, Marillac appreciated the damage done to France's relations with the Protestant powers by the persecution of Huguenots. He also pointed to the burden of taxation and to ecclesiastical abuses. 'I believe', he said, 'that there are two . . . pillars . . . upon which are based the security of the king's estate: the integrity of religion and the benevolence of the people. If they are strong, it is not necessary to fear that obedience be lost.' Both pillars, Marillac argued, were under serious threat. Weakness in the religious pillar had usually been corrected by a General Council, but since the pope could not be made to summon one, a national council should be called by the king. The support of the people could be regained only by hearing and remedying their complaints at a meeting of the Estates-General. To hold the obedience of his subjects, the king would have to explain his policies and the problems of the crown in such an assembly.

Many historians, writing under the influence of the contemporary writer Régnier de La Planche, have interpreted the speeches of Monluc and Marillac as an attack on the Guises. Yet both prelates had close ties with them. They had almost certainly been briefed to defend the government and their proposals coincided with its policy since March. The only criticism of the government during the Fontainebleau assembly came from Admiral Coligny, who on 23 August submitted two petitions – one to the king, the other to his mother – from the Protestants of Normandy, acting on behalf of all their French co-religionists. While protesting their loyalty, they begged to be allowed to worship freely pending a General Council. As for the Cardinal of Lorraine, he proposed that disturbers of the peace should be punished, but not loyal dissenters who went unarmed to hear sermons and sing psalms and who abstained from mass. Backing the demand for a meeting of the Estates-General, he agreed to set up an enquiry into church corruption in preparation for a future general or national council. This met with the assembly's approval and the king formally summoned a meeting of the Estates-General at Meaux on 10 December.

The Huguenots, meanwhile, continued to press the claims of the princes of the blood against the Guises. They published several pamphlets affirming that foreigners were excluded from government by the Salic law and by custom. Catherine, however, was unwilling to dismiss the Guises, for this would have left her at the mercy of Montmorency, whom she disliked, and of the Bourbons. Early in August the king of Navarre held a council meeting at Nérac which was attended by François Hotman, the eminent Protestant jurist from Strassburg, and Théodore de Bèze, Calvin's lieutenant in Geneva. It drew up a remonstrance in which historical precedents were used to back up the claims of the princes of the blood and to attack Guise tyranny. Meanwhile, Huguenots elsewhere in France resorted to arms. The younger Maligny captured Lyon and might have stayed there if Navarre had not ordered him to withdraw. Condé called on several great lords, including Anne de Montmorency and François de Vendôme, Vidame de Chartres, to assist him. Montmorency refused, but the vidame promised to serve Condé against everyone save the king, his brothers and the queens. After his letter had been intercepted, the vidame was sent to the Bastille. Fearing Protestant violence, Catherine appealed for help to Philip II and the duke of Savoy. At the same time Francis II ordered Navarre to bring Condé to court so that he might explain why he had been raising troops. Catherine tried to drive a wedge between Montmorency's followers and the Bourbons by disclosing that the vidame had been arrested as a result of information supplied by the constable and his son Damville.

The king of Navarre, forced to choose between obedience and rebellion, decided to bring Condé to court. On 31 October, however, Condé was arrested at Orléans and thrown into prison. As a peer of the realm he was entitled to be judged by his fellow peers in the parlement, but the Guises, fearing his acquittal, set up a special tribunal made up of magistrates, royal councillors and knights of the Order of St Michael. Catherine was afraid that a death sentence passed on Condé would destroy any hope of a settlement with the Huguenots. On 26 November he was found guilty of *lèse-majesté*, but two of his judges – L'Hôpital and du Mortier, both servants of the queen mother – failed to sign the sentence. This gained time just as the king fell seriously ill. Having suffered fainting fits earlier in the month, Francis passed out during vespers on 17 November. His physicians found a fistula in his left ear for which they knew no cure. Meanwhile, delegates to the Estates-General were arriving in Orléans. The queen mother, fearing that in the event of her son's death the estates might hand over power to the princes of the blood, reacted skilfully. On 2 December she summoned Navarre and, in front of the Guises, reproached him for all the plots hatched by the Bourbons. He protested his innocence and, as a gesture of goodwill, offered to cede to Catherine his right to the regency. She promptly accepted this offer, which Navarre was made to confirm under his signature. In exchange, he was promised the title of lieutenant-general of the kingdom. Catherine also bought off the Guises by exculpating them for Condé's imprisonment. She explained that only the king had ordered it, whereupon Navarre agreed to kiss the Guises. On 5 December, before any further action could be taken against Condé, Francis II died.

The Estates-General of Orléans, 13 December 1560–31 January 1561

Francis II's death obliged the Guises to step down from their position of authority in the state: his brother, who now took the throne as Charles IX, was only ten years old, so a regent had to be appointed. By custom the first prince of the blood should have been chosen as regent, but Navarre had forfeited his right to do so by his recent conduct. In the meantime, the deputies to the Estates-General had gathered at Orléans.

The Estates-General had not met since 1484 when the deputies had been elected by a common assembly of the three estates in each *bailliage* or *sénéchaussée*. Past historians have suggested that in 1560 the three estates met separately to choose their representatives and that a system of indirect suffrage was introduced to allow the peasantry to be represented. Both notions are wrong. In 1560 the three estates usually met together to elect their representatives as they had done in 1484, and in many parts of France, particularly in the south, the peasants were not convoked. The 116 deputies of the clergy included nine archbishops or bishops, nineteen abbots and priors, 47 archdeacons, deans and canons, and only seven parish priests. The second estate was dominated by lesser nobles, few of whom could boast of a higher title than *seigneur*. Lawyers and royal officials shared control of the third estate.

The Estates-General opened at Orléans on 13 December with a lengthy speech from L'Hôpital. They had been called, he said, to remedy the divisions in the kingdom for which religious differences were mainly to blame. 'It is folly', he said, 'to hope for peace, repose and friendship among people of different faiths.' Community of belief was a stronger bond, in his judgement, than ties of blood or race. A Frenchman and an Englishman sharing the same faith were closer in affection and friendship than two men of different faiths living in the same town and under the same lord. L'Hôpital did not believe that religious dissidents should be wiped out, but warned that freedom of conscience could easily lead to religious anarchy. They should wait, he said, for the decision of a free and holy council. Turning to the Catholics, L'Hôpital reminded them that the sword was powerless against the spirit. 'We must henceforth assail our enemies with charity, prayer, persuasion and God's word, which are the proper weapons for such a conflict . . . Gentleness will achieve more than severity. And let us banish those devilish names – "Lutheran", "Huguenot", "Papist" – which breed only faction and sedition; let us keep only one name: "Christian".' To those who used religion as a cover for sedition L'Hôpital showed no pity: they deserved to be driven out of the kingdom even more than lepers or victims of plague. He ended his speech by calling on the king's subjects to assist him in his needs.

L'Hôpital has been acclaimed as an early champion of religious toleration, but it was only a second best for him. What he really wanted was Christian unity, not the coexistence of two or more faiths. As a statesman, however, he realized that religious unity could not be imposed without upsetting the domestic peace. He looked for administrative, rather than doctrinal, solutions of France's internal crisis. As he was to tell the *parlementaires* in June 1561, religion had to be separated from politics. L'Hôpital consistently stressed the need for national unity and espoused the cause of toleration, not for moral or philosophical reasons, but because he saw it as the only way of preserving peace at a time when agreement through compromise was unattainable.

Many deputies of the third estate had been instructed to demand that the crown's debt be cleared by a confiscation of church wealth and that the princes of the blood be admitted to the king's council. Following the king's death, however, they were expected in some quarters to appoint a regent, but they were not sure that their powers allowed them to do this. Catherine, for her part, was afraid that a new round of elections would produce an assembly devoted to Navarre's interests. The deputies were consequently told by the government that their original powers remained valid. On 21 December the *Conseil privé* ruled on the administration without consulting them: Catherine was appointed regent with sweeping powers. She was forty-one years old and free of any compromising commitment to either of the rival houses of Guise or Bourbon. Her chief aim was to uphold the independence of the throne and, in its pursuit, she tried to maintain a fine, if at times uneasy, balance between the two families, favouring each in turn. Since the Guises had recently dominated the government, Catherine now turned to the Bourbons to establish an equilibrium. Navarre was appointed lieutenant-general of the kingdom, but given relatively minor responsibilities.

On 1 January 1561 the estates gave their views on how the government should deal with its current difficulties. Speaking for the clergy, a canon lawyer challenged the king's right to touch the church or dogma. Instead of allowing heretics to have churches, he should forbid his subjects to have any dealings with Geneva and other countries infected with heresy. The nobility's spokesman complained of abuses by the ecclesiastical courts and demanded freedom of worship for nobles, not, it seems, as a human right, but as a privilege attached to their order. The third estate condemned clerical ignorance and avarice. The three orders were only agreed about one thing: their refusal to give the crown any money. On 13 January, L'Hôpital admitted a public debt of 43 million *livres* – four times the crown's annual revenue. The deputies were unmoved. After ten days of debate, the third estate declared itself powerless to grant any tax increases, and the nobility and clergy were equally unco-operative.

Three days later, at the closing session of the estates, L'Hôpital listed the sacrifices which the government expected from the nation: the third estate should grant an increase of the *taille* for six years and the clergy should redeem for the king all the domain, *aides* and *gabelles* which had been alienated. Since the deputies did not feel authorized to grant any supply, the chancellor invited them to return to their *bailliages* and consult their constituents. He asked them to reassemble at Melun in a few months' time but not in such large numbers; each *gouvernement* needed to send only one deputy of each order with a clear brief.

On the same day the crown issued the Ordinance of Orléans, covering a host of topics under the general heading of 'the reform of justice'. In particular, it called for the suppression of all offices created since the reign of Louis XII, for a ban on judicial pluralism and on close relatives sitting on the same magisterial bench. Article 106 called on judges to dispense justice impartially and not to allow the king's poor subjects to be exploited and oppressed by their feudal lords. The ordinance made no concession to the second estate's demand that a third of royal offices be reserved to its use. It reflected L'Hôpital's belief in the need for a reorganized bureaucracy and an improved judiciary. He set out to suppress corruption and to define judicial boundaries. One of his main objectives was to get rid of venal judicial offices whose number had increased dramatically during the first half of the century. L'Hôpital believed that venality promoted corruption among judges and undermined administrative efficiency; it also deprived the king of control over his own officials. He also disapproved of the transmission of offices within the same family.

L'Hôpital was keen to reduce papal interference in the affairs of the French church, and this aim too was reflected in the Ordinance of Orléans. It restored the system of electing archbishops and bishops which had been abolished by the Concordat of 1516. Electors were to suggest three names to the king who was to pick one, subject to papal approval. Annates (payment to Rome of the first year's revenue from a see or benefice) were suspended completely. A clause banning clerical absenteeism confirmed earlier royal letters patent, which had ordered all prelates with certain exceptions to return to their dioceses by September on pain of confiscation of their temporalities. Almost every provision of the ordinance prescribed for disciplinary sanctions the seizure of ecclesiastical revenues. The government assumed that it had the right to confiscate ecclesiastical temporalities when the clergy had violated royal edicts.

The Huguenot Lent, 1561

On 28 January 1561, Catherine issued *lettres de cachet* which confirmed and also modified the Edict of Romorantin. It was described as an act of clemency upon the king's accession. All religious prisoners were to be released and all heresy cases suspended, even those against people who had assembled in arms or provided money. In other words, Catherine used her new powers to pardon participants in the Tumult of Amboise, except the leaders. Significantly, pastors were not excluded from the amnesty, as they had been in the original edict. The regent's conciliatory policy caused the Huguenots to believe that she was coming over to their side. The second Calvinist national synod, meeting at Poitiers on 10 March, drew up a memorandum for the next session of the Estates-General. It called for the establishment of a royal council capable of enforcing royal edicts and decided to appoint representatives at court who were to act as a pressure group for the Reformed church.

In the kingdom at large the pace of Protestant expansion quickened perceptibly in 1560–61. The Huguenot population of Rouen, for example, grew to around 15,000, or 15–20 per cent of the city's total population, before the end of 1561. In February and March 1560, Calvinists held public gatherings in Rouen for the first time, and in May groups of people were singing psalms each night in the streets. When the Spanish ambassador visited Rouen in July, he was amazed to see regular gatherings of 3000 to 4000 Protestants outside the cathedral listening to preachers. In November 1561 they felt sufficiently strong to hold their *prêche* publicly in the Halles. When the Cardinal of Bourbon visited Rouen, he was subjected to 'thousands of insults'. Calvinists mocked the Host, calling it a 'god of paste', and refused to adorn the façades of their houses in honour of the Blessed Sacrament, as was the custom on the feast of Corpus Christi. Similar disrespect was shown to saints' images and to the crucifix: both were allegedly hung upside down from the public gallows in August 1560 and a statue of the Virgin on the wall of the archbishop's palace was frequently attacked. Immodest celebrations of religious festivals were disrupted. The Rouen Calvinists also boldly snatched some of their co-religionists from the clutches of the law.

The situation was echoed elsewhere. In Troyes, the arrival of the minister Jean Gravelle marked the start of the local church's 'wonder year'. In May 1561 open-air services were held in the rue du Temple and the cemetery of Saint-Panthaléon in spite of attempts by the local *bailli* to stop them. At Etampes, Melun, Meaux and Chartres, Calvinists held services in the open or created other disturbances. In various parts of Normandy, Catholic churches were sacked by mobs. But it was in the Midi that the Huguenots really made their presence felt. No fewer than thirty-eight pastors preached Lenten sermons in Saintonge. A royal official wrote of his alarm at Protestant excesses in Guyenne since the start of Lent. In Agen, churches were sacked and set alight. The Parlement of Toulouse complained of armed assemblies in Rouergue, Quercy, Lower Languedoc and Armagnac. Catholic preachers were being ousted from their pulpits and replaced by pastors. On 23 March the estates of Languedoc petitioned Catherine for freedom to worship. In the diocese of Nîmes, two hundred churches were reported to be in ruins; in Provence and Dauphiné, the story was much the same. Even allowing for exaggeration by witnesses, French Protestantism was becoming an irresistible force in the spring of 1561.

The rapid political changes at the centre of government since the death of Francis II seriously undermined royal authority in the provinces. 'The kingdom was as if without a king . . . Justice lost all its force', wrote a Rouennais. As censorship was relaxed, works of propaganda flowed ever more swiftly into France from the Genevan presses. Protestant sympathizers, who had so far hesitated about joining the Reformed church, now felt sufficiently confident to do so. Calvinists interpreted the surge of new recruits to their cause as a sign of divine approval. Their optimism found expression in a poem, *The True Bulls-Eye of the Archers Who Aim at the Popeinjay*, and in a popular song entitled 'Regrets and Adieu to the Pope'. An extremely popular woodcut illustration conveyed the same triumphalist mood. Called *The Great Marmite Overturned*, it showed a stewpot containing all the riches of the Roman church being toppled by a shaft of light from Heaven, bearing the Holy Scriptures, and also by the fires which had consumed the Protestant martyrs.

A letter written to Calvin by an anonymous pastor describes his visit to the trade fair of Guibray in Normandy during August 1561. He was surprised to see placards against the mass being hawked openly and vociferously among the stalls. Priests who tried to silence the vendors were quickly surrounded by a hostile crowd. After hesitating for a time, the pastor began to preach daily to an audience that grew steadily: he estimated the Sunday crowd at 5000 to 6000. That night the *compagnons de boutique* began to sing psalms in front of their stalls. Some Parisian makers of rosary beads responded with profane songs and when they refused to be silent, Huguenot zealots drove them off. Several hundred Protestants moved systematically through the fair, swords in hand, 'reforming' any activity not to their liking.

The official organs of the Reformed church in Normandy shared Calvin's disapproval of sedition. The provincial synod, at its meeting in 1560, had affirmed its opposition to acts of iconoclasm, while the consistory of Rouen condemned any violent acts by its members, but such pronouncements could not stop the violence. The concern for public order shown by the urban élite who dominated the consistory was not necessarily shared by their social inferiors. In Rouen alone at least nine incidents, described as 'tumults', 'riots' or 'seditions', took place in 1560 and 1561.

The 'Huguenot Lent' of 1561 was bound to lead to a Catholic backlash. Various parlements delayed registering the edicts of toleration or amended their wording to reduce or nullify their effect. The Parlement of Paris, for example, tampered with the Edict of Romorantin and ordered houses used for Protestant assemblies and services to be razed to the ground. Meanwhile, fanatical Catholic preachers stirred public indignation by hurling abuse at the Huguenots, whose nocturnal conventicles were denounced as sexual orgies. They were also accused of gluttony, simply because they denied the need for fast days and for abstinence in Lent, and charged with sedition because they boycotted ceremonies which the people viewed as promoting amity and concord. Insults soon led to blows. At Rennes a royal official warned that public order could not be guaranteed as long as a certain Jacobin friar was allowed to inflame the people.

The Triumvirate, 7 April 1561

Early in 1561, Antoine de Navarre, taking umbrage at his brother's continued detention, demanded more effective powers and attempted to drive the duc de Guise from court. He threatened to leave with the constable and the Châtillons unless he got his way. But the regent resisted his demand, and the king persuaded Montmorency not to desert him. Rather than be isolated, Navarre remained at court. Condé was acquitted on all charges, released from prison on 8 March 1561, and soon admitted to the king's council. On 25 March, Navarre was confirmed as lieutenant-general of the kingdom and formally renounced his claim to the regency.

Angered by these developments, the Guises returned to their estates pending the king's coronation. The constable too made no secret of his displeasure. He objected to the wayward sermons of Jean de Monluc, who had been been invited by Catherine to preach at court, and protested by attending the strictly orthodox sermons which a Jacobin friar was giving to the court's domestic staff. Here Montmorency and Guise met by chance. They decided to bury their differences and were soon joined by Marshal Saint-André. On Easter Monday, 7 April, they formed an alliance, known as the Triumvirate, for the defence of the Catholic faith. Its promoter was Cardinal Tournon. Catherine's reaction was to draw closer to Navarre and his friends. A Genevan pastor called Merlin, whom Coligny had invited to preach in his apartment at court, began holding public meetings near the château.

On 19 April the government tried to pour oil on troubled waters by issuing an edict at Fontainebleau banning the use of the terms 'Huguenot' or 'papist'. The right to enter houses in pursuit of illegal assemblies was restricted to magistrates, and the earlier edict, ordering the release of prisoners of conscience, was reaffirmed. But the new edict was sent to local authorities without having been submitted to the parlement for registration. This offended the *parlementaires*, who threatened to call the chancellor to account. Far from cooling the situation, the edict caused Catholics to think that Catherine was turning Protestant; yet she was probably less concerned with religion than with politics. Writing to her daughter, she accused the Guises of plunging the kingdom into chaos. She also resisted their efforts to marry off their niece Mary Stuart to Philip II's son, Don Carlos. Catherine suggested that Philip might detach Antoine de Bourbon from the Protestant cause by giving him back Spanish Navarre or another territory, such as Siena or Sardinia. The Triumvirs were, in the meantime, being urged by the Spanish ambassador Chantonnay to come to terms with Navarre who had been seen at mass.

On 15 May, Charles IX, aged eleven, was crowned at Reims. The Cardinal of Lorraine used the occasion to speak to the regent. He protested at the spread of Protestantism and complained of judges who seemed to think that they had to tolerate Protestant assemblies. He suggested that the king should call an Assembly of Notables in order to draw up a law forbidding religious innovations. On 11 June the seigneur d'Esternay presented a petition to the king on behalf of the Huguenots, asking for permission to expound their confession of faith, and to recall foreign exiles under safe-conduct. They also demanded an end to persecution, protection from outrages, the release of prisoners, permission to hold services in public and to have churches or *temples*. To obviate the charge of sedition, they offered to admit royal observers at their services.

Acting on a complaint from the clergy, Catherine consulted the parlement as well as the princes and members of the king's council in a series of meetings in Paris between 23 June and 14 July 1561. According to Pasquier, she put forward a motion that the people should either follow the Roman Catholic faith or quit the kingdom with permission to sell their property. Her proposal was carried by a bare majority of three. The only tangible result of the discussions was another edict which seemed to take away with one hand what it gave with the other. It banned all Protestant worship, public or private, yet continued to deny the parlements' right to judge heresy cases and made banishment the maximum penalty for simple heresy, pending the outcome of a general or national council. The death penalty for heresy was ruled out and a complete pardon offered for all offences, both religious and seditious, committed since Henry II's death. By forbidding magistrates to hound religious dissidents in the privacy of their homes, the edict seemed to contradict its own ban on private religious meetings. Not surprisingly, it satisfied no one and seems not to have been implemented.

The 'Contract of Poissy', 21 September 1561

On 27 August 1561 the Estates-General met at Saint-Germain-en-Laye. After the opening session, the deputies divided into two groups: the nobility and third estate met at Pontoise, and the clergy at Poissy. The lay estates launched a vigorous attack on the clergy's wealth; only the confiscation of the church's revenues, they believed, would serve to clear the public debt. Religious foundations, in their opinion, had been set up originally by the people and were therefore national assets which could be legitimately applied to the needs of the state. The following proposal was advanced: a general sale of church temporalities would yield at least 120 million *livres*. Out of this sum, 42 million would be used to reimburse royal creditors; 48 million would be re-invested so as to provide the clergy with an annual income of 4 million *livres*; and 30 million would be invested in trading ventures, which would provide the king with an annual revenue of 500,000l. This would help pay for border fortifications and the army. The clergy would be allowed to buy back its property at the highest price paid by the last purchaser.

The clergy's representatives at Poissy were naturally alarmed by the proposal. They countered it by making an enormous sacrifice. Under an agreement known as the Contract of Poissy (21 September 1561), they undertook to pay to the crown over six years 1,600,000l. for the redemption of royal domain and indirect taxes which had been alienated. Thereafter, over ten years, they would clear the king's debt in respect of the *rentes sur l'Hôtel de Ville de Paris*, to the tune of 7,650,000l. The French church committed itself for the first time to paying the crown an annual subsidy.

The Colloquy of Poissy, July–October 1561

Catherine could choose one of three courses of action to solve France's religious problem. First, she could revive the policy of persecution, but this had failed to check the growth of Protestantism. Secondly, she could join the Huguenots, but this would bring her into conflict with the Triumvirate and set off a civil war. Thirdly, she could try to heal the religious differences among the king's subjects by means of a national council or colloquy. In the end, this was the course she decided to pursue with the support of a group of moderates, including L'Hôpital, Jean de Monluc, the Cardinal of Lorraine and the king of Navarre. The inclusion of Lorraine among the moderates may be surprising, since he was a Guise and had championed religious persecution; he certainly supported the idea of a national council, but the notion that he also favoured a colloquy has been disputed. A national council did not imply participation by Calvinist ministers, whereas a colloquy did. What Lorraine really wanted, it seems, was a General Council to which the German Lutherans would be invited, not a national council in which Protestants and Catholics would debate their differences on equal terms. Pius IV had recalled the Council of Trent in November 1560, but Catherine, while signifying her acceptance of it, pressed on with her own plans. The Gallican assembly at Poissy was meant to choose prelates to go to Trent, but the agenda also mentioned 'several things of great importance' about which the regent wished to consult the prelates – evidently a reference to the religious troubles in France. On 25 July, Catherine indicated that the assembly was open to 'all subjects' wishing to be heard.

On 31 July 1561, Charles IX opened the national council at the Dominican convent in Poissy, near Saint-Germain-en-Laye. It was attended by the royal family, the princes of the blood, the king's council, six cardinals, more than forty archbishops and bishops, twelve theologians and many canon lawyers. A majority of the prelates were rigidly orthodox, yet all but five accepted the government's proposal that the Huguenots should be allowed a hearing. The national council thus became a colloquy. Besides their party at court, the Protestants were represented by twelve ministers assisted by some twenty laymen. De Bèze, whom Geneva had sent in response to a royal invitation, led the Protestant delegation. A skilled diplomat, polished orator and nobleman, he was well suited to dealing with court protocol. Though his faith was as firm as Calvin's, he was more conciliatory in respect of form, and at an early meeting with the Cardinal of Lorraine offered some hope of compromise. The aim of the colloquy was not toleration, but concord. Toleration was rarely expressed in the sixteenth century outside the writings of theorists like Sebastien Castellio. Far more common was the ideal of religious compromise based on mutual concession. The edicts of toleration issued by the French crown were merely temporary steps pending the restoration of Christian unity. The Colloquy of Poissy was an attempt to eliminate the need for toleration by finding a doctrinal compromise satisfactory to both Catholics and Protestants. But the gulf between them was too wide to be bridged. While the Catholic prelates assumed that the Protestants had come to be instructed and judged, the latter were intent on defending their doctrinal principles.

The first full-length oration of the colloquy was delivered by de Bèze. After outlining the beliefs shared by both sides, he turned to their differences and especially their divergent interpretations of the Eucharist. 'We say', he declared, 'that His body is as far removed from the bread and the wine as heaven is from the earth.' This provoked cries of 'he has blasphemed!' from the prelates, who had so far listened in silence. An ambassador reported that 'the faces of all those who were within the hall changed colour and it was remarked that even Coligny covered his eyes with his hands.' Yet

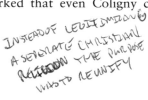
INSTEAD OF LEGITIMISING
A SEPARATE CHRISTIAN
RELIGION THE PURPOSE
WAS TO REUNIFY

the colloquy continued. The morning after de Bèze's oration, the prelates conferred on their next move. Opinions were divided, but in the end Lorraine was unanimously chosen to reply to de Bèze. The Calvinists warned the king that if the prelates usurped the role of judges, they would be closing the door to further conversation. Their exasperation was soon assuaged by the arrival of Peter Vermigli, alias Peter Martyr. A Florentine and an ex-Augustinian, he had become a Protestant by 1542 and, five years later, Regius Professor of Divinity at Oxford. His writings included numerous commentaries on Scripture and a *Loci communes* or systematic theology. In 1556 he had become a pastor in Zürich. But he was now old and fixed in his views. Martyr apparently attended the colloquy at the suggestion of Catherine. Their purposes, however, were far apart: she wanted the peaceful reform of the church with the support of the prelates; he stressed the duty of the prince to reform the church.

On 16 September, Lorraine delivered his reply to de Bèze. The substance of his speech was relatively accommodating, yet de Bèze was unimpressed. 'Never have I heard such impudence, such ineptitude...' he said, 'the old arguments a thousand times refuted ... moved me to nausea.' De Bèze also poured scorn on the efforts being made at Poissy to bring the Confession of Augsburg into the debate. The first attempt had been made by the Lutherans themselves. Navarre had long been in contact with the German princes through his special envoy, François Hotman. They had shown an interest in the French national council and Christopher duke of Württemberg had invited Navarre to sponsor the confession in France. Shortly after Lorraine's speech on 16 September, Navarre decided that it would be desirable to have Lutheran representatives at the colloquy. He issued an official invitation to which the duke of Württemberg and the Elector Palatine answered positively.

On 15 September the Society of Jesus, which had long been suspect on account of its Ultramontanism, was formally admitted to France by the prelates at Poissy. This was consistent with a change of attitude on the part of the Holy See. Whereas Paul IV had been hostile to the order, Pius IV wished it well. In November 1561 he wrote to Philip II: 'Among all the religious orders ... the Society of Jesus deserves to be embraced with special love by the Holy See.' A few days later Ippolito d'Este, Cardinal of Ferrara, and Diego Lainez arrived as emissaries from Rome with the aim of frustrating the colloquy. The cardinal knew France well, having been an influential figure at the court of Francis I. He was also a diplomat and used his talents to entice Catherine towards the Council of Trent and the vacillating king of Navarre towards Catholicism. Lainez was the general of the fledgling Society of Jesus. He was uncompromisingly committed to Rome and the Council of Trent.

On 22 September the government, responding to a petition from the Calvinists, altered the form of the colloquy. Henceforth twelve Calvinists would meet as many Catholics in private. The king would be absent and, perhaps to encourage a more conciliatory atmosphere, most prelates would also stay away. But once again the Eucharist proved the overwhelming obstacle in the path of conciliation. An attempt by Lorraine to persuade the Calvinists to subscribe to the Confession of Augsburg seemed a conciliatory move, but it may have been a cunning ploy to split the Protestants. Either way, it failed, and an intemperate speech by Lainez, attacking the legality of the national council, further antagonized the Calvinists. Late in September, Catherine made a last attempt to save the colloquy by modifying its composition. This time five theologians from each side were appointed to confer on the Eucharist, but they still could not agree. On 13 October the national council dissolved itself. Its results were not wholly negative, for the clergy had agreed to grant the crown an annual subsidy and a fairly comprehensive programme of church reform had been enunciated, but the regent's principal aim – conciliation between Catholics and Huguenots – had not been achieved.

De Bèze did not return to Geneva immediately. Instead, he preached at the French court, while other Calvinist pastors did so in the kingdom at large. They scored a notable victory by converting Antonio Caracciolo, bishop of Troyes, to their faith. Their followers too became more aggressive. As both sides gathered arms, the Venetian ambassador reported that a 'great fear' was sweeping across the kingdom. Yet Catherine still hoped for conciliation. On 24 October she asked Rome to sanction the taking of communion in both kinds by the laity. Other concessions to the Huguenots were urged by Jean de Monluc, Jean de Saint-Gelais and Cardinal Châtillon. Their demands were not well received in Italy, where the Council of Trent had reopened on 18 January 1562 without a single French prelate in attendance.

Meanwhile, Catherine called to Saint-Germain a small group of councillors and *parlementaires* who, apart from Saint André and Montmorency, had been carefully chosen for their moderation. The result was the famous Edict of Saint-Germain (17 January 1562), commonly known as the Edict of January, which allowed the Huguenots to gather for worship in the countryside but not inside walled towns. This move naturally infuriated Catholic zealots; yet their outcry was less violent than might have been expected, for they had known for a long time that Catherine was working towards partial toleration. The impact of the edict was also softened for them by the king of Navarre's announcement that he had become a Catholic. His conversion deprived the Huguenots of a royal kinsman who by rights should have been the regent.

At the eleventh hour Catherine decided to hold another colloquy, this time at Saint-Germain. A wide-ranging agenda, covering more than strictly disciplinary matters, was outlined by the chancellor, but the discussion never got beyond the first item. Its failure sealed Catherine's disenchantment with theological debates. A few days later she ordered a team of French bishops, led by Lorraine, to set off for Trent. Now that a national council had proved useless, Catherine was forced to pin her hopes of peace on a general one. But the fathers at Trent would only accept conciliation on their own terms, and their deliberations only served to widen the gulf between Catholics and Protestants. The failure of the Colloquy of Poissy marked 'the waning of moderation and irenicism, the breakdown of communication, the loss of contact, the hardening of religious estrangement' (Nugent).

The First Civil War, 1562–3

Following the Edict of January, the Guises retired to their estates and immersed themselves in local politics, flatly refusing invitations to return to court. But the Cardinal of Lorraine was more determined than ever to achieve a rapprochement with the German Lutherans. He contacted Christopher duke of Württemberg, who keenly agreed to meet his old friend the duc de Guise at Saverne in the near future. Christopher sent Guise two printed editions of the Württemberg confession and urged him to seek the truth in Scripture. Meanwhile, Lorraine delivered a course of sermons in Reims, which Hubert Languet described as almost Lutheran in tone. By mid-November the cardinal had rejoined his brothers at Joinville.

The four Guise brothers met the duke of Württemberg and four Lutheran theologians, including Johann Brenz, at Saverne on 15 February 1562. Christopher's only object was to commend his own faith to the Guises and to plead for toleration for French Calvinists. Lorraine was prepared to go to almost any lengths to reach an understanding with the Lutherans. On 16 February he preached a sermon in which he insisted that Christ was man's only mediator with God and, having thus prepared for the abandonment of the Invocation of Saints, he advanced towards Justification by Faith by teaching that trust was not to be placed in good works. In another sermon, Lorraine declared that God should only be adored as He exists in Heaven, a formula making it possible to abandon worship of the Host while retaining transubstantiation.

On the 17th, Brenz spoke his mind on the mass at Lorraine's invitation. In his reply, the cardinal said that in eucharistic processions worship of the Host had gone too far: simple reverence for the Sacrament and kneeling at communion were alone necessary. He even agreed that the mass was merely an act of commemoration of Christ's sacrifice on the Cross, not itself a sacrifice. He thought an agreement with the Lutherans on the church hierarchy was feasible. Dismissing the Council of Trent as powerless to rescue Christendom from disunity, the cardinal waxed eloquent on the eirenic possibilities of the Confession of Augsburg. He maintained that if the Calvinists at Poissy had been less intransigent, an accord would have been possible. The duke of Württemberg suggested that the experiment of Poissy should be revived, while Brenz urged Lorraine to advance the Word of God in France and to shield the Protestants from persecution. Lorraine solemnly swore that he had never condemned any man for his faith, not even Du Bourg. Christopher promised to spread the good news throughout Germany, whereupon all four Guises pledged themselves not to persecute Protestants openly or secretly.

Next day, Lorraine proposed a colloquy in Germany between Catholics and Lutherans. He begged the duke of Württemberg to solicit the support of other Lutheran princes, asserting that he could win the consent of the pope and the emperor. At the same time, he prophesied that the victory of the Tridentine decrees would cause bloodshed on a large scale. As they left Saverne, the Guises again took a solemn pledge against persecution and vowed to dedicate their energies to the cause of Christian unity.

The conference at Saverne has been interpreted by some historians as an attempt by the Guises to drive a wedge between the Lutherans and the Calvinists. But if Evennett is right, it needs to be related to Lorraine's opposition to the resumption of the Council of Trent. The cardinal genuinely believed that this would inflame the situation in France by destroying any hope of concord between Catholics and Protestants, whereas his initiative might keep open the possibility of religious compromise.

The massacre at Vassy, 1 March 1562

Ten days after the meeting at Saverne, the duc de Guise set off from Joinville for Paris, accompanied by members of his family, noblemen and servants. At Vassy, a walled town situated within his domain, he stopped to attend mass at the parish church. Nearby stood a barn where a large number of Calvinists had gathered for worship. What happened next is unclear, for contemporary accounts are biased. According to one version, Guise, on learning that some 500 Calvinists were worshipping close by, decided to remonstrate with them. Some of his companions reached the barn ahead of him. As they burst through the door they were invited to join the congregation, but instead they shouted: 'Mort-Dieu, kill them all!' and were duly thrown out. While some Calvinists barricaded the entrance to the barn, others climbed scaffolding over the porch and started pelting the duke and his men with stones which they had stored for just such an occasion. Some noblemen were struck, including Guise. Furious, they opened fire on the

Calvinists with arquebuses, and entered the barn after breaking down the
door. Worshippers who tried to flee by clambering on to the roof were shot
down 'like pigeons'; others were made to walk between two lines of Guise's
men and hacked down. The massacre left about thirty dead and more than
a hundred wounded.

Exactly what happened at Vassy will never be known. There was wrong
on both sides. Under the Edict of January, the Protestants were forbidden
to hold services within walled towns. On the other hand, Guise was not
supposed to interfere with a private service. The Calvinists were also at
fault in throwing stones at him and his men, an action hardly consistent
with feudal etiquette; but Guise overreacted criminally by opening fire on
them. Under the most recent edict, the worst punishment prescribed for a
religious dissenter was exile, not death.

Though Vassy was not a large town, its Reformed church was a flourishing one. A few months before the massacre, the bishop of Châlons had
attempted to persuade the inhabitants to live as good Catholics, but he had
been challenged by the local pastor and driven out of the town under a
volley of abuse. The dowager duchess of Guise, Antoinette de Bourbon,
disliked the presence of heretics so near to her residence at Joinville and
on lands forming part of the dowry of her granddaughter, Mary Stuart. So
the massacre could have been premeditated, but the evidence is against this.
It made nonsense of the pledges given by the Guises at Saverne, destroying
all their hopes of circumventing the Council of Trent by securing a rapprochement with the German Lutherans. Almost certainly it was the overreaction
of a hot-headed nobleman who felt that his authority had been impugned
by his vassals and probably failed to measure the consequences. Vassy has
been called 'the Sarajevo of the Civil Wars' (Evennett).

The aftermath of Vassy

Paris was still reeling from the effects of the quarrel between the crown
and the parlement over registration of the Edict of January when news of
the massacre was received. The Catholic population, which had been infuriated by the edict and had been restless ever since, was of course delighted,
while the Protestants feared that the outrage was only the start of a new
campaign of terror. The regent, meanwhile, was with the court at
Montceaux. Steps had to be taken to ensure peace in the capital. Marshal
Montmorency, the local governor, ordered the Reformed church to suspend
its services, but the pastors refused. They saw no reason for giving way to
the Catholics, and urged the governor to enforce the king's edicts. Meanwhile Condé, who had remained in Paris, called a meeting of Protestant
nobles to advise on means of opposing the threat from Guise. Some militants

wanted to march against him and force a showdown, but moderates, including de Bèze, favoured a judicial appeal to the government. This opinion prevailed and a deputation was accordingly sent to the regent. Even so, on 10 March, Condé warned all the Reformed churches of France that they could expect to be treated as cruelly as the church at Vassy had been, and ought to take steps to defend themselves and assist any churches that might come under attack. According to La Noue, Condé's manifesto caused many Protestant nobles to gather arms and horses.

Meanwhile the Huguenot deputation arrived at Montceaux with a demand that Guise be brought to justice. Catherine explained that she had ordered him to give up his march on Paris; she also promised to see justice done, and it seems that the government did order a formal enquiry into the Vassy massacre. However, while de Bèze and the other Protestant deputies acted legally, the Paris pastor Le Maçon, alias La Rivière, urged the other churches of the kingdom to muster their forces in preparation for war.

On 12 March, Guise arrived at Nanteuil, not far from Montceaux. He had been ordered by the regent to come to court, but on the 13th he was persuaded by Montmorency and Saint-André to go to the defence of Paris which was being threatened by Condé. Three days later, the Triumvirs (Montmorency, Guise and Saint-André) entered the capital with 2000 to 3000 troops. Guise was acclaimed by the Parisians as the 'hero of Vassy', and the *prévôt des marchands* offered him twenty thousand troops and two million in gold to pacify the kingdom. Guise modestly replied that he left that responsibility to the king of Navarre and the regent, whom he was bound to obey as the king's subject. Condé, for his part, had become the leader of the Protestants following Navarre's defection. Each day nobles arrived in Paris to place themselves under his command. He led his followers to a public service just as the Triumvirs were entering the capital. The two processions passed each other in silence, their respective leaders exchanging salutes with the pommels of their swords.

Catherine still hoped to find a way out of the crisis through compromise. She appointed Condé's brother Charles, who as a cardinal and a Bourbon seemed acceptable to both sides, as governor of Paris. He and the presidents of the parlement decided that Guise and Condé should both leave Paris (17 March), but the *prévôt des marchands* persuaded Guise to remain, and Condé also decided to stay put. The Triumvirs painted a grim picture of the situation and invited Navarre to come and see it for himself. Tensions were certainly running high. On 20 March a bloody riot took place when a Catholic crowd tried to exhume a Protestant who had been buried in the Cemetery of the Innocents. Navarre then arrived, and on Palm Sunday he and the Triumvirs took part in a triumphal procession. Later that day, speaking to the parlement, he praised the Triumvirs for restoring order to the capital. Yet Pasquier tells us that the Palm Sunday processions were scenes of 'chaos and confusion' in which 'pistol shots and cannon served as carillons'.

The queen mother, who was now at Fontainebleau, began to woo Condé. Between 16 and 26 March she wrote him four letters recommending herself, her children and the kingdom to his protection. She promised never to forget his services and to ensure that he was suitably rewarded. The prince, meanwhile, left Paris, where his position had become untenable; but he missed an opportunity of seizing control of the government. Instead of going to Fontainebleau and getting hold of the regent and her son, he went to Meaux, leaving the way clear for his opponents to act as he himself should have done. On 27 March the Triumvirs, with a large force of cavalry, came to Fontainebleau and urged Catherine to return to Paris. She begged Navarre to respect her freedom and he seemed about to give way, when Guise appeared and stiffened his resolve. On 31 March, Catherine and her children were effectively kidnapped and taken to Paris, but the regent made the best of the situation. She blamed the Protestants for her plight and claimed that her letters to Condé had been misunderstood. Ridiculing the suggestion that she and her son were prisoners, she now assumed the leadership of the Catholic party under the tutelage of the Triumvirs.

Condé's rebellion, 8 April 1562

On 2 April 1562 a group of Protestant nobles led by Condé seized the town of Orléans, and six days later the prince issued a manifesto claiming that he had taken up arms to free the king and his mother and to ensure respect for the Edict of January and the religious peace which Guise had flouted. But the parlement, to whom the manifesto was addressed, replied that the king and his mother were free and that edicts were always provisional and designed to prevent religious disturbances, not to innovate in matters of faith. If the Edict of January had not been enforced, then redress lay with the king, not with his subjects acting on their own authority. Meanwhile the Huguenots captured Angers, Tours, Blois and the middle reaches of the Loire. On 27 April, baron des Adrets took Valence by surprise, and three days later Lyon, the second city of the kingdom, fell to the rebels.

Alarmed by this turn of events, the Triumvirs allowed Catherine more scope. She retired to Montceaux in May 1562 and negotiated with the Huguenots, who demanded nothing less than the enforcement of the Edict of January and the removal of the Triumvirs. Catherine then talked directly to Condé, but failed to make any headway. Jean de Monluc proposed that the prince might offer to go into foreign exile with his followers. Such a move, he suggested, by showing the purity of Condé's intentions would silence his opponents. The prince was ready to oblige but his followers indignantly refused to quit the land of their birth.

In the meantime, violence spread to many parts of France. At Sens, on 12 April, a crowd of Catholic pilgrims, responding to the preaching of a fanatical friar, destroyed the Protestant temple. Many Huguenots were massacred and their bodies thrown into the Yonne. They floated downstream into the Seine and eventually to Paris where they were seen passing under the bridges. At Tours in July, two hundred Huguenots were bludgeoned to death or drowned in the Loire. In Maine, terrible atrocities were committed by troops under the sieur de Champagne.

A particularly brutal champion of law and order was Blaise de Monluc, who recorded his experiences much later in his *Commentaires* (1592). As the king's lieutenant-general in Guyenne, he kept the peace for five years at the cost of much bloodshed. He was accompanied everywhere by two executioners who administered summary justice at his bidding. Michelet's description of Monluc as 'a man of blood' is amply justified by the testimony of the *Commentaires*. He began by executing a rebel leader. The victim begged to be spared but Monluc grabbed him by the throat, saying: 'You rogue! How dare you ask for mercy when you have disobeyed your king!' He then threw him on to a stone cross where he was instantly felled by a blow so violent that part of the cross was smashed. Later in life, as he reflected on this deed, Monluc showed some remorse, but he soon set it aside: 'If I had not acted thus', he writes,'I would have been mocked and if I had not always trailed a gun behind me, the lowliest village consul would have shut his door in my face, for everyone wanted to be master.'

The catalogue of Monluc's crimes is a long one. Let a few examples suffice. At Fumel in 1562 he ordered thirty or forty Protestants to be hanged or broken on the wheel without trial. At Villefranche-en-Rouergue he intervened when two royal commissioners failed to act promptly and hanged some miscreants from the town-hall windows. At Gironde he hanged some eighty Huguenot prisoners of war from the pillars in the market hall. At Monségur in August 1562 he presided over the garrison's massacre. Among the victims was a certain Captain Héraud, who had served Monluc with distinction in Italy. He expected that his life would be spared, but Monluc made a point of killing him. 'I knew his valour,' he writes, 'and this was the cause of his death, for I felt sure, knowing him to be very headstrong and wedded to that faith [Protestantism], that he would never join us.' In September 1562 he ordered the inhabitants of Terraube to be slaughtered. So many bodies were heaped inside a deep well that those on top could be touched easily. Cruelty, according to Monluc, was essential to the effective conduct of war. He boasted that his passage through Guyenne could be easily plotted on account of the bodies he had left hanging from trees. 'One man hanged', he declared, 'is more effective than a hundred killed in battle.'

On 13 July 1562, Protestants were outlawed by the parlement. A decree allowed anyone to slaughter them with impunity. According to the *Histoire ecclésiastique*, peasants left their fields and artisans their workshops and turned into tigers and lions, while women took up arms alongside them. Huguenots, too, went on the rampage. On 27 May they smashed images of the Last Judgement around the west door of Bourges cathedral. Wherever Huguenots got the upper hand, they destroyed religious images and stripped altars of all their adornments. They melted down chalices and church bells, turning them into coin and cannon respectively. Not even tombs were spared. At Craon the entrails of Anne de la Trémoïlle were tipped out of their urn and spread all over the pavement. At Cléry the tomb of Louis XI was destroyed, and at Vendôme the Bourbon tombs suffered a similar fate.

As the violence spread, Catherine looked to foreign help: she appealed to the pope, the duke of Savoy and Philip II of Spain. The Huguenots, for their part, looked to Elizabeth I of England. Religion apart, she had sound political reasons for responding favourably to their appeal. Her title to the English throne was being challenged by Mary Stuart, the Guises' niece. Elizabeth also wanted to recover Calais, which the peace of Cateau-Cambrésis had ceded to France for eight years. On 20 September at Hampton Court, Condé's envoys accepted her terms: she promised them 100,000 crowns and 6000 troops in exchange for the port of Le Havre which was to be exchanged for Calais even before the eight years were up. But the treaty was a miscalculation by Elizabeth, for all patriotic Frenchmen, both Protestant and Catholic, were much offended by it.

The Huguenots also raised troops in Germany. On 22 September 1562, d'Andelot returned to France with mercenaries, called 'reiters', who were cavalry armed with flintlock pistols. They were relatively new to warfare and soon became notorious for their lack of discipline, and brutality. 'These [reiters] are always ready to fight,' wrote Hotman, 'but in all other matters they obey no one and behave with great cruelty. They pillage everything and this does not satisfy them. They destroy everything including the wines and the harvests.'

The tide of war soon turned in favour of the Catholics, at least in the Loire valley, where they recaptured Blois. In Languedoc and Guyenne the Huguenots conquered some important towns, but failed to capture Toulouse. As a first step towards retaking Orléans, the Triumvirs crossed the Loire and seized Bourges (31 August), thereby cutting Huguenot communications between Orléans and the south; and on hearing about the Protestant talks with England, they attacked Rouen before any English troops could arrive to relieve the city. As they were besieging it, on 15 October, the king of Navarre was severely wounded and replaced as commander by the constable. Being anxious to spare Rouen the horrors of a sack, Catherine offered its defenders generous terms, but to no avail. On

26 October, therefore, the royal troops entered the city and for three days indulged in a frenzy of pillage, murder and rape. Though fatally wounded, Navarre lived long enough to taste the fruits of victory: he was carried through the city on a litter, but died a few days later on a boat at Les Andelys. Condé declared himself lieutenant-general of the kingdom, but the government resolved to replace Navarre with the Cardinal of Bourbon.

The battle of Dreux, 19 December 1562

After the fall of Rouen many royal troops were sent home for the winter, though garrisons were maintained in towns around Orléans. Guise was hoping to confront the English, who had arrived in Le Havre on 4 October, but he had to change his plan when Condé left Orléans and marched on Paris. As he approached the capital, the inhabitants were once again seized by panic, and Guise hurried to their assistance. Condé hoped to reach Paris first, but lost precious time capturing various towns on the way. He also allowed himself to be lured into fruitless talks with the queen mother. Consequently, Guise won the race and Condé had to alter his plans: on 9 December he veered towards Normandy in the hope of joining the English; but ten days later he found his way barred three miles south of Dreux by a large army commanded by Montmorency. Two hours elapsed before battle was joined. According to La Noue, this was because no battle between French armies had been fought for a century: everyone had friends or brothers on the other side, and there was reluctance to shed the blood of kinsmen and to open the first act of an inevitable tragedy. Less sentimental observers thought that Montmorency did not want to leave his strong position and that the Huguenots were fearful of the artillery fire they would encounter if they attacked. About noon, as the Huguenots moved westward, the constable launched an attack on their flank which was repulsed. On the other hand, a cavalry charge by the Protestants was successful on the eastern half of the battlefield. Montmorency, fighting in the front line in spite of his seventy years, was unhorsed, slightly wounded and taken prisoner. Fatal casualties among his following included the young duc de Nevers and Annebault, son of the late admiral. Some fugitives fled as far as Paris, where they reported that the constable had been taken prisoner and his army routed. Catherine is alleged to have said: 'In that case we shall have to learn to say our prayers in French.'

Meanwhile, on the western side of the field things had gone differently. Condé was faced here by a big phalanx of Swiss infantry and to the right of it by Saint-André's corps. He decided to break through the Swiss line and attack Saint-André from the flank and rear. In the event, the Swiss recoiled but held together. Part of Saint-André's *gendarmerie* was sent to relieve them, but they were routed by Condé's reiters. Aumale, the brother of Guise, was wounded; Montbéron, the constable's youngest son, was killed. Condé then seems to have lost his head. Determined to pierce the Swiss line at whatever cost, he sent in his landsknechts, but the Swiss, their fury aroused, drove them off. Condé then ordered his cavalry to charge, but it too was unsuccessful. At this juncture Guise, who had been standing by, suddenly emerged from woods with his troops, while Saint-André led a charge. The Huguenot line collapsed; Guise and Saint-André routed the Germans whom the Swiss had beaten off. 'These were the most cowardly lot of landsknechts who came into France during the forty years of war', wrote a Huguenot. With a handful of gendarmes and reiters, Condé charged, but his horse was killed and he himself taken prisoner. 'It was the act of a hero of romance, not of the general of an army' (Oman). As La Noue commented, the battle of Dreux was unique in that the commanders-in-chief on both sides were taken prisoner.

Guise and Saint-André imagined that the battle was won, but as dusk fell a large body of cavalry, which Coligny had assembled behind a hedge, suddenly appeared. Confused fighting ensued which lasted into the dark hours. Saint-André was captured and shot dead soon afterwards by a certain Bobigny whom he had wronged in the past. But Coligny's horse failed to dislodge the Catholic infantry from among houses and trees where they had taken cover. After several attempts he ordered a retreat. In a dispatch written soon afterwards he claimed that he had lost only 140 horse and 2200 foot, with the 5000 landsknechts who had surrendered. This was certainly an underestimate, but a Catholic claim that 6000 Huguenots had been left on the field may also be doubted. Twenty-two Huguenot standards, found after the battle, were sent to the king and hung in Notre-Dame cathedral. Almost all Condé's German infantry had been captured and a large number were sent home on parole, unarmed and bearing white staves in token of submission. The rest entered the king's service. Retaining complete control of his movements, Coligny sent his surviving infantry under d'Andelot to strengthen the garrison in Orléans, taking with them the captured constable, while he himself rode with his cavalry into Normandy. Here he captured Caen and other places, but he was running out of cash and his urgent appeals for help to Queen Elizabeth fell on deaf ears. By the end of February his reiters were 'in such rage for their money that he could scarce keep them together'. They were destroying villages regardless of religion.

Guise, who was now the only effective Triumvir, assumed command of the royal army. Instead of pursuing Coligny, he decided to tighten his hold on the Loire valley: on 5 February he laid siege to Orléans.

Two provincial towns: Rouen and Toulouse

The history of the Wars of Religion is bewildering in its complexity: it cannot be easily understood by simply describing events at the political centre. In recent years historians have focused their attention on certain urban centres: in particular, Philip Benedict has studied Rouen and Mark Greengrass, Toulouse.

In Rouen, news of the massacre of Vassy and its aftermath caused alarm among the Protestants, who began to mount an armed guard around their assemblies. In April, two captains who had come to raise troops for the crown were driven away, and soon afterwards the local *bailli*, who was a Guisard, was besieged in the castle. As Catholics looked on, too stunned to resist, the Huguenots secured the gates to the city and changed the night watch to safeguard their military control. But their coup was originally defensive: Catholics still shared in the debates of the town council, and the parlement continued to sit. Some mendicants fled, but the clergy continued to celebrate mass. Appeals for calm by the Protestant ministers and elders failed however to deter zealots from taking direct action. Early in May bands of armed Huguenots set about destroying Catholic churches and their contents. They also burst into Catholic homes, seizing their arms. Catholic merchants, officials and priests fled to neighbouring towns, and on 10 May the parlement suspended its sittings. Catholic services also ceased. On 4 July a new all-Protestant council was voted into office and a 'Council Established by the People' began to function.

Catherine de' Medici, in the meantime, opened talks with the rebels. She hoped they would admit royal officials into the city in return for a promise of lenience, but they demanded the revocation of the commission recently given to the duc d'Aumale, Guise's brother, as lieutenant-general in Normandy. The Triumvirs, however, would not give way. On 28 May, Aumale appeared before Rouen and ordered the gates to be opened. When the inhabitants refused, he began a siege. Soldiers who came to Rouen's defence proved to be an unruly mob. They robbed the inhabitants when they were not carrying out pillaging raids on nearby towns. Early in August some *parlementaires* set up a skeleton court at Louviers which embarked on a campaign of terror against Huguenots. The authorities in Rouen retaliated by persecuting Catholics: they imprisoned some, forced others to profess publicly the Reformed faith, and seized the property of those who had left the city.

As the king's armies were victorious in central France, the Rouennais turned abroad for help. On 15 August a deputy of the city and the Vidame de Chartres left for England to negotiate with Queen Elizabeth. Three weeks later, as the royal army pushed north of Bourges, the Rouennais appealed to Elizabeth to save their city 'that is and wishes to render itself yours'. These talks led to the Treaty of Hampton Court (20 September) whereby the Huguenots handed over Le Havre to Elizabeth in return for the promise of 6000 troops to aid Rouen and Dieppe. The treaty was not universally popular among the Huguenots, some of whom protested by leaving Rouen. Their doubts were to prove justified, for on 4 October, when 200 Scots arrived, the city was being besieged by 30,000 royal troops under the king of Navarre.

Once a fort commanding Rouen from the south-east had been captured by the king's army, the city's fall seemed imminent. Catherine pressed for a negotiated settlement, but Protestant zealots within the city backed the commander's decision to continue resistance. On 21 October the king's army launched an assault and five days later breached the city's wall. The royal captains tried to avert a sack by promising their men a bonus, but they were not to be bought off so cheaply. Bursting into the city, they slaughtered the inhabitants without regard to sex, age or religion. Not even Catholic churches were spared. Merchants converged on Rouen from as far away as Paris to buy the soldiers' booty at bargain rates. According to the Spanish ambassador, the sack left a thousand dead.

Rouen's capitulation was followed by the restoration of Catholic rule. The *parlementaires* returned from Louviers and set up a new town council without a single Protestant member. Yet this did not mark the end of Protestantism in the city. Many Huguenots decided to remain, and at the end of the first civil war, when the Edict of Amboise allowed those who had fled to return and to worship freely again, their congregation soon picked up. The baptismal registers for 1565–6 suggest a larger community than that which had existed before the war. Other Protestant congregations in Normandy also grew in strength between 1561 and 1564. What is more, Huguenots had not given up hope of making converts and even of returning to power. They resumed psalm-singing in public, and the printer Abel Clémence turned out many religious works on a secret press in the city. In 1566 an attempt was made to elect several Huguenots to the city's council. But the sack of Rouen confirmed Catholics in believing that Huguenots were seditious and socially harmful. They were repeatedly blamed for the city's economic ills. The events of 1562 also had the effect of checking the advance of Protestantism in Rouen. The local congregation grew in size, yet it attracted few converts and became more inward-looking, and consequently more suspect, to the world outside.

Toulouse was a large town of 40,000 inhabitants. Its municipal government comprised eight *capitouls*, who were elected each year. Like Rouen, the city was the seat of a *parlement*. Relations between the two bodies were tense on the eve of the civil wars. Whereas the *capitouls* responded favourably to Catherine de' Medici's policy of toleration towards Huguenots, the parlement obstructed its implementation and blocked the enforcement of the tolerant Edict of January 1562. Meanwhile, a Reformed church was established in the city. Early in 1561 conventicles were being held in the houses of notables, and during the summer they moved to the squares in the warm evenings. By 1562 they were meeting outside the walls and the first *temple* was erected. A consistory appeared in March staffed by solid citizens.

Various incidents occurred during Lent 1562. The most serious was an attempt by priests to snatch the body of a Protestant merchant's wife so as to give it a Catholic burial. They clashed with the mourners and a riot ensued that lasted two days, leaving several Protestants dead or wounded. A truce was patched up, but it lasted barely a month, as the *capitouls* lost control of the military situation. The Catholics had various caches of arms in the city and they drew strength from the arrival of some two hundred nobles, who came to serve in the *ban et arrière-ban*. Toulouse also found itself caught up in the national crisis that followed the massacre of Vassy and Condé's rebellion at Orléans. Pierre Hunault, sieur de Lanta, who had gone to Paris on city business, called on the prince and was instructed to take Toulouse for the Protestants. But the parlement was warned of the plot by the duc de Guise and by Monluc, the king's lieutenant in Guyenne. The Huguenots, realizing that they had been forestalled, seized the town hall, occupied parts of the university and erected barricades in the streets. On 13 May fighting broke out between thousands of Catholics and Protestants. The battle soon spread to a wide area. The Catholics, who were more than twice as numerous, used four large moveable towers to cover themselves from Huguenot snipers. On 15 May they set a whole district alight, destroying more than two hundred houses. Protestants who had hidden in a sewer were flushed out and thrown into the Garonne. Ten churches and monastic houses, but not the cathedral, were captured by the Huguenots. The parlement threw its weight on the Catholic side: five or six judges toured the streets urging people to murder Protestants and sack their homes. The *capitouls* were replaced by the parlement's nominees, yet only a minority were actually Huguenots. The main Huguenot leaders were the pastor, consistory and captains.

The sustained violence of the uprising shocked contemporaries. As the revolt progressed, pressure for a pogrom of Protestants grew. Suspects ran the risk of being lynched by Catholic mobs. Pillage was a feature from the start. The parlement licensed the burning of Protestant bookshops. The homes of rich merchants on both sides were ransacked. The total cost of the insurrection was estimated (conservatively) at 20,000 *écus*. The final truce came on 16 May, when the defeated Huguenots were allowed to leave the city, but the safe-conduct given to them proved worthless. Many were butchered by gangs of peasants who had gathered in the neighbouring countryside. More Protestants were killed outside Toulouse's walls than within. The estimate of 3000 or 4000 dead given by the *Histoire ecclésiastique* may not be far from the truth.

The Protestants had failed to capture Toulouse for several reasons. They had lost the element of surprise, and military help which they had expected from outside never materialized. They also ran out of gunpowder and food, and were hampered by crowds of women and children who had gathered in the university and town hall. Above all, they were a minority who could not match the violence of the Catholics.

Rites of violence

The history of France in the second half of the sixteenth century is an appalling catalogue of violence which calls for an explanation, for it had a character of its own which can be related to the denominational conflict. Historians who simply see it as an expression of underlying socio-economic conditions miss its ritualistic significance, which has recently been investigated by historians like Natalie Zemon Davis and Denis Crouzet.

Religious violence, Davis suggests, had at least three main goals: first, 'the defence of true doctrine and the refutation of false doctrine through dramatic challenges and tests'. Thus a crowd of image-breakers shouted to the people of Albiac in 1561, 'Look, they are only animal bones' as they displayed relics seized from a monastery. In Angers a Catholic crowd paraded a French Bible at the end of a halberd. 'There's the truth hung', they cried. 'There's the truth of the Huguenots, the truth of all the devils.' Then, throwing it into the river: 'There's the truth of all the devils drowned.' A more frequent goal was that of ridding the community of pollution. 'The Calvinists have polluted their hands with every kind of sacrilege men can think of', wrote a theologian in 1562. Catholics firmly believed that the nocturnal conventicles of Calvinists were sexual orgies, while Calvinists pointed at the lewdness rampant among the Catholic clergy. The mass was to them a defilement of the sacred, as was the worship of images. Pollution was seen by both sides as a danger to the community since it provoked God's wrath, as manifested in storms, floods and epidemics. Catholics also worried about offending the Virgin Mary or the saints. Thus many acts of violence may be seen as acts of purification: for Catholics, the extermination of heretical 'vermin' was socially beneficial, and Protestants viewed the purging of priestly 'vermin' in the same way. A third goal of religious violence was to replace government. If a magistrate failed to wield the sword in defence of the faith or to punish idolaters, then a crowd did so for him. Some riots ended with the alleged wrongdoers being marched off to jail. For example, in 1561 some Parisian Calvinists, fearing an attack on their services, took fifteen Catholics 'bound like galley slaves' to the Châtelet prison. Crowds also took their victims to places of official execution, as in Paris in 1562, when a printer was dragged to the Marché aux Pourceaux for burning. Sometimes riots were intended to hasten a judgement or to protest about one that was deemed excessively harsh or lenient. Thus in Montpellier in 1569, a Catholic crowd forced the judge to sentence a prominent Huguenot to death, then hanged him outside his own house. At Marsillargues in 1561, Protestants who had been set free by royal decree were rearrested by a Catholic mob and burned in public. Calvinist crowds also imagined that they were acting for the authorities when they destroyed churches and their contents, while Protestant artisans who broke into churches at Agen in 1561, destroying the altars and images, declared: 'If one tarried for the Consistory, it would never be done.'

Crowds convinced themselves of the legitimacy of their actions, partly because clerics or royal officers sometimes acted with them, albeit unofficially. In Lyon in 1562, Pastor Jean Ruffy helped to sack the cathedral, sword in hand, and in Rouen in 1560, priests and parishioners broke into the houses of Protestants who had failed to honour the Corpus Christi procession. At Agen in 1561, the town's executioner was among the iconoclasts. 'It is my office to burn', he declared, as he set the statues alight. In the absence of official participants, crowds may have derived their legitimation from sermons. For instance, a Protestant preacher at Sens allegedly told his audience that they would be doing God a great service by exterminating the papal vermin. Iconoclastic riots in Gien and Rouen occurred on 3 May 1562 immediately after sermons had been preached on Deuteronomy 12: 1–3: 'And ye shall overthrow their altars, and break their pillars and burn their groves with fire; and ye shall hew down the graven images of their gods, and destroy the names of them out of that place'. Calvin and other pastors did not approve of iconoclasm, but they seemed to understand it, perhaps because they saw the hand of God in it. Catholic preachers took a similar line: they blamed the king's defeat at Saint-Quentin on his toleration of heretics. People were also accustomed to taking the law into their own hands. Royal edicts encouraged them to hunt down criminals, and laymen were authorized by canon law to perform priestly duties in an emergency. Protestant laymen preached before Reformed churches were set up. Some Calvinists were prepared, if need be, to defend their faith independently of a magistrate.

Religious riots should not be identified with food riots. For example, the Toulouse riots during the first five months of 1562 occurred when grain prices were the same as or lower than in the previous two years. Grain was more abundant than in 1557, when there was no religious riot. The Catholic attack on the conventicle in the rue Saint-Jacques (see above p. 241) also took place when grain was plentiful and cheap. Religious violence usually took place during religious worship or ritual and in the space used by one or both groups for sacred purposes. Often, though not always, it was an extension of ritual, prompted by some religious event, such as a baptism, a funeral, the celebration of mass or a Protestant preaching. Such incidents, however, tended to be trivial by comparison with the explosions of violence that accompanied processions. The Corpus Christi parade, for instance, offered Protestants the chance to demonstrate their disrespect and Catholics a pretext to attack them. In Lyon in 1561, the cry went up: 'For the flesh of God, we must kill all the Huguenots!' A Protestant procession of armed men and women in dark clothes, singing the Psalms, seemed to Catholics like an affront to the church and its sacraments. It was an occasion for children to throw stones, for insults to be exchanged and for fighting. When two rival processions met, as happened in Sens in 1562, the result could be a massacre. Particularly provocative were popular Catholic festivals when dancing, masks, banners, costumes and music filled the streets. Such an event caused a riot in Lyon in 1565. At Pamiers in 1566, a dance turned into a bloody encounter between Huguenots and Catholics. One dancer said: 'It's a long time since I was up to my elbows in Huguenot blood.'

As with liturgical rites, there were differences between Catholic and Protestant rites of violence. According to the Protestant *Histoire ecclésiastique*, the Calvinists attacked only property, whereas Catholics drew blood. This claim contains a grain of truth: Protestants did kill and Catholics did destroy property, but the former did excel as iconoclasts, not only because Catholic churches were more numerous than *temples* and contained more sacred objects, but also because Protestants regarded the wrongful use of material objects as doctrinally dangerous. For Catholics the persons of heretics themselves threatened the unity of the body social. Each side also had its favourite human targets. For Protestants, they were priests, monks and friars; for Catholics, the death of any heretic was a social cleansing.

How far were the riots motivated by class hatred? Instances can be found of religious rioters expressing a social grievance, but the overall picture is not one of the poor attacking the rich. In Davis's opinion, Catholic and Protestant movements in cities up to 1572 cut vertically through the social structure, though each had a distinctive occupational distribution. Only the poorest – the unskilled, the day-labourers and the unemployed – were neither among the killers nor their victims: they turned up after the massacres to strip the corpses of their clothes. Only when the rioters were peasants did social antagonisms appear.

Rites of violence derived their pattern from various sources: the Bible, the liturgy, the action of political authority and the traditions of popular folk justice. Destruction by fire or water had a clear religious significance: both are purifying agents. The water flowing in the rivers that received Protestant corpses was holy, the fire that destroyed Protestant houses was

We don't want our identity to be challenged

This is some serious hatred, maybe natural to religious disagreement!

like the burning of incense. Protestants tortured and killed Catholics, but were not interested in their corpses. Catholics, on the other hand, liked to humiliate the Protestant dead. They would drag their bodies through the streets, disembowel them and cut off their genitals. Protestants threw the Host to the dogs, roasted the crucifix on a spit, used holy oil to grease their boots, and smeared human excrement on baptismal fonts. Both sides used techniques derived from folk justice. Thus Catholic crowds led Protestant women through the streets wearing muzzles or a crown of thorns. Victims on either side would be made to ride backward on an ass. Certain rites persuaded the killers that their victims were vermin, not human beings.

low

A high percentage of the religious rioters were artisans, though crowds sometimes included people from the lower orders. More often they encompassed merchants, notaries, lawyers and clerics. The leaders were sometimes artisans, but were frequently a mixed group. Iconoclastic riots, unless carried out by Protestant nobles and their troops, were usually led by the *menu peuple*, but notables led the rioters into the church of Saint-Médard in Paris in 1561. City women and teenage boys figured prominently in the disturbances. Women tended to be most violent towards other women. Adolescent males and boys aged between ten and twelve were prominent in both Catholic and Protestant crowds. In Lyon and Castelnaudary in 1562, children stoned Protestants on their way to worship and in several towns of Provence, Catholic youths stoned Protestants to death and burned them. In Poitiers in 1559 and 1562, Protestant youths took the lead in smashing statues and overturning altars.

The crowds were often organized. Targets were listed and means of identifying friends devised (for example white crosses on Catholic doors in Mâcon in 1562). Existing organizations (confraternities among Catholics, units of the militia or craft groupings for both Catholics and Protestants) might underpin the disturbances. New organizations were also set up, such as the band of the sieur de Flassans in Aix in 1562. He organized a troop of *menu peuple* and monks to seek out Protestants and kill them. They wore rosaries and plumed hats, sang anti-Huguenot songs, carried a flag adorned with the papal keys, and were led by a Franciscan carrying a tall wooden cross.

Unlike many historians, Davis sees the religious violence of sixteenth-century France as normal rather than pathological. The crowds assumed the role of the authorities with a view to defending the faith or purifying the religious community. They saw their actions as legitimized by various features of political and religious life as well as by the group identity of the people involved. Although the targets and character of violence differed somewhat between Catholics and Protestants, in both cases it was linked to worship. It drew upon a store of punitive and purifying traditions current in sixteenth-century France. Even in the most extreme cases, the crowds

Public violence is legitimized by belief that they are purifying, acting on behalf of authorized, identity

were not mindless: they were defending a cause and believed that they were acting lawfully. Their violence had a structure that was both dramatic and ritualistic.

Fascinating as it is, Davis's interpretation of religious violence needs cautious handling. In Toulouse, for example, the revolt of May 1562 certainly had ritualistic elements, especially at the beginning; but as the violence grew they were submerged by the normal practices of civil war. As Greengrass writes:

> Bodies were dumped in the river Garonne, sewers in the city were scoured out, *quartiers* were set alight, not as ritual cleansings and purification of the city but as a natural recourse in the strategy of urban warfare when the prisons were full and the sewers offered some refuge. The greater violence perpetrated by the Catholics was not necessarily an expression of their outrage at the desecration of their religious symbols and their failure to find Protestant ritual objects to attack in return; it was the inevitable result of a sectarian conflict in a confined space in which Catholics outnumbered Protestants and had the assistance of professional soldiers to whom killing came easily.

Civil war was not just a macabre ballet.

Crouzet's contribution to the debate on violence in sixteenth-century France rests on an exhaustive analysis of printed contemporary sources. They suggest that the violence expressed a state of mental anguish which had begun to grip people in the 1520s – he calls it a 'civilization of anguish' (*civilisation de l'angoisse*). The idea that the world was about to end was confirmed and sustained by almanacs and prognostications (like those of Nostradamus). Heretics were seen, along with a rich array of portents, including monstrous births and heavenly apparitions, as harbingers of the Last Judgement. Preachers and pamphleteers called on the people to unite against the forces of evil. But Calvin stood outside this eschatological frenzy: he rejected judicial astrology, prognostication, divination and millenarianism. He did not see holy power as immanent in the world, fighting the forces of darkness. For Calvin, world order comes from the laws of nature which are imposed by the Creator. He has predestined its shape and man's salvation in ways which transcend our understanding. Calvinist theology was the alternative to anguish.

The desire to rid the world of heresy, according to Crouzet, was only one aspect of a more fundamental urge to be the conduit of God's wrath, to feel part of God's immanence in the Last Days. Children were prominent in the violence because they were seen as Christ-like bearers of God's blessing. The gruesome cruelties inflicted on Protestants were not sadism, as we understand it, for the victims were seen as non-human devils. Calvinist violence, by contrast, was human, rationalistic and cool: its aim was to achieve the Protestant Reformation. It began by attacking images, then

[handwritten margin note: BELIEF THAT THE APOCALYPSE WAS UPON THEM PROVOKED THEM TO ACT]

other aspects of holy power. Huguenots set out to desacralize traditional religion and to free the people from its ruses. Behind their policy lay a perception of radical change, a sense that the world could be made new. But the sacral monarchy of France stood in the way of change, so Protestant violence contained an impulse towards regicide. This was expressed early on in the attempted assassination of Henry II by a Protestant in 1558 (see above, p. 243) and in the popular description of Charles IX as 'a kinglet of shit' overheard by Monluc in 1562. Royal shrines were also a target for Protestant vandals early in the civil wars. However, this impulse towards regicide was for a time concealed. Calvin and the pastors at the early national synods were obsessed with the dangers to order posed by iconoclasm and desacralization. They preached passive acceptance of what Providence decreed. God sent trials and tribulations to test the faithful. At the same time, the aristocratic leaders of the Protestant movement stressed that they were fighting *for* the king against the evil Guisards who held him prisoner. Following the massacres of St Bartholomew's day in 1572, the tensions within the Huguenot movement were released and the impulse towards regicide was to find an outlet in the writings of the monarchomachs.

The Edict of Amboise, 19 March 1563

On 18 February 1563 the duc de Guise was returning from a camp inspection at Orléans when he was shot three times in the shoulder. He died a few days later. His assassin was Poltrot de Méré, a Huguenot nobleman from Saintonge, who was captured and put on trial. The duke's assassination was enormously important politically, for his eldest son, Henri prince de Joinville, was only a boy of thirteen. Two of the duke's brothers, Aumale and the Grand Prior, died a few days later; a third, Elbeuf, was besieged in Rouen; and the fourth, the Cardinal of Lorraine, was away at the Council of Trent. The Guises were thus as leaderless as were the Bourbons and the Montmorencies. The way was clear for Catherine de' Medici to take over the government. But Coligny was still fighting, Orléans was holding out and, in Languedoc, Antoine de Crussol, who had been given the task of pacifying the province, was apparently busy carving out a principality for himself. Peace was urgently required to check the formation of pockets of resistance and even of small Huguenot states within the kingdom. As negotiators, Catherine used the two chief prisoners of war, Montmorency and Condé. Ideally, the latter would have liked to see a return to the Edict of January 1562, but he valued his personal freedom even more. So he signed the Peace of Amboise (19 March 1563), which guaranteed freedom of conscience but regulated rights of worship according to social status. Noblemen with rights of high justice were allowed complete freedom of

Calvinist preaching and worship on their estates, while those with inferior rights of jurisdiction could worship within their homes. Protestant worship was allowed in all towns held by the Huguenots before 7 March and in one town in each *bailliage*. It was forbidden in and around Paris. Property confiscated from the Catholic church was to be restored.

The peace was highly unpopular among the Catholic powers of Europe. The pope, the emperor, the king of Spain and the duke of Savoy sent ambassadors to Charles IX to protest about it. Yet many Huguenots were angered by the settlement, viewing it as a sell-out by Condé. Coligny accused him of inflicting more damage on the Reformed churches than their enemies had done in ten years. Calvin denounced the prince as 'a wretch who had betrayed God out of vanity'. By allowing social criteria to determine the legality and distribution of Protestant worship, he had taken care of his own interests and those of the upper nobility while showing a complete disregard for Huguenots of a lower social standing. The Reformed faith had been made to look like an aristocratic religion, and conversions suffered accordingly. In Rouen, as we have seen, their number declined. For the sake of his own position, social and political, Condé had compromised the future of his church and his party.

20

The Fragile Peace, 1563–6

The first civil war had cleared the way for Catherine de' Medici to impose her authority. The king of Navarre and the duc de Guise had both been killed, and the heads of their respective houses were too young to be a nuisance: Henri de Bourbon was nine years old and Henri de Lorraine, thirteen. The last of the Triumvirs, Montmorency, was getting old and had been chastened by his misfortune at Dreux. Condé was tired of fighting and anxious to assume the place at court formerly occupied by the king of Navarre. Thus the queen mother was allowed four years in which to govern the kingdom as she wished.

The recapture of Le Havre, 30 July 1563

The Peace of Amboise called Queen Elizabeth's bluff. When she sent troops to occupy Le Havre, she declared that her action was prompted solely by the wish to wrest Charles IX from the tyranny of the Guises and the Huguenots from that of the papists. In reality, she wanted to recover Calais in exchange for Le Havre. The queen viewed the Peace of Amboise as a betrayal of Huguenot promises, and in April made known her displeasure to Condé's envoy. At first Catherine remained aloof, as though these exchanges were not her concern, but eventually she did intervene, precipitating a breakdown of the relations between Elizabeth and her former allies. The arrogance of the French envoy, the seigneur d'Alluye, scandalized William Cecil, who directed England's foreign policy; and Elizabeth allegedly sent a sharp note to Catherine telling her that she had not seized Le Havre to assist Charles IX or anyone else, but to be avenged for the injuries she had suffered at the hands of the French, in particular their capture of Calais which was hers by right. Be that as it may, Catherine rallied troops of both religions against Elizabeth, and Montmorency, assisted by Condé, besieged Le Havre which surrendered on 28 July 1563. Elizabeth never trusted the Huguenots again. Neither she nor Catherine wanted war, but Elizabeth, out of spite, dragged out the peace talks for eight months. Eventually, under the Treaty of Troyes, France retained Calais in return for a payment of 120,000 crowns.

Charles IX's majority declared, 17 August 1563

The age of majority for a king of France had been fixed at fourteen by an ordinance of Charles V. Catherine's son, Charles IX, was only thirteen, but she was anxious to have him proclaimed of age, as a king commanded more obedience than a regent. She may also have wished to deny Condé the chance of becoming lieutenant-general of the kingdom. The council decided that Charles, being in his fourteenth year, was old enough to rule, and his majority was proclaimed on 17 August 1563, not in the Parlement of Paris, as might have been expected, but at a *lit de justice* held in the Parlement of Rouen. What is more, the declaration was linked to a formal confirmation of the Edict of Amboise. By linking the two laws and submitting them to the Parlement of Rouen for registration, the chancellor hoped to secure speedy registration of the Edict of Amboise without having to face the remonstrances which the Parlement of Paris would undoubtedly have submitted. L'Hôpital was also breaking new ground constitutionally by establishing the precedent that a *lit de justice* could be held in any parlement, not just in Paris. As the Spanish ambassador Chantonnay pointed out, this was a deliberate move to detract from the authority and pre-eminence of the Parlement of Paris, which the chancellor and the queen mother disliked because of its opposition to their policy. By persuading Charles IX to hold his *lit de justice* in a provincial parlement, L'Hôpital challenged the doctrine according to which the parlements were united under the oldest and most illustrious one. Instead, he was proposing that all of them were united in 'one class' under the king.

At the ceremony, which was attended by Catherine, the princes, the constable, marshals of France and many royal councillors, the young monarch commanded his subjects to keep the peace and forbade any of them to seek military or financial assistance abroad. The chancellor announced the annexation of Calais to the domain and praised Charles V's wisdom in providing for the early termination of regencies, which had always proved troublesome. He explained that Charles expected to be obeyed universally while reserving his mother's right to command. L'Hôpital also reminded the *parlementaires* that their role was to administer justice fairly and castigated them for their partisanship, judicial miscarriages and greed. Believing, as he did, that all privileges granted by the king had force only during his

lifetime, the chancellor rejected the notion that *parlementaires* were protected by a law superior to the king. The doctrine of irremovability from
office, he asserted, did not confer on the judges immunity for their actions.
He reminded them that they were accountable to the king.

After the First President's reply, the ceremony of homage took place.
Catherine formally handed over the government to her son. As she was
about to make her obeissance, he left his throne and, cap in hand, assured
her that she would continue to rule 'as much or more than ever'. Each of
the great dignitaries then came to the king, bowed deeply and kissed his
hand. The doors of the parlement were thrown open and a proclamation
was read out, calling on all the king's subjects to lay down their arms. Only
nobles were allowed to keep them in their homes, and neither they nor
their servants were allowed to carry firearms. Only the king's soldiers were
exempted from this ban. Usually the crown disbanded its troops after a
campaign, but not on this occasion. Part of the infantry was retained and
assigned to a corps called *enseignes de la garde du roi*.

The Parlement of Paris was, of course, offended by the proceedings in
Rouen. It refused to register the declaration of the king's majority and
objected to the confirmation of the Edict of Amboise, complaining that the
linkage turned the edict into a permanent law and implied recognition of
the two religions. The parlement also asked for Parisians to be allowed to
keep their arms which, it alleged, they had taken up to defend the king
and by his command. Although Charles IX received these remonstrances
graciously, he chose to ignore them. When the parlement created more
difficulties, he lost his temper. He ordered it to send him representatives at
Meulan (24 September) and gave them a dressing down. Their job, he said,
was to administer justice to his subjects, not to act as his mentors, as
protectors of the kingdom or as custodians of Paris. So effective was this
rebuke that the parlement complied with the king's wishes on 28 September.
In November, L'Hôpital, in an address to the parlement, expounded on the
proper relations between the king and the judges. Their role, he declared,
was to exercise the king's judicial authority, not to question his laws, picking
some and discarding others. He accused them of giving encouragement
to 'bold and wicked spirits' by their remonstrances against the edicts of
pacification.

Catherine de' Medici's efforts at conciliation

The queen mother does not seem to have understood why the Triumvirs
had rebelled. On 19 April 1563 she spoke with pride of the Edict of January
and with disdain of the Edict of Amboise which, in her judgement, had
done nothing more to assist the Catholics. She blamed the Guises, who had

'tried to be kings', for all France's current ills. Catherine failed to see that her policy of religious toleration was interpreted by Catholics as undermining their faith and political hegemony. She was an incorrigible optimist, who underestimated the task facing her. The religious passions which the civil war had inflamed were not easily assuaged, and the popular mood in Paris was particularly feverish. The late duc de Guise was worshipped by Parisian Catholics as a martyr for their faith. When Poltrot de Méré was executed on 18 March, the onlookers fell upon his remains like wild beasts and dragged them through the streets before tearing them to pieces. Next day the capital turned out in force to escort the duke's coffin on its last journey to Joinville. At Notre-Dame there was much weeping and lamentation as a preacher noted for his attacks on heretics delivered the duke's funeral oration. In another pulpit, Artus Desiré gave his own gloss on Christ's words to his disciples: 'Let him who has no sword sell his tunic in order to buy one.' Despite the peace, Parisians would not lay down their arms.

It was in the midst of this highly charged atmosphere that Catherine tried to conciliate the rival factions. She hoped that Paris would set an example to the rest of the kingdom. In June 1563 she and the king stayed with Condé in Paris. As they crossed the city in his company, the people seemed happy enough, but soon afterwards, as Condé's wife left the capital, her coach was attacked by hundreds of armed Parisians and one of her escort was killed. Suspecting a Guise plot, Condé threatened to leave the court and Catherine had difficulty dissuading him. A few days later she announced his reconciliation with the duc de Nemours and the Cardinal of Guise. But on 1 January 1564 another violent incident enraged the Catholics. As Charry, an officer of the king's guard and a Catholic, was crossing a bridge in Paris, he was murdered by three men. One of them was Chastelier-Portout, Coligny's standard-bearer, and another, Mouvans, a Huguenot leader from the Midi. The murder was probably a private act of vengeance (Charry had killed Chastelier-Portout's brother fourteen years earlier), but Catholics blamed d'Andelot and Coligny for the crime.

Soon afterwards, Catherine settled a far more serious dispute. Under torture, Poltrot de Méré had implicated Coligny in the murder of the duc de Guise, then retracted his accusation only to repeat it. On 12 March the admiral protested his innocence, but he also admitted that he would not have dissuaded anyone from murdering Guise who, he understood, had been plotting to kill him. Writing to Catherine, he was more candid still. His protestation of innocence, he explained, implied no regrets on his part over the duke's death; it was, he thought, the best thing that could happen to the kingdom and, above all, to himself and his house. The Guises, for their part, demanded justice and began arming themselves. Fearing a renewal of civil war, Catherine evoked the matter to the king's council, but both parties wanted to be judged only by the king or his mother. Charles IX defused the situation temporarily by postponing a decision on the case for three years. Both parties were to abstain from any judicial or armed action in the meantime.

In the kingdom at large the peace was only patchily applied. Protestant noblemen continued to plunder churches and seize ecclesiastical property. Wherever they were dominant, as in Poitou, they refused to hand back benefices that had been secularized. Catholics, for their part, attacked Huguenots returning home under cover of the peace accord. In some provinces hired assassins were engaged to eliminate Huguenots.

At first the government relied on the existing administrative and judicial bodies to enforce the pacification. By April 1563, however, the crown had become convinced that only someone of high status, such as a prince or a Marshal of France, would be able to disarm the belligerents. Charles IX therefore decided to send the four Marshals of France on tours on inspection. They were instructed to call before them royal and municipal officials and to find out from them how the Edict of Amboise was being applied, to listen to complaints from Catholics and Protestants and to provide remedies. To assist the marshals Charles IX appointed twenty-eight commissioners drawn from the *conseil privé* or the Parlement of Paris. They were expected to enforce the amnesty for acts of war, to restore property which had been arbitrarily confiscated, to find a site for Protestant worship in each *bailliage* and to inspect local crown officials. The crown's reliance on the Marshals of France did not necessarily ensure a smooth return to peace. Thus Gaspard de Saulx-Tavannes, the king's lieutenant-general in Burgundy, allowed the Catholic inhabitants of towns to remain under arms and to continue guarding their gates on the ground that national security was at stake. By so doing, he retained armed control of the towns and was able to monitor the return of Huguenots. Another marshal who interpreted his duties in a partisan way was Henri de Montmorency-Damville. He proved so aggressively Catholic during his tour of Languedoc in 1563 that Charles IX had to order him to curb his zeal. A contentious issue facing the royal commissioners was the choice of sites for Protestant worship. Huguenots naturally wanted to be allocated an accessible site, while Catholics wanted to see their services removed as far as possible from their own. Many Catholic towns sought exemption from the edict on the ground that they were frontier towns and that confessional co-existence would undermine national security. Huguenots often complained that the sites allocated to them were too remote or their access too dangerous. Once they had left a walled town, they could find themselves at the mercy of hostile bands of peasants, and, on their return, they were liable to be set upon by urban mobs. Complaints over sites of worship often led to lengthy lawsuits. Burial sites were another contentious issue. At Tours, for example,

Huguenots were accused of burying their dead on church land. At Mâcon, Tavannes granted them a site outside the town provided that not more than eight gathered there at one time, that they abstained from religious services, sermons and hymn singing, and that they buried their dead at dawn. Catherine de' Medici urged the king's lieutenants to enforce the peace, while, at the centre of government, she tried to balance the parties. Lists of royal councillors in 1563–7 contain the names of sixteen Catholics, six Protestants and some twenty moderates. The latter's numerical superiority truly reflected the government's policy of elevating the king's authority above the religious factions and making it the arbiter of their disputes.

The Gallican church and the Council of Trent

The civil war did not rule out all hope of reuniting the churches through dialogue. After the rebuffs she had suffered at Poissy and Saint-Germain, Catherine de' Medici no longer believed that a dialogue was possible in France, but she did not despair of a solution being found by a General Council of the church as long as certain conditions were met: she believed that it should be a new council, not simply a continuation of the Council of Trent; that it should assemble in a venue acceptable to Protestants; and that its agenda should not be imposed by the papacy. Catherine did not understand the dogmatic differences separating the parties and therefore imagined that a reform of church discipline would be enough to bring them together. A key figure in promoting concord was Charles, cardinal of Lorraine, whom Protestant legend has so completely misrepresented. Seemingly unaware of the severe harm done to relations with the German Lutherans by the Vassy massacre, he still hoped to reach some dogmatic compromise with them. Following his return to Paris on 23 April 1562, he decided to attend the Council of Trent. He wanted it to reform the church, especially the system of collating to benefices, but the instructions he received from Catherine went much further. He was to demand communion in both kinds and the use of French in church services. He was also to back the demands of the German Protestants, should they attend the council, as long as they did not contradict the Word of God, and to seek an accord on clerical marriage and on confiscated church property. On 19 September 1562 Charles IX asked some 60 French prelates to go to Trent, but very few were willing to travel in the midst of civil war. In the end, Lorraine, who led the French delegation, was accompanied by twelve bishops, three abbots and eighteen theologians. Their coming was viewed with apprehension in Rome, where Lorraine was regarded as a dangerous churchman who talked to heretics and criticized the papacy. On 23 November he delivered a speech to the council in which he blamed the moral corruption of the church, particularly the bishops, for the grim situation in France. He made no secret of the fact that he regarded discussion of divine law by the council as a waste of time and urged it not to present an aggressive face to the Protestants. Lorraine's speech was clearly intended to reassure them. Writing to Montmorency on 23 November, he still hoped that the council might solve the religious troubles in France, but events were to frustrate his optimism.

On 2 January 1563 the French presented certain Articles of Reform to the council. They proposed the suppression of various papal dispensations which were commonly granted in return for money. To set an example, the French crown offered to give up *confidences* and *commendes*, whereby secular clergy and even laymen were able to draw monastic revenues. Lorraine and all the Gallican theologians refused to acknowledge the pope's absolute power over the universal church, as this implied his superiority over the General Council.

Lorraine, as we have seen, had for long sought a rapprochement with the German Lutherans. He had expressed some radical opinions in various sermons on the eve of the Vassy massacre, and even afterwards tried to win over the Lutherans. But his attitude changed after the murder of his brother and the Peace of Amboise. The goodwill he had shown towards Reformers suddenly vanished. In September 1563 he visited Rome, and in his absence the papal legates at Trent put forward proposals curbing the powers of secular princes in ecclesiastical matters. They seemed to be aimed mainly at France, where the crown had been trying for centuries to take over ecclesiastical jurisdiction. The French ambassador, Arnaud du Ferrier, complained that the legates were attacking the Gallican liberties and the authority of the Most Christian King. He expressed surprise that they should talk of reforming, even of excommunicating, princes who were divinely appointed and to whom obedience and respect were owed. Having delivered his protest, the ambassador retired to Venice. After his return from Rome, Lorraine persuaded the legates to drop their clumsy proposals, but he failed to persuade the French ambassador to return to Trent.

The doctrinal decrees of the Council of Trent, by reaffirming the traditional tenets of the Roman church and excommunicating heretics, confirmed the division of Christendom. But the council's decrees on discipline were less binding, and were accepted, rejected or modified by the secular powers as they thought fit. France rejected them because they implied the surrender to the Holy See of all the authority, jurisdiction and rights of patronage which her king claimed over the Gallican church. When Lorraine returned home from Trent he tried to get the Tridentine decrees published in France. They were hotly debated by the *Conseil privé* and by the presidents of the parlement. L'Hôpital spoke so strongly against their publication that Lorraine challenged him to drop his mask and openly embrace the new religion; the chancellor retorted that the cardinal ought to know who had trampled on the Edict of January at Vassy.

When the pope summoned seven French bishops to Rome on suspicion of heresy, the French government objected strongly. He had no right, it claimed, to remove the accused from their own country and to have them tried by judges who had not been appointed by the king of France and were not answerable to the parlement on appeal. The government protested even more strongly when Pius IV decided to depose the queen of Navarre. Catherine reminded him that he had no authority over kings and queens and could not dispose of their lands as he wished, particularly if those lands were held of the French king.

Catherine de' Medici and the Huguenots

The Huguenot leaders misunderstood Catherine's policy, imagining that she was about to revert to the tolerant regime that had prevailed at Saint-Germain on the eve of the civil war. But she was a pragmatist. Knowing that most Frenchmen were strongly attached to the Catholic faith, she understood that it would be hazardous to concede more to the Huguenots than they had already received in the Edict of Amboise. De Bèze had no illusions about her policy. After his return to Geneva in May 1563, he praised the tolerance of Charles IX and his brothers, but said nothing about their mother. Calvin accused her of stirring up the Catholic fanatics in Paris, and of using 'hidden tricks' to frustrate the good decisions of the king's councillors, particularly the chancellor's. 'It is the last straw for a people,' wrote de Bèze, 'to be ruled by a woman, particularly one of that kind.'

During 1563 the government made life more difficult for the Huguenots. The Edict of Vincennes (14 June) forbade them to trade on Catholic feast days, and an important 'Declaration and Interpretation' (14 December) clarified certain ambiguities in the Edict of Amboise. The rule, which had allowed Huguenot worship in one town per *bailliage* and in all towns where it had existed before 7 March, was now restricted to towns which the Huguenots had occupied by force and where Protestantism had been practised openly. The ban on trade on Catholic feast days was confirmed, and Protestant butchers were forbidden to work on fast days. Monks and nuns, who had left their religious houses during the recent troubles, were ordered to return there or to leave the kingdom, even if they had married. Parisian Protestants were forbidden to go to neighbouring *bailliages* for worship. They were to bury their dead at night without attendants and under the supervision of the civic watch. Not more than four or five persons were to attend their baptisms. Although clearly aimed at safeguarding public order, these measures were seen by the Huguenots as confirming their inferior legal status.

The Huguenots viewed as treasonable Catherine's efforts to reconcile their leaders with the Guises. They also viewed as a threat a royal decree of 13 January 1564 allowing heads of households in Paris to keep their arms. Catherine wrote to Coligny, vehemently denying a rumour that the government was planning to attack the Huguenots. She reminded him of the orders she and her son were giving each day to magistrates, while admitting that they were not always obeyed. She urged Coligny to reassure his co-religionists that the edict of pacification would be rigorously enforced.

L'Hôpital is often given credit for the crown's policy of moderation, but Catherine's role should not be underestimated. She loved power, as her voluminous correspondence testifies, and paid close attention to both policy-making and administrative detail. Though an able minister, L'Hôpital lacked the diplomatic finesse of Catherine and stood almost alone: Catholics suspected him of being a Huguenot sympathizer, and Huguenots often distrusted him as a former henchman of the Guises. He depended entirely on uncertain royal favour and was able to keep his position only for as long as long as Catherine was inclined to follow his policy.

The court of Catherine de' Medici

The queen mother once recalled that Francis I used to say that two things were necessary to live at peace with the French and to retain their love: they had to be kept happy and occupied with some honest exercise; other-wise they were likely to follow more dangerous pursuits. Catherine, it seems, made a conscious effort to divert the nobility from civil strife by keeping it entertained at her court. Among its principal adornments were Catherine's ladies-in-waiting, numbering about eighty, whom she recruited from the noblest houses of France. A selection of those, who regularly accompanied Catherine on her progresses and diplomatic errands, became known as her 'flying squadron' and were allegedly used by her to seduce courtiers for political ends. According to Jeanne d'Albret, the court of France was a sink of iniquity, where women, not men, made the sexual advances. But her testimony may be subject to caution. As an austere Huguenot, Jeanne doubt-less wished to protect her son from the temptations of Catherine's circle, however innocent. Morally, the French court was probably no worse than any other major court of the time. Its social conventions are easily misunder-stood today. According to the duc de Bouillon, it was a custom of the court in the 1560s for a young nobleman to be given a 'mistress' who would introduce him to high society and its code of manners. 'I cannot disapprove of this custom,' he wrote, 'for as much as one only saw, heard and did

good, youth then being more desirous than today [under Henry IV] to do
nothing improper.' Maybe Brantôme had this in mind when he described
Catherine's court as 'a veritable earthly Paradise and a school of all honesty
and virtue, France's ornament'.

Catherine's court was notable for its lavish entertainments, like those
staged at Fontainebleau in February and March 1564. Not a day passed
without a spectacle of some kind: a military parade led by great noblemen, a
cavalcade of nymphs, a joust or tournament, tilting at the ring, a magnificent
banquet accompanied by music performed by sirens perched on fountains
in the palace gardens, an audition of Ronsard's *Eglogues* and a performance
of the *Beautiful Ginevra*, a tragi-comedy adapted from *Orlando Furioso* in
which the royal children took part along with princes and princesses of the
blood, great lords and ladies. Masques were also performed in which gods
and goddesses sang the praises of the king and his mother.

The royal tour of the kingdom, March 1564–May 1566

In an effort to restore the king's authority in full, Catherine took Charles
IX on an extended tour of his kingdom: she hoped that the sight of the
young king would revive loyalty to the monarchy after the damage it had
sustained in the religious troubles. She also wanted to restore France's
international prestige by meeting foreign rulers, especially her son-in-law,
Philip II of Spain. The progress began on 13 March 1564, when several
thousand people, accompanied by a multitude of beasts of burden and a
veritable army, set off from Fontainebleau. Although the court's itinerary
had probably been mapped out in advance, some of its stops were, it seems,
chosen at short notice. The means of transport varied according to the
status of the travellers. The king and his mother travelled either by coach
or litter or they rode horses, as did most of the nobles. Where rivers were
navigable, boats were used, but the rank and file always went on foot. The
court's speed of travel was leisurely by modern standards: the van often
reached its destination before the rearguard had left the last stop. Nor did
the court necessarily travel as one body or even along the same road. Its
members would part company, take short cuts, travel across fields and meet
up along the way. Halts varied in length: some were for one night only,
others might last a week and some occupied several weeks. Among reasons
for such variations were the king's health (he fell ill twice), bad weather,
the state of the roads, and feast days. In overall charge of the progress was
the Constable of Montmorency, who kept discipline, issued instructions to
town governors, and rode ahead of the main company to see that everything
was ready for the king's reception.

After stopping at Sens, scene of a massacre of Protestants in 1562, the royal caravan arrived at Troyes, where the peace treaty with Elizabeth was signed. The progress enabled Charles IX to carry out an inspection of his local officials. He required them to give an account of their activities and to receive his instructions. The success of the pacification depended on their willingness to apply it everywhere. The king accused his judges at Troyes of not pulling their weight and warned them that they would be replaced by others unless their performance improved. From Troyes the court moved on to Bar-le-Duc to attend the baptism of Catherine's first grandchild, Charlotte-Catherine, the daughter of Charles III duke of Lorraine and Claude de France. Habsburg observers, remembering Henry II's invasion of Germany in 1552, wondered if there was an ulterior motive for the king's progress into Lorraine. They were much relieved when the court turned south and entered Burgundy. On 22 March the king made his entry into Dijon, whose governor, Gaspard de Saulx-Tavannes, a veteran of many campaigns, staged a military pageant of such verisimilitude that Catherine was petrified with fear.

One of the aims of the progress was undoubtedly to curb the independence so often shown by the provincial parlements and municipal authorities. At Dijon on 23 May, Henri duc d'Orléans, acting in the name of his brother the king, sent for the parlement's registers and for information on the municipal authority from the lieutenant-general of the province. Next day, Chancellor L'Hôpital checked the publication of the Edict of Amboise and examined each lawsuit recently tried by the court to ensure that its decisions were in line with its powers. The crown intervened in the affairs of almost every town visited by the court on its progress, but it was not invariably in support of the Catholic cause. Wherever possible, the king tried to strike a balance between the religious parties. From Chalon, the court travelled by boat to Mâcon, where it was joined by Jeanne d'Albret, queen of Navarre. She was in mourning for her late husband, Antoine de Bourbon, and accompanied by eight Calvinist ministers as well as a military escort, necessitated, so she claimed, by the lawless activities of Monluc and the Spaniards.

In the course of the progress foreign dignitaries attached themselves to the court, but only two – the papal nuncio and the Spanish ambassador – stayed throughout the progress. Nobles also tagged on or dropped off as they pleased. Political or religious affiliations determined their movements. For example, as long as the court was in Lorraine or in territories dominated by the Guises, the principal Huguenots absented themselves. The king's council accordingly fell under the influence of Catholics, the party of moderation being represented only by the constable and the chancellor. This may explain why measures restricting Protestant worship were taken by the council during the progress, though they may have been intended simply to avoid trouble.

The next major stop was Lyon, a city with a large Protestant community. The constable, riding ahead of the king, took charge of the city's fortifications, artillery and keys before giving it a royal garrison. As a further safeguard, Protestant services were forbidden for the duration of the royal visit. This ban was soon extended to other towns still to be visited by the court. Its sojourn in Lyon was accompanied by pageants and celebrations in which members of the city's important Italian and German colonies took part. The king also fraternized with prominent bourgeois. He stayed with Pierre Teste, a rich spice-merchant, dined with the banker Thomas Gadagne at his château of Beauregard, and visited the banker Albisse del Bene at his château of Perron. In July he resumed negotiations with members of the *Grand Parti*, and in August signed an agreement with the imperial towns for the repayment of loans by German merchants. While the court was in Lyon, it was joined by Emmanuel-Philibert, duke of Savoy, and his wife Marguerite. Pleased as Catherine was to see her sister-in-law again, she refused to hand Pinerolo and Savigliano back to the duke.

A terrible epidemic of plague, which allegedly killed 25,000 people, forced the court to leave Lyon on 8 July. It moved to Crémieu where an important edict was issued on 14 July regarding the towns of the kingdom. L'Hôpital believed that municipal independence had got out of hand. Nearly half the 'good towns' had fallen into Protestant hands in 1562, but the government was not concerned with them alone. Under the Edict of Crémieu, the choice of municipal magistrates in the principal towns was given to the king. The elective system was not abolished, but electors were required to submit two lists of candidates for municipal office to the king, leaving him to make the final choice. This was a major step in the subordination of towns to royal control. Not even Louis XI had included all the towns in a single ordinance; he had picked them off individually.

The court's next halt was Roussillon, a château belonging to Cardinal Tournon, where on 4 August, Charles IX ruled on the application of the Edict of Amboise. Protestant worship beyond the limits prescribed in the edict was to be punished by heavy fines and confiscations of property. Married priests were to leave their wives on pain of banishment. On the other hand, royal officials were to see that Protestant worship took place only in the permitted areas. On 15 August the court continued its journey. Travelling down the Rhône valley, it reached Romans, then Valence. On 5 September the king's council examined a complaint from the Huguenots of Bordeaux about breaches of the peace. Charles IX ordered Burie and Monluc, the lieutenants of the governor of Guyenne, to observe it. After a short break to allow the king to recover from a chill, the court went on to Montélimar (14 September), Orange (22 September) and Avignon, where Charles was the guest of the papal vice-legate. On 16 August he moved on to Salon de Crau, where he and his mother called on the elderly Nostradamus.

The king gave him 200 *écus* and made him a royal councillor and his physician. The old man prophesied in return that the king would live as long as the constable.

On 23 October the royal caravan arrived at Aix-en-Provence, whose parlement remained bitterly opposed to the recent pacification. All the parlements had been troublesome since 1562. The Edict of Amboise had been registered at Bordeaux, Rouen, Toulouse and Dijon, but they had delayed its publication and had refused to reinstate Protestant councillors. Aix was unique in its refusal even to register the edict. Protestant worship was also effectively banned in its *ressort*. Charles IX was accordingly obliged to assert his authority: he suspended the parlement, replacing it by a commission of Parisian *parlementaires* and members of the *Grand conseil*.

The next stage of the progress was less contentious. The king was welcomed at Brignoles by girls dancing the *volta* and *martingale*. As he travelled through Provence, he was able to admire its distinctive flora, including orange and palm trees, pepper and cotton plants. He was also given a practical lesson in Roman history among the province's Roman remains. On 3 November, at Toulon, Charles took a trip out to sea on one of Elbeuf's galleys. At Marseille, a staunchly Catholic city where Catherine had been married thirty years before, he took another sea trip. The king and his companions also took part in a mock naval battle disguised as Turks. After leaving Marseille, Charles crossed the Camargue, where he saw flamingoes. On 16 November the court reached Arles, where it remained for three weeks on account of floods. The king visited Les Alyscamps, the famous avenue of Roman sarcophagi, and watched bullfights in the Roman arena. Meanwhile, his mother and the chancellor tried to persuade the provincial estates to accept the pacification. After crossing the Rhône by means of a pontoon bridge at Tarascon, the court visited the Pont du Gard. At Nîmes, a staunchly Protestant town, the king was accorded an entry notable for its ingenious mechanical devices. On 1 January, after celebrating Christmas in Montpellier, the royal party set off for Toulouse, but at Carcassonne it was held up for ten days by snow.

Throughout the progress the king and his mother remained in close touch with Paris. Out of 413 letters written by Catherine during the tour of the kingdom, 110 were sent to Parisians: Marshal Montmorency, governor of Paris and the Ile-de-France, received 74, the mayor and *échevins* 22 and the parlement 14. Catherine was mainly interested in the maintenance of order and in her building operations, particularly at the Tuileries. While she was in Toulouse, grim news reached her from the capital. François de Montmorency, the governor, had refused to let the cardinal of Lorraine enter the city with an armed escort. The cardinal had defied the order, whereupon Montmorency had dispersed his escort by force, forcing Lorraine to seek shelter in a merchant's house. The Guises assembled their forces, and Coligny brought 500 Protestant horse into Paris to support the governor. To avert a new civil war, Catherine ordered the Guises and the admiral to leave the capital, but only the latter obeyed.

On 11 March, after forty-six days in Toulouse, the royal caravan took to the road again. Travelling through Montauban and Agen, it came to Bordeaux. On 12 April, Charles IX held his *lit de justice* in the parlement and the chancellor used the occasion to reprimand the judges. 'All this disorder stems from the contempt in which you hold the king and his ordinances which you neither fear nor obey except at your own pleasure.' The parlement, he explained, had no right to interpret the law; only the king could do so; its only right was to remonstrate. The king, L'Hôpital continued, was the supreme lawgiver; the parlement was merely a regional court, which could not acquire national status. Its members, concerned as they were with purely local matters, were wrong to think of themselves as wiser than the king, the queen and the king's council who had to look after the entire kingdom. The chancellor reaffirmed the king's determination to impose the edict of pacification.

The same treatment was meted out to all the parlements visited on the progress. Only Grenoble and Rennes escaped. An epidemic of plague kept the king away from Grenoble, and in August 1565 he was prevented from going to Rennes by 'great seditions' in towns along the Loire valley. Even before he arrived in a *ville de parlement*, contacts were established between the parlement and royal ministers. At Bordeaux, the constable called on the parlement eleven days before the king's entry, and in the following weeks the chancellor, royal councillors and masters of requests attended the court's sessions. On 18 May, a fortnight after the king had left Bordeaux, the chancellor returned to the parlement and carefully examined its registers in order to assess the conduct of its members. However, the crown was not always critical of the provincial parlements. While insisting on their obedience, it sometimes helped to strengthen their authority. For example, at Bordeaux the king silenced a campaign of denigration against the First President, Lagebaston, waged by extreme Catholics in Guyenne. The crown also supported the provincial parlements against the pretensions of the Parlement of Paris.

The court remained in Bordeaux for twenty-three days, leaving on 3 May for Bayonne, where Catherine hoped to meet her daughter Elisabeth, now queen of Spain. At Mont-de-Marsan it waited two weeks for confirmation that Elisabeth was on her way. On 31 May, Catherine went to Bayonne in disguise to oversee preparations for her daughter's reception. Charles followed on 3 June; six days later, Henri duc d'Orléans left to meet his sister in Spain and escort her back to France.

The Franco-Spanish meeting in Bayonne, between 15 June and 2 July 1565, was the diplomatic climax of the progress. Catherine hoped to strengthen her son's monarchy by forging closer links with Spain. For months she had urged Philip II to meet her and, after many delays and at the urging of the prince of Eboli, he had reluctantly agreed. But as preparations got under way, a ministerial reshuffle took place in Spain: Eboli lost power to the duke of Alba. A veteran of the Habsburg–Valois struggle, he was hostile to France and even more to the Huguenots, who supported Philip's own heretics in the Low Countries. Alba's influence effectively destroyed any prospect of a rapprochement with France. Philip eventually decided not to attend the meeting himself, but allowed his wife to go with an escort led by Alba. The duke was instructed to persuade Catherine to ban all Protestant worship in France, to expel all pastors within a month on pain of death, to publish the Tridentine decrees, and to oblige royal servants to swear a Catholic profession of faith. Catherine, for her part, was mainly interested in arranging profitable marriages for her children. In particular, she wanted Marguerite to marry Philip's son Don Carlos, and the duc d'Orléans to marry Juana, Philip's sister. In both cases she hoped that Philip would give part of his dominions as dowries.

Although the Bayonne interview had been prepared with meticulous care as to protocol, the political and religious aims of the two sides were so contradictory that no progress was possible. Alba replied to Catherine's proposals by lecturing her on the evils of tolerance and by suggesting that she should put her house in order. To Charles IX he spoke of war and hunting, and whenever possible he encouraged the more fanatical Catholics, notably Blaise de Monluc. On two points, however, he was adamant: the present alliance required no new marriages and the Huguenots should not be invited to a national council. Catherine's only satisfaction was to see her daughter again; otherwise the meeting turned out to be a pointless charade. Ironically, however, it seriously alarmed Europe's Protestants, who believed that it portended a crusade against them. When the St Bartholomew's day massacre occurred seven years later, they convinced themselves, contrary to all reason, that it had been planned in Bayonne.

The progress offered the king a chance to make contact with the provincial nobility. Wherever the court stopped, nobles came forward to meet him. At Troyes, for example, he was greeted by the nobility of Champagne and Brie. At Niort, the sieur de Soubise, the Protestant defender of Lyon in 1562–3, came to see him with 'a very fine band, including many of the most important nobles of Poitou'. From the beginning, the king summoned nobles to meet him in the chief town of each *gouvernement*, but he did not want them to be too numerous. When he learned that a very large number were waiting for him in Toulouse, he ordered their dispersal. In return for gifts of offices and favours, Charles hoped to win the nobles' loyalty. On four occasions during the progress, he and his mother acted as godparents to a noble infant. One was Monluc's daughter,

Charlotte-Catherine. Charles was also willing to admit important nobles to his council, but new admissions had to be suspended in June 1564 as the council was becoming too large. Even more important were admissions to the Order of St Michael: nine knights were created at Valence in August 1564 and at least 31 at Toulouse in February 1565, but the crown had to be careful not to devalue the order. In April 1565, Charles suspended creations until the number of knights had been reduced to fifty. Membership of the order remained a rare honour. The knights enjoyed direct access to the monarch and often attended meetings of his council. On 18 May 1565 the king, fearing new 'associations', asked all the princes, governors, knights of the order, seigneurs and captains to swear to obey his ordinances. The oath was sent to absentees for their signature. In October 1563 a similar oath had been demanded of all municipal councillors and public administrators. Thus did the progress aim to rebuild the unity of the kingdom on a network of *fidélités*.

From Bayonne, the French court travelled through Angoumois and Saintonge to Nantes, where Charles dined with André Ruiz, a wealthy merchant who, along with his son, lent money to the crown over a long period. Then, after stopping at Châteaubriant, the court reached Angers in November 1565 and sailed up the Loire to Blois. Then it crossed Berry and came to Moulins, former capital of the dukes of Bourbon, where it spent three months (December 1565–March 1566). The government had planned to cap its programme of administrative and judicial reform with a great ordinance and, to this end, Catherine had called an Assembly of Notables which opened on 24 January 1566. It comprised princes of the blood, royal councillors, great officers of state, and the First Presidents of six parlements. For the first time since 1564 the Guises and the Châtillons met face to face, and the queen mother worked hard to bring them together. On 29 January the king formally acquitted Admiral Coligny of responsibility for the assassination of the duc de Guise, and Catherine persuaded the Cardinal of Lorraine and the admiral to embrace. The constable also persuaded his son François to make his peace with Lorraine.

In his opening address to the notables, the chancellor excused himself for speaking bluntly. He drew a clear distinction between law-making and the administration of justice. The king, he said, could not allow those, who had merely the right of publishing laws, to interpret them. This power belonged only to the law-maker, namely the prince. L'Hôpital once again pointed to judicial corruption as the underlying cause of the nation's troubles. He denounced the proliferation of laws, overlapping jurisdictions, the multitude of venal offices and unproductive litigation. He spoke of earlier times when laws had been few and simple, and foreigners had chosen to plead their suits in France. Since the reign of Charles VII, L'Hôpital declared, private greed and ambition had taken over the judiciary. Yet the king's justice was not there to be bought and sold. Appeals and evocations ought to be limited. There should be fewer presidial courts, and cases should be judged by ambulatory courts rather than static ones far from where the cases had arisen. Municipal authorities, L'Hôpital also declared, were corrupt; their powers should be given to royal officers.

Most of the points made in the chancellor's speech were echoed in the Ordinance of Moulins (February 1566), one of the major legislative texts of the French monarchy. Its eighty-six articles covered many aspects of government: justice, law and order, administration, hospitals, ecclesiastical benefices, trade guilds and confraternities. Its overriding purpose was to strengthen and extend royal authority. Thus it forbade parlements to remonstrate more than once after the king had ordered a new law to be registered. Towns possessing criminal jurisdiction were allowed to keep it, but their civil jurisdiction was transferred to royal judges. Governors, who had taken advantage of the recent troubles to enlarge their powers, were cut down to size: they were forbidden to issue letters of pardon, to authorize markets and fairs, to raise taxes on their own authority, to evoke lawsuits from the ordinary courts or to meddle in judicial matters. The ordinance abolished superfluous presidial courts, revised court procedures, and limited or defined appeals. In the financial administration, the number of *généralités* was cut down from seventeen to seven, alienated domain was to be redeemed and the number of duplicate office-holders under the system of *alternatif* was to be reduced. None of the cuts in the judicial administration was to apply until an office-holder died, when his salary was to be distributed to his colleagues. The ordinance banned gratuities, nepotism and pluralism. It also provided for a more effective examination of candidates' qualifications for office. Although the ordinance remained a dead letter, it served as a launching pad for future attempts to reform the government of the kingdom.

At the winter ended, the court left Moulins for the Auvergne. It stopped on 31 March at the Mont-Dore, then returned north by way of Clermont, La Charité, Auxerre and Sens. On 1 May 1566, Catherine and the king were back in Paris. Peace seemed to have returned to the kingdom. The end of fratricidal conflict had been symbolized at Aix on 21 October 1564 when a pine tree from which many Huguenots had been hanged was cut down by the king's command. Letters written by Catherine during the progress are full of optimism. In March 1565 she wrote: 'All things are as peaceful here as we may hope; the further we go, the more is obedience established, and the damage time had brought in the form of disorder and confusion to the minds of many people is purged and cleansed so I hope that with God's help all things will revert to their original state.' In August 1565 she rejoiced to see Huguenots and papists dancing together. That autumn she wrote: 'How much I would like to see this kingdom revert to the state it was in when the mere sight of a white wand was enough for the whole kingdom to obey the king ... The king, *Monsieur* my son, has the will to restore it to that state and I hope, if God allows him to live, that he will succeed.'

Admiral Coligny and Florida

On 6 January 1566 the Spanish ambassador informed Philip II: 'The son of Jean Ribaut and two other captains have gone directly to the admiral to complain of the defeat they have suffered in Florida.'

Ever since 1550, Philip had been repeatedly urged to occupy Florida, but he only decided to do so in December 1557 and took a further two years to organize an expedition. A large number of men, women and children, led by Tristán de Luna y Arellano, left Vera Cruz in December 1559 and settled at Pensacola, but they did not find it congenial and in July 1561 moved to Hispaniola. Florida thus remained in the same juridical position as Canada: both had been occupied, then evacuated. If past occupation was the test of present ownership, then Florida belonged to Spain as much as Canada did to France. If, on the other hand, Francis I had been correct in regarding only permanent occupation as the test, then both territories were still 'up for grabs'.

Frenchmen knew almost nothing about Florida. They may have remembered that Verrazzano believed that somewhere between Florida and Canada there existed an isthmus linking the Atlantic to the Pacific. They would also have heard stories about Cibola, a land somewhere in the southeast of North America where gold and precious stones were so plentiful as to be used in everyday objects. Such tales must have appealed to some of the more adventurous French noblemen, who felt at a loose end now that the Italian wars were over. Among them would have been Huguenots from the coastal provinces of Normandy and Brittany.

Admiral Coligny was drawn to the notion of a French colony overseas where Huguenots might worship freely, and Florida seemed a suitable place for it. Having been expelled from Brazil by the Portuguese, the French hoped to find an alternative area in the New World with a climate less harsh than that which Cartier's men had experienced in Canada and with prospects of enrichment. Florida offered such an alternative, for it was at present unoccupied by any European power. Of course, Philip II was unlikely to allow the French to establish themselves in a territory which commanded the strait through which Spanish treasure ships passed on their way back from Mexico to Spain. But the admiral welcomed a confrontation, which he believed might be the solution of France's domestic strife. A war with Spain might serve to unite all Frenchmen – Catholics and Huguenots – in a common struggle against the foreigner.

Coligny's colonial venture consisted of three expeditions between 1562 and 1565. The first was a reconnaissance, whose direction was entrusted to Jean Ribault, a Huguenot sea-captain from Dieppe. His second-in-command was Goulaine de Laudonnière, a Protestant nobleman from Brittany. Accompanied by 500 soldiers, mostly Huguenots, they set off from Le Havre in two ships on 18 February 1562 and made landfall on 29 April in Florida. They entered the mouth of the St Johns river, encountered some friendly Indians, and erected a stone column to mark Florida's annexation to France. Ribault then explored the coast, naming the successive rivers he encountered after French ones until he reached St Helena Sound. He set up a second column, then returned to the entry he called Port Royal and built a fort, called Charlesfort in honour of the king. Ribault then returned to France, leaving about thirty men behind under Captain La Pierria. They were led to expect reinforcements in the following year. Meanwhile, they were meant to explore the area near their camp.

On arrival in Normandy, Ribault was caught up in the first civil war. He helped his co-religionists to defend Dieppe against the king's army, then retired to England where, in May 1563, he published *The Whole and True Discoverye of Terra Florida*, an English version of his report to Coligny. This aroused the interest of Queen Elizabeth and some of her courtiers. Thomas Stukely, a young adventurer, decided to assist the French in the hope of self-enrichment. He set out in July 1563 without Ribault, who was for a time imprisoned in the Tower of London. But Stukely never got to Florida: he preferred instead to plunder ships of any nation as they approached the English Channel.

Meanwhile, in Florida, Ribault's companions waited in vain for reinforcements. They alienated the Indians on whom they depended for supplies and, as they became hungry, turned mutinous and murdered their captain. They built a small ship and set off for France, but ran out of food and began eating each other. The survivors were rescued by an English privateer and taken to France where they reported the failure of the first French outpost in Florida. In May 1564, Philip II sent Rojas, governor of Cuba, to wipe out the French colony. He found one of the French columns and the house at Charlesfort and, after destroying both, returned to Havana.

Yet Coligny remained hopeful of planting a French colony in Florida. After the Peace of Amboise, in March 1563, he sent another expedition under Laudonnière, consisting of three ships and three hundred men. It reached Florida on 25 June 1564 and set up a fort called La Caroline (again in honour of the king). Among the settlers was a painter, Jacques le Moyne de Morgues, who made a visual record of the new land for home consumption. But the settlers still refused to grow their own food and allowed themselves to be drawn into tribal warfare among the Indians. They also started squabbling over religion. Those who were committed Huguenots deplored the absence of any minister who might cater for their spiritual needs. They gathered to sing psalms and read Scripture. The others were more interested in looking for gold. Discipline broke down and Laudonnière was imprisoned for a time. After his release he had four mutineers executed. In June 1565 the settlers decided to return to France if relief did not arrive soon. By early August they had a ship of 80 tons and two pinnaces of 15 tons each and an ample supply of grain, but shortly before they were due to leave Sir John Hawkins arrived with four ships. He offered to take them home, but they refused. Laudonnière did, however, buy a ship from Hawkins, who also left him some supplies before departing.

On 28 August, Ribault reappeared at the head of a third expedition. This time he was accompanied not only by soldiers, but by artisans and peasants with their wives and children. Laudonnière stood down, leaving Ribault to command the colony. Meanwhile, Philip II appointed Pedro Menéndez de Aviles to lead an expedition against the French. Menéndez knew the coast of Florida well and had an implacable hatred of heretics. He left Spain with ten ships and 2600 men. They reached Florida on 28 August, as Ribault was arriving further north, and founded a settlement at San Augustin. On 20 September, after marching overnight through swamps, Menéndez took La Caroline by surprise. He spared the lives of the women and children and of six musicians, but slaughtered 132 men. Laudonnière, however, managed to escape and returned to France, where he was coolly received at court in March 1566. Menéndez, meanwhile, destroyed every trace of heresy at La Caroline. He thought he had accomplished his mission when he was informed that a number of Frenchmen, including Ribault, had fled and been shipwrecked along the coast of Florida. These men were now rounded up. They offered Menéndez a ransom, but he demanded their unconditional surrender. He dropped a hint that he might be merciful, but had them all butchered, except for a handful of Catholics. 'I had Juan Ribao and all the rest put to the sword,' he wrote to Philip II on 15 October, 'considering it to be necessary to the service of God and of Your Majesty.' It was the end of Coligny's attempts to colonize Florida.

21

The Second and Third Civil Wars, 1566–70

In May 1566, Catherine de' Medici believed that peace had been restored in France. She dismissed the duke of Alba's pessimistic forecasts as wishful thinking. 'I truly believe', she wrote, 'that some people are very unhappy to see so much pacification.' But the religious troubles could not be contained within national frontiers. Calvinism had become an international force: it had reached other parts of Europe, particularly the Netherlands where its preachers were attracting huge and growing popular audiences. A fall in trade caused by a war in the Baltic, and an unusually harsh winter, had produced much suffering and unrest in the textile towns of the southern provinces. Politically, too, the situation in the Netherlands was fraught. Since Philip II's departure in 1559, the government had been in the hands of his half-sister, Margaret of Parma, who had to cope with a strong aristocratic opposition. As yet, however, it was not essentially religious: its main concern was to defend local and noble privileges against the authoritarianism of the Spanish monarchy. It included Catholics and Calvinists and was, therefore, different from the opposition in France which was essentially Calvinist. Like Catherine, Margaret tried to temporize, but the more she conceded, the more the opposition demanded. Meanwhile, in Spain, Alba's ascendancy caused Philip to pursue a hard-line policy towards heresy. As the 'iconoclastic fury' swept across the southern Netherlands in the summer of 1566, he decided to send the duke of Alba with an army to restore order.

Philip planned to send his forces by way of Provence, Dauphiné and Burgundy. The prospect horrified Catherine, who believed that it would set France alight once more. Eventually the Spanish army followed a different route beyond France's eastern border. Even so, Catherine took no chances: she strengthened the French garrisons in Piedmont, Picardy and the three bishoprics of Metz, Toul and Verdun. After assembling an army in Milan,

Alba began to march north in June 1567: he crossed the Mont-Cenis, then advanced through Franche-Comté, Lorraine and Luxemburg. Many people thought he would attack Geneva, but, in fact, he only skirted its walls without firing a shot. When Charles IX levied 6000 Swiss mercenaries to defend his kingdom, the Spanish ambassador told him that he had nothing to fear: Alba was going to Flanders simply to put down its rebellion. He arrived in Brussels on 22 August and soon afterwards set up the notorious Council of Troubles, also known as the 'Council of Blood', which began a regime of terror. It tried more than 12,000 people, of whom more than a thousand were executed.

The Second Civil War, 1567–8

The court of France heaved a sigh of relief when Alba reached Brussels. Catherine had no taste for war and, as a goodwill gesture, she had sent 6000 sacks of grain to the duke's army on its northward march. The Huguenots, on the other hand, were disappointed that a Franco-Spanish conflict had not occurred, for it would have given them a pretext to send military assistance to their co-religionists in Flanders. They were seriously alarmed by Alba's savage campaign of repression, and wondered whether it was the opening shot in a more general crusade against Protestantism, planned by Alba and Catherine during their meeting in Bayonne eight years earlier. Their suspicions were enhanced by Charles IX's retention of the 6000 Swiss mercenaries after the threat to his kingdom had been lifted. When Condé and Coligny asked for the Swiss to be sent home, the constable gruffly replied: 'What do you expect us to do with these well-paid Swiss except use them?'

It was in anticipation of a new campaign of persecution by the government that the Huguenot leaders met at the château of Valléry in the Yonne. They decided, according to La Noue, 'to try and expel M. the cardinal of Lorraine from the court, who many imagined to be continually pressing the king to ruin all those of the Religion'. In other words, they planned to repeat the Tumult of Amboise. By seizing the king's person, the plotters hoped not only to get rid of Lorraine, but also to give Charles IX a new council which Huguenot grandees would dominate. Once the decision had been taken, messengers were sent out to inform the Protestant communities, who were by now extremely well-organized. Soon small groups of armed Huguenots were making their way, as covertly as possible, to Rosay-en-Brie, the plotters' rendezvous.

The court was residing nearby at the château of Montceaux. At first Catherine and her ministers shrugged off rumours of troop movements in the neighbourhood, but a report that a Protestant army was marching on

Lagny was taken seriously. On 26 September the king and his mother fled to Meaux, the nearest fortified town, and called to their aid the Swiss troops stationed at Château-Thierry. But even Meaux was deemed unsafe, so early on 28 September the court left, strongly escorted by the Swiss. They were followed by Huguenot cavalry, who tried to close in several times but were deterred from attacking by the Swiss pikemen. Charles IX eventually reached Paris safely, albeit tired, famished and angry. The Huguenots, La Noue writes, 'aroused the indignation and hatred of the king against those who had forced him to retire to Paris fearfully and in haste, so that he never trusted them again'. The plot also changed Catherine's attitude. Abandoning her policy of moderation, she told the Spanish ambassador that she hoped soon to imitate Alba's 'holy decision' in France.

The 'surprise of Meaux' was part of a general uprising. While negotiating with the government, the Huguenots prepared to invest the capital. On the night of 1 October they burned a dozen or more windmills outside Paris. The inhabitants, fearing a full-scale attack and readily believing rumours that Protestant agents were preparing to set fire to the city, rushed to take up arms. Catholics broke into Protestant homes to find the arsonists. A few Protestants who had not fled were maltreated or killed. In many respects this was a dress rehearsal for the St Bartholomew's day massacre five years later. One of its key symbols appeared at this time. According to Pasquier, anyone who did not put a white cross on his hat was at risk of being killed.

Elsewhere in France the Protestants consolidated their position. They seized a number of towns, including Montereau, Nîmes and Orléans. At Nîmes on 30 September there was a terrible massacre, known as the *Michelade*. Catholic notables, monks and priests were herded into the courtyard of the bishop's palace and butchered in cold blood. The dead and the dying were tossed into wells. Altogether some eighty people died.

Catherine was horrified to see the kingdom reverting to the troubles which she had worked so hard to eradicate. Before resorting to force, she sent L'Hôpital, Vieilleville and Morvillier to Condé's headquarters at Saint-Denis to find out what the rebels wanted. The king offered them a full pardon if they would lay down their arms, but they wanted Charles to disband the Swiss, expel the Guises from court, allow unrestricted freedom of Protestant worship, reduce taxes, get rid of Italian financiers and call the Estates-General. Only the estates, claimed the rebels, had the authority to remedy the nation's ills 'for the French monarch had from the beginning been tempered by the authority of the nobility and of the communities of the provinces and great towns of the kingdom'.

Condé's demands were backed up by propaganda. In two manifestos he explained that he only wanted the king to call the Estates-General and 'to relieve his poor subjects by restoring all things to their original condition and splendour'. He proclaimed his desire for toleration, forbidding 'all those of his company to anger, provoke or molest anyone of any religion, touching either their goods or persons on pain of death, but to live in friendship and to treat each other gently in accordance with the king's edicts'. Some Huguenots were dismayed by the undenominational character of Condé's demands; but, as he explained, he and the nobility had been obliged to assume the defence of *all* the people regardless of religion. If they were to be relieved of unfair impositions, all differences between them had to be laid aside. In other words, Condé saw the 'duty of revolt' as indivisible. All the nobility and the princes of the blood shared the obligation of defending the public interest.

The prince's terms were unacceptable. Though Catherine continued to negotiate with the rebels for a little while longer, she prepared to use force. She sought the help of Philip II, the duke of Savoy and duke Cosimo of Florence. While the duc de Nevers raised several companies of light cavalry in Piedmont, Catherine recruited more Swiss troops. She also looked everywhere for funds. She stopped the repayment of a large debt to the duke of Ferrara and obtained the pope's permission to raise cash from the sale of church goods or from the levy of a half-annate on the kingdom. Pius V sent her 25,000 *écus* and offered her 6000 soldiers.

On 7 October, Charles IX replied to the demands of the Huguenot leaders in the time-honoured fashion. He sent out a herald, preceded by a trumpeter, to their headquarters at Saint-Denis and summoned them by name to appear before him unarmed or be charged with rebellion. Thinking that they had perhaps overstepped their rights, the Huguenot leaders now asked merely for the Edict of Amboise to be restored permanently. But Montmorency told them that it had never been intended as more than provisional and that the king was entitled to do as he liked with his edicts. The negotiations ended there. The constable was now extremely hostile towards the Huguenots. Signifying approval of Alba's repression, he suggested that Philip II and Charles IX should make common cause against their respective rebels. Any French ones who fell into his hands, he said, would have their heads struck off.

The battle of Saint-Denis, 10 November 1567

Despite Catholic forebodings, the Protestants did not try to enter Paris. The firearms, rocks and chains which the Parisians had prepared were not needed. But they were soon threatened with famine. Having cut off entrances to the capital, the Huguenots planned to starve it into submission. Paris had not yet recovered from the inter-war scarcity, and the inhabitants became increasingly angry as the negotiations dragged on through October and their food supplies dwindled. Much of their anger was directed at

Marshal Montmorency and his father the constable, who had charge of the city's defence. They were accused of treachery when the garrison of Charenton, a point through which much of the city's grain supply flowed, capitulated to the Huguenots. According to de Thou, if the king had not been in the capital there would have been a general rising. The threat of such an upheaval forced the constable to act. His troops made several sorties which allowed Paris to be provisioned.

Presuming too much on the procrastination of the aged constable (he was 74 years old), Condé detached d'Andelot with horse and foot to the left bank of the Seine and another force under Montgomery to capture Pontoise. Learning of this, the constable marched out of Paris on 10 November and advanced on Saint-Denis. Condé managed to get his troops into battle array, but could not recall d'Andelot in time, much less Montgomery. The prince, however, made up in self-confidence what he lacked in men. As the enemy approached, he took up a prepared position. His plan was to let the enemy come on to his chosen ground, then to charge as they came under fire from his arquebusiers. The royalists took a very long time to emerge from the capital's northern gates and form up outside its walls, and it was afternoon when the two armies collided. As the royalist horse tried to outflank the squadrons of Coligny and Genlis, they were thrown into disorder by volleys from marksmen hidden in trenches. Coligny and Genlis charged, driving the assailants back against their infantry. Montpensier, on the royalist right, held firm, but the Paris militia retreated towards Montmartre. Condé then successfully charged the constable's *gendarmes*. Montmorency broke the jaw of a Scotsman who had called on him to surrender, but at the same instant a pistol shot shattered his spine. Marshal Montmorency carried his father to the rear. A furious cavalry mêlée followed in which neither side had much advantage, but Condé was finally compelled to sound the retreat. As dusk fell, the Huguenots rallied in front of Saint-Denis, while the royalists assembled on the battlefield. They had won a technical victory, but had lost their commander-in-chief.

The constable was still alive when he was taken to Paris, but the famous surgeon Ambroise Paré could do nothing to save him. On 11 November, Charles IX and his mother paid Montmorency a last visit. He died next day, and, although Catherine did not grieve overmuch, she did arrange for him to be given an almost royal funeral. His embalmed body lay in state for several days at the Hôtel de Montmorency, as masses were said for his soul. Nearby, on a bed of honour, lay his effigy. After more religious services, his heart was taken to the convent of the Celestins for burial near that of his old master, Henry II. An enormous procession accompanied the constable's body to Notre-Dame on 25 November, when a funeral oration was preached on the text: 'I have fought the good fight'. From Notre-Dame it was taken to the church of St Martin at Montmorency for burial. On the way, it was deposited for a time at the foot of Henry II's tomb at Saint-Denis. The constable's death generated a flood of versification in praise of his eight decades of life, his eight battles and his eight wounds. His magnificent mausoleum, designed by Jean Bullant and bearing an inscription by Ronsard, was destroyed in the French Revolution. The bronze *priants* are lost, but the *gisants* in white marble of the constable, in full armour, and his wife are now in the Louvre.

In the Protestant Midi, the battle of Saint-Denis was celebrated as a victory. Thanksgiving services were held and a public holiday declared. A popular song treated the constable's death as a sign of God's backing for the Protestant cause; yet his death played into the hands of Catholic extremists. For although he had always been a staunch Catholic, he had helped to counter the influence of the Guises who now came into their own. As Henri, the third duke, was only eighteen, it was his uncle, the Cardinal of Lorraine, who assumed the headship of the family. He set about ingratiating himself with the queen mother and her favourite son, Henri duc d'Anjou. Lorraine soon became all-powerful: 'He alone', reported Norris, the English ambassador, 'does all in everything.'

The constable's replacement as commander-in-chief was made difficult by the jealous rivalries existing among the court nobility. To avoid causing offence to anyone, Catherine left the constableship vacant and appointed Anjou as lieutenant-general of the kingdom. But as he was still too young and inexperienced, she gave him a general staff representing the different factions. The Guises were represented by the duc de Nemours, a prince of the house of Savoy who had recently married Anne d'Este, widow of the second duc de Guise. As he was renowned for his valour and likely to enhance the popularity of the Guises, Catherine tried to counterbalance his influence by appointing as another of Anjou's helpers the duc de Montpensier, a Catholic Bourbon. Finally, as a sop to the moderates and to the Montmorencys, she made Artus de Cossé a marshal of France.

The Peace of Longjumeau, 28 March 1568

Condé was now in a difficult situation. Reinforcements which he was expecting from the south had not turned up, and he obviously could not besiege Paris with only 6000 men, especially as Spanish troops were on their way from the Netherlands to assist the king. The prince accordingly decided to move east to join the German reiters which John Casimir, the Count Palatine, had raised for him. On 4 November he decamped and, after picking up levies from Poitou and Orléans at Montereau, moved slowly across Champagne and Lorraine. Nemours wanted to pursue the rebels and crush them before they could join up with the Germans, but he was obstructed by Cossé. Condé was thus able to link up with the German reiters, some 6000 strong, on 16 January 1568. With this increased strength he turned east and laid siege to Chartres, before whose walls he was joined by a large body of Gascons and other Huguenots from the south.

Catherine wanted to bring the war to an end, but public opinion in Paris opposed any settlement. According to Norris, the Parisian magistrates offered her large bribes to continue fighting. He reported in January that her negotiations had to be kept secret for fear of offending the Parisian bourgeois, who had contributed 600,000 francs to the war effort. They wanted to eliminate the Huguenots once and for all. A pamphlet published in February said that it was morally and tactically wrong to treat with 'seditious rebels' who aimed at the 'entire subversion and ruin of the state'. It described rebellion as a cancer which needed to be cut out, and warned that a negotiated peace would result in the king being despised and exposed to the threat of more rebellions.

Both sides, however, were exhausted financially. 'Only the bourgeoisie and the *gens de longue robe* still have money', wrote the Venetian ambassador. 'It is difficult for the King to obtain money without force. In addition to these troubles with his subjects, the King has lost all his credit with foreign merchants and cannot raise an *écu* outside his kingdom without giving collateral.' The crown was unable throughout the civil wars to raise enough money to pay its army beyond about two months. In the 1560s and 1570s the army's peacetime cost was 4.8 million *livres*, that is to say about 40 per cent of the crown's gross annual revenue of between 10 and 14 million *livres*. But the crown also had to settle debts left over from earlier wars, which in 1560 amounted to 40 million *livres*, so that even in peacetime it could not live within its means. In wartime, the royal budget came under additional pressure as the army was much enlarged. In January 1568 its total cost rose above 1.3 million *livres* per month. The annual cost of around 18 million *livres* far exceeded the king's normal income. In wartime, this tended to fall sharply as the collection of taxes became more difficult. By resorting to various expedients, such as loans bearing a heavy rate of interest, the crown managed to pay most of its army for the first three or four months of the second civil war. However, by February 1568 it faced bankruptcy. Condé too was bankrupt: his troops were unpaid and on the verge of mutiny. He added conditions to his earlier demands. He wanted peace terms to be confirmed by all the parlements and certain towns – he named Boulogne and Calais – to be given to the Protestants as guarantees of the government's good faith. The royal negotiators rejected these demands as impugning the king's honour. Charles also refused to make the edict of 1563 perpetual and protested at the political and military organization of the Huguenots 'insomuch as his liberty remaining, the King shall never be assured in his realm'. In the end, the Huguenots accepted the Peace of Longjumeau (28 March) whereby the Edict of Amboise was confirmed without any of the subsequent restrictions, and Charles agreed to pay the reiters. They were to leave the kingdom at once, while he undertook to disband his own troops later. Condé was criticized by many Huguenots for placing so much trust in the king's word.

The peace was never seriously observed by either side. Its significance has not always been understood by historians. It has been called 'the little peace' and interpreted as a genuine peace move by the crown, whereas it was almost certainly a trap designed to bring about the destruction of the Huguenot leadership. La Noue, in his memoirs, calls it 'this wicked little peace', describing it as the worst for the Huguenots of all the peace treaties signed during the wars. He shows that it was forced on Condé and Coligny by their followers. Their army was melting away even during the siege of Chartres as the unpaid infantry deserted and nobles drifted home in order to protect their families from attacks by their Catholic neighbours. Finding themselves virtually defenceless, the Huguenot leaders settled for peace and disbanded most of their forces. They believed that the crown would do likewise, but this did not happen: the Catholics remained under arms. This marked a significant departure from past practice. Hitherto, the crown had normally reduced its army after a peace treaty, thereby placing itself at a disadvantage when the peace collapsed. Mobilizing its forces was a long and complicated process during which the Huguenots could seize the initiative. This did not happen after Longjumeau, when it seems that a conscious decision was taken by the crown not to demobilize in spite of the parlous state of its finances. Coligny was less favorably inclined than Condé towards the peace. He suspected, correctly as events were to show, that it would be used by the crown to avenge the *Surprise de Meaux*.

The Catholics were soon preparing for a new round of hostilities. Tavannes, the governor of Burgundy, formed a league called the Confraternity of the Holy Ghost (*Confrérie du Saint Esprit*) in which churchmen, nobles and wealthy bourgeois pledged themselves to defend the Catholic church in the service of the king. 'Without using coercion [Tavannes] gave orders for the enrolment of men-at-arms and the collection of money, created warders, spies and messengers, in imitation of the Huguenots, in order to discover their machinations. The oath subscribed to justified this design. Each parish in Dijon paid its men for three months, and each town contributed 200 horse and 250 footmen.' In April 1568 the Brotherhood of the Catholics of Chalon-sur-Saône was formed. In May a similar association was created in Berry and confirmed at Bourges by the archbishop. A month later a league for the defence of the Catholic church and the maintenance of royal authority in the house of Valois 'so long as it shall govern in the Catholic and Apostolic religion' appeared in Champagne under the auspices of the duc de Guise. The nobility, bishop and clergy of Troyes took an oath to this league on 25 June. One month later, Beauvaisis formed a league to the same end, then Maine and Anjou. In Toulouse an earlier league was revived in September 1568 under the patronage of the Cardinal of Armagnac and led by a priest who attacked the Protestants in his sermons with a crusader's zeal. The new league was, in fact, called The Crusade and its members wore a white cross. Small towns followed the example set by large ones: at Anduze the churches formed a Catholic union and the movement spread into Lower Navarre. A league formed at Saint Palais to oust Calvinist preachers was speedily suppressed by Jeanne d'Albret.

In France generally the peace was followed by many serious incidents. In Paris, Catholic preachers warned of dire consequences if the king did not cease to support false prophets. The Huguenots, they said, would destroy France if they were not exterminated first. Protestant houses were sacked and Huguenots who dared to return to the city were assaulted. On 7 August the English ambassador wrote: 'More have been murdered since the publishing of the peace than were all these last troubles.' In Rouen a mob forced its way into the parlement on the day the peace was registered, causing the councillors to flee; it then turned on Huguenots, killing many and destroying their property. In Toulouse the parlement tried and executed the bearer of the king's instructions to publish the edict, disregarding a royal safe-conduct. At Auxerre the royal garrison seized 50,000 écus which Coligny had sent to the reiters and a nobleman despatched to claim the money was murdered by command of the town governor. Coligny was understandably furious. Writing to Catherine, he promised to do everything in his power to stop the strife, but warned: 'If we are forced to defend the freedom of our consciences, our honour, lives and goods, we shall not be so easily defeated as the cardinal of Lorraine boasts each day.'

Lorraine, it seems, was the moving spirit behind a number of anti-Huguenot conspiracies. On 29 March, six days after the peace, he and other leaders of the Guise faction, meeting in secret at the Louvre, agreed to observe the peace only until the Huguenots had been disarmed and then to seize Orléans, La Rochelle and other Huguenot strongholds. By some means, Cardinal Châtillon learned of the plot and informed his cousin Marshal Montmorency. At the same time it was leaked to Condé from another source. When Charles IX was asked for an explanation, he denied all knowledge of the matter and accused Lorraine of acting treasonably. He wrote to Condé, promising 'good and sincere' observance of the peace treaty.

The Edict of Longjumeau was unpopular among both Protestants and Catholics. In the Midi people could not understand why Condé had agreed to confirm the highly unpopular Edict of Amboise. Local chroniclers viewed the peace as a trap laid by the government for the Protestants. No one disarmed. The Protestants refused to hand over towns (Montauban, Sancerre, Albi, Millau and Castres) which they had occupied during the war.

La Rochelle, which had declared for Condé on 9 January 1568, admitted the governor, Guy Chabot de Jarnac, but not his military escort.

The Huguenots also continued to show concern for their co-religionists in the Netherlands. Here the situation was getting steadily worse, as Alba continued his regime of terror. William of Orange had escaped to Germany, where he prepared to free his countrymen. In April 1568 he published the first of a series of manifestos in which the religious quarrel was presented as essentially a pretext by Philip II to attack the people's rights. Disclaiming any disloyal intentions, William blamed Philip's evil councillors for his country's wrongs. While he assembled an army of volunteers and mercenaries, his brother Louis of Nassau launched a preliminary invasion of the Netherlands but, having been poorly prepared, it soon came to grief. An invading force was to be provided by French Huguenots, but as soon as Catherine got wind of this she ordered Marshal Cossé to intercept them. The Huguenots were cut to pieces at Saint-Valéry, and their captain, Cocqueville, was captured and executed. Catherine ordered other captured Frenchmen to be executed or sent to the galleys. On 5 June 1568, Alba retaliated for the invasion by having sixty people executed in Brussels, including Egmont and Hoornes, two of the highest nobles in the land. Louis of Nassau then suffered a crushing defeat at Jemmingen. Early in September, William of Orange invaded the Netherlands near Liège only to be defeated by Alba on 19 October, whereupon he retired into France 'tired and worn out and half dead with hunger' with the remnants of his army. Catherine offered him free passage into Germany and, ignoring protests from Spain, sent him money and supplies. In January 1569, William returned to Germany after disbanding his troops.

The Third Civil War, 1568–9

Following the Peace of Longjumeau, Condé and Coligny retired to Noyers and Tanlay respectively. While the government claimed to be committed to the peace, Catherine, it seems, plotted to capture the Huguenot leaders. She sent a verbal message to Tavannes, the governor of Burgundy, to besiege Noyers and capture Condé. Though a Catholic and a client of the Guises, Tavannes was wily enough to insist on written instructions clearing him of all personal responsibility, for laying hands on a prince of the blood was no trifling matter. He summoned troops from the Loire valley and, taking his time, prepared to encircle Noyers; but, having fought with Condé in Italy, he arranged for him to be warned. He sent scouts into the vicinity of Noyers on whom were found cryptic messages, such as 'the stag is at bay', 'the hunt is being prepared' or simply 'hurry'.

The two Protestant commanders heeded the warning. The deaths of

Egmont and Hoornes seemed to foreshadow the fate being prepared for them by the French government. Soon afterwards they made a secret alliance with William of Orange against 'the evil councillors who have caught the ears' of their respective kings and promised that whoever got rid of tyranny first would help the other to do so. That is how William and Louis of Nassau came to take part in the third of France's civil wars. However, the reciprocal obligation assumed by the Huguenot leaders to assist the Dutch rebels had serious implications for Franco-Spanish relations. Protestant historians have blamed the government of Charles IX for the renewal of civil war, but he may be fairly said to have acted not only according to his right, but also to prevent the union of the Huguenot and Dutch causes. France was not yet ready to espouse an openly anti-Spanish policy.

Condé and Coligny escaped from Noyers on 23 August with their families and about 150 soldiers. After a hazardous journey lasting four weeks, they reached La Rochelle in mid-September. They were joined on the way by so many Huguenots with their chattels that Coligny compared their journey to the flight from Egypt of God's chosen people. As they crossed the Loire, they sang Marot's translation of Psalm 114. On 28 September the Huguenot leaders were joined at La Rochelle by Jeanne d'Albret and her son Henri, who had outwitted Monluc when he tried to prevent them leaving Nérac. In her *Mémoires*, Jeanne wrote: 'I delivered my son [to] M. his uncle, so that, under the tutelage of the latter's prudence and valour, he would learn the task to which God has called him, and in order that later, when his age and means permit, he will be able to use them, and his life, in the service of his God, of his King and of his blood.' The presence of the queen of Navarre and her son in La Rochelle revived the old feudal relationship between the Protestant Midi and the house of Albret. Monluc shrewdly noted that Jeanne was urging Condé to concentrate his military operations in the south. In his judgement, she was hoping to build up a large, independent principality for her son centred on Guyenne. Signs soon confirmed his opinion. Early in 1569, Condé and Henri de Navarre began issuing written commands under their joint signatures to towns under Protestant control, authorizing them to levy taxes from all the inhabitants, including Catholics, to help pay for the war. The Parlement of Toulouse vetoed such levies, describing them as robbery, but they were raised just the same.

La Rochelle was an excellent base whence the Huguenots could communicate by sea with their friends in England or the Netherlands. On the landward side the town was almost impregnable, and the Huguenots made it even more so by conquering towns and villages commanding its approaches. In the meantime the Protestant Midi rallied to the cause. A Huguenot army numbering 25,000 men under two captains, Mauvans and Jacques d'Acier, marched on Poitou from the south. A royal force under Montpensier tried to intercept them south of Poitiers. A minor battle was fought on 26 October in which Mouvans was killed, but d'Acier's army got through to La Rochelle.

Meanwhile, the crown threw down the gauntlet. On 25 September an edict proscribed the Reformed faith, banished its pastors and excluded Protestants from public offices and the universities. As far back as July the government had tried to secure papal permission to alienate church lands worth 200,000 *écus* per annum. The pope eventually agreed to the alienation of lands worth half this amount provided the proceeds were used to fight the Protestants. The debate over the new measures produced a serious clash in the king's council on 19 September between the Cardinal of Lorraine and L'Hôpital. The chancellor protested at the revocation of the Edict of January and refused to seal the ordinance giving effect to the papal bull in France. Lorraine accused L'Hôpital of hypocrisy; the chancellor retorted with a sarcastic reference to Guise administrative practices. Only the intervention of Marshal Montmorency prevented Lorraine from seizing L'Hôpital's beard. In his rage, the cardinal turned to Catherine and blamed the chancellor's policy of toleration for all the kingdom's woes. If L'Hôpital were held by the parlement, said the cardinal, his head would not remain on his shoulders for twenty-four hours. On 28 September, L'Hôpital was dismissed from office and replaced by Birague, a protégé of the Guises, who promptly sealed the anti-Protestant legislation.

The battle of Jarnac and the death of Condé, 13 March 1569

In the spring of 1569 the main royal and rebel armies faced each other along the River Charente. Condé and Coligny hoped to link up with another Huguenot army which had been levied in the south, but before they could do so, Tavannes, who was the effective commander of the royal army, crossed the river at Châteauneuf, taking the admiral by surprise. Condé, who commanded the 'battle' near Jarnac, hastened to the admiral's rescue. As was his wont, he charged impetuously and broke through the enemy ranks, but was attacked on his flank by royalist cavalry. The prince, who had a broken leg, surrendered, but one of Anjou's guards, called Montesquiou, shot him in the head. It is possible that Condé's murder was part of a comprehensive strategy by the government to wipe out the Huguenot leadership. Next to fall was d'Andelot, who died, possibly of poisoning, at Saintes on 7 May 1569. 'You see, my son', Catherine wrote to the king, 'how God helps us for he causes them to die without a blow being struck.' She did not baulk, it seems, at using assassination to destroy the Huguenot leadership. Evidence of her complicity in various attempts to poison Coligny and La Rochefoucauld is not easily discounted. When the Spanish ambassador advised her in April to sound the death knell for the admiral, d'Andelot and La Rochefoucauld, she replied that she had already done so: three days before she had offered 50,000 *écus* for the admiral's murder and 20,000 or 30,000 for that of the other two.

After the battle of Jarnac, Jeanne d'Albret presented the young prince de Condé and her own son, Henri de Navarre, to the Huguenot army. They were mere boys, aged fifteen and sixteen respectively, yet were acknowledged as the new leaders. Their presence in the army conferred a kind of legitimacy on the Protestant rebellion, for as princes of the blood they had a better right to govern than the king's advisers. The effective leader of the Huguenots, however, was Admiral Coligny, and this was why Catherine was so keen to see him eliminated. On 12 July the parlement declared the office of admiral vacant and early in August it confiscated all the property of the Huguenot leaders, depriving them at the same time of their offices. In September, Coligny was sentenced to death by the parlement, a price of 50,000 *écus* being placed on his head. On 9 October one of his chief captains, called Mouy, was murdered by Louviers de Maurevert, a former servant of the Guises. He had planned to kill the admiral, and was to try again in August 1572, two days before the massacre of St Bartholomew's day.

The tactical impact of the battle of Jarnac was negligible. The royalists tried to capture Cognac, then Angoulême, but failed. Lacking heavy artillery, they had to be content with minor conquests (Mucidan, Aubeterre, Bergerac). Coligny meanwhile reorganized his forces, which had only been marginally reduced at Jarnac as the infantry had not been used. He rested his hopes on the German troops – 6000 reiters and nearly as many landsknechts – levied by the Elector Palatine and commanded by Wolfgang duke of Zweibrücken. Nearly 250 miles separated this army from Coligny and the risk of interception by the royalists was high, but Wolfgang was an astute general. He eluded Nemours and Aumale, who were waiting for him on the Meuse, by marching through Montbéliard and Franche-Comté. After sacking Beaune, Wolfgang crossed the Loire at La Charité (20 May), but died on 11 June shortly before his army linked up with the admiral's at Saint Yriex.

The royalist army was larger than its rival, but its morale was low. The troops felt that their victory at Jarnac had been wasted and that the Germans should not have been allowed to slip past them. War-weary nobles were deserting in large numbers. Five weeks after Coligny's junction with the Germans, he defeated a small royalist force near La Roche l'Abeille, capturing Strozzi, colonel-general of the infantry. But he took few prisoners and caused hundreds of peasants to be massacred. Aubigné admits that his fellow Protestants behaved 'like devils incarnate' during the third civil war. Following his success, Coligny wanted to take Saumur, but was persuaded to besiege Poitiers instead. This proved to be a big mistake, for the siege lasted from 24 July until 7 September. The king's army, in the meantime, received reinforcements sent by the pope, Florence and Spain. By late June it comprised about 8000 horse and 16,000 foot. The strength of the Huguenot army was roughly the same, though it probably had more infantry.

The battle of Moncontour, 3 October 1569

Coligny eventually took up a position near Moncontour, where he thought he could accept a defensive battle with advantage; but a flanking movement by Tavannes obliged him to fight on different ground. Battle was not joined for some time, however. The royalists had a slight numerical advantage over their rivals. Castelnau gives Anjou and Tavannes 7000 horse, 18,000 foot and 15 field-pieces; Tavannes credits the admiral with 7000 horse, 16,000 foot and 11 guns. Protestant sources acknowledge only 18,000 men on their side (6000 horse and 12,000 foot) and put the royalist cavalry up to 8000. Both armies had a surprisingly high proportion of foreign mercenaries: the royalists had 6000 Swiss infantry, 3000 or 4000 Italian infantry, and of cavalry 3000 reiters, 800 Italians and a few hundred Walloons. The Huguenots still had 4500 reiters left over from the 6000 originally brought by Zweibrücken and some 4000 landsknechts.

Among sixteenth-century battles, Moncontour is particularly difficult to follow, but its main features are reasonably certain. The two armies were divided, as at Dreux, into two corps – the vanguard and the 'battle' – not three as of old. The two halves were roughly of equal strength, and they fought not in a single line, but in several. In addition there was a reserve on the royalist side. The vanguard or right wing of the royalist army was led by Montpensier and the 'battle' by Anjou. On the Huguenot side, Coligny commanded the vanguard or left wing, and Louis of Nassau the 'battle'. Before the fighting began, however, the admiral ordered Nassau to send some of his reiters to strengthen the van. Foolishly, Nassau came over in person, leaving the 'battle' without a commander just as the royalists attacked.

The action was essentially a cavalry mêlée. Coligny was so badly wounded by a pistol shot that he had to retire. His command was taken over by Nassau. On the other side, Anjou was unhorsed and only saved by his personal guard. Matters were still undecided and the field was full of broken squadrons, rallying in disorder and making inconclusive charges, when Tavannes brought up the Swiss infantry and the cavalry reserve under Cossé and Biron. Nassau charged the Swiss, but failed to break them. The reiters executed their regular manoeuvre – the *caracole* – but were driven off by the cavalry reserve. At this point the Huguenots gave up the fight. Their cavalry left the field, abandoning the landsknechts. The Swiss, seeing their professional rivals isolated, fell upon them with ferocious glee and slaughtered them in cold blood. Many Germans allegedly fell on their knees, crying out, 'Bon Papiste, bon Papiste, moy!' but no quarter was given. About half the Huguenot infantry were massacred; the rest escaped. The royalists lost very few infantry, but more cavalry than the Huguenots.

The Peace of Saint-Germain, 8 August 1570

The victory filled Catherine de' Medici with joy. She was happy, she declared, that God had allowed her son to be the instrument of such a glorious deed. The real victor, however, was Tavannes. He wanted to pursue and annihilate the enemy, but was persuaded by Anjou's captains to embark on the piecemeal capture of strongholds around La Rochelle. Niort soon fell, but Saint-Jean-d'Angély held firm. By 2 December, when the garrison surrendered, winter had begun and the royal army started melting away. All that the royalists had gained from their victory at Moncontour was a large part of Poitou. La Rochelle, Angoulême and Cognac remained in enemy hands.

Having recovered from his wound, Coligny crossed the Charente, overran Guyenne and joined his lieutenant Montgomery, who had recently conquered Béarn. The admiral spent the winter in the south, practically unmolested and helped by disagreements among the local Catholic leaders. Damville, the governor of Languedoc, refused to support Monluc, who wanted to crush the admiral before he could be reinforced from Béarn. While the two men quarrelled, Coligny's army swept through the Toulousain, destroying the country homes of Catholic magistrates and bourgeois. In March 1570 he stood outside Carcassonne, but refrained from sacking the town; instead he plundered the countryside around Narbonne and penetrated Roussillon. After burning down villages around Montpellier, his troops spent some time in Nîmes, recuperating from their exertions.

On 16 April the admiral began a spectacular march across France. With 3000 cavalry and as many arquebusiers mounted on nags, he marched across the Vivarais and into Burgundy. On 18 June his men sacked the abbey of Cluny. At Arnay-le-Duc, near Autun, on 27 June he ran into a large army commanded by Marshal Cossé, but gave it the slip under cover of darkness. Finally, after picking up guns and reinforcements at Sancerre and La Charité-sur-Loire, Coligny marched on Paris in the hope of securing a speedy and advantageous peace.

Intermittent peace talks had taken place during the war, but the Huguenots wanted more than just freedom of conscience. They insisted on freedom to worship and required guarantees that a new peace would be firm. Concessions were, of course, opposed by the Cardinal of Lorraine and his international backers, Spain and the pope. By February 1570, however, nearly all the king's council wanted a settlement. By early May, Lorraine, whose influence was slipping, had come to regard a settlement as inescapable. His fall in July was probably sealed by the disgrace of his nephew the duc de Guise, who had dared to woo the king's sister Marguerite. By 11 August the cardinal had left the council.

Catherine had other reasons for wanting peace. She was annoyed with Philip II, who had hardly lifted a finger to help her and was now obstructing her matrimonial designs. His queen, Elisabeth de Valois, had died on 3 October 1568, and Catherine had hoped that he might marry her sister Marguerite, but Philip was seeking the hand of the emperor's elder daughter whom Catherine wanted for Charles IX. The queen mother's tit for tat was to make peace with the Huguenots on 8 August at Saint-Germain-en-Laye.

The Edict of Saint-Germain has been called 'a Calvinist charter'. That is an exaggeration: Protestantism was still banned at court and in Paris. But the edict marked a distinct advance on its predecessors, for Protestants were granted four security towns (*places de sûreté*) – La Rochelle, Montauban, La Charité and Cognac – for two years. They were allowed freedom of conscience throughout the kingdom and freedom of worship where it had taken place before the war: in two towns per *gouvernement* and in the homes of nobles with rights of high justice. Huguenots were also to be admitted to all universities, schools and hospitals; they were to have their own cemeteries, and were given certain judicial privileges to protect them from biased judgements by the parlements. All confiscated property and offices were to be handed back. The edict baffled many Catholics, who did not think that the Huguenots were in a sufficiently commanding position to exact such favourable terms. Monluc complained that they had gained 'by writings' what they had lost by fighting.

The St Bartholomew's Day Massacres, 1572

The Peace of Saint Germain and the fall of the Guises cleared the way for a reconciliation between the crown and the Huguenots. Two important marriages were planned to facilitate this: the first between the king's sister Marguerite de Valois and the young Huguenot leader Henri de Navarre, and the second between the king's brother Henri d'Anjou and Elizabeth I of England. But Catherine de' Medici's enthusiasm for these marriages was not shared by all the parties concerned. Among the Huguenots there was little support for the Navarre marriage: Jeanne d'Albret was not sure that it was in her son's best interests, while Admiral Coligny opposed it. He would have preferred a marriage between Navarre and Elizabeth of England, but she saw no advantage to herself in such an arrangement. As for the Anjou marriage, it was unexpectedly resisted by the duke himself: he thought he would be dishonoured by marrying Anne Boleyn's daughter, who was regarded as a bastard by the Catholic world.

In 1571, while Catherine worked to bring her matrimonial schemes to fruition, the idea of a French military intervention in the Netherlands on the side of the Dutch rebels was being strongly promoted in France. William of Orange, their leader, had left France to prepare an invasion of the Netherlands, but his brother, Louis of Nassau, and many Dutch exiles had stayed behind. They organized raids on Spanish shipping from their base at La Rochelle and, with Huguenot help, they prepared an attack on the Netherlands from the south which would coincide with an invasion by William from the east. Such an expedition, however, required the backing of the French government. King Charles IX had so far shown more interest in hunting than in affairs of state, but he had become jealous of the military reputation his brother Anjou had gained in the third civil war, and was attracted by the idea of meddling in the Netherlands while Philip II of Spain was tied down by a serious revolt in Andalusia. The negotiations that were taking place for an Anglo-French marriage opened up the possibility of English co-operation in a Dutch enterprise. On 19 July 1571, Charles IX attended two secret meetings, the first at the château of Lumigny and the second, soon afterwards, at Fontainebleau. Nassau attended the second meeting and possibly the first as well. The outcome was a plan to partition the Netherlands between France, England and the Empire. But English co-operation depended on the negotiations for an Anglo-French marriage being successful, and Anjou ensured their collapse by insisting on exercising his Catholic faith in England, a condition wholly unacceptable to Elizabeth and her ministers.

Coligny favoured a war against Spain in the Netherlands and it was mainly for this reason that he was persuaded to return to court in August 1571. He was warmly welcomed by the king at Blois on 12 September, admitted to his council and given 150,000 *livres* as well as a lucrative abbey. However, the admiral's standing at court was less secure than these favours would suggest. The king was trying to emancipate himself from his mother's tutelage, but her influence remained paramount. She distrusted Coligny and opposed his warlike designs on Spain. Yet she needed his support for the Valois–Navarre marriage, which she saw as the keystone of a reconciliation of the religious parties in France. At first Coligny opposed the match, fearing that it might lead to Henri de Navarre's abjuration; later he accepted it as the prerequisite to war with Spain. The king's weakness and Catherine's distrust were not Coligny's only problems. Most Frenchmen regarded him as a rebel and a heretic, and the Guises (with Spanish backing) looked for any chance to ruin him. In November it was reported that they were gathering funds and followers in Paris. The Huguenots countered this move by gathering round Coligny at Châtillon. France seemed on the brink of yet another civil war, but the threat was narrowly averted. In March 1572, Charles IX again cleared Coligny of any guilt for the murder of the duc de Guise, but the vendetta was not so easily suppressed. Only the admiral's blood could satisfy the Guises.

By 8 October the king had given his approval to an armed intervention by France in the Netherlands, but his mother got the decision rescinded. News of the Spanish victory over the Turks at Lepanto (7 October) confirmed her in her reluctance to go to war with Philip II. Even so, Nassau and the other Dutch exiles in France stepped up their preparations for an attack on the Netherlands. On 1 April 1572 the Dutch 'Sea Beggars' captured Brill and on 14 April, William of Orange declared war on Spain. Nassau pressed Charles IX to support the rebels, but he felt unable to go against the wishes of his mother and councillors, save for Coligny. So Nassau acted alone. Towards the end of May he and some Huguenot confederates captured the towns of Valenciennes and Mons. Coligny again pressed the king to enter the war, but on 7 June, Charles forbade his subjects to cross the Dutch border in support of Nassau. In mid-July he allowed a small army of Huguenots (300 to 400 horse and 3000 foot) to march to the relief of Mons. Although the king swore that the expedition had been mounted against his wishes and in defiance of his strict prohibition, no one was deceived, least of all the duke of Alba. He treated the Huguenot raid as an act of aggression and dismissed Charles's statements as mere hypocrisy. Unfortunately for Charles, the expedition proved a fiasco. On 17 July the French force was taken by surprise and crushed before it could reach Mons. Its captain, Genlis, was taken prisoner and on him was found a letter from Charles promising aid to the rebels. 'I have in my hands a letter from the king of France', wrote Alba to Philip II, 'which would astound you if you could see it . . . I have seen nothing like it in my whole life.'

The Genlis affair made it all the more necessary for Coligny to intervene in the Netherlands in support of the prince of Orange. He still enjoyed the king's favour and informed William that he would soon come to his aid. After a brief visit to Châtillon in late July, the admiral returned to Paris to promote his war plan, trusting in the king's continued favour and Huguenot support. He pointed to the dangers that France would face if Orange were defeated, and also to the restlessness of his followers. According to Tavannes, he said that he could not restrain them and that the choice facing Charles IX lay between war with Spain and civil war. But Coligny faced the resolute opposition of Catherine, who not only opposed war with Spain but resented the admiral's influence with her son. She feared that if Coligny got his way nothing would stop him gaining supreme power at her expense. The papal legate, Salviati, shared this view: France, he believed, would fall prey to the Huguenots if she went to war with Spain. On 9 and 10 August the king's council opted for peace, yet soon afterwards 3000 Huguenots assembled near Mons, and Alba asked for an explanation. Coligny also assembled an army of 12,000 arquebusiers and 2000 horsemen. Catherine viewed these developments with alarm and, in league with the Guises, may have decided to get rid of Coligny.

In the meantime, negotiations regarding the Valois–Navarre marriage moved towards a happy conclusion. On 2 March 1572, Jeanne d'Albret, who had so far resisted Catherine's invitation to visit the court, arrived at Blois. She despised the court's pleasure-loving ways and regretted her future daughter-in-law's refusal to become a Calvinist, yet the marriage contract was signed on 11 March. Jeanne, however, never saw the outcome, as she died in Paris on 9 June. Poison was inevitably suspected, but the cause of death was tubercular pleurisy. In spite of her death, preparations for the wedding continued, though time was lost waiting for a papal dispensation for a mixed marriage, which neither Pius V nor his successor Gregory XIII seemed willing to grant. The atmosphere in Paris became highly charged as Huguenot noblemen, carrying arms and wearing distinctively austere clothes, converged on the capital. The Guises also arrived with their large clientèle and took up residence at the Hôtel de Guise and in houses belonging to the clergy. At the same time fanatical preachers urged the Parisians to gain their salvation by slaughtering the heretics. Perhaps the most inflammatory was Simon Vigor, the *curé* of Saint-Paul in the Marais – a Parisian pastor once described him as 'a true bellows of Satan'. In all his Paris sermons (of which more than 140 have been published), Vigor underlined the threat posed by heresy not only to individual salvation but to the entire social order. God, he said, would punish those who allowed it to exist and would do so collectively as well as individually. He prophesied torrents of blood if the Valois–Navarre wedding took place 'for God will not suffer this execrable coupling'. Wild talk of this kind was in tune with a surge of popular discontent, which was in part provoked by a steep rise in the cost of food but more probably by the favourable terms conceded to the Huguenots in the peace of Saint-Germain. Having lost the third war, their leaders were strutting about Paris as if they had been the victors.

Paris and the Huguenots

The massacre of Saint Bartholomew's day has traditionally been seen as a unique event in the history of the Wars of Religion, and one for which the government of Charles IX has been blamed. Yet, as recent studies have underlined, it can only be explained satisfactorily as the culmination of a long series of popular disturbances in the French capital. Huguenots had been violently attacked by Catholics over many years.

A particularly dramatic incident occurred in January 1569, when Philippe and Richard Gastines were arrested on a charge of holding a Protestant service in their house in the rue Saint-Denis. Their arrest prompted a riot, in which fifty people were allegedly killed. 'The Huguenots were so hated', wrote Claude Haton, the priest-diarist of Provins, 'that if the king and the authorities had let them have their way, there would not have been one in the whole city who was not attacked.' In July the Gastines were hanged, their property confiscated and their house demolished. On the site a monument, a stone pyramid surmounted by a cross, was erected to symbolize the triumph of orthodoxy: it soon became a symbol of Parisian opposition to any kind of religious toleration. A clause of the edict of Saint-Germain required the demolition of all such monuments, but the Parisians would not allow the cross to be torn down. Eventually, it was removed under an armed guard to the Cemetery of the Innocents. Even so, there were disturbances. The *Golden Hammer*, a house on the Pont Notre-Dame whose owner had allegedly lobbied for the cross to be removed, was attacked by a mob. The city sent troops to restore order and several arrests were made, but the prisoners were set free by an angry crowd. Later the *Golden Hammer* came under renewed attack and a neighbouring Huguenot house, the *Pearl*, was sacked.

The anger generated by the affair of the cross of Gastines persisted into the new year. Although the city repaired the *Golden Hammer* and the *Pearl*, passers-by continued to deface them. The king pressed for justice to be done, but to little effect: some minor participants were punished, but the main culprits evaded arrest. The parlement, in its report to the king, blamed the rioting on poor people – labourers, women and children. Historians have also looked for *agents provocateurs*, perhaps Spain or the Guises. But as Barbara Diefendorf has shown, if such agents were involved, they merely 'took advantage of already present, long-festering hatreds and encouraged their expression'.

It seems that Charles IX failed to understand the mood of the capital. The removal of the cross of Gastines was only one grievance of the Parisians among several. Not all were religious; some were economic. The effects of war, bad harvests and high prices were causing much hardship. Yet, following the peace of Saint-Germain, the king demanded 600,000 *livres* from the Parisians with which to pay off the mercenaries who had come to the aid of the Huguenots. Parisians claimed that they could not afford to meet the royal demand; they also resented the reason given for the tax as well as extravagance at court. The king eventually agreed to take only half the tax, yet collecting it still proved difficult. In January 1572, Charles waived the last 100,000l. on condition that the balance of 50,000l. was paid at once. In order to scrape together even this amount, the city threatened to seize the property of defaulters or to quarter troops on them. By May the king was asking for another 200,000 *livres*.

Charles IX also resorted to fiscal expedients, notably the *rentes sur l'Hôtel de Ville*. Wealthy citizens were coerced into buying annuities which they did not want. As public confidence in the *rentes* evaporated, the king turned to private financiers (*partisans*), who were mostly Italian. In return for cash they acquired *rentes* and drew the interest until they decided to dispose of them. Charles, in the meantime, continued to borrow, while ever more tenuous sources of income were assigned to the payment of the *rentes*. The Hôtel de Ville was left to collect the funds with which to pay the interest. Parisian *rentiers* were afraid that the system would soon collapse, destroying their investments.

Under the Peace of Saint-Germain, offices, which had been taken from Huguenots and given to Catholics, had to be returned to their former owners. Since the crown had no money, Catholics who were dispossessed could expect little or no compensation. Similarly, people who had taken over houses which Huguenots had vacated during the second civil war were now required to hand them back. They were promised compensation from the proceeds of a tax on re-entry to be levied on the Huguenots, but they probably got nothing. Catholics were promised first call on new leases as they became available, but this was not enough to quell their resentment of a peace treaty which seemed to favour rebels rather than the king's loyal subjects.

The potent combination of religious and economic grievances alienated the Parisians from the government. They were prepared to forgive Charles IX on account of his youth, but they blamed his mother who, they believed, still held the reins of power. In March 1570 a Franciscan preacher claimed that 'the kingdom had fallen to the distaff' and that 'the distaff should be burned'. As an Italian, Catherine could expect no sympathy from a fiercely xenophobic population. In 1565 a Venetian reported that Italians could not venture into the streets of Paris in safety. Early in 1572 they were accused of ritually murdering children, whose blood, it was alleged, was needed to cure the duc d'Anjou of a secret illness. Some said that Catherine also required the blood of innocents.

On his return to court in September 1571, Coligny had been given, as we have seen, a handsome pension and readmitted to the king's council. Parisians naturally concluded that he was exercising an undue and pernicious influence on the young king. N. M. Sutherland has suggested that this was not so: that Charles resisted much of Coligny's advice and temporized over issues that concerned him specially. The admiral, moreover, spent only five weeks at court between September 1571 and August 1572, so his influence cannot have been as great as historians have commonly assumed; but the perception of contemporaries may have been different: noting that the Guises had left the court just as Coligny returned and that Charles IX was insisting on the strict enforcement of the Peace of Saint-Germain, they drew their own conclusion. It was also Coligny who had asked for the removal of the cross of Gastines. The news that the king's sister was about to marry the Huguenot prince of Navarre increased suspicion that Protestants controlled the court. So did rumours of a possible French invasion of the Netherlands. When a Huguenot army led by Nassau captured Valenciennes and Mons in May 1572, the rumours seemed confirmed. Charles IX, it was alleged, had secretly backed the enterprise and been promised Flanders in the event of a Protestant victory. He was apparently keen to exploit Habsburg difficulties and unite his subjects in a foreign war, but Parisians did not share his enthusiasm: they foresaw that a war in the Netherlands would worsen their economic problems. They were also shocked by the idea of their king allying with heretics to fight another Catholic ruler.

The wedding of Henri de Navarre and Marguerite de Valois was celebrated on 18 August in the cathedral of Notre-Dame. It was followed by four days of glittering festivities taking the form of tournaments, banquets, balls and ballets which stood in sharp contrast to the poverty afflicting many Parisians. Coligny, meanwhile, pressed the king to commit himself firmly to a war in the Netherlands and to the strict application of the Edict of Saint-Germain. 'My father,' replied Charles (using his courtesy title for Coligny), 'please allow me four or five more days to enjoy myself; then I promise, on my faith as king to satisfy you and your co-religionists.' Did the king mean what he said? He had been playing a double game for some time and now seemed closer to his mother and the Catholic camp.

On 22 August 1572, as Coligny was walking from the Louvre to his residence, the Hôtel de Béthisy, an arquebus was fired at him from the upper window of a house. The bullet shattered his left index finger and fractured his left forearm. The assailant managed to evade capture by the admiral's escort. His identity is uncertain, but he was probably Charles de Louviers, seigneur de Maurevert. Historians have usually regarded him as a royal agent, but he may have acted on his own account, either to pay off a private score or in response to public clamour for the elimination of the Catholics' 'public enemy number one'. However, the house from which the shot was fired belonged to the Guises, as did the horse on which the assailant fled from the scene.

As news of the attempted assassination spread through Paris, Huguenot leaders gathered at the bedside of their stricken leader. Later the king himself came, accompanied by his mother and several courtiers. Charles promised to avenge the crime. A judicial enquiry held on 23 August implicated Henri duc de Guise. Meanwhile the city authorities took steps to restrain the Parisians, who were keen to vent their hatred of Protestants. The admiral chose to stay put in spite of the dangerous environment. In response to his request for a bodyguard, the king gave him fifty arquebusiers.

It is unlikely that the attack on Coligny was the opening shot in a campaign against the Huguenots generally. Even if it had succeeded it would have been a tactical error, for they would have been alerted to the danger facing them. The admiral's followers would probably have left Paris and started a new civil war. But the plot having misfired, Coligny refused to leave the capital, trusting the king's promise to track down and punish the would-be assassin. The other Huguenot leaders remained with him, feeding off each other's anger and threatening revenge. According to Tavannes, the king and his council, at a meeting in the Louvre on 23 August, decided that civil war had become inevitable and that 'it was better to win a battle in Paris, where all the leaders were, than to risk it in the field and fall into a dangerous and uncertain war'. Tavannes's memoirs, which were written by his son long after the events described, are not necessarily trustworthy, but Catholics did fear a Huguenot uprising after the attack on Coligny. Rumours of a plot to murder the king and his family and to sack Paris were rife, and Charles IX must have remembered that the Huguenots had once tried to capture him at Montceaux; the notion of a pre-emptive strike to ward off such a plot may well have appealed to him. We can at any rate

[margin note: ASSASSINATION ATTEMPT ON ADMIRAL COLIGNY]

be certain that in the afternoon or evening of 23 August, Charles decided to wipe out the Huguenot leadership. Prime responsibility for the mass slaughter was given to the king's Swiss and French guards and to those of the duc d'Anjou serving under the ducs de Guise and d'Aumale and other Catholic captains.

The part played by the municipal authorities is less clear. It was evidently in order to avert a Huguenot uprising that the *prévôt des marchands*, Jean Le Charron, was summoned to the Louvre late on 23 August. The king ordered him to take all necessary steps to secure the city: he was to keep the gates locked, immobilize boats on the right bank of the Seine, distribute arms to the militia and bourgeoisie and dispose of the city's artillery outside the Hôtel de Ville. The municipal register hints at additional instructions given to Le Charron by the king, which historians have interpreted as ordering the massacre that followed. This view is supported by some contemporary memoirs, but they are not necessarily accurate. Be that as it may, Le Charron transmitted the king's orders to his municipal colleagues on his return to the town hall, but they were not passed on to the captains of the militia till early next morning, so they would not have had time to summon their men, distribute weapons and issue orders before the massacre began.

It is said to have started before dawn, say around 4 AM, when members of the king's guard, led by the duc de Guise and other Catholic noblemen, broke into the Hôtel de Béthisy, murdered Coligny and tossed his body out of a window. The duke wiped blood off the admiral's face, saying, 'It's him; I recognize him', then kicked the body. One of Guise's followers cut off Coligny's head and took it to the royal palace to show it to the king and queen mother. It was later embalmed and sent to Rome to be displayed to the pope and the cardinals. Meanwhile, a Catholic mob mutilated the admiral's headless corpse and dragged it through the streets for three days (as they had done to his effigy some years before). It was then hanged at the gibbet of Mautfaucon like any common criminal, and crowds flocked to see it. Eventually the admiral's remains were cut down and secretly buried. His cruel end ensured him a place in the pantheon of Protestant martyrs. It became a centrepiece of many Protestant pamphlets, which portray Coligny as a good Christian and a committed Protestant who was murdered primarily for his faith.

The tocsin of Saint-Germain-l'Auxerrois allegedly rang as the admiral was being murdered, but there is uncertainty about this. The attack on the Hôtel de Béthisy, which was resisted by Huguenot nobles, doubtless caused a commotion. Residents in the neighbourhood, aware of the rumours of an imminent Huguenot rising, would have reacted, and their terror and confusion would have soon spread like wildfire across the city. A similar situation had occurred in 1567, when the Huguenots had set alight windmills on the edge of Paris, but this time the violence was far worse. It is possible too that Parisian Catholics were encouraged to set upon their Protestant neighbours by words spoken by Guise. As he left the Hôtel de Béthisy, he was overheard urging his men to continue the slaughter of Huguenots as they were obeying the king's command. His words 'transformed private passions into public duty' (Diefendorf). Many Parisians were all too willing to believe that the king had at last thrown his authority on the side of God's purpose of national purification.

At 11 AM on 24 August, Le Charron called on the king to complain of the bloodshed and destruction sweeping through the capital, which hardly suggests that he had been ordered to unleash the massacre. That afternoon, in response to a royal command, he called a halt to the 'pillaging, sacking of houses and murders'. For nearly a week, however, the slaughter continued. From the district of Saint Germain l'Auxerrois and the Louvre, where the king's guard dispatched the Huguenot nobles attendant upon Henri de Navarre and the prince de Condé, the massacre spread south and east in the city. Protestant sources contain horrific accounts of the atrocities committed. The deaths of Huguenot women are commonly described in more detail than those of men. Children are described witnessing their parents' death. Thus the youngest daughter of Nicolas Le Mercier was dipped 'stark naked in the blood of her massacred father and mother, with horrible threats that, if ever she became a Huguenot, the same would happen to her'. In telling such stories Protestants evidently wanted to dehumanize their persecutors, but they were not necessarily lying or exaggerating, for the massacre repeated on a larger scale incidents that had already occurred in the religious wars, when women had been dragged by the hair through the streets and thrown into the Seine. Such violent acts were often drawn from a store of punitive and purificatory traditions current in sixteenth-century France. Magisterial roles were acted out in many Huguenot deaths: the burning of a bookbinder mimicked the execution traditional for heresy, just as the mutilation of Coligny's body was a confused ritual of humiliation as well as the parodying of royal justice.

Among the first non-noble victims of the St Bartholomew's day massacre were wealthy Huguenot merchants like Mathurin Lassault, the queen mother's jeweller, and Nicolas Le Mercier, who had already been attacked at the time of the cross of Gastines affair. Other victims included Philippe Le Doux and his wife, who was about to give birth to her twenty-first child. She was stabbed in the abdomen and her half-born babe left to die in the gutter. Le Doux's assailant was Pierre Coullon, a neighbour and less successful professional rival. One suspects that greed and jealousy often helped to fuel the violence, as did alcohol. Many of the murderers and looters were certainly drunk, which may explain some of their more barbaric acts. But the violence was not simply vindictive: it was used by the Catholics to force their victims to recite Catholic prayers or go to mass. Goulart tells us of the murder of Antoine Mulenchon who had refused to 'invoke the Virgin Mary and the saints and to renounce his religion'. Sometimes, too, there was extortion. Jean Lot, for example, won a reprieve for his life by promising to pay a ransom of a thousand *écus*.

What role did the Parisian militia play in the massacre? According to the historian J.-L. Bourgeon, Charles IX had lost control of the capital to the bourgeois militia, consisting of 5000 well-armed men led by some 150 captains. Each captain was responsible for mobilizing a *dizaine*, which in territorial terms was little more than a main street and its immediate neighbourhood. Being in close touch with the inhabitants, they could best harness opposition to the crown's fiscal and religious policies. But whom did they obey? Bourgeon points to various possible leaders, including the former *prévôt des marchands* Claude Marcel, but does not rule out the possibility that the captains took their cue ultimately from the duc de Guise. Another historian, Barbara Diefendorf, does not attach the same degree of cohesion to the militia and indicates that relatively few captains played an active role in the massacre. Significantly, they were the same men who had committed acts of violence earlier in the religious wars. One of them, Thomas Croizier, boasted of having killed more than 400 men single-handed on St Bartholomew's day. A close reading of even the Protestant sources suggests that the highest city officials remained aloof from the killing and may have tried to restrain it.

Not all Parisian Catholics turned into murderers. While some remained quietly in their homes, others tried to protect their Huguenot friends and neighbours. Thus Philippe Duplessis-Mornay was sheltered first by the host of the *Golden Compass*, where he had taken rooms for the royal marriage, then by his family's notary. His future wife, Charlotte d'Arbaleste, was protected by various Catholics until her escape from Paris. Renée Burlamaqui and her two children were helped by several Catholics, including the duc de Guise. It seems that it was a minority of Parisians who took part in the violence; the rest stayed behind closed doors. Even so, many approved of the killing. When an old hawthorn bush in the Cemetery of the Innocents suddenly sprang to life, they proclaimed this to be a miracle indicating God's pleasure at the destruction of Coligny and his friends.

News of the massacre was speedily carried to Rome by special messengers. For some time the Curia had been putting pressure on the French government to act decisively against heresy. It now seemed to have responded positively, and the new pope, Gregory XIII, held a *Te Deum*. This was followed by a more elaborate ceremony of celebration at the French church of St Louis in Rome under the direction of the Cardinal of Lorraine. A special commemorative medal was struck by the pope with his profile on one side and, on the reverse, an angel carrying a cross and superintending the killing of Coligny and his friends. Vasari was commissioned to paint frescoes celebrating the massacre in the *Sala Regia of the Vatican* palace (the room is no longer regularly shown to visitors!). At the same time the pope showed a genuine pastoral concern: he gave instructions to his nuncio in France that the French clergy should welcome wandering Protestants back into the church.

Was the St Bartholomew's massacre premeditated? Many contemporaries, both Catholic and Protestant, were convinced that it was. The Cardinal of Lorraine, for one, was keen that his own family should take credit for the massacre and intimated that it had been planned by the Guises and was expected. Protestants like Goulart were also sure that the massacre had been planned, perhaps for years, and the charge of premeditation became a staple of Protestant propaganda. Goulart claimed that the planning had begun in 1570 with the Edict of Saint-Germain, whose generous terms had been cleverly designed to lull the Protestants into a false sense of security. The French government had encouraged the Dutch rebels so as to lure Coligny and other Huguenot leaders to Paris, ostensibly to make final plans for launching an anti-Spanish campaign, but in reality to arrange for their killing. The idea of premeditation found support in a pamphlet by a papal courtier, Camillo Capilupi, called *The stratagem of Charles IX, King of France, against the Huguenots, rebels against God and his servants*. Capilupi claimed to know of several documents proving that the massacre had been planned by the French government, yet modern research has signally failed to turn up this evidence.

The idea that the massacre was premeditated has its supporters among some present-day historians. Bourgeon, for example, has suggested that Spain and most probably Tridentine Rome were behind the plot to kill the admiral. Its significance, in his judgement, far transcended 'a vulgar settling of accounts between rival feudal clans'. Bourgeon believes that Alba, who undoubtedly favoured assassination as a political weapon, was the prime mover in the plot to eliminate Coligny, and the fact that the Spanish ambassador first pointed the finger of blame at the king of France reinforces his conviction. Bourgeon does not think that the decision to kill the Huguenot leaders could have been taken without thought for the consequences. 'Despite its unfolding in two stages (22 and 24 August),' he writes, 'nothing, it seems, was less improvised than the St Bartholomew ['s day massacre]: which does not mean that it was intended to be as brutal and traumatic.' He believes that the elimination of the Huguenot leadership was meant to be the opening shot in a campaign orchestrated by Spain to force a complete change of royal policies in France: the annulment of the Navarre marriage, the abrogation of the Edict of Saint-Germain, the return to power of the Guises, the exclusion of Huguenots from the king's council, parlements and other bodies, a curb on taxation, the abandonment of French interference in the Netherlands and a realignment of French diplomacy in line with that of Philip II and Gregory XIII. While Bourgeon does not believe a massacre on a large scale was part of this plan, he points to powerful pressure groups which were preparing to force Charles IX to abandon his policies. As supporting evidence, he points to the judicial strike launched by the parlement on 19 August and to the huge propaganda exercise mounted by an army of *curés* and fanatical preachers. The truth, alas, will never be known. Nor shall we ever know who advised Charles IX to order the destruction of the Huguenot leaders: Catherine de' Medici, Anjou, the comte de Retz and the duc de Guise have all been variously accused. The only certainty is that in the afternoon or evening of 23 August it was agreed by the king and his advisers that the Huguenot leaders must die.

The provincial massacres

The St Bartholomew's day massacre was not limited to Paris. The violent example set by the capital was soon followed in other French towns, notably La Charité, Meaux, Bourges, Saumur, Angers, Lyon, Troyes, Rouen, Bordeaux, Toulouse and Gaillac. In most of these towns the violence followed almost immediately upon receipt of the news of the massacre in Paris; in a few it spread into the first week of October. In some towns the killing was cold-blooded and methodical: the authorities rounded up the Huguenots and dispatched them one by one; in others, the initiative came from below as mobs took to looting and butchery. But everywhere, it seems, the killers believed that they were doing the king's bidding. Without this confidence in the legitimacy of their actions, the provincial death toll – estimated at around 3000 – would probably have been lower.

For a long time chroniclers believed that Charles IX had ordered the provincial massacres, but the available documentary evidence does not support this; in fact, there are numerous letters from the king expressly ordering his lieutenants to stem the tide of violence. On 24 August he wrote to his chief provincial governors announcing the assassination of the Huguenot nobles at court, which he blamed on their long-standing rivalry with the house of Guise. He urged them to apply the Edict of Saint-Germain. On 27 and 28 August more letters were sent out by the king, this time urging his officers in the Midi to be on their guard lest the Huguenots rise up in reaction to the Parisian massacre. Charles informed those elsewhere in France that he had himself ordered the execution of the Protestant leaders in order to avert a plot which they had been preparing against him. At the same time he stressed that the mass violence, which had broken out since, contradicted his orders. He urged the authorities everywhere to maintain or restore calm. Sixteenth-century Calvinists regarded these letters as a smokescreen intended to conceal the king's real commands which secret messengers delivered by word of mouth. But the available documentary evidence shows that magistrates everywhere tried conscientiously to carry out the instructions contained in Charles's letters of 24, 27 and 28 August.

However, the king seems at first to have hesitated about the orders he should issue and dispatched verbal instructions to a few provincial officials at least, ordering them to deal sternly with the Huguenots in their areas. He soon countermanded them, but his hesitation may well have cost lives by playing into the hands of Catholic extremists who were bent on killing Huguenots. In Bordeaux, for example, a massacre was touched off by the mayor, Charles de Montferrand, who appeared before the city's magistrates brandishing a list of prospective Huguenot victims which, he claimed, had been handed to him by the king. The list was almost certainly spurious, but Charles IX's failure to make his opposition to violence clear from the start may have given plausibility to de Montferrand's claim. The local magistrates consequently made no attempt to stop him and his henchmen slaughtering Huguenots.

An important reason for the king's hesitation was undoubtedly the pressure exerted upon him by Catholic extremists. Such men, notably the Guises, had been advocating the mass extermination of Huguenots since 1560. Here and there they had even tried to carry it out, but they had been restrained by the government. Now it may have looked as if Charles IX was coming round to their view, and some did not wait for his decision before rushing off to the provinces with the news that he had ordered a general massacre. The following letter which Henri duc d'Anjou, the king's brother, commissioned an agent to write to the governor of Saumur, suggests that he, for one, wanted the massacre to be extended:

> The Admiral and all the Huguenots in Paris have been killed, and it is the will of His Majesty that Huguenots everywhere should meet the same end. So, if you have ever desired to serve the king and Monsieur, you must go at once to Saumur with all your supporters and kill any Huguenots you find there . . . And having done that, you must go to Angers and help the captain of the château do the same thing there . . . You must use the utmost diligence in this affair so as not to lose any time whatsoever.

Similar directives reached other towns. At Troyes, for example, the seigneur de Ruffec urged the guards at the town gates to exterminate all the Huguenots as he himself was about to do in his own *gouvernement* of Angoulême. A similar message was carried to Nantes by the duc de Montpensier, but the mayor did not pass it on to the town council for more than a week. By the time a general assembly met, Charles IX's letter ordering calm to be preserved had arrived. The assembly accordingly voted measures to safeguard the Protestants and no incidents followed.

Why did towns react so differently to the news from Paris? Philip Benedict has pointed to certain features common to those where violence occurred in 1572. Nearly all were towns where anti-Protestant sentiment had been fanned by events in the first decade of civil war. In all the Huguenots formed a minority, albeit a significant one, and in all they had been systematically debarred from exercising political power since the end of the earlier civil wars. In Rouen, Orléans, Lyon, Meaux and Bourges power had been seized in 1562 by a Protestant faction representing only a minority of the population, and it had since reverted to the Catholic majority. Gaillac had seen massacres by Catholics in 1562 and by Protestants in 1568. Toulouse and Bordeaux were Catholic enclaves in strongly Calvinist territory. In all of these towns, except perhaps Bordeaux and Rouen, the violence was characterized by a large amount of mob involvement and brutal excesses. In four other towns (La Charité, Angers, Saumur and Troyes) the killing was begun by small groups of soldiers and municipal officials, often acting in a quasi-judicial way; the mob joined in later, if at all, and there was little looting, pillaging or ritual brutality. At Angers the massacre was carried out almost single-handed by Monsoreau, governor of Saumur, who went from house to house dispatching leading Huguenots; he was joined later by a mob, but calm was soon restored by the municipality.

In many French towns there were no massacres. The Huguenots were briefly imprisoned, mainly for their own protection, and many were so alarmed by the reports coming out of Paris that they returned to the Catholic faith. Local authorities, acting out of loyalty to the crown or out of fear that anti-Huguenot violence might suddenly turn into an indiscriminate attack on the rich, managed to protect the Huguenots from harm. Many towns which were spared violence lacked a sizeable Huguenot minority. They were of three kinds: first, Huguenot strongholds (like La Rochelle, Montauban, Nîmes) where the Protestant authorities kept the Catholic population under control and forestalled any threat to their own safety by expelling or denying entry to any military official representing the king; secondly, relatively tolerant towns, like Rennes, where interdenominational relations had been quiet in the preceding civil wars; and thirdly, bastions of Catholicism, like Reims, where the Guises were dominant and where Protestants were too few and insignificant to be worth slaughtering.

The effects of the massacres on the French Reformed church

The Parisian Huguenots, it seems, offered little resistance to the massacre. Most of them were dragged out of their beds unawares and killed before they could group together in self-defence. But their attitude also owed much to their faith, as exemplified by the martyrdom of Pierre de La Place, a president of the *Chambre des comptes*, which Goulart first recounted in his *Mémoires de l'estat de Charles neufiesme* (1578). Early on 24 August, La Place was warned of the massacre that was taking place. His first inclination was to escape, but finding no Catholic neighbour willing to offer him shelter, he stayed at home and undertook his normal Sunday routine. He gathered his family and servants and led them in prayer. After reading a passage from the Bible and a commentary by Calvin, he prepared them and himself 'to endure all sorts of torments, even death, rather than do anything contrary to the honour of God'. Next day, La Place was called before the king, but he was prevented from reaching the Louvre by the street violence. He asked for and was given an armed escort, but he had no sooner left his house than he was lynched by a mob. La Place's martyrdom exemplified the Huguenots' trust in the promise of salvation, their acceptance of suffering as a trial imposed by God and their belief in the need to suffer under the cross.

Many Huguenots were persuaded to abjure their faith by the sheer magnitude of the massacre: they refused to believe that God was prepared to allow such a slaughter of His children. One who lapsed was the pastor Hughes Sureau Du Rosier. 'I began to see it [the massacre]', he wrote, 'as evidence of the indignation of God, as if He had declared by this means that He detested and condemned the profession and exercise of our religion as if He wished entirely to ruin this church and favour instead the Roman.' Later Du Rosier repented, blaming his lapse on the devil and on his own weakness of character. He reverted to Protestantism, but was never fully reintegrated into the French Reformed church and ceased to be a minister.

The expectation that French Protestants would return to the Catholic church was high at court, where the young princes of Navarre and Condé, the nominal leaders of the Huguenot movement, had survived the massacre. Charles IX offered them one of three choices: the mass, death or life imprisonment. Navarre seemed willing to abjure, but Condé was defiant. He said that he would never become a Catholic and left the other choice to God's decision. A cell at the Bastille was allegedly prepared to receive him. But the resistance of the two princes did not last long. They were not helped by the conversion of Du Rosier, who was given the task of persuading them to follow his example. Soon afterwards the princes were received into the Catholic church. On 3 October, Henri had to write a letter to the pope asking for forgiveness; on 16 October he issued an edict re-establishing Catholicism in Béarn. Thereafter he behaved as if the massacre had never taken place, walking and talking with Guise and others who had murdered his companions.

The princes and Du Rosier were not the only Huguenots in Paris to lapse. A contemporary reported soon after the massacre that 5000 had abjured.

Ten years later, Jean de L'Espine said that the French churches had lost more than two-thirds of their members and this estimate is borne out by documents concerning the community in Rouen. The Catholic parish registers reveal a flood of rebaptisms of Calvinist children, marking their reintegration into the Catholic fold. Many adult Huguenots submitted to a formal ceremony of abjuration in the cathedral. They were made to renounce their faith in writing and to endorse any legal punishment they might have incurred for their beliefs. The account books of several churches record monetary donations made by Huguenots 'reduced' to becoming Catholics. Such documents indicate that at least 3000 Protestants in Rouen formally became reconciled to the Roman Catholic church.

Other Huguenots in Rouen preferred to emigrate. England was their preferred destination. A census of aliens taken in Rye on 4 November reveals the presence of 174 Rouennais, not counting those who had already passed through the port on their way to other English destinations. The emigration was still going on six weeks after the massacre. The so-called 'Walloon' congregation in Southampton became predominantly French after 1572. Other refugees from Rouen may have gone to Zeeland, while a handful risked the perilous overland journey to Geneva. They had to run the gauntlet of Guise's men who patrolled the roads of eastern France looking for Huguenots fleeing to Germany or Switzerland.

Catholic observers hoped that the massacre had destroyed the Protestant church in France. Even the king hoped that Protestantism was on the verge of extinction: he banned all Calvinists from royal offices as a spur to future conversions. Reformed services ceased in Rouen. Catholic hopes, however, were soon dashed. The chain of Protestant strongholds across southern France and up the west coast into Poitou ensured the survival of Protestantism as well as the continuation of the civil wars. Yet it had suffered a crippling blow from which it never recovered. When Rouen's Reformed church rose from the ashes after the pacification of July 1573, it was but a shadow of its former self. Its recovery was painfully slow. Only a handful of Huguenots dared to return from exile in October 1574; most remained wary of royal assurances of protection. The congregation which began to meet regularly in 1578 was a fraction of its size in the mid-1560s. In 1579, the first full year in which services were held regularly, only 70 baptisms took place – barely a tenth of the number in 1565. The church grew steadily in the next six years, but even in 1584 there were only 115 baptisms. The numerical collapse since 1565 was dramatic: from a community of 16,500 souls it had sunk to one of 1500 to 3000 and the decline was permanent. Even after the end of the religious wars in 1594 the Reformed church never regained its old strength. The massacre of St Bartholomew's day may not have been wholly to blame: the harsh anti-Protestant measures taken during the second and third civil wars certainly prompted defections; but the massacre was undoubtedly the principal reason for the numerical collapse of Rouen's Protestant community.

The sieges of La Rochelle and Sancerre

Although the St Bartholomew's day massacres had wiped out many Huguenot nobles, and Navarre and Condé were effectively prisoners, there remained enough of the lesser nobility to work out a new defensive strategy, both military and political. Protestant defiance was most pronounced in the south of France, particularly Languedoc, a region far from Paris and traditionally noted for its combination of religious heterodoxy and political dissent. Much of the province, including the cities of Nîmes and Montauban, were in Protestant hands at the time of the massacres; other parts were controlled by Catholics who were at least prepared to tolerate Protestantism. Nearer to Paris a number of towns were also under Huguenot control, the most important being La Rochelle, a port on the Atlantic coast which had close relations with Protestant England and the Dutch rebels against Spain. During the third religious war it had been the Protestant headquarters and in 1571 had played host to a particularly important Huguenot synod. Another Protestant centre, albeit a much smaller one, was Sancerre in Berry. Both towns came under pressure from the government to submit to certain demands and, when they refused, came under attack from royal forces. The shift of military operations to south of the Loire worked to the disadvantage of the crown, which kept its artillery mainly in Paris or along the northern and eastern borders of the kingdom. Transporting it beyond the Loire proved difficult as communications were poor.

More is known about the siege of Sancerre than that of La Rochelle because of a remarkable account written by Jean de Léry, the Calvinist minister who in 1558 had accompanied the Huguenot expedition to Brazil. In addition to giving an almost day-by-day account of the siege, he provides an extraordinary description of the famine which befell the inhabitants. Sancerre never lacked wine, but its meat and bread ran out, and Léry describes the alternatives resorted to by the inhabitants: first, horses, asses and mules, then cats, dogs, rats and mice, followed by leather and parchment. Instead of wheat, the people fed on grasses and roots, some of which turned out to be poisonous. He instances one case of cannibalism: a vinedresser and his wife who ate their infant daughter. Léry's account was designed to encourage similar heroism elsewhere: it showed that Protestants were prepared to accept extreme deprivation and to risk agonizing deaths in defence of their faith.

Politically, the siege of La Rochelle was far more important than that of Sancerre. A few weeks after the St Bartholomew's day massacre the people of La Rochelle refused to admit Marshal Biron, whom the king had appointed as their new governor. Charles IX asked François de La Noue, a Huguenot captain who had just been released from captivity in Flanders, to negotiate with the Rochelois. They refused to do so, but at the same time invited La Noue to become their leader. He accepted their offer after obtaining the king's consent and thus found himself in the curious situation of being simultaneously Charles IX's emissary and leader of the rebels. As they showed no willingness to obey the king's wishes, Biron was ordered to take La Rochelle by force. The marshal laid siege to the town and in February 1573 was joined by a large army under the command of the king's brother, Henri duc d'Anjou. Charles's younger brother, François duc d'Alençon, was also there, as were the princes of Navarre and Condé, the dukes of Guise and Aumale, and many other nobles who had taken an active part in the St Bartholomew's day massacre. But they lacked unity. From the beginning of the siege they quarrelled over tactics; some were even suspected of wanting to help the enemy.

Historians have sometimes suggested that it was in Anjou's camp outside La Rochelle and more specifically in Alençon's entourage that the *Politiques* – a party of moderate nobles dedicated to the peaceful solution of France's religious problem – originated. But no such party was formed at this stage. True, Alençon was annoyed because he had not been given a military command. So far he had only made his mark as one of Elizabeth I's suitors, and he was madly envious of Anjou's military reputation. As a prince of the blood and second in line to the throne, he was the obvious rallying point for other nobles who felt disgruntled for a variety of reasons. Religion was not necessarily one of them – as de Thou says, they were 'all dissatisfied, but for different reasons' – so they can hardly be said to have formed a party with any clear political or religious objective.

Rumours of treason and rebellion were rife in Anjou's camp. The Malcontents were reported to be secretly in league with the defenders of La Rochelle and with the comte de Montgomery, who had fled to England after the massacre and was said to be preparing an expeditionary force to relieve La Rochelle. The malcontents were allegedly planning to stage a *coup d'état* the moment Montgomery arrived. Rumour also had it that Alençon and Navarre were planning to murder Anjou. No one knows if there is any truth in these stories. The only certainty is that Alençon allowed himself to become associated with a group of noblemen who for a variety of reasons were dissatisfied with the government of Charles IX.

In the event, the siege was not disrupted and lasted throughout the spring of 1573. La Rochelle's resistance had been stiffened by the arrival of refugees from the St Bartholomew's day massacres. The most prominent was La Noue, who led the defenders on a number of sorties while trying at the same time to persuade them to lay down their arms. Eventually he returned to the royal camp and helped to negotiate the final settlement of the conflict in July 1573. Meanwhile, the main burden of resistance fell on the mayor of La Rochelle and the other elected officials. At times the entire population was mobilized, including women who pelted the royal troops with stones and other missiles from the ramparts. The defenders also included fifty-four refugee ministers in addition to three who normally resided in the town. They served as chaplains to the troops and visited the sick and wounded. When peace talks were under discussion, they insisted that La Rochelle should not treat separately from the other Protestant communities. They wanted nothing less than full toleration of Protestant services, sacraments and rites.

La Rochelle had to endure a fierce bombardment by Anjou's guns (they fired a total of 12,790 volleys) and repulsed several assaults by his troops. The town was quite well fortified. Only a small part of its wall could be attacked from firm ground; the rest was protected by moats filled with sea-water. Beyond the wall lay salt marshes and waterways. The royalists tried to deny the inhabitants access to the sea by sinking a carrack at the entrance to the harbour. But this move was largely ineffectual, as La Rochelle had plentiful food stocks and small vessels continued to slip out to sea to catch fish. In May, however, more than three hundred Rochelois signed a petition calling for peace.

The siege of La Rochelle has been described as 'the most important and decisive military episode of the entire period of the early wars of religion' (J. B. Wood). While demonstrating the growing military difficulties faced by the crown, it also undermined the army's morale and effectiveness. Royal casualties incurred during the siege were out of all proportion to the results obtained. If the effects of sickness and desertion are taken into account, they may have numbered about 12,000. The casualty rate among the officers was especially high at 73 per cent. Even allowing for France's buoyant population, the crown would have been hard put to make up such losses rapidly. The siege also drained the kingdom of guns and munitions faster than they could be stockpiled. The treasury, too, was seriously depleted. From the mid-1570s onwards the crown could no longer afford large-scale military operations. A year was about as long as the king could afford to fight; hence the brevity of the later civil wars. Pitched battles were abandoned in favour of sieges. 'In this process', writes Wood, 'the resistance of La Rochelle was more than a beacon of hope and a sign from the heavens for the Protestants . . . It was a harbinger of the type of military stalemate that was to characterize the final decade and a half of the civil wars'.

Curiously, La Rochelle was saved by events in eastern Europe. Sigismund-Augustus, king of Poland, the last representative of the Jagiellon dynasty, had died on 7 July and France was afraid that his throne would pass into Habsburg hands. Catherine de' Medici, who had already tried to marry

Anjou off to two queens, now strove to make him king of Poland. She sent Jean de Monluc, the eloquent bishop of Valence (and brother of Marshal Monluc), to the Polish diet to press her son's candidature. He arrived almost at the same time as news of the massacre in Paris. Polish Protestants, who formed a significant minority, were shocked, as were Catholics who, save for a few bishops, favoured religious toleration. Monluc tried to play down Anjou's involvement with the massacre and blamed the Parisian mob for the bloodshed. Fortunately for the duke, there were serious objections to his main rivals for the Polish throne – the Russian Tsar Ivan the Terrible, and the Austrian archduke Ernest. Among the advantages which the electors hoped to gain by voting for the French prince were the friendship of France's ally the Ottoman sultan, and French subsidies for the building of a Baltic navy. On 10 May, after almost a month of intensive electioneering by the representatives of the various candidates, the archbishop-primate of Poland announced the result: 'Our king is the most illustrious duke of Anjou.' But the election was not unconditional. Five days after the declaration Monluc had to subscribe to two documents, the *Pacta conventa* and the *Articuli Henriciani* which regulated relations between the king and the senate and proclaimed freedom of conscience and worship. The *Articuli* abolished the principle of hereditary succession to the Polish throne. The king was required to consult the senate on all public matters, he was to be assisted by a council of four senators, renewable every six months, and was required to confirm all the nobility's privileges. If he broke the *Articuli*, the nobility would be free to rise against him.

Henri d'Anjou received the news of his election as king of Poland at his camp outside La Rochelle on 29 May. It offered him a good excuse to end the siege honourably, for he could not fight the Huguenots and keep faith with his new Polish subjects. He cared little about Poland as such, but liked the idea of being a king in his own right instead of living in his elder brother's shadow. On 17 June, Polish ambassadors arrived at La Rochelle and arranged for a coronation at sea with gun salvoes and fireworks. Soon afterwards Henri agreed terms with the Rochelois. These were not particularly generous: Protestant worship was allowed in La Rochelle, but only in private houses and buildings. Protestant nobles were allowed to hold Calvinist services in their homes, but only baptisms and weddings attended by no more than ten people. The same concessions were extended to the other Protestant strongholds of Montauban and Nîmes.

On 22 August, almost a year to the day after the massacre of St Bartholomew, Polish ambassadors called on Henri d'Anjou at the Louvre. A few days later he reluctantly subscribed to the conditions which the Polish Diet had laid down. As the bishop of Poznań explained to him: 'You will be powerless to do harm and all powerful to do good.' When Henri hesitated before signing, another Polish delegate exclaimed: 'Either you will swear or you won't rule.' On 10 September the duke took a solemn oath as king of Poland at Notre-Dame; four days later he made his entry into Paris. The city gave him a statue in silver gilt and enamel of Mars riding a chariot pulled by two white horses. On 2 December, Henri took leave of his mother and of members of the court of Lorraine at Blamont at the start of his Polish odyssey. It was to last till June 1574 when he left Cracow as a quasi-fugitive to succeed his brother on the French throne.

The 'United Provinces of the Midi'

While the armies of Charles IX were trying to reconquer Sancerre and La Rochelle, the Huguenots seized several towns in Languedoc and the governor, Henri de Montmorency-Damville, was ordered to pacify the area. Political activity was also intense among the Huguenots, especially in the south. Their leaders swore a solemn oath of union, and assemblies of Huguenots met more or less spontaneously in late 1572 and 1573 at Réalmont, Millau, Montauban, Castres, Uzès and Nîmes. Rules laid down at these meetings determined the constitution of an independent state. Especially important were the assemblies of Montauban (August 1573) and Millau (December 1573) which envisaged a federal state. Supreme authority was vested in the Estates-General, an occasional body made up of representatives from each province which had sworn allegiance to the Protestant union. The executive authority was a Protector, who had charge of military affairs and was assisted by a permanent council. Jean Delumeau has given the name of 'the United Provinces of the Midi' to the new federation, but this name is seriously misleading as it implies an analogy with the republican constitution adopted by the Dutch rebels, whereas the Huguenots remained consistently loyal to the idea of monarchy. They described the aim of the constitution they adopted in December 1573 as 'the glory of God, the advancement of Christ's reign, the good and service of the crown and the common repose of this kingdom'. The delegates at Millau in July 1574 vehemently denied that they had ever thought of deserting their natural lord, the king. The founders of the 'Provinces of the Union' did not plan to create a separate state, only to reform the existing one. Their federation enjoyed a high degree of autonomy, albeit under the king. As Greengrass has shown, the reluctance to alienate permanently the property rights of the Catholic church, even during periods of open warfare, 'reflects an underlying conservative royalism within the Huguenot cause'.

Each province was allowed a considerable measure of autonomy within the federation: it was administered by a chamber, meeting periodically, a permanent executive council and a military commander for the region. A similar degree of independence was accorded to the towns and villages: the municipal officers were empowered to administer local affairs, enforce law and order and control taxation. Justice was left in the main to magistrates of the *bailliages* and *présidiaux*, who were for the most part early converts to Protestantism. Cases on appeal were judged by special courts – one for each of the five provinces of the union – with an equal number of Protestant and Catholic judges. The Huguenot state was funded out of taxes normally paid to the crown, the salt-tax, confiscated ecclesiastical revenues and extraordinary levies on Huguenot churches. These revenues were administered by a federal controller, federal receivers and provincial controllers: the larger towns had their own controllers and receivers.

The new French 'state within the state' resembled in some respects the Dutch United Provinces: both were federations in which military authority was exercised by a high-ranking nobleman controlled by a permanent executive, and by a federal assembly, meeting periodically, in which the provinces of the union were all represented. But there was also much that was traditional in the Huguenot state, for the towns and villages of southern France had a long tradition of self-government. The provincial assemblies of the Huguenots were also comparable to the old provincial estates and *états particuliers*. It is likely that, except for an increase in taxation, local people did not see any great change between the new regime and the old, especially since the personnel remained essentially unchanged. Yet the new state was revolutionary, since the federal assembly or Estates-General appointed the Protector, who exercised powers (the fixing and distribution of taxes, the appointment of ambassadors and generals, the making of laws) which hitherto had belonged exclusively to the king of France.

The effectiveness of the new state was restricted by geographical factors and internal divisions. Only the Huguenots living south of a line drawn roughly from Grenoble in the east to Saint-Jean-d'Angély in the west were part of it: those living further north were excluded, even if they did sometimes send representatives to the southern assemblies. What is more, within the Huguenot state itself there were many large towns (Toulouse, Bordeaux, Marseille, Avignon, Aix and Agen) which lay outside its control. Provence, the Toulouse region and many small areas near the Pyrenees remained Catholic. Constant friction also disturbed relations between the great nobles who led the military operations and members of the assemblies and councils. The Protectors were, first, the prince de Condé, then Henri de Montmorency-Damville (who was a Catholic ally of the Union from 1574 to about 1579), and finally Henri de Navarre (who escaped from the French court in February 1576). These strong men did not take kindly to being controlled by an assembly dominated by Calvinist pastors and men of the robe. They were even less submissive to a permanent council whose *raison d'être* was to control their actions. When Navarre became heir presumptive to the throne in 1584, relations became even more strained. The Assembly of La Rochelle (1588) had to amend the membership and powers of the permanent council. Henceforth it was to consist of ten members, who would meet three times a week at Navarre's residence and discuss with him all the Union's affairs.

23

Literary Responses

The political and religious troubles which befell France in the second half of the sixteenth century inevitably affected every aspect of French life, prompting various responses. Many of the participants in the civil wars were moved to express their feelings of outrage, compassion or elation in a literary form. Others sought to justify their actions, to explain the current situation or to advocate remedies for the constitutional sickness which was afflicting the body politic.

Military autobiography

The French nobility in the sixteenth century had the reputation of despising intellectual pursuits. In 1577, François de l'Alouëte, in a treatise largely devoted to the nobility, blamed the decline of its power and influence on its loss of public positions. For this he blamed the nobles themselves who, preferring pleasure, vanity and ignorance, had made themselves unfit for responsibility. To remedy this state of affairs some commentators urged the nobles to educate themselves. David Du Rivault (1596) attacked the old idea that learning was unaristocratic and demeaning. Greek and Roman nobles, he said, were proficient in both arms and letters, and their decline came only when they neglected one or the other. One writer urged French nobles to learn letters so that they might immortalize the deeds of their ancestors by writing them up. Such a message was bound to appeal to a generation keen that its achievements should not be lost to posterity. If a nobleman felt uneasy about taking up the pen in place of the sword, he could take comfort from the example of Julius Caesar, who had combined a brilliant military career with literary activity. 'The greatest captain that ever lived', wrote Blaise de Monluc, 'was Caesar, and he has led me the way, having himself written his own commentaries, and being careful to record by night the actions he performed by day.'

Already during the first half of the sixteenth century a number of French noblemen had produced autobiographies. While Marshal Florange recorded his own deeds of heroism in his *Memoirs*, Guillaume du Bellay, seigneur de Langey, set out to write a history. He lived at a time when French historical writing was coming of age. While Claude de Seyssel was translating into French the histories of Thucydides, Xenophon and Diodorus Siculus, French editions of Caesar's *Commentaries* and Livy's *Decades* were being published. A translation of Suetonius appeared in 1520 and one of Sallust in 1528. In 1518 there appeared a Latin history of France which was modelled on the pattern of classical historians, especially Livy. Its author was Paolo Emilio of Verona, who had come to France at the invitation of Louis XII. His history was continued to the death of Francis I by Arnoul Le Ferron.

Du Bellay was undoubtedly influenced by the new historiographical trends. He wrote his history in Latin and called it the *Ogdoades* because it was divided into eight books as against Livy's ten. His many public duties stood in the way of his writing, but he was given strong encouragement by the king, including access to the royal archives. In effect du Bellay became Emilio's successor as the official historian of the reign, and he approached his task in a truly scientific spirit: questioning eyewitnesses, gathering reports and memoranda and delving into private and public archives. On the king's advice, he dropped Latin in favour of French, but his work was unfinished at his death in 1543. Its completion was entrusted to his younger brother Martin, who was first and foremost a soldier. By adding his own reminiscences to Guillaume's work, he produced a blend of history and memoirs spanning the years 1513 to 1547.

The Peace of Cateau-Cambrésis ended the Italian wars and with them died an age full of echoes of the chivalric past. For the rest of the century France was torn apart by civil strife and the golden age of Francis I and the 'Preux de Marignan' was eclipsed by the horrors inflicted by Frenchmen on each other, culminating in the massacre of St Bartholomew's day. A by-product of this new situation was a spate of memoirs, many of which were intended not only to glorify their authors but also to defend them against charges or criticism. The memoirs of the period also reflect the sudden changes of fortune that could dash a reputation overnight. Examples of the new genre of memoir-writers are Blaise de Monluc, Jean de Saulx-Tavannes, François de La Noue, Agrippa d'Aubigné and Brantôme.

Blaise de Monluc was born in 1501. Gascony, his native province, was reputed to be fertile only in soldiers. Monluc's military career began in the declining years of chivalry. His account of his early experiences in the Italian wars reflects the enthusiasm that animated the young noblemen who

ventured across the Alps. Under Henry II, Monluc attached himself to the
rising star of François duc de Guise, and in 1554 he was given his greatest
charge: the defence of Siena. Following the Peace of Cateau-Cambrésis,
Monluc fell on hard times, like many other soldiers. He thought of joining
the Huguenots in south-west France, but in the end saw that his interest
lay in upholding the Catholic cause. His decision owed little or nothing to
religious conviction. As the king's lieutenant-general in Guyenne, he kept
the peace for five years at the cost of great bloodshed. The portrait that
emerges from Monluc's memoirs is of a man blindly loyal to his king:
service is all that matters to him, leaving him little scope for inner conflict
or metaphysical speculation.

Monluc had enemies at court and was accused of excessive brutality,
gross corruption and of being a rapist (*forceur de filles*). He was certainly
a great sinner, even on his own admission, but that did not deter him from
defending himself stoutly. At the age of seventy he was disfigured by an
arquebus shot and forced to wear a mask for the rest of his life. On being
relieved of his governorship, he turned into a lonely and embittered old
man. He died in 1577.

Monluc used his retirement to write his memoirs, calling them
Commentaires in imitation of Caesar. He hoped to be read by other soldiers,
not by scholars who, in his opinion, had enough historians to serve them.
He offers his fellow captains advice on discipline, on relations with their
troops, on the need to show their worth in action. Monluc warns them
against the dangers of gambling, drink, avarice and wenching. The
Commentaires (1592) are a storehouse of military examples for 'young
soldiers': they contain advice on tactics, strategy, fortification and leadership. They show the growing importance of the hand gun: while condemning
it as an 'accursed engine', Monluc has learnt to use it effectively. He
approves of the wheel-lock pistol, which the German reiters brought into
general service in the 1550s, and on the subject of artillery his judgement
is more balanced than that of other commentators at the time. The cannon,
he writes, 'begets more fear than harm'. He echoes the commonly held
distrust of foreign mercenaries – 'a native militia is the true and only way
to have a good army on foot (as the Romans did)' – yet he can see a
difficulty: not all Frenchmen are as warlike as the Gascons.

The *Commentaires* were dictated by an old man relying on his memory.
Consequently, the work is full of digressions, repetitions and descriptions
of trivial incidents, yet they are extremely vivid. Monluc was a born racont-
eur: he could bring the past to life. His *Commentaires* 'deserve to hold their
place in the first rank of narrative sources for the history of France and
Italy in the sixteenth century' (P. Courteault).

Another soldier of the civil wars who turned memorialist in old age was
Jean de Saulx, seigneur de Tavannes. He was the son of Gaspard de Saulx,

marshal of France and a member of the council that decided on the
St Bartholomew's day massacre. According to Jean, his father was 'so lacking in vanity that he refused memoirs to those who wanted to immortalize
his name'. It thus fell to Jean to ensure that Gaspard's name and achievement
were not forgotten. He also wanted to confound the malice and lies of some
and the flattery and ignorance of others, especially Huguenots, who tried
to destroy the memory of Gaspard's achievement by presenting the battles
of Ceresole, Renty, Jarnac and Moncontour as 'minor encounters'. Jean,
who was eighteen when his father died, could recall witnessing some of the
major events in Gaspard's career. In compiling his memoirs he used his
father's papers and interspersed them with long digressions consisting of
his own reminiscences and moral reflections. The memoirs of Tavannes are
partly historical, partly philosophical. The historical part is the more valuable: Jean sees the rivalry of the houses of Guise and Montmorency as the
root cause of France's troubles and blames Henry II for allowing it to
develop. His memoirs throw valuable light on the role of the upper nobility
in the formation of the Catholic League. By contrast, the philosophical
section is haphazardly arranged and poorly written, yet it does illuminate
some military questions as well as the attitudes and customs of the nobility.

Memoir-writers stood on both sides of the religious fence in the French
civil wars. While Monluc and Tavannes were Catholics, François de La
Noue and Agrippa d'Aubigné were Protestants. La Noue was born in 1531.
Though educated with a view to becoming a soldier, he was well-read in
the classical historians, Scripture, the Church Fathers, and contemporary
writers such as Calvin, Rabelais and Bodin. It was soon after 1559 that La
Noue became a Protestant. Yet he remained on good terms with the duc
de Guise and accompanied Mary Stuart to Scotland in 1560. With the
outbreak of the first religious war, he served under Condé and fought at
Dreux. In the second war he lost an arm which was replaced by an iron
one – hence his nickname *bras de fer* (Ironarm). In spite of his profession,
La Noue hated war; he also deplored the disunity among Frenchmen. In
1572 he fought in the Low Countries and, later, was given the impossible
task of persuading his co-religionists to surrender La Rochelle to the king.
In the end, he took command of the town's defences and was subsequently
chosen to command the Huguenots of western France. In 1578 he followed
the duc d'Alençon to the Low Countries and in 1580 was taken prisoner
by the Spaniards. His captivity lasted five years. Philip II offered to release
him if he would allow himself to be blinded: understandably, La Noue
refused. He was eventually set free thanks to Guise intercession. In 1589
he fought for Henry III against the League and was promised the first
marshalship of France to fall vacant, but the promise was forgotten. Under
Henry IV, La Noue served in various parts of France. He was fatally
wounded in 1591, as he led an assault on a Breton town.

La Noue wrote his *Discours politiques et militaires* during his five years' imprisonment in Limbourg. His purpose differed from that of Monluc and Tavannes. They had wanted to record their own exploits or those of their kinsmen; La Noue says little about himself. In fact, his *Discours* are not primarily autobiographical. His personal recollections form only the twenty-sixth part of the book. The rest is concerned with various matters: moral, religious, political, economic and military. The *Discours* are addressed to La Noue's fellow nobles and officers and are intended to warn them of the dangers facing France and to point to the remedies available to them.

La Noue believed that the army, like much else in France, had degenerated since his youth: its discipline especially had crumbled away. Two monsters, he claims, are devouring France: *la picorée* (pillage) and massacre. He argues in favour of military reform within the means available, advocating a revival of the feudal levy and the creation of a standing infantry 2500 strong. He is critical of the traditional way of using cavalry, favouring compact blocks instead. Regarding fortification, he thinks earthworks are cheaper and more effective than the elaborate structures favoured by Italian military engineers. By saving money on one fortress, he says, ten could be built. But La Noue's memoirs are about far more than military matters. They are especially remarkable for their tolerance and humanity. La Noue, it has been said, 'did not know how to hate'. Although he was a zealous Protestant, he never forgot that Jesus had shed His blood for all Christians, not just a few, and that Frenchmen were all brothers regardless of creed.

From a strictly literary standpoint the most distinguished military autobiographer thrown up by the Wars of Religion was Agrippa d'Aubigné, who is best known for his *Histoire universelle* and the long poem *Les Tragiques*. Born in 1552, he was brought up in the Protestant faith and given a good education: he was allegedly proficient in Latin, Greek, Hebrew and French by the age of six. Two years later he and his father were riding through Amboise when they saw the heads of the recently executed plotters. 'My child,' said the father, 'to avenge those honourable men you must not spare your life, as I shall not spare mine; spare it and you will earn my curse.' In 1563, d'Aubigné became an orphan. With only a small fortune he completed his studies, first at Orléans, then at Geneva, and at sixteen entered upon a military career. He fought at Jarnac and entered the service of Henri de Navarre. He shared the latter's enforced stay in Paris after the massacre of St Bartholomew until Henri made his escape in 1576. During the next seventeen years d'Aubigné served him loyally, but relations between them were sometimes strained, as d'Aubigné frequently remonstrated with Henri about his behaviour. In 1588, d'Aubigné captured the town of Maillezais and became its governor. Henry IV's conversion to Catholicism shocked him deeply. He felt that Henry had betrayed the Protestant cause and never trusted him again, but the king's assassination in 1610 left him grief-stricken. In 1620 he fled to Geneva, where he spent the last years of his life. In spite of his advanced age, he acted as military adviser to the governments of Geneva, Berne and Basel, and offered his services to Protestant princes. He died in 1630.

The *Sa Vie à ses enfants* (His life for his children) was written in 1629. D'Aubigné did not want it published, but his wishes were overruled in 1729. The book reads well and, if allowance is made for certain lapses of memory and a tendency to self-glorification, it is on the whole trustworthy. It also reveals d'Aubigné's complex character: self-confident, vain, obstinate, rough and quarrelsome, but also chivalrous, loyal, honourable and capable of warmth and tenderness. Unlike much sixteenth-century writing, *Sa Vie à ses enfants* is brief and to the point. This is partly due to the author's concise style, but also because he had already written his *Histoire universelle*. The two works are complementary. The history offers vivid descriptions of events which d'Aubigné had witnessed, but it tries to be impartial, for he did take seriously his responsibilities as a historian. This may explain why later he felt the urge to give a less inhibited account of his life. *Sa Vie à ses enfants* underlines his personal contribution to the Protestant cause. It invites the reader to examine the author's mistakes, while repeatedly pointing to his glory and martial genius. At the same time, it reveals another side of his character: his remorse over deeds of cruelty, his willingness to forgive enemies, his compassion towards the poor. The personal apologetics so characteristic of Renaissance autobiographies are also diminished by d'Aubigné's frequently stated conviction that all the tribulations of his life are the work of Providence.

By comparison with d'Aubigné, the high-minded Protestant hero Pierre de Bourdeille, abbé de Brantôme, may seem to epitomize the frivolous decadence of the Valois court; but his life was not devoid of seriousness. In spite of his abbey, Brantôme was a soldier and a courtier; he never took holy orders. Born about 1539 into a noble family of Périgord, his childhood was spent at the court of Marguerite de Navarre. After studying at Paris and Poitiers, he travelled to Italy. In 1560 he returned to France and made his first appearance at court. He spent the next fourteen years fighting on the Catholic side in the civil wars, in attendance at court or in travel. In 1574 his military career ended as his duties of gentleman of the king's chamber kept him at court. Two events then altered his life: he lost the king's favour and was badly injured in a riding accident. It was to overcome the frustration of being bedridden for four years that he took up the pen. He also needed to voice his resentment: twenty-five years of loyal service to the crown had gained him little, yet he had seen men whose merits he rated lower than his own rise in wealth and honour. Maybe he had only himself to blame, for he was reputed to be 'extremely violent, difficult to live with and of too intransigent a temper'.

Brantôme's writings look like biographies, but are heavily autobiographical. The best known are the *Dames galantes* and the *Grands capitaines*.
The first takes the form of conversational anecdotes intended to amuse.
Brantôme's role in each story is enigmatic, yet he repeatedly affirms that
he is writing only what he has seen and heard. In the *Dames galantes* he
delights in exposing the private, erotic truths behind the public and chivalric
image of his courtly contemporaries. But he is also proud to be living in
what he regarded as the greatest age in French history, and his *Grands
capitaines* sets out to trace the evolution of that greatness. He sees this as
a kind of graph, rising sharply after 1515, levelling off in the 1550s and
gently declining between 1560 and 1580. Brantôme's own life followed this
pattern. War was for him the vocation of the aristocracy; his golden age
was the reign of Henry II:

> Such was the court of that great king, whose reign may be compared with
> the empire of Caesar Augustus . . . but there was a difference: that of Caesar
> flourished after a war whereas that of our king flourished in war. With the
> coming of peace it lost its splendour, richness and fruitfulness as a consequence
> of his unfortunate death. His reign and court may be justly called the delight
> of our age, but since his death France's misfortune.

The poetry of conflict

Perhaps the most important literary response to the massacre of
St Bartholomew is a poem by Agrippa d'Aubigné called *Les Tragiques*. He
began writing it in 1577, but it was not published till 1616. The poem
consists of some 9300 verses and has been dismissed as tedious, monotonous
and shapeless. Yet the seven books into which it is divided do have a
structure: each has a heading and a theme. The first, *Misères*, focuses on
France's sufferings. We hear the cries of war victims and are made to share
the pain of peasants in a countryside laid waste. D'Aubigné felt genuine
compassion for humble folk and admired nature. Earth in his poem accuses
man of ingratitude. It also lashes out at France's feckless rulers, cursing
two monsters from Hell: Catherine de' Medici, the new Jezebel, and the
Cardinal of Lorraine, Achitophel. The second book, *Les Princes*, is a violent
diatribe against the Valois. After an attack on evil councillors, mercenary
preachers and 'court charlatans', it rounds on the sickly and ferocious
Charles IX and on the foppish Henry III with his heavy make-up and strings
of pearls which cause onlookers to wonder whether they are seeing 'a man
queen or a woman king'. An allegorical debate ensues between Fortune and
Virtue: each proffers advice to a provincial nobleman newly arrived at
court. *La Chambre dorée* denounces the corruption and severity of the

parlement's judges. God descends from heaven to visit the palace which is built of human bones and ashes. The vices of the judges are presented as grotesque allegorical creatures. *Les Feux* describes a procession of martyrs to the heavenly Jerusalem, among them Anne Du Bourg, Gastines and Bernard Palissy. *Les Fers* opens with an altercation between God and Satan and with the transformation of the Angel of Light into a serpent. The main events of the Wars of Religion are then evoked, including the St Bartholomew's day massacre, 'the tragedy that effaces all the rest'. Charles IX, seized with remorse, is horrified to see crows blackening the roof of the Louvre. The old man Ocean awakes from peaceful slumber with a start at the sight of blood in the water pouring from France's rivers. *Vengeance* shows God punishing the persecutors of His church, in a tedious enumeration of divine chastisements from the time of Cain onwards. *Jugement* brings to a logical conclusion the struggle between God and Satan. D'Aubigné launches a final onslaught on apostates in his own religious camp, on the bloody cities that will share Jerusalem's fate and on Antichrist. He engages in a long theological discourse over the Resurrection in which the influence of neoplatonism is detectable, but soon the reader is borne aloft to a magnificent vision of the Last Judgement towards which all parts of the poem have been converging. *Les Tragiques* ends with an ecstatic vision of d'Aubigné, unable to fathom the mysteries of eternity, being reduced to the silence of a mystic whose soul is possessed by God.

Les Tragiques defies straightforward literary classification. It is strongly dramatic in character, the tone throughout relentless in its urgency and indignation. Violent scenes are presented as though by an eyewitness who arrests the reader's attention with such exclamations as 'See here!' or 'Look!' The poem allows no room for debate; the facts, it assumes, speak for themselves and call for action. Its opening lines are: 'Since we must attack the legions of Rome . . .' In the language of Huguenot polemics the meaning is obvious: Rome is the Whore of Babylon, the seat of all vices, the scourge of the true church. The poem appeals to God for revenge and judgement. *Les Tragiques* portrays the unhappy lot of a people, the struggle between the wicked and the good, and, on a higher level, between God and Satan and the final judgement whereby good conquers evil. The present is dramatically linked to future salvation: every Christian must choose between vice and virtue and opt for the 'narrow door' which alone leads to heaven. There is also a strong historical element in d'Aubigné's poem. He judges the present as a witness. Though reasonably accurate, his account is at times distorted by partisan zeal. The present bears continual witness to 'the judgement and power of God'. Some of the poem's most moving passages occur when history is transformed into epic. D'Aubigné is a genius at creating myths, like the *Chambre dorée* and the old man Ocean. Nature for him is not peopled with pagan deities, yet it has a personality that can reproach man for his cruelties and also sympathize with his sufferings. Every epic needs heroes, and those of *Les Tragiques* are the numerous Calvinist martyrs. The poem also contains satire. In *Les Princes*, Juvenal is evoked, elsewhere Rabelais. But the satire is also biblical, being reminiscent of Amos and Ezekiel. At the same time, d'Aubigné can pray to God with as much fervour as the prophets. Through him something of the literary beauty of the Old Testament has passed into the French language. He reminds one of Dante or Milton without being their equal, for his poetry lacks craftmanship; it contains too many speeches, debates, apostrophes and lists. But whatever its flaws may be, *Les Tragiques* stands as a magnificent testimony to the sufferings and hopes of the French Huguenots. Never has the spirit of revolt in France been more poignantly expressed.

On a strictly literary level, D'Aubigné and other Protestant writers were reacting to court poetry, notably that of Ronsard. But he too wrote religious and polemical pieces, though these were mostly written in 1562 and 1563. Ronsard remained silent about the St Bartholomew massacre. His polemical pieces were at first published separately, then gathered together and published in 1567 under the title of *Discours*. They are usually referred to as *Discours des misères de ce temps*. The first poem, which is dedicated to Catherine de' Medici, describes the calamities of the civil war, expresses confidence in her ability to pacify the warring parties and, should she fail, urges her to punish the rebels. The second poem is a more specific attack on the Huguenots and Calvinist theology. The *Remontrance au peuple de France* vehemently criticizes Protestant reliance on individual interpretation of the Bible and the supplanting of knowledge by 'Opinion', who is the daughter of 'Imagination' (i.e. Fantasy). Opinion visits Luther and persuades him to declare war on the pope and the church, causing bloodshed, discord and fratricide. Ronsard's last substantial poem replies to the invectives of two Huguenot preachers. They had accused him of many sins, including paganism, immorality and of writing bad poetry. Ronsard replies to each accusation, sometimes playfully, sometimes vehemently. He defends his faith, gives an account of his daily activities and reaffirms the value of poetry as distinct from oratory. Unlike d'Aubigné, who felt no need to defend his faith, Ronsard sets out to refute the Protestant position on biblical exegesis, the sacraments and so on. By so doing he inevitably weakens his own polemical position; he may be accused of looking back in time. The massacre of St Bartholomew, it has been suggested, 'marked a symbolic, though not historical, dividing line between the possibility of reasonable argument in a space separate from action, and its impossibility. In literary terms, the massacre divides the conventional court poetry of Ronsard from the hyperbolic, self-consciously transgressive battle cries of d'Aubigné' (U. Langer).

Montaigne and stoicism

Not all Frenchmen in the 1570s allowed themselves to be drawn into political activism or resistance. The massacres of 1572 were followed by a revival of stoic doctrines among French humanists, among whom the most famous is Michel de Montaigne. In 1570 he sold his office of councillor in the Parlement of Bordeaux and retired to his château. There he set up an inscription at the entrance to his study celebrating his decision to withdraw from 'the servitude of the court and of public employments' and soon began writing the *Essays* on which his literary fame rests. The first two books were published in 1580 and it was chiefly as a stoic moralist that Montaigne became influential. He shared with other stoics of his day the concept of Fortune as an inscrutable goddess, capricious and ultimately overwhelming in her power, and preached the need to remain steadfast in the face of Fortune's changeability.

Montaigne has sometimes been presented as a religious sceptic. This view rests mainly on the longest of the *Essays*: the 'Apology for Raymond Sebond', a fifteenth-century Spanish theologian who wrote a *Natural Theology*, which Montaigne had translated at the request of his father. Sebond presents Nature as a book, given to us, like the Bible, to reveal the existence of God. It is a theology based on reason, not faith. Although Montaigne calls his essay an apology, it is in effect a refutation. It argues that man is presumptuous to think of himself as the noblest of God's creatures, since animals have as much practical reason, while man's theoretical reason is unreliable and its conclusions are uncertain. Montaigne poses the question: 'What do I know?' and replies that 'reason does nothing but go astray in everything, especially when it meddles with divine things.' Divine reason, Montaigne argues, is totally outside our reach; God moves in mysterious ways and is not in any way hedged by our human reason. All we can do is to recognize this fact and live with it. Yet Montaigne, while distrusting reason, seems to trust faith. Man's *being*, he claims, is always in flux: it never *is*. It is 'of the nature of our senses', he writes, 'to be misled and deceived. Because they do not know what *being* is, they take *appears to be* for *is*.' But Time is movement: only God is timeless; only He *is*. Without Him man cannot rise above humanity. 'He will rise if God proffers him – extraordinarily – His hand; he will rise by abandoning and disavowing his own means, letting himself be raised and pulled up by purely heavenly ones. It is for our Christian faith, not that Stoic virtue of his, to aspire to that holy and miraculous metamorphosis.'

Montaigne's scepticism was limited to the possibility of achieving proof in religious belief; it existed alongside a seemingly sincere Christian faith. In his *Essay* on Prayer he is contemptuous of people who simply mouth the words without understanding them. There are, he thinks, too many prayers; the only one that really matters is the one given to us by God:

> If it depended on me, I would like to see Christians saying the Lord's Prayer as a grace before and after meals, when we get up and go to bed and on all those special occasions where we normally include prayers, saying it always if not exclusively . . . It is the only prayer that I say everywhere: instead of varying it I repeat it . . .

When Montaigne visited Rome he listened with pleasure to the Lenten sermons and went on pilgrimage to some of the principal shrines. In his *Journal de voyage* he expresses admiration for the Jesuits, complimenting them on their efficient services, and in his *Essay* on Prayer he declares his intention to write nothing contrary to the doctrine of 'the Catholic, Apostolic and Roman church in which I was born and in which I die'. He even submits his ideas 'to the judgement of those to whom it belongs to direct not only my actions and my writings, but my thoughts'.

Yet Montaigne was not a conventional Catholic. Even his commitment to Christianity seems doubtful in places, for he writes: 'We are Christians in the same way as we are either Périgourdins or Germans.' Pure faith, he thinks, is idealistic and impossible: it is custom, usage and milieu which determine our religious conduct. This concept of relativity runs through much of the 'Apology', but is also to be found elsewhere in the *Essays*. For example, in 'Of cannibals' he mentions a conversation he had in Rouen with three Brazilians. Other nations, he affirms, are not barbarous, only different; yet we judge their faults while being blind to our own. Montaigne admires the superiority of unspoiled natural men in Latin America; they are not corrupted by our laws or by a government such as ours. He distrusts the supernatural. For example, he does not share the Catholic view that miracles are a divinely sanctioned suspension of nature's laws. His view is that 'miracles depend on our ignorance of nature, not on nature itself'. An event is described as miraculous on account of its strangeness, but it may not appear so to other observers in a different setting. In other words, our judgement is ethnocentric and so is our view of Providence. He is vehemently critical of anthropomorphism – the ascribing of a human form to God – which he blames on 'a mere and egregious sottishness or drunkenness of man's wit'.

> We are all cramped and confined inside ourselves. We can see no further than the end of our noses . . . When frost attacks the vines in my village my parish priest talks of God being angry against the human race: in his judgement the Cannibals are already dying of the croup! At the sight of our civil wars, who fails to exclaim that the world is turned upside down and that the Day of Judgement has got us by the throat, forgetting that many worse events have

been known in the past and that in thousands of parts of the world they are having a fine old time!

Turning to witches, Montaigne does not condemn them out of hand, as does Bodin: without denying their existence, he wonders if human reason is capable of detecting them. He would rather give them the benefit of the doubt than persecute them. 'I am of St Augustine's opinion that in matters difficult to verify and perilous to believe, it is better to incline towards doubt than certainty . . . it is to put a very high value on your surmises to roast a man alive for them.'

Montaigne was not a political theorist, but he could not be indifferent to the political and religious questions which were tearing his nation apart. He knew that much was wrong in French society. For example, he deplored the sale of judicial offices: 'What is more uncouth than a nation where, by legal custom, the office of judge is openly venal and where verdicts are simply bought for cash.' Yet he did not like change. 'For the Rule of Rules,' he writes, 'the general Law of Laws, is that each should observe those of the place wherein he lives . . . it is greatly to be doubted whether any obvious good can come from changing any traditional law whatever it may be, compared with the evil of changing it; for a polity is like a building made of divers pieces interlocked together, joined in such a way that it is impossible to move one without the whole structure feeling it.' 'Once the great structure of the monarchy is shaken by novelty and its interwoven bonds torn asunder – especially in its old age – the gates are opened as you wish to similar attacks.' 'The Christian religion', Montaigne continues, 'bears all the signs of the highest justice and utility, but none is more obvious than the specific injunction to obey the powers that be and to uphold the civil polity.' Obedience, in his view, is the first law of God.

In politics, as in religion, Montaigne was acutely aware of the limitations of human reason. 'To speak frankly, it seems to me that there is a great deal of self-love and arrogance in judging so highly of your opinions that you are obliged to disturb the public peace in order to establish them, thereby introducing those many unavoidable evils and that horrifying moral corruption which, in matters of great importance, civil wars and political upheavals bring in their wake – introducing them moreover into your own country.' Too much of a pragmatist to favour any one type of constitution, he believed that different regimes suited different societies through the power of custom and that monarchy was best for France. He was amused by the controversy over its nature and limits, which seemed to him to be of no practical use – 'fit for nothing but the exercise of our wit' – yet he did not regard monarchy as 'sacrosanct, inviolable and holy'. The king, in his judgement, was a human being like any other: 'even if we sit on the highest throne in the world, we are still sitting on our own bottom.' Yet if

Montaigne took an unmystical view of monarchy, he still believed that force of custom had made it the only viable regime for France and that in the interest of all its subjects it should be obeyed. The Protestant rebels, he believed, were being blindly selfish: 'Their discretion hath no other choice but what pleases them and furthers their cause, which I had especially observed in the beginning of our distempered factions and factious troubles.'

As a moderate man Montaigne must be a royalist in the sense that obedience to the king *qua* king overrides the king's particular defects as a human being.

The Huguenot theory of resistance

Until the last years of his life Calvin firmly adhered to the doctrine of non-resistance. It was the subject's sacred duty, he asserted, to obey the ruler (or magistrate) even if he was 'a very wicked man utterly unworthy of all honour'. For those who ruled unjustly or incompetently had been appointed by God 'to punish the wickedness of the people'. But in the 1550s, Calvin may have moved closer to acceptance of a constitutional theory of resistance. In a letter to Coligny of 16 April 1561 he recalled that he had strongly condemned resistance, albeit with a major reservation: 'I admitted, it is true, that if the princes of the blood demanded to be maintained in their rights for the common good, and if the courts of the *parlement* joined them in their quarrel, then it would be lawful for all good subjects to lend them armed resistance.' In his *Homilies on the first book of Samuel*, Calvin endorsed the view that if the supreme magistrate failed in his office, the inferior magistrates had the right 'to constrain the prince in his office and even to coerce him' in the interest of upholding good and godly government. Yet even in the 1560s he continued to rule out the possibility of resistance by individual citizens or the body of the people.

In France, Calvin's followers began by avoiding any direct confrontation with the government of Catherine de' Medici: they pinned their hopes on achieving a measure of religious toleration. But toleration, as we have seen, failed to carry the day. After the massacre of Vassy in March 1562, the prince of Condé issued a declaration in which he justified his armed uprising by accusing the Guises of usurping the lawful government. His purpose, he declared, was 'to uphold the observation of the edicts and ordinances of the king's majesty'. However, as violence continued and Catherine gave up her efforts at conciliation, the Huguenots found it increasingly difficult to maintain that they were simply defending the government against the Guises. In a second manifesto, Condé accused it of perverting the constitution. Similar arguments were used in many anonymous Huguenot pamphlets published in 1567 and 1568. But it was the massacre of

St Bartholomew's day and the role played by Charles IX and his mother in that tragic event which made it impossible for the Huguenots to continue justifying their armed insurrection in terms of defending the monarchy. For the king had, on his own admission, ordered the slaughter of the Huguenot leaders, even if he had not sanctioned the mass slaughter of their followers. The Huguenots could no longer profess loyalty to a monarchy that had instigated so foul a deed. No longer could they draw a line between the king and his 'evil counsellors'. The hands of both were equally bloodstained.

As La Rochelle and other Huguenot towns threw off their allegiance to the crown, they had to find a new justification for armed resistance. All the Huguenot writers believed that, ever since the massacre of Vassy, the Catholics, inspired mainly by the Cardinal of Lorraine, had been planning to wipe out the Protestants. Catherine de' Medici, they alleged, had been a party to the plot at least since her meeting with the duke of Alba at Bayonne in 1565. Permeating the Huguenot pamphlets of the 1570s was a myth strongly tinged with xenophobia. The recent massacres were interpreted as a manifestation of the queen mother's Italianism. 'Among all the nations,' wrote Henri Estienne, 'Italy carries off the prize for cunning and subtlety, so it is in Italy with Tuscany, and in Tuscany with Florence.' Catherine was seen as a disciple of Machiavelli, the quintessential Florentine, whose spectre had begun to haunt Protestant Europe. She was accused of having brought up her children on Machiavelli's *Prince*. Her son, the duc d'Anjou, it was said, carried a copy of the work in his pocket, and the massacre was the direct application of its precept to commit all necessary cruelties in a single blow. Innocent Gentillet, a Huguenot who fled to Geneva after the massacre, published in 1576 his *Anti-Machiavel*, a lengthy and furious tirade which helped to create the legend of Machiavelli as the author of textbooks for tyrants. He blamed him directly for the French government's 'infamous vices' and, by so doing, helped the Huguenots to present their resistance as a necessary and legitimate act of self-defence.

Many of the Huguenot pamphlets which appeared after the massacre of 1572 continued the tradition of straightforward diatribes, but instead of limiting their attacks to the Guises they extended them to the royal family. Such a pamphlet was *Le Reveille-matin des François et de leurs voisins*. As the title implies, it was addressed not only to Frenchmen but also to their foreign neighbours. It also appeared in three languages – Latin, French and German – and had a multiple authorship. The work consists of two dialogues. The first takes place between friends (called the Historian, the Politician and so on) who have recently fled from France. The Historian gives an account of the rise of Protestantism in France since Luther's time, giving special attention to the religious wars and the events leading up to the St Bartholomew's day massacre. His rambling narrative, punctuated by anecdotes, prayers and poems, is abruptly ended by the prophet Daniel, who offers a daring solution to France's problems. In addition to an armed alliance of Protestant powers, pledged to assist each other, he lays down forty laws and ordinances for the government of France which amounts to her dismemberment. Every Protestant community, Daniel says, must set up its own administration, consisting of a mayor and a council of twenty-four, elected annually, and of larger councils meeting less regularly. Each community must appoint a general to lead its forces and must set up a public treasury with powers to collect and disburse funds. Ecclesiastical discipline must be imposed by a minister and elders, whom the secular authorities must support. Catholics must supply 'food, ammunition and money' by way of taxation. No community should trust the existing government which has broken faith repeatedly; even rule by a foreign prince may be preferable and ought to be seriously considered. As J. H. M. Salmon has indicated, there are strong resemblances between Daniel's proposal and the network of political assemblies set up by the Huguenots of Languedoc in 1574. As for the second dialogue, it relates to travels all over western Europe by the Historian and the Politician. After an excursus into the religious politics of England, they report their success in spreading news of the recent massacres and in begging assistance for the French Protestant cause. The *Reveille-matin* ends with an appeal to all Frenchmen, whatever their religion, to overthrow tyranny and to reassert their ancestral rights.

Another Huguenot treatise which appeared after the St Bartholomew's day massacre is called the *Politique*. It takes the form mainly of a dialogue between a man (Archon) and a woman (Politie). In the course of their discussion, Politie insists that a king and his laws cannot be obeyed if they are unjust, and that no laws are more unjust than those which force the people into impiety. If this situation drives people into rebellion, so be it, but Politie denies the right of resistance to private individuals. It belongs, she says, to the 'inferior powers' – people who, by virtue of their office, have elected the prince and may therefore depose him. But the *Politique* goes beyond restating this classic Calvinist argument by affirming that the inferior agents have a right to lead resistance on behalf of the true faith. The argument is couched in terms that reflect the situation of the Huguenots under Charles IX and is supported by many instances of rulers who have been legitimately deposed, from the kings of the Old Testament to Mary Stuart. Yet the *Politique* admits that revolt, even when legal, may not be the wisest course of action. The legitimate causes for revolt are then examined by the author, and Catholicism is presented as in itself a violation of divine law. Archon warns kings to stop persecuting true believers; otherwise they may lose their thrones and reputations. In several passages the *Politique* comes close to saying that no Catholic ruler should be obeyed and no Protestant one disobeyed.

The *Politique* was an avowedly Protestant tract and this may explain why it was not published separately or widely circulated: the Huguenots could not afford at this stage to alienate support from outside their own movement. It was included with other pamphlets in the *Mémoires* of Simon Goulart. Also in this collection was the *Discours de la servitude volontaire*, which was neither Protestant nor written after the massacre. The author was Etienne de La Boëtie, a young nobleman and Montaigne's closest friend, who may have composed it about 1548. The *Discours* is a meditation on why people accept the rule of tyrants and are willing to live in 'voluntary slavery'. Tyranny, La Boëtie asserts, is made possible by the acceptance of the people, yet they do not need to accept it. They have the power to overthrow any government that proves tyrannical. La Boëtie does not explain how this is to be done or by whom; nor does he indict a specific tyrant. To contemporary readers of Protestant polemics, the target must have seemed obvious: Charles IX and members of his family, particularly his mother and the duc d'Anjou. Much to the chagrin of Montaigne, who deplored the appropriation by Protestant propagandists of his friend's essay, it had a compelling immediacy for its readers after the 1572 massacres.

Another anonymous treatise of the period under review is the *Discours politiques des diverses puissances establies de Dieu au monde*. This has been described as 'the most revolutionary of all, presenting a more anarchic theory of resistance than any other work of Huguenot political thought' (Q. Skinner). Kingdon, however, thinks that the *Discours* 'develops its argument in prose far more measured and considered than that of many of the pamphlets'. It presents 'a reasoned argument for strong monarchic government and displays considerable skepticism about recourse to inferior magistrates for help in organizing resistance'. Yet the *Discours* does make a strong and uncompromising appeal for resistance to a tyrant, leading if necessary to tyrannicide. It rejects the idea that tyranny must be endured as a punishment sent by God, like plagues or famines. No one, the author declares, deserves a more glorious reputation than a tyrant's assassin. In discussing the various sorts of tyranny, the author is especially critical of government by women, who in his opinion are by nature unfit to rule. He does not single out Catherine de' Medici or the massacres – in fact, there is nothing specifically Protestant about the *Discours* (even its attack on the papacy could have been written by a Gallican). What makes it distinctive is its advocacy of tyrannicide.

In addition to such works the Huguenots produced pamphlets containing more reasoned and considered political argument. Even after 1572 they were anxious to repudiate as far as possible the populist and insurrectionary elements in Calvinist political thought. Although their main concern was to call their membership to arms, they also needed to look outside their own religious ranks for support, for they were a vulnerable minority and likely to remain so. If they were to survive they needed to recruit allies

outside their own ranks, possibly among moderate Catholics who disapproved of the brutal methods used by the Valois. To appeal to such
people, or at least not to alienate them, the Huguenots had to find a non-
sectarian justification for their resistance.

The first to appear of a new series of works of Huguenot political theory
was François Hotman's *Francogallia* (1573). On the surface, this is a work
of antiquarianism: it deals with Gauls, Romans and Franks and carefully
avoids contemporary historians and events. But its dedication indicates
clearly its relevance to the contemporary situation. Deploring the fact that
for twelve years France has been torn apart by civil conflict, Hotman
assumes that her ancient constitution remains valid for his own time. He
follows Seyssel's opinion that the crown is subject to three bridles: *police*,
religion and justice. All France's current problems, Hotman argues, are the
result of an attack by Louis XI on her ancient constitution: the crown had
usurped the functions that had been originally exercised by the people,
acting through their representatives in the estates. According to Hotman,
the king was originally elected by the people's representatives, who retained
the power to control his actions. He was only 'the magistrate of the whole
people': they could make or unmake him. Here was a historically-based
theory of popular sovereignty which the Huguenots could use to discredit
the government of the Valois and to gain wide support for their revolution.

Hotman's view of the French constitution served the Huguenot cause by
implying a criticism of Valois rule, but it did not go far enough. What
the Huguenots required was a condemnation of the monarchy's actions,
especially its policy of religious persecution, which would serve to justify
resistance. But as Quentin Skinner has shown, the existing tradition of
radical Protestant thought could not satisfy this need. As a way out of
their dilemma, Huguenot theorists turned to the scholastic and Roman
law traditions of radical constitutionalism. They abandoned the traditional
Protestant notion of God thrusting man into political subjection as a punishment for his sins, and instead began to argue that the original and fundamental condition of the people is one of natural liberty. By so doing they released
themselves from the Pauline doctrine that the 'powers that be are ordained
of God', and inferred that legitimate political authority must originate in
the free consent of all the people.

Du droit des magistrats sur leurs subjets ('On the right of magistrates
over their subjects') was written by Théodore de Bèze, Calvin's principal
lieutenant and successor at the head of the international Reformed church.
He published it anonymously in 1574 in Germany, where he joined the
prince de Condé after he had escaped from the French court and reverted
to Protestantism. In form, *Du droit des magistrats* is a scholastic treatise
which discusses some ten propositions. The first is that only God is to be
obeyed without exception. All rulers owe their power to Him, yet they

should be obeyed only if their commands are consonant with His; any command that is irreligious or iniquitous must be disobeyed. De Bèze then considers whether subjects must presume that the laws that govern them are just. While conceding that rulers cannot be expected to justify every one of their laws, the subjects must follow their consciences in deciding whether to obey those laws. De Bèze indicates that an irreligious or iniquitous command must be disobeyed even if this exposes the subject to punishment. If the command has come from an inferior magistrate the subject can appeal to the sovereign, but if the sovereign himself has issued it, the subject has no recourse: he cannot rise up in spontaneous revolt and may have to face martyrdom or exile. Yet de Bèze offers another option. Magistrates, he argues, are created for the benefit of the people, and governments which do not recognize this principle are tyrannies. Some tyrants are usurpers, others are tyrants by practice, that is to say tyrants who have assumed power lawfully. Usurpers may be resisted by every means, including assassination by private individuals, but resistance to tyrants by practice needs justification.

De Bèze devotes more than half his treatise to the question of how far subjects may resist a tyrant who has acquired power lawfully. He distinguishes three kinds of subjects: private individuals, inferior magistrates, and officials of the central government who share responsibility for selecting and controlling the sovereign. The private individual is forbidden to resist by the Gospel; he can only disobey. As for inferior magistrates, de Bèze distinguishes two types: aristocrats and elected municipal officials. Both share power with the sovereign in legally specified areas which cannot be encroached upon. If the sovereign violates the agreed division of responsibilities, he can and must be resisted. So too must a sovereign who tries to force an inferior magistrate to apply an irreligious or iniquitous command. An inferior magistrate who fails to resist such a tyrant may be punished by God. If he has the right and duty to resist his sovereign, the official who has helped select that sovereign has an even more compelling reason to monitor his deeds. Power comes ultimately from the people and those who mediate that power as electors of the sovereign must ensure that the power is used properly; if it is not, then they must withdraw it by deposing the sovereign. De Bèze supports his argument by using evidence taken from Roman law and sometimes feudal law. He shows that the relationship between ruler and subject is contractual, carrying mutual obligations by the parties involved: if the ruler defaults on his obligations, the subject is not bound to obey him.

De Bèze evidently shared Hotman's belief that the Estates-General was the best source of relief from the tyranny of the house of Valois. But what is the subject to do if the tyrant refuses to convene the estates? De Bèze suggests that he should appeal to the inferior magistrates in the hope that they may convene the estates or band together to resist the tyrant and appeal for help to foreign well-wishers if necessary. Finally, de Bèze considers the limits of lawful resistance. High taxes are not enough in themselves, he thinks, to warrant resistance; only if they are part of an attempt to overthrow the fundamental laws of the kingdom would they qualify. Subjects should also negotiate with their prince before resorting to armed resistance. Turning finally to religious persecution, de Bèze argues that true religion cannot be imposed; it can only be spread by preaching and teaching of the Gospel. Any attempt to prevent its establishment can justifiably be resisted. Once the true religion has been established, it can and should seek the government's protection against 'the bloody whore of Rome'.

The one Calvinist work which rivalled de Bèze's treatise in influence was the *Vindiciae contra tyrannos* (Defence of liberty against tyrants) which is usually attributed to Philippe Duplessis-Mornay, though Hubert Languet may have written the first draft, leaving Mornay to publish it after revision. Be this as it may, the work was planned as early as 1575 but not published until 1579. In form the *Vindiciae* is a scholastic treatise organized around four basic questions: 1) Must subjects obey a prince who commands something against the law of God? 2) Is it lawful to resist a prince who wishes to break the law of God and to ruin the church? 3) Is it lawful to resist a prince who oppresses the state? 4) May neighbouring princes rescue the subjects of tyrants? The answers given to these questions are 'No' to the first and 'Yes' to the other three. In explaining these answers the author develops a distinctive theory of two contracts: the first between God and the people, including the ruler; the second between the ruler and his subjects. Each contract carries mutual obligations. If a king breaks the law of God he loses divine support as expressed by the leaders of His church, and a king who breaks his promises to his subjects loses their obedience.

In answering the third question, the author of the *Vindiciae* parts company with the resistance theory previously developed by Calvinist thinkers. Royal power, he asserts, rests on popular consent which, being conditional, can be revoked. Turning to the matter of tyranny, he draws the classic distinction between usurpation and practice. The first does not present any problem: a usurping tyrant can be resisted by anyone. But the tyrant by practice is not so easily dealt with. An abuse of power on his part does not release private subjects from their obedience; but the officers of the kingdom are obliged to resist. Here the author draws an analogy with Roman civil law. Just as the co-tutors of a minor are obliged to restrain or replace a principal tutor who misuses the property of their joint charge, so the inferior officials of a monarchy are obliged to restrain or replace a king who oppresses his people. The *Vindiciae* distinguishes two kinds of official: those with a local or regional responsibility (like provincial governors or town mayors) and those with national responsibilities (peers of the realm, marshals). The *Vindiciae* says little about the Estates-General.

Jean Bodin and absolutism

The revolutionary movement which was set off by the St Bartholomew's day massacre provoked an ideological rejoinder in the form of Bodin's doctrine of absolute and indivisible sovereignty. Bodin was born at Angers about 1530 into a well-to-do bourgeois family. While still a boy he entered the Carmelite order and was sent to Paris to study. Here he was trained in the old scholastic methods and became familiar with the writings of Aristotle, but he seems to have preferred the New Learning, as taught in the collège des Quatres Langues. It was probably here that he acquired his knowledge of Greek and Hebrew literature and his platonism. After he had been freed from his vows, he went to Toulouse where he spent ten years studying and teaching the civil law. In 1561 he entered the Parlement of Paris as a barrister. Meanwhile, he embarked on an enquiry into universal law, which he thought was best approached through historical study. In 1566 he published his *Methodus ad facilem historiarum cognitionem* (The method for the easy comprehension of history). In this work he aimed to establish what experience had shown to be the best and most enduring forms of law, but he soon became more interested in forms of government. In 1571 he joined the household of the duc d'Alençon as master of requests and councillor. This brought him into contact with the world of diplomacy. He accompanied Alençon to England and, in 1583, to the Low Countries.

Meanwhile, in 1576, he published his *Six Books of the Republic* for which he is best remembered today. Almost immediately afterwards Bodin's career took a downward turn – nothing to do with the work itself but a consequence of his conduct as a deputy at the Estates of Blois, his first and only appearance in public life. In an assembly dominated by the Catholic League, he urged that a peaceful solution be found to the religious problem. He upheld the right of the third estate to dissent from the recommendations of the two privileged orders and opposed the alienation of royal domain as a means of fundraising for the war. His intervention cost him the favour of Henry III. When Alençon died, Bodin left Paris and took up an office in the presidial court of Laon, where he spent the rest of his life. Even in retirement his intellectual activities were sustained. In his *Novum Theatrum Naturae* (1594) he set out to describe the universal system of nature, and his unpublished *Heptaplomeres* was a search for the principles of a universal religion. It was also in Laon that Bodin composed his *Demonomania* (1580), a study of the influence of good and evil spirits 'which more than any other [book] reanimated the witch-fires throughout Europe' (H. Trevor-Roper).

The opening sentences of Bodin's *Republic* betray its original plan. He starts by defining the republic as 'the rightly ordered government of a number of families and of those things which are their common concern, by a sovereign power'. Bodin's concern is to establish first, what a state is and the ends for which it exists; then to discuss the practical policies needed for their accomplishment. The massacre of St Bartholomew seems to have affected Bodin's political thinking, as is revealed by comparing the *Republic* with his *Methodus*. Whereas in 1566 he had expressed confidence in the stability of the French monarchy, in the *Republic* he warns of the impending wreck of the ship of state. He suggests that the captain and the crew are now so exhausted that the time has come for the passengers to lend them a hand. 'That is why for my part,' he writes, 'being unable to do anything better, I have undertaken this discourse of the commonwealth.' He denounces two kinds of men who have 'profaned the sacred mysteries of political philosophy'. The first are the disciples of Machiavelli who have allegedly extolled impiety and injustice; the second are men 'who under pretence of exemption from burdens and popular liberty make subjects rebel against their natural prince and open the door to a licentious anarchy, which is worse than the greatest tyranny in the world'. Bodin mentions no names, but is evidently thinking of the Huguenot resistance theorists or monarchomachs. The purpose of his *Republic*, he explains, is to correct their dangerous errors.

Though France was Bodin's immediate concern, he aimed to arrive at a universal science of politics. He followed in the *Republic* the same procedure as in the *Methodus*: namely, induction from known facts about the contemporary world, as provided by travel books, contemporary histories and diplomats, and from the facts of past history. 'For acquiring prudence', Bodin writes, 'nothing is more important or more essential than history, because episodes in human life recur as in a circle, repeating themselves.' The same method had been used by Machiavelli, but Bodin's values were very different. Unlike the Florentine, he was not just concerned with the techniques of successful government; he aimed to uncover the proper order of human society as revealed by natural reason and the law of God.

Bodin's political thought is rooted in the law of God as revealed in the Old Testament. Along with Calvin and the early reformers, he believed that the state originated in the Fall. It is necessary because of man's wickedness. But Bodin sees it as a means of protecting liberty and property, two rights sanctioned by divine law. He defines natural liberty as the perfect freedom to live as one pleases, subject only to the law of reason. This is qualified when a man becomes a citizen by the obligation to obey the ruler, but, unlike the Huguenot resistance theorists, Bodin does not make that obligation depend on the citizen's consent. As for private property, he defends it as sanctioned by divine and natural law.

Bodin defined a tyrannical government as one under which liberty and property of the subject are arbitrarily invaded; and a lawful government as one in which the ruler or rulers respect and guarantee them. He did not share Calvin's view of the state as merely a machinery to punish sin. A true state (*droit gouvernement*) is for him one in which men are disciplined to virtuous activity directed to the apprehension of eternal truth. But Bodin did not believe that it was the state's duty to establish 'true religion' or to compel submission to any given church. In his view, any beliefs are better than none, and only toleration can promote piety.

Having defined the ideal state, Bodin focuses on the structure of the state. He follows Aristotle in regarding the family group, not the individual, as the state's essential component. Being convinced that men need discipline to correct their factious and rebellious spirits, he wants to see the father's authority strengthened even to the extent of having power of life and death over his dependants. Bodin thus conceived of the state in terms of power. Its distinguishing mark is sovereign power which is necessarily perpetual and absolute, for anyone who can impose any time limits or restrictions on its competence must be the true sovereign and the apparent sovereign only an agent. Bodin rejected the Roman theory that *imperium* is inherent in the community and conferred by it on the ruler. He denied that consent to government was any part of natural liberty or that the obligation to obey depended on that consent being given. His ideas on the origin of political authority derived not from Roman law but from Scripture: all power is of God; all right to command is therefore independent of the consent of the subjects.

The characterization of the sovereign in terms of power is one of Bodin's most original conceptions; it marks a break with the traditional view of kingship, enshrined in so many coronation oaths, of the king as the fountain-head of justice. While agreeing that all jurisdiction derived from the king, Bodin does not even include the exercise of jurisdiction among the attributes of sovereignty. His view of this matter, it seems, had changed since 1566. The list of attributes given in the *Methodus* comprises: appointing high magistrates and defining their office; ordaining and abrogating laws; declaring war and peace; hearing final appeals and exercising the power of life and death. In the *Republic*, Bodin declares that anything that a sovereign prince passes on to a subject is *ipso facto* not an attribute of sovereignty. The rights of jurisdiction, the appointment of magistrates, the infliction of penalties, the award of honours and the taking of counsel are not marks of sovereignty. There is only one such attribute from which all the others derive and that is the power to make law. So long as the king was regarded as the embodiment of justice, the obligation to obey could be deemed as conditional on justice being done; once the king was conceived of as an absolute and independent power, the usual grounds for disobedience and revolt were denied.

However, Bodin's definition of the state included the idea of right as well as of power. In a rightly ordered society the law should conform to equity.

If the ruler is absolute in relation to the subject, he is not so in relation to God. To God, as the author of his authority, he is answerable in all things. The sovereign is not, therefore, a law unto himself but the instrument of divine will. For government to be efficient, three things are needed: counsel, execution and assent. The state thus needs a 'senate' or council to advise the sovereign, a magistracy with rights of jurisdiction and estates which provide means of communication between the subjects and the sovereign. The 'senate' and the estates, though desirable, are not essential, but the sovereign cannot do without the magistracy to which he delegates rights of jurisdiction. It is on the magistrate rather than the sovereign that the regular functioning of the state depends.

Bodin reduces Aristotle's six types of state to three: monarchy, aristocracy and democracy. Aristocracy is the rule of a minority group; democracy that of a majority of the whole group. Bodin rejects as impossible Aristotle's mixed constitution, which was much admired in the sixteenth century. Absolutism, he maintains, is indivisible. Of the three kinds of state, Bodin favoured monarchy, believing that commands must come from a single will. He thought democracy was the least stable form, because the majority of men include the ignorant, passionate and gullible. Aristocracy was insecure because it was always threatened by internal dissensions. His preferred form was a monarchy governed democratically: that is, where the king consults the estates and all subjects are eligible for office. The estates exist simply to provide subjects with an opportunity to present their requests. The only active role left to them is to give consent to taxation, but even here the king may dispense with such consent in times of necessity. Bodin concludes that the sovereignty of the monarch, far from being diminished by the estates, is exalted by their presence, since it is then that his sovereignty is explicitly recognized. But Bodin did not think it possible to establish at will any form of government since this was determined by environment or, as he writes, 'climate'.

By the time of his death in 1596, Bodin was already famous. His *Republic* became an extremely influential text, yet it ceased to be widely read after the mid-seventeenth century, almost certainly because of its literary short-comings. Still, there is no denying Bodin's originality as a thinker. He has been justly acclaimed as 'the undisputed intellectual master of the later sixteenth century' (Trevor-Roper).

24

Fraternal Discord, 1573–83

The election of Henri duc d'Anjou as king of Poland in May 1573 and his departure from France in the following December had raised the hopes of his younger brother, François duc d'Alençon. He assumed that he would succeed Henri as lieutenant-general of the kingdom, but was opposed by the Guises who had always linked him with the Montmorencys. Alençon was close to Marshal François de Montmorency and during the winter of 1573–4 he tried repeatedly to gain the support of the marshal's brother, Henri de Montmorency-Damville, the governor of Languedoc. Rumours also circulated at court of an impending alliance between Alençon and William of Orange, the leader of the Dutch rebels. In November 1573, Charles IX received a request from the seigneur de Maisonfleur, a former agent of Alençon who had joined Orange's service, to send the duke with an army to aid the Dutch rebels. Charles did not wish to antagonize Spain by such a move, but he was prepared to give the Dutch covert assistance in the form of a subsidy, the first instalment of which was paid to Louis of Nassau, Orange's brother, when the French court was at Blamont.

In January 1574, Charles IX promised to appoint Alençon as lieutenant-general, but the Guises immediately set about discrediting him and his friend Marshal Montmorency. In the Louvre on 16 February, Henri duc de Guise attacked the sieur de Ventabren, one of Alençon's gentlemen, claiming that Ventabren had been hired by Montmorency to assassinate him. Although the charge was never proved, Montmorency was persuaded to leave the court and Charles IX, breaking his promise to Alençon, appointed Charles duke of Lorraine, Guise's cousin, as lieutenant-general of the kingdom. The choice of Lorraine was apparently the queen mother's, for she feared that if Alençon were appointed he would use the position to seize the throne in the event of Charles's death, taking advantage of Anjou's absence in Poland.

These developments added fuel to the conflict at court. Moderate Protestants and Catholics could no longer look to Marshal Montmorency for
leadership, and young nobles who had enjoyed his protection looked for
patronage elsewhere. A number turned to Alençon, whose status as a prince
of the blood outweighed his youth and inexperience. Among the nobles
who gathered around him were the princes of Navarre and Condé, Méru,
Thoré, Marshal Cossé, the seigneur de Montaigu, the comte de Coconas
and the seigneur de La Mole. Historians have often described them as
Politiques, but they were too inexperienced and disorganized to constitute
a party. Although many did favour religious coexistence, religion seems to
have been less important to them than their own private ambitions. The
word *politique* was, in any case, seldom used before 1584 and then pejor-
atively.

Two plots at court, March–April 1574

On the night of 27–28 February 1574 the court fled in confusion from
Saint-Germain-en-Laye to Paris after Protestant troops had been spotted in
the château's vicinity. Their aim, it was alleged, was to free Alençon and
Navarre so that they might escape to the Netherlands, but the plot was
bungled. The sieur de Guitry, who had brought the troops prematurely,
was captured and disclosed under questioning that the plot had been aimed
not at the king but at the Guises. When Alençon was questioned, he confirmed that it was aimed at the Guises, who had prevented him from
obtaining a position of responsibility in the government. Chancellor Birague
wanted Alençon and Navarre to be executed as traitors, but Charles IX
would not take such a drastic step; instead the princes were put under heavy
guard and on 24 March were made to sign an oath of loyalty.

In April, as Montmorency was persuaded to return to court, a second
plot was leaked to the queen mother. The plan this time was for Alençon
and Navarre to escape from the court at Vincennes to Sedan, where Turenne
would meet them with 300 cavalry. Charles immediately placed the two
princes and Montmorency under even heavier guard and arrested some fifty
alleged plotters, including La Mole and Coconas. Under interrogation, La
Mole denied any knowledge of the plot, but Coconas indicated that its
scope had been much larger than hitherto suspected. Two days later Alençon
and Navarre were questioned. The former claimed that he had only wanted
to reach the Netherlands, while Navarre confessed that he and Alençon
had feared a repetition of the St Bartholomew's day massacre. Birague again
urged the king to execute the two princes, but Charles decided to spare
them. They made public apologies and asked the king to receive them as
faithful servants. La Mole and Coconas, however, were tried and executed

on 30 April. On 4 May marshals Montmorency and Cossé were imprisoned in the Bastille.

Henry III's accession

On 30 May 1574, Charles IX, who had been very sickly for some time, died. His mother Catherine de' Medici declared herself regent until such time as the new king, Henry III, returned from Poland. Alençon and Navarre were made to sign another oath of loyalty. As heir presumptive to the throne, Alençon was under less pressure to leave the court, but his relations with the Huguenots remained a source of concern in extreme Catholic circles.

The political situation in France and the threat of foreign intervention by Elizabeth of England, William of Orange and the German princes called for Henry III's speedy return, but he would not be rushed. He was in Cracow on 15 June when news reached him of his brother's death. Three days later, he slipped away at night with a few companions, abandoning his Polish throne and subjects. He rode full tilt to the Austrian border, and on 24 June reached Vienna where the emperor received him magnificently; but an even grander welcome awaited him in Venice. He entered the city on board a galley, escorted by the *Bucintoro* and hundreds of richly decorated gondolas. Among the entertainments offered to the king were fireworks, regattas, banquets, concerts, a solemn *Te Deum* at the basilica of San Marco, balls and a tour of the Arsenal. With such a display of power and wealth, Venice hoped to tighten her alliance with France which seemed to offer the best protection against the threat of Spanish domination, already weighing heavily in other parts of Italy. Henry was easily seduced by the Serenissima: he spent lavishly on jewels and perfumes by day and tasted less innocent pleasures by night. From Venice, he made his way across northern Italy by way of Ferrara and Mantua, reaching Turin on 12 August. His mother, meanwhile, was kept waiting. Henry did not even answer her letters, leaving her without news for a month. He knew from past experience that she was good at coping with emergencies.

On 8 August, Catherine and the rest of the French court, including Alençon and Navarre, left Paris to meet Henry in Lyon. He made his belated entry into the city on 6 September, and one of his first acts was a public show of amity with Alençon and Navarre. They were allowed to come and go as they pleased, yet continued to be closely watched. The court remained in Lyon for several months, while the situation in the rest of France took a downward turn. Some of Henry's councillors urged him to make concessions to the Huguenots, but Catherine, the Cardinal of Lorraine and Chancellor Birague persuaded him to use force. Four armies were assembled:

one, commanded by the duc de Montpensier, was already fighting in Poitou, another under the comte de Retz would go to Provence; a third under the prince-dauphin (the son of Montpensier) was to occupy the Rhône valley; and Henry III himself took charge of operations against Damville.

Damville was ordered to disband his army and either go to the king in Lyon or retire to Savoy without prejudice to his property. His reply was a manifesto, issued on 13 November, which blamed foreigners in the king's council for all the kingdom's woes. He accused them of conspiring to deny the nobility access to offices and dignities, and of condemning the king's subjects to living like wild beasts. They were sending two armies into Provence, one under a foreigner (Retz) and the other under an ex-iconoclast (Uzès). They had wanted Damville's assassination, but this was not why he had taken up arms. He had done so in response to appeals from 'the princes of the blood, officers of the crown and peers of the realm' and also from all the French provinces. As an officer of the crown, a native Frenchman and a descendant of 'Christians and barons of France', he felt impelled to seek a remedy for their ailments.

From Lyon, Henry and his mother travelled to Avignon. Here Catherine tried to negotiate with Damville, but he suspected that she only wanted to detach him from his Huguenot allies. While the king took part in penitential processions through the streets of Avignon, Damville consolidated his defences in Languedoc. He also called the provincial estates, a move which Henry promptly countered by calling them to Villeneuve. Meanwhile, Damville bombarded Saint-Gilles with such gusto that his guns could be heard thirty kilometres away in Avignon. At the same time, representatives of the Protestant churches and Catholic associates met at Nîmes to seal their union and make arrangements for the administration of the southern and central provinces, in effect setting up a state within the state.

While Damville was consolidating his position, Condé spent the winter of 1574–5 in Heidelberg negotiating with John Casimir, the youngest son of the Elector-Palatine Frederick III. As long ago as 1567, John Casimir had offered to assist Coligny with money and troops, and he was now again willing to aid the Huguenots. Although Frederick preferred diplomacy to direct military intervention in France, he gave John Casimir the means to hire mercenaries for Condé. In return for their help, the Elector and his son hoped eventually to gain control of the sees of Metz, Toul and Verdun, which the French had taken over in 1552. Condé also looked for assistance from England, and although Elizabeth was not prepared to enter into a formal treaty, she did send Frederick money to assist the Huguenots. What this Protestant alliance was aiming at is not altogether clear. It probably did not intend to attack Henry III directly, but it must have hoped to oblige him to concede at least freedom of conscience to all his Protestant subjects. The alliance may also have hoped to enhance its legitimacy by gaining the support of a prince of the blood. With Alençon or Navarre at its head it might eliminate the Guises, make peace in France and then free the Low Countries from Spanish control.

On 10 January, Henry III left Avignon for northern France. He had signally failed to impose his authority on the Midi and suffered a further humiliation outside Livron, a town which Bellegarde was vainly besieging for him. A crowd of women hurled abuse at the royal party from the top of the town walls as it travelled past them. On 13 February 1575, Henry was crowned at Reims and, on the following day, he married Louise de Vaudémont, a princess from Lorraine whose beauty had attracted his notice at the time of his leaving for Poland. Meanwhile, in the west, Montpensier managed to capture a number of small towns commanding the approaches to the Protestant stronghold of La Rochelle, but he failed to seize the île de Ré, which would have threatened the town's seaward communications. As war seemed to be getting him nowhere, Henry tried to negotiate. On 11 April 1575 he received a deputation from Damville. The king explained that he had come from Poland with open arms, intending to embrace all his subjects equally without religious discrimination, but he became angry when the deputies presented sweeping demands. They asked for freedom of Protestant worship throughout the kingdom, bipartisan lawcourts in all parlements, secure towns, the release of the two imprisoned marshals, the calling of the Estates-General, rehabilitation of the victims of St Bartholomew's day and punishment of the murderers. Henry was only prepared to offer freedom of Protestant worship in the *places de sûreté* and in two towns *per gouvernement*. Catherine informed the delegates that her son would never revert to the Edict of January. An assembly of the Union was then called by Damville to consider the king's response, and this resulted in another deputation being sent to him. This laid down two prerequisites to any further talks: freedom of Protestant worship throughout France and the liberation of the two marshals.

In the meantime, fighting continued in many parts of France, but its character was changing. Large armies were no longer involved. Instead, forces of a few thousand men, each under a captain, were mounting surprise attacks on towns and villages, springing ambushes or causing mayhem in the countryside. Pillage, rape and the exacting of ransoms were the order of the day; religion seemed to matter less to the combatants than settling old scores or satisfying private ambition or lust. Among the bolder captains was Montbrun, who led the Huguenots in Dauphiné. He even plundered Henry III's baggage train as it travelled to Avignon, and routed a large force of Swiss mercenaries. But fate caught up with him: he was captured, tried by the Parlement of Grenoble and executed.

Alençon's intrigues

During the summer of 1575 there were disturbances in Paris following the murder of a student by an Italian. Before long a mob of students rampaged through the university quarter beating up Italians, while pamphlets and placards denounced their presence in the government. Chancellor Birague was particularly unpopular. Alençon took advantage of this situation. He had still not been appointed lieutenant-general of the kingdom, and had now fallen out with Navarre. On 15 September he slipped out of Paris. Henry III at once assumed that his brother was planning to join the forces which Condé and John Casimir had been gathering in Germany. He ordered the duc de Nevers to bring him back, thereby causing much merriment at court as Nevers was lame. Alençon, meanwhile, reached Dreux, where he issued a manifesto which complained about royal policies without directly attacking the king; it asked for the removal of foreigners from court, for a religious peace pending a church council and for a meeting of the Estates-General. All three demands had already been made by Damville in November.

Alençon's escape from court coincided with a threat of foreign invasion. By now Condé and John Casimir had signed a treaty. Condé agreed to provide 16,000 troops for an invasion of France in return for a monthly subsidy and promised John Casimir the governorship of Metz, Toul and Verdun once the war was over. Early in October, Thoré led a force of 2000 German reiters into Champagne. The prospect of a link-up between the invaders and the rebels in the west and south of France was even more alarming now that Alençon was free, for as heir presumptive to the throne he could give the coalition an appearance of legality if he put himself at its head. Wishing to avert this at all cost, Henry sent their mother to negotiate with him. The first meeting took place at Chambord (29–30 September). The duke asked for the release of marshals Montmorency and Cossé, which Henry reluctantly conceded, but peace depended on Catherine agreeing to further demands. She was not helped in her delicate task by some of the king's advisers, who thought that she was being duped. She warned Henry against repeating the error of Louis XI, who had been persuaded to fight his brother instead of seeking a reconciliation and had eventually been forced to accept worse terms.

On 10 October, Thoré was defeated by Guise at Dormans, but Catherine could not relax until she had signed a seven-month truce with Alençon at Champigny (21 November). As a guarantee for the truce, he was granted five towns (Angoulême, Niort, Saumur, Bourges and La Charité), while Condé was promised Mézières. Freedom of worship was granted to the Protestants in all the places already under their control and in two other towns *per gouvernement*. The sum of 500,000 *livres* was to be paid to the reiters, who were not to cross the Rhine. The queen mother hoped that the truce would lead to a lasting peace; but the governors of Angoulême and Bourges refused to hand over their charges to Alençon. Moreover, he had no control over the actions of Condé and John Casimir. In December their army, numbering some 20,000 men, was standing by in Lorraine. On 9 January it crossed the Meuse at Neufchâteau, taking Henry III completely by surprise. He had not prepared for war and watched helplessly as the invaders swept through Burgundy, leaving a trail of destruction in their wake. They then pushed into the Loire valley and made for a rendezvous chosen by the confederates in the plain of Limagne.

Catherine hoped that Alençon would stay neutral, but he saw something to be gained by siding with the invaders. Most of the towns which he had been promised in the truce of Champigny were refusing to admit his men. In December, he accused Birague of trying to poison him and used this as a pretext to repudiate the truce. He went to Villefranche where Turenne joined him with 3000 arquebusiers and 400 horse. The situation was grim for Henry III. On 5 February 1576 it was aggravated further when Henri de Navarre escaped from court. On reaching the town of Alençon, he formally abjured Catholicism in favour of his original Calvinist faith.

The Peace of Monsieur, 6 May 1576

Within a fortnight of Navarre's escape, a delegation representing him, Alençon, Condé and Damville presented a remonstrance of 93 articles to Henry III. It demanded the free exercise of the Protestant religion throughout France, the creation of bipartisan courts (*chambres mi-parties*) in all the parlements, a number of fortified towns (*villes de sûreté*), and payment of the German reiters. Alençon asked for the duchy of Anjou, Navarre for certain rights and privileges in Guyenne, and Condé for the town and castle of Boulogne. Henry III lacked the resources needed to oppose the forces ranged against him. Alençon and Condé joined forces at Moulins, where they met envoys from Navarre and Damville. John Casimir and most of his reiters were at a camp nearby. Navarre and his troops were in Poitou.

For a time Alençon dithered. He was afraid of mortally offending his brother by marching on Paris and was also fearful of the demands a victorious Protestant army might make. Condé, John Casimir and Turenne gave him an ultimatum: unless he decided to march by a fixed date, they would act without him. On 9 April 1576, Alençon issued another declaration. 'We have decided', he said, 'to exploit the means that God has given us to win by force the peace and tranquillity that we could not achieve by way of reason.' Henry III was left with no choice but to seek peace. Once again he entrusted negotiations to his mother. She left Paris on 26 April with the king's reply to the princes' recent remonstrance, met them at Chastenoy, near Sens, and conceded virtually all their demands. Henry would not allow free Protestant worship within ten leagues of Paris, but even on this he had to give some ground: the distance was reduced to two leagues. The resulting Edict of Beaulieu was proclaimed on 6 May and registered by the parlement a week later. It became known as 'the Peace of Monsieur' (the title given to the king's younger brother) because everyone guessed that it had been forced on the king by Alençon.

The edict's preface expressed the king's desire to bring his subjects together in perfect concord and peace. Catholicism was to be restored in areas where it had been suppressed by the Huguenots; Protestants were to observe Catholic feast-days; and the Protestant religion was to be referred to as 'the so-called reformed religion' (*religion prétendue reformée*) in all official documents and pronouncements. In the main, however, the edict was remarkable for its generosity to the Huguenots. Under the Edict of January 1562 they had been allowed to worship anywhere except in towns, and under the Edict of Amboise of 1563 freedom of Protestant worship had been limited to nobles with superior rights of justice and in a suburb of the main town of each *bailliage* or *sénéchaussée*. Now, for the first time, Huguenots were given freedom of worship throughout France except within two leagues of Paris or the court. They were also allowed to build churches (*temples*) anywhere except within two leagues of the capital. The validity of marriages entered into by priests who had turned Protestant was recognized, and Huguenots were to be admitted to all professions, as well as to schools and hospitals.

For the first time, too, bipartisan courts (*chambres mi-parties*), comprising judges of both religions, were to be established in every parlement to ensure fair play in cases involving Catholics and Protestants. All sentences passed on troublemakers, or people alleged to be so, since the reign of Henry II were rescinded and their victims rehabilitated. The massacre of St Bartholomew was described as a 'crime' and the king gave public expression to his remorse. Families of the victims were exempted from taxation; Coligny was rehabilitated posthumously and his children recovered their property, while the descendants of exiles were recognized as French and subjects of the king. Eight *villes de sûreté* were granted to the Huguenots: two each in Languedoc, Guyenne, Dauphiné and Provence. Under secret articles, the king gave La Charité-sur-Loire to Alençon and Péronne to Condé. Finally, Henry III promised to call a meeting of the Estates-General within six months and to intercede secretly with the pope and the Inquisition on behalf of religious feedom. In separate letters patent, Alençon was allowed to add the duchies of Anjou, Touraine and Berry to his apanage. He was also given an annual pension of 100,000 *écus*. He now became known as duc d'Anjou, which had been Henry's title before his accession to the throne.

The Edict of Beaulieu, however, did not automatically rid France of foreign troops. On 6 May, Henry III wrote to du Ferrier: 'All that is required is money to rid my kingdom of the oppression and ruin of war.' Only by satisfying John Casimir's demands could he get rid of the reiters. John Casimir wanted 1,700,000 *livres* by 7 June and also some old debts to be settled. The *surintendant des finances* Bellièvre made frantic efforts to raise the necessary cash by means of loans, which had to be secured in various ways. Hostages had to be surrendered and jewels or plate pawned. On 1 June, Henry asked Emmanuel-Philibert of Savoy to lend him 300,000l. He also asked Charles III of Lorraine for a loan of 2 million *livres* and the Cardinal de Guise for one million florins. Alençon informed Bellièvre that 'Duke Casimir, whom I have just seen, is unwilling to depart or to allow his troops to leave unless he is given what he has been promised.' The king's financial situation could not have been worse. Madame de Nemours had offered to lend him money she had borrowed from an Italian financier, but he wanted a French province as security. He was offered four dioceses instead but refused them; nor would he accept Brittany. Henri de Guise and his nephews offered silver plate as security for a loan of 100,000l. from a certain sieur Nouveau. 'Whichever way we look,' Morvillier wrote to Bellièvre, 'we see nothing but despair.' On 30 June, Henry informed Bellièvre that Cardinal de Guise had offered 2 million *livres* and 100,000 more in the form of silk and woollen cloth, but this would need to be obtained from the merchants of Rouen who might prove difficult. The king was caught between the rapacity of the reiters and the greed of the moneylenders. 'I can assure you', he wrote, 'that if I could extricate myself at the cost of my own blood I would not spare myself, given my strong desire to rid my kingdom of ruin and desolation.' On 5 July, Bellièvre reached an agreement with John Casimir for the evacuation of his troops from the kingdom. The reiters were to be paid two months' wages before they left France. On 20 July six hostages went to the court of Lorraine at Nancy, but two refused to be handed over to John Casimir. His response was to seize Henry III's envoys, Bellièvre and Harlay, as hostages. 'We would never have thought', Catherine wrote, 'that duke Casimir would have shown so little respect to the king, my son, who has treated him so well.'

The Peace of Monsieur provoked widespread indignation among Catholics, who regarded it as a 'sell-out' to the Huguenot party. Placards denouncing it appeared all over Paris and the king had to hold a *lit de justice* to ensure the edict's registration by the parlement. Henry III was acutely conscious of the shame and humiliation he had incurred as a result of the peace. He even arranged for the bells of Notre-Dame to be silenced as a *Te Deum* was celebrated. He also turned against the bishop of Senlis, who had assisted Catherine in the negotiations, and refused to see her for two months. In a letter to Pope Gregory XIII of 20 May, he admitted his distress and powerlessness. Once again the crown had shown its inability to defeat the Huguenot war machine, which was altogether more efficient and better resourced than its own. Many Catholics began to see that only by forming themselves into a party would they ever be able to defend their cause effectively. Already under Charles IX, armed associations or confraternities had been set up in Guyenne, Languedoc and Champagne; also in Angers and Bourges. Tavannes had wanted to give the Catholics of his province an organization modelled on that of the Huguenots. Thus in 1576 an anti-Huguenot league was formed which felt no compunction about choosing a popular figure as leader. It soon became clear that the Guises would take advantage of the assertion that the king was betraying both France and the 'true faith'. As early as December 1575, Catherine had warned Henry of the danger facing his authority; she had urged him to plant loyal servants in all the provinces. At the same time, the English ambassador reported that Henri de Guise was showing himself a great deal in Paris and seizing every chance of enhancing his popularity.

The Catholic League, which eventually became known as the Holy League (*Sainte Union*), was prompted by the article in the Peace of Monsieur which had granted Condé the governorship of Picardy as well as the fortified town of Péronne. Jacques d'Humières, the town's governor, refused to hand it over and formed a league of Picard nobles and soldiers to prevent Condé from taking it by force. At the same time he called on all the princes, nobles and prelates of the kingdom to form a holy and Christian union against the heretics. Such a league, he indicated, would need foreign help. Henry III reprimanded d'Humières for his initiative. No one, he said, was a better Catholic than himself; he had been forced to make concessions to the Huguenots in order to restore peace to his kingdom. Writing to Bellièvre on 14 June, he used the word 'league' for the first time to describe the newly formed association of Picard towns, which had now been joined by Amiens, Abbeville, Saint-Quentin, Beauvais and Corbie. The Venetian ambassador reported that the League was being fomented by Philip II, who was anxious to prevent Condé from residing so near to the Low Countries. From Picardy, the League soon spread to the rest of France. Meanwhile, Guise issued a declaration which may be regarded as the founding document of the Holy Catholic League. It stated that the Catholic princes, lords and nobles aimed to implement the law of God in its entirety, to uphold Catholic worship and to maintain the king 'in the state, splendour, authority, duty, service and obedience owed to him by his subjects, albeit without prejudice to such decisions as would be taken by the Estates-General'. It was necessary, the declaration continued, to restore to the provinces and estates the rights, franchises and liberties that they had in the time of King Clovis and to enlarge them, if possible, under the League's protection. All Catholics were to join it and provide it with arms and men according to their individual capacity; anyone who stayed neutral would be treated as an enemy. Members of the League would assist each other, judicially or militarily. They would swear to obey any leader chosen to accomplish the League's sacred mission.

Before publishing its programme, the League sent Jean David, a lawyer in the parlement, to seek papal approval. On his return from Rome, however, he was murdered and on his body was found a memo containing a plan for the deposition of the Valois dynasty and its replacement by the Guises, as descendants of Charlemagne. The Huguenots made capital out of this discovery, claiming that it was a summary of minutes taken at a consistory presided over by the pope. The claim was patently absurd, but the memo alerted Henry III to Guise ambitions. The tenor of the document was clear: while the Capetians were a discredited house, the Guises, as descendants of Charlemagne, were perfectly suited physically and spiritually to fight and destroy the heretics. David had been well received in Rome, and Gregory XIII was certainly aware of the League's existence. People rallied round Henri de Guise from all parts of France. Lists of members among the bourgeois and magistrates of Paris were drawn up and circulated. Among the League's chief recruiting agents were the mendicant friars and the Jesuits. The Hôtel de Guise was at the centre of a web spun across the kingdom. The soul of the conspiracy was Guise's sister Catherine, who had been supplanted in the king's affections by Marie de Clèves. She never forgave Henry, and, having married the elderly duc de Montpensier, spent the next fifteen years plotting the king's downfall. It was probably at the Hôtel de Guise and the Hôtel de Montpensier that much of the League's propaganda, aimed at demonstrating the Carolingian credentials of the Guises, and mercilessly lampooning Henry and his favourites, was produced.

One of Henry III's main objectives in 1576 was to detach his brother Anjou from his alliance with the Huguenots and the moderate Catholics or *Politiques* in the Midi. Indeed, there are reasons for thinking that the Peace of Monsieur had been primarily intended to achieve this: several months later the queen mother told Nevers that she and the king had signed the peace only 'to get back Monsieur, not to re-establish the Huguenots' and Henry made similar statements. In the face of the League's threat to his authority, he tried to win over his brother by pointing to the danger posed to the Valois dynasty by Guise ambitions. Anjou proved responsive. He was receiving advances from the Catholic provinces in the Low Countries and the prospect of a foreign crown caused him to break off his alliance with the Huguenots and seek Henry III's backing. The brothers were reconciled at Ollainville in mid-November 1576. Although the king hated Anjou, he received him honourably.

The Estates-General of Blois, December 1576–March 1577

The mounting defiance of the Catholic opposition to the peace forced Henry III to act: he decided to put himself at its head. The success of this policy was put to the test at the Estates-General of Blois in December 1576. Although the Huguenots had been demanding a meeting of the estates since 24 August 1572, they were almost completely excluded when that meeting actually took place as a result of their refusal to take part in the elections, claiming that in many areas they had been rigged by the parish priests. They also complained of undue pressure by the local authorities and of threats by Catholic leagues, though in many provinces, particularly in the south and south-west, a fair number of Huguenots would have been elected if they had only stood. In the event, Monsieur de Mirambeau, a nobleman from Saintonge, was the only Huguenot elected.

As the deputies gathered in Blois, Henry III ordered the establishment of armed leagues in every part of his kingdom. He laid down the rules on 2 December. In each province a force of armed and mounted men was to be set up and the necessary funds for its upkeep raised. The governors would be assisted by the six chief men of the province, and in each *bailliage* or *sénéchaussée* one or two noblemen, or others of requisite substance and loyalty, would be picked to advise on what was needed. Catholics who refused to join the association would be regarded as enemies of God, king and country, and condemned to suffer every indignity and misfortune. This provision was evidently intended to oblige moderate Catholics – both Malcontents and *Politiques* – to rally to the king's standard. Finally, he assured peaceful Protestants that their freedom of conscience (but not, by implication, freedom of worship) and their lives and property would be respected, provided they complied with whatever he decided after the meeting of the Estates-General.

In his opening address on 6 December, Henry expressed his desire for peace among his subjects and paid fulsome tribute to his mother for all that she had done to ensure the kingdom's wellbeing. He promised to devote himself unsparingly to the noble task of eradicating abuses and restoring order. The king was followed by the chancellor, who showed that peace was essential to the success of reforms and asked for the necessary funds. The sentiments expressed by Henry and his chancellor may seem at variance with the policy of setting up armed leagues in the provinces, but the discrepancy was more apparent than real. By assuming the leadership of the Catholic League, Henry was effectively denying that role to Guise, and by setting up a national militia he was freeing himself from the need to hire foreign mercenaries whose cost was prohibitive. He certainly wanted to go back on the Peace of Monsieur, but he could not place his cards on the table too soon. Having called the Estates-General supposedly to seek their advice, it would have been impolitic of him to present them with a *fait accompli*.

Next day, the third estate appointed Le Tourneur, a lawyer in the parlement as its spokesman; the clergy chose Pierre d'Espinac archbishop of Lyon, and the nobility chose the baron de Sennecey. The first two were to become zealous members of the Catholic League and were known to be clients of the Guises. The estates held many meetings to consider their response to the king, and rumour was rife. On 11 December, Mirambeau asked him if it were true that a new massacre of Protestants was being planned. Henry indignantly denied the rumour, and on 13 December sent a formal rebuttal to all provincial governors. His greatest wish, he repeated, was for all his subjects to live in peace and harmony. That same day, the three orders asked him to accept as definitive any unanimous decision which they might take. He refused to endorse such a blatant infringement of his authority, yet agreed to submit to the estates the names of councillors who would examine their *cahiers*. This had never been allowed before. The presence among the estates of an element hostile to royal absolutism was demonstrated on 9 December when a deputy proposed the establishment of an executive body whose decisions would be given effect even without the king's approval. Under pressure from the Guise lobby, the clergy and nobility backed the proposal, but it was turned down by the third estate. All that Henry could do to counter these attacks on his authority was to put on a show of Catholic zeal. He decided to incite the three orders to propose the restoration of religious unity in the kingdom. Many deputies, even zealous Catholics, feared that this might provoke a new war with the Huguenots. But this was what Henry secretly desired; he wanted the estates to bear responsibility for breaking the peace so that they would be morally bound to grant him subsidies.

On 19 December the nobility decided in favour of religious unity and of measures against Protestant pastors and nobles who offered them shelter. Three days later, the clergy voted unanimously for the suppression of Protestantism. It suggested that the three estates should present a unified *cahier*, but the third estate was divided. Jean Bodin, the deputy for Vermandois, opposed a suggestion that all the king's subjects should be Catholics. He pleaded for peace until a church council – general or national – could settle the religious question. In the end he had to accept a watered-down version of the original proposal. The third estate as a whole demanded the suppression of Protestant worship, both public and private, and the banishment of all pastors and consistory members. This satisfied Henry III. At a council meeting on 29 December, he explained that he had signed the Peace of

Monsieur simply to get back his brother and to drive the reiters and other foreign troops out of France. He said that he hoped to restore the Catholic religion to the place it had occupied under his predecessors and promised never again to break the oath he had sworn at his coronation. Some councillors, including Bellièvre, warned him of endless war with the Protestants which he was risking by his policy, but he would not listen. However, in order to carry it out he needed money.

In effect, hostilities had already begun, for the Protestants expected to gain nothing from the Estates-General. In Provence and Dauphiné they were openly fighting and winning ground. But before reacting, Henry wished to be seen to be in the right. He therefore persuaded the estates to send envoys to Condé, Navarre and Damville with an invitation to come to Blois in order to discuss the religious situation with him. Condé rejected the invitation outright. Navarre replied courteously, but asked the estates to reconsider their demand for religious unity. The duc de Montpensier, who had once been a harsh persecutor of Huguenots, returned from his mission to Damville a changed man. He had been so moved by the pleas for peace, which he had encountered from suffering peasants all along the way, that he urged all three estates to embrace religious toleration.

The estates, meanwhile, displayed an extreme reluctance to assist the king financially. He was at his wits' end: he could not pay the wages of his Swiss troops or maintain the traditional life-style of his household, but the deputies at Blois seemed unconcerned. The clergy and nobility invoked their rights of exemption, while the third estate pleaded poverty. In the end, the clergy relented under pressure from the cardinals of Bourbon and Guise and offered the king 450,000 *livres*. But his attempt to raise an additional 300,000 by alienating crown lands was foiled by the third estate, including Bodin, who defended the law of inalienability with vigour. 'They won't help me with their [money]', complained Henry, 'and they won't let me help myself with mine; it's too cruel.'

The king's predicament was compounded by the League's distrust. The Picard nobles would only swear his oath of association on condition that their franchises and privileges were respected. When Jacques d'Humières tried to take control of Amiens, he was refused entry, and the king had to allow the citizens to be exempt from membership of the League in return for a payment of 8000 *livres*. All this was profoundly discouraging for Henry. He had opted for war not out of religious fanaticism, but in order to efface the humiliation of the Peace of Monsieur, to stand up to the Guises and to obtain money from the estates. He now had war, but uncertain support from the League and virtually no money. On 2 March he and his council took another look at the question of religious unity. While Nevers remained intransigent, the queen mother, who disapproved of her son's policy, pressed for peace. Religious unity, she said, would only be achieved if the kingdom were preserved, not destroyed by civil war. Henry now began to share this opinion. If there was to be war, he hoped that it would be brief.

The only bright spot for Henry was his reconciliation with Damville in March 1577. On Catherine's advice, Henry wrote to the marshal on 6 March offering him the marquisate of Saluzzo and its dependencies, if he would hand over the towns he was holding without prejudice to his governorship of Languedoc. Catherine also wrote beguiling letters to him and won over his wife, Antoinette de La Marck. Damville accordingly renewed his allegiance to the king and deserted his Huguenot allies.

The Peace of Bergerac, 17 September 1577

To sustain an army, Henry reckoned that he needed at least two million *livres*. He hoped to get 1,200,000 from forced loans on the fortified towns and the rest from the *taille*, with an additional million from a clerical tenth. The towns begged for exemption, were slow to pay or refused outright, yet the king did manage to raise twenty companies of *gendarmerie*, sixty of infantry and twenty-four cannon. However, he had only enough money to keep them in the field for a month.

Without the support of the German reiters or the alliance of Anjou and Damville, the Huguenots had become vulnerable, except in the south of France where they remained strongly entrenched. In the Loire region, Henry gave his brother Anjou the task of recapturing the small town of La Charité, which the Huguenots had recently taken by surprise. It was besieged on 25 April and surrendered on 2 May, whereupon the town was sacked by the royal troops. Henry gave Anjou a hero's welcome when he returned to court, and on 9 May, Catherine organized a sumptuous banquet for the duke at Chenonceaux. Court beauties appeared topless and with flowing hair 'like brides', while the king, trimly corseted and heavily perfumed, wore a pink and silver gown sparkling with jewels. On 28 May, Anjou rejoined the army as it laid siege to Issoire in Auvergne. The town's governor, Chavignac, was warned of the dire consequences of resistance, but he stood firm. Henry instructed Anjou to punish the town severely for its disobedience and his instructions were duly carried out after it capitulated on 12 June. 'Most of the town', de Thou writes, 'and all its riches were reduced to ashes.' Countless women were raped. On 19 July, Anjou was given another hero's welcome at court, this time at Poitiers. In the eyes of the Huguenots his hands were now as bloodstained as those of his mother and brother. They never trusted him again.

Anjou was now free to push west or south, but the king, not wishing to see his brother add to his laurels, recalled him to court and gave command of the army to the duc de Nevers, while Mayenne was ordered to take Brouage. The king's army by now had dwindled to fewer than two thousand men. As it threatened Limoges, Nevers complained that his ammunition had run out. He was also told that the royal treasury could not afford to pay his troops. Yet the war was far from won. Many Protestant strongholds remained intact, and Navarre and Condé were still at large with the bulk of their forces. When they captured Brouage, on the Atlantic coast, and began receiving aid from England, Henry decided to seek terms. He instructed Montpensier on 6 August to make peace without referring back to him, which would only waste time. The Edict of Poitiers, which confirmed the Peace of Bergerac (17 September), limited the concessions which the Huguenots had been granted in the Peace of Monsieur. Freedom of Protestant worship was restricted to the suburbs of only one town *per bailliage* and to towns held by the Huguenots on 17 September. The exclusion zone around Paris was enlarged. Half the bipartisan courts were abolished and the proportion of Huguenot magistrates serving in the remainder was reduced to one-third. But the Huguenots were allowed to keep eight 'secure towns' for six years. Catholic worship was to be reinstated throughout the kingdom. All leagues and confraternities on both sides of the religious divide were banned. The settlement was an attempt by the king to reassert his authority – he called it 'his peace' as distinct from the earlier one which had been Monsieur's – and it was to give his subjects seven years of more or less unbroken peace.

Anjou and the Dutch revolt

The fragile Peace of Bergerac was soon threatened by developments in the Low Countries. After the Spanish governor-general, Don John of Austria, had captured Namur on 24 July, the Dutch rebels redoubled their efforts to gain Anjou's support. The last thing Henry III wanted, however, was to be dragged into a war with Spain by his brother. He forbade his subjects to take any part in the Dutch revolt, yet Anjou remained in touch with the Dutch rebels. Meanwhile his position at the French court became intolerable, as his followers, led by Bussy d'Amboise, exchanged verbal abuse and blows with the king's favourites or *mignons*. On 10 January 1578, Bussy challenged one of them to a duel involving 300 men on either side. The king banned the fight, but not a day passed without brawls between members of his household and Anjou's servants. The quarrels reached an absurd climax when the king burst into his brother's bedchamber one night and accused him of plotting treason. The misunderstanding was soon cleared up, yet Anjou felt insecure. He also wished to be free to advance his prospects in the Low Countries. On 14 February, therefore, he escaped from court with the connivance of his sister Marguerite, and began raising troops in his apanage at Angers. The duke was accompanied by rowdy supporters who soon disgraced themselves. At a banquet offered by the local bishop, they became the worse for drink and threw food, furniture, silver plate, even people, out of the windows of the banqueting hall. Such behaviour did little to enhance the reputation of courtiers among ordinary people.

Henry III was deeply disturbed by his brother's flight. He was afraid that public opinion would read into it the start of a new civil war, but the duke assured the parlement, Damville, Navarre and Condé that his loyalty to the crown was firm and that he upheld the Peace of Bergerac. Henry, in the meantime, tried to restore harmony to his court, but even after Anjou's departure tensions remained. On 27 April three *mignons* fought a duel with three of Guise's followers, two being killed on either side. The king's favourite Caylus took nearly a month to die of his wounds and Henry offered the surgeons 100,000 francs if they could save his life. He visited him every day and when Caylus eventually died, Henry cut off his hair and removed his earrings and kept them as mementoes. He gave his *mignons* a magnificent tomb. According to L'Estoile, the king's conduct on this occasion further damaged his reputation while enhancing that of the Guises.

Anjou, in the meantime, offered to lead an army into Hainault in exchange for some border towns, but his troops were little better than a rabble. Henry III tried to stop them marching north, while Catherine lectured Anjou on the dangers facing the kingdom if he persisted in his enterprise. The duke explained that he could not ignore cries for help which were reaching him from the Low Countries. On 12 July he arrived at Mons and informed William of Orange that he had come to assist the States-General in their just quarrel. A month later he signed a treaty with them. In exchange for his military assistance over three months, the States appointed him 'Defender of the liberty of the Netherlands against the tyranny of the Spaniards and their allies'; but this title conveyed no authority. The States also promised to consider him as Philip II's possible successor. Anjou, for his part, had to swear to protect the rights of Dutch Protestants and not to attempt to separate the Catholic provinces from the rest. The Dutch, however, did not wish to substitute a French tyrant for a Spanish one, and such hopes as they had placed in Anjou's help soon evaporated as his unpaid troops began to desert, ravaging the countryside in their homeward path. In the autumn of 1578, Anjou reopened his marriage negotiations with Elizabeth of England. She indicated that she would never marry someone she had not met, and Henry and Catherine encouraged Anjou to go to England so as to remove him from the Low Countries. On 5 January 1579 he wrote to Villeroy, justifying his Dutch expedition. He explained that he could not return to the French court because he was regarded by everyone there as a 'common criminal'.

Although the kingdom was now officially at peace, the reality, especially in the south, was closer to anarchy. In Provence the comte de Carcès, the king's lieutenant, opposed the comte de Suze, whom the king had appointed as provincial governor. In Guyenne the governor, Henri de Navarre, was opposed by his lieutenant, Marshal Biron. In Languedoc, Coligny, the governor of Montpellier, resisted the provincial governor, Damville. Meanwhile, Huguenot soldiers attacked castles and churches as well as merchants and travellers. As Henry III disliked travel, he left the task of imposing his authority on the south to his mother. She met Henri de Navarre and Damville, signed a treaty with the Huguenots at Nérac (28 February 1579) and presided over the estates of Languedoc. Wherever Catherine passed, she urged mutual understanding, while stressing the need to obey the king above all. Her physical energy was widely admired, and she did prevail upon the troublesome comte de Suze to resign. But the situation in the Midi remained precarious and the presence at the court of Nérac of Navarre's frivolous wife Marguerite did not make for stability. Her amorous intrigues, which rivalled those of her husband, prompted her brother Henry III to mock the court of Navarre, which gave the Huguenots in the south a pretext for renewing hostilities. However, it was in the north that the so-called 'Lovers' War' – the seventh of the Wars of Religion – began, when Condé seized the small border town of La Fère in November 1579. Fighting then broke out in the south, and Navarre first made his mark as a military leader by storming Cahors in May. However, the Protestants of the Midi were divided, a majority preferring to keep the peace. Anjou was also opposed to the war, which threatened his plans in the Netherlands. In November 1580 he negotiated the Peace of Fleix, which confirmed the treaties of Bergerac and Nérac. The Huguenots were allowed to retain their surety towns for another six years, except Cahors which they had to give back.

Having settled the latest civil war, Anjou hoped that Henry III would back his enterprise in the Netherlands by giving him adequate funds. But the king and his mother were most anxious to avoid a conflict with Spain, so Anjou received only minimal support from his brother. In August he seized Cambrai, but was soon forced back to the Channel coast. He visited England in October and made a pact with Elizabeth, but she indicated that she had no intention of marrying him. On returning to the Netherlands, Anjou assumed the title of duke of Brabant. By October 1582 he was desperate. 'Everything is falling apart in ruin', he wrote, 'and the worst part of it is that I was given hopes which had led me too far to back down now.' An attempt by him to seize Antwerp in January 1583 ended disastrously. The following October he returned to France for good. Even if he had been properly funded, his personal failings would probably have produced the same result.

25

Henry III and his Court

The last of the Valois kings was tall, like his father and paternal grand-father, and in his youth he was slim. But in the course of his brief life (he was 38 at his death) he aged prematurely: his hairline receded and he put on weight. Yet he retained an air of distinction. He had beautiful hands and his bearing was praised for its nobility and grace. Unlike some of his courtiers, he had refined manners. His voice was agreeably soft. He never swore, but he could be hot-tempered. On one occasion he kicked a magistrate who had been accused of corruption. At a council meeting in 1584 he had to be restrained from drawing his sword against Michel de Seurre.

Sartorial excess had become the fashion at court. Courtiers liked to cover themselves with jewels, embroidery and other accessories. About 1590, dandies wore doublets with four sleeves, two being for use and two, trailing behind like wings, merely for show. Henry III was a dandy. At the Estates-General in 1576 he wore a doublet and breeches covered with gold and silver braid, yet soon afterwards he appeared dressed all in black with only a single jewel pinned to his cloak. In time, he abandoned bright colours in favour of black or grey and preferred a turned-down collar of white linen to the broad ruff which made the wearer's head look like that of St John the Baptist on a platter.

The king was also fastidious. The attention which he gave to his personal hygiene, in particular to his hair, was imitated by his companions but mocked by contemporary observers as effeminate. A critic like Thomas d'Embry, in a work called *L'Isle des hermaphrodites nouvellement descou-verte* (The newly discovered island of hermaphrodites), made fun of court-iers who used soap and a white tooth-powder. Their table forks and sweetmeat boxes also came in for ridicule, as did their unwonted use of nightclothes.

In 1574 the staff of Henry III's household included seventeen physicians, six barbers and eighteen surgeons. Ten years later their number had been reduced to nine, eight and nine respectively, reflecting Henry's low opinion of doctors. He was once ordered to insert his foot into the jaw of a newly killed ox as a cure for a leg abscess. Given such treatment, it is not surprising that he was seldom healthy. Early in his reign he suffered acutely from indigestion. He also had sciatica (1575) and gout (1579). He was above all fearful of the stone, which usually led to an extremely painful, and almost invariably fatal, operation. To avert such a fate, Henry took the waters at the spas of Bourbon-Lancy and Pougues. Thermal treatment, however, was not a universal cure. In 1579, Henry developed a painful ear abscess. It burst of its own accord, but left him partially deaf. This abscess and others, which developed later on the king's hand and leg, were probably tubercular. Poor health helped to undermine his authority, for people assumed that his reign would be brief.

Henry III was also thought to be impotent, yet his queen had a miscarriage shortly after his coronation and it is possible the appalling treatment she received on that occasion prevented her from bearing children thereafter. However, Henry may have contracted a venereal disease, for he was allegedly treated with mercury. Physicians at the time were inclined to diagnose many ailments as the *mal de Naples* (syphilis) and Henry's trouble may have been nothing other than a urogenital disorder of tubercular origin. Whatever the cause, he failed to produce any progeny, and in 1582 suffered a kind of nervous breakdown after convincing himself that his kingdom would be plunged into a succession crisis and all his efforts to give it peace and reform would be nullified.

Henry's character bewildered contemporaries. As duc d'Anjou he had been a successful soldier. He had won the battles of Jarnac and Moncontour and had laid siege to La Rochelle, but after his Polish excursion and his accession to the throne, he became apparently indolent and pleasure-loving. The public failed to understand his dislike of army life and his realization that domestic peace would not be achieved through violence. Although basically an intellectual, Henry was a good sportsman, provided he was in the right mood. He was exceedingly temperamental. Thus he would hunt intensively for a few days, then stop. Similarly, he would play tennis or some other ball-game, but only briefly. Having been trained in the use of arms by renowned Italian masters, he was an accomplished jouster. Henry's other hobbies were equally transient. After losing 30,000 *écus* gambling in 1579, he never gambled again and two years later expelled the marquis d'O from his presence for being an incorrigible gambler. In 1585, Henry took to playing *bilboquet* (cup-and-ball), which had become very popular at court and in Paris. He also liked to make cut-outs from illuminated manuscripts, which he would paste on to coloured backgrounds. More lasting was his fondness for small lapdogs, an interest which he shared with members of his family and court. In 1586 there were at least three hundred lapdogs in his household. The king received and offered them as gifts. Unlike Charles IX, Henry disliked animal fights.

Henry's intellectual gifts were recognized by contemporaries. Jacques Amyot, who had been his tutor, compared him to his grandfather, Francis I. They were equally intelligent, he thought, but, unlike Francis, Henry had the patience to listen, read and write. At the age of sixteen he had had to interrupt his education in order to serve as lieutenant-general of the kingdom, but he had resumed his studies afterwards. In Poland he had been taught Latin and Italian by Jacopo Carbonelli, and after his return to France had continued to study. He talked to Giordano Bruno about memory. Henry read a great deal and was a fine public speaker. He would spend several hours each day examining state papers, writing numerous letters (he had 64 secretaries in 1574, 71 in 1584), reading and taking notes.

Nowadays Henry is perhaps best remembered for his *mignons*. The word *mignon* in the sixteenth century was not pejorative; it meant simply a familiar or companion. Henry's *mignons* were young noblemen of his own generation. At first there were four of them: O, Saint-Sulpice, Caylus and Maugiron. Henry wrote to them in a spirit of comradeship, yet did not allow them to forget that he was their master. They were succeeded by Saint-Luc, Joyeuse and Epernon (better known originally as La Valette) who aroused jealousy because of the political influence which they derived from their friendship with the king.

Henry's relationship with his *mignons* was not homosexual, as is commonly thought. The phrase used by him in a letter to Caylus ('I kiss your hands with all my affection') means nothing more than it says: overstatement was chararacteristic of the epistolary style of the time. Far from being effeminate, the king's *mignons* were skilful swordsmen, who in duels risked their lives and those of others. Historians have misinterpreted L'Estoile's description of the return of Henry and his *mignons* to Paris in October 1577: the phrase '*maintien fardé*' does not mean that they were plastered with make-up, simply that they were affected in manner. L'Estoile's descriptions of court entertainments in 1576 and 1577 in which Henry appeared disguised as an Amazon have also been misinterpreted. It was not uncommon for men taking part in court festivals to dress up as women. The Amazonian disguise symbolized chastity and courage. At Bayonne in 1565, when Henry was still a child, he took part in a mock battle between Amazons and other women, all being men in disguise.

The court

In a famous letter, probably written to Henry III on 8 September 1576, Catherine de' Medici urged him to bring more formality into his court. She explained that she wished to restore the kingdom to its former dignity and splendour. In so doing she seems to have been preaching to the converted, for Henry was temperamentally a loner, who wished to distance himself as far as possible from the hurly-burly of the court. Unlike his predecessors, he disliked open-air pursuits, especially hunting, and travelled far less than his predecessors, preferring to reside most of his time in Paris or Blois, except for regular breaks lasting a week or so spent in privacy at Ollainville, Saint-Germain, Vincennes or Madrid. On 10 September 1574 he ordered the Grand Master to restore to his household the order which had existed under Francis I and Henry II. The king's efforts to reform the household took place in three stages: September 1574, August 1578 and January 1585.

Soon after the king's arrival in Lyon in September 1574, he introduced a number of changes to the court's daily routine. He began by abandoning his *lever* in the presence of the great nobles. Secondly, instead of meeting the *conseil des affaires* in the morning, he shut himself up with his mother and the chancellor. Thirdly, at dinner, he insisted on the gentlemen of the chamber being hatless as they served him. He refused to be spoken to and ordered a barrier to be erected around his table to keep the public at a distance. These changes upset many people. Some noblemen left the court in disgust; others derided the novelties which the king had imported from Poland to set himself apart from the rest of humanity. The rumpus was such that Henry had to back-track: he readmitted the *grands* to his *lever*, removed the barriers from around his table and granted after-dinner audiences. The French king had always been more accessible to his subjects than other European monarchs. By his actions, Henry III had repudiated a familiarity which his great nobles had come to regard as theirs by right.

In August 1578, Henry tried again to regulate his household, this time in a written document. As in 1574, he did away with the public *lever*. A restricted council meeting, called *les Affaires*, was held each morning and the king attended the council of state only once a week. After *les Affaires* he attended mass publicly, as his predecessors had done from time immemorial. He then dined in public without barriers and served by his household staff. The pages were bareheaded and archers surrounded the royal table to prevent courtiers from approaching the king or speaking to him. Two features of the regulation were quite new: never before in France had the king's timetable been fixed with such clocklike precision; and admissions to his chamber had never been given a strict order of precedence. Now, courtiers could only approach him in carefully regulated phases. Thus the day began with the king standing in his *cabinet* with his valets and barber. Then, before he was officially wakened (i.e. dressed), only princes, great officers of the crown and councillors might enter his chamber. After the king had signalled that he was awake, he was joined in his *cabinet* by members of the *conseil des affaires*, while the rest of the courtiers stayed in the chamber. Simultaneously, the gentlemen of the chamber entered the antechamber. The king then asked for his cloak and sword and, leaving his *cabinet*, walked through his entire apartment to the chapel accompanied by his lords. In other words, privilege was now attached less to the room into which courtiers were admitted than to the moment at which they entered.

In 1582 specific rulings were added to the regulation of 1578. The most important concerned reform of the council, but two others should be noticed here. First, the king invited a dozen courtiers to share a round table with him informally every Sunday. Secondly, the chief steward was instructed to lay two places at the *bas-bout* of the king's table, one of which was to be permanently reserved for the duc de Joyeuse or the duc d'Epernon. Such favouritism was not unprecedented, but never before had the names of the beneficiaries been written into a household regulation.

In 1585, Henry III issued a general regulation, which he had partly written in his own hand. A printed version was circulated to courtiers on 1 January. Unlike the regulation of 1578, this one revolutionized protocol at the French court by reshaping the king's apartment and controlling the circulation of courtiers within it. The king's chamber (*chambre royale*) was now to be reached through four rooms: the great hall (*salle du roi*), the antechamber (*antichambre*), the chamber of state (*chambre d'état*) and the audience chamber (*chambre de l'audience*). Such a suite of rooms existed in Roman palaces from the beginning of the century, though Henry may have got the idea from Spain, where Philip II's *aposento* was reached through four rooms. However, it seems that in France the new scheme was soon dropped, for Louis XIV's apartment before 1684 consisted of only one antechamber between the king's chamber and the guardroom (*salle des gardes*), as it had been under Henry II.

The circulation of courtiers through the royal suite was strictly regulated in 1578. Before waking-up time, only the dukes of Joyeuse and Epernon and the valets were allowed to enter the closet, or *cabinet*, where the king was dressing. No one could enter the king's chamber, and courtiers were distributed according to rank in the four preceding rooms. Then, when the king let it be known that he was awake, each group of courtiers moved forward one room. The greatest nobles thus entered the king's chamber, but only members of the *conseil des affaires* were admitted to the closet. The king, still in his closet, then called for his *collation*, thereby giving the signal for another forward movement of the courtiers from room to room. It was now the turn of royal councillors, great officers of the crown, the king's chief physician and so on to enter the king's chamber. Finally, as the king asked for his cape and sword and entered the chamber before going to mass, a last move forward took place in the antechambers.

The 1578 regulation also laid down strict though less revolutionary rules governing the king's meals, the manner of laying his table and the procession of dishes from the kitchens; and the provision of barriers around the royal table was revived. The origin of the new protocol may again have been Spanish, for the French were much influenced by usages at Philip II's court. It was from there, for example, that they borrowed the practice of hand-kissing. Yet there were differences. At Philip's court the movement of court-iers was determined not by the time of day but by social rank. The king could also avoid public notice for weeks on end, whereas Henry III walked through his apartment each day on his way to a public mass. Once again, there is uncertainty as to how far the 1578 protocol was actually applied. It was certainly remembered for a long time and is cited at the head of all accounts of French royal ceremonial published later in the *ancien régime*. It seems to be the origin of that strange mixture of decorum and familiarity which typified the court of Versailles till 1789.

The Palace Academy

The academies that were set up in France in the second half of the sixteenth century were part of a tradition reaching back to the Platonic Academy, which existed in fifteenth-century Florence and is associated with thinkers such as Marsilio Ficino and Pico della Mirandola. Neoplatonism aimed at reconciling not only religion and philosophy but all religions, for underlying the syncretism of the Florentine Academy was the idea of a continuous religious tradition linking Christianity with the religions of antiquity. Neo-platonism, as we have seen, reached France during the late fifteenth century, exerting a powerful influence on Lefèvre d'Etaples, Marguerite de Navarre and other representatives of the *Pré-Réforme*. Thus, when Jean Dorat began to instruct the poets of the Pléiade in esoteric doctrine at the collège de Coqueret in the 1550s, he was continuing a well-established tradition. The Pléiade was an unofficial academy. The first official one was founded in 1570 by Jean-Antoine de Baïf, who had been one of Ronsard's fellow students at the collège de Coqueret. He was the son of Lazare de Baïf, Francis I's ambassador in Venice, who had kept his master in touch with literary and artistic, as well as political, developments. It was Lazare who built a superb mansion in the rue des Fosses-Saint-Victor, in Paris, which became the home of the first French Academy.

Charles IX formally approved Baïf's foundation, the aim of which was to revive 'both the kind of poetry and the measure and rule of music anciently used by the Greeks and Romans'. The Academy admitted two sorts of members: 'composers, singers and players'; and auditors, who were to subsidize its activities. Appended to the royal letters patent were the Academy's statutes, which paid careful attention to the business side of the venture and to the detailed regulation of the concerts. However, the Academy was far more than a series of concerts organized under royal patronage. Its activities had an underlying moral purpose. The letters patent state: 'where music is disordered, there morals are also depraved, and where it is well ordered, there men are well disciplined morally'. In other words, Charles IX hoped to foster good morals among his subjects by sponsoring a revival of ancient poetry and music. Neoplatonism, however, included all the arts and sciences within music, and we know that the scope of Baïf's Academy was truly encyclopaedic. Apart from music and poetry, its studies included natural philosophy, mathematics, painting, languages, even military discipline and gymnastics. And it was for this reason that its foundation was opposed by the University of Paris.

It is often claimed that, under Henry III, poetry and music were ousted from the Academy in favour of eloquence and philosophy, but this is incorrect. Henry's encouragement of philosophy was not new, since the Academy's programme had been encyclopaedic. His innovation was to invite some of the academicians to dispute before him on questions of moral and natural philosophy in his own private apartments at the Louvre. These meetings became known as the Palace Academy. The king, it seems, also attended Baïf's Academy, where proceedings included music.

From February 1576 until September 1579, poets, scholars and philosophers gathered in Henry's presence to discuss matters unconnected with current affairs. Yet the essential purpose of these meetings was to equip the king intellectually and morally for the tasks of kingship. La Primaudaye, in dedicating his *Académie française* to the king, recalled that 'republics are blessed only if kings philosophize or if philosophers govern'. In realizing this Platonic ideal, Henry hoped to fill gaps in his education. Astronomy and cosmology were the main topics under discussion during the first eighteen months of the Academy's existence, while the last lectures were devoted to eloquence. In short, the proceedings of the Academy covered all aspects of scholastic philosophy, but excluded the mechanical arts. The Palace Academy brought together most of the literary and scholarly personalities of the day, including Ronsard, Guy du Faur de Pibrac, Jean-Antoine de Baïf and the king's favourite poet, Philippe Desportes. Doron, his Latin tutor, Pontus de Tyard, an Italianizing poet, and Jacques Davy du Perron were among the regular participants. Others who attended were Amadys Jamyn, the courtier-poet, two physicians, Miron and Cavriana, and Agrippa d'Aubigné. Female members of the Academy included Claude Catherine de Vivonne, the wife of Marshal de Retz, who knew Greek, Latin and Italian, and Cabriana de La Guyonnière, renowned for her wit. Among provincial members were Scévole de Saint-Marthe from Poitiers and Robert Garnier from Le Mans.

Although Henry III once expelled du Perron from court for proposing to argue against the existence of God as effectively as he had done the opposite, speech at the Academy seems to have been relatively free. Henry was looking for instruction, not flattery. Although interested in astronomy, he did not share his mother's enthusiasm for astrology. According to d'Aubigné, he disliked the way she allowed herself to be exploited by 'false magicians'. Generally, the speeches delivered before the Academy were strongly Christian in tone, but humanism dictated the choice of topics and the often ponderous classical allusions with which the speakers liked to enrich their contributions. Henry and his academicians looked for ways of disciplining such human passions as anger.

From the start of Henry's reign, the academicians had to pursue their studies under the shadow of an impending storm which eventually broke and overwhelmed them. Etienne Pasquier was one of several people who criticized the king for continuing to patronize culture at such a time:

> If ever a prince had good cause to fear it was then; nevertheless this new king, as though he were living in the tranquillity of a profound peace, instead of putting on his armour, on the one hand began to learn grammar and the Latin language from Doron (whom he afterwards made counsellor in the Privy Council) and on the other hand exercised a kind of concert and academy with Pibrac, Ronsard, and other *beaux esprits* who met on certain days and discoursed upon some subject which they had previously arranged. This was certainly a noble and worthy enterprise, but not fitting considering the affairs which the king then had on hand.

Henry III's religiosity

As Henry returned from Poland in 1574, he passed through Germany, Italy and Savoy. Wherever he went, especially in Venice, he was fêted as a man of high destiny. In the Milanese he had several conversations with Carlo Borromeo, the future saint, who gave him a crucifix containing a piece of the True Cross. Borromeo seems to have made a deep impression on the king, to whom he may have imparted the need to appease God's wrath by a new outpouring of religious fervour. An emphasis on penitence was an important aspect of post-Tridentine Catholicism, as was the necessity of good works. In 1580, Borromeo told du Ferrier, the French ambassador in Venice, that penitential reform was the only remedy for France's disorders. The ambassador passed on the advice to Henry, who replied that his desire was to relieve his subjects of the miseries and calamities which were afflicting them by doing penance for his own sins and vices.

Penitential confraternities were common in Italy; they also became conspicuous in Paris under Henry III. In 1583 he established a confraternity of White Penitents at the Augustinian house. Among their penitential observances, public processions loomed large. On such occasions they wore a robe of white holland cloth shaped like a sack with a knotted girdle and a hood covering the head and face, except for two slits for the eyes. The king was himself a member, as were many courtiers, *parlementaires* and prominent bourgeois. Music of high quality accompanied the processions.

Another of Henry III's foundations was the Order of the Holy Spirit. He was especially devoted to the Holy Spirit on account of coincidences with his own life: he was born, elected king of Poland and became king of France on the day of Pentecost. While he was in Venice he was presented with a manuscript containing the statutes of an Order of the Holy Spirit which had been founded in Naples in 1352 by Louis of Taranto. His own order was inaugurated in 1578 by a splendid religious ceremony which followed upon two days of concerts. In his letters patent founding the order, Henry prayed God 'to grant us the grace of soon seeing all our subjects reunited in the faith of the Catholic religion and living for the future in good fellowship and concord with one another under the observance of our laws and in obedience to us and our successors'.

Henry encouraged the foundation of hospitals and other charitable institutions. Notable among them was the *Maison de Charité Chrétienne*, a combined orphanage, school, hospital and pharmacy founded by the apothecary and art-lover Nicolas Houel. Attached to it was a garden in which medicinal plants were grown, and the orphans were instructed in their use and in the relief of the sick poor. There was also a hospital in which wounded soldiers were cared for and taught useful handicrafts. In 1575 the king founded the *Confrérie de Sainte Cécile* in the church of the Grands Augustins. The statutes laid down that a Low Mass would be said by a monk every Sunday and that he would offer prayers for the king and for the union of the Catholic and Christian church. Every year there was to be a High Mass with special music and a procession. All the musicians in France were to be invited to send their compositions so that new talent might be discovered and rewarded.

In December 1583, Henry III set up at Vincennes a confraternity of 'Hieronymites'. It consisted initially of twelve members who were courtiers and ecclesiastics, including the dukes of Joyeuse, Mercoeur and Aumale; the counts of Maulevrier and Bouchage; the bishops of Auxerre, Nevers and Angers; and Cardinal de Vaudémont. They were given cells in the forest of Vincennes in which they made retreats from time to time. On such occasions they wore a friar's habit and observed a strict rule. The

Hieronymites were closely associated with another royal institution, created in 1584. This was the *Congrégation de l'Oratoire de Notre Dame de Vie Saine*, which was located in a priory that Henry had acquired. The members, who were partly lay and partly clerical, included all the Hieronymites and several members of the Palace Academy, including Desportes and du Perron.

Sacred oratory was an important activity of the congregation at Vincennes. The king himself preached on the feast of St Jerome; but among the sermons preached at Vincennes, only those of Du Perron survive. One of them shows that the king wanted the spiritual discourses to be academic in character. Literary men as well as ecclesiastics were called upon to deliver them. The Palace Academy was thus 'transposed to the plane of a sacred academy' (Yates), its purpose being to combat heresy 'with spiritual arms'. Among the other orators were the humanist Jacques Amyot and the poet Philippe Desportes. Bishops who lectured included the notorious Guillaume Rose, who later became one of the Catholic League's most savage preachers against the king. Another speaker was Father Edmond Auger, the king's Jesuit confessor, who translated the *Imitation of Christ* into French. Another of his devotional works was entitled 'Spiritual sugar to sweeten the bitterness of the sharp miseries of his time'. Auger introduced from Italy a method of preaching aimed at stirring the souls of an audience by playing on three 'tones': the first calmly described Man's Fall and Christ's descent from Heaven to deliver him; the second called fervently on the Christian to look towards the Saviour; and the third called on the people to repent and shed tears for their sins so that God might give them grace in this world and glory in the next. Such an operatic approach to preaching evidently drew its original inspiration from Quintilian's treatise on oratory.

Henry III's extravagant devotionalism was grist to the mill of his opponents. Following his flight from Paris in 1586, the Parisian mob, urged on by fanatical preachers, broke into the royal park at Vincennes and sacked the king's oratory. They seized a pair of candlesticks adorned with satyrs which served the League's propaganda. A pamphlet was published entitled 'The Sorceries of Henri of Valois and the oblations which he made to the devil in the wood at Vincennes'. On Ash Wednesday in 1589, Guincestre, one of the League's most violent preachers, produced one of the candlesticks from his sleeve as proof of the king's devil-worship. Yet, as we know, satyrs were a common feature of sixteenth-century candlesticks. Following the king's assassination, a Parisian mob destroyed everything of his that it could lay its hands on, including the tombs of the *mignons* and a large painting depicting Henry surrounded by the knights of the Holy Spirit.

In recent years, historians have shown more understanding of Henry's religiosity. It sprang from a temperament that was mystical and contemplative, which led him genuinely to believe that the problems with which his kingdom was being plagued could best be solved by spiritual means. The decorations on the bindings of some of his religious books, notably a Psalter with its flames of the Holy Spirit, skeletons, coffins, torches, bells and candlesticks, are revealing of his obsessively penitential brand of faith. Yet it cannot be explained simply in terms of Henry's character. His devotionalism was the final stage in the evolution of the French academies which had begun with the Pléiade, and it heralded the mystical revival of early seventeenth-century Catholicism.

A notable event in the history of the French academic movement was the funeral of Ronsard on 24 February 1586. This took place in the chapel of the collège de Boncourt and was attended by a distinguished company drawn from the court, the parlement and the university. A special mass, composed by Jacques Mauduit, linked the event to Baïf's Academy, while the funeral oration, delivered by the young poet and future cardinal Jacques Davy du Perron, tied it to the present. His oration, stressing Ronsard's role as a great Catholic champion, caused a great impression which lasted into the age of Louis XIV. It harked back to Du Perron's speech at Vincennes and through that to the discourses of the Palace Academy, and reflected 'the atmosphere of the academic enclopaedia in which all pursuits of the mind culminate on a poetic plane of vision' (Yates). The tribute to Ronsard was twofold: he was given not only the earthly glory of a noble Roman who had served the state virtuously, but also the Christian crown of glory and immortality in Heaven. The funeral, however, marked the end of an epoch. Soon afterwards, all that the ceremony stood for was apparently swept away by the ruinous tyranny of the League. Yet if the academies themselves disappeared, their influence lived on and helped to shape the task of reconciliation and reconstruction under Henry IV.

Court festivals and entertainments

As Henry III travelled less than his predecessors, he took part in far fewer royal entries. Whereas Charles IX and Catherine de' Medici had been offered at least 108 entries during their 'grand tour' of France, Henry took part in only four during his entire reign: at Lyon (6 September 1574), Reims (11 February 1575), Orleans (15 November 1576) and Rouen (13 June 1588). While the Lyon entry made use of the traditional heroic imagery, that of Reims stressed the role of the king as peacemaker. The Orleans entry needs to be seen as part of an attempt by the king to reaffirm his authority in opposition to the party led by his brother, Alençon. As for the Rouen entry, it followed Henry's expulsion from Paris in May 1588 (see below p. 449). He looked to Normandy and its riches to back the authority of his favourite Epernon whose dismissal was being demanded by the League. Aquatic displays performed in the entry recalled the warlike imagery

used in 1574. But if Henry was not particularly interested in sustaining the
crown's traditional ties with the various urban elites, he did call upon his
favourites to act in his name. Thus in the 1580s the dukes of Joyeuse and
Epernon (successively governors of Normandy) took part in various entries.
Epernon was acclaimed in Rouen in 1588 as 'being possessed of the king's
ear, favour and authority'. While Henry III relied on his favourites to represent him in towns, he himself indulged public ceremonies of a more
religious kind, designed to underline the special bond linking him to the
Almighty. He took part personally in no less than five *Te Deums* in Paris
between 1576 and 1587 and ordered another six although he did not attend
them himself.

But if Henry III distanced himself ceremonially from the mass of his
subjects, he aimed to turn his court into a place dedicated to the daily
exaltation of his own majesty. In 1581 the court marshalled all its resources
– poets, artists, musicians and mechanics – to celebrate the marriage of the
king's favourite, the duc de Joyeuse, with the queen's sister, Marguerite de
Lorraine. The festivities, described as 'magnificences', lasted for about a
fortnight, a different spectacle being offered almost daily. Such entertainments were derived from the world of medieval chivalry. French and Burgundian chivalry had been renowned for its splendid trappings and the
'magnificences' continued that tradition, adding to it the learning and
refinement of the Renaissance. The exercises of chivalry became exercises
in poetic declamation with musical accompaniment, carefully staged and
costumed. They were the genesis of a new art form – the *ballet de cour* –
which in turn was to develop into opera.

The Joyeuse 'magnificences' were the culmination of a series of entertainments perfected at the Valois court earlier in the century. Catherine de'
Medici was doubtless keen to express the artistic gifts she had inherited
from her Florentine ancestors; and it is possible that she tried to promote
religious concord and loyalty to the crown by staging festivals and inviting
Catholics and Huguenots to take part in them as she did at Fontainebleau
in 1564. One day, for example, three sirens swimming in a canal greeted
Charles IX with a song written by Ronsard. It told how the nymphs and
gods which had filled the woods under Henry II had been chased away by
the civil wars, and looked forward to their return under Charles. As Neptune
approached in a chariot pulled by four sea-horses, a rock opened, disclosing
a nymph who recited verses to the king. The entertainments at Fontainebleau were diversified by tournaments and jousts in allegorical settings
in which the king and nobles took part. One was a combat in which six
knights, led by the prince de Condé, defended a castle against six others,
led by the king.

In 1565 fêtes were held at Bayonne to celebrate Catherine's reunion with
her daughter, the queen of Spain. The combination of tournament and

dramatic allegory had perhaps never been so splendid. One tournament was preceded by a 'Triumph of the Four Elements', another by the entry of Venus and Cupid on chariots accompanied by singing Mercurys. In yet another, all the provinces of France were allegorically represented. There was also a water-carnival with whales and Neptune and his sea-horses.

In Paris in 1572 fêtes were held to celebrate the wedding of Henri de Navarre and Marguerite de Valois. One was 'The Paradise of Love' in the Salle Bourbon. The action began with an assault on Paradise by knights errant (Navarre and his Huguenot companions) who wanted to carry off twelve nymphs. They were repulsed by three defenders (Charles IX and his brothers) and thrown into Hell. Mercury and Cupid then descended from heaven, singing words by Ronsard. After the royal brothers had been harangued by Mercury, they danced with the nymphs, after which the knights errant were set free. On 31 August there was a tilting match between Amazons, led by the king, and Turks, led by the king of Navarre. Huguenot writers later viewed the entertainments as a sinister prelude to the massacre of St Bartholomew; but similar fêtes had taken place earlier without leading to bloodshed.

At the spectacular fête put on in celebration of the marriage on 24 September 1581 of the duc de Joyeuse and Marguerite de Lorraine, about seventeen entertainments were given: tournaments in allegorical settings, a water fête, an equestrian ballet and a wonderful fireworks display. Elaborate temporary buildings, designed by the best artists of the day, were erected in the streets and squares and the various shows were accompanied by music acclaimed as 'the most harmonious that had ever been heard'. According to L'Estoile, the king paid Ronsard and Baïf two thousand crowns each for verses and music which they provided for the occasion.

The dominant artist employed for the Joyeuse 'magnificences' was Antoine Caron, who was assisted by Germain Pilon. Jean Dorat was the humanist designer of their works. Ronsard and Desportes wrote verses. The influence of Baïf's Academy was also present, as Baïf himself and the musician Claude Le Jeune contributed 'verses and measured music' (*vers et musique mesurée*). The 'effects' of Le Jeune's music were compared by contemporaries to those of 'ancient music'. They caused one gentleman 'to take up arms, swearing loudly that he felt absolutely impelled to rush to fight someone'; then, as the music turned to the subphrygian mode, he reverted to being 'quite tranquil'.

According to a manuscript programme, there was to be a combat on foot between the king and the dukes of Guise, Mercoeur and Damville on 19 September. The subject of their fight was Love. The programme describes the action: 'They will enter on a rock at the base of which Love will be bound, beneath the King's feet. The musicians, dressed in some elegant antique fashion, as men and women, will sing insults to Love, with menacing gestures, as though to shake him, pinch him, bind him, and injure him in other ways.' Le Jeune's music, called *La Guerre*, was countered by Ronsard's verse. The performance was evidently a musical dramatization of Petrarch's *Trionfi* with the king's band representing the 'Triumph of Chastity'.

The programme for 24 September was a combat between Henry III and the dukes of Guise and Mercoeur. The king's 'entry will have the form of a marine triumph, being in a great ship, before which there will be two or three rocks like little floating islands, on which will be Tritons and Sirens playing various instruments and sorts of music, with drums, to excite and accompany the King's triumph'. The *Airs* of Le Jeune contain the musical accompaniment to this scene. The song 'O Reine d'honneur' is like an incantation aimed at drawing down the influences of fortunate stars on the monarchy.

Another evening entertainment is described in the programme as follows: 'The twelve torch-bearers will be men and women disguised as trees . . . the golden fruits of which will carry lamps and torches.' This was probably the setting for another Baïf–Le Jeune song, called 'L'un émera le violet' which has been called 'a solar incantation'. Jean Dorat in his *Epithalame ou Chant nuptial* describes the festivities in which he had a hand. He probably helped to design the schemes of the visual decorations and to write the inscriptions in verse under the pictures and on the triumphal arches. He describes two 'arcades' erected for a nocturnal tournament: one, dedicated to the newly-weds, shone like the full moon; the other, dedicated to the king, was like a flaming sun. Echoing the sun–moon theme, were the white and yellow liveries of the twenty-eight combatants. The arcades were connected with a *théâtre pompeux*: a great amphitheatre in which were 'cabinets', representing the planets and constellations. Among these artificial heavens were allusions to Catherine de' Medici's Rainbow, to Henry III's Three Crowns and to the twin stars of Castor and Pollux. The theatre was designed by Louis de Montjosieu, a protégé of Joyeuse. It seems to have served as the background for a dramatic entry by the king as the Sun in a sun-chariot, prefiguring Louis XIV as the 'Sun-king'.

The most famous of the Joyeuse 'magnificences' was the *Ballet comique de la reine*. It was offered by the queen, who employed different poets and musicians from those who had been engaged for the other entertainments. Yet the music aimed at producing 'effects', while the plot and themes also constitute an invocation of cosmic forces in aid of the French monarchy. The theme was the transference of power from the hands of the enchantress Circe into those of the royal family who watched the performance. At one end of the hall was the garden of Circe before whom passed men who have been turned into beasts. The action opened with the escape of a gentleman from Circe's garden. After crossing the hall, he implored the king to deliver the world from the sorceress. In the mythological drama that ensued, Circe was not immediately defeated, though in the end she did succumb to superior powers. The 'golden vault' (*voute dorée*) on the left of the hall represented the celestial world. It contained singers and players who were divided into ten *concerts de musique*.

The elemental world of nature, represented by sirens and satyrs, was under Circe's control. She was only defeated by an alliance of the virtues and Minerva with the celestial world, expressed through ballets based on symbolic geometrical figures and danced by the queen, the bride and other ladies. When the Four Cardinal Virtues entered, wearing star-spangled robes, they appealed to the gods to descend from heaven. The music of the 'golden vault' replied to their music, and it was at this point that the celestial world began to get the upper hand of Circe. Her defeat was assured by the descent of Jupiter sitting on an eagle. This had been signalled by a loud clap of thunder and was accompanied by the 'most learned and excellent music that had ever been sung or heard'. The words sung to this music would have reminded spectators of the message of peace already conveyed by the display in Montjosieu's amphitheatre. Jupiter was not just a mythological figure; he was a 'fortunate star' brought down by powerful music to protect France from the horrors of war and to strengthen and bless her monarchy.

Royal patronage of the arts under the last Valois

As compared with the artistic patronage of Francis I and Henry II, that of the last three Valois kings seems paltry. Francis II was too short-lived to accomplish anything. Charles IX did at least have one ambitious project in mind. He acquired extensive lands on the banks of the River Andelle and called on Jacques Androuet Du Cerceau to build him a palace there. It was to be called Charleval, and the plan, which survives, shows that it was intended to be vast. Henry III was more interested in the theatre, music and dancing than in architecture and painting. He did have a favourite architect in Baptiste Androuet Du Cerceau and was generous to some churches and religious houses in Paris. For example, he gave 2000 *écus* for the completion of the church of Saint-Etienne-du-Mont. Among religious orders, he was generous especially to the Capuchins and the Feuillants. When the church of the Cordeliers burnt down in 1580, he helped to pay for the rebuilding of the choir.

Henry's principal architectural achievement was the Pont-Neuf in Paris. The idea of linking the *bourg* Saint-Germain with the right bank of the Seine can be traced back to the reign of Charles V, but it was Henry who

first took it up seriously. He appointed a commission in 1577 to draw up
a plan, the architects concerned being Du Cerceau and Pierre des Illes. The
first stone was laid by the king on 31 May 1578. The funeral of the *mignons*
Caylus and Maugiron took place that same day and rumour had it that the
king intended to call the bridge the *Pont des Pleurs* (Bridge of Tears).
Initially, a bridge without houses was planned. A grand decorative scheme
proposed by the commission survives in a painting at the Musée Carnavalet.
It shows two triumphal arches, a cluster of obelisks and a central pavilion
halfway across the bridge. These may not have been purely ornamental
features: as Sauval has suggested, they would have obstructed a march by
rebels on the Louvre. The plan, however, was abandoned, perhaps because
of cost. Instead, a bridge with two rows of houses upon it was built. All
that remains today are the round towers above each pile and a row of
bearded masks.

The Pont-Neuf was incomplete when Henry III was assassinated. Would
he have built more, but for the political upheavals of his reign? This is
possible, but we should not assume, as is commonly done, that the Wars
of Religion were a time of architectural stagnation. A considerable amount
of building took place in various parts of France, but the main royal impetus
came from the queen mother, Catherine de' Medici, who seems to have
longed to build in France palaces comparable to those she had known in
the Florence of her childhood. She employed some outstanding architects,
notably Philibert de l'Orme and Jean Bullant, but started more schemes
than she could ever finish.

Following the death of her husband Henry II, in 1559, Catherine abandoned the old royal palace of the Tournelles, which had become painful to
her. She had it destroyed and sold off the site. In 1563 she decided to build
a new residence close to the Louvre, but outside the walls of Paris. This was
the Tuileries, named after a tile-factory formerly on the site. As architect,
Catherine chose Philibert de l'Orme, who had been dismissed as *Surintendant* after Henry's death. If we are to believe an engraving by Du Cerceau,
the Tuileries was intended to be a vast palace with three courtyards, the
two smaller ones being divided by large oval halls. But Blunt has cast doubt
on the accuracy of this engraving. Almost certainly, de l'Orme planned a
smaller palace based on a single courtyard with pavilions on either side. In
fact, little of this scheme was built, for de l'Orme died on 5 January 1570
and two years later Catherine stopped the work, allegedly after a fortune-
teller had warned her that she would die in the parish of Saint-Germain.
This story, however, is suspect, for Catherine continued to visit the Tuileries
frequently, as, for example, in 1573 when she received the ambassadors
who had come to offer the Polish crown to her son. She may have given
up building the Tuileries for economic reasons or because it was too
vulnerable to attack. For whatever reason, it remained unfinished. Much

of it was pulled down under Louis XIV and the rest was destroyed in 1871.

According to Du Cerceau, Catherine decided before 1576 to connect the Louvre with the Tuileries. The first part of this link was the *Petite Galerie*, designed by de l'Orme or Lescot. But only the ground floor was built, in part or completely, in Catherine's lifetime. At some time after de l'Orme's death, work also started on a pavilion at the southern end of the incomplete de l'Orme wing of the Tuileries. The architect of this structure was Jean Bullant, who evidently planned to extend the Tuileries to the Seine, where a gallery might be run towards the southern extremity of the *Petite Galerie*.

In 1572, Catherine began looking for the site of a new residence within the walls of Paris, but she wanted one big enough to contain gardens. Having purchased the Hôtel Guillart, near the church of Saint-Eustache, she swept away a whole built-up area to make way for her new palace. With the pope's permission, she moved the Filles Repenties, an order dedicated to reclaiming girls from prostitution, to another house in the rue Saint-Denis, then demolished the convent, except for the chapel. Catherine also bought and demolished the Hôtel d'Albret and other houses in the vicinity. On their site, Jean Bullant built a new palace, called Hôtel de la Reine. It has disappeared except for a tall, fluted Doric column whose decoration bears witness to Catherine's grief over the loss of her husband; it was not just a memorial: it seems to have been used as an observatory by Catherine's famous astrologers.

Outside Paris, Catherine's architectural activity was mainly focused on two châteaux: Saint-Maur-des-Fossés and Chenonceaux. She purchased Saint-Maur from the heirs of Cardinal du Bellay and employed de l'Orme to complete it. He added two pavilions at each end of the main *corps de logis*. On the garden side, the pavilions were joined by a terrace carried by a *cryptoporticus*. Saint-Maur was unfinished when de l'Orme died. Some time after 1575 another project was advanced by an unidentified architect: he doubled the pavilions on the garden side, raised them by two storeys and crowned them with high-pitched roofs. Two additional arches were built over the *cryptoporticus* and this part of the building was given a colossal, not to say grotesque, pediment. But this too was carried out only in part, and the house seems not to have been habitable till the next century.

In 1560, Catherine forced Diane de Poitiers to exchange Chenonceaux for Chaumont, but it was not until 1576 that she assigned large revenues to building work at Chenonceaux. This consisted of two galleries on the bridge which Bullant almost certainly designed. A drawing and engraving by Du Cerceau show a vast scheme which Catherine allegedly planned for Chenonceaux, but this may have been no more than a fantasy. Du Cerceau 'sometimes inserted in his book designs embodying ideas which he himself would have liked to see carried out rather than those of the actual designer of the building in question' (Blunt).

Catherine was not only a great, if capricious, builder; she was also a notable collector. This is borne out by an inventory of the moveables at the Hôtel de la Reine drawn up in August 1589, after her death. By then she had already given to her granddaughter, Christina of Lorraine, the famous Valois tapestries, now at the Uffizi. But some notable tapestries remained, notably a series of twenty-four, bearing her device and coat of arms, which has been identified with the first weaving of the *Story of Artemisia*. Apart from the tapestries, the contents of the Hôtel de la Reine included, on the ground floor, 25 maps 'drawn by hand' of different parts of the world, more than 135 pictures and several works of sculpture. On the first floor were portraits of all sorts, 341 in all, many of them by Pierre and Come du Monstier and Benjamin Foulon, Catherine's official painters. There were 259 pieces of Limoges ware. One room had walls covered in costly Venetian mirrors. Catherine's study was lined with cupboards decorated with landscapes and filled with varied objects: leather fans, dolls, caskets, a stuffed chameleon, Chinese lacquer, numerous games and pious objects. Hanging from the ceiling were seven stuffed crocodiles and many stags' heads. Around the room were a collection of minerals, some terracotta statuettes and four small cannon. In a cupboard Catherine kept a collection of books and a set of architectural plans. Altogether she owned about 4500 books, including 776 manuscripts. Her printed books were at Saint-Maur. Finally, the inventory lists many costly fabrics, furniture of ebony inlaid with ivory and 141 pieces of china, probably from Bernard Palissy's workshop.

By comparison with architecture, painting stood at a low ebb in late sixteenth-century France. Only two painters emerge as recognizable personalities: Antoine Caron and Jean Cousin the younger. Exaggerated claims have been made for Caron's work. He was not a particularly gifted artist, but he is of great historical interest on account of the themes which he chose to paint. These are of three kinds: allegorical subjects recalling the festivities at Henry III's court; massacre paintings; and paintings which express the astrological preoccupations of Catherine de' Medici and her circle. Caron was employed by the crown in various capacities. He worked under Primaticcio at Fontainebleau and, in the 1570s, was much concerned with the decorations of various public ceremonies and festivities. The spirit and symbolism of such events are well conveyed by Caron's painting of *Augustus and the Sybil* (Louvre, see cover picture). This shows a city *en fête*, decorated with temporary structures of the kind erected for entries and festivals. In the middle are two large twisted columns, probably an allusion to the Temple at Jerusalem, surmounted by a crown and linked by a festoon upon which an eagle is perched. From the festoon hangs the motto: *Pietas Augusti*. This, as Yates has argued, 'must surely be a version of the imperial device of Charles IX'. He himself, as Augustus, is kneeling before the Tyburtine Sybil, who points to a vision of the Virgin and Child. In other words, the Most Christian King is being promised a universal empire based on the Holy Land, as in the prophecies of Guillaume Postel.

About 1560, Caron was commissioned by Nicolas Houel to make various designs for a series of tapestries in honour of Catherine de' Medici. They illustrate the story of Artemisia II, who is remembered for her grief at the death of her husband, Mausolus prince of Caria (352–350 BC). She built the Mausoleum of Halicarnassus in his memory, defeated his enemies and brought up his children, five of whom became kings. Each of Caron's drawings (there are 44 in all) has a border showing the arms of France and of the Medici with the motto: *Ardorem extincta testantur vivere flamma.* Catherine's tears, though abundant, were not enough to extinguish the flame of her love for Henry II. Also visible in the borders are scythes, shattered mirrors, scattered pearls and floods of tears. The tapestries themselves were not woven till the reign of Henry IV who set up a tapestry factory in Paris which later became the Gobelins.

Caron is best known for his massacre paintings. He did not invent the genre. According to the *Histoire ecclésiastique*, in 1561, five years before Caron painted his *Massacre of the Triumvirs* (Louvre), three large paintings illustrating massacres in ancient Rome were brought to the French court and purchased by great nobles, including the prince de Condé, who had one in his room for the Huguenots to see. Caron's painting is a 'veritable anthology of Roman monuments' (Hautecoeur), but we should not assume that he knew Rome at first hand. He borrowed extensively from the engravings of Antoine Lafréry, a Franche-Comtois who had settled in Rome in 1540. The purpose of Caron's massacre paintings is unclear: was he condemning violence or glorifying it? As a Catholic working for the crown, it is unlikely that he was getting at the French Triumvirs. Perhaps he was expressing fear of a possible Protestant triumvirate. What is certain is that Caron became closely associated with the League and that his pictures carried political messages that would have been clear to contemporaries. His *Abraham and Melchisedech* has been interpreted as a critical commentary on Mayenne's defeat at Arques (see below p. 455)

No brief survey of French art during the Wars of Religion should fail to mention the sculptor Germain Pilon. In 1558 he was paid for eight statues for de l'Orme's tomb of Francis I which have since disappeared, and in 1560 he worked for Primaticcio on the monument for the heart of Henry II. Between 1563 and 1570 he worked under Primaticcio on the tomb of Henry II and Catherine de' Medici. No large-scale work by Pilon survives from the 1570s, but he was very active at this time making portrait busts and medals. His marble busts of Henry II, Francis II and Charles IX (Louvre), and the bronze of Charles IX (Wallace Collection, London), suggest that he was closely acquainted with contemporary Italian sculpture.

His portrait medals representing Henry II and his sons are remarkable for their psychological insight and technical brilliance.

During the 1580s, Pilon was mainly concerned with two schemes: groups for the Valois chapel and tombs of the Birague family. Catherine de' Medici planned to set up Henry II's tomb in the central space of a chapel which Primaticcio was to build for her at Saint-Denis. At the same time, she asked Pilon to prepare groups for the smaller chapels. The fragments that survive of his *Resurrection* (Louvre and church of Saint-Paul-Saint-Louis) show Pilon's indebtedness to Michelangelo. His *St Francis in ecstasy* (church of Saint-Jean-Saint-François) looks forward to the Baroque in the open gesture of the arms and hands. More impressive still are Pilon's works for the Birague chapel in the church of Sainte-Catherine-du-Val-des-Ecoliers, Paris. They were badly damaged in the eighteenth century, but three are preserved at the Louvre. Before his death in 1583, Chancellor Birague commissioned from Pilon the tomb of his wife, Valentine Balbiani. Her marble recumbent effigy shows the sculptor's virtuosity in carving detail and its richness contrasts with the grimness of the *gisant* on the sarcophagus below. The chancellor's bronze effigy is quite different. He is shown kneeling at a prie-dieu with his robes forming a long train behind him. While the surface of the metal has been deliberately left rough and unpolished, the head and the hands show intense observation and great directness of rendering.

26

The Catholic League, 1584–92

On 10 June 1584 the duc d'Anjou died of tuberculosis, taking with him the hope which many Frenchmen had placed on his succession to the throne; for Henry III had no son and seemed unlikely ever to have one. This left the Huguenot leader, Henri de Navarre, as heir presumptive to the throne under the Salic law, a prospect which filled Catholics with alarm. Navarre was invited by Henry to come to court and abjure his faith, but refused. This grave situation led to the creation of a new league for the defence of the Catholic faith. In September 1584, Henri duc de Guise, his brothers, the duc de Mayenne and Cardinal de Guise, and two other noblemen founded an association at Nancy aimed at excluding Navarre from the throne. They tried to win the support of Pope Gregory XIII, but he was unwilling to encourage a movement hostile to Henry III, whose Catholic credentials were unimpeachable. Philip II of Spain, on the other hand, could not forgive the house of Valois for the support it had given, however imperfectly, to the Dutch rebels. He therefore allowed his agents to sign the Treaty of Joinville with Guise (31 December 1584). The parties undertook to defend the Catholic faith and to extirpate Protestantism from France and the Netherlands. They recognized Navarre's uncle, the Cardinal de Bourbon, as the lawful heir to the throne. The decrees of the Council of Trent were to become 'fundamental laws' in France. The future king was to renounce France's alliance with the Turks and stop French privateering against Spanish shipping. Philip agreed to subsidize an armed rising by the League.

Military operations began immediately. While Guise captured Chalon, Mayenne took Dijon, Mâcon and Auxonne. As governors of Champagne and Burgundy respectively, they rallied their supporters and set about recruiting some more. In Brittany, Normandy and Picardy, other members of the Guise family – Mercoeur, Elbeuf and Aumale – stirred up agitation.

Soon much of northern and central France passed under Guise control and Cardinal de Bourbon was taken to Reims in anticipation of his crowning. Yet the assistance, military and financial, which Guise had been promised by his allies failed to materialize, and he might have run into serious difficulties if Catherine de' Medici had not prevented the king from acting swiftly to restore his authority. Why she did so is unclear: she may have been reacting to the power exercised at court by Henry III's favourite, Epernon. Whatever the motive, her intervention allowed reinforcements to reach Guise in time. On 31 March 1585 the Leaguers published at Péronne a manifesto which explained why 'the cardinal de Bourbon, the princes, peers and lords of the cities and communities' were opposing those who threatened to subvert the Catholic religion and the state. The manifesto stressed the risk of persecution which faced Catholics in the event of a Huguenot becoming king. It denounced recent warlike acts by Protestants and urged Catholics to prepare for a new civil war. The king's ministers Joyeuse and Epernon were accused, without being named, of paving the way to the throne for a heretic and of depriving other nobles of powers and titles in order to secure for themselves complete control of the armed forces. The manifesto also called for the abolition of all taxes and extraordinary subsidies introduced since the reign of Charles IX and for triennial meetings of the Estates-General. Historians are divided over their interpretation of the Péronne manifesto. While Crouzet sees it as the expression of a mystical urge among Catholic nobles to save society, Jouanna believes that the defence of their own material interests mattered at least as much to them. They could reasonably fear exclusion from royal favour in the event of a Protestant becoming king.

Under threat of invasion by foreign mercenaries in the pay of the League, Henry III hired troops in Switzerland and prepared to defend Paris against a surprise attack. At the same time, he looked for a diplomatic solution to the crisis. Once again he relied on his mother's good offices. She began talks with the Leaguer princes at Epernay on 9 April, but they used them simply to consolidate their military position. They asked for several surety towns and insisted on the king issuing a new edict against heretics which they would enforce. On 7 July the Treaty of Nemours was signed. It was profoundly humiliating for Henry, who undertook to pay the troops which had been raised against him. He also conceded a number of surety towns to the Leaguers. The lion's share went to the duc de Guise, whose clients also received favours, pensions and governorships. As commander-in-chief of the royal armies, Guise was free to raise troops and grant promotions. By accepting such a settlement Catherine discarded the policy of national unity and the principle of religious liberty which she had championed for twenty-five years. As for the Huguenots, they were left with no choice but to fight for survival. An edict arising out of the treaty banned Protestant worship and ordered all pastors to leave the kingdom at once. Their flocks were allowed six months in which to abjure or go into exile. Protestants were debarred from all public offices and were to hand over the surety towns they held. Setting aside the Salic law, the edict also deprived Navarre of his rights to the French throne. Henry III held a *lit de justice* on 18 July to get the edict registered – against his better judgement, for he confided privately that the edict would bring only ruin to his kingdom and subjects.

Navarre, meanwhile, was appalled by the Treaty of Nemours. Half of his moustache, he said, had turned white when he had heard about it. In several letters to Catherine he said that he could not be party to a peace settlement made without him. 'I am bound to oppose with all my strength', he declared, 'those who wish to cause the ruin of the crown and house of France.' He was pressed by two of the king's ministers to abjure, but refused. On 10 August 1585 he and Condé met Damville near Lavaur and renewed the alliance between the Protestants and the 'united Catholics'. In a joint manifesto they accused the house of Lorraine of seeking 'to extinguish the house of France and to take its place'. While affirming their belief that Protestantism was indestructible, Navarre and Condé promised to respect Catholics and their faith 'having always believed that consciences should be free'. The Protestant leaders and Damville reaffirmed their loyalty to the crown and explained that they had no option but to fight the Leaguers who were its enemies. Already in May, Navarre had sent an agent to England and Germany to obtain aid, but he was so short of cash that he was reduced to offering lands by way of payment.

Henry III may have hoped to get round the Treaty of Nemours in the same way as he had evaded the Peace of Monsieur, but the situation was different now. Guise had the support of the Catholic nobility and also of a number of towns, including Paris. There were many reasons for the popular support gathered by the League. The prospect of a Protestant reaching the throne struck genuine fear into the hearts of many town-dwellers. In the League they found the realization of a Christian ideal whose triumph would ensure their salvation. It also held out the hope of a change of regime. The reforms which had been promulgated in the Ordinance of Blois (1579) had so far been largely ineffective: justice was as badly administered as ever, civil war was endemic, pillaging by soldiers was rife, taxes were becoming heavier, and the venality of offices continued to flourish. Furthermore, the price of bread had doubled between 1578 and 1586, causing much hardship among the urban masses. All this, in addition to the personal unpopularity of Henry III and his *mignons*, played into the hands of Guise and his allies.

Among towns that supported the League, Paris was the most radical. It set up its own organization, which became known as the Sixteen (*les seize*) after the number of districts in the capital from which members of the central committee were elected. The Parisian League was set up late in 1584 by Charles Hotman, sieur de La Rocheblond, and three clerics: Jean Prévost, Jean Boucher and Mathieu de Launoy. They nominated other Catholic zealots and respectable Parisians to join them. The recruitment was carefully done, each new member being required to take an oath of secrecy and loyalty. Even so, a royal agent, Nicolas Poulain, managed to infiltrate the movement and kept the king informed of what was taking place. His testimony shows that from the beginning a close relationship existed between the Sixteen and the duc de Guise. While the Sixteen penetrated all the major institutions in Paris, including the parlement, the other sovereign courts, the Châtelet and the university, arms were being transported at night to the Hôtel de Guise, the duke's residence in the capital. A propaganda campaign comprising hundreds of printed pamphlets warned the people that the Huguenots were planning a massacre as well as Navarre's accession to the throne. Meanwhile, an agent was sent to various towns with a request for financial help for the Catholic reconquest of the kingdom. Historical opinion is divided over the aims of the Parisian League. Barnavi sees it as a movement by urban notables of middling rank against the monopoly of major offices enjoyed by a relatively few noble families; Descimon as an attempt by urban officials to restore traditional institutions in local government which had suffered from the crown's excessive advancement of the Robe; and Crouzet as an attempt to establish a mystical union with God at a time of impending disaster for the world.

Henry III looked to the Catholics to pay for the war which they were forcing on him. On 11 August 1585 he asked the municipality of Paris for 200,000 *écus*, at the same time informing the parlement that he would no longer pay its judges. The king explained that, if he had kept the peace so far, it was not out of disloyalty to the Catholic faith but because he realized how difficult it would be to break it. He made it clear that he was not prepared to face ruin alone and warned Cardinal de Bourbon that he would have no scruples about helping himself to church revenues.

Pope Sixtus V issued a bull on 9 September, depriving Henri de Navarre and the prince de Condé of their rights to the French throne. Henry III refused to publish it since it breached the Salic law, but copies were circulated among the general public. Shocked Gallicans were reminded of the deposition of the Emperor Henry IV by Pope Gregory VII in the eleventh century. The Leaguers, on the other hand, could not contain their joy. Protestants were naturally indignant. François Hotman, writing in Geneva, denounced the pope's action in a pamphlet called *Brutum fulmen Papae Sixti V* (Pope Sixtus V's idiotic thunderbolt). On 11 October, Henri de Navarre, using the pen of Duplessis-Mornay, formally protested to the parlement and other bodies. Meanwhile, on 1 October, Damville issued a manifesto. His policy, he declared, was to keep the peace, to place his trust in a future council, to uphold the laws of the kingdom and the rights of princes of the blood. Thanks to their alliance with Damville, the Huguenots managed to strengthen their position in Guyenne and Languedoc. In Dauphiné, Lesdiguières recaptured several towns; in Poitou, Condé repulsed an invasion led by Mercoeur, but he then laid siege to Brouage. On being defeated by Henri de Joyeuse (the *mignon*'s brother), Condé fled to Guernsey.

On 7 October 1585, Henry III issued an edict even harsher for the Huguenots than that of 18 July. They were now branded as traitors whose goods were to be sold for the king's benefit, and were allowed only six months in which to abjure or go into exile. All Condé's followers were to be hunted down and their property seized. Navarre responded on 30 November by ordering the confiscation of property belonging to noblemen and churchmen who had joined 'the enemies of the state'. Writing to Catherine de' Medici, he spoke with contempt of the pope's bull. The papacy, he warned, was using religion as a pretext to dispose of the French crown as it wished. Henry III might find himself being deposed.

Both sides appealed to public opinion before coming to blows. On 1 January 1586, Navarre wrote to the three estates. He reminded the clergy of their Christian duty to keep the peace. 'If you prefer a battle to a debate, a conspiracy to a council,' he wrote, 'so be it. May the blood that will be spilt be on your heads.' Turning to the nobles, Navarre showed that the kingdom's honour was at stake. How could they allow its fate to be decided from outside by the pope? He deplored in advance the loss of noble blood which France needed to defend herself against foreign aggressors. 'I love you all,' he said. 'I feel myself dying and weakening in your blood.' No one had ever spoken like this since the start of the troubles. Navarre's letter to the third estate was similarly compassionate. 'I complain to you', he said, 'not on my account, but on yours. I am complaining that I cannot defend myself without causing innocent people to suffer. I am a born Frenchman. I sympathize with your woes. I have tried to exempt you from civil wars and I will never spare my life to cut them short.' Such persuasive pleading needed to be countered by the League. One of its founders, Louis Dorléans, warned French Catholics not to believe Navarre's professions of tolerance. In a work called *Avertissement des catholiques anglais aux François catholiques*, an English Catholic warns his French co-religionists that, if they allow a heretic to become king, they will suffer the same persecutions as English Catholics are suffering under Elizabeth. They would do better to find a Spaniard, a Tartar, a Muscovite or a Scythian as long as he is a Catholic. If Henry III chose a heretic to succeed him, Dorléans did not doubt that the people would rise in fury like the sea in a storm, which engulfs captain, crew and ship.

Propaganda alone could not win a war; money was needed to pay for arms. When the clergy met in October, the king required Bellièvre to show

that four armies were needed to fight the Huguenots and that their maintenance would cost two million *livres* per month. The clergy reluctantly agreed
to the sale of church lands worth 50,000 *écus* per annum. The bishop of
Paris was sent to Rome by Henry III in order to get papal permission for
a more substantial sale of church property. Sixtus V agreed to an alienation
of 100,000 *écus* in two instalments. This angered the clergy who felt that
their traditional exemption from taxation was being impugned. Henry III
threatened to hold a *lit de justice* to enforce publication of the bull. Before
any proceeds of the sale could reach his coffers, however, war with the
Huguenots got under way. If the politico-military situation in south-west
France was confused, along the north-east border it was clear enough:
measures had to be taken to stop an invasion by German reiters. Early in
March 1586 the king gave Henri de Guise command of fifty companies of
infantry and 5000 to 6000 cavalry. Another army under Marshal d'Aumont
was sent to Auvergne and Languedoc, while Biron fought Condé, who
by now had returned from Guernsey and within two months had seized
Saint-Jean-d'Angély.

However, Henry III showed no inclination to fight in earnest. If de Thou
is to be believed, the king had given secret orders to certain trustworthy
governors to fight only half-heartedly. Underestimating the League's fanaticism, he still hoped that it would make peace. On 26 April he pandered to
it by publishing another harsh edict against the Huguenots. Yet on the
approach of Holy Week, the king went on a religious retreat to Chartres.
Meanwhile, fighting continued. Mayenne and Biron captured Monségur
and Lusignan respectively for the king. But his generals were criticized at
court for being lethargic. Henry III tried to silence criticism by giving commands to his two favourites, Joyeuse and Epernon. The former was sent to
Auvergne and Languedoc; the latter to Dauphiné and Provence. The king
may not have wanted to fight Navarre himself, knowing that he might need
his alliance in the future.

Both sides in the civil war were desperately hard up. On 16 June, Henry
went to the parlement to secure registration of twenty-seven fiscal edicts, a
legislative avalanche which infuriated Parisians. Placards insulting the king
and his mother soon appeared all over the capital. Meanwhile, Navarre
managed to obtain assistance in England. After offering 50,000 crowns,
Elizabeth doubled that amount on learning of Parma's successes against the
Dutch rebels. The money was paid to John Casimir, regent of the Palatinate,
who also received a subsidy from the Danish king. He undertook in return
to raise an army of 8000 reiters and infantry to assist the Huguenots.

As the threat of a German invasion grew, Catherine de' Medici again
offered her services as negotiator. But she was obstructed on every side,
notably by the pope who warned her that Henry would never reign in peace
unless heresy were extirpated from his kingdom. The League, too, opposed

a settlement. Its preachers in Paris accused the king of dealing in secret with Navarre and of deliberately impeding the war effort. In September, Henri de Guise and the cardinals of Guise and Bourbon met at the abbey of Ourscamp, near Noyon. They decided to reject any peace, to stand by the anti-Huguenot edict and to act independently of Henry III. Meanwhile, the queen mother tried to persuade Navarre to negotiate. Despite her age (67) and poor health (chronic catarrh and rheumatism), Catherine soldiered on through the winter, putting up in unsafe lodgings and braving bandit-infested roads. Eventually, Navarre agreed to meet her at the château of Saint-Brice, near Cognac, but he was only playing for time, pending the arrival of John Casimir's reiters. Although Henry III knew that the talks were futile, he would have welcomed a truce of two or three years. But Navarre asked for more time in which to consult the Protestant churches. On 13 March, Catherine returned to Chenonceaux empty-handed.

In the meantime, Catholic opinion in France was outraged by news of the execution in England of Mary Queen of Scots. She was instantly elevated to the rank of Catholic martyr and a veritable torrent of abuse, directed at the English Jezebel and her Huguenot allies, poured out of the League's pulpits and presses. On 13 March, Henry III caused a solemn mass to be sung in Mary's memory, but Catholics expected more from him. Having failed to save Mary's life, he seemed unwilling to avenge her death. He was accused of having betrayed her. A rumour circulated in Paris that 10,000 Huguenots were concealed in the suburbs, waiting for a signal to avenge the St Bartholomew's day massacre by slaughtering the Catholic population. In February, Henry III shut himself up in the Louvre after learning of a plot by the League to kidnap him and force him to hand over power. On 15 March another plot to remove him came to light. Guise, who was defending the Champagne border, was not to blame – indeed, he warned the Sixteen not to act without him and they duly complied. Meanwhile, they offered Henry an army of 24,000 men, paid for by the Leaguer towns and under commanders of their own choice, to defend the kingdom against the German reiters. At the same time, a new oath was proposed for members of the League whereby their obedience to the king was made conditional on his acting as a true Catholic. They were more than ever determined not to accept Navarre as heir to the throne. If Henry III died, it wanted the Cardinal de Bourbon to be considered by the Estates-General as a possible successor on account of his faith and personal qualities.

Henry III had lost control of the kingdom. The Guises were acting as they pleased: Guise besieged Sedan and Jametz, towns belonging to the duc de Bouillon, while Aumale seized a number of towns in Picardy. In May, Catherine de' Medici had talks in Reims with Guise and Cardinal de Bourbon. They agreed to extend a truce recently signed with Bouillon, but refused to hand over the towns of Doullens and Le Crotoy to the duc de

Nevers, whom the king had appointed as governor of Picardy. Early in July, Henry met Guise at Meaux and tried to persuade him to make concessions to the Huguenots, but he refused. Although the duke made a great show of obedience to the king, his real master, as he admitted to Mendoza on 12 June, was Philip II of Spain. 'I regard His Catholic Majesty', he wrote, 'as the common father of all Catholics and of myself in particular.'

The 'War of the Three Henrys'

In August 1587, Henry III unexpectedly announced that he would take the field at the head of his army. He left Paris on 12 September and took up a position on the Loire with the aim of preventing a link-up of the German relief army and the Huguenots. The relief army, numbering some 35,000 men (20,000 Swiss, 10,000 German reiters and 2000 to 3000 Frenchmen under Bouillon), had by now invaded France. They marched south in good order and mainly at night. Their objective was not Paris but the rich granaries of Beauce and Poitou. By mid-October they had reached Briare; only the Loire stood between them and the king's army.

Meanwhile, Henry sent Joyeuse to fight Navarre in the west. The royal favourite was keen to prove that he, not Guise, was the true champion of the Catholic cause. On 18 October, Joyeuse learned that Navarre was about to cross the River Dronne near Coutras in the hope of joining the reiters. The two opposing armies were of roughly equal strength, but the Huguenot troops were hardened veterans, whereas Joyeuse's cavalry was made up of inexperienced young noblemen. The Protestant guns started the battle by wreaking havoc among Joyeuse's infantry. His cavalry – 'the most resplendent ever assembled in France' – then advanced towards the enemy. After waiting till the last moment, Navarre's cavalry charged. It broke through the extended royalist line at several points, throwing Joyeuse's cavalry into disorder. Some fled, others, including Joyeuse, were cut down. At the end of the day, the Catholics had lost about 2500 men to the Protestants' 500 or so. Navarre had scored a crushing victory, but instead of following it up by joining the German invasion force, he let his army break up and went to Béarn to lay captured Catholic standards at the feet of his mistress, Corisande d'Andoins. As Sully put it, 'All the advantage of so famous a victory floated away like smoke on the wind.' Navarre was a fine cavalry leader, but no strategist. Meanwhile the relief army, after failing to cross the Loire, advanced westward towards the Beauce, but it was in poor shape and its various components broke apart. The reiters set off on their own, only to be defeated twice – at Vimory (26 October) and Auneau (24 November) – by Guise, who had been shadowing them. Meanwhile, the Swiss came to terms with Henry III. They agreed to go home in return for four months' pay, supplies, and equipment worth 50,000 *écus*. On 8 December the Germans surrendered to Henry III: they agreed to leave in return for cash and under the protection of a strong escort. Guise felt cheated of the fruits of victory; he had hoped to annihilate the Germans on their return through Lorraine.

On 23 December, Henry III returned in triumph to Paris. He attended a *Te Deum* at Notre Dame and organized a splendid funeral for Joyeuse. The plaudits of the crowd, however, could not hide the fact that the only victorious commanders of the recent war had been the king's enemies: Guise and Navarre. The League's preachers in Paris praised Guise's bravery without which 'the ark would have fallen to the Philistines'. The 'Sorbonne' decreed that a ruler whose conduct was not acceptable could be lawfully deposed. The pope, for his part, complained that the money which he had allowed the king to raise had been used to subsidize the destroyers of his kingdom.

Henry III now provoked the League's fury by giving to Epernon offices previously held by Joyeuse. Guise had wanted the governorship of Normandy as a reward for defeating the Germans, but the favourite became governor of Normandy and Admiral of France. He was also appointed governor of Angoumois, Aunis and Saintonge, in place of César de Bellegarde, who had been killed at Coutras. He became the chief target of the League's propaganda: as Pasquier noted, Henry's appointment of Epernon lost him more nobles than at Coutras. Epernon was also accused by the League of robbing the kingdom. His personal wealth may not have been as large as the Leaguers imagined, but it had been built up within a decade. It was impossible to know the true extent of the king's gifts to favourites because of the secrecy that shrouded them. Protestant propagandists alleged that, between 1547 and 1580, the kings of France had spent only 927 million *livres* out of 1453 million which they had levied in taxes. The fact that the royal coffers were now empty meant that the king was either lying about his penury or had been cheated. The conviction that Epernon was leading the kingdom to its doom caused Pierre d'Espinac, archbishop of Lyon, to join the League. He wrote a pamphlet in which Epernon was likened to Piers Gaveston, Edward II's ill-fated favourite.

The League's propaganda was largely directed by the duc de Guise's sister, the duchesse de Montpensier. According to L'Estoile, the king ordered her to leave Paris but she refused 'and even had the impudence to say . . . that she carried at her belt the scissors which would give the third crown to Brother Henry of Valois. Her preachers also gave sermons more violent and full of invective than ever, against the authority of the king.' Henry, meanwhile, continued to live outrageously. On 12 February, writes L'Estoile, 'the king prolonged the fair at Saint-Germain for six more days, at the request of some ladies, and went there every day, seeing and allowing infinite and villainous acts by his *mignons* and courtiers, especially outrages

to the women and girls they encountered. Every night he attended parties
... with girls ... in various quarters of the city, dancing, laughing ... and
dining sumptuously ... He also held masquerades and balls just as if the
times were those of greatest peace, and as if there were no war and no
League in France.' On 4 and 9 March, Henry gave magnificent funerals to
Anne and Claude de Joyeuse. A commemorative medal was struck bearing
the inscription: *Victima pro salvo domino, fit in aethere sidus.* Having given
his life to save the king, Joyeuse had become a star in the firmament. In
the meantime, news reached Paris of Condé's death, which some people
ascribed to poison. While the Huguenots mourned their best leader, the
League lit bonfires in celebration.

The Day of the Barricades, May 1588

Early in 1588, Guise and the other principal Leaguers, meeting at Nancy,
drew up a list of demands for the king. They demanded Epernon's dismissal,
the acceptance of Guise tutelage in the fight against heresy, and publication
of the decrees of the Council of Trent. Though Sixtus V was anxious to
reconcile Guise with Henry III, the duke did not want a settlement that
would downgrade his own role. He overran the territory of the duc de
Bouillon, who had just died, and again blockaded Sedan. Meanwhile
Aumale, who effectively controlled Picardy, tried to stir up trouble for
Epernon in Normandy. 'We must henceforth be king,' Henry III wrote to
Villeroy, 'for we have been the valet for too long.' But he lacked the means
to impose his authority. The League, meanwhile, harassed Epernon with
encouragement from Spain. Philip II instructed his ambassador, Mendoza,
to harm the favourite by every possible means. 'The people of France,'
writes L'Estoile, 'poisoned by the false words of the League, hated this man
to death, and called him the chief of the Navarrists and *Politiques*.' During
the spring of 1588 several attempts were made to assassinate Epernon,
causing the king to tighten security at the Louvre.

Political tension in Paris was aggravated by economic problems. France
was feeling the effects of nearly thirty years of civil war. Since 1586 the
cost of food had risen steadily and beggars were flocking into the capital
from the countryside. In August, 'the poor people of the countryside, dying
of hunger, went about in gangs and cut the half-ripe grain in the fields,
then ate it on the spot ... in spite of the measures taken by those who
owned the fields. Sometimes they threatened to eat [the owners] too, if they
would not allow them to eat the grain.' The crisis continued through the
winter of 1586–7. Parisian bourgeois were each asked to contribute 7 *livres*
16 *sols* per annum to the upkeep of the poor. On 3 June 1587 a *setier* of
corn cost 30 *livres* at the Halles. On 22 July there was a popular rising

against bakers. In the spring of 1588 the fiscal demands of the government fuelled popular unrest in the capital, but such troubles occurred elsewhere as well. A royal attempt to regulate guilds caused a popular revolt in Troyes and the plundering of houses owned by Italian merchants. In December 1586 some twenty Norman villages refused to pay the *taille* and other taxes.

Tension between the king and Guise exploded in May. The duke, as we have seen, had been forbidden by the king to enter Paris, but he chose to defy the ban in response to an invitation from the Sixteen. Accompanied by a few nobles, he called on Catherine de' Medici, who took him in her own coach to the Louvre. Guise tried to justify his conduct to the king, who chose not to arrest him. At night on 11 May, however, Henry introduced troops into the capital and posted them in various strategic places. His purpose, it was said, was to round up Guise's supporters and execute them as an example to the rest. The Parisians did not take kindly to this infringement of the capital's traditional right of self-defence. Crowds poured into the streets and erected barricades. The royal troops came under attack from the mob, while ministers sent out by Henry to assist them ran into trouble. At first Guise did nothing to appease the mob, but eventually he rode through the streets in response to an appeal from the king. Such was his popularity that he managed to bring the troops to safety; but the Parisians remained under arms. On 13 May, Henry III slipped away from the capital unnoticed, ending the Day of the Barricades. The Parisians suddenly became aware that they had become rebels. Guise wrote to the king regretting his departure, which had prevented a settlement. A deputation of hooded penitents and thirty-five Capuchins called on Henry at Chartres; he received them courteously, but conceded nothing. Deputations sent by other Parisian bodies were no more successful, though Henry was conciliatory towards the parlement, knowing that it was basically loyal. 'I want people to know', he said, 'that I have as much spirit and courage as any of my predecessors. Since my accession, I have used no rigour or severity towards anyone. You know this and can bear witness to it; but I do not want my clemency and gentleness to be abused.'

On 14 May the Bastille surrendered and Guise appointed a new governor, Bussy-Leclerc. The king's supporters on the town council either fled or were dismissed. Elections were announced for 18 and 20 May, thereby marking a return to more democratic ways, but voting was by voice alone, so that non-Leaguers were effectively debarred. Predictably, the leader of the Sixteen, La Chapelle-Marteau, was elected as *prévôt des marchands* and took an oath to the duc de Guise as representing the heir to the throne, Cardinal de Bourbon. Four new *échevins* – all of them merchants – were also Leaguers. Guise, in the meantime, occupied various towns around Paris so as to safeguard its supplies in the event of a confrontation with the king. This, however, did not occur, largely because of Catherine de' Medici's mediation. In the end, Henry III accepted nearly all the League's demands in a new Edict of Union: he dismissed Epernon, reaffirmed the Treaty of Nemours, recognized Cardinal de Bourbon as heir-presumptive to the throne, bestowed new governorships on the Guises, and appointed Henri de Guise as lieutenant-general of the kingdom. Yet in Paris, measures were taken to defend the city against attack by royal forces. The militia was purged, following elections in July with candidates chosen from lists drawn up by assemblies in each *quartier*. As a result, the militia fell into the hands of the Parisian populace.

The Estates-General of Blois, 1588

Henry III was playing for time. While resisting all attempts to lure him back to the capital, he prepared to avenge his recent humiliation and was cheered by news of the defeat of the Spanish Armada. On 8 September he surprised everyone by sacking his ministers, perhaps because they had supported the queen mother's conciliatory policy towards the Guises. The king chose to rely on young, hard-working men who owed nothing to Catherine, including the *surintendant* François d'O; the *contrôleur-général*, Chenailles; the Keeper of the Seals, Montholon; and two new secretaries of state, Ruzé and Revol. Henry also called a meeting of the Estates-General. He tried to influence the elections, but most of the deputies supported the League. The presidents of the three estates – cardinals de Bourbon and de Guise for the clergy, the comte de Brissac for the nobility and La Chapelle-Marteau for the third estate – were prominent Leaguers. The main areas of disagreement between the king and the majority of deputies were taxation and the nature of royal authority.

The king's financial predicament played into the hands of the League. It was able to exploit his failure to pay the salaries of office-holders and the interest owing to holders of annuities (*rentes*). By 1585 office-holders were owed more than a year's salary, and arrears of *rentes* amounted to over four million *livres*. After the Day of the Barricades, revenues normally assigned to such payments were diverted by Henry III towards paying for the war against the League. The aggrieved interests of office-holders and *rentiers* undoubtedly increased support for the League. On 12 August 1588 the *Chambre des comptes* demanded the appointment of new ministers who would conduct the king's financial affairs efficiently and honestly. It asked that contractual obligations should be met before revenues were assigned to other expenses. The court also complained that financial ordinances were not being applied. On 19 December, Henry had to agree to the creation of an extraordinary financial tribunal (*chambre de justice*) whose 24 members were to be chosen from a list of one hundred elected by the Estates.

Despite Henry's conditional acceptance of some of the estates' fiscal demands, members of the third estate remained truculent. Monarchs, they claimed, owed their authority to the estates. 'Why then', asked the deputies, 'should the decisions we take in this assembly be controlled by the king's council?' Henry suspected that the third estate was being manipulated by aristocratic members of the League. He was also convinced that Guise had encouraged the duke of Savoy's invasion, in October, of the marquisate of Saluzzo, which was under French occupation. Although in the past Henry had often seemed weak, he now showed himself to be ruthless. On 23 October, Guise was lured to the king's chamber in the château of Blois and brutally murdered by the Forty-five, Henry's bodyguard. Next day the duke's brother, Cardinal de Guise, was also murdered, while other prominent Leaguers and members of the Guise family were gaoled, including Cardinal de Bourbon. Henry claimed that he had acted in self-defence: the Guises, he said, had plotted his deposition and death. The estates wound up their business quietly, but in parts of France controlled by the League news of the murders set off an explosion of grief and anger. Most of the towns north of the Loire sided with the League, and there were pockets of resistance in the south (including Toulouse and Marseille). A number of provincial governors did so too, among them Guise's younger brother, Charles duc de Mayenne, who became the effective leader of the League's aristocratic wing.

Nowhere was the reaction to the murders at Blois more strongly felt and expressed than in Paris, where preachers cried out for vengeance on 'the new Herod'. Within a few hours pamphlets circulated exalting the martyrdom of the Guises. Their cousin, the duc d'Aumale, was appointed governor by the town assembly. A new revolutionary body, the Council of Forty, emanating from the sixteen districts, was added to the municipal council. It was made up of twelve clergymen, including six bishops, seven noblemen and twenty-four of the third estate. The council repudiated its allegiance to the blood-soaked tyrant of Blois, a measure ratified by the Sorbonne. On 7 January 1589 it released Frenchmen from their obedience to the king and called on them to take up arms. It also sought papal approval for its action. The murder of a cardinal was, of course, a heinous crime in the eyes of the church, and in May, Sixtus V summoned Henry to Rome to explain his conduct under threat of excommunication.

Meanwhile, a new administration was set up in Paris. Special committees of nine members in each district elected representatives to a council of the Sixteen. The houses of *Politiques* were searched, and taxes imposed on the rich 'for the defence of the Catholic religion'. At the same time the mob attacked royal images. At the church of the Augustins, a picture of Henry III and the Order of the Holy Spirit was destroyed, as were the tombs of his *mignons* in the church of Saint-Paul. The parlement, too, came under fire. On 16 January a group of men, led by Bussy-Leclerc, broke into the hitherto inviolate *Grand' Chambre* and carried off to the Bastille the First President, Achille de Harlay, and two of his colleagues. Brisson was appointed in place of Harlay and other vacancies were filled by Leaguers. The Châtelet, too, was purged, Mathieu de La Bruyère becoming *lieutenant civil*. Packed as it now was, the parlement unanimously recognized Cardinal de Bourbon as King Charles X of France, but, as he was the king's prisoner, decisions had to be taken in his name.

The arrival in Paris of the duc de Mayenne complicated the political situation. Although he lacked the charm and charisma of his murdered brother, he was politically astute and had built up a strong clientèle in his *gouvernement* of Burgundy. When he entered Paris with an army on 12 February, he was acclaimed as a saviour and appointed lieutenant-general of the kingdom by the Sixteen, but he refused to allow democracy free rein. He promptly modified the General Council of the Union and the Council of Forty by adding to their members fourteen of his own friends. Mayenne also reserved to himself all political decisions. He set up his own administration, consisting of a council of state, a keeper of the seals and secretaries of state. In exchange for large ransoms, he secured the release of the magistrates from the Bastille.

Political thought of the League

Few Catholics before 1560 challenged the king's right to full obedience and complete sovereignty, but their mood changed dramatically in 1576 following the Peace of Monsieur, which many regarded as far too generous to the Huguenots. They began to cast doubt on Henry III's interest in rooting out heresy. The manifesto of the Catholic League, set up in 1576, contained a number of clauses which went far beyond its stated aim of defending the Catholic church. One called for 'the restoration to the provinces and their estates of their ancient rights, pre-eminences, freedoms, and liberties such as they were in the time of King Clovis'. While swearing obedience to Henry III and his successors, the Leaguers agreed to resist, by force if necessary, *anyone* who refused to accept their stated principles. When the Estates-General met in 1576, an attempt was made to turn the Catholicism of the monarchy into a 'fundamental law' of the kingdom, and this led to a protracted discussion of the 'fundamental laws' in Catholic writings of the next twenty years. Almost everyone agreed that the laws were a body of custom by which France had been governed since Pharamond, the legendary king of the Franks, but their number and scope were controversial. The lack of precise definition enabled the League to argue that it was a 'fundamental law' that the king of France should always be a Catholic.

When the Protestant leader Henri de Navarre became heir to the throne in 1584, the Leaguers searched French history and law for evidence by which Navarre might be excluded in favour of his uncle, Cardinal de Bourbon. Many pamphlets between 1585 and 1588 concentrated on the law of succession. Some argued that the Salic law was void, others that the cardinal was the true heir to the throne because of the law of proximity in blood. But there was little radical thinking in the writings of the League before May 1588.

The event that unleashed the full force of Leaguer radicalism was the murder in December 1588 of Guise and his brother, the cardinal. The Sorbonne, as we have seen, authorized Frenchmen to take up arms against the king, and Parisian preachers defended regicide. Thus Pierre-François Pigenat, *curé* of Saint-Nicolas-des-Champs, called on the people to avenge Guise by shedding the blood of the tyrant, Henry III. Another priest, Jean Gincestre, said that he would not scruple to kill the king. Julien de Moranne recalled in a pamphlet that, in Merovingian times, Bodillon had killed King Childeric II. 'Will there not be found in France a Bodillon', he asked, 'who will avenge the wrong done ... to a most valiant prince ... by a coward more despicable than Childeric ever was?'

An outspoken advocate of tyrannicide was Jean Boucher, *curé* of Saint-Benoît. As the 'one-eyed king of Paris', he played a leading role in the city's administration from 1589. Though an erudite and eloquent preacher, he frequently resorted to calumny and coarseness. In his *De justa Henrici tertii abdicatione* (August 1589), Boucher argues the case for regarding Henry III as a tyrant who may be deposed, even killed. He gives scant attention to the origin of the state, but suggests that kingship is a human institution created by the people for their own convenience. They have transferred sovereignty to the king in a contract between God and the people. The king is bound by this contract, and the people, in order to ensure its observance, retain power over him. While acknowledging that hereditary succession has become the normal method by which French kings ascend the throne, Boucher points to the coronation oath as a vestige of the monarchy's elective character. In spite of current appearances, the people, in his view, still hold sovereign power; their assemblies can depose a king and wage war on him. Even a private individual may strike down a king who has been declared a tyrant and deposed by a national body or by the pope. Boucher's discussion of tyrannicide ranges more widely than any Protestant work of the time. He charges Henry III with ten major crimes, each enough to warrant his deposition. It is for the pope, as the supreme judge of Christendom, writes Boucher, to release Henry's subjects from their obedience; if he fails to do so, the people of France must act against the tyrant.

The assassination of Henry III, 1 August 1589

On 5 January 1589, Catherine de' Medici died leaving Henry III isolated. He was caught between the forces of the League to the north and east and those of the Huguenots in the south. The king controlled three towns on the Loire (Tours, Blois and Beaugency), Bordeaux, and the provinces of Berry and Dauphiné. He badly needed a powerful ally, but reconciliation with Mayenne was unthinkable. Henry was also desperately short of money, for his loss of political control in northern France had entailed a loss of revenues. In order to pay for the war, he was reduced to pawning crown jewels to financiers. On 17 February 1589 he secured a loan of 1.2 million *livres* from the Elbene brothers, but his credit rating was too low to attract larger loans. He was only able to borrow quite small sums from members of his entourage. Only by allying with Henri de Navarre could he hope to carry on the fight. On 26 April the two Henrys signed a truce; four days later, at Plessis-lez-Tours, they sealed their accord. Combining their armies, they marched on Paris, capturing Senlis and Pontoise on the way. As they laid siege to the capital – Henry III at Saint-Cloud and Navarre at Meudon – a frenzy of anti-Valois sentiment exploded in Paris. Processions invoked the help of the Almighty; preachers clamoured for the extermination of Henry III as an agent of Satan. Among those who heard the message was a young Dominican friar called Jacques Clément. On 1 August he made his way from Paris to Henry's camp. Claiming that he carried a message from some of the king's friends in the capital, he was admitted to the royal presence. The king, who was sitting on his close stool, invited Clément to come nearer, whereupon the friar stabbed him in the abdomen. A few hours later Henry died; he was the first king of France to die at the hands of one of his subjects, a clear indication of how far the mystique of monarchy had collapsed since 1572. One of Henry's last acts was to recognize Navarre as his heir, but he also warned him that only by becoming a Catholic would he gain the throne.

News of the king's assassination caused jubilation in Paris. It was seen by many Catholics as the completion of the sacred mission which the massacre of St Bartholomew had only partially accomplished. Henry's demise seemed to remove the last obstacle in the path of a Catholic triumph in France. Clément was 'canonized' by the League's propagandists. Boucher added several chapters to his *De justa Henrici tertii abdicatione*. After praising Clément as a martyr for the true faith – 'a new David has killed Goliath; a new Judith has killed Holofernes' – he turns briefly to the question of Henry's successor. Brushing aside Navarre's candidacy, he calls on the estates to meet swiftly and elect the Cardinal de Bourbon as king. From now on, the political writings of the League addressed themselves to the succession question. An important contribution to this debate was *De justa reipublicae Christianae in reges impios et haereticos auctoritate* (1590) by Guillaume Rose. It is the most comprehensive treatment of political theory of all Leaguer writings and comes down heavily on the side of popular sovereignty. Obedience to the king is made to depend on his observing the contract by which he was raised. In particular, he must rule in a Christian manner, and this excludes any heretic from the throne; a heretic who tries to occupy it is a tyrant subject to the appropriate penalties. Calvinists, the author contends, are worse than pagans or Turks, and their leader Henry of Navarre can never be 'The Most Christian King'.

Under the Salic law, Henri de Navarre succeeded Henry III as King Henry IV, but his Protestantism made him unacceptable to the League. On 7 August the parlement, acting under pressure from the League, recognized Cardinal de Bourbon, who was still in prison, as King Charles X. The Protestant army may have recognized Henry IV unconditionally, but the Catholic army at Saint-Cloud did not. There were heated arguments among the Catholic commanders on 2 and 3 August. François d'O conveyed their terms to Henry: he was to abjure his faith, banish all Protestant worship in France and reserve all offices to Catholics. Henry refused, but next day he accepted modified terms: he promised to protect the Catholic faith and to take religious instruction from a national council which he would summon within six months. Protestant rights would be guaranteed pending a peace settlement which would define their extent. Towns and fortresses captured from the rebels would be placed under Catholic control. The new king promised also to punish those who had plotted Henry III's assassination and to protect his servants. Having accepted these terms on 4 August 1589, the Catholic captains recognized Henry IV as king. They asked him to call a meeting of his followers within two months to discuss state affairs pending a meeting of the Estates-General. They also asked for an envoy to be sent to Pope Sixtus V to explain their action, and they pledged their lives to drive out or exterminate all rebels and enemies.

Anxious as Henry was to gain the loyalty of all Frenchmen, he was not entirely successful. Protestant zealots, like La Trémoïlle, withdrew their troops from the camp at Meudon, while some of the Catholics at Saint-Cloud preferred to join the League rather than sign the accord. Other Catholics (including Nevers and Epernon) retired to their estates and *gouvernements*, and awaited developments. As soldiers deserted rather than serve a heretical monarch, the royal army besieging Paris dwindled in size from 40,000 men to 22,000. Henry could not maintain the siege and retired to Normandy pursued by the duc de Mayenne, who declared that he would either throw him into the sea or bring him back to Paris in chains. On 21 September 1589, however, Mayenne was defeated by Henry at Arques, near Dieppe. Meanwhile in Paris, the militia prepared to defend the city against another attack by Henry IV. It came at dawn on 1 November, when he launched a general assault. His troops overran the *faubourg* Saint-Germain, killing 800 militiamen in bitter street fighting. From the belfry of Saint-Germain-des-Prés, Henry saw that he would not be able to break through the city's medieval wall and when Mayenne returned with reinforcements, the king decided to retreat. He moved to Tours, where news reached him that Venice had recognized him as king – the first Catholic power to do so.

Henry's victory at Arques proved to be a turning-point for the League. Provincial leaders who had previously ignored Mayenne's call for Catholic solidarity became even less inclined to follow him after his defeat. Provincial separatism and personal jealousy, which had long divided the Leaguers, became even more influential. Consequently, Mayenne's dependence on Spain and the papacy for funds and arms increased. Informal talks which took place between Henry IV and leaders of the League between 1589 and July 1593 were merely used by each side to gain time rather than to secure peace. Loyalist Catholics were naturally anxious that Henry should convert to the Catholic faith, but some of Mayenne's advisers felt that papal approval of his conversion should first be secured. In August 1589 the duc de Luxembourg called on Pope Sixtus V in Rome. News of Henry IV's victory at Arques had made the pope more receptive to some kind of accommodation with the king. He made a major concession by invalidating Henry's 1572 conversion to Catholicism, which meant that the king was no longer a relapsed heretic, but a misbeliever capable of instruction. But Sixtus's willingness to compromise was not shared by his legate in France, Cardinal Caetani, who threw his whole weight behind the League. He persuaded its prelates to boycott an assembly of the clergy which met in Tours in February to discuss the king's instruction. Anticipating the policies of Pope Gregory XIV, the legate threatened to excommunicate anyone who came into contact with Henry or his agents.

Instead of going into winter quarters, Henry IV now conducted a successful military campaign in Normandy. He wrested from the League all the major towns in the province save Rouen and Le Havre. At Ivry, on 14 March 1590, he routed Mayenne's army, but instead of following up this victory he wasted time in fruitless talks. Though Henry's military successes would not have been possible without Catholic support, he now felt less inclined to convert. He was confident that he would soon capture Paris, but the capital proved a tougher nut to crack than he had anticipated. Henry cut off the city's food supplies and fired his guns into it at random from the hills of Montmartre and Montfaucon, but his Catholic allies persuaded him not to storm the capital lest he should undermine his image as a benevolent monarch. By August some Catholic loyalists were afraid that if he conquered Paris by force he would be less likely to convert. This reluctance to bring the Parisians to their knees helped them to resist.

By now Mayenne's prestige had sunk so low that his rival, the duc de Nemours, assumed command of the Parisian league and became the darling of the Sixteen. He was assisted by a formidable trio of Guise ladies – the mother, widow and sister of the murdered duke – who helped to galvanize resistance. Parish priests also stirred the people from their pulpits, while the papal legate and the Spanish ambassador Mendoza provided money. Nemours disposed of more troops than Henry, but he was also faced with the problem of feeding a large population (300,000?) swollen by refugees from the surrounding countryside. In April, the city had only one month's supply of corn in hand. Rationing was introduced and a close watch kept on bakers, but prices soared. Empty houses were demolished to provide fuel for the mercenaries.

As the siege began on 7 May, the 'Sorbonne' promised a martyr's crown to anyone who died fighting heresy. A famous painting shows a procession on 14 May of armed monks and laymen. A similar procession, on 3 June, brought together 1300 armed monks, priests and students. But arms could do nothing against famine. According to L'Estoile, 30,000 people died in July alone – the figure is probably exaggerated, but loss of life was evidently considerable – and hunger began to undermine the will to resist: demonstrators cried out for 'peace or bread'. On 2 August, the bishop of Paris and the archbishop of Lyon tried to persuade Henry to lift the blockade. On 1 September a convoy of food reached the capital from Dourdan and Spanish troops, sent by Parma, stood nearby. On 11 September, after another fruitless assault, Henry again withdrew.

Meanwhile, Parisians began to detach themselves from the hard line pursued by the Sixteen. Following the death of Cardinal de Bourbon in May 1590, Mayenne, who returned to Paris on 17 September, claimed the throne for himself; at the same time arguments tracing descent of the house of Lorraine from Charlemagne were revived. Mayenne's young nephew, Charles duc de Guise, was favoured by most Parisian Leaguers, while a group more vocal than numerous supported Philip II of Spain or a member of his family. Several Leaguer clerics, it seems, adhered to the medieval concept of a *respublica christiana*; they could see nothing wrong in calling on a foreign Catholic prince to save the faith in France. Spain looked for an arrangement that would include the Infanta Isabella Clara Eugenia, Henry II's granddaughter.

The siege of Rouen

Having failed to seize Paris, Henry IV turned his attention to Rouen, which had suddenly become the focal point of international politics. Elizabeth I wanted him to concentrate his military efforts in Normandy so that the

Channel coast should not fall under the domination of the League and Spain. In July she and Henry agreed to mount a joint expedition against Rouen, the English force being commanded by the earl of Essex. The city's inhabitants prepared feverishly to defend themselves; as the enemy approached the suburbs were set alight, but, lacking a decisive advantage in manpower and artillery, the attackers tried to starve Rouen into submission. In April 1592, as Spanish tercios sent by Parma arrived on the scene, Henry and Essex lifted the siege.

Rouen was safe, but its population had suffered grievously. Parish registers show that the death rate rose dramatically during the siege and continued thereafter; by early 1593 nearly three times as many people had been buried as in a normal year. Nearly all were victims of famine or plague. This crisis brought to a head four years of economic hardship. Ever since fighting began, the volume of trade entering and leaving Rouen was 15–35 per cent of the pre-1588 levels. The decline in trade brought hardship to the town's artisans. Unprecedented cuts had to be made in the taxes levied on some of the city's products, while the number of new masters received into the weavers' and goldsmiths' guilds fell to an all-time low. Although people from the surrounding countryside sought shelter within Rouen's walls, the number of baptisms declined by 15 per cent between 1579–86 and 1587–94. Emigration was largely responsible: foreign merchants and royalist officials left, apprentices fled abroad in search of work, and established artisans moved to nearby towns to ply their trades in peace. As people left, rents fell and houses were left empty. In the surrounding countryside conditions were worse still, for military operations prevented peasants from working. Villages sued for a diminution of the *taille* because their crops and livestock had been requisitioned, their houses burned down or their money extorted by bands of soldiers. The English in 1591 had brought no supplies and were given virtually free rein to live off the countryside. The destruction caused a significant drop in the income of Rouen's ecclesiastical institutions and of its élite of *officiers* and merchants. The town was also obliged to import Baltic grain, while the inhabitants had to forage in nearby woods for fuel they could no longer afford to buy. The ultimate effect of the crisis was to undermine enthusiasm for the League: people began to long for a king who could restore order.

Paris under siege: the Sixteen

By the end of 1592, Henry IV's main objective – the capture of Paris – seemed as far removed as ever. By now, Nemours had been replaced as governor by the sieur de Belin, who was an opportunist. The Sixteen began to fear a treasonable surrender of the capital. A small group (La Chapelle-

Marteau, Acarie, Bussy-Leclerc) decided to prevent such a possibility. Taking advantage of Mayenne's absence, they accused the parlement of scandalous lenience after it had acquitted a certain Brigard, who had been accused of secret dealings with the royalists. On 15 November the parlement's president, Barnabé Brisson, was arrested, taken to the Petit Châtelet, summarily tried and hanged. Two other magistrates suffered the same fate. Terror became the order of the day. Lists of *Politiques* circulated. Each name was preceded by a letter: 'C' for *chassé* (expelled), 'D' for *dagué* (stabbed) or 'P' for *pendu* (hanged). Such excesses provoked a reaction. Mayenne was appalled by the execution of the three magistrates. On 28 November he returned to Paris and a few days later had four of the Sixteen hanged at the Louvre. Bussy-Leclerc fled after surrendering the Bastille and the General Council of the Union was dissolved. These events have been described as a 'Mayennist Thermidor', but they may have demonstrated rather the failure of the Sixteen to keep in step with public opinion in Paris at large.

In recent years historians have tried to unravel the complexities of the situation in Paris between 1585 and 1594. In particular they have asked the question: who were the Sixteen? L'Estoile portrays them as men of low birth whose violence stemmed from hatred and greed. By contrast, he presents the *Politique* royalists as respectable, law-abiding citizens; but this neat division is both partisan and simplistic. To a degree, it reflects the extant documentation: whereas the Sixteen were ultimately defeated and their papers destroyed or tampered with, their victorious rivals were able to preserve theirs. The historian Barnavi has described the Sixteen as 'a political party in the sense in which we would understand it today, that is to say, a forceful organization which fights for power over a wide area and is internally and structurally strong, possessing a programme at a national level, a political ideology and, almost, a social doctrine transcending all social orders'. But as Greengrass has argued, 'it is difficult to conceive of any group possessing the means – even if it had the pretensions – to totality within its [Paris's] walls', given the capital's ancient traditions and its compartmentalized political and social life. Parisian support for the League was overwhelming on the Day of the Barricades because the king, by introducing professional soldiers into the city, had provoked a common reaction among different groups of people. Thereafter, the Sixteen's hold on the capital was never complete. Some parishes may never have fallen under their spell; nor could the Sixteen rely on the complete loyalty of the bourgeois militia. Some elections to the posts of captain and colonel of the militia after May 1588, far from being dominated by the Sixteen, showed respect to local magistrates. In 1588, following the imprisonment at court of the *prévôt des marchands*, Paris found itself without a constituted authority. The Sixteen consequently elected a General Council of the Union so that Mayenne's authority as lieutenant-general might be validated. The General Council, however, was short-lived; thereafter the existence of a central committee of the Sixteen is very shadowy.

Until 1 August 1589 the Sixteen were obsessed with the idea of deposing Henry III, but after his assassination other issues came to the fore: notably the role of Spain and the papacy in the kingdom's affairs, the succession to the throne, the nature of monarchy and fear of social disorder. Such concerns were reflected in the abundant pamphlet literature produced in Paris during the time of the League. Denis Pallier has shown how a group of 120 printers, representing different levels of wealth, assisted the League's activities by flooding the market with pamphlets aimed at conditioning Parisian public opinion. Their total output was staggering for the time: in 1589 they were publishing nearly one new title per day. Much of this propaganda was strongly religious, for, as Pallier writes, 'while taking into account the political aspect of the wars, it is impossible to overlook the religious upheaval.' He also demonstrates the limitations of the League's censorship. As the printers suffered economic damage during the siege of Paris, the tone and content of their pamphlets became distinctly more moderate than the sermons of the League's preachers. By advocating a return to peace and to the old social order they doubtless helped to open the gates of Paris to Henry IV.

The social composition of the Paris League has been exhaustively analysed by Robert Descimon, using genealogical and notarial records. He offers detailed profiles of 225 adherents of the League. The vast majority were notables (*honorables hommes*) of some standing. Lawyers and merchants were numerically preponderant. In other words, the Sixteen were recruited mainly from the social crust, though not the 'upper crust'. The traditional idea, promoted by their contemporary rivals, that they were from the common people is mistaken. They were also mainly Parisians: 143 out of 185 were born in Paris of Parisian parents. Three were born outside France and only 28 outside the Ile-de-France. Ninety-five (42.2 per cent) were probably aged between 45 and 55 in 1591: in other words, they were reaching late adolescence when the civil wars began. A further 71 (31.5 per cent) were aged between 35 and 45 in 1591: these had never known peace as children. Although slightly younger than the merchants, the lawyers were nevertheless men of standing and experience. The Sixteen were not juvenile hot-heads.

Two historians (Drouot and Mousnier) have suggested that the League was a movement of bourgeois who felt excluded from offices which, having become venal, were the monopoly of a restricted number of families. But Descimon's analysis of the Paris Leaguers does not bear this out. The Sixteen were socially stable before 1588 and a minority achieved a degree of social advancement. The League's lawyers and merchants, far from being deprived, were able to arrange good marriages and provide excellent dowries and portions for their children. True, an urban nobility (*noblesse de ville*) was beginning to detach itself from the rest of urban society, but this trend was still in its infancy. Thus the idea that the League was part of a conflict between two groups of bourgeois competing for offices and power does not carry conviction. Other aspects of the movement were probably more important. In Paris it was undoubtedly a response by citizens attached to certain democratic traditions of local government reaching back to the Middle Ages against moves by the monarchy to impose its authority. The League was also a profoundly religious movement aiming at the triumph of Catholicism. It has been called 'the *curés*' revolt'. Parish priests were certainly among its activists and some may have hoped to set up a theocratic government. Yet even allowing for their influence as preachers, they never succeeded in controlling the movement: the laity marched alongside the clergy but remained a distinct component.

Economic decline and social unrest

The wars of the League from 1585 until 1596 caused much distress throughout France. Grim mortality statistics for towns like Rouen and Nantes and equally disturbing price indices for Paris, Lyon, Toulouse and other towns cannot be explained simply in economic terms. There may have been a recession, but war made it worse. France's overseas trade was severely disrupted. Catholic ports on the Atlantic coast were blockaded by Huguenot privateers so that merchants had to give up trading. Only strongly fortified Protestant ports, like La Rochelle, prospered. In the Mediterranean, Spain controlled navigation across the Golfe du Lion. Marseille was cut off from its hinterland by enemy troops and its trade was also damaged by duties imposed by the crown on foreign imports. Lyon lost its pre-eminence as a banking and printing centre. The number and value of letters of exchange issued by the Bonvisi bank declined sharply after 1583. In northern France, textile exports from Brittany and Normandy to England and other countries collapsed. As cloth production in Amiens declined after 1586, imports of English cloth into France increased. The Dutch, too, broke into French markets. From 1587, Dutch ships bringing grain, salt, fish and cloth came regularly to Rouen, Bayonne and Saint-Malo. In the Midi, cloth production aimed at the Levant trade also declined. The wine trade suffered as well. Quantities of wine shipped through Bordeaux in the 1590s were less than a third of what they had been thirty years before.

France also experienced monetary instability at this time. Gold began to appreciate rapidly in value and silver to depreciate in relation to the *livre tournois*. Subsidies paid by Spain to the League and to her troops in France boosted monetary inflation by flooding the country with silver specie. This, in turn, provoked price rises in basic commodities. The situation was made worse by the minting of substandard coins by both sides in the war as a way of paying their armies. By 1590 there were more than twenty mints, many of which produced small silver coins with a face value far above their actual silver content. Many mint-masters took advantage of this speculative climate to line their own pockets. In certain areas copper coins from Germany began to supplant French coinage, but as they were vulnerable to clipping, they soon became discredited. Some coins ceased to be legal tender and villages found themselves without cash.

Plague became more virulent in the last two decades of the century, often spread by armies whose movements were unstoppable. In some towns the plague of 1586-7 was the worst of the century. Other diseases – malaria, smallpox and influenza – also claimed many victims. Such afflictions, like floods and other natural disasters, were commonly regarded as signs of divine wrath and consequently prompted large demonstrations of public penance, usually processions. Plague was often associated with famine which could be the result of one or more bad harvests. The years from 1584 to 1591 were particularly bad. A change of climate may have been to blame. Historians have called the late sixteenth and the early seventeenth century 'the little ice-age'. A fall of only one degree centigrade in the average summer temperature was enough to reduce the farm growing season by more than thirty days. When harvests failed, bread prices soared to a level that was beyond the reach of most poor families. Since the cultivation of alternative staples was in its infancy, no cheap food was available and many people starved to death. Those who survived a famine often succumbed to disease. A sequence of bad harvests could wipe out an entire generation, creating a recurring void in the demographic statistics.

War, too, could cause famine as soldiers ate what they needed and burned the rest. The German troops who invaded France in 1587 cut a swathe through Lorraine, Burgundy and Beauce, pillaging and stealing. Agrippa d'Aubigné in *Les Tragiques* describes the plight of a wounded and starving peasant from Périgord who has seen his wife and children slaughtered by marauding troops. The worst offenders, according to a Venetian observer, were the lesser nobles who led the soldiers and enriched themselves by extracting ransoms under threat of violence. Their actions caused bitter resentment, which was shared by small market towns, many of which were besieged and sacked, some more than once.

The fall in agricultural production is reflected in the returns of tithes to churches. In the Paris region the yield from tithes began to fall after 1570 and even more after 1585. In the Norman Vexin it declined by about 25 per cent during the wars of the League. In Burgundy it was about the same. A report from Autun in 1596 shows a fall of 50 per cent in the number of taxpayers in many villages. Beasts of burden had been seized and could not be replaced. Communities which had borrowed money to buy off soldiers had to sell their commons to settle their debts. Some peasants survived by becoming share-croppers; others sold up to local townsmen, nobles or more prosperous peasants. Rural society became increasingly divided between an élite of *laboureurs* and *fermiers* and a mass of cottagers, share-croppers and wage-labourers.

Rural discontent was bound sooner or later to explode into open revolt. Organized unrest occurred in Provence (1578), the Rhône valley (1579) and Normandy. Peasants of either faith took part. Often led by the smaller towns, they demanded lower taxes, proper representation in the provincial assemblies, an end to unfair tax exemptions and the right to act against noble brigands. In each movement we find evidence of hostility to the local nobility. The closing stages of the wars of the League were accompanied by widespread popular risings. In July 1589, Norman peasants, called *Gautiers* (after the village of La Chapelle-Gautier), attacked the château of La Tour, near Falaise. Soon afterwards they came into conflict with the royal army led by the duc de Montpensier. A large number of peasants – perhaps as many as 3000 – were slaughtered, while the rest surrendered or took flight. In Perche in 1590, a peasant militia opposed the forces of Henry IV. Again the rebels suffered heavy losses when royalist forces stormed the village of Ronnel. In Brittany the peasants, crushed by unending war, followed the League's army like hungry wolves. At Vitré they ambushed a Huguenot army and virtually destroyed it. Eventually, the peasants were crushed by the prince de Dombes who reduced them parish by parish, using fire and sword. According to a contemporary, almost all lower Brittany was in revolt. 'The peasant communes being armed have colonels and popular tribunes who lay down the law to the nobles who live in the areas.' At Roscanou, near Quimper, thousands of peasants broke up an aristocratic wedding party. The château was set alight and, as the occupants fled, sixty were lynched by the rebels; even the bride had her neck pierced by a pitch-fork. The Breton peasants were finally crushed by royalist forces at Cahaix in November 1590. Further south, in Comminges, peasants set out 'to rally and declare war on the nobility and seize the fortified towns of the countryside'. Their enemies, as in Normandy, were the Leaguer nobles who terrorized the area. The most serious peasant uprisings took place in Burgundy (the *Bonnets rouges*, 1594, 1597), in the Velay (1595) and above all in the south-west (the *Croquants*, 1593–5).

The *Croquants* first rose in the *vicomté* of Turenne in 1593. Soon their movement spread to the whole of Guyenne. Initially the rebels called them-selves *Chasse-voleurs*, because their chief aim was to stop the theft of live-stock by noble captains. Later they called themselves *Tard-avisés* (Latecomers). They were afraid that they would be made to pay for the favours which Henry IV was heaping on the Leaguer nobles and towns. The historian of the revolt, Y.-M. Bercé, has argued that it was an essentially anti-fiscal rebellion, not an expression of class antagonism; but he has been vigorously challenged by Henry Heller, who believes that 'the "Croquant" upheaval was 'at bottom a challenge to the nobility on the part of the peasantry and the small-town bourgeoisie.' A clear line of demarcation is not easily drawn between heavy taxation and aristocratic oppression. True, the *Croquants* did initially call on their social superiors to lead them, but some of their pronouncements had a distinctly social dimension. One called on the peasants 'to take up arms and raze to the ground many châteaux belonging to those who stole the cattle and beefstock of their neighbours'. The secretary of the town council of Périgueux reported: 'They openly speak of destroying the nobility and being free of everything.' An observer in Limousin recalled that 'they threatened the nobility, held them up to ridicule and the towns also ... In fact, they terrorized and scared many and it seemed as if the world had turned upside down.' As the Parlement of Toulouse noted, aristocratic oppression was a major cause of the revolt. According to J. H. M. Salmon, the demands of the *Croquants* were 'in no sense those of a social revolutionary, but they indicate clearly enough that the peasantry were engaged in a conscious struggle with the *noblesse*, and that, while they did not intend to recast the structure of society, they wanted to modify its balance.'

The Triumph of Henry IV,
1593–1610

On 26 January 1593 the Estates-General – 128 deputies in all – met in Paris. The majority resented the pressure being exerted by Spain in support of the candidature to the French throne of Philip II's daughter, Isabella Clara Eugenia. The presence of the Spanish ambassador and the proximity of Spanish troops were to prove counter-productive to the Infanta's cause. Meanwhile, Henry IV invited the estates to negotiate with him, albeit without acknowledging their legality. His proposal, though resisted by the more extreme Leaguers, was accepted by the estates as a whole. Talks began at Suresnes on 29 April and a truce was agreed; but the succession question remained unsolved. On 20 June the estates formally rejected the Infanta's candidature, but it was still on the cards that a Guise would be chosen as king. However, the parlement condemned in advance any attempt to confer the crown on a foreign prince, thereby effectively ruling out the Guises – as Lorrainers they were deemed to be foreign. By its timely action, the parlement not only confirmed the hereditary nature of the French monarchy, but also reasserted its own constitutional authority which the estates had almost usurped.

Henry IV, in the meantime, was being instructed by theologians in the Catholic religion. On 16 May he announced his decision to abandon the Protestant faith, and on 25 July he solemnly abjured in the abbey at Saint-Denis. His conversion removed the League's main reason for excluding him from the throne, yet doubts remained as to his sincerity. An outspoken sceptic was Jean Boucher who, early in August, preached a series of sermons subsequently published under the title *Sermons de la simulée conversion* (Sermons on the simulated conversion). France, he argued, as a Christian state must have a Christian ruler. Henri de Navarre, as an excommunicate, could not be considered. Since no bishop could absolve someone whom the pope had excommunicated, Henry remained a heretic. The estates were therefore bound to elect a genuine Catholic as ruler.

The end of the League

Henry's abjuration was the signal for many town governors to declare their loyalty to him, but it did not come cheap. 'Treaties of capitulation' contained clauses which excluded Protestants from worship within a town and confirmed the office-holders whom Mayenne had appointed. Henry's followers, whose offices had been taken over by Leaguers, were promised compensation. Sometimes, too, Henry agreed to settle a town's debts, to remit its arrears of *taille* and to exempt it from tax for some years. Huge sums were also paid to noblemen. As Sir George Carew remarked, 'Those, who hazarded their lives and fortunes for settling the crown upon his head, [the king] neither rewardeth nor payeth; those who were of the League against him, he hath bought to be his friends and giveth them preferments.' According to Sully, Henry spent between 30 and 32 million *livres* in treaties 'for the recovery of the kingdom'. He was accused of demeaning the monarchy by paying out such bribes, but, as he told Sully, he would have had to pay ten times more to achieve the same result by the sword.

Normally a king of France was crowned at Reims, but as that town was still in enemy hands, Henry used Chartres instead. His coronation took place amidst the usual pomp on 27 February 1594. During the ceremony, he promised *inter alia* to 'expel from all lands under my jurisdiction all heretics denounced by the church'. Many large towns rallied to him, but, in Paris, he continued to be opposed by radical elements. Mayenne, however, had left the capital and the governor, Charles de Cossé-Brissac, had been won over to the royalist cause. On 22 March, Henry's forces converged on the capital from three directions. The gates were opened from within and a chain across the Seine was lifted. Meeting with little resistance, the royal troops converged on the city centre. At 6 AM, Henry entered Paris and attended mass at Notre-Dame, then watched the departure of 3000 foreign troops from the capital. He allegedly called out to their Spanish captains: 'My compliments to your master, but do not come back.'

Only a small number of Leaguers in Paris – about 120 – refused to submit to the new regime and were accordingly proscribed. Brissac became a marshal of France and François d'O succeeded him as the capital's governor. On 28 March the parlement and the other sovereign courts were formally re-established, and on the 30th a decree cancelled all legislation passed since 29 December 1588 'to the prejudice of the authority of our kings and royal laws'. Over Easter the king went out of his way to demonstrate his orthodoxy: he washed the feet of the poor on Maundy Thursday, visited the sick at the Hôtel-Dieu, freed some prisoners on Good Friday and touched 660 people for the King's Evil on Easter Sunday. Soon afterwards he won over the Faculty of Theology. In September 1595 he reached an agreement with the pope, promising, in return for Clement VIII's absolution, to recognize the insufficiency of his abjuration, to publish the decrees of the Council of Trent, to restore Catholicism in Béarn and to appoint only Catholics to high office.

The next task facing Henry was to rid France of the Spanish invader. He declared war on Spain in January 1595 and, early in June, moved to Burgundy, which had been invaded by a Spanish army from north Italy. On 5 June the royal cavalry met the Spanish vanguard near Fontaine-Française. Though heavily outnumbered by the enemy, Henry led two furious charges which carried the day. Mayenne was so disgusted with his Spanish ally that he decided to come to terms with Henry. The battle, in addition to being a tactical triumph, enabled Henry to consolidate his hold on Burgundy. Early in September he made his entry into Lyon.

In northern France, however, the Spaniards under the count of Fuentes launched a new offensive. While Henry was still in Lyon, Fuentes attacked Cambrai. Henry asked the United Provinces to send troops and appealed to the parlement to register his fiscal edicts, but the Dutch troops were slow in coming and the parlement was unco-operative. Cambrai fell in October; whereupon Henry, after assembling a large army, laid siege to La Fère, the last Spanish outpost south of the Somme. Meanwhile, the Spaniards captured Calais and soon afterwards Ardres. Early in 1596, however, Mayenne was reconciled with the king, and the dukes of Epernon and Joyeuse soon followed suit. As the duc de Guise had come over in January, only the duc de Mercoeur among the great nobles remained obdurate.

In March 1597 the Spaniards took Amiens by surprise. Henry IV expressed his feelings in a letter to Gaspard de Schomberg, comte de Nanteuil: 'I am not only unwell, but also assailed by so many problems and burdens that I hardly know which saint to invoke in order to lead me out of this unfortunate situation.' The king was desperately short of money to pay his troops. The municipality of Paris and sovereign courts were asked for a once and for all grant to aid him, but they were only prepared to offer 360,000 *livres* – far short of the king's requirement of 3.6 million *livres* with which to raise an army and of 450,000l. per month to pay for its upkeep.

By June, Henry had thrown a series of forts linked by trenches around Amiens, and by the end of August he had some 20,000 infantry, 3000 cavalry and 45 cannon. The Spanish garrison was numerically far inferior, and on 3 September its commander was killed. On 19 September the Spaniards surrendered. Henry wanted to march on Arras, but his army had largely deserted, so he spent the winter preparing to reconquer Brittany, where Mercoeur – the last of the Leaguer nobles – was holding out. Although the duke had ruled the province since 1582, he had failed to build it up as an autonomous power. Seeing the futility of resistance, he agreed to recognize Henry's authority and surrendered Nantes and other towns in return for suitable compensation.

The Edict of Nantes, 13 April 1598

From the time of his abjuration in July 1593, Henry's relations with his former co-religionists had deteriorated. Successive Protestant assemblies at Sainte-Foy (1594), Saumur (1595) and Loudun (1596) had seen the development of an increasingly intransigent group. By 1597 they had become so alienated from the king that they refused him assistance to recapture Amiens. By the spring of 1598, however, Henry's situation had much improved. He had recaptured Amiens and was negotiating peace terms with Spain. Mercoeur had abandoned his lone resistance in Brittany. So the Huguenots were induced, after some hard bargaining, to accept the Edict of Nantes.

The edict consisted of four separate documents: 92 general articles, 56 secret articles and two royal *brevets*. The 92 articles generally reaffirmed the provisions of earlier edicts. Liberty of conscience was conceded and Protestant worship allowed under three headings: 1) on the estates of Huguenot nobles, 2) at two places in each *bailliage* to be decided by royal commissioners and 3) wherever the Huguenots could prove that it had been openly practised in 1596 and 1597. Article 27 removed the religious qualification from the right to acquire or inherit any office, and bipartisan courts (*chambres mi-parties*) were to be set up in the parlements to judge lawsuits involving Protestants. However, Huguenots were not allowed to impose taxes, to build fortifications, to levy troops or to hold political assemblies.

The 56 so-called 'secret articles' were not really secret: they attempted to harmonize the general articles with specific promises which had been made to certain towns, like Paris or Toulouse, exempting them from heretical services within their walls and immediate suburbs. Some clauses dealt with the establishment of Protestant universities and the training of ministers. The two *brevets* were in some ways the most important feature of the edict, as they granted Protestants a limited degree of military and political independence. One *brevet* provided for the payment of stipends to Protestant pastors from public funds; the other allowed the Huguenots to hold for eight years all the towns which they occupied in August 1597 and arranged for annual royal payments to their garrisons.

The edict encountered stiff opposition from the parlement, as the king might have expected. On 7 February 1599 he called its members to the Louvre and made a remarkable speech. 'You see me here in my study', he said, 'and I am speaking to you, not in royal attire with cape and sword (like a prince addressing foreign ambassadors), but dressed like the father of a family, in a doublet, speaking frankly to his children.' His aim, he explained, was pacification which was in the judges' interest as well as his own.

> I have secured peace abroad and I desire peace at home. You must obey me, if only because I am king and all my subjects owe me obedience, particularly members of my parlement. To some I have restored the homes from which they were banished; to others I have given back the faith they had lost. If obedience was due to my predecessors, it is all the more due to me because I have established the state which is mine by inheritance and by conquest. The members of my parlement would not be in their place but for me.

He reminded the magistrates of their past disloyalty.

> I am aware that there have been intrigues in the parlement, and preachers urged to talk sedition, but I shall take care of such people without expecting any help from you. That road led to the barricades and by degrees to the late King's assassination. I shall not go that way; I shall nip in the bud all factions and all seditious preaching; and I shall behead all those who encourage it. I have leapt on to the walls of towns; surely I can leap over barricades, which are not so high.

Henry then explained that he had acted on the advice of his ministers, who all believed that the edict was essential to the state's well-being. He urged his audience to think about his words and to do as he wished.

Three weeks later the Edict of Nantes was registered by the Parlement of Paris, but the other parlements also had to be cajoled by the king. By degrees he got his way. Toulouse registered the edict on 19 January 1600; Dijon in the same month; Bordeaux on 7 February; Rennes on 23 August. As Grenoble had conformed on 27 September 1599, only Rouen remained. It held out on certain details till 1609. But even after the edict had become legally binding, it needed to be applied. Teams of commissioners – some Protestant, others Catholic – were accordingly sent to the provinces. In areas like Burgundy, where the League had been strong, they were resisted by the local estates. A difficult matter was the selection of sites for Protestant worship; another was the siting of Protestant *temples* in the suburbs of towns.

The Edict of Nantes was not essentially new: it formed part of the long series of religious edicts reaching back into the sixteenth century and incorporated some of their provisions. The essential difference was that it lasted longer, largely because of war-weariness on both sides of the religious divide. The edict was only a truce which enabled Protestants and Catholics to live side by side within the state pending the end of the religious schism.

Neither side regarded it as permanent. It fell far short of what many Protestants wanted: it did not put them on the same footing as Catholics. It did
not create a 'state within the state', as is sometimes said, because the two
brevets on which this claim rests were personal promises made by Henry
IV which did not bind his successors. By paying the Protestants for their
churches and garrisons, he bought their loyalty and bound them more
closely to the monarchy. At best, the edict made them a privileged group
within the realm, but one that remained heavily dependent on royal favour.

The Peace of Vervins, 2 May 1598

While Henry IV was in Brittany dealing with Mercoeur, two of his most
trusted agents, Bellièvre and Brûlart de Sillery, negotiated a peace treaty
with Spain. It was signed at Vervins on 2 May 1598. It laid down that all
towns captured by either side since the Peace of Cateau-Cambrésis in 1559
should be returned: France had to give back Cambrai, but recovered Ardres,
Calais, Doullens and other places. The fate of the marquisate of Saluzzo,
which the duke of Savoy had seized in 1588, was referred to papal arbitration, but Clement VIII, after some feeble efforts on his part, abandoned
the responsibility. In 1599, Duke Charles-Emmanuel decided to negotiate
directly with Henry. He was received at Fontainebleau, but said that he
had not come to surrender the marquisate. Eventually the Saluzzo question
was submitted to a committee chaired by the Patriarch of Constantinople,
and on 27 February 1600 an agreement was reached. The duke promised
to surrender Saluzzo by 1 June or to cede other territories, but soon afterwards he sought Spanish aid to defend Saluzzo. By early July Henry realized
that he had been duped. He gathered a large army at Lyon, and on 11
August declared war on Savoy. As French troops invaded the duchy, capturing several towns including Chambéry, the pope intervened, and on 17
January 1601 a new treaty was signed. Henry gave up Saluzzo, but received
Bresse, Bugey, Valromey and Gex. Opinions were divided as to the merits
of this treaty. Villeroy and others thought Henry should have kept Saluzzo,
while Sully was satisfied with the acquisition of territories that were more
valuable fiscally. The loss of Saluzzo deprived France of the power to
counterbalance Spanish influence in northern Italy. On the other hand, the
duke of Savoy surrendered the *pont de Grésin*, part of the vital 'Spanish
road' used by Spanish troops marching to the Netherlands from north Italy.
Henceforth, France was able to cut it almost at will, so that the Spaniards
had to look for an alternative route to the north through the Grisons.

Elizabeth I did not like the Peace of Vervins. She urged Henry IV to
undermine Spanish power by assisting the Dutch rebels. Her words were
not lost on him: from 1598 onwards he sent them substantial sums as

secretly as possible. Sometimes, too, he allowed French troops to be recruited to serve their cause. Such levies contravened the Treaty of Vervins, but Henry chose to ignore Spanish protests. He tried also to stir up trouble for Spain in the Mediterranean. In January 1601 he encouraged the Turks to attack the coasts of Calabria and Sicily, and fomented unrest among the Moriscos in Spain. The 'cold war', however, was not one-sided. Spanish agents were constantly promoting disloyalty among the French nobility. Marshal Biron and the dukes of Guise and Bouillon were in the pay of Spain. From 1601 onwards, Nicolas L'Hoste, Villeroy's secretary, supplied the Spanish government with information about sensitive French diplomatic moves. The English agent Winwood did not believe that real peace between France and Spain had ever existed after 1598. In his view, each country was 'attending the opportunity who can first get the start on the other'. In July 1601, Philip III ordered the arrest of members of the French ambassador's staff after a brawl with Spaniards in Valladolid. Henry retaliated by banning French trade with Spain. Three years later there was more trouble when Philip imposed a tax of 30 per cent on all imports into his dominions. Henry reacted in February 1604 by again banning trade with Spain and her colonies. However, this proved so damaging to both countries that in October the ban was lifted, as was the Spanish levy.

Sully's administration

Henry IV's achievement is inextricably linked to the career of his principal minister, Maximilien de Béthune, sieur de Rosny, duc de Sully. He was born on 13 December 1559 into an impoverished noble family. His parents had both become Protestants and he himself, having been brought up as a Protestant, remained loyal to his faith throughout his life. After surviving the massacre of St Bartholomew's day in Paris, he entered the service of Henri de Navarre and served the Huguenot cause with bravery and distinction during the religious wars. He was wounded at Ivry and even more seriously at the siege of Chartres. Artillery and military engineering were his principal expertise, and his guns contributed significantly to the victory at Coutras.

When the *surintendant des finances*, François d'O, died on 24 October 1594 a financial council (*conseil des finances*) was established. For two or three years Nicolas de Harlay, sieur de Sancy, was the effective head of the financial administration. In February 1595 the First President of the *Chambre des comptes* warned Henry IV that his finances were in a sorry state. The king, he said, was spending too much on gifts; Henry III's creditors were being reimbursed for fictitious loans; provincial governors were misusing their financial powers. Above all, the president opposed the sale of offices as a means of raising revenue. It would pile up trouble for the future, he explained, for the crown, after selling the offices cheaply, would incur the permanent burden of paying salaries to their holders. The sale of offices also encouraged people with money rather than merit to acquire them. The parlement was equally critical of the financial administration. It refused to register fiscal edicts and asked for a special commission to investigate alleged misappropriation of *rentes* payments.

Rosny's influence only began to be felt in July 1596. As yet he had less experience of financial matters than his older colleagues, but his drive and determination mattered more to the king than technical expertise. In September 1596, Henry, under the pressure of necessity, sent commissioners to various *généralités*, supposedly to inspect them, but in reality to raise funds. Rosny, who was allocated the *généralités* of Orléans and Tours, came back with cartloads of money. He had seized revenues intended for payment of the sovereign courts: they protested loudly, but Henry was too pleased with the results of Rosny's mission to question his methods.

On 4 November 1596 an Assembly of Notables met in Rouen to consider various reform proposals put forward by members of the *Conseil des finances*. Two have survived. The first, drawn up by Pomponne de Bellièvre, suggested a reduction of expenditure on the royal household, on pensions, on the army, on *rentes* and on the salaries of office-holders, the repurchase of royal lands and *aides*, an increase of indirect taxes, and a reduction in the number of exemptions from the *taille*. Bellièvre also advocated the creation of two bodies to administer royal funds: a *Conseil du bon ordre* to deal with funds intended for the payment of *rentes*, salaries to office-holders, and other contractual obligations, and a *Conseil des finances* for all other revenues. The other set of proposals, which Rosny submitted, did not constitute a coherent programme. He suggested levying new taxes on a variety of products, a duty on mines, taxes on exports, an extension of the *droit de régale*, the revocation of certain exemptions from the *taille*, and devaluation of the currency.

The notables, in effect, approved the major part of Bellièvre's plan, and the measures taken by the *Conseil des finances* early in 1597 took their advice into account. On 10 March a new indirect tax – the *pancarte* or *un sol pour livre* – was levied on all merchandise sold in towns, but it proved so unpopular that it had to be abolished on 10 November 1602. On 21 May a *Conseil particulier* was set up to administer funds for the payment of *rentes*, salaries to office-holders and other contractual obligations. Bellièvre's triumph, however, was short-lived, for after the Spaniards had captured Amiens on 11 March 1597, Henry IV devoted all his energies to recapturing it. He turned to Rosny for assistance. To pay for the siege, Rosny proposed various expedients: a creation of offices, a loan to be levied on the 'better-off' (*aisés*), postponing the settlement of certain debts, and a *crue* on salt. On 8 May 1597 an extraordinary financial tribunal (*chambre de justice*) was established, ostensibly to prosecute corrupt financial officials, but in reality to raise money. Rather than face a trial, the officials offered compositions to the government in the form of non-refundable loans. In June, the tribunal was wound up and a general amnesty given to all the officials concerned. These measures enabled the king to supply his army with victuals and ammunition. On 25 September, Amiens was recaptured.

Henceforth Rosny's rise was unimpeded. By June 1598 he was regarded as head of the financial administration. The office of *surintendant des finances*, which had been suppressed at d'O's death, was revived and given to Rosny, and he soon acquired other responsibilities. He was appointed *grand voyer de France* (1599), *grand maître de l'artillerie* (1599), *surintendant des fortifications* (1599), captain of the Bastille (1602), *surintendant des bâtiments* (1602), governor of Poitou (1603). In 1606 he became duc de Sully and a peer of France. As from 1602–03 he ran what would today be four separate ministries: finance, supply, defence and culture. However, he was mainly important as the effective head of the king's council.

In the late sixteenth century the council assumed different forms in accordance with the different kinds of business it conducted. There was a *Conseil des finances* and a *Conseil des affaires*. Sully sat in both. As he gained control of the financial administration, the *Conseil des finances* became less important. Policy, both domestic and foreign, was directed by the *Conseil des affaires*, but major decisions were taken by an inner group of four members called *Conseil étroit*. Apart from Sully, they were Pomponne de Bellièvre (appointed chancellor in 1599), Nicolas de Neufville de Villeroy (secretary of state for foreign affairs and war) and Nicolas Brûlart de Sillery (who took over the seals from Bellièvre in 1605 and replaced him as chancellor in 1607). However, the government was dominated by Sully and Villeroy, who, despite their differences of temperament, age, religion and social background, worked quite well together.

During the last decade of Henry IV's reign, Sully's influence on French policy was preponderant. He controlled an enormous administrative machine, employing a large staff. A workaholic, who got up each day at 4 AM and kept to an exacting schedule, he loved figures, statistics, balance-sheets and reports, and from his headquarters at the Arsenal kept tabs on everything. One of his chief aims was to strengthen royal authority by methods which had been to some extent anticipated in the sixteenth century, notably under Henry III. They comprised a tightening of controls and regulations, a reduction of the powers of local representative assemblies, the multiplication of commissioners and *intendants* and the creation of special courts to curb financial abuses. Under Sully, the king's council issued a large number of decrees (*arrêts*). Letters which he sent to the *trésoriers généraux de France* at Caen between 1599 and 1610 show how closely he watched them. He also intervened in the *pays d'états*. Sully regarded the provincial estates as enemies of the Crown, and would doubtless have tried to suppress them if they had not been so popular. He did attempt to undermine their effectiveness by structural reforms. In January 1603 eight *élections* were created in Guyenne. This had been done before, but only temporarily as a means of extracting compositions from the estates. The aim now was political, not financial: it was to weaken them. Despite their fierce opposition, the edict was registered by the Parlement of Bordeaux (April 1604), but the *élus* were not established until 1609 and the system of *élections* was not extended to other *pays d'états* under Henry IV although he and Sully had manifested their wish to apply it to the whole kingdom.

Russell Major has examined in detail the treatment meted out to the provincial estates by Henry IV and Sully. By 1610 the *élus* were functioning in the newly acquired provinces of Bresse, Bugey and Gex and throughout Guyenne. In other *pays d'états*, however, the estates survived in spite of Sully's wish to destroy them. In Languedoc he was overruled by the king, who owed his throne to the governor, Montmorency, more than to any other man. The duke was a powerful magnate who disposed of a formidable aristocratic clientage, and too much royal interference in the province against his wishes might have provoked a serious revolt. The estates were also united in defending their privileges. Henry had to be equally cautious in Provence, as the estates had invited the duke of Savoy to intervene during the religious wars and their loyalty could not yet be taken for granted. By 1609 the threat of a new conflict with Spain made it inadvisable to tamper with the privileges of a border province. In Dauphiné the estates were so divided over sharing the burden of taxation that the government had to raise taxes without their consent, yet Henry received very little revenue from them: such taxes as were raised were used to meet local needs. They were often levied by the duc de Lesdiguières who was lieutenant-governor of the province. His hold on Dauphiné was such that Henry and Sully thought it prudent not to interfere more than necessary. In Burgundy the duc de Biron, the governor, supported the estates in their efforts to secure lower taxes and other concessions, while in Brittany royal officials were almost non-existent. In 1604, Sully suggested creating a bureau of finances in the province, but Henry did not act on his suggestion, perhaps because the estates agreed to help redeem the royal domain. But they made their assent conditional on controlling the collection of the relevant tax. Sully was never able to impose uniformity of tax collection on the whole kingdom.

Henry IV's relations with the towns were hardly less important than those with the provincial estates. At first he had to tread cautiously, particularly in respect of Leaguer towns which had not recognized him as king until he had abjured his Protestant faith in 1593. He confirmed their privileges and even hinted that he might extend them. Once he had been recognized, however, his policy became more aggressive. In December 1595, for instance, Henry replaced the mayor of Lyon and twelve *échevins* by a *prévôt des marchands* and four *échevins*. The *prévôt* and two of the *échevins* were nominated by him. Lyon's municipal government thus became identical with that of Paris and became the model for other towns. Henry also intervened in other ways to win the co-operation of municipal officials. When Nantes refused to elect his choice as mayor and suggested three possible alternatives, Henry lost his temper. 'I will be obeyed in this', he wrote. 'If not, I will find both reason and means to be obeyed.' Sully felt sure that municipal governments were thoroughly corrupt and was determined to audit their accounts and have their debts verified before they were settled. Municipal officials resented such investigations, regarding them as a breach of their privileges. They frequently clashed with Sully. The officials whom the king imposed on the towns were doubtless loyal to the crown, but their influence on their fellow-citizens could be limited. As a result, royal directives were sometimes ignored and delaying tactics used, as in the case of the *pancarte*. To recover part of his losses Henry increased the *taille* by 400,000 *livres*. In other words, the towns had succeeded in shifting more of the burden of taxation on to the countryside.

An effective way for the king and Sully to intervene in the running of the kingdom was to dispatch commissioners who could be revoked at will. The habit of sending out such agents – usually drawn from the élite corps of *maîtres des requêtes de l'hôtel* – had developed during the sixteenth century. Such men were more likely to serve the king dutifully than royal office-holders who, having bought their offices, were immovable. The commissioners were so amenable that they were gradually given wider powers over a longer period. Under the name of *intendants de justice, police et finances* they were to become the pillar of royal absolutism under Louis XIII and Louis XIV. They exercised the king's civil authority alongside the provincial governors who were his military representatives. Already under Henry IV, some remarkable commissioners were sent into the provinces. One was Raymond de Bissouze or Viçose, a man of Portuguese origin, who represented the king in Guyenne from 1594 until 1611 and also conducted tours of inspection in other provinces of the Midi. Similar duties were carried out by Miles Marion in Languedoc and Antoine Le Camus in Normandy. In Lyon there was an uninterrupted series of commissioners: Méry de Vic (1597–1600), Eustache de Refuge (1601–07) and Guillaume de Montholon (1607–17). Lyon had neither parlement nor provincial estates. Its governor was, therefore, all powerful, and it was to counter his authority that Henry kept an *intendant* permanently at his side.

Sully's most remarkable achievement was to place the monarchy on a sound financial footing. For the first time in living memory the royal budget achieved a surplus: it stood at perhaps 15 million *livres* in 1610. But, as

Richard Bonney has demonstrated, this was partly achieved by operating an undeclared bankruptcy. Sully did not even try to repay in full the royal debt which stood at around 147 million *livres* in 1598. Part of it was owed to the Swiss. Henry had used the siege of Amiens as an excuse for delaying their repayment. In March 1599 they threatened to break off their alliance unless they received their due, which in 1602 stood at 36 million *livres*. In October, Henry promised to pay them 1.2 million *livres* annually until the debt was paid off, which would have taken thirty years without taking into account any new interest charge; yet by 1607 the French government claimed that the debt had been reduced to 16.7 million *livres*. This had been achieved not by actual payments but by 'compositions' with private creditors unwilling to wait thirty years to be paid. Swiss captains often accepted as little as one-seventh of their due. Smaller foreign debts were treated in a similar way. Under the Treaty of Hampton Court (July 1603) one-third of France's subsidy to the Dutch rebels was set against her English debt which was thus paid off by 1613. Marie de' Medici's dowry helped to offset Henry IV's debt to her uncle, the Grand Duke of Tuscany, which stood at 3.5 million *livres* and remained unpaid at Henry's death. The same was true of debts to German towns and princes and to French nobles who had left the League.

The *rentiers* continued to suffer under Henry IV, as they had under Henry III. By 1605 some had received no interest payments for nineteen years and their arrears totalled 60.8 million *livres*. In March 1599, Sully ordered an investigation of *rentes* created since 1560. This revealed fraud, and in August 1604 he decided to stop the payment of arrears and to reduce the rate of interest on current payments. Some *rentes* were to be abolished, others bought out cheaply by the government. These proposals were so vigorously resisted that they had to be modified: the stop on arrears remained, but the repurchase scheme was dropped. No permanent solution was found to the burden of *rentes* on the royal purse, though Sully did stabilize their payment.

To achieve a budgetary surplus, Sully needed to increase revenues and cut expenses. He did both. In 1596 the deficit on the current account stood at 18 million *livres*. This included a debt of more than 1.8 million *livres* to revenue farmers, which Sully allegedly paid between 1598 and 1605. Once peace had returned, he increased the annual rent to 4.6 million *livres* by 1605. The yield from indirect taxes greatly increased under Sully, though this was partly due to more effective collection. Even so, it was only 16.5 per cent of total revenues between 1600 and 1604 and 19.1 between 1605 and 1609; but more taxes were levied than were actually paid into the Treasury, for some office-holders' salaries were paid directly by the revenue farmers. The yield from indirect taxes reflected an improvement in the economy after 1600. Agricultural and urban rents rose in real terms and manufacturing production (textiles, for example) reached pre-war levels.

The burden of direct taxes remained heavy. In the *pays d'élections* they contributed an average of 49.6 per cent of total revenues between 1600 and 1604 and 31.5 per cent between 1605 and 1609. Again, the amount received by the Treasury was often less than had been levied, as revenues were assigned locally to royal creditors. The total levy of direct taxes in any one year under Sully probably never exceeded 16.2 million *livres* or fell below 13.5 million.

One of Sully's chief aims was to obtain a predictable income. He helped to achieve this by creating the *droit annuel* (also called *Paulette*) in 1604. This was a kind of insurance premium payable by office-holders to exempt them from the notorious forty-day rule. In return for an annual charge equivalent to one-sixtieth of the value of an office, its holder could resign it, even shortly before death. The measure may have been intended to remove offices from the patronage of powerful nobles and make them dependent on royal favour; but the immediate fiscal advantage probably outweighed the long-term political one. Previously, royal income from offices had been unpredictable; now it became regular and could be farmed out. It yielded on average 7.2 per cent of total revenues between 1600 and 1604 and 7.8 per cent between 1605 and 1609.

After 1607, Sully tried to resume crown lands and other revenues which had been alienated during the civil wars. Crown lands, it was said, had been sold off far below their market value. Sully entered into fifty-one contracts with financiers, which he hoped would retrieve royal assets worth more than 40 million *livres*, but the scheme came to nothing as it required long-term stability which could not be sustained. Other measures taken by him were less demanding. Financial courts (*chambres de justice*), set up in 1597, 1601, 1605 and 1607, imposed fines on some financiers (some were too important to be thus molested). In 1601 they brought in 600,000 *livres*. Sully wanted that figure raised to 1.2 million in 1607, but this sum was not easily achieved. At the same time, he kept royal expenditure under close scrutiny. It was just under 20 million *livres* per annum between 1600 and 1604; and only 30 million between 1605 and 1609.

Sully and the king's works

Sully held three offices which gave him overall control of public works under Henry IV. As *grand voyer de France* he was responsible for roads and waterways and also town-planning; as *surintendant des fortifications* he had to reorganize the frontier defences; and as *surintendant des bâtiments* he looked after the royal palaces. Although distinct in theory, all three departments drew on the same pool of engineers and contractors and called for similar standards in respect of contracts.

Until the reign of Henry IV, most of the technical specialists employed on public works in France had been foreigners. Under Sully a growing number of French technicians were employed, among them Jean Errard (fortification expert), Claude Chastillon (civil engineer), Jacques Alleaume (mathematician), Salomon de Brosse (architect) and Bénédit de Vassalieu and Jean de Beins (cartographers). Sully also tried to ensure accurate book-keeping, to regularize relations between government and contractors, and to tighten royal control of public works. Two major principles were enshrined in a number of conciliar decrees: annual budgeting and careful adjudication of state contracts.

The religious wars had left France's communications in a sorry state. Many bridges had been destroyed, either deliberately for tactical reasons or because they had collapsed under the weight of artillery. Traditionally, their upkeep was left to the *trésoriers de France* or, in towns, to *voyers particuliers*. There was no central direction. It was to remedy this deficiency that Henry IV appointed Sully as *grand voyer de France* in September 1599. To carry out his duties, he was authorized to appoint a lieutenant in each *généralité* of the kingdom. This official was expected to visit his *généralité* twice a year: in February, to draw up estimates of work to be done; in September–October, to inspect work done in the summer. In November the lieutenants had to report to Sully on repairs outstanding. They were also expected to investigate tolls. In general, Sully managed to impose his authority in the *pays d'élections*; he was less successful in the *pays d'états*. Some main roads were repaired, notably in Poitou, and new ones opened up. Bridges were built or repaired. However, Sully concentrated his main effort on waterways, which offered the easiest, safest and cheapest form of transport. He planned a network of canals to link the Mediterranean with the Atlantic, the Channel and the North Sea. However, he was only able to start work on the *canal de Briare*, a relatively modest yet technically demanding project which was completed in 1642 after an interruption in 1611.

As *surintendant des fortifications*, Sully improved France's frontier defences. The traditional type of town wall was a high curtain wall, broken here and there by round towers. Though useful against lightly-armed robber bands, it could not withstand a modern artillery bombardment. The Italians were the first to develop the bastion, a type of fortification designed to resist siege guns. By the late sixteenth century many Italian towns had fine bastioned traces, and the Spaniards had completed several fortresses in the Low Countries. In France the north-eastern frontier had been extensively fortified in the 1540s, but the other frontiers could offer little resistance to attack except for Brouage, Grenoble and La Rochelle. Nor was the administrative structure effective. Until the reign of Francis I the towns themselves had undertaken the construction and upkeep of their walls.

Then, during the wars with Charles V, the royal treasury had begun to make contributions, but the king's treasurers shared the allocation of funds with the captain and mayor of each town. Each held a key, and the chest containing the fortification-money could not be opened without all three. Sully set about reforming this system as from 1604. He established a network of local officers, whom he supervised closely. In each great frontier province of the east – Picardy, Champagne, Dauphiné and Provence – he appointed an *ingénieur du roi* who had as his deputy a *conducteur des desseins*. The *ingénieur* had to note down, as he travelled round the province, work to be undertaken the following year. When this had been approved by the governor, contracts were put out to tender and, once completed, the work was measured up and the account settled by the *ingénieur*.

The *ingénieurs* were apprenticed like other artisans. In the course of their construction work they drew up maps, thereby making an important contribution to provincial cartography. A magnificent map of Picardy and Artois was drawn by Jean Martellier, *conducteur des desseins* for the *ingénieur* Jean Errard. Work in that province yearly consumed 250,000 *livres*. A fine example of Errard's style is the citadel of Amiens, a handsome pentagon showing an acute angle between the wall and the bastion's flank. The other sites in Picardy which took most money were Calais and Doullens. Errard also worked on fortifications in Burgundy and planned new fortifications at Bayonne. In Champagne the *ingénieur* was Claude Chastillon, and his deputy Bartolomeo Ricardo (naturalized in 1609 as Barthélemy Richard) was probably the last of a long line of Italian engineers who had worked for kings of France. The fortification of Champagne was extensive, costing annually about 75,000 *livres*. In Dauphiné the annual expenditure was about 100,000l. Jean de Beins, working under the supervision of the duc de Lesdiguières, made considerable additions to the citadel of Grenoble and also drew maps of Savoy, Dauphiné and part of Languedoc. In Guyenne expenditure on fortifications was low: about 30,000 *livres* annually. In general, the Atlantic and Channel coasts up to Picardy received little attention from Sully and even the great works on the eastern frontier were soon outdated, but the organization of a sound administrative system and the founding of numerous engineering dynasties offered Henry IV's successor a sturdy instrument with which to face a renewed Habsburg threat.

Henry IV and his private life

In 1600, Robert Dallington wrote the following description of Henry IV: 'This king . . . is about 48 years of age, his stature small, his hair almost white, or rather grisled, his colour fresh and youthful, his nature stirring and full of life, like a true French man.' Henry was certainly active. He would hunt by day, gamble in the evening and wench at night. Yet he was frequently unwell. Apart from frequent colds and bouts of indigestion, his teeth tortured him. More serious were the venereal infections contracted in his youth which culminated in October 1598 in a high fever – the worst, as he recalled, since a pleurisy which had laid him low in 1589. An attack of gonorrhea later that month gave rise to an alarming heart condition which left Henry feeling depressed. In 1602 he began to suffer from attacks of gout which lasted for the rest of his life.

The king was anything but fastidious. His clothes were often worn, even dirty, and he never washed. He reputedly stank like carrion, but was not alone among his contemporaries to consider bathing dangerous. A change of linen was regarded as the best form of cleanliness. Henry's clothes were not all filthy. He had several dozen shirts 'made of fine linen, woven with thread of gold and silk, and many colours at the cuffs, collars and seams'. In October 1602, at a reception for Swiss envoys, he wore a splendid outfit 'with a priceless diamond-crusted plume in his black and white hat, and a sash of the same colour, also covered with diamonds'.

Henry was highly intelligent: far-sighted, quick-witted, decisive and skilled at choosing subordinates. His *bons mots* were famous, though he lived to regret some of his quips. He disliked pomposity and long speeches, and dispatched his daily business speedily. He saw no need for long discussions with ministers: he knew what he wanted and quickly decided how to get it. His voluminous correspondence bears ample witness to his intellectual gifts. His education, however, was not perfect: although as a child he had been taught Greek and Latin, his command of languages was poor.

The tumultuous private life of Henry IV has become legendary. He fully merited his nickname of *Vert Galant*. His sexual appetites were insatiable and yet he had no recognized heir as late as 1599, for his marriage to the equally dissolute Marguerite de Valois had been a disaster. He had not seen her since 1582 and wished to divorce her in order to marry his mistress, Gabrielle d'Estrées. Henry's councillors feared the political consequences of such a match, but he would not listen. He put on Gabrielle's finger the diamond ring with which he had symbolically married France at his anointing; but she died soon afterwards. Though grief-stricken, Henry soon threw himself into a 'bout of wenching' remarkable even by his standards. He began to chase Henriette d'Entragues in earnest, while paying court to several other handsome ladies. His friend, the financier Sébastien Zamet, placed his Parisian house at Henry's disposal for his assignations.

In October 1599 the parlement formally asked the king to marry a princess 'worthy of half his bed'. Various foreign princesses, including some German ones, were suggested as possible candidates, but Henry was not interested. If he married a German, he said, he would feel that he had a wine-barrel in his bed. However, he did make advances to Princess Maria, niece of the Grand Duke of Tuscany, who was very rich. Meanwhile, negotiations for the king's divorce had been going well. On 17 December the annulment of his marriage was formally proclaimed by the archbishop of Arles. By January 1600 the contract for Henry's marriage to Maria was settled, her dowry being fixed at the enormous sum of 600,000 *écus* of which 250,000 were used to cancel his debt to the Grand Duke. The marriage itself was celebrated in Florence in October 1600 with the sieur de Bellegarde acting as Henry's proxy.

From May onwards Henry wrote regularly to his new wife without, however, giving up his affair with Henriette d'Entragues, who was now marquise de Verneuil. Maria embarked at Leghorn on 19 October and travelled to Marseille in a beautiful Tuscan galley, escorted by sixteen other galleys. From Marseille she travelled to Lyon by way of Avignon and Aix. Wherever she passed she was welcomed by happy crowds and triumphal arches. In Lyon she was joined by Henry, and the royal couple went through another marriage ceremony before going to Paris. Marie (as we may now call her) entered the capital on 7 February. In September she gave birth to a son, the future Louis XIII. The event caused much rejoicing in France as there had not been a Dauphin for eight years. He was the kingdom's guarantee against a new civil war on Henry's death. The king proved an affectionate father. By 1606 he had nine children: three by the queen, three by Gabrielle d'Estrées, two by Henriette d'Entragues and one by Charlotte des Essarts. They were brought up together despite the queen's resistance. Perhaps understandably, she did not show the children much affection.

Henry's patronage of the arts

Henry was very interested in the visual arts. His taste in painting was essentially down to earth: he enjoyed lifelike portraits and intelligible allegories. The eroticism favoured by the Valois monarchs gave way to romantic dreaming of a more forthright, even rather coarse, kind. Three artists – Ambroise Dubois, Toussaint Dubreuil and Martin Fréminet – formed the second School of Fontainebleau. Although their mannerism was more Flemish than that of their predecessors, they continued to drew inspiration from Italian writers. Though Henry may not have been a discerning connoisseur, he deserves credit for saving Francis I's unique collection of masterpieces from destruction. At Henry's accession they were mouldering away in the humid atmosphere of the baths at Fontainebleau. He removed them to a drier place – too late, alas, to save them all – and appointed a curator, the first of his kind in France, to look after them.

Henry also encouraged sculptors and medallists, but it was architecture that really aroused his enthusiasm. Unlike the Valois monarchs, he did not start buildings and leave them unfinished. He undertook no new residence, but took existing buildings in hand, completed those that were unfinished and only made additions where necessary. At first he confined his attention to royal châteaux; later he took up town-planning, especially in Paris.

The Louvre was among the first royal palaces to claim the king's attention. By February 1601 it had become so dilapidated that Marie de' Medici thought at first either that it could not be the royal palace or that the French were making fun of her. Henry thought of quadrupling its size, but as this would have entailed a great destruction of neighbouring houses, he was satisfied with lesser modifications. He completed the *Petite Galerie* and carried out Catherine de' Medici's idea of linking the Louvre to the Tuileries by a gallery, 450 metres long, running alongside the Seine. The ground floor was occupied by artists' lodgings and the upper floor by an immense hall that could serve for festivities or as a playroom for the Dauphin. Unfortunately, little survives of the interior decoration undertaken at this time. This had formerly been left to the discretion of the artists, but in 1600, Antoine de Laval presented a treatise to Sully, who as *surintendant des bâtiments* was responsible for the king's works. It suggested that in future paintings should represent incidents from French history. The *Petite Galerie* was decorated in this way and became known as the *Galerie des rois*. The painter chiefly responsible was Jacob Bunel whom Sully also employed at the Arsenal. At Fontainebleau, Henry completed Primaticcio's work in the *Cour de la Fontaine*, rebuilt the east side of the *Cour ovale*, giving it a central domed gateway, turned the chapel of the Trinity into a handsome royal church with a painted vault by Fréminet, and between 1606 and 1609 added a large stable court.

Saint-Germain-en-Laye was another palace favoured by Henry, but only for short stays. As the old château, where the king's children were brought up, was a rather dreary building, he focused his attention mainly on the *Château Neuf* which de l'Orme had built as an annex for Henry II. It was now enlarged by the addition of galleries and pavilions at either end, while the hillside between it and the Seine was elaborately landscaped with five terraces and as many allegorical fountains. The huge retaining walls contained grottoes adorned with seashells, mother of pearl and so on and within them were automata: moveable figures of bronze or brass operated by water and designed by the Francini, the best Italian water-engineers of the day, whom the king had invited to France in 1598. There were also water-jets intended to catch unwary visitors, especially ladies, by surprise. Henry IV carried out repairs on other châteaux, notably at Villers-Cotterêts and Saint-Léger. The château of Montceaux-lès-Meaux was extended, probably by Salomon de Brosse.

Henry IV's interest in replanning Paris marked a new departure in French royal patronage. Francis I had experimented with urbanism, but only in respect of new towns like Le Havre or Vitry-le-François. In Paris, the crown had sponsored only bridges. In 1601, Henry IV announced his intention to reside in Paris and to make it as beautiful as possible. He began by developing the site of the Tournelles, which Catherine de' Medici had laid waste. He gave part of the land to Sully and set up a silk factory close by. Then in 1605 he decided to create a square which Parisians might use as a *promenoir* or as a setting for public spectacles. As completed, it was closed on all sides except the south and lined with identical pavilions of brick with stone quoins, each consisting of four bays, two storeys and a high roof. The ground floor consisted of an arcaded cloister. Two of the pavilions were built by the king, the rest by private individuals, who were given the land in return for an undertaking to build according to the set plan and for an annual rent to the crown. The project, which was rapidly completed, proved a great success. The Place Royale became a favourite abode of bankers and rich office-holders. Many were Sully's officers who found the square convenient on account of its proximity to the Arsenal. It survives, much altered, as the Place des Vosges. The buildings were completed in 1612, but the architect's identity is unknown.

Henry also completed the Pont-Neuf, and added an embankment round the Ile de la Cité, terminating in a triangular square. This too was lined with identical houses built of brick and stone. The square, called Place Dauphine, was left open at one end, and Marie de' Medici commissioned an equestrian statue of her husband to close the vista. She wanted Jean de Bologne to do it, but as he was too old, the commission was given to Pietro Tacca and Pierre de Franqueville. It was Marie's gift to Paris and was put up four years after Henry's death. Unfortunately, the delightful unity of the Place Dauphine has suffered from additions made by generations of greedy landlords. In 1608, Henry learnt that the Grand Prior of the Temple was about to sell some land on the north-east side of the city, yet within the wall of Charles V. Denying him a free hand as to the use of the land, Henry ordered another square. This was to back on to the wall, to be semi-circular in shape and to have uniform pavilions separated by roads radiating from a central gateway in the wall. The square was to be called Place de France and each road was to be named after a French province. The scheme, however, never left the drawing-board, as Henry was assassinated before it could be carried out.

While all this royal activity had been going on, the municipal authorities had not been idle. Several important building schemes were completed and Sully set about cleaning up the capital, which was notoriously filthy. The famous traveller Thomas Coryat thought the streets were the most unkempt he had ever encountered. Sully tried to correct this by organizing a service to remove rubbish, by paving certain streets and by ensuring a supply of water. The rubbish removal service was so strongly opposed that it had to be dropped after eighteen months. The laying of *pavé* went ahead more smoothly, but supplying water raised serious difficulties. Many private individuals had connected their pipes to the common conduit, so that public fountains went short. To increase the general supply of water, Sully saw to the construction in 1604 of four pumps on the Pont-Neuf which were the work of a Fleming, Jean Lintlaër, and fed the conduits of Paris. Sully also sought fresh sources of water outside Paris. He was particularly anxious to bring it to the university quarter on the left bank. By 1623 the aqueduct of Arcueil, which was probably designed by Jacques Alleaume and Salomon de Brosse, was delivering water to Paris.

Economic recovery

Ten years of peace inevitably helped to revive the French economy. Agriculture, it seems, recovered fastest, helped by some good harvests between 1604 and 1609. Coryat encountered only one village in 1608 'exceedingly ransacked and ruinated by means of the civil wars'. Tithe returns point the same way. Salt consumption increased dramatically and grain prices fell, encouraging diversification into other crops such as maize, vegetables, vines and oil. The rural revival is reflected in Olivier de Serres's *Théâtre d'agriculture* (1600), which went through five editions under Henry IV and became the standard textbook for substantial French farmers during the *ancien régime*. It taught them how to rebuild a *seigneurie*, choose land, run a farm and cultivate an orchard, a vineyard or a meadow, as well as advising on new crops and new techniques.

The urban revival was more variable. Some towns never regained the prosperity they had enjoyed before the wars. In Toulouse, the woad industry failed to compete with indigo. Lyon ceased to be the pre-eminent business centre it had once been, though it did acquire a significant silk industry. Marseille regained some of its commercial importance by importing raw silk from the Levant. It received encouragement from Henry IV who built a fleet to combat piracy in the Mediterranean and signed an advantageous commercial accord with the sultan in May 1604. Along the Atlantic seaboard prosperity focused mainly on the smaller ports of Saint-Malo, Brest and La Rochelle which exploited the valuable trade in grain and cloth with Spain. From the same ports overseas ventures were mounted. Henry set up trading companies with the East Indies in 1604 and Canada ('New France') in 1605.

Sully's achievements as *grand voyer* assisted the economic revival. While new bridges facilitated the movement of goods within the kingdom, improved rivers and canals linked landlocked parts of France to the Atlantic coast. As *surintendant des finances*, he assisted the recovery by stabilizing the currency. In an important edict of September 1602 he restored the *livre tournois* as the basic accounting unit and devalued it against gold and, to a lesser extent, silver. The edict was strongly resisted by the sovereign courts and the Paris mint, and the devaluation may not have been enough to restore the competitive edge to French exports.

Sully believed that only an industrial revival would solve France's monetary problems. He persuaded the king to appoint a controller of mines and one of commerce in 1601–02, and to establish a 'council of trade' (*conseil du commerce*) to look into and to sponsor industrial projects. The first controller of commerce was Barthélemy de Laffemas, who, at the Assembly of Notables of 1596, had pressed for a large-scale manufacturing initiative. The council of trade became very active. It held 150 meetings and examined numerous industrial projects, submitting detailed reports to the king's council. The council successfully promoted the making of silk in Lyon and subsequently in Tours and around Montpellier and Nîmes. The king himself encouraged the cultivation of silkworms by planting mulberry trees in his gardens. Such activities reduced the need to import silk; under Henry IV such imports fell to one-sixth of their pre-war value. Other textile ventures comprised fine textiles in Rouen, tapestry at the Gobelins factory in Paris, gold and silverpoint at the Louvre and muslin in Reims. Metallurgy, however, remained weak.

Historians once believed that agriculture and finance interested Sully more than commerce and industry. It is true that in 1602 he raised certain objections to the establishment of a silk factory, but by 1603 he had fallen in with the scheme. He worked with other members of the council for the general establishment of foreign merchants and artisans in France. Regulations concerning the corn trade, which have been used as evidence of his 'free trade' sympathies, were merely an application of the time-honoured principle of restricting exports in time of dearth and of opening the customs after good harvests. Not only was Sully not opposed to Laffemas over royal regulation of trade and industry, their views and interests often coincided. Like Laffemas, Sully tried to encourage inventors. When he described 'tillage and pasture' as the two breasts (*mamelles*) of France, he was not seeking to exclude or subordinate all other economic activities. He shared the enthusiasm of Laffemas and others for the establishment of industries by the state and sympathized with 'free trade' only when it benefited the treasury. Far from despising merchants, he numbered them with peasants and artisans among the four classes whose labours permitted the glories of the clergy, nobility and other privileged groups in society.

Aristocratic unrest

Although the crown's financial position improved after 1598, the political damage caused by the Wars of Religion could not be repaired overnight. Even after peace with Spain in April 1598, great nobles remained troublesome. Henry IV's reign was punctuated by plots which drew encouragement and financial support from France's enemies. Unrest continued to feed on doubts regarding the succession to the throne. The direct Bourbon line was not assured until the birth of the future Louis XIII in 1601, and was not secure till the birth of his brother Gaston in April 1608. Even their claims did not go unchallenged, for the validity of Henry IV's divorce in 1599, and therefore the legitimacy of Marie de' Medici's children, remained controversial. Henry IV's relationship to his predecessor was so remote that some princes of the blood considered their claim to the throne to be at least as good as his. Such doubts and ambitions were nurtured by the Habsburgs, ever anxious to exploit opportunities of weakening France, if only to keep her out of Italy or the Netherlands.

In January 1601, Marshal de Biron admitted that he had been in touch with Spanish agents for some time. Henry forgave him, hoping that he would now be loyal, but the incorrigibly ambitious Biron was soon organizing a rebellion. In February 1602 several hundred gentlemen in Auvergne and Gascony were reported to be conspiring with Savoy and Spain. In March one of Biron's agents, Jacques de La Fin, betrayed the conspiracy to the king. Henry and his council continued to write to Biron about routine administrative matters as if nothing were amiss, but on 14 May the king asked the marshal to come to court in order to clear himself of various accusations. Next day, Henry wrote to a friend: 'Every day I discover the greatest evil-doings, perfidies, ingratitudes and plots against me which you could ever believe.' When Biron visited Fontainebleau in mid-June he proclaimed his innocence, but he and the comte d'Auvergne were arrested and sent to the Bastille. Towns were enjoined to be watchful and Marshal de Lavardin was sent to Burgundy, Biron's province, to keep the peace and to shadow a Spanish army near France's eastern border. Biron's indictment before the parlement was extremely damaging; nor did he help himself by behaving like a wild animal. He was found guilty and on 31 July was beheaded in the Bastille.

Henry IV was at first ready to believe that Philip III of Spain had known nothing of Biron's conspiracy, but it soon became clear that he had been deeply implicated. Even more disturbing was a report that some leading French nobles had also been involved. Henry was unwilling to bring charges against all of them – he even set free the comte d'Auvergne to please his sister Henriette d'Entragues – but he could not overlook evidence against the duc de Bouillon. The prestige he had gained as Henry's lieutenant-general during the civil wars, his extensive lands in south-west France and, above all, his principality of Sedan on the German border made him a powerful rallying point for discontented noblemen. He was, moreover, allied to German Protestant princes through his brother-in-law, Frederick IV of the Palatinate. In November 1602, Henry invited Bouillon to come to court to explain himself, but the duke went to Languedoc instead. Posing as a Protestant martyr, he hoped to capture a number of towns with Spanish money and bring in an army of German and Swiss mercenaries. However, he failed to drum up Protestant support within France, for his clientage was held together by faction rather than religion. Eventually he moved to Sedan, where he remained for some months. In March 1606, Henry marched on Sedan with an artillery train. He anticipated a siege, but Bouillon surrendered without a fight on 1 April in return for a pardon and confirmation of his offices.

Another conspiracy had taken place in 1604, this time revolving around the ambitions of the king's mistress, Henriette d'Entragues. She wanted her son by the king to be heir to the throne and with the help of her father and brother, the comte d'Auvergne, she enlisted Spanish support. However, news of the plot leaked out. François d'Entragues and Auvergne were imprisoned, tried and sentenced to death. But except for Auvergne, who was imprisoned until 1616, Henry treated the conspirators leniently. Entragues was allowed to retire to his château at Malesherbes and Henriette to hers at Verneuil. The king even legitimized her son.

In July 1605 reports reached Henry of aristocratic unrest in Limousin and Périgord. He sent the governor of each province to deal with the trouble, and went himself to Limoges. In mid-October he reported that all strongholds in the area had surrendered and nearly all the nobles had assured him of their loyalty. After his departure, the governor of Quercy rounded up a number of troublemakers and executed five of them. The unrest was apparently connected with earlier aristocratic plots. In the opinion of the *Mercure françois*, the rebels wanted merely 'to fish in troubled waters, and while seeming to act for the public good to grow fat on the spoils of the poor people'.

Clouds of war

According to Sir George Carew, Henry IV 'studiously avoideth all occasion of war, especially when he doubteth to find any strong opposition'. Yet the king did mobilize three times between 1600 and 1610. We have already noted his invasion of Savoy in August 1600 and that six years later he moved on Sedan against Bouillon. On both occasions a settlement was soon reached, but a far more dangerous situation developed in 1609.

In 1607 the Catholics of the imperial free city of Donauwörth complained to the emperor of being harassed by the Protestant majority in the city. After Maximilian of Bavaria, acting on the emperor's orders, had occupied it, there was a hardening of religious divisions in Europe. On 16 May 1608 an Evangelical Union was formed which soon comprised nine princes and seventeen imperial cities. In March 1609 the duke of Cleves, Jülich, Mark and Berg died, leaving no issue. His duchy was situated between the United Provinces and their allies among the German princes. If it were to fall into Habsburg hands, as Donauwörth had recently done, the security of the United Provinces would be threatened. The Emperor Rudolf II summoned the various claimants to appear before him; in the meantime, he ordered his cousin Leopold to occupy the duchy. In July, after the claimants had refused to accept Rudolf's adjudication, he ordered the duchy's sequestration. In December hostilities began between Leopold and two important Lutheran claimants.

Henry IV's council was divided as to what course of action to take. Sully and Jeannin favoured the use of force, while Villeroy advised caution. Henry, for his part, was hesitant: he was not ready for war and was told in September 1609 that the German princes were not prepared to dislodge Leopold by force. However, on 29 November the young prince de Condé fled to Brussels with his wife Charlotte, a beautiful girl of fifteen whose favours the king had hoped to enjoy. Condé's flight threw Henry into a frenzy: he threatened to march on the Netherlands at the head of 50,000 men unless Condé and the princess were returned. Soon afterwards the Evangelical Union decided to attack the Habsburgs in Jülich. Meanwhile, Henry and his ministers decided to invade Flanders in the spring; but, except for the duke of Savoy, Henry's allies refused to commit themselves.

By May all was ready. A main force of 30,000 men was about to invade the Netherlands from Champagne. In the south, the duc de La Force was ready to attack Spanish Navarre with 10,000 men, and in the south-east, Lesdiguières was about to lead 15,000 men into Italy. On 14 May, however, Henry IV was assassinated. Instead of the planned offensive, a small French army marched to Jülich. In September the Habsburgs in the duchy capitulated and in 1614, at Xanten, a compromise was reached concerning the succession.

Historians are divided as to Henry's motives in 1610. Many cannot believe that he was ready to declare war over Condé and Charlotte. Geoffrey Parker states that the refusal of the Spanish authorities in Brussels to repatriate Condé 'was certainly not the *casus belli*'. Henry's chief aim, he argues, was to preserve his influence in Germany which had waned since the formation of the Evangelical Union. A brisk campaign in Cleves in support of the Protestant cause would have demonstrated French power to his former clients. Buisseret, on the other hand, thinks that Condé's flight was the main reason for the king's action. 'Henry's judgement', he writes, 'was always defective when Venus had the upper hand, never more so than in this his last passion.' What seems certain is that Henry's death saved his reputation. Had he invaded the Netherlands, he might have been sucked into a major conflict with the Habsburgs and his efforts to reconstruct France after her civil wars would have been nullified.

Assassination

Henry IV is often regarded as the most popular king of France; yet some twenty attempts were made on his life in the course of his reign. In August 1593, Pierre Barrière came to Melun to kill him allegedly with the encouragement of the Jesuits: the king, who had not yet been absolved by the pope, was still regarded by many Catholics as a lapsed heretic. In December 1594 he was stabbed by Jean Chastel, a law student. The blow, however, merely injured his lip and broke a tooth. Chastel was duly executed and the Jesuits, who were wrongly implicated in his crime by the parlement, were expelled from the kingdom for a time. In 1596 a Flemish Dominican called Ridicauwe came to France with the intention of killing Henry. He and a Capuchin called Langlet helped the Spaniards to take Amiens by surprise.

So Henry was never out of danger. Fanatical Catholics continued to cast doubt on the sincerity of his conversion and to believe that he was an agent of Satan. On the afternoon of 14 May 1610 the king was travelling in his coach from the Louvre to the Arsenal. With him were Epernon and two other courtiers. The day was fine and the coach's awnings had been taken down to allow them to see the street decorations for the queen's entry into Paris the next day. Suddenly, the coach was brought to a standstill by a traffic jam in the rue de la Ferronnerie. As the footmen ran on to clear a passage, a big red-headed man jumped alongside the coach and stabbed the king three times through the open carriage window. One blow grazed a rib, another pierced the king's lung and cut the aorta. Blood gushed from Henry's mouth as he lost consciousness. The coach returned in haste to the Louvre, but the king died before it could reach there. Meanwhile the assassin, called Ravaillac, was detained. Questioned under torture, he claimed that he alone was responsible for his crime. On 27 May he was taken to the Place de Grève where he was put through an atrocious ordeal before being torn apart by horses.

Political assassinations nearly always give rise to conspiracy theories and many have been advanced to explain Henry IV's death; none has been proved. Almost certainly Ravaillac acted alone. He believed that the king had failed in his duty towards God by not turning the Huguenots into

Catholics. He also felt sure that Henry was preparing to make war on the pope and consequently on God. In short, Ravaillac was unhinged, but he was not alone in regarding Henry as a tyrant whom an individual could lawfully kill. His action was backed by a body of political theory which had evolved during the Wars of Religion. Henry IV paid heavily for his decision to follow the path of religious compromise.

Conclusion

To what extent had Henry IV arrested the decline which France had experienced since the mid-sixteenth century? Our judgment needs to sort fact from fiction. History offers many examples of greatness conferred by assassination. Whether Henry would have been called '*Henri le grand*' if he had not fallen victim to Ravaillac's knife seems doubtful. He had certainly accomplished a great deal: he had gained the throne without shedding too much blood and had given his subjects a decade of relative peace by conceding the Edict of Nantes. The respite had been used by his minister, Sully, to shore up the royal finances, and the reign ended with a budgetary surplus of 15 million *livres*. Yet, as we have seen, the king was preparing for war at the time of his assassination. It is likely that if he had lived longer France would have been plunged into a war with the Habsburgs which would soon have used up the king's war fund at the Bastille. Henry's reputation, apart from its enhancement through assassination, was deliberately inflated by the memoirs which Sully wrote, under the title of *Sage et royales oeconomies d'état . . . de Henri le grand*, after his enforced retirement from public life in 1611.

Henry IV's assassination plunged France into a political crisis similar to that of 1559 following Henry II's accidental death. Both kings were in their prime; both left male heirs who were too young to rule. As Louis XIII was only eight years old, his mother, Marie de' Medici, became Regent. Like Catherine de' Medici before her, she suffered from three disadvantages: she was a woman, she lacked experience of government and she was a foreigner. Marie had been described as 'jealous, quarrelsome and stupid'. She did not know how to govern and allowed herself to be ruled by advisers. As a devout Catholic and a friend of Spain, she listened to former Leaguers, such as Villeroy and Jeannin, and turned against Sully. As a Protestant, he did not commend himself to Marie, and he opposed her policies, notably her generosity towards nobles. He was also unwilling to compromise with the new power behind the throne, Concino Concini and his wife, Leonora Galigaï.

On 26 January 1611 Sully resigned. Soon afterwards a new financial commission was established. It was dominated by Pierre Jeannin, Sully's erstwhile rival, who, as controller-general, exercised the same powers as a *surintendant des finances*. In effect, France was now ruled by Brûlart de Sillery, Villeroy and Jeannin – the so-called *barbons* or 'greybeards'. As members of the nobility of the robe, they were poorly equipped to stand up to the nobility of the sword. Concessions seemed to them preferable to a renewal of civil war. Consequently, the change of régime was accompanied by a 'loosening of the purse strings, an outpouring of pensions and gifts that was unprecedented since 1594.' (Bonney) Between 1610 and 1614 the Regent spent at least ten million *livres* on magnates, such as Condé, Mayenne, Conti and Nevers. In January 1612 the *Chambre des comptes* protested at the increase in gifts and pensions since Henry's death. It warned that if expenses continued to rise, the reserve fund at the Bastille would soon be used up and the crown would have to increase taxes. Pensions and gifts, which had averaged 3.4 million *livres* per annum in 1605–09, rose to an average of 6.5 million per annum between 1610 and 1614. By focusing on immediate rather than long-term needs, the government did succeed in securing four years of civil peace.

Henry IV may have pacified the kingdom; he had not solved the perennial problem of aristocratic disloyalty. He had had to face several conspiracies in the course of his reign, and they continued during the Regency and beyond. In 1614 Condé once again raised the standard of revolt. He claimed in a manifesto that only a meeting of the Estates-General would prevent the state from collapsing. He resented Concini's control of patronage and objected to the proposed marriage of Louis XIII to Anne of Austria, the daughter of Philip III of Spain. The government agreed to defer the marriage till the king's majority and to call the Estates-General. It also paid Condé 450,000 *livres* to cover his expenses as a rebel. By the time the Estates-General met in 1614 the royal finances were much less healthy than they had been four years earlier. Jeannin admitted a deficit of 3.7 million, which in reality was probably nearer 8.8 million. The third estate put forward the 'most far-reaching criticism of the financial administration since the manifestos of the Catholic League' (Bonney), but in the short term its impact was negligible. In May 1615 the Parlement added its voice to the complaints. It denounced 'the insatiable greed of those who have . . . the direction and handling of affairs'. Yet the government did nothing to curb Concini's malign influence. In July 1615 he was given the task of suppressing the revolt of the princes. On 9 August Condé published another manifesto. His rhetoric against the proposed Spanish marriage and in favour of the religious status quo secured him an alliance with the Protestant leadership.

Protestantism had lost much of the strength which it had mustered during the Wars of Religion. Many Protestant nobles had followed the king's example by becoming Catholics. Yet the Huguenots remained a force to be reckoned with, especially in the south of France. The Edict of Nantes remained effective – at least on paper – for eighty-seven years; it did not finally liquidate France's religious problem. Protestant churches were not put on the same footing as the Catholic church. After Henry IV's death the sums which he had promised to the Protestant churches each year soon ceased to be paid regularly and became only occasional after 1630. The edict gave the Huguenot communities security, but circumscribed their influence. Henceforth, they had to defend the privileges which they had been granted by the edict against constant erosion by the Catholics. However, they did so in the lawcourts, rather than by taking up arms. 'Open war was replaced by cold war' (E. Labrousse).

Although religious toleration did become part of the everyday life of some Frenchmen, powerful pressure groups wanted to see a return to religious uniformity. Convocations of Catholic clergy, meeting every five years, repeatedly denounced the Edict of Nantes and tried, with growing success, to restrict its application. Missions by Catholic priests or friars moved into areas with a large Huguenot population, while Catholic clergy seized every chance of legal quibbling over the privileges conceded to the Huguenots by the edict. The Parlements also objected to the edict, seeing it as a private treaty between the king and a few of his subjects, which had no place in French law. Catholics also resented the fact that Huguenots were now competitors in the pursuit of royal offices as well as in other professions and trades. In short, much tension continued to exist between the two faiths. It was fomented by Catholic polemicists who accused the Huguenots of being 'republicans'. Their doctrine was said to be incompatible with monarchy. French Protestantism was presented as an outpost of the 'Calvinist International'.

The Edict of Nantes did not end the religious wars. They began again as a result of Louis XIII's decision to apply it to Béarn, which meant imposing Catholicism on the region. In 1621 the Protestant Assembly of La Rochelle divided France into eight circles, nominating a military governor chosen from the high nobility in each. The pattern of the past was being repeated; only this time the prospective war was defensive. Its aim was to preserve the privileged status of the Huguenot minority. The new cycle of religious wars lasted seven years, and its duration can be ascribed to the tenacity of such Huguenot towns as Montauban and, above all, La Rochelle; also to the leadership of the duc de Rohan. The war ended in 1629 with the peace of Alès which deprived the Huguenots of their political and military privileges, while allowing them to practise their faith. Yet pressure on them to become Catholics continued until Louis XIV revoked the Edict of Nantes in 1685.

It is difficult to believe that Henry IV and Sully could have cured the ills, which had brought France almost to her knees, in the course of a mere decade. In many parts of France the ruins left by the religious wars had still not been removed by the time new troubles arose under Louis XIII. As late as 1631, for example, the small town of Barcelonne in the Gers, which in 1591 had been almost entirely destroyed by troops of the League, had not yet been rebuilt or repopulated. Pastoral visitations also indicate the extent of the damage suffered by the church during the wars. In 1611 twenty-two churches in sixty-six parishes visited by the bishop of Nîmes were completely destroyed, twenty-four were partially so and the rest were in a poor condition. The situation in the dioceses of Rieux and Tarbes was similar.

In eastern France recovery from the recent troubles was also very slow. The *cahiers de doléances* submitted by parishes in the *bailliage* of Troyes to the Estates-General of 1614 throw light on conditions in Champagne. As a border region, it was regularly overrun by armies, even in peacetime. Henry IV's preparations for the siege of Sedan in 1606 had seriously disrupted local trade. He had also imposed heavy taxes on towns to pay for the bribes which he had paid out to leaders of the League. The king's demands coincided with a sharp fall in agricultural and industrial production. At Provins, in 1600, only four looms were still working out of a total of 1,600! In the *cahiers* villagers complained that townsmen were trying to shift on to them the burden of maintaining town walls, bridges and roads. Of course, they may have exaggerated their own woes in order to claim relief from taxation, but the crown itself formally acknowledged the hardships faced by many village communities. Peasants, who had been driven from the land by heavy debts and inability to pay the *taille*, were helping to swell the throngs of beggars and vagabonds who drifted into towns in search of alms and food. The population of France also showed little sign of recovery from the combined ravages of war, plague and famine. In the words of Le Roy Ladurie: 'the powerful upsurge of the early sixteenth century was well and truly checked after 1560–70 ... The watershed in 1570 proved definitive. After 1600, in spite of the return of peace, one no longer finds the wild exuberance, the joyful demographic frenzy of the reigns of Louis XII, Francis I and Henry II'.

All in all, then, Henry IV's reign marked a respite in the period between the wars of the League and the outbreak of the Thirty Years War rather than a period of rapid or sustained recovery. That there was a measure of recovery is undeniable. But all the conditions – political, social, economic and religious – which had led to civil war remained more or less unchanged. But for war weariness on all sides, the so-called recovery under Henry IV would almost certainly not have occurred. The kingdom remained divided religiously, though the Huguenots were now less powerful than they had been before 1572. The nobility still had the potential to cause trouble at home if its ambitions were not satisfied. Aristocratic plots continued under Louis XIII, culminating in the Fronde of the Princes. At the other end of the social scale, the potential for unrest also remained. The return of peace had given the peasants some material relief; but they still had to bear the heaviest burden of taxation and their livelihood remained precarious. Peasant unrest, which had exploded in different parts of France in the 1580s and 1590s, subsided under Henry IV, but soon broke out again with greater ferocity. From 1630 until the end of Louis XIII's reign rural unrest was endemic in France. It culminated in the revolt of the *Croquants* which, starting in May 1636, soon covered a huge area of western France. So it seems that the decline of France which had begun around 1559 did not end with the reign of Henry IV. Sir Thomas Overbury, who visited France in 1609, expressed the foreboding that many Frenchmen probably felt at the time: 'Sure it is that the Peace of France, and somewhat that of Christendome it selfe, is secured by this Princes life: For all Titles and Discontents, all factions of Religion there suppresse themselves till his Death; but what will ensue after; what the rest of the House of Bourbon will enterprise upon the Kings Children, what the House of Guise upon the House of Bourbon; what the League, what the Protestants, what the Kings of Spaine, and England, if they see a breach made by civill Dissension, I chuse rather to expect then Conjecture, because God hath so many wayes to turne aside from humaine fore-sight, as hee gave us a testimony upon the Death of our late Queen'.

Bibliographical Essay

Abbreviations used for journal titles

AESC	*Annales: Economies, sociétés, civilisations*
A du M	*Annales du Midi*
AHR	*American Historical Review*
AR	*Archiv für Reformationsgeschichte*
BEC	*Bibliothèque de l'Ecole des Chartes*
BHR	*Bibliothèque d'humanisme et Renaissance*
BIHR	*Bulletin of the Institute of Historical Research*
BM	*Burlington Magazine*
BSHPF	*Bulletin de la Société de l'histoire du protestantisme français*
EHQ	*European History Quarterly*
EHR	*English Historical Review*
Econ. HR	*Economic History Review*
ESR	*European Studies Review*
FH	*French History*
FHS	*French Historical Studies*
GBA	*Gazette des Beaux Arts*
HES	*Histoire, économie, et société*
HJ	*Historical Journal*
J EccH	*Journal of Ecclesiastical History*
JES	*Journal of European Studies*
JMH	*Journal of Modern History*
JWCI	*Journal of the Warburg and Courtauld Institutes*
PHSL	*Proceedings of the Huguenot Society of London*
P& P	*Past and Present*
RA	*Revue de l'Art*
RH	*Revue historique*
RHMC	*Revue d'histoire moderne et contemporaine*

RQH   *Revue des Questions historiques*
SCJ   *Sixteenth-Century Journal*

Books in French were published in Paris unless otherwise noted.

General works

The essential starting-point for research into the history of sixteenth-century France is H. Hauser, *Les sources de l'histoire de France XVIe siècle*, 4 vols (1906–16). This can be complemented by P. Caron and H. Stein, *Répertoire bibliographique de l'Histoire de France*, 6 vols (1923–38), then by the *Bibliographie annuelle de l'histoire de France*, published since 1953 by the Comité français des sciences historiques. A most useful reference work is G. Cabourdin and G. Viard, *Lexique historique de la France d'Ancien Régime* (2nd edn, 1981). The nearest French equivalent to the Dictionary of National Biography is the *Dictionnaire de biographie française*, which is as yet far from complete. A very useful collection of documents is P. Hamon and J. Jacquart, *Le XVIe siècle* (Archives de la France, ed. J.Favier, vol. 3, 1997).

General surveys

Unquestionably the best text-book in French is Arlette Jouanna, *La France du XVIe siècle, 1483–1598* (1996). Excellent analytical surveys in English are H. A. Lloyd, *The State, France and the Sixteenth Century* (London, 1983); D. Potter, *A History of France, 1460–1560: The Emergence of a Nation State* (London, 1995). See also *La France de la fin du XVe siècle – Renouveau et apogée*, ed. B. Chevalier and P. Contamine (1985), and J. Jacquart, 'La France du milieu du XVe siècle à la fin du XVIe siècle' in *Civilisations, peuples et mondes*, vol. 4, *La Renaissance*, ed. R. Mousnier (1966), 195–243. J. S. C. Bridge, *A History of France from the Death of Louis XI* (Oxford, 1931–6) provides narrative detail on the period up to 1515. Still useful are H. Lemonnier, *Les Guerres d'Italie. La France sous Charles VIII, Louis XII et François Ier (1492–1547)* (vol. 5 of *Histoire de France*, ed. E. Lavisse, 1903) and his *Henri II, la lutte contre la Maison d'Autriche, 1519–1559* (1983 reprint from same) and J.-H. Mariéjol, *La Réforme et La Ligue: L'Edit de Nantes (1559–1598)* (1983 reprint from vol. 6 of same). See also my own *French Renaissance Monarchy: Francis I and Henry II* (rev. edn. London, 1996) and F. J. Baumgartner, *France in the Sixteenth Century* (London, 1995).

Four surveys of the Wars of Religion are G. Livet, *Les Guerres de religion (1559–1598)* (1962); M. Pernot, *Les Guerres de religion en France, 1559–1598* (1987); Mack P. Holt, *The French Wars of Religion, 1562–1629* (Cambridge, 1995); and my own *The French Wars of Religion, 1559–1598* (rev. edn, London, 1996). An extremely useful collection of documents translated into English is offered by D. Potter (ed.), *The French Wars of Religion* (London, 1997). A most informative reference work, including a lengthy interpretative essay, is A. Jouanna, J.Boucher, D. Biloghi and G. Le Thiec, *Histoire et dictionnaire des Guerres de Religion* (1998). R. Briggs, *Early Modern France, 1560–1715* (Oxford, 1977; revised edn. 1998) is an analytical essay, particularly strong on the economy and society. J. H. M. Salmon,

Society in Crisis: France in the Sixteenth Century (London, 1975) is mainly concerned with the post-1559 period. Two textbooks by Janine Garrisson, *Royaume, Renaissance et Réforme, 1483–1559* (1991) and *Guerre civile et compromis, 1559–1598* (1991), have been clumsily combined in an English translation under the title: *A History of Sixteenth-Century France, 1483–1598. Renaissance, Reformation and Rebellion* (London, 1995). The author is a leading authority on French Protestantism, but is less sure-footed on other aspects.

Secondary works

These fall into two categories: 1) those which have a bearing on the whole or a substantial part of the period covered by this book and 2) those concerned with a specific reign or event. The first are thematically listed below:

Army and Navy

P. Contamine, *La Guerre au moyen âge* (2nd edn, 1986) has a useful bibliography. For the organization of the French army see *Histoire militaire de la France*, ed. A. Corvisier: vol. 1, *Des origines à 1715*, ed. P. Contamine (1992). Among Contamine's other works, the following should be noted: *Guerre, état et société à la fin du moyen âge: Etudes sur les armées des rois de France, 1337–1494* (1972). See also F. Lot, *Recherches sur les effectifs des armées françaises des guerres d'Italie aux Guerres de Religion, 1494–1562* (1962); H. Michaud, 'Les institutions militaires des guerres d'Italie aux guerres de religion', *RH*, 258 (1977), 219–43; and three essays in *Passer les monts. Français en Italie-l'Italie en France*, ed. J.Balsamo (1998): P. Hamon on the funding of the Italian wars (pp.25–37); J-M.Sallmann, on the evolution of military technology during the wars (pp. 59–81), and J.Jacquart on some famous captains (pp.83–90). D. Potter, *War and Government in the French provinces: Picardy 1470–1560* (Cambridge, 1993) provides a detailed analysis of the organization of military power in a key border province. The most important recent contribution to the military history of the Wars of Religion is J.B.Wood, *The King's Army: Warfare, Soldiers and Society during the Wars of Religion in France, 1562–1576* (Cambridge, 1996). Unfortunately it is confusingly structured and mangles many French place-names. The same author's 'The royal army during the early Wars of Religion, 1559–1576' in *Society and Institutions in Early Modern France*, ed. Mack P. Holt (Athens, GE, 1991) is a useful summary. My own *The French Civil Wars* (London, 2000) tries to set the military story in its socio-political and religious contexts. C. Oman, *A History of the Art of War in the XVIth Century* (London, 1937) remains useful for its descriptions of battles. It should be used in conjunction with P. Pieri, *Il Rinascimento e la crisi militare italiana* (Turin, 1952). The standard work on the French navy remains C. de La Roncière, *Histoire de la marine française*, 6 vols (1899–1932).

Art, Architecture, Music

The fundamental survey is A. Blunt, *Art and Architecture in France, 1500–1700* (Harmondsworth, 1953). The most recent synthesis is A. Chastel, *L'Art français: temps modernes, 1430–1620* (1994). A stimulating survey is H. Zerner, *L'Art de la Renaissance en France; l'invention du classicisme* (1996). Among many beautifully illustrated books, I. Cloulas and Michèle Bimbenet-Privat, *Treasures of the French Renaissance: Architecture, Sculpture, Paintings, Drawings* (New York, 1997) is outstanding. Architecture has been particularly well served by recent research. Many of its fruits are to be found in the series called *De Architectura*, created in 1981 by A. Chastel and J. Guillaume and published by Picard, which contains papers given at the biennial conferences of the Centre d'Etudes Supérieures de la Renaissance of the University of Tours. F. Gebelin, *Les Châteaux de la Renaissance* (1927) and *Les Châteaux de France* (1962) have been to some extent superseded by J.-P. Babelon, *Châteaux de France au siècle de la Renaissance* (1989). *Le Château en France*, ed. J.-P. Babelon (1986) contains chapters by leading specialists. The essential guide to French art in the sixteenth century is the catalogue of the exhibition held at the Grand Palais, Paris, in 1972, devoted to the School of Fontainebleau. This was organized by Sylvie Béguin, whose many authoritative writings include *L'Ecole de Fontainebleau: le maniérisme à la cour de France* (1960). There are also many important articles in the *Actes du colloque international sur l'Art de Fontainebleau, 1972*, ed. A. Chastel (1975). K. Woodbridge, *Princely Gardens: The Origins and Development of the French Formal Style* (London, 1986) is a scholarly survey of an aspect of contemporary design all too often ignored. H. M. Brown, *Music in the Renaissance* (Englewood Cliffs, NJ, 1976) is the best introduction to French music of the period. A lively, non-technical account is I. Caseaux, *French Music in the Fifteenth and Sixteenth Centuries* (Oxford, 1975). F. Dobbins, *Music in Renaissance Lyons* (Oxford, 1994) shows how Lyon's cosmopolitan environment fostered intense musical activity.

Biographies

A number of biographies are relevant to several chapters of this book and are most conveniently listed here. For the reign of Francis I and in some cases beyond, they include J. Jacquart, *Bayard* (1987); E. Fournial, *Monsieur de Boisy* (Lyon, 1996); C. A. Mayer and D. Bentley-Cranch, *Florimond Robertet, (?-1527), homme d'état français* (1994), A. Buisson, *Le Chancelier Antoine Duprat* (1935), P. Jourda, *Marguerite d'Angoulême*, 2 vols (1930); A. Lebey, *Le Connétable de Bourbon* (1904), V.-L. Bourrilly, *Guillaume du Bellay, seigneur de Langey* (1905); M. François, *Le Cardinal François de Tournon* (1951); F. Decrue, *Anne de Montmorency grand maître et connétable de France à la cour, aux armées et au conseil du roi François Ier* (1885). For the second half of the century the following should be noted: F. Decrue, *Anne de Montmorency, connétable et pair de France sous les rois Henri II, François I et Charles IX* (1889); Nancy L. Roelker, *Jeanne d'Albret, 1528–1572* (Cambridge, MA, 1968); J. Delaborde, *Gaspard de Coligny, amiral de France*, 3 vols (1882); and J. Shimizu, *Conflict of Loyalties: Politics and Religion in the Career of Gaspard de Coligny, Admiral of France, 1519–1572* (Geneva, 1970). J. Garrisson,

Marguerite de Valois (1994) is less reliable than Eliane Viennot, *Marguerite de Valois, histoire d'une femme, histoire d'un mythe* (1993).

Economic and Social

The best general introduction is *Histoire économique et sociale de la France*, ed. F. Braudel and E. Labrousse: vol. 1, *L'Etat et la ville*, ed. P. Chaunu and R. Gascon (1977). F. Mauro, *Le Seizième Siècle européen: aspects économiques* (1966) is also useful. For a round-up of recent research and a comprehensive bibliography, see F. Bayard and P. Guignet, *L'Economie française aux XVIe, XVIIe et XVIIIe siècles* (1991).

Information on France's population in this period is fragmentary, as shown in P. Goubert, 'Recent theories and research in French population between 1500 and 1700' in D.V. Glass and D.E.C. Eversley, (eds), *Population in History: Essays in Historical Demography* (London, 1965), 457–73. The standard work is *Histoire de la population française*, ed. J. Dupâquier, 2 vols (1988). Regional studies include A. Croix, *Nantes et le pays nantais au XVIe siècle* (1974) and E. Baratier, *La Démographie provençale du XIIIe au XVIe siècle* (1961).

The essential starting-point for a study of rural life is *Histoire de la France rurale*, ed. G. Duby and A. Wallon, vol. 2: 1340–1789. The classic study of the peasantry is E. Le Roy Ladurie, *Les Paysans de Languedoc* (1966; abridged English trans., Urban, Ill., 1974). Also seminal is J. Jacquart, *La Crise rurale en Ile-de-France, 1550–1670* (1974). Important articles by the same author, many concerned with the peasantry, are brought together in his *Paris et l'Ile-de-France au temps des paysans (XVIe–XVIIe siècles)* (1990). See also A. Leguai, 'Les révoltes rurales dans le royaume de France du milieu du XIVe siècle à la fin du XVe siècle', *Le Moyen Age*, 88 (1982), 49–76. The problems of the peasantry during the religious wars are highlighted by J. Jacquart in *Henri III et son temps*, ed. R. Sauzet (1992), 277–84. On peasant unrest see Y.-M. Bercé, *Croquants et nu-pieds. Les soulèvements paysans en France du XVIe au XIXe siècle* (1974). His *The History of Peasant Revolts: The Social Origins of Rebellion in Early Modern France* (Oxford, 1990) is a savage abridgment of his monumental *Histoire des Croquants*, 2 vols (1974).

A good introduction to the nobility is provided by J.-M. Constant, *La Vie quotidienne de la noblesse française aux XVIe–XVIIe siècles* (1985) which derives from his thesis: *Nobles et paysans en Beauce aux XVIe et XVIIe siècles* (Lille, 1981). G. Huppert, *Les Bourgeois Gentilshommes* (Chicago, 1977) argues that a 'third class', neither *noblesse* nor *bourgeoisie*, played a pivotal role in the social structure of the *ancien régime*. L. Bourquin, *Noblesse seconde et pouvoir en Champagne aux XVIe et XVIIe siècles* (1994) focuses on the political and military role of the provincial nobility in an area of high strategic importance. Arlette Jouanna considers the concept of 'nobility' in *L'Idée de race en France au XVIe siècle (1494–1614)*, 3 vols (1976) and *Ordre social: mythe et réalités dans la France du XVIe siècle* (1977). F. Billacois, *Le Duel dans la société française des XVIe–XVIIe siècles* (1986, English trans., New Haven, CT., 1990) seeks to explain the reasons for the duelling mania. A *gentilhomme-campagnard* who has left a unique day-to-day account of his activities comes under scrutiny in Madeleine Foisil, *Le Sire de Gouberville: un gentilhomme normand au XVIe siècle* (1981). A number of useful essays are contained in *Sociétés et Idéologies des Temps Modernes. Hommage à Arlette Jouanna*, ed. J.Fouilleron, G. Le Thiec and H. Michel. 2 vols (Montpellier, 1996) and *Le Second ordre: l'idéal nobiliaire*, ed. Chantal Grell and A. Ramière de Fortanier (1999), notably J.-M.Constant, 'Étude de la noblesse protestante en France pendant les guerres de religion: difficultés et problèmes'(pp. 43–53), N. Le Roux, 'Élites locales et service de la Couronne au XVIe siècle: l'exemple de la noblesse de Touraine' (pp. 153–67). Important works in English include J. Dewald, *Aristocratic Experience and the Origins of Modern Culture: France 1570–1715* (Berkeley, CA, 1993), Ellery Schalk, *From Valor to Pedigree: Ideas of Nobility in the Sixteenth and Seventeenth Centuries* (Princeton, NJ, 1986); Kristen Neuschel, *Word of Honor: Interpreting Noble Culture in Sixteenth-Century France* (Ithaca, NY, 1989) and J. Russell Major, *From Renaissance Monarchy to Absolute Monarchy: French Kings, Nobles and Estates* (Baltimore, MD 1994).

For urban life see *Histoire de la France urbaine*, ed. G. Duby, vols 2 and 3 (1981). B. Chevalier, *Les Bonnes Villes de France du XIVe au XVIe siècle* (1982) is first-rate. *Villes, bonnes villes, cités et capitales: Mélanges offerts à Bernard Chevalier*, ed. M. Bourin (Tours, 1989) is a wide-ranging *Festschrift*. The introduction of P. Benedict (ed.), *Cities and Social Change in Early Modern France* (London, 1989) offers an admirable overview of French towns from the sixteenth century to the Revolution. On Paris, see especially J.-P. Babelon, *Paris au XVIe siècle* (1986). The ruling urban élite is examined in B. Diefendorf, *Paris City Councillors in the Sixteenth Century: The Politics of Patrimony* (Princeton, NJ, 1983). Among older works the following deserve to be noticed: A. Franklin, *Paris et les Parisiens au seizième siècle* (1921) and Pierre Champion, *L'Envers de la tapisserie* (1935); *Paganisme et Réforme* (1936) and *Paris au temps des Guerres de Religion* (1938). Among works on individual towns, the following are important: R. Boutruche, *Bordeaux de 1453 à 1715* (Bordeaux, 1966); B. Chevalier, *Tours ville royale, 1326–1520* (1975); B. Rivet, *Une Ville au XVIe siècle: Le Puy en Velay* (Le Puy en Velay, 1988), and R. Schneider, *Public Life in Toulouse, 1463–1789* (Ithaca, NY, 1989).

The economic boom of the late-fifteenth and early-sixteenth centuries was essentially commercial and industrial. On trade, see E. Levasseur, *Histoire du commerce de la France*, 2 vols (1911); P. Boissonnade, 'Le mouvement commercial entre la France et les îles britanniques au XVIe siècle', *RH*, 134 (1920), 193–228; 135 (1920), 1–27; M. Brésard, *Les Foires de Lyon aux XVe et XVIe siècles* (Lyon, 1914); F. Braudel, *Capitalism and Material Life, 1400–1800*, trans. M. Kochan (London, 1973); G. K. Brunelle, *The New World Merchants of Rouen, 1559–1630* (Ann Arbor, 1991); R. Collier and J. Billioud, *Histoire du commerce de Marseille*, vol. 3: 1480–1599 (1951); E. Coornaert, *Les Français et le commerce international à Anvers*, 2 vols (1961); E. Trocmé and M. Delafosse, *Le Commerce rochelais de la fin du XVe siècle au début du XVIIe* (1952); G. Caster, *Le Commerce du pastel et de l'épicerie à Toulouse de 1450 environ à 1561* (Toulouse, 1962); H. Lapeyre, *Une Famille de marchands, les Ruiz: contribution à l'étude du commerce entre la France et l'Espagne au temps de Philippe II* (1955). J.U. Nef, *Industry and Government in France and England, 1540–1640* (Ithaca, NY, 1957) focuses on the question of state regulation or its absence. On guilds, see E. Coornaert, *Les Corporations en France avant 1789* (2nd edn, 1968); on banking, R. Doucet, 'La banque en France au XVIe siècle', *Revue d'histoire économique et sociale*, 29 (1951), 115–

23; F. Bayard, 'Les Bonvisi, marchands-banquiers à Lyon, 1575–1629', *AESC*, 26 (1971), 1234–69; on prices, P. Goubert, 'Sur le front de l'histoire des prix au XVIe siècle', *AESC*, 165 (1961), 791–803. The standard work on the currency and its fluctuations is F.C. Spooner, *L'Economie mondiale et les frappes monétaires en France, 1493–1680* (1956). The importance of Lyon as a commercial and banking centre is reflected in several works, notably R. Gascon, *Grand Commerce et vie urbaine au XVIe siècle: Lyon et ses marchands*, 2 vols (1971). Natalie Zemon Davis, *Society and Culture in Early Modern France* (London, 1975) draws heavily on the Lyon archives. She deals with strikes, poor relief, women, youth societies and printing. Her *Fiction in the Archives: Pardon Tales and their Tellers in Sixteenth-Century France* (Stanford, CA, 1987) analyses crime stories told by men and women to their judges in order to escape the gallows. Letters of remission are also the main source for C. Gauvard, *'De grâce espécial': crime, état et société en France à la fin du moyen âge*, 2 vols (1991). See also D. Potter, 'Rigueur de justice: Crime, Murder and the Law in Picardy, Fifteenth to Sixteenth Centuries', *FH*, vol. 11 (1997), p.265–309.

On poverty and poor relief see J. P. Gutton, *La Société et les pauvres: l'exemple de la généralité de Lyon, 1534–1789* (1971) and *La Société et les pauvres en Europe (XVI–XVIIe siècles)* (1974). The Parisian poor are examined in B. Geremek, *The Margins of Society in Late Medieval Paris* (Cambridge, 1987). See also Barbara B. Davis, 'Reconstructing the poor in early sixteenth-century Toulouse', *FH* 7 (1993), 249–85; R.A. Mentzer Jr, 'Organizational endeavour and charitable impulse in sixteenth-century France: The care of Protestant Nîmes', *FH* 5 (1991), 1–29.

Government Central and Local

The standard work on governmental institutions in sixteenth-century France is R. Doucet, *Les Institutions de la France au XVIe siècle*, 2 vols (1948). G. Zeller, *Les Institutions de la France au XVIe siècle* (1948), though briefer, is sometimes more perceptive. Better still, being right up-to-date and judicious, is B. Barbiche, *Les institutions de la monarchie française à l'époque moderne (XVIe–XVIIIe siècle)* (1999). J.H. Shennan, *Government and Society in France, 1461–1661* (London, 1969) is a good introduction supported by documents. See also the review article by R. Bonney on 'Precursors of the modern state', *FH* 3 (1989), 466–78.

P. S. Lewis, *Later Medieval France: The Polity* (London, 1966) is a subtle essay concerned with the interplay of society and government. D. Richet, *La France moderne: l'esprit des institutions* (1973) is a brilliant short essay. E. Le Roy Ladurie explores the same territory, albeit less critically, in *L'Etat royal, de Louis XI à Henri IV (1460–1610)* (1987). Two remarkable studies tracing the evolution of the monarchical idea are Colette Beaune, *Naissance de la nation française* (1985; English trans. *The Birth of an Ideology: Myths and Symbols of Nation in Late-Medieval France*, Berkeley, CA, 1991) and J. Krynen, *L'Empire du roi. Idées et croyances politiques en France XIIIe–XVe siècle* (1993). Marc Bloch, *Les Rois thaumaturges* (1961; English trans. *The Royal Touch*, 1973) remains the classic exposé of the miraculous powers ascribed to the kings of France and England. Following in the footsteps of E. H. Kantorowicz, *The King's Two Bodies. A Study in Medieval Political Theology* (Princeton, NJ, 1957), R. E. Giesey has probed the ideology of kingship in *The Royal Funeral Ceremony in Renaissance France* (Geneva, 1960), *The Juristic Basis of Dynastic Right to the French Throne* (Philadelphia, 1961) and *Cérémonial et puissance souveraine. France, XVe–XVIIe siècles* (Cahiers des Annales, 41, 1987). The symbolism associated with enthronement is examined in R. A. Jackson, *Vivat rex: Histoire des sacres et couronnement en France, 1364–1825* (Strasbourg, 1984; English trans. *Vive le roi! A History of the French Coronation from Charles V to Charles X* (Chapel Hill, NC, 1984). See also R. Descimon, 'Les fonctions de la métaphore du mariage politique du roi et de la république en France, XVe–XVIIIe siècle', *AESC*, 47 (1992), 1127–47. A first-rate survey of recent research on the institution of monarchy in early modern France is *La Monarchie eutre Renaissance et Révolution, 1515–1792*, ed. J. Cornette (2000).

The only general study of the royal court is J.-F. Solnon, *La Cour de France* (1987). Royal entries are discussed by J. Chartrou, *Les Entrées solennelles et triomphales à la Renaissance (1484–1551)* (1928) and L. M. Bryant, *The King and the City in the Parisian Royal Entry Ceremony: Politics, Ritual and Art in the Renaissance* (Geneva, 1986). Mounting criticism of the court is investigated by P. M. Smith, *The Anti-Courtier Trend in Sixteenth-Century French Literature* (Geneva, 1966). On the royal council, see M. Harsgor, *Recherches sur le personnel du conseil du roi sous Charles VIII et Louis XII* (Paris IV thesis, 4 vols, Lille, 1980). A useful essay is J.A. Guy, 'The French king's council, 1483–1526', in R.A. Griffiths and J. Sherborne (eds), *Kings and Nobles in the Later Middle Ages* (New York, 1986). R. Mousnier, *Le Conseil du roi de Louis XII à la révolution* (1970) is disappointing as it consists mainly of short biographies of councillors, some of them quite well-known (Philippe Hurault, G. Bochetel, A. Gouffier and G. Budé). The chancery is exhaustively treated in H. Michaud, *La Grande Chancellerie et les écritures royales au XVIe siècle* (1967). For the masters of requests, whose number grew sharply during the century, see M. Etchechoury, *Les Maîtres des requêtes de l'hôtel du roi sous les derniers Valois (1553–1589)* (Geneva, 1991). On royal secretaries, see A. Lapeyre and R. Scheurer, *Les Notaires et secrétaires du roi sous les règnes de Louis XI, Charles VIII et Louis XII, 1461–1515*, 2 vols (1978); and S. Charton-Le Clech, *Chancellerie et culture au XVIe siècle: les notaires et secrétaires du roi de 1515 à 1547* (1993). For the later period see N.M. Sutherland, *The French Secretaries of State in the Age of Catherine de Medici* (London, 1962).

E. Maugis, *Histoire du Parlement de Paris de l'avènement des rois Valois à la mort d'Henri IV*, 3 vols (1913–16) remains essential; J.H. Shennan, *The Parlement of Paris* (London, 1968; revised edn. Stroud, Glos., 1998) is a succinct account of the court's political and judicial functions. Nancy Lyman Roelker, *One King, One Faith. The Parlement of Paris and the Religious Reformations of the Sixteenth Century* (Berkeley, CA, 1996) is a posthumous work which promises more than it delivers. On the *lit de justice*, Elizabeth A.R. Brown and R.C. Famiglietti, *The Lit de Justice. Semantics, Ceremonial and the Parlement of Paris, 1300–1600* (Sigmarinen, 1994) is more reliable than Sarah Hanley, *The Lit de Justice of the Kings of France* (Princeton, NJ, 1983), which argues that the institution did not exist before 1527 and was suspended in the late sixteenth century. These views are refuted by myself in 'Francis I and the "Lit de Justice": A legend defended', *FH* 7 (1993), 53–74; and by M.P. Holt, 'The king in Parlement: the *lit de justice* in sixteenth-century France', *HJ* 31 (1988), 507–23.

On royal finance, a useful guide is M. Wolfe, *The Fiscal System of Renaissance France* (New Haven, CT, 1972). See also M. Antoine, 'L'administration centrale des finances en France du XVe au XVIIe siècle', *Francia*, 9 (1980), 511–33. The basic study of royal taxation remains J.J. Clamageran, *Histoire de l'impôt en France*, 3 vols (1867–76), but its figures are sometimes suspect. For the later period R. Bonney, *The King's Debts: Finance and Politics in France, 1589–1661* (Oxford, 1981) is essential. See also M. Wolfe, 'French views on wealth and taxes from the Middle Ages to the Old Regime', *Journal of Economic History*, 26 (1966), 466–83. Taxation at the provincial level is examined in P. Dognon, 'La taille en Languedoc de Charles VII à François Ier', *A du M* (1891), 340–65; L. Scott Van Doren, 'War taxation, institutional change and social conflict in provincial France – the royal *Taille* in Dauphiné, 1494–1559', *Proceedings of the American Philosophical Society*, 121 (1977), 70–96. On the *gabelle*, see J.-C. Hocquet, *Le Sel et le pouvoir de l'an mil à la Révolution française* (1985). On royal expedients, see P. Cauwès, 'Les commencements du crédit public en France: les rentes sur l'hôtel de ville du XVIe siècle', *Revue d'économie politique*, 9 (1895), 97–123; B. Schnapper, *Les Rentes au XVIe siècle* (1957). On the sale of offices, the standard work is R. Mousnier, *La Vénalité des offices sous Henri IV et Louis XIII* (2nd edn, 1971), which traces the practice further back than the title suggests.

An important aspect of local government is illuminated by R. Harding, *Anatomy of a Power Elite: The Provincial Governors of Early Modern France* (New Haven, CT, 1978). On the same subject see B. Chevalier, 'Gouverneurs et gouvernements en France entre 1450 et 1520', *Francia* 9 (1980), 291–307. Royal administration at a lower level is examined in B. Guénée, *Tribunaux et gens de justice dans le bailliage de Senlis à la fin du moyen âge (vers 1380–vers 1550)* (Gap, 1962); and A. Bossuat, *Le Bailliage royal de Montferrand (1425–1556)* (1957).

The leading authority on representative institutions in early modern France is J. Russell Major. His *From Renaissance Monarchy to Absolute Monarchy: French Kings, Nobles and Estates* (Baltimore, MD, 1994) is a mature commentary on views expressed in earlier works of which the most important are *Representative Government in Early Modern France* (New Haven, CT, 1980); *Representative Institutions in Renaissance France, 1429–1559* (Madison, WI, 1960) and *The Deputies to the Estates-General in Renaissance France* (Madison, WI, 1960). The only general account of the Estates-General remains G. Picot, *Histoire des Etats-généraux*, 4 vols (1872).

International Relations

Much useful information on France's relations with other powers is contained in works on contemporary foreign rulers. For England, see J.J. Scarisbrick, *Henry VIII* (London, 1968); D.M. Loades, *The Reign of Mary Tudor* (London, 1979); and R.B. Wernham, *Before the Armada. The Growth of English Foreign Policy, 1485–1588* (London, 1966) and his *After the Armada: Elizabethan England and the Struggle for Western Europe, 1588–1595* (Oxford, 1984). For Spain and the Holy Roman Empire, see K. Brandi, *The Emperor Charles V*, trans. C.V. Wedgwood (London, 1939); M.F. Alvarez, *Charles V: Elected Emperor and Hereditary Ruler* (London, 1975); M.J. Rodríguez-Salgado, *The Changing Face of Empire: Charles V, Philip*

II and Habsburg Authority, 1551–1559 (Cambridge, 1988); L. Febvre, *Philippe II et la Franche-Comté* (1912); W. S. Maltby, *Alba. A biography of Fernando Alvarez de Toledo, third duke of Alba, 1507–82* (Berkeley, CA, 1983); G. Parker, *The Army of Flanders and the Spanish Road, 1567–1659* (Cambridge, 1972) and *The Grand Strategy of Philip II* (New Haven, CT, and London, 1998). For the papacy, see L. von Pastor, *The History of the Popes*, trans. F.I. Antrobus and R.F. Kerr, 23 vols (London, 1891–1933).

Religion

An up-to-date account of the French church at the close of the Middle Ages is J. Chiffoleau, 'La religion flamboyante (*c.*1320–*c.*1520)' in *Histoire de la France religieuse*, ed. J. Le Goff and R. Rémond, vol. 2 (1988). See also two volumes in the *Histoire de l'Eglise*, ed. A. Fliche and V. Martin: E. Delaruelle, E.-R. Labande and P. Ourliac, vol. 14: *L'Eglise au temps du Grand Schisme et de la crise conciliaire* (1964) and R. Aubenas and R. Ricard, vol. 15: *L'Eglise et la Renaissance* (1951). On the episcopate, see M.C. Péronnet, *Les Evêques de l'ancienne France* (Paris IV thesis, 2 vols, Lille, 1977) and F.J. Baumgartner, *Change and Continuity in the French Episcopate: The Bishops and the Wars of Religion, 1547–1610* (Durham, NC, 1986). For a study in depth of a single diocese in southern France see Nicole Lemaitre, *Le Rouergue flamboyant: le clergé et les fidèles du diocèse de Rodez, 1417–1563* (1988). A.N. Galpern, *The Religions of the People in Sixteenth-century Champagne* (Cambridge, MA, 1976) explores the social history of popular belief, taking note of artistic evidence.

Secondary works relevant to certain chapters

Chapter 1

The sources used in this chapter are mainly cited in the general section above.

Chapters 2 and 3

The best account of Charles VIII's reign is Yvonne Labande-Mailfert, *Charles VIII et son milieu (1470–1498): La jeunesse au pouvoir* (1975), but it is almost entirely concerned with the king's Italian adventure. An abridged version is entitled *Charles VIII. Le vouloir et la destinée* (1986). On his minority, see P. Pélicier, *Essai sur le gouvernement de la dame de Beaujeu (1483–1491)* (1882). On Brittany, A. Dupuy, *Histoire de la réunion de la Bretagne à la France*, 2 vols (1880); B.A. Pocquet du Haut-Jusse, 'Les débuts du gouvernement de Charles VIII en Bretagne', *BEC* 115 (1957), 138–55. On Anne of Brittany, see E. Gabory, *Anne de Bretagne, duchesse et reine* (1941).

Charles VIII's invasion of Italy is described in H.F. Delaborde, *L'Expédition de Charles VIII en Italie, histoire diplomatique et militaire* (1888) and I. Cloulas, *Charles VIII et le mirage italien* (1986). Italian perceptions of Charles VIII as liberator and oppressor are discussed in D. Weinstein, *Savonarola and Florence: Prophecy and Patriotism in the Renaissance* (Princeton, NJ, 1970). See also J.-P.

Seguin, 'La découverte de l'Italie par les soldats de Charles VIII, 1498–1515', *GBA* 50.

Chapter 4

By comparison with Charles VIII or Francis I, Louis XII has been poorly served by historians, though his reign is covered by many of the general works listed above. Only two biographies deserve a mention: B. Quilliet, *Louis XII, père du peuple* (1986) and F.J. Baumgartner, *Louis XII* (Stroud, 1994). See also H. Lloyd, 'Louis XII: Medieval king or Renaissance monarch?', *History Today* 42 (1992), 17–23. In the nineteenth century, Maulde La Clavière produced several works of value for the study of the reign, but no full biography. His *Histoire de Louis XII*, 3 vols, deals with the house of Orléans only up to 1498. His other works include *La Diplomatie au temps de Machiavel*, 3 vols (1892–3) and *Jeanne de France, duchesse d'Orléans et de Berry* (1883). On the king's chancellor, see E. de Ganay, *Un Chancelier de France sous Louis XII: Jehan de Ganay* (1932). See also M. Shearman, 'Pomp and circumstances: Pageantry and propaganda in France during the reign of Louis XII, 1498–1515', *SCJ* 9 (1978), 15–32. A volume of conference papers entitled *Passer les Monts. Français en Italie-l'Italie en France (1494–1525)* , ed. J. Balsamo (1998) contains one on Louis XII's Milanese entries (Luisa Giordano) and another on Noël Abraham, a little-known royal propagandist (R. Cooper). Domestic reform under Charles VIII and Louis XII is usefully examined in C.W. Stocker, 'Judicial reform and Renaissance monarchy', *Proceedings of the Western Soc. for French History*, 3 (1975), 13–22.

Chapter 5

The fundamental work on the period which French scholars like to call the 'Pre-reformation' is A. Renaudet, *Préréforme et humanisme à Paris pendant les premières guerres d'Italie (1494–1517)* (1953). On the conciliar movement and its impact on France, see N. Valois, *La France et le Grand Schisme d'occident* (1902); V. Martin, *Les Origines du Gallicanisme*, 2 vols (1939); P. Imbart de la Tour, *Les Origines de la réforme*, vol. 2 (2nd edn, 1944); H. Jedin, *A History of the Council of Trent*, vol. 1 (London, 1957); and A. Renaudet, *Le Concile gallican de Pise-Milan. Documents florentins, 1510–1512* (1922). On the episcopate, see M. Piton, 'L'idéal épiscopal selon les prédicateurs français de la fin du XVe et du début du XVIe siècle', *Rev. d'hist. ecc.* 61 (1966), 77–118, 393–423. On the reform of monastic orders, see B. Chevalier, 'Le cardinal d'Amboise et la réforme des réguliers' in B. Chevalier and R. Sauzet (eds), *Les Réformes. Enracinement socio-culturel* (Colloque de Tours, 1982) (1985); M. Godet, 'Jean Standonck et les frères mineurs' in *Archivium franciscanum historicum* (1909), 398–406, and 'Capitulation de Tours pour la réforme de l'Eglise de France (12 Nov. 1493)', in *Revue de l'histoire de l'église de France*, 9 (1911), 175–96, 336–48. H. Martin, *Le Métier de prédicateur en France septentrionale à la fin du moyen âge, 1350–1520* (1988) presents a synthesis of some 2800 careers and investigates some 770 sermons. Larissa Taylor, *Soldiers of Christ: Preaching in Late Medieval and Reformation France* (Oxford, 1992) deals mainly with late-medieval orthodox sermons whose doctrinal message contains few surprises.

Chapter 6

Most biographies of Francis I are popular works of no historical value. Among older works two should be noticed: P. Paris, *Etudes sur François Premier*, 2 vols (1885), which refutes some traditional yarns about the king's private life, and C. Terrasse, *François Ier, le roi et le règne*, 3 vols (1945–70), which presents a rose-tinted view of the reign. The two most recent studies are J. Jacquart, *François Ier* (rev. edn, 1994) and my own *Renaissance Warrior and Patron: The Reign of Francis I* (Cambridge, 1994), a largely rewritten and more lavishly illustrated version of my *Francis I* (Cambridge, 1982). A revised version, translated into French, is called *Un prince de la Renaissance: François Ier et son royaume* (1998). Various projections of the kingly image until 1520 are brilliantly illuminated by Anne-Marie Lecoq, *François Ier imaginaire: symbolique et politique à l'aube de la Renaissance française* (1987). See also her 'La symbolique de l'état. Images de la monarchie des premiers Valois à Louis XIV' in P. Nora (ed.), *Les Lieux de mémoire*, vol. 2: *La Nation* (1986). On the king's reputation, see my ' "Born between two women": Jules Michelet and Francis I', *Renaissance Studies*, 14 (2000), 329–43. On the Marignano campaign, see A. Spont, 'Marignan et l'organisation militaire sous François Ier', *RQH*, 22 (1899), 59–77; M.-F.Piéjus 'Marignan, 1515: échos et résonances' and Anne Denis '1515: Il Serenissimo Francesco, roi de France, duc de Milan' in *Passer les monts. Français en Italie-l'Italie en France (1494–1525)*, ed. J. Balsamo (1998), pp.245–76. On franco-imperial relations see M. Mignet, *Rivalité de François Ier et de Charles-Quint*, 2 vols (1875). On the imperial election see M. François, 'L'idée d'empire en France à l'époque de Charles-Quint', *Charles-Quint et son temps* (1959); L. Schick, *Un grand homme d'affaires au début du XVIe siècle, Jacob Fugger* (1957) and H. Cohn,'Did bribes induce the German electors to choose Charles V as Emperor in 1519?' in *German History*, 19 (2001) pp. 1–27. On the Concordat of Bologna, see my 'The Concordat of 1516: A Re-assessment', *Univ. of Birmingham Hist. Journal* 9 (1963), 16–32, repr. in *Government in Reformation Europe*, ed. H. J. Cohn (London, 1971); J. Thomas, *Le Concordat de 1516: ses origines, son histoire au XVIe siècle*, 3 vols (1910); G. Loirette, 'La première application à Bordeaux du Concordat de 1516: Gabriel et Charles de Grammont (1529–30), *A du M* 68 (1956). On the Field of Cloth of Gold, see J.G. Russell, *The Field of Cloth of Gold* (London, 1969); and S. Anglo, *Spectacle, Pageantry and Early Tudor Policy* (Oxford, 1969) and idem. in *Fêtes et cérémonies au temps de Charles-Quint*, ed. J. Jacquot (1960). Anglo-French relations after 1520 are examined in P. Gwynn, 'Wolsey's foreign policy: The conferences of Calais and Bruges reconsidered', *HJ* 23 (1989), 735–72; and J. Russell, 'The search for universal peace: The conferences of Calais and Bruges in 1521', *BIHR* 44 (1971), 162–93. See also *François Ier et Henri VIII. Deux princes de la Renaissance (1515–1547)*, ed. C. Giry-Deloison (Lille, n.d.) which contains papers given at a conference at the French Institute, London, in May 1991. Among them is a useful piece by the editor on Henry VIII as Francis I's pensioner. V.-L. Bourrilly delves into Franco-Turkish relations in 'La première ambassade d'Antonio Rincon en Orient, 1522–23', *RHMC* 2 (1900–1), 23–44.

The king's often strained relations with the parlement are examined in R. Doucet, *Etude sur le gouvernement de François Ier dans ses rapports avec le Parlement de Paris*, 2 vols (1921–6), a fine work which the author, alas, never completed. A magnificent survey of the reign's financial history is P. Hamon, *L'Argent du roi: les finances sous François Ier* (1994) to which the author has now added an equally impressive sequel: '*Messieurs des finances*'. *Les grands officiers de finance dans la France de la Renaissance* (1999). This traces the careers of 121 leading fiscal officials between 1527 and 1547. Sales of titles of nobility are examined by J.-R. Bloch, *L'Anoblissement en France au temps de François Ier* (1934).

Chapter 7

The role of the faculty of theology of the university of Paris is illuminated by two works by J.K. Farge, *Orthodoxy and Reform in Early Reformation France: The Faculty of Theology of Paris, 1500–1543* (Leiden, 1985) and *Biographical Register of Paris Doctors of Theology, 1500–1536* (Toronto, 1980). On humanism in France see A. Renaudet, *Humanisme et Renaissance* (Geneva, 1958). See also the chapter by J.-C. Margolin in *The Impact of Humanism on Western Europe*, ed. A. Goodman and A. Mackay (Harlow, 1990). *Humanism in France at the end of the Middle Ages and in the Early Renaissance*, ed. A.H.T. Levi (Manchester, 1970) contains contributions by E.F. Rice on humanist Aristotelianism, R.R. Bolgar on humanism as a value system, and G. di Stefano on Greek studies. F. Simone, *Il Rinascimento francese. Studi e ricerche* (Turin, 1961; abridged English trans. G. Gaston Hall, London, 1961) traces the medieval roots of the movement in France. Also useful is *French Humanism, 1470–1600*, ed. W.L. Gundersheimer (London, 1969) with contributions by A. Renaudet, Eugene F. Rice Jr., and L. Febvre. Margaret Mann, *Erasme et les débuts de la réforme française, 1517–1536* (1934) is an important early work by the distinguished Erasmian scholar better remembered as Margaret Mann Phillips. Erasmus's letters are to be found in his *Opus epistolarum*, ed. P.S. and H.M. Allen, 8 vols (Oxford, 1906–34). P.E. Hughes, *Lefèvre: Pioneer of Ecclesiastical Renewal in France* (Grand Rapids, Mich., 1984) is a good account of Lefèvre d'Etaples's career. *Jacques Lefèvre d'Etaples (1450?-1536)*, ed. J.-F. Pernot (1995) contains important conference papers on Lefèvre and his contemporaries. See also H. Heller, 'The evangelicism of Lefèvre d'Etaples', *Studies in the Renaissance*, 19 (1972), 43–77. For Guillaume Budé, see L. Delaruelle, *Etude sur l'humanisme français, Guillaume Budé, les origines, les débuts, les idées maîtresses* (1907); D.O. McNeil, *Guillaume Budé and Humanism in the Reign of Francis I* (Geneva, 1975), Marie-Madeleine de La Garanderie, *Christianisme & lettres profanes: Essai sur l'humanisme français (1515–1535) et sur la pensée de Guillaume Budé* (1995) and G. Gadoffre, *La Révolution culturelle dans la France des humanistes: Guillaume Budé et François Ier* (Geneva, 1997). Some useful essays, notably one by F. Lestringant on the myth of Francis I and another by Jean Dupèbe on François Olivier, the humanist chancellor, are contained in *Humanism and Letters in the Age of François Ier*, ed. P. Ford and G. Jondorf (Cambridge, 1996). Important essays on the *lecteurs royaux* and on Budé's part in their creation are contained in *Les Origines du Collège de France (1500–1560)*, ed. M. Fumaroli (1998). New light on the origins of the college is shed by J.K. Farge, *Le Parti conservateur au XVIe siècle. Université et Parlement de Paris à l'époque de la Renaissance et de la Réforme* (1992). See also A. Chastel,'François Ier et le Collège de France' in *Culture et demeures en France au XVIe siècle* (1989). All these works remain indebted to the pioneering work of

Abel Lefranc, notably his *Histoire du Collège de France depuis ses origines jusqu'à la fin du premier Empire* (1893) and his 'La fondation et les commencements du Collège de France' in *Le Collège de France(1530–1930)*, a volume celebrating its quatercentenary.

Two excellent accounts in English of the early French Reformation are M. Greengrass, *The French Reformation* (Oxford, 1987) and the chapter by D. Nicholls in *The Early Reformation in Europe*, ed. A. Pettegree (Cambridge, 1992). Despite its age P. Imbart de la Tour, *Les Origines de la Réforme*, 4 vols (1905–35) remains useful. Lucien Febvre, *Au Coeur religieux du XVIe siècle* (1957) contains his seminal essay: 'Une question mal posée: Les origines de la réforme française et le problème des causes de la réforme'. Recent research into the origins of religious dissent in France has taken a close look at socio-economic factors. Examples are D. Nicholls, 'Social change and early Protestantism in France: Normandy, 1520–60', *ESR* 10 (1980), 279–308; 'The nature of popular heresy in France, 1520–1542', *HJ* 26 (1983), 261–75; 'The social history of the French Reformation: Ideology, confession and culture', *Social History*, 9 (1984), 25–43; and H. Heller, 'Famine, revolt and heresy at Meaux, 1521–25', *AR* 68 (1977), 133–57. A recent overview is provided by D. Crouzet, *La genèse de la Réforme française, 1520–1562* (1996). T. Wanegffelen, *Ni Rome, ni Genève. Des fidèles entre deux chaires en France au XVIe siècle* (1997) seeks to identify those Christians who fell between the increasingly restrictive orthodoxies imposed by the rival churches. In *Une difficile fidélité. Catholiques malgré le concile en France, XVIe–XVIIe siècles* (1999) he examines the plight of Catholics who refused to toe the uncompromising line prescribed by the church authorities.

Lutheranism's impact on France is assessed in W. G. Moore, *La Réforme allemande et la littérature française* (Strasbourg, 1930). See also D. Hempsall, 'Martin Luther and the Sorbonne, 1519–21', *BIHR* 46 (1973), 29–36, and his 'Measures to suppress "La Peste Luthérienne" in France, 1521–2' in *BIHR* 49 (1976), 296–9; also F. Higman, *Censorship and the Sorbonne* (Geneva, 1979). M. Veissière, *L'Evêque Guillaume Briçonnet (1470–1534)* (Provins, 1986) is a documentary biography of one of the most controversial figures of the time.

Chapter 8

The best account of the battle of Pavia is J.-P. Mayer, *Pavie 1525. L'Italie joue son destin pour deux siècles* (Le Mans, 1998). The superb series of tapestries by Bernard van Orley depicting moments in the battle is examined by Nicola Spinosa and others in *La Bataille de Pavie* (Réunion des Musées nationaux, 1999). The foreign policy of Louise of Savoy as regent is examined in G. Jacqueton, *La Politique extérieure de Louise de Savoie* (1892). The king's refusal to cede Burgundy following his release is examined by H. Hauser, 'Le traité de Madrid et la cession de la Bourgogne à Charles-Quint', *Revue bourguignonne* 22 (1912). For his escape attempt see C. Paillard, 'Documents relatifs aux projets d'évasion de François Ier ainsi qu'à la situation intérieure de la France', *RH* 8 (1878), 297–367. On the parlement's role during the king's captivity, see R. Doucet, *Etude sur le gouvernement de François Ier dans ses rapports avec le Parlement de Paris*, vol. 2 (Algiers, 1926); C. W. Stocker, 'The politics of the Parlement of Paris in 1525', *FHS* 8 (1973), 191–212, and my 'Francis I and the "Lit de Justice": a "legend" defended', *FH* 7 (1993), 53–83. Evidence of Parisian discontent at this time is given in my 'Francis I and Paris', *History* 56 (1981), 18–33.

Chapter 9

On the Grande Rebeyne see R. Gascon, *Grand Commerce et vie urbaine au XVIe siècle: Lyon et ses marchands* (1971), vol. 2, 768–74; and on social unrest at Meaux, H. Heller, *The Conquest of Poverty: The Calvinist Revolt in Sixteenth Century France* (Leiden, 1986). On the king's ransom, see P. Hamon, 'Un après-guerre financier: la rançon de François premier', *Etudes champenoises* (1990–7), 9–20 and 'L'honneur, l'argent et la Bourgogne. La rançon de François Ier', *Revue française d'histoire des idées politiques* 1 (1995), 9–38. Francis's relations with the German Protestants are carefully examined in V.-L. Bourrilly, 'François Ier et les Protestants: les essais de concorde en 1535', *BSHPF* 49 (1900), 337–65, 477–95, 'Lazar de Baïf et le landgrave de Hesse', *BSHPF* (1901). On Anglo-French relations, see his 'François Ier et Henri VIII: l'intervention de la France dans l'affaire du divorce', *RHMC* 1 (1899), 271–84. On Savoy, see J. Freymond, *La Politique de François Ier à l'égard de la Savoie* (Lausanne, 1939)

The king's response to the growth of heresy is considered in my 'Francis I, "Defender of the Faith"?' in *Wealth and Power in Tudor England*, ed. E. W. Ives, R. J. Knecht and J. J. Scarisbrick (London, 1978). V.-L. Bourrilly and N. Weiss, 'Jean du Bellay, les Protestants et la Sorbonne', *BSHPF* 52 (1903), 97–127, 193–231; 53 (1904), 97–143 investigates the tensions between them. See also C. Schmidt, *Gérard Roussel, prédicateur de la reine Marguerite de Navarre* (Strasbourg, 1845). On Calvin's early career see Q. Breen, *John Calvin: A Study in French Humanism* (Grand Rapids, MI, 1931); F. Wendel, *Calvin* (London, 1965); T.H.L. Parker, *John Calvin* (London, 1975) J. Bouwsma, *John Calvin: A Sixteenth-Century Portrait* (Oxford, 1988) and D.Crouzet, *Jean Calvin* (2000). On the Affair of the Placards, see L. Febvre, 'L'origine des Placards de 1534', *BHR* 7 (1945), 62–72. R. Hari, 'Les placards de 1534' in *Aspects de la propagande religieuse*, ed. G. Berthoud *et al.* (Geneva, 1957) and especially G. Berthoud, *Antoine Marcourt* (Geneva, 1973).

Chapter 10

On Francis I's court, see my 'The court of Francis I', *ESR* 8 (1982), 1–22. Exciting new light on the court derived mainly from hitherto untapped Italian archives is shed by Monique Chatenet, *La Cour de France au XVIe siècle: architecture et vie sociale* (2002). Leonardo da Vinci's activities in France, see C. Pedretti, *Leonardo da Vinci: the Royal Palace at Romorantin* (Cambridge, MA, 1972); J. Guillaume, 'Léonard de Vinci, Dominique de Cortone et l'escalier du modèle en bois de Chambord', *GBA* 1 (1968), 93–108; 'Léonard de Vinci et l'architecture française', *RA* 25 (1974), 71–91, and 'Léonard et l'architecture' in *Léonard de Vinci ingénieur et architecte* (Montreal, 1987); L. H. Heydenreich, 'Leonardo da Vinci, Architect of Francis I', *BM* 94 (1952), 277–85. On Blois, see A. Cosperec, *Blois: la forme d'une ville* (1994). A fascinating letter from the Gonzaga archives is discussed by M. Hamilton Smith, 'François Ier, l'Italie et le château de Blois', *Bulletin monumental*,

147 (1989), 307–23. Monique Chatenet, *Le Château de Madrid au bois de Boulogne* (1987) revives a palace which disappeared in the eighteenth century. See also her 'Le coût des travaux dans les résidences royales d'Ile-de-France entre 1528 et 1550', in A. Chastel and J. Guillaume, (eds), *Les Chantiers de la Renaissance* (1991), 115–29; 'Une demeure royale au milieu du XVIe siècle: La distribution des espaces au château de Saint-Germain-en-Laye', *RA* 81 (1988), 20–30 and 'Le logis de François Ier au Louvre', *RA* 91 (1992), 72–4. Another scholarly reconstruction is Sylvie Béguin, J. Guillaume and A. Roy, *La Galerie d'Ulysse à Fontainebleau* (1985). The interior decoration at Fontainebleau is examined in *La Galerie François Ier au château de Fontainebleau*, a special number of the *RA* (1972). Literature on the *Galerie François Ier* is voluminous. The ingenious theories advanced by D. and E. Panofsky in 'The iconography of the Galerie François Ier at Fontainebleau', *GBA*, 6th ser. 52 (1958), 113–90 have been disproved. Important new light is thrown on the various stages in Fontainebleau's construction by Françoise Boudon and J. Blécon, *Le Château de Fontainebleau de François Ier à Henri IV: Les bâtiments et leurs fonctions* (1998). Their findings are summarized in my 'Francis I and Fontainebleau', the *Court Historian* 4 (1999), 93–118. For an illuminating interpretation see H. Zerner, *L'Art de la Renaissance en France* (1996), pp. 66–88. See also his *The School of Fontainebleau* (1969) which is concerned with etchings and engravings.

Francis I's collection of works of art is examined by Janet Cox-Rearick, *The Collection of Francis I: Royal Treasures* (New York, 1995) and by Cécile Scailliérez, *François Ier et ses artistes dans les collections du Louvre* (1992). See also her *François Ier par Clouet* (1996) and Cox-Rearick, 'Sacred to profane: diplomatic gifts of the Medici to Francis I', *Journal of Medieval and Renaissance Studies* 24 (1994), 239–58. The iconography of Andrea del Sarto's paintings for the king is critically examined by S. Béguin,'A propos des Andrea del Sarto au musée du Louvre', *Paragone* 477 (1989), 3–22. Artistic agents who helped the king to build up his collection are studied by M. G. de La Coste-Messelière, 'Battista della Palla, conspirateur, marchand ou homme de cour?', *L'Oeil* 129 (1965), 19–24, 34; Caroline Elam, 'Art and diplomacy in Renaissance Florence', *Royal Society of Arts Journal* (1988), 1–14 and 'Art in the service of liberty: Battista della Palla, art agent for Francis I', *I Tatti Studies – Essays in the Renaissance* 5 (1993), 33–109; and J. Adhémar, 'Aretino: Artistic adviser to Francis I', *GBA*, 6th ser. 30 (1946), 5–16.

Several fine studies exist of artists employed by Francis. They include S.J. Freedberg, *Andrea del Sarto*, 2 vols (Cambridge, MA, 1963); J. Shearman, *Andrea del Sarto*, 2 vols (Oxford, 1965), K. Kusenberg, *Rosso* (1931), E.A. Carroll, *Rosso Fiorentino: Drawings, Prints and Decorative Arts* (Washington, DC, 1987) – this work contains an extensive bibliography; P. Mellen, *Jean Clouet* (London, 1971); and L. Dimier, *Le Primatice, peintre, sculpteur, et architecte des rois de France* (1900) and *Le Primatice* (1928). J. Pope-Hennessy, *Cellini* (London, 1985) is a magnificent work which ranges further than the artist's highly entertaining autobiography. The first truly critical examination of Francis I's own poetry is *François Ier: Oeuvres poétiques*, ed. J.E. Kane (Geneva, 1984). On his principal court poet see C.A. Mayer, *Clément Marot* (1973) and *La religion de Marot* (Geneva, 1960); and P.M. Smith, *Clement Marot, Poet of the Renaissance* (London, 1970). L. Febvre, *Amour sacré, amour profane: autour de l'Heptaméron* (1944) shows that the two loves were not perceived as incompatible at the time. See also his seminal study *Le Problème de l'incroyance au XVIe siècle: la religion de Rabelais* (1947; English trans. Cambridge, MA, 1985). The standard work on Rabelais is M. Screech, *Rabelais* (London, 1979). J. Plattard, *The Life of François Rabelais*, trans. L.P. Roche (London, 1963); G. Demerson, *Rabelais* (1991) and Madeleine Lazard, *Rabelais l'humaniste* (1993) are useful.

The art of printing under Francis I is examined by E.A. Armstrong in *Robert Estienne, Royal Printer* (Cambridge, 1954; rev. edn, 1986) and *Before Copyright: The French Book-Privilege System, 1498–1526* (Cambridge, 1990). On the king's library see Ursula Baurmeister and M.-P. Laffitte, *Des livres et des rois: la bibliothèque royale de Blois* (1992) and M.-P. Laffitte and F. Le Bars, *Reliures royales de la Renaissance. La Librairie de Fontainebleau* (1999). A. Hobson, *Humanists and Bookbinders* (Cambridge, 1989) is a fine piece of scholarship shedding much light on the handsome bindings ordered by Francis and especially Henry II.

Chapter 11

V.-L. Bourrilly, *Guillaume du Bellay* (1905); M. François, *Le Cardinal François de Tournon* (1951) and F. Decrue, *Anne de Montmorency, grand maître et connétable de France à la cour, aux armées et au conseil du roi François Ier* (1885) are vitally important in respect of the last ten years of the reign. For foreign policy see also V.-L. Bourrilly, 'Le cardinal Jean du Bellay en Italie', *Revue des études rabelaisiennes* 5 (1907), 246–53, 262–74. On relations with the Turks, see *Négociations de la France dans le Levant (1848–60)*, ed. E. Charrière (4 vols, 1848–60); J. Ursu, *La politique orientale de François Ier* (1908); V.-L. Bourrilly, 'L'ambassade de La Forest et de Marillac à Constantinople (1535–38)', *RH* 76 (1901), 297–328; G. Zeller, 'Une légende qui a la vie dure: les capitulations de 1535', *RHMC* 2 (1955). M.E. Emerit, 'Les capitulations de 1535 ne sont pas une légende', *AESC* 19 (1964), 362–3.

G. Procacci, 'La Provence à la veille des guerres de religion, 1535–45', *RHMC* 5 (1958) offers a Marxist view of peasant unrest in the wake of Charles V's invasion. On fiscal reform the work of P. Hamon (cited above) now supersedes all previous studies. On the annexation of Brittany see J. de La Martinière, 'Les états de 1532 et l'Union de la Bretagne à la France', *Bulletin de la Société polymathique du Morbihan* (Vannes, 1911), 177–93. The ordinance of Villers-Cotterêts still awaits a proper study, particularly in respect of its enforcement. Aspects are considered in J.H. Langbein, *Prosecuting Crime in the Renaissance* (Cambridge, MA, 1974); A. Esmein, *A History of Continental Criminal Procedure*, trans. J. Simpson (London, 1914); A. Croix, *Nantes et le pays nantais au XVIe siècle* (1974); H. Hauser, *Ouvriers du temps passé* (1927) and N.Z. Davis, 'A trade union in sixteenth-century France', *Econ.HR* 19 (1966), 48–69.

Francis's relations with the German Protestant princes are examined by J.-D. Pariset, *Les Relations entre la France et l'Allemagne au milieu du XVIe siècle* (Strasbourg, 1981); J.-Y. Mariotte, 'François Ier et la Ligue de Smalkalde', *Revue suisse d'histoire* 16 (1966), 206–42; and D. Potter, 'Foreign policy in the age of the Reformation: French involvement in the Schmalkaldic War, 1544–47', *HJ* 20 (1977), 525–44.

Francis's quarrel with the parlement of Rouen is described in A. Floquet, *Histoire du Parlement de Normandie*, 7 vols (Rouen, 1840). On the rise of court faction see, in addition to the biographies by F. Decrue and M. François (listed above, page 499): E. Dermenghem, 'Un ministre de François Ier: la grandeur et la disgrace de l'amiral Claude d'Annebault', *Revue du XVIe siècle* 9 (1922), 34–50; E. Desgardins, *Anne de Pisseleu, duchesse d'Etampes et François Ier* (1904); C. Porée, *Un Parlementaire sous François Ier: Guillaume Poyet, 1473–1548* (Angers, 1898); and A. Martineau, 'L'amiral Chabot, seigneur de Brion (1492?–1542)', in *BEC* (1883), 77–83. On the imperial invasion of 1544, see C. Paillard, *L'Invasion allemande de 1544* (1884) and A. Rozet and J.-F. Lembey, *L'Invasion de la France et le siège de Saint-Dizier par Charles-Quint en 1544* (1910).

On the fight against heresy, see N. Weiss, 'La Sorbonne, le Parlement de Paris et les livres hérétiques de 1542 à 1546', *BSHPF* 34 (1885), 19–28. A major victim of persecution is studied in R.C. Christie, *Etienne Dolet, the Martyr of the Renaissance* (London, 1880). His martyrdom is used by D.R. Kelley in *The Beginning of Ideology: Consciousness and Society in the French Reformation* (Cambridge, 1981) as one of eight apologues taken to reflect private and public consciousness at the time. D. Nicholls, 'The theatre of martyrdom in the French Reformation', *P. & P.* 121 (1988), 49–73, shows that martyrdom often proved counterproductive and was used more sparingly than is often assumed. On the Waldensian heresy, see G. Audisio, *Les Vaudois du Luberon: Une minorité en Provence (1460–1560)* (Mérindol, 1984) and his *Procès-Verbal d'un massacre: Les Vaudois du Luberon (avril 1545)* (Aix-en-Provence, 1992), 377–92. English readers may use his *The Waldensian Dissent. Persecution and Survival, c.1170–c.1570* (Cambridge, 1999). E. Cameron, *The Reformation of the Heretics: The Waldenses of the Alps, 1480–1580* (Oxford, 1984) disagrees with Audisio on some major issues and is more reliable on Italy than on Provence. The Vaudois also come within the purview of M. Venard's massive tome, *Réforme protestante, Réforme catholique dans la province d'Avignon au XVIe siècle* (1993), which ranges across a much wider religious spectrum than its title suggests.

Chapter 12

Excellent general surveys of the political ideas of the period are Q. Skinner, *The Foundations of Modern Political Thought*, 2 vols (Cambridge, 1978); J. H. Burns (ed.), *The Cambridge History of Political Thought, 1450–1700* (Cambridge, 1991); and W. F. Church, *Constitutional Thought in Sixteenth-Century France* (Cambridge, MA, 1941).

Two major contemporary texts are Claude de Seyssel, *La Monarchie de France*, ed. J. Poujol (1961), which exists in an English translation by J.H. Hexter with a commentary by D.R. Kelley (New Haven, CT, 1981), and G. Budé, *L'Institution du Prince*, edited by C. Bontems in *Le Prince dans la France des XVIe et XVIIe siècles*, ed. C. Bontems, L.-P. Raybaud and J.-P. Brancourt (1965).

For a definition of absolutism, see R. Bonney, 'Absolutism: What's in a name?', *FH* 1 (1987), 93–117, and his *L'Absolutisme* (1989). For the view that it predominated in sixteenth-century France, see P. Mesnard, *L'Essor de la philosophie politique au XVIe siècle* (2nd edn, Paris, 1951), J. W. Allen, *Political Thought in the Sixteenth Century* (London, 1928) and G. Pagès, *La Monarchie d'ancien régime en*

France (1946). On specific thinkers see J.-L. Thireau, *Charles Du Moulin (1500–1566)* (Geneva, 1980) and Howell A Lloyd, 'Constitutional Thought in Sixteenth-Century France: The case of Pierre Rebuffi', *FH*,8 (1994), 259–75. Historians of provincial France have long stressed the practical limits of royal absolutism in this period: see H. Prentout, *Les Etats provinciaux de Normandie*, 3 vols (Caen, 1925) and P. Dognon, *Les Institutions politiques et administratives du Pays de Languedoc du XIIIe siècle aux Guerres de Religion* (Toulouse, 1895). Among present-day historians, J. Russell Major is the chief critic of a French Renaissance monarchy that was absolute. In addition to his works listed above under 'Government central and local', see his 'The Renaissance monarchy: A contribution to the periodization of history', *The Emory University Quarterly* 13 (1957), 112–24. D. Parker, *The Making of French Absolutism* (London, 1983) argues in favour of a monarchy that was 'both absolute and limited'. D. Hickey, *The Coming of French Absolutism: The Struggle for Tax Reform in the Province of Dauphiné, 1540–1640* (Toronto, 1986) demonstrates how the crown became involved in provincial jurisdictions as it tried to resolve a struggle over the *taille*.

Chapter 13

I. Cloulas, *Henri II* (1985) is the best biography now available. For English readers, F.J. Baumgartner, *Henry II King of France 1547–1559* (Durham, NC, 1988) can be recommended. L. Romier, *Les Origines politiques des guerres de religion*, 2 vols (1913–14) draws on the Este archives in Ferrara: the first volume is concerned with Henry II's Italian policies, the second with his struggle with the Protestants. On Anglo-French relations, see D.L. Potter, 'The treaty of Boulogne and European diplomacy, 1549–50', *BIHR* 55 (1982), 50–65; and G. Zeller, *La Réunion de Metz à la France (1552–1648)*, 2 vols (Strasbourg, 1926) which focuses on Henry's occupation of the bishoprics of Metz, Toul and Verdun. On religious persecution, see N. Weiss, *La Chambre ardente, étude sur la liberté de conscience sous François Ier et Henri II, 1540–1550* (1989) and D. El Kenz, *Les bûchers du roi. La culture protestante des martyrs (1523–1572)* (1997). On royal institutions, see M. Antoine 'Un tournant dans l'histoire des institutions monarchiques: le règne de Henri II', *Colloque franco-suédois* (1978) and 'Institutions françaises en Italie sous le règne de Henri II. Gouverneurs et intendants (1547–1559)', *Mélanges de l'école française de Rome*, 94 (1982). F. Bardon, *Diane de Poitiers et le mythe de Diane* (1963) is mainly concerned with the idealized portrayal of Diane in art.

Chapter 14

For Pierre Lescot's work at the Louvre, see D. Thomson, *Renaissance Paris: Architecture and Growth, 1475–1600* (London, 1984). The imperial message conveyed by the Louvre's iconography is discussed by V. Hoffmann, 'Le Louvre de Henri II: un palais imperial', *Bulletin de la Société de l'Histoire de l'Art français, année 1982* (1984), 7–15. See also M. Jenkins, 'The imagery of the Henri II wing of the Louvre', *Journal of Medieval and Renaissance Studies* (1977), 289–307. On sculpture, see Pierre du Colombier, *Jean Goujon* (1949) and H. Lemonnier, 'Jean Goujon et la Salle des Cariatides au Louvre', *GBA* (1906), 177–94. The portraiture of François

Clouet is surveyed in E. Moreau-Nélaton, *Les Clouet et leurs émules*, 3 vols (1924) and *Les Clouet et la cour des rois de France* (catalogue of exhibition at the Bibliothèque nationale, Paris, 1970). The cult of ancient Rome is a major theme running through Margaret McGowan's *Ideal Forms in the Age of Ronsard* (Berkeley, CA, 1985). In addition to the poet himself, she explores architecture, painting and dance in order to recreate the period's cultural and intellectual climate. See also her *The Vision of Rome in Late Renaissance France* (New Haven, CT, and London, 2000) and *L'Entrée de Henri II, Rouen, 1550* (Amsterdam, 1974). I.D. McFarlane, *The Entry of Henri II into Paris, 16 June 1549* (Binghamton, NY, 1982) contains a facsimile of the original festival book. On poetry, see R. Lebègue, *Histoire de la poésie française de 1560 à 1630* (1947) and M. Vianey, *Le Pétrarchisme en France au XVIe siècle* (Montpellier, 1909). The significance of Jean Dorat is stressed in F. Yates, *The French Academies of the Sixteenth Century* (London, 1988). M. Simonin, *Ronsard* (1990) is the latest addition to the poet's extensive bibliography.

Chapter 15

On Anglo-French relations, see D.L. Potter 'The duc de Guise and the fall of Calais 1557–58', *EHR* 118 (1983), 481–512, and C.S.L. Davies, 'England and the French war, 1557–9', in J. Loach and R. Tittler (eds), *The Mid-Tudor Polity, c.1540–1560* (London, 1980), 159–85. The peace of Cateau-Cambrésis is examined in L. Romier 'Les guerres d'Henri II et le traité de Cateau-Cambrésis (1554–9)', *Mélanges d'archéologie et d'histoire* 30 (1910), 1–50; A. de Ruble, *Le Traité de Cateau-Cambrésis (2–3 avril 1559)* (1889) and in R. Romano, 'La pace di Cateau-Cambrésis e l'equilibrio europeo', *Rivista Storica Italiana* (1949), 526–50. On the revolt in Guyenne, see J.-C. Gigou, *Révolte de la Gabelle en Guyenne, 1548–49* (1906) and J. Powis, 'Guyenne 1548: The crown, the province and social order', *ESR* 12 (1982), 1–15. On the financial situation, see R. Doucet, 'Le grand parti de Lyon au XVIe siècle', *RH* 171 (1933), 473–513.

The role of Genevan missionaries in France is examined in R.M. Kingdon, *Geneva and the Coming of the Wars of Religion in France, 1555–1563* (Geneva, 1956). There are also a number of important articles on France in his *Church and Society in Reformation Europe* (London, 1985). Protestantism and its institutions in southern France receive detailed attention in Janine Garrisson, *Protestants du Midi, 1559–1598* (Toulouse, 1981); her more popular books, *L'Homme protestant* (1980) and *Les Protestants au XVIe siècle* (1988), are also recommended. On the religious crisis in Paris, see F. Aubert, 'A propos de l'affaire de la rue Saint Jacques (4–5 septembre 1557)', *BSHPF* 73 (1947). The same event is used by D.R. Kelley in his *The Beginning of Ideology* (already cited, page 513), 91–128. Royal legislation against Protestants is critically examined in N.M. Sutherland, *The Huguenot Struggle for Recognition* (New Haven, CT, 1980). See also her *Princes, Politics and Religion, 1547–1589* (London, 1984). The early persecution of Protestants in the Midi is considered by R.A. Mentzer Jr in 'The legal response to heresy in Languedoc, 1500–1560', *SCJ* 4 (1973), 19–30; 'Heresy suspects in Languedoc prior to 1560: Observations on their social and occupational status', *BHR* 39 (1977), 561–9; and 'Heresy proceedings in Languedoc, 1550–1560', *Proceedings of the American Philosophical Society* (1984).

Chapter 16

Excellent outlines and bibliographies are to be found in P. Chaunu: *L'Expansion européenne du XIIIe au XVe siècle* (1960) and his *Conquête et exploitation des nouveaux mondes (XVIe siècle)* (1969). Still excellent on French activities is C.-A. Julien, *Les Voyages de découverte et les premiers établissements* (1948). Also first-rate are D.B. Quinn, *North America from Earliest Discovery to First Settlements* (New York, 1978); S. E. Morison, *The European Discovery of America: The northern Voyages, AD500–1600* (New York, 1971); and B. Penrose, *Travel and Discovery in the Renaissance, 1420–1620* (Cambridge, MA, 1952). *La France et la mer au siècle des grandes découvertes*, ed. P. Masson and M. Verge-Franceschi (1993), is rich in information on shipbuilding, harbours and maritime personnel in the sixteenth century. Only 70 pages of E. Taillemite, *Marins français à la découverte du monde. De Jacques Cartier à Dumont d'Urville* (1999) concern the sixteenth century. They are chronological narratives quoting liberally from various accounts of voyages written by participants.

Early French contacts with Brazil are described in P.L.J. Gaffarel, *Histoire du Brésil français au seizième siècle* (1878). For the impact on the motherland, see J.-M. Massa, 'Le monde Luso-Brésilien dans la joyeuse entrée de Rouen' in *Les Fêtes de la Renaissance*, ed. J. Jacquot and E. Konigson (1975), vol. 3, 105–16. On Villegaignon, see T.Wanegffelen, 'Rio ou la vraie Réforme: la "France antarctique" de Nicolas Durand de Villegagnon entre Genève et Rome' in *Aux temps modernes: naissance du Brésil* (Actes du colloque franco-brésilien, Sorbonne, March 1997, pub. 1998), pp. 159–75. See also L. Peillard, *Villegagnon, vice-amiral de Bretagne, vice-roi du Brésil* (1991). The career of Verrazzano is described in two well-documented works: L.C. Wroth, *The Voyages of Giovanni da Verrazzano, 1524–1528* (New Haven, CT, 1970) and M. Mollat du Jourdin and J. Habert, *Giovanni et Girolamo Verrazano navigateurs de François Ier* (1982). On Thevet, the best work is F. Lestringant, *André Thevet, cosmographe des derniers Valois* (Geneva, 1991). See also his *L'Expérience huguenote au Nouveau Monde (XVIe siècle)* (Geneva, 1996) and *Le Huguenot et le sauvage. L'Amérique et la controverse coloniale en France au temps des guerres de religion (1555–1589)* (1990).

On the French in North America, see *1492–1992. Des Normands découvrent l'Amérique* (Rouen, 1992) and Raymonde Litalien, *Les explorateurs de l'Amérique du Nord* (1993) On Canada, see M. Trudel, *Histoire de la Nouvelle-France. 1. Les vaines tentatives, 1524–1603* (Montreal, 1963) and, more briefly, *The Beginnings of New France, 1524–1663* (Toronto, 1973). On Cartier, see G. Lanctot, *Jacques Cartier* (Montreal, 1947) and F. Braudel, *Le monde de Jacques Cartier. L'aventure au XVIe siècle* (1984).

Chapter 17

Fluctuations of grain prices are recorded in M. Baulant and J. Meuvret, *Prix des céréales extraits de la mercuriale de Paris*, 2 vols (1940–62). See also M. Baulant, 'Prix et salaires à Paris au XVIe siècle: Sources et résultats', *AESC* 31 (1976), 954–995; on wages, see her 'Le salaire des ouvriers du bâtiment à Paris de 1400 à 1726', *AESC* 26 (1971), 463–93. H. Hauser, 'The French Reformation and the French people', *AHR* 4 (1899), 217–27, was the first attempt to link early Protestantism with economic depression. Hauser has found a zealous disciple in H. Heller, who argues for a similar connection in *The Conquest of Poverty. The Calvinist Revolt in Sixteenth-Century France* (Leiden, 1986) and *Iron and Blood: Civil Wars in Sixteenth-Century France* (Montreal, 1991). His views are at variance with those of P. Benedict in *Rouen during the Wars of Religion* (Cambridge, 1981). Natalie Z. Davis, focusing on the printing industry in Lyon in *Society and Culture in Early Modern France* (1975), also sees 'no significant correlation between socioeconomic position and religion in the period up to 1567', but she does see one between vocation and religion. A unique poll of religious opinion in Troyes in 1563 is analysed by Penny Roberts in 'Religious conflict and the urban setting: Troyes during the French Wars of Religion', *FH* 6 (1992), 259–78.

The fortunes of the nobility have attracted considerable attention from historians recently. For the traditional notion of a nobility in decline, see L. Romier, *Le Royaume de Catherine de Médicis*, 2 vols (1922); G. Roupnel, *La Ville et la campagne au XVIIe siècle* (1955); H. Drouot, *Mayenne et la Bourgogne: Etude sur la Ligue (1587–1596)*, 2 vols (1937); P. de Vaissière, *Gentilshommes campagnards de l'ancienne France* (1925) and D. Bitton, *The French Nobility in Crisis, 1560–1640* (Stanford, CA, 1969). This notion is refuted by J.B. Wood, *The Nobility of the Election of Bayeux, 1463–1666: Continuity through Change* (Princeton, NJ, 1980). See also his 'The decline of the nobility in sixteenth and early seventeeth-century France: Myth or reality?', *JMH* 48 (1976) and J. Russell Major, 'Noble income, inflation, and the Wars of Religion in France', *AHR* 86 (1981), 21–48. Other kindred studies include M. Greengrass, 'Property and politics in the sixteenth century: The landed fortune of the constable Anne de Montmorency', *FH* 2 (1988), 371–98; D. Crouzet, 'Recherches sur la crise de l'aristocratie en France au XVIe siècle: les dettes de la maison de Nevers', *HES* 4 (1987), 7–50; D. Potter, 'The Luxembourg inheritance: The House of Bourbon and its lands in Northern France during the sixteenth century', *FH* 6 (1992), 24–62; and W. A. Weary, 'The house of La Trémoïlle, fifteenth through eighteenth centuries: Change and adaptation in a French noble family', *JMH* 49 (1977). The traditional view of a conflict between sword and robe is challenged by J. Dewald, *The Formation of a Provincial Nobility: The Magistrates of the Parlement of Rouen, 1499–1610* (Princeton, NJ, 1980).

Aristocratic clientage has attracted close attention from historians in recent years. On this see Y. Durand, *Hommage à Roland Mousnier: clientèles et fidélités en Europe à l'époque moderne* (1981); also J. Russell Major, 'The crown and the aristocracy in Renaissance France', *AHR* 69 (1964), 631–45; and ' "Bastard Feudalism" and the kiss: Changing social mores in late medieval and early modern France', *Journal of Interdisciplinary History* 17 (1987), 509–35; Sharon Kettering, 'Clientage during the Wars of Religion', *SCJ* 20 (1989), 221–39; 'Gift-giving and patronage in early modern France', *FH* 2 (1988), 131–4; 'Patronage and kinship in early modern France', *FHS* 16 (1989), 409–18, and 'Friendship and clientage in early modern France', *FH* 6 (1992), 139–58; M. Greengrass, 'Noble affinities in early modern France: The case of Henri I de Montmorency', *EHQ* 16 (1986), 275–311; J.M. Davies, 'Family service and family strategies: The household of Henri duc de Montmorency, ca. 1590–1610', *Bulletin of the Society for Renaissance Studies* 3 (1985), 27–43; M.P. Holt, 'Patterns of *clientèle* and economic opportunity at court during the Wars of Religion: The household of François, duke of Anjou', *FHS* 13 (1984), 305–22.

On the role of women, see Sharon Kettering, 'The patronage power of early modern French noblewomen', *HJ* 32 (1989), 817–41. The power which they exercised in various spheres of human activity is the subject of *Royaume de fémynie. Pouvoirs, contraintes, espaces de liberté des femmes de la Renaissance à la Fronde*, ed. K. Wilson-Chevalier and E.Viennot (1999). The key role played by marriage in aristocratic family strategy is explored by Joan Davies, 'The politics of the marriage bed: Matrimony and the Montmorency family, 1527–1612', *FH* 6 (1992), 63–95. Arlette Jouanna examines the motives behind aristocratic unrest in *Le Devoir de révolte: la noblesse française et la gestation de l'état moderne, 1559–1661* (1989).

Protestant conversions among the nobility are discussed by J. Garrisson in *Protestants du Midi, 1559–1598* (Toulouse, 1981), 22–8. On the role of nobles in Geneva, see R.M. Kingdon, *Geneva and the Coming of the Wars of Religion in France, 1555–1563* (Geneva, 1956), 6–7. The role of women in assisting the spread of Protestantism is discussed in N.L. Roelker, 'The appeal of Calvinism to French noblewomen in the sixteenth century', *Journal of Interdisciplinary History*. 2 (1971–2), 391–413, and 'The role of noblewomen in the French Reformation', *AR* 63 (1972), 168–95. See also J. Garrisson, *Protestants du Midi*, 47–9; and especially Natalie Z. Davis, 'City women and religious change' in *Society and Culture in Early Modern France* (London, 1975), 65–95.

Chapter 18

Two works by Lucien Romier give detailed narrative accounts of events under Francis II and Charles IX: *La Conjuration d'Amboise* (1923) and *Catholiques et Huguenots à la cour de Charles IX* (1924). Other treatments of the Amboise conspiracy are H. Naef, *La Conjuration d'Amboise* (Geneva, 1922); L.-R. Lefèvre, *Le Tumulte d'Amboise* (1949); J. Poujol, 'De la Confession de Foi de 1559 à la Conjuration d'Amboise', *BSHPF* 109 (1973), 158–77; and N.M. Sutherland, 'Queen Elizabeth and the Conspiracy of Amboise, March 1560', *EHR* 81 (1966), 474–89. On the Guises, see J.-M. Constant, *Les Guise* (1984), which is heavily indebted to R. de Bouillé, *Histoire des ducs de Guise*, 4 vols (1849) and H. Forneron, *Les ducs de Guise et leur époque*, 2 vols (1877). See also Stuart Carroll, *Noble Power during the French Wars of Religion. The Guise Affinity and the Catholic Cause in Normandy* (Cambridge, 1998), a study based on archival research which traces the links between high politics and popular confessional groups. On Antoine de Bourbon, see N.M. Sutherland, 'Antoine de Bourbon, king of Navarre and the French crisis of authority, 1559–1562' in *French Government and Society, 1500–1850. Essays in Memory of Alfred Cobban*, ed. J. F. Bosher (London, 1973), 1–18. On Catherine de' Medici, see the biographies by I. Cloulas, (1979); J. H. Mariéjol (1920); J. Héritier (1959); P. van Dyke (New York, 1922) and my own *Catherine de' Medici* (1998) which tries to be fair to the lady without whitewashing her. N.M. Sutherland, *Princes, Politics and Religion, 1547–1589* (London, 1984) contains two essays on Catherine. On Michel de L'Hôpital, Seong-Hak Kim, *Michel de L'Hôpital. The Vision of a Reformist Chancellor during the French Religious Wars* (Kirksville, MS, 1997) argues that L'Hôpital was as 'a rare blend of pragmatist statesman and idealist reformer'.D. Crouzet, *La Sagesse et le malheur. Michel de L'Hospital chancelier de France* (1998) is a difficult but rewarding work. Calling itself an 'introspective biography', it suggests that even at the height of the troubles L'Hôpital continued to believe in the possibility of a return to Christian unity. See also Sylvia Neely, 'Michel de L'Hospital and the *Traité de la réformation de la justice*: A case of misattribution', *FHS* 14 (1986), 339–66. The best account of L'Hôpital's politics remains J.H.M. Salmon, *Society in Crisis: France in the Sixteenth Century* (London, 1975), 51–62. *Discours pour la majorité de Charles IX et trois autres discours*, ed. R. Descimon (1993) gives four of the chancellor's speeches. See also J. Russell Major, *The Estates General of 1560* (Princeton, NJ, 1951).

On the Colloquy of Poissy, see H.O. Evennett, *The Cardinal of Lorraine and the Council of Trent* (Cambridge, 1930); D. Nugent, *Ecumenism in the Age of the Reformation: The Colloquy of Poissy* (Cambridge, MA, 1974); and N.M. Sutherland, 'The cardinal of Lorraine and the *Colloque* of Poissy, 1561: A reassessment', *J. Ecc.H.* 28 (1977), 265–89. On the edict of January, see A.-C. Keller, 'L'Hospital and the Edict of Toleration of 1562', *BHR* (1952), 301–10. Essential reading on the French crown's conciliar policy is A. Tallon, *La France et le Concile de Trente (1518–1563)* (Rome, 1997).

Chapter 19

Recent scholarship has focused on the Wars of Religion as they affected various towns. P. Benedict, *Rouen during the Wars of Religion* (Cambridge, 1981) and B. Diefendorf, *Beneath the Cross: Catholics and Huguenots in Sixteenth-Century Paris* (Oxford, 1991) are excellent. W. Kaiser, *Marseille au temps des troubles: morphologie sociale et luttes de factions, 1559–1596* (1992), being heavily statistical, is less easily digested. Penny Roberts, *A City in Conflict: Troyes during the Wars of Religion* (Manchester, 1996) focuses on the fortunes of the Protestant minority in a town situated within the Guise orbit, using a rich, and still unpublished, contemporary source, Nicolas Pithou's 'Histoire ecclésiastique de l'église de Troyes'. An important regional study is M.Cassan, *Le Temps des guerres de religion: Le cas du Limousin (vers 1530- vers 1630)* (1996). On the massacre of Vassy, see H. Forneron, *Les Ducs de Guise et leur époque* (1893), vol. 1, 306–26, and L. Romier, *Catholiques et Huguenots à la cour de Charles IX* (1924), 318–27. The Parisian reaction to this event is well described in Diefendorf, *Beneath the Cross*, 62–3. The atrocities committed by Blaise de Monluc are described in his *Commentaires*, ed. P. Courteault, 3 vols (1911–25). Extracts in English are to be found in *The Valois–Habsburg Wars and the French Wars of Religion: Blaise de Monluc*, ed. I. Roy (London, 1971). Monluc's career as a soldier and writer is authoritatively examined in P. Courteault, *Blaise de Monluc, historien* (1908). See also my 'The sword and the pen: Blaise de Monluc and his *Commentaires*', *Renaissance Studies* 9 (1995), 104–18. On the treaty of Hampton Court, see N.M. Sutherland, 'The origins of Queen Elizabeth's relations with the Huguenots, 1559–1562', *PHSL* 20 (1966 for 1964), 626–48. For the sack of Rouen in 1562, see Benedict, *Rouen during the Wars of Religion*, 101–3, and for events in Toulouse, M. Greengrass, 'The anatomy of a religious riot in Toulouse in May 1562', *J Ecc. H* 34 (1983), 367–91; and J.M. Davies, 'Persecution and Protestantism: Toulouse, 1562–1575', *HJ* 22 (1979),

31–51. What were the goals of popular religious violence? The question is posed by Natalie Z. Davis in her essay on 'The Rites of Violence' in *Society and Culture in Early Modern France* (London, 1975), 152–87. D. Crouzet, *Les Guerriers de Dieu: la violence au temps des troubles de religion*, 2 vols (Seyssel, 1990) has been described as 'nothing less than a complete reinterpretation of the religious history of the French sixteenth century'. Its mammoth bibliography lists sixty-five pages of printed primary sources alone. Olivier Christin examines the roots of confessional violence in *Une révolution symbolique. L'iconoclasme huguenot et la reconstruction catholique* (1991). In *La paix de religion. L'automisation de la raison politique au XVIe siècle* (1997) he considers the various attempts at religious co-existence in France, Switzerland and the Empire. On the assassination of the second duc de Guise, see N.M. Sutherland, *Princes, Politics and Religion, 1547–1589* (London, 1984), 139–55, and P. de Vaissière, *De Quelques assassins* (1912).

Chapters 20 and 21

Many of the events in these chapters are covered by works listed above, particularly H. O. Evennett on *The Cardinal of Lorraine and the Council of Trent* and L. Romier, *Catholiques et Huguenots à la cour de Charles IX* (1924). The entry of Charles IX and his queen into Paris in 1571 is described in F. A. Yates, *Astraea: The Imperial Theme in the Sixteenth Century* (London, 1975), 127–48. For the court of Catherine de' Medici see J.-H. Mariéjol, *Catherine de Médicis (1519–1589)* (1920), J. Héritier, *Catherine de Médicis* (1940), I. Cloulas, *Catherine de Médicis* (1979) and my own *Catherine de' Medici* (London, 1998). The marvellous series of festivals, which she organized, inspired the famous tapestries now in the Uffizi. They are interpreted controversially in F. Yates, *The Valois Tapestries* (2nd edn, 1975). The queen mother's extensive progress through France is described in P. Champion, *Catherine de Médicis présente à Charles IX son royaume (1564–1566)* (1937) and is given the full *Annaliste* treatment in J. Boutier, A. Dewerpe and D. Nordman, *Un Tour de France royal: Le voyage de Charles IX (1564–1566)* (1984). See also V.E. Graham and W. McAllister Johnson, *The Royal Tour of France by Charles IX and Catherine de Medici: Festivals and Entries, 1564–66* (Toronto, 1979).

On Ribault, see H. P. Biggar, 'Jean Ribaut's discoverye of Terra Florida', *EHR* 32 (1917), 253–70.

On the *Michelade* of Nîmes, see R. Sauzet, *Chroniques des frères ennemis: Catholiques et Protestants à Nîmes de XVIe au XVIIIe siècle* (Caen, 1992). The *Actes du Colloque L'Amiral de Coligny et son temps (Paris, 24–28 octobre 1972)* (1974) contain many papers of variable quality on all aspects of his eventful political and military career. Ambroise Paré, who served as royal surgeon for forty years, is carefully studied in Paule Dumaître, *Ambroise Paré, chirurgien de quatre rois de France* (1986).

Chapter 22

On the situation in Paris on the eve of the massacre see B. Diefendorf, 'Les divisions religieuses dans les familles parisiennes avant la Saint-Barthélemy', *HES* 7 (1988), 55–78; 'Prologue to a massacre: Popular unrest in Paris, 1557–1572', *AHR* 90

(1985), 1067–91; 'Simon Vigor: A radical preacher in sixteenth-century Paris', *SCJ* 18 (1987), 399–410; and her *Beneath the Cross* (cited above, p. 519). Also L. Mouton, 'L'affaire de la croix de Gastine', *BSHPF* 56 (1929), 102–13; D. Richet, 'Aspects socio-culturels des conflits religieux à Paris dans la seconde moitié du XVIe siècle', *AESC* 32 (1977), 764–89.

The massacre itself remains highly controversial. The documentary evidence is examined in N.M. Sutherland, 'Le massacre de la Saint-Barthélemy: La valeur des témoignages et leur interprétation', *RHMC* 38 (1991), 529–54. The government of Charles IX is blamed by Janine Estèbe (now Garrisson), *Tocsin pour un massacre: la saison des Saint-Barthélemy* (1968) and her *La Saint-Barthélemy* (1976). N.M. Sutherland, *The Massacre of St Bartholomew and the European Conflict, 1559–1572* (London, 1973) places the event in its international context. She exculpates Catherine de' Medici, as does J.-L. Bourgeon, *L'Assassinat de Coligny* (Geneva, 1992), who blames the Guises, Spain and Tridentine Rome. See also his 'Les légendes ont la vie dure: A propos de la Saint-Barthélemy et de quelques livres récents', *RHMC* 34 (1987), 102–16; 'Pour une histoire, enfin, de la Saint-Barthélemy', *RH* 282 (1989), 83–142; 'Une source sur la Saint-Barthélemy: l'histoire de Monsieur de Thou relue et décryptée', *BSHPF* 134 (1988), 499–537, and 'La Fronde parlementaire à la veille de la Saint-Barthélemy', *BEC* (1990), 17–89. *The Massacre of St Bartholomew*, ed. A. Soman (The Hague, 1974) comprises various reappraisals and cites two contemporary Italian accounts, one anonymous, the other by Tomaso Sassetti. D. Crouzet, *La Nuit de la Saint-Barthélemy: Un rêve perdu de la Renaissance* (1994) argues that it was a 'crime of love'. See also his 'La nuit de la Saint-Barthélemy: confirmations et compléments' in *Le Second ordre: l'idéal nobiliaire*, ed. Chantal Grell and A. Ramière de Fortanier (1999), pp.55–81. The massacre's wider impact is examined in P. Benedict, 'The St Bartholomew's massacres in the provinces', *HJ* 21 (1978), 201–25. See also his 'Catholics and Huguenots in sixteenth-century Rouen; the demographic effects of the religious wars', *FHS* 9 (1975), 209–34. The decline of Protestantism in France is quantified in his 'The Huguenot population of France, 1600–1685: the demographic fate and customs of a religious minority', *Transactions of the American Philosophical Society* 81, pt 5 (1991). On the siege of Sancerre, see Geralde Nakam, *Au Lendemain de la Saint-Barthélemy, guerre civile et famine. Histoire mémorable du siège de Sancerre de Jean de Léry (1573)* (1975).

Chapter 23

Useful introductions to the literature of the period are J. Cruickshank, *French Literature and Its Background*, vol. 1 (Oxford, 1968); R. Aulotte, *Précis de littérature française du XVIe siècle: La Renaissance* (1991); *A New History of French Literature*, ed. D. Hollier (Cambridge, MA, 1989) and I.D. McFarlane, *A Literary History of France: Renaissance France, 1470–1589* (London, 1974).

On the attitude of nobles to writing, see D. Bitton, *The French Nobility in Crisis, 1560–1640* (Stanford, CA, 1969), 47–9. See also my 'Military autobiographies in sixteenth-century France', in *War, Literature and the Arts in Sixteenth-Century Europe*, ed. J. R. Mulryne and Margaret Shewring (London, 1989), 3–21. Texts discussed in this chapter are *Mémoires du maréchal de Florange, dit le jeune aventu-*

reux, ed. R. Goubaux and P. André Lemoisne, 2 vols (1924); *Mémoires de Martin et Guillaume du Bellay*, ed. V.-L. Bourrilly and F. Vindry, 4 vols (1908–19); *Commentaires de Blaise de Monluc*, ed. P. Courteault, 3 vols (1911); *Oeuvres complètes de Pierre de Bourdeille, seigneur de Brantôme*, ed. L. Lalanne, 11 vols (1864–82); Brantôme, *Les Dames galantes*, ed. M. Rat (1960); F. de La Noue, *Discours politiques et militaires*, ed. F.E. Sutcliffe (Geneva, 1967); Agrippa d'Aubigné, *Sa Vie à ses enfants*, ed. G. Schrenk (1986); *Les Tragiques*, ed. J. Bailbé (1968); Ronsard, *Discours des misères de ce temps*, ed. J. Baillou (1949). On these writers see V.-L. Bourrilly, *Guillaume du Bellay* (1905); P. Courteault, *Blaise de Monluc, historien* (1908); H. Hauser, *François de La Noue* (1892); S. Rocheblave, *Agrippa d'Aubigné* (1910); K. Cameron, *Agrippa d'Aubigné* (Boston, 1977); Madeleine Lazard, *Agrippa d'Aubigné* (1998); A.-M. Cocula-Vaillières, *Brantôme* (1986); R.D. Cottrell, *Brantôme: The Writer as Portraitist of his Age* (Geneva, 1970); Madeleine Lazard, *Pierre de Bourdeille, Seigneur de Brantôme* (1995); M. Simonin, *Pierre de Ronsard* (1990); *Ronsard the Poet*, ed. T. Cave (London, 1973); E. Armstrong, *Ronsard and the Age of Gold* (Cambridge, 1968); D. Wilson, *Ronsard, Poet of Nature* (Manchester, 1961). The *Essays* of Montaigne are now available complete in a fine translation by M. Screech (Penguin Classics, London, 1987). See also Madeleine Lazard, *Michel de Montaigne* (1992); D.G. Coleman, *Montaigne's Essais* (London, 1987) and M.C. Smith, *Montaigne and Religious Freedom: The Dawn of Pluralism* (Geneva, 1991).

On the Huguenot theory of resistance, see Q. Skinner, *Foundations of Modern Political Thought*, vol. 2 (Cambridge, 1978); R.M. Kingdon, *Myths about St Bartholomew's Day Massacres, 1572–76* (Cambridge, MA, 1988), which focuses on the collection of pamphlets assembled by the Calvinist pastor Simon Goulart under the title *Mémoires de l'estat de France sous Charles IX*; D.R. Kelley, *François Hotman: A Revolutionary's Ordeal* (Princeton, NJ, 1973); and M. Yardeni on 'French Calvinist political thought, 1534–1715' in *International Calvinism*, ed. M. Prestwich (Oxford, 1985). The texts themselves include F. Hotman, *Francogallia*, Latin text by R.E. Giesey; trs. J.H.M. Salmon (Cambridge, 1972); T. de Bèze, *Du Droit des magistrats*, ed. R. M. Kingdon (Geneva, 1970); and *Vindiciae, contra tyrannos*, ed. G. Garnett (Cambridge, 1994).

On Bodin and absolutism, see R. Bonney, 'Bodin and the development of the French monarchy', *Transactions of the Royal Historical Society*, 5th ser. 40 (1990), 43–61. The central thesis of J. Franklin, *Jean Bodin and the Rise of Absolutist Theory* (Cambridge, 1973) is that Bodin's absolutism was as unprecedented as the doctrine it opposed. Before the 1570s the mainstream of the French tradition had been tentatively constitutionalist. Bodin, *On Sovereignty*, ed. J. Franklin (Cambridge, 1992), consisting of four books from his *Six livres de la République* (Paris, 1583, repr. Aalen, 1961) also has a useful bibliography. N. O. Keohane, *Philosophy and the State in France: The Renaissance to the Enlightenment* (Princeton, NJ, 1980) argues that until the end of the sixteenth century elements distinctive of absolutist thought were used interchangeably with those we associate with constitutionalism. See also J. H. M. Salmon, 'Bodin and the monarchomachs' in *Renaissance and Revolt: Essays in the Intellectual and Social History of Early Modern France* (Cambridge, 1987), 119.

Chapter 24

The best account of the career of Charles IX's troublesome younger brother is M.P. Holt, *The Duke of Anjou and the Politique Struggle during the Wars of Religion* (Cambridge, 1986). See also J. Boucher, 'Autour de François duc d'Alençon et d'Anjou, un parti d'opposition à Charles IX et Henri III', in *Henri III et son temps*, ed. R. Sauzet (1992). The duke's involvement in the Netherlands is chronicled in P. Geyl, *The Revolt of the Netherlands, 1555–1609* (5th edn, London, 1980) and G. Parker, *The Dutch Revolt* (London, 1977), and his courting of Elizabeth I in W. T. MacCaffrey, 'The Anjou match and the making of Elizabethan foreign policy', in *The English Commonwealth, 1547–1640*, ed. P. Clark et al. (Leicester, 1979). Links between the Huguenots and the Dutch rebels are examined in H. G. Koenigsberger, 'The organization of revolutionary parties in France and the Netherlands in the sixteenth century', *JMH* 27 (1955), 335–51.

On Montmorency-Damville, see Claude Tiévant, *Le Gouverneur de Languedoc pendant les premières guerres de religion (1559–1574): Henri de Montmorency-Damville* (1993), but it really antedates work by J. M. Davies, M. Greengrass and R. Harding. On the *Politiques*, see F. Decrue de Stoutz, *Le Parti des politiques* (1890). On Bellièvre, see Olivier Poncet, *Pomponne de Bellièvre (1529–1607). Un homme d'état au temps des guerres de religion* (1998), a work of exemplary scholarship.

The Estates-General of Blois in 1576 have been studied from several angles. See M. Greengrass, 'A day in the life of the Third Estate, Blois, 26th December 1576', in *Politics, Ideology and the Law in Early Modern Europe: Essays in Honor of J. H. M. Salmon* (Rochester, NY, 1994) and his 'The Project for the "Taille Egalée" at the Estates-General of Blois, 1576–77' in *Le Second ordre: l'idéal nobiliaire*, ed. Chantal Grell and A. Ramière de Fortanier (1999), pp. 169–81; also M.P. Holt, 'Attitudes of the French nobility at the Estates General of 1576', *SCJ* 18 (1987), 489–504; M. Orléa, *La Noblesse aux états généraux de 1576 et de 1588* (1980); O. Ulph, 'Jean Bodin and the Estates General in 1576', *JMH* 19 (1947), 289–96; R. Crahay, 'Jean Bodin aux états généraux de 1576', in *Assemblee di stati e istituzioni rappresentativi. Convegno internazionale* (Perugia, 1983), 85–120; and J.-M. Constant, 'Le langage politique paysan en 1576: les cahiers de doléances des bailliages de Chartres et de Troyes' in *Représentation et vouloir politiques autour des Etats généraux de 1614*, ed. R. Chartier and D. Richet (1982) and 'Les idées politiques paysannes: étude comparée des cahiers de doléances (1576–1789)', *AESC* 37 (1982), 717–27.

Chapter 25

The best recent biography of Henry III is P. Chevallier, *Henri III, roi Shakesperien* (1985). For his youth, see P. Champion, *La Jeunesse de Henri III*, 2 vols (1941–2). Jacqueline Boucher's monumental *Société et mentalités autour de Henri III* (Lyon II thesis, 4 vols, Lille, 1981) seeks to redeem the king's reputation. It is summed up in the same author's *La Cour de Henri III* (Rennes, 1986). Several useful essays are contained in R. Sauzet (ed), *Henri III et son temps* (1992). Henry's reputation is further considered by D. Potter, 'Kingship in the Wars of Religion: The reputation of Henri III of France' *EHQ* 25 (1995),485–528 and by K. Cameron, *Henri III: Maligned or Malignant King?* (Exeter, 1978) and his 'Henri III – the antichristian king', *JES* 4 (1974), 152–63. See also S. Anglo, 'Henri III: some determinants of vituperation' in K. Cameron, (ed.), *From Valois to Bourbon* (Exeter, 1989). On the king's favourites, see the brilliant thesis by N. Le Roux, *La Faveur du roi. Mignons et courtisans au temps des derniers Valois* (Seyssel, 2000); also P. Champion, 'Henri III: la légende des mignons', *BHR* 6 (1939), 494–528. Henry's religiosity is viewed sympathetically in F.A. Yates, *The French Academies of the Sixteenth Century* (rev. edn, London, 1988). See also A. Lynn Martin, *Henri III and the Jesuit Politicians* (Geneva, 1973) and R.J. Sealy, *The Palace Academy of Henry III* (Geneva, 1981). The etiquette at Henry's court is examined in M. Chatenet, *La Cour de France au XVIe siècle: architecture et vie sociale* (2002) and 'Henri III et "l'Ordre de la Cour". Evolution de l'étiquette à travers les règlements généraux de 1578 et 1585', in *Henri III et son temps*, ed. R. Sauzet, 133–9. See also D. Potter and P.R. Roberts, 'An Englishman's view of the court of Henri III, 1584–5: Richard Cook's "Description of the Court of France" ', *FH* 2 (1988), 312–26 and Jacqueline Boucher, 'L'évolution de la maison du roi: des derniers Valois aux premiers Bourbons', *XVIIe siècle* 137 (1982), 359–79. For Henry's patronage of the arts see my 'Royal patronage of the arts in France, 1574–1610' in *From Valois to Bourbon*, ed. K. Cameron (Exeter, 1989). On the art of Antoine Caron, see G. Lebel, 'Notes sur Antoine Caron et son oeuvre', *Bulletin de la Société de l'Histoire de Paris et de l'Ile de France* (1940), 7–34; and J. Ehrmann, *Antoine Caron, peintre des fêtes et des massacres* (1986). See also Margaret McGowan, *The Vision of Rome in Late Renaissance France* (New Haven & London, 2000). On sculpture, see *Germain Pilon et les sculpteurs français de la Renaissance*, ed. G. Bresc-Bautier (1993). The 'Magnificences' for the marriage of the duc de Joyeuse and religious processions in 1583–4 are critically examined by F.L. Yates in *Astraea* (cited above, p. 520), 149–207.

Chapter 26

The Catholic League has received much historical attention in recent years. An excellent recent survey is J.-M.Constant, *La Ligue* (1996). The classic study of the movement outside Paris remains H. Drouot, *Mayenne et la Bourgogne*, 2 vols (Dijon, 1937). See also M. Greengrass, 'The *Sainte Union* in the provinces: The case of Toulouse', *SCJ* 14 (1983), 469–96; and N. Le Roux, 'The Catholic nobility and political choice during the League, 1585–1594: The case of Claude de La Châtre', *FH* 8 (1994), 34–50. An excellent introduction to the Parisian league is M. Greengrass, 'The Sixteen: Radical politics in Paris during the League', *History* 69 (1984), 432–9. The social composition of the movement is examined in E. Barnavi, *Le Parti de Dieu: Etude sociale et politique des chefs de la Ligue parisienne* (Louvain, 1980) and R. Descimon, *Qui étaient les Seize? Mythe et réalités de la Ligue parisi-enne (1585–1594)* (1983). Barnavi and Descimon are joint authors of a more popu-lar work: *La Sainte Ligue, le juge et la potence* (1985). See also R. Descimon, 'La Ligue à Paris (1585–1594): une révision', *AESC* 37 (1982), 72–111, and A. Ramsay, *Liturgy, Politics and Salvation* (Rochester, NY., 2000). The role of preachers is stressed in A..Lebigre, *La Révolution des curés: Paris, 1588–94* (1980). On Spanish involvement in the League's activities, see De Lamar Jensen, *Diplomacy and Dogma-*

tism: Bernardino de Mendoza and the French Catholic League (Cambridge, MA, 1964). See also his 'French diplomacy and the wars of religion', *SCJ* 5 (1974), 22–46.

Aspects of the eschatological mood which gripped the Catholic masses in the 1580s are described in D. Crouzet, 'Recherches sur les processions blanches, 1583–1584', *HES* 4 (1982), 511–63 and 'La représentation du temps à l'époque de la Ligue', *RH* 270 (1983), 297–88. See also R.R. Harding, 'The mobilization of confraternities against the Reformation in France', *SCJ* 11 (1980).

The huge output of pamphlets published in Paris under the League is closely examined in D. Pallier, *Recherches sur l'imprimerie à Paris pendant la Ligue (1585–1594)* (Geneva, 1976). Such pamphlets have been used by Myriam Yardeni, *La Conscience nationale en France pendant les guerres de religion (1559–1598)* (Louvain, 1971). She concludes that a national consciousness was 'very strong'.

The political ideas of the League are examined in F.J. Baumgartner, *Radical Reactionaries; the political thought of the French Catholic League* (Geneva, 1976). See also F.S. Giese, *Artus Desiré, Priest and Pamphleteer of the Sixteenth Century* (Chapel Hill, NC, 1973) and Cromé, *Dialogue d'entre le maheustre et le manant*, ed. P.M. Ascoli (Geneva, 1977). J. Powis, 'Gallican liberties and the politics of later sixteenth-century France', *HJ* (1983), 515–30, suggests that most Gallicans (e.g. De Thou, L'Estoile) were committed to upholding royal authority in defence of order rather than compromising with the Protestants, as some historians (W.J. Bouwsma, G. Huppert and C. Vivanti) have suggested.

Henry III's efforts to clear his name in Rome after the Blois murders and Guise countermoves are investigated in R. Cooper, 'The aftermath of the Blois assassinations of 1588: Documents in the Vatican', *FH* 3 (1989), 404–26. Regional perspectives are offered by M. Greengrass, 'The Later Wars of Religion in the French Midi', in *The European Crisis of the 1590s*, ed. P. Clark (London, 1985), 106–34; E. Le Roy Ladurie, *Carnival: A People's Uprising at Romans 1579–1580* (London, 1980); and J.H.M. Salmon, 'Peasant revolt in the Vivarais (1575–80), *FHS* 11 (1979), 1–28.

Chapter 27

An excellent survey of the reign is M. Greengrass, *France in the Age of Henry IV: The Struggle for Stability* (rev. edn, London, 1994). A succinct biography, particularly good on the military aspects, is D. Buisseret, *Henry IV* (London, 1984). J.-P. Babelon, *Henri IV* (1982) is a good synthesis. Janine Garrisson, *Henry IV* (1984) is particularly informative on the king's early life in Béarn. R. Mousnier, *L'Assassinat d'Henri IV* (1964, English trans., London, 1973) measures the king's record against the theory of tyrannicide. The protracted negotiations leading to his abjuration are closely followed by M. Wolfe, *The Conversion of Henry IV: Politics, Power and Religious Belief in Early Modern France* (Cambridge, MA, 1993). See also his 'Piety and political allegiance: The Duc de Nevers and the Protestant Henri IV, 1589–93', *FH* 2 (1988), 1–21. The three best studies of Sully are D. Buisseret, *Sully* (London, 1968), B. Barbiche, *Sully* (1978) and B. Barbiche and Ségolène de Dainville-Barbiche, *Sully* (1997). The *Oeconomies Royales de Sully*, ed. D. Buisseret and B. Barbiche, 2 vols (1970–88) is the best edition of his memoirs. See also E. H. Dickerman, 'The man and the myth: Sully and the *Economies Royales*', *FHS* 7

(1972), 307–31. The Association Henri IV 1989, based at the château of Pau, has celebrated the fourth centenary of the king's accession by publishing five volumes of conference papers under the general title of *Avènement d'Henri IV quatrième centenaire*.

D.J. Buisseret examines various aspects of the reign in: 'Les ingénieurs du roi Henri IV', *Bulletin de géographie* 75 (1964), 13–84; 'The French Mediterranean fleet under Henry IV', *The Mariner's Mirror*, i (1964), 297–306; 'The communications of France during the reconstruction of Henry IV', *EHR*, 2nd ser. 18 (1965), 43–53; 'A stage in the development of the intendants: the reign of Henry IV', *HJ* 9 (1966), 27–38. The quatercentenary of the Edict of Nantes in 1998 has produced a large crop of books and articles, including B.Cottret, *1598. L'Edit de Nantes* (1997), J.Garrisson, *L'Edit de Nantes* (1998), *Coexister dans l'intolérance. L'Edit de Nantes (1598)*, ed. M.Grandjean and B. Roussel (Geneva, 1998); *L'Edit de Nantes: sa genèse, son application en Languedoc*, ed. A. Jouanna and M. Perronet (Montpellier, 1999), and *Paix des Armes, paix des âmes*, ed. P. Mironneau and Isabelle Pébay-Clottes (2000). On the execution of the edict, see Elisabeth Rabut, *Le Roi, l'église et le temple. L'éxécution de l'édit de Nantes en Dauphiné* (Grenoble, 1987). S. Annette Finley-Croswhite, *Henry IV and the towns. The Pursuit of Legitimacy in French Urban Society, 1598–1610* (Cambridge, 1999) argues that Henry 'mastered urban France with a policy of lenient pacification'. The arts under Henry IV have been the subject of a conference at Fontainebleau in 1990. The proceedings, published under the title *Avènement d'Henri IV quatrième centenaire. Colloque V. Fontainebleau 1990* (Pau, 1992), include contributions by leading scholars. On the king's foreign policy, see *La Paix de Vervins, 1598* , ed. Claudine Vidal and Frédérique Pilleboue (Vervins, 1998). The king's achievement was celebrated by an exhibition held at Pau and Paris in 1989–90. The catalogue entitled *Henri IV et la reconstruction du royaume* (1989) is superbly illustrated. Henry's encouragement of town-planning is thoughtfully examined in Hilary Ballon, *The Paris of Henry IV. Architecture and Urbanism* (Cambridge, MA, 1991).

H. Heller, *Labour, Science and Technology in France, 1500–1620* (Cambridge, 1996) provides a fascinating account of little known public and private initiatives taken during the Wars of Religion to revive France's economy, which Henry IV sought to widen and develop.

Glossary

aides	A range of indirect taxes, mainly on wine.
aisés	The upper level of urban society. The well-to-do.
alternatif	The system of selling one office to two persons, each of whom performed the duties for six months.
annates	The first year's income of an ecclesiastical benefice, paid to the papal curia.
arrêt	A formal judgement pronounced by a court.
Assembly of Notables	A consultative national assembly drawn from the clergy, office-holders and municipal governments usually by personal summons from the king.
Aumône générale	A municipal system of poor-relief, as at Lyon.
aventuriers	French volunteer infantrymen.
bailliage	The basic unit of royal administration at the local level, administered by the *bailli*.
ban et arrière-ban	The feudal levy.
Basoche	An Abbey of Misrule whose members were law clerks attached to a parlement. It was a kingdom in miniature with its own judicial and administrative machinery. By the fifteenth century the members (*basochiens*) had begun to perform satirical plays.
'battle'	The centre body of any army drawn up in order of battle.
brevet	An act by which the king confers a certain privilege.
Bureau des pauvres	A secular department for poor relief.
Cahiers/Cahiers de doléances	See *doléances*.
censier	A written record of a tenant's obligations to his lord.
Chambre ardente	The popular name given to the chamber of the Parlement of Paris created in 1547 to try cases of heresy.

chambre mi-partie	A chamber within a parlement comprising an equal number of Catholic and Protestant judges, who were to try cases between members of the two faiths. Also called *chambre de l'édit*.
château	A royal palace or aristocratic country house as distinct from a castle or *château-fort*.
Châtelet	The two courts of the royal *prévôté* of Paris (*Grand Châtelet* and *Petit Châtelet*).
collation	Institution to an ecclesiastical benefice when the ordinary (commonly the bishop) is himself the patron.
committimus	A privilege whereby a lawsuit could be evoked to a higher court, such as the *Chambre des requêtes* of the Parlement of Paris.
compagnies d'ordonnance	The armoured cavalry of *gens d'armes* (hence their other name, *gendarmerie*) in which the nobility of the sword served.
Confession of Augsburg	A statement of Lutheran beliefs presented to the German Diet of Augsburg in 1530. Its chief author, Melanchthon, tried to be conciliatory in its phraseology.
confraternity	An association of masters and artisans formed to celebrate the feast of a trade's patron saint and to participate in religious and public ceremonies.
Conseil des affaires	Inner ring of the king's council; also called *Conseil secret*.
Conseil d'état	The king's council in its widest form.
Conseil privé	The king's council (also called *Conseil des parties*), specializing in judicial business.
Constable of France	The highest military officer under the king.
crue	A direct tax in addition to the *taille* or *taillon*.
curé	A parish priest.
Curia regis	The royal court in the early Middle Ages before some of its components (e.g. the parlement) detached themselves and became fixed in Paris.
décharge	A royal warrant authorizing a payment.
décime	A tax levied by the clergy on all of its members for the purpose of paying a *don gratuit* (free gift) to the king.
dérogeance	Rule under which a nobleman who engaged in a demeaning occupation, notably trade, lost his status and privileges.
doléances	Complaints submitted to the king by a representative body.
douane	A customs house.
droit annuel	Another name for the *Paulette*.
échevin	An alderman in a municipal government.
élections	Courts responsible for the local administration of the *taille* and other taxes; also the areas where they functioned. The officials in charge were called *élus*.

épargne	Central treasury founded by Francis I in 1523. Its full name is *Trésor de l'épargne*.
Estates-General *(Etats-généraux)*	The national representative body, comprising elected representatives of the three orders of clergy, nobility and third estate. During the Wars of Religion they met in 1560–61, 1561, 1576–7, 1588–9 and 1593.
Etats particuliers	Representative assemblies held in a few regions within the *pays d'états*.
évocation	The process whereby the king transferred a lawsuit from one court to another or to his council.
expectative	A papal mandate conferring the expectation of an ecclesiastical benefice.
faubourg	The peripheral district of a town, lying outside its walls.
finances extraordinaires	The king's extraordinary revenue, drawn from taxation.
finances ordinaires	The king's ordinary revenue, drawn mainly from his demesne.
gabelle	A tax on salt levied on a variable basis in five out of six areas of France, the sixth (Brittany) being exempt.
Gallicanism	A school of thought according to which the French church was held to be in certain respects free from papal control.
gendarmerie	Another name for the *compagnies d'ordonnance*.
généralité	Originally one of four fiscal areas, each one administered by a *général des finances*. In 1542 the *généralités* were subdivided into sixteen *recettes-générales*, subsequently called *généralités* (as distinct from *pays d'états*). As from 1552 they were run by officials called *trésoriers généraux*.
généraux des finances	Senior officials, who before 1523 administered the king's extraordinary revenues.
gens des finances	The collective name for the king's chief financial officials before 1523: the *généraux des finances* and *trésoriers de France*.
gentilhomme campagnard	A member of the rural nobility.
gouvernement	A provincial governorship.
Grand' Chambre	The principal chamber of the Parlement de Paris.
Grand Conseil	A judicial offshoot of the king's council. It became an independent sovereign court in 1497, but continued to follow the king on his travels.
Grand Parti	A syndicate of Lyon bankers formed in 1555 to consolidate royal debts by means of regular amortisement.
Grands Jours	Courts composed of magistrats drawn from the parlements sitting in various provinces for a limited period.
Greek cross	A cross with four equal arms.
grenier à sel	A warehouse in which salt was kept under the system of *gabelle*. The official in charge was a *grenetier*.

herms	Three-quarter-length figures on pedestals used as decorations in Renaissance architecture.
Humanism	The programme of classical studies practised by certain scholars of the Renaissance (humanists) and the ideology stemming from that programme.
in commendam	The practice of allowing an individual to draw the income of an ecclesiastical benefice during a vacancy. The individual might be a layman, in which case he would be *ipso facto* debarred from performing the duties.
Juges-délégués	A special tribunal comprising two *parlementaires* and two theologians, set up in 1525 on the pope's authority to judge cases of heresy; abolished in 1527.
lance	A unit within the *gendarmerie*, comprising one man-at-arms and two archers sharing eight horses. A standard company of horse consisted of 40 *lances*. By the 1530s this meant in practice 40 men-at-arms and 60 archers. Each *lance* also had pages, usually young noblemen in training.
landsknechts	German mercenary infantry.
langue d'oc	The dialect spoken in southern France during the Middle Ages and in certain areas of the south till the nineteenth century. Also called *occitan*.
langue d'oïl	Dialect spoken in northern France during the Middle Ages, the ancestor of modern French.
lettre de jussion	Royal command to the parlement demanding immediate and unqualified registration of legislation.
lieutenant	A local magistrate; also used to designate the deputy of a provincial governor.
lieutenant criminel	A local magistrate serving in the court of a *bailliage*.
lieutenant-général du royaume	A title conferring general command of the kingdom. It was given in 1557 to François duc de Guise; in 1561 to Antoine de Bourbon; and in 1588 to Henri duc de Guise. During the League, the duc de Mayenne became lieutenant-general of the state and crown of France.
lit de justice	Personal attendance by the king in the parlement, usually to enforce registration of legislation.
loggia	Gallery open on one or more sides, sometimes pillared.
machicolation	A projecting gallery built on the outside of a castle tower with openings in the floor through which boiling oil, missiles, etc., could be dropped on an enemy.
maîtres des requêtes de l'hôtel	Officials attached to the royal council and under the chancellor's control.
mannerism	A controversial stylistic term applied to artistic products of the High Renaissance. It is a calculated, highly sophisticated style, founded on supreme technical competence.

mentalités	A term much used by the present generation of historians to describe contemporary attitudes and perceptions.
menu peuple	The lowest level of urban society, comprising manual workers and domestic servants.
mignon	One of Henry III's favourites.
Nominalism	A school of thought regarding universals or abstract concepts as mere names, without any corresponding realities.
notables	Important bourgeois in the magistracy and municipal government. The term is used less specifically in 'Assembly of Notables'.
office	A permanent government post (as distinct from a commission, which was temporary). It was often sold and entailed some degree of ennoblement.
Order	In classical architecture, a column with the base (usually), shaft, capital and entablature decorated and proportioned according to the Doric, Ionic, Corinthian or Composite mode.
ordinance (*ordonnance*)	A law or edict.
parlement	The highest court of law under the king, also responsible for registering royal edicts and with administrative duties. In addition to the Parlement of Paris, there were seven provincial parlements (Aix-en-Provence, Bordeaux, Dijon, Grenoble, Rennes, Rouen and Toulouse), which in theory were subordinate to it, but which in time acquired similar powers within their own jurisdictional areas (*ressorts*).
parlementaire	Any magistrate serving in a parlement.
Parties casuelles	A special treasury set up by Francis I to receive the proceeds from the sale of offices.
parvis	Open space in front of a church: e.g. the parvis of Notre Dame in Paris.
Paulette	The *droit annuel*, a tax upon venal office created in 1604, which gave security to office-holders and their heirs. It was named after Charles Paulet, sieur de Corbéron, who headed the group of financiers which proposed the measure. The tax was initially farmed out to him.
pays d'élections	Provinces in which taxation was levied by the *élus* on orders from the king's council.
pays d'états	Provinces in which taxation was levied by the local estates (e.g. Languedoc, Brittany, Burgundy and Provence) as distinct from the *pays d'élections*.
pediment	In classical architecture, a low-pitched gable, straight-sided or curved, above a portico, door or window.

pilaster	A shallow pier or rectangular column projecting only slightly from a wall.
place de sûreté	A fortified town which the Protestants were allowed to garrison. Under the Peace of Saint-Germain (1570) they obtained four such towns (La Rochelle, Cognac, La Charité and Montauban) for two years. The number was raised to eight in the Peace of Monsieur (1576) and to about 100 in the Edict of Nantes (1598).
police	In sixteenth-century France this meant more than just keeping the peace. It referred to all established administrative procedures.
Politique	Someone of moderate persuasion during the civil wars, equally opposed to extreme Protestantism or fanatical Catholicism and supporting the crown.
provision	The practice whereby the papacy nominated to vacant benefices over the head of the normal patron.
Premier président	The presiding magistrate in a parlement.
présidiaux	Courts set up in 1552 between the provincial parlements and the *bailliage* courts.
Prévôt de l'hôtel	Official in charge of keeping law and order at the royal court.
Prévôt des marchands	The mayor of Paris.
procureur	A solicitor. In every royal court there was a *procureur du roi*, known in the parlement as the *procureur-général*.
quartenier	An official heading the administration of one of the sixteen districts (*quartiers*) of Paris.
Realism	The scholastic doctrine of the objective or absolute existence of universals (abstract concepts) of which Thomas Aquinas (1225–74) was the chief exponent.
Receveur des parties casuelles	See *Parties casuelles.*
Receveur ordinaire	A receiver of royal revenue.
reiters	German mercenary cavalry, usually armed with pistols.
remonstrances	Objections or grievances submitted to the king, verbally or in writing, by a parlement, usually in response to a legislative proposal.
rente	A government bond issued on the security of municipal revenues. A *rentier* was someone living off such an investment.
reservation	The action on the part of the pope of reserving to himself the right of nomination to a vacant benefice.
Sacramentarianism	A body of Protestant thought, held mainly by Zwingli and his followers, which rejected the doctrine of the Real Presence of Christ in the Eucharist.
sacre	Literally, the consecration of a new French king; more loosely, his coronation.

Salic law	One of the so-called 'fundamental laws' of the French monarchy, whereby females were excluded from the succession to the throne.
Scholasticism	The characteristic method of teaching in medieval universities. Also its Christian philosophy with its strong dependence on Aristotelian texts and commentaries. Almost synonymous with medieval, as distinct from Renaissance, thought.
Sea Beggars	Dutch Calvinist rebels against Spain who operated mainly at sea.
Secrétaires des finances	Officials who prepared and countersigned royal correspondence. From them evolved the four *secrétaires d'état* in 1547.
seigneurie	The basic economic unit in rural France. The obligations of tenants to the seigneur involved a complex of rights, services and dues. A seigneur enjoyed rights of jurisdiction of varying degrees (called 'high', 'middle' and 'low' according to the severity of the penalties prescribed) within his lands, albeit subject to appeal to a royal court.
sénéchaussée	Another name, used mainly in southern France, for a *bailliage*. The equivalent to a *bailli* was a *sénéchal*.
setier	A measurement of capacity.
Sorbonne	Strictly, one of the colleges of the University of Paris. Commonly used to describe the Faculty of Theology.
sovereign courts	High courts, such as the Parlement of Paris, which had originally formed part of the king's court (*Curia regis*).
strapwork	Decoration consisting of interlaced bands and forms similar to fretwork or cut leather.
stucco	Plasterwork.
Surintendant des finances	The king's chief minister of finance. The title was held by François d'O (1578–94) and by Maximilien de Béthune, baron de Rosny, later duc de Sully (1598–1611).
Syndic	A person chosen to look after the interests of a group or corporation. The office of Syndic of the Faculty of Theology of the University of Paris was created in May 1520 to oversee the faculty's meetings and affairs, although the dean still officially presided.
taille	The principal direct tax, levied in two ways: the *taille personnelle*, levied on the unprivileged in the north, and the *taille réelle*, levied on non-noble land in the south.
taillon	An addition to the *taille* introduced under Henry II.
thaumaturgical	Pertaining to the working of miracles, more specifically the healing of the sick.
Tournelle criminelle	Chamber of criminal justice in the parlement.

Trésoriers de l'épargne	See *épargne*.
Trésoriers de France	Four officials who before 1523 administered the king's ordinary revenues.
Valet de chambre	A title conferring membership of the king's household. It was purely honorific and entailed no domestic duties.
vicomté	In local government a jurisdiction below the *bailliage* and equivalent to a *prévôté*.
Vidame	Title given in the Middle Ages to a bishop's temporal representative, who commanded his troops. By the sixteenth century it seems to have survived as an honorific title only in respect of Chartres.
ville-franche	A town exempt from the *taille*.

Genealogies

The house of Guise-Lorraine

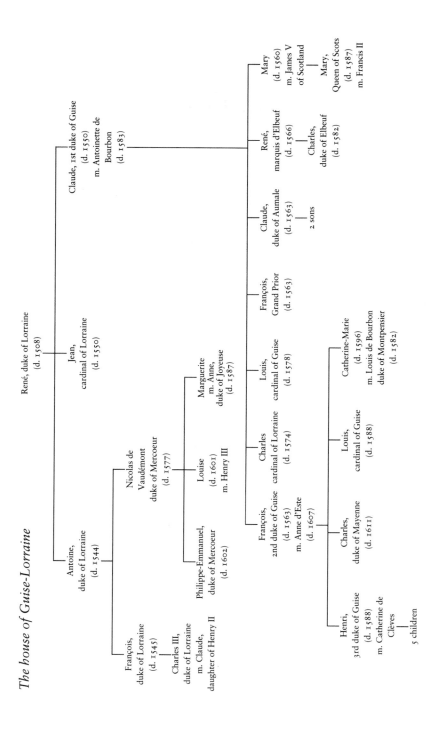

René, duke of Lorraine
(d. 1508)

Antoine,
duke of Lorraine
(d. 1544)

Jean,
cardinal of Lorraine
(d. 1550)

Claude, 1st duke of Guise
(d. 1550)
m. Antoinette de
Bourbon
(d. 1583)

François,
duke of Lorraine
(d. 1545)

Charles III,
duke of Lorraine
m. Claude,
daughter of Henry II

Nicolas de
Vaudémont
duke of Mercoeur
(d. 1577)

Philippe-Emmanuel,
duke of Mercoeur
(d. 1602)

Louise
(d. 1601)
m. Henry III

Marguerite
m. Anne,
duke of Joyeuse
(d. 1587)

François,
2nd duke of Guise
(d. 1563)
m. Anne d'Este
(d. 1607)

Charles
cardinal of Lorraine
(d. 1574)

Louis,
cardinal of Guise
(d. 1578)

François,
Grand Prior
(d. 1563)

Claude,
duke of Aumale
(d. 1563)

2 sons

René,
marquis d'Elbeuf
(d. 1566)

Charles,
duke of Elbeuf
(d. 1582)

Mary
(d. 1560)
m. James V
of Scotland

Mary,
Queen of Scots
(d. 1587)
m. Francis II

Henri,
3rd duke of Guise
(d. 1588)
m. Catherine de
Clèves

5 children

Charles,
duke of Mayenne
(d. 1611)

Louis,
cardinal of Guise
(d. 1588)

Catherine-Marie
(d. 1596)
m. Louis de Bourbon
duke of Montpensier
(d. 1582)

The later Valois

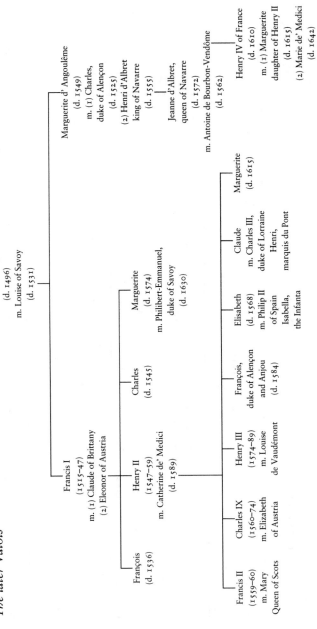

Charles, count of Angoulême
(d. 1496)
m. Louise of Savoy
(d. 1531)

Marguerite d' Angoulême
(d. 1549)
m. (1) Charles,
duke of Alençon
(d. 1525)
(2) Henri d'Albret
king of Navarre
(d. 1555)

Francis I
(1515–47)
m. (1) Claude of Brittany
(2) Eleonor of Austria

Jeanne d'Albret,
queen of Navarre
(d. 1572)
m. Antoine de Bourbon-Vendôme
(d. 1562)

François
(d. 1536)

Henry II
(1547–59)
m. Catherine de' Medici
(d. 1589)

Charles
(d. 1545)

Marguerite
(d. 1574)
m. Philibert-Emmanuel,
duke of Savoy
(d. 1630)

Henry IV of France
(d. 1610)
m. (1) Marguerite
daughter of Henry II
(d. 1615)
(2) Marie de' Medici
(d. 1642)

Francis II
(1559–60)
m. Mary
Queen of Scots

Charles IX
(1560–74)
m. Elizabeth
of Austria

Henry III
(1574–89)
m. Louise
de Vaudémont

François,
duke of Alençon
and Anjou
(d. 1584)

Elisabeth
(d. 1568)
m. Philip II
of Spain
Isabella,
the Infanta

Claude
m. Charles III,
duke of Lorraine
Henri,
marquis du Pont

Marguerite
(d. 1615)

The house of Montmorency

Guillaume de Montmorency
(d. 1531)

Anne de Montmorency
constable
(d. 1567)
m. Madeleine of Savoy

(2) Gaspard I de Châtillon
(d. 1522)

Odet, cardinal,
bishop of Beauvais
(d. 1571)

Gaspard II (Coligny)
admiral
(d. 1572)
m. Charlotte
de Laval
(d. 1568)

François d'Andelot
colonel-general
(d. 1569)

François de Châtillon
(d. 1591)

Louise
(d. 1620)
m. (1) Charles de Teligny
(2) William of Orange

Gabriel
(d. 1562)

Guillaume (Thoré)
(d. 1592)

Charles (Méru)
admiral
(d. 1612)

Louise de Montmorency
(d. 1547)
m. (1) Ferry de Mailly

Madeleine
(d. 1567)
m. Charles, count of Roye
(d. 1552)

Charlotte
(d. 1567)
m. François de
la Rochefoucauld

Eléonore de Roye
(d. 1564)
m. Louis I,
prince of Condé

Henri I (Damville)
(d. 1614)
m. (1) Antoinette
de La Marck
(2) Louise
(d. 1598)

François,
marshal,
governor of Ile-de-France
(d. 1579)

Eléonore
m. François
de la Tour,
vicomte de Turenne

Jeanne
m. Louis de
la Trémoïlle
duke of Thouars

The house of Bourbon-Vendôme

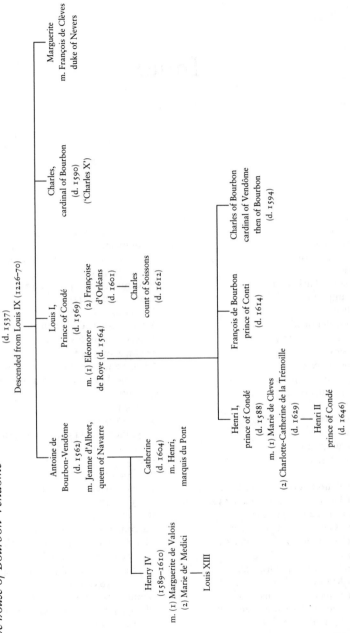

Charles de Bourbon-Vendôme
(d. 1537)
Descended from Louis IX (1226–70)

Antoine de
Bourbon-Vendôme
(d. 1562)
m. Jeanne d'Albret,
queen of Navarre

Louis I,
Prince of Condé
(d. 1569)
m. (1) Eléonore
de Roye (d. 1564)

(2) Françoise
d'Orléans
(d. 1601)

Charles,
cardinal of Bourbon
(d. 1590)
('Charles X')

Marguerite
m. François de Clèves
duke of Nevers

Charles
count of Soissons
(d. 1612)

Catherine
(d. 1604)
m. Henri,
marquis du Pont

Henry IV
(1589–1610)
m. (1) Marguerite de Valois
(2) Marie de' Medici

Louis XIII

François de Bourbon
prince of Conti
(d. 1614)

Charles of Bourbon
cardinal of Vendôme
then of Bourbon
(d. 1594)

Henri I,
prince of Condé
(d. 1588)
m. (1) Marie de Clèves
(2) Charlotte-Catherine de la Trémoille
(d. 1629)

Henri II
prince of Condé
(d. 1646)

Index